DICTIONARY OF
COMPUTING

FIFTH EDITION

Dictionary Titles in the Series

Specialist Dictionaries:

Dictionary of Accounting	0 7475 6991 6
Dictionary of Banking and Finance	0 7475 6685 2
Dictionary of Business	0 7475 9680 0
Dictionary of Economics	0 7475 6632 1
Dictionary of Environment and Ecology	0 7475 7201 1
Dictionary of Hotels, Tourism and Catering Management	1 9016 5999 2
Dictionary of Human Resources and Personnel Management	0 7475 6623 2
Dictionary of ICT	0 7475 6990 8
Dictionary of Marketing	0 7475 6621 6
Dictionary of Medical Terms	0 7475 6987 8
Dictionary of Military Terms	1 9038 5620 5
Dictionary of Nursing	0 7475 6634 8
Dictionary of Science and Technology	0 7475 6620 8

English Language:

Easier English Basic Dictionary	0 7475 6644 5
Easier English Basic Synonyms	0 7475 6979 7
English Study Dictionary	1 9016 5963 1
Easier English Student Dictionary	0 7475 6624 0
English Thesaurus for Students	1 9016 5931 3

Check your English Vocabulary Workbooks:

Business	0 7475 6626 7
Computing	1 9016 5928 3
English for Academic Purposes	0 7475 6691 7
PET	0 7475 6627 5
FCE +	0 7475 6981 9
IELTS	0 7475 6982 7
TOEFL®	0 7475 6984 3

Visit our website for full details of all our books
http://www.bloomsbury.com/reference

DICTIONARY OF
COMPUTING

FIFTH EDITION

S.M.H. Collin

BLOOMSBURY

www.bloomsbury.com

Originally published by Peter Collin Publishing

Fifth edition published 2004
Fourth edition published 2002
Third edition published 1998
Second edition published 1994
First published in Great Britain 1988

Bloomsbury Publishing Plc
38 Soho Square, London W1D 3HB
© Copyright S.M.H. Collin, 1988, 1994, 1998, 2002
This edition © copyright Bloomsbury Publishing Plc 2004

British Library Cataloguing-in-Publication Data

A catalogue record for this book is available from the British Library

ISBN 0 7475 6622 4

Text processing and computer typesetting by Bloomsbury
Printed and bound in Italy by Legoprint

Text Production and Proofreading
Lesley Brown, Stephen Curtis, Howard Sargeant, Megan Thomson, Katy
McAdam, Joel Adams, Daisy Jackson, Charlotte Regan

Preface

This dictionary provides the user with a comprehensive range of the vocabulary used in the field of computing. It covers all aspects of computing, including hardware, software, peripherals, networks and programming, as well as many applications in which computers are used, such as the Internet or desktop publishing. It also describes the latest developments in networks, the Internet, communications, programming, multimedia, processor design and storage technology.

Each headword is explained in clear, straightforward English. Examples are given to show how the words and phrases can be used in context. General comments about particular items of interest, complex ideas or hardware or software applications are given in separate boxes. Quotations from magazines and journals are given to show how the words are used in real text.

The dictionary includes a number of product names and company names. The trademarked names that are included are those that are judged to be of de facto importance to users or important in the development of computer technology.

Pronunciation

The following symbols have been used to show the pronunciation of the main words in the dictionary.

Stress has been indicated by a main stress mark (') and a secondary stress mark (ˌ). Note that these are only guides, as the stress of the word changes according to its position in the sentence.

Vowels		*Consonants*	
æ	back	b	buck
ɑː	harm	d	dead
ɒ	stop	ð	other
aɪ	type	dʒ	jump
aʊ	how	f	fare
aɪə	hire	g	gold
aʊə	hour	h	head
ɔː	course	j	yellow
ɔɪ	annoy	k	cab
e	head	l	leave
eə	fair	m	mix
eɪ	make	n	nil
eʊ	go	ŋ	sing
ɜː	word	p	print
iː	keep	r	rest
i	happy	s	save
ə	about	ʃ	shop
ɪ	fit	t	take
ɪə	near	tʃ	change
u	annual	θ	theft
uː	pool	v	value
ʊ	book	w	work
ʊə	tour	x	loch
ʌ	shut	ʒ	measure
		z	zone

A

A¹ /eɪ/ *symbol* the hexadecimal equivalent of the decimal number 10

A² /eɪ/ *abbr* ampere

A: used in some operating systems to denote the first disk drive on the system

Å *abbr* angstrom

abandon /ə'bændən/ *verb* to clear a document, file or work from a computer's memory without saving it ○ *Once you have abandoned your spreadsheet, you cannot retrieve it again.*

abb. add. *abbr* abbreviated addressing

abbreviated address /ə,briːvieɪtid ə'dres/ *noun* (*in a network*) a user name that has fewer characters than the full name, making it easier to remember or type in or faster to decode

abbreviated addressing /ə,briːvieɪtid ə'dresɪŋ/ *noun* the use of abbreviated addresses. Abbr **abb. add.**

abbreviated installation /ə,briːvieɪtid ,instə'leɪʃ(ə)n/ *noun* the installing of new hardware or software without restoring the previous backup settings of the operating system

abbreviation /ə,briːvi'eɪʃ(ə)n/ *noun* a short form of a word, command or instruction ○ *Within the text, the abbreviation proc is used instead of processor.*

ABD *abbr* Apple Desktop Bus

abend /'æbend/ *noun* an unexpected stoppage of a program that is being run, caused by a fault, error or power failure ○ *An interrupt from a faulty printer caused an abend.* Also called **abnormal end, abnormal termination**

abend code /'æbend kəʊd/ *noun* a special number, generated by the operating system, that identifies the type of error that has caused a particular problem

abend recovery program /,æbend rɪ'kʌv(ə)ri ,prəʊgræm/ *noun* a piece of software that will reload a program or system software and restart it at the point at which an abend occurred

aberration /,æbə'reɪʃ(ə)n/ *noun* **1.** distortion of a light beam or image caused by defects in the optical system **2.** distortion of a television picture caused by a corrupt signal or incorrect adjustment

ablation /ə'bleɪʃ(ə)n/ *noun* a method of writing data to an optical storage device in which a laser burns a hole or pit, representing digital bits of data, into the thin metal surface of the storage device

> COMMENT: A laser burns a hole or pit (which represents digital bits of data) into the thin metal surface of the storage device.

abnormal end /æb,nɔːm(ə)l 'end/ *noun* same as **abend**

abnormal termination /æb,nɔːm(ə)l ,tɜːmɪ'neɪʃ(ə)n/ *noun* same as **abend**

abort /ə'bɔːt/ *verb* to end a process in the event of a malfunction occurs by switching the computer off manually or by an internal feature ○ *The program was aborted by pressing the red button.*

aborted connection /ə,bɔːtɪd kə'nekʃ(ə)n/ *noun* a connection to a network or online service that has not been shut down correctly

abort sequence /ə'bɔːt ,siːkwəns/ *noun* a unique sequence of bits that indicates that the transmission will be terminated because of a fault, error or power failure

About... /ə'baʊt/ a menu selection in the SAA CUA front end that tells you who developed the program and gives copyright information

above-the-fold /ə,bʌv ðə 'fəʊld/ *adjective* referring to the part of a webpage that is seen by all users who call up the page, because they do not have to scroll down to read it. Compare **below-the-fold**

ABR /,eɪ biː 'ɑː/ *noun* a service provided by an ATM network that tries to provide the bandwidth requested by a customer, though it cannot guarantee to do so. Full form **available bit rate**

AB roll /ˌeɪ 'biː ˌrəʊl/ *noun* (*in a multi-media application*) a sequence of two video or music segments that are synchronised so that one fades as the second starts

ABS /ˌeɪ biː 'es/ *noun* a programming instruction that returns the magnitude of a number without the number's sign ○ *The command ABS(-13) will return the answer 13.* Full form **absolute function**

absolute address /ˌæbsəluːt ə'dres/ *noun* **1.** a computer storage address that directly, without any modification, accesses a location or device ○ *Program execution is slightly faster if you code only with absolute addresses.* Compare **indexed address 2.** a computer storage address that can only access one location ▶ also called **actual address, machine address**

absolute addressing /ˌæbsəluːt ə'dresɪŋ/ *noun* the locating of a data word stored in memory by the use of its absolute address

absolute assembler /ˌæbsəluːt ə'semblə/ *noun* a type of assembly language program designed to produce code that uses only absolute addresses and values

absolute cell reference /ˌæbsəluːt sel 'ref(ə)rəns/ *noun* a spreadsheet reference that always refers to the same cell, even when copied to another location

absolute code /'æbsəluːt kəʊd/ *noun* binary code that directly operates the central processing unit, using only absolute addresses and values. Also called **actual code, basic code**

absolute coordinates /ˌæbsəluːt kəʊ'ɔːdɪnəts/ *plural noun* coordinates that describe the distance of a point from the intersection of axes

absolute device /ˌæbsəluːt dɪ'vaɪs/ *noun* an input device such as a tablet or mouse that returns the coordinates of a pointer within specified axes

absolute error /ˌæbsəluːt 'erə/ *noun* the value or magnitude of an error, ignoring its sign

absolute expression /ˌæbsəluːt ɪk'spreʃ(ə)n/ *noun* (*in assembly language*) the value of an expression that is not affected by program relocation

absolute function /ˌæbsəluːt 'fʌŋkʃən/ *noun* full form of **ABS**

absolute instruction /ˌæbsəluːt ɪn'strʌkʃən/ *noun* an instruction that completely describes the operation to be performed, requiring no other data

absolute loader /'æbsəluːt ˌləʊdə/ *noun* a program that loads a section of code into main memory

absolute maximum rating /ˌæbsəluːt 'mæksɪməm ˌreɪtɪŋ/ *noun* a statement of the maximum values or limits of a system

absolute positioning /ˌæbsəluːt pə'zɪʃ(ə)nɪŋ/ *noun* the position of an object in relation to a point of origin

absolute priority /ˌæbsəluːt praɪ'ɒrɪti/ *noun* (*in the OS/2 operating system*) the priority of a process that cannot be changed by the operating system

absolute program /ˌæbsəluːt 'prəʊɡræm/ *noun* a computer program written in absolute code

absolute time /'æbsəluːt taɪm/ *noun* (*in CD-audio*) the length of time that an audio disc has been playing

absolute value /ˌæbsəluːt 'væljuː/ *noun* the size or value of a number, regardless of its sign ○ *The absolute value of – 62.34 is 62.34.*

absorb /əb'zɔːb/ *verb* to take in light, liquid or a signal

absorptance /əb'zɔːptəns/ *noun* a measure of how completely an object or substance absorbs radiant energy. Opposite **reflectance**

absorption /əb'zɔːpʃən/ *noun* the power loss of a signal when travelling through a medium, due to its absorptance

abstract data type /ˌbstrækt 'deɪtə ˌtaɪp/ *noun* a general data type that can store any kind of information

A-bus /eɪ bʌs/ *noun* the main internal bus in a microprocessor

ac *abbr* academic organisation (NOTE: used in email and website addresses)

AC *abbr* alternating current

ACAP /ˌeɪ siː eɪ 'piː/ *noun* an email system developed to work with the IMAP4 email protocol to provide extra features such as management of an address book. Full form **application configuration access protocol** (NOTE: It was originally termed IMSP (Interactive Mail Support Protocol).)

ACC /ˌeɪ siː 'siː/ *noun* the most important internal CPU storage register, containing the data word that is to be processed ○ *Store the two bytes of data in registers A and B and execute the add instruction –*

the answer will be in the ACC. Full form

accumulator

accelerated graphics port /ək
ˌseləreɪtɪd 'græfɪks ˌpɔːt/ *noun* full
form of **AGP**

acceleration time /əkˌseləˈreɪʃ(ə)n
taɪm/ *noun* **1.** the time taken for a disk
drive to spin a disk at the correct speed,
from rest ○ *Allow for acceleration time in
the access time.* **2.** the total time between
an access instruction's issue to a peripheral
and the transfer of the data

accelerator board /əkˈseləˌreɪtə
bɔːd/, **accelerator card** /əkˈseləˌreɪtə
kaːd/ *noun* a circuit board that carries a
faster or more advanced version of the
same processor that runs your computer.
Adding an accelerator board to your computer makes it run faster.

accelerator key /əkˈseləˌreɪtə kiː/
noun a key that, when pressed together
with another, carries out a function that
would otherwise have to be selected from
a menu using a mouse ○ *Instead of selecting the File menu then the Save option, use
the accelerator keys Alt and S to do the
same thing and save the file.*

accept /əkˈsept/ *verb* to establish a session or connection with another computing device

acceptable use policy /ək
ˌseptəb(ə)l juːz 'pɒlɪsi/ *noun* a set of
rules that describe what a user can write or
do on the Internet without offending other
users. Abbr **AUP**

acceptance sampling /əkˈseptəns
ˌsaːmplɪŋ/ *noun* the testing of a small random part of a batch to see if the whole
batch is up to standard

acceptance test /əkˈseptəns test/
noun a test to check that a piece of equipment will perform as required or will reach
required standards

acceptance testing /əkˌseptəns
'testɪŋ/ *noun* the performing of an acceptance test

access /ˈækses/ *noun* **1.** the fact of being able to reach or use something ○ *to
have access to the computer room* **2.** the
fact of being allowed to use a computer
and read or alter files stored in it. This is
usually controlled by a security device
such as a password. □ **to deny access** to
refuse access to a circuit or system for rea-
sons of workload or security ■ *verb* to call
up data which is stored in a computer ○

*She accessed the employee's file stored on
the computer.*

access arm /ˈækses aːm/ *noun* a mechanical device in a disk drive used to position the read/write head over the correct
track on a disk ○ *The access arm moves to
the parking region during transport.*

access authority /ˈækses ɔːˌθɒrəti/
noun permission to carry out a particular
operation on data

access-barred /ˌækses 'baːd/ *adjective* prevented from accessing particular
data

access category /ˈækses ˌkætəg(ə)ri/
noun a category that defines which files or
data a user can access and which he or she
cannot

access channel control /ˌækses
ˌtʃæn(ə)l kənˈtrəʊl/ *noun* (*in a Token-
Ring network*) the set of protocols that
manage the data transfer between a station
and a medium access control

access charge /ˈækses tʃaːdʒ/ *noun* a
cost due when logging onto a system or
viewing special pages on a bulletin board

access code /ˈækses kəʊd/ *noun* a series of characters or symbols that must be
entered to identify a user before access to
a computer is permitted

access control /ˈækses kənˌtrəʊl/
noun a security device such as a password
that only allows selected users to use a
computer system or read files

access control byte /ˌækses kən
ˈtrəʊl baɪt/ *noun* (*in a Token-Ring network*) a byte following a start marker in the
token that indicates if the station can access the network

access controller /ˈækses kən
ˌtrəʊlə/ *noun* (*in CD-i*) an electronic device that transfers image data to the video
controller

access control list /ˌækses kənˈtrəʊl
lɪst/ *noun* full form of **ACL**

access counter /ˈækses ˌkaʊntə/
noun ♦ **counter**

access head /ˈækses hed/ *noun* the
part of a disk drive that moves to the correct part of the disk's surface and reads information stored on the disk

access hole /ˈækses həʊl/ *noun* an
opening in both sides of a floppy disk's
casing allowing the read-write head to be
positioned over the disk's surface

accession number /əkˈseʃ(ə)n
ˌnʌmbə/ *noun* a number in a record that

shows in which order each record was entered

access level /'ækses ˌlev(ə)l/ *noun* a predefined access category (NOTE: The lowest access level might allow the user to only view data, the highest access level allows a user to do anything.)

access line /'ækses laɪn/ *noun* a permanently connected communications line between a terminal and a computer

access log /'ækses lɒg/ *noun* a file on a website server computer that contains a record of every visitor to the website, showing when a person visited and which pages he or she viewed ○ *The access log is invaluable – we produce graphs of the pages that are most popular using an access log analyser program.*

access mechanism /'ækses ˌmekəniz(ə)m/ *noun* a mechanical device that moves an access arm over the surface of a disk

access method /'ækses ˌmeθəd/ *noun* **1.** a means used for the internal transfer of data between memory and display or peripheral devices. Differences in the methods used are often the cause of compatibility problems. **2.** a set of rules that allows a device to send data onto a network. Token passing and CSMA/CD are two methods commonly used in a local area network.

access method routines /'ækses ˌmeθəd ruːˌtiːnz/ *plural noun* software routines that move data between main storage and an output device

access name /'ækses neɪm/ *noun* a unique name that identifies an object in a database

access number /'ækses ˌnʌmbə/ *noun* the telephone number that a computer dials up in order to be connected to an Internet service provider or other network provider

accessor /'æksesə/ *noun* a person who accesses data

accessory /ək'sesəri/ *noun* an extra, add-on device, e.g. a mouse or printer, that is attached to or used with a computer ○ *The printer comes with several accessories including a soundproof hood.* (NOTE: The plural is **accessories**.)

access path /'ækses pɑːθ/ *noun* a description of the location of a stored file within the directory structure of a disk

access path journalling /ˌækses ˌpɑːθ 'dʒɜːnəlɪŋ/ *noun* the process of recording changes to an access path in case of malfunction

access period /'ækses ˌpɪəriəd/ *noun* a period of time during which a user can access data

access permission /'ækses pə ˌmɪʃ(ə)n/ *noun* a description of all the access rights for a particular user

access point /'ækses pɔɪnt/ *noun* a test point on a circuit board or in software, allowing an engineer to check signals or data

access privilege /'ækses ˌprɪvɪlɪdʒ/ *noun* the status granted to a user that allows him or her to see, read or alter files

access provider /'ækses prəˌvaɪdə/ *noun* same as **ISP**

access rights /'ækses raɪts/ *plural noun* the rights of a particular user to access a particular file or data object

access time /'ækses taɪm/ *noun* **1.** the total time that a storage device takes between the moment the data is requested and the return of the data ○ *The access time of this dynamic RAM chip is around 200nS – we have faster versions if your system clock is running faster.* **2.** the length of time required to find a file or program, either in main memory or a secondary memory source

access unit /'ækses ˌjuːnɪt/ *noun* (*in a Token-Ring network*) a wiring concentrator

accidental /ˌæksɪ'dent(ə)l/ *adjective* which happens by accident ○ *Always keep backup copies in case of accidental damage to the master file.*

accordion fold /ə'kɔːdiən fəʊld/, **accordion fanfold** *noun* method of folding continuous paper, one sheet in one direction, the next sheet in the opposite direction, allowing the paper to be fed into a printer continuously with no action on the part of the user. Also called **fanfold**

account /ə'kaʊnt/ *noun* (*in a network or online system*) a record of a user's name, password and rights to access a network or online system ○ *If you are a new user, you will have to ask the supervisor to create an account for you.* ■ *verb* to keep track of how much time and resources each user of a network or online system uses

accounting package *noun* a piece of software that automates a business's accounting functions ○ *We now type in each transaction into the new accounting pack-*

age rather than write it into a ledger. Also called **accounts package**

account name /əˈkaʊnt neɪm/ *noun* the unique name of a user on a network or online system ○ *John Smith's account name is JSMITH.*

accounts package /əˈkaʊnts ˌpækɪdʒ/ *noun* same as **accounting package**

accumulate /əˈkjuːmjʊleɪt/ *verb* to gather several things together over a period of time ○ *We have gradually accumulated a large databank of names and addresses.* (NOTE: accumulates – accumulating – accumulated)

accumulator /əˈkjuːmjʊleɪtə/, **accumulator register** *noun* full form of **ACC**

accumulator address /əˈkjuːmjʊleɪtə əˌdres/ *noun* an address accessed by an instruction held in the ACC

accumulator shift instruction /əˌkjuːmjʊleɪtə ˈʃɪft ɪnˌstrʌkʃən/ *noun* a command to shift the contents of an ACC left or right by one bit

accuracy /ˈækjʊrəsi/ *noun* **1.** the extent to which something is correct or true **2.** the extent to which a person avoids errors **3.** the total number of bits used to define a number in a computer (NOTE: The more bits allocated the greater the accuracy of the definition.)

accuracy control character /ˌækjʊrəsi kənˈtrəʊl ˌkærɪktə/ *noun* a code that indicates whether data is accurate or whether the data should be disregarded by a particular device

ACD /ˌeɪ siː ˈdiː/ *noun* a specialised telephone system that can handle lots of incoming calls and direct them to a particular operator according to programmed instructions in a database. Full form **automatic call distribution**

ACDI *abbr* asynchronous communications device interface

ACF *abbr* advanced communications function

ACH /ˌeɪ siː ˈeɪtʃ/ *noun* an automated network that links banks together and enables them to handle payments made from one bank to another through electronic points of sale and withdrawals from cashpoints. Full form **automated clearing house**

achromatic colour /ˌeɪkrəʊmætɪk ˈkʌlə/ *noun* a grey colour within the range between black and white displayed by a graphics adapter

ACIA /ˌeɪ siː aɪ ˈeɪ/ *noun* a circuit that allows a computer to transmit and receive serial data using asynchronous access. Full form **asynchronous communications interface adapter**

ACK /ˌeɪ siː ˈkeɪ/ *noun* a signal that is sent from a receiver to indicate that a transmitted message has been received and that it is ready for the next one ○ *The printer generates an ACK signal when it has received data.* Full form **acknowledge**

Ackerman's function /ˈækəmənz ˌfʌŋkʃən/ *noun* a recursive function used to test the ability of a compiler to cope with recursion

acknowledge /əkˈnɒlɪdʒ/ *noun* full form of **ACK** ■ *verb* **1.** to tell a sender that a message or letter has been received **2.** to send a signal from a receiver to show that a transmitted message has been received (NOTE: acknowledges – acknowledging – acknowledged)

acknowledge character /əkˌnɒlɪdʒ ˈkærɪktə/ *noun* a special code sent by a receiver to indicate to the transmitter that the message has been correctly received

acknowledged mail /əkˌnɒlɪdʒd ˈmeɪl/ *noun* a function that signals to the sender when an electronic mail message has been read by the recipient

ACL /ˌeɪ siː ˈel/ *noun* a security system that has a list of user names and passwords that is checked by the operating system to find out if a particular user is allowed to access or use a resource or feature of the shared computer or network. Full form **access control list**

acoustic /əˈkuːstɪk/ *adjective* referring to sound

acoustic coupler /əˌkuːstɪk ˈkʌplə/ *noun* a device that connects to a telephone handset, converting binary computer data into sound signals to allow it to be transmitted down a telephone line

COMMENT: The acoustic coupler also converts back from sound signals to digital signals when receiving messages. It is basically the same as a modem but uses a handset on which a loudspeaker is placed to send the signals rather than direct connection to the phone line. It is portable and clips over both ends of a normal telephone handset. It can be used even in a public phone booth. The acoustic coupler has generally been replaced by a direct cable link from the computer's modem to the standard telephone socket.

acoustic delay line /əˌkuːstɪk dɪˈleɪ laɪn/ *noun* an outdated data storage method that delays data in the form of sound pulses as they travel across a medium

acoustic feedback /ə,kuːstɪk 'fiːdbæk/ *noun* ♦ **feedback**

acoustic hood /ə'kuːstɪk hʊd/ *noun* a soundproof cover put over a line printer to cut down its noise

acoustic memory /ə,kuːstɪk 'mem(ə)ri/ *noun* same as **acoustic store**

acoustic panel /ə,kuːstɪk 'pæn(ə)l/ *noun* a soundproof panel placed behind a device to reduce noise

acoustic store /ə'kuːstɪk stɔː/ *noun* an outdated form of regenerative memory that uses an acoustic delay line. Also called **acoustic memory**

ACPI /,eɪ siː piː 'aɪ/ *noun* a software system that allows the operating system to configure compatible hardware automatically. Full form **advanced configuration and power interface**

acquisition /,ækwɪ'zɪʃ(ə)n/ *noun* the accepting, capturing or collecting of information

Acrobat ♦ **Adobe Acrobat**

ACS /,eɪ siː 'es/ *noun* a computer linked to a network that controls several dial-up modems and allows remote users to connect to the server using a modem link and gain access to the network. Full form **asynchronous communication server**

action /'ækʃən/ *noun* (*in a SAA CUA front end*) a user event, e.g. pressing a special key, that moves the cursor to the action bar at the top of the screen

action bar /'ækʃən bɑː/ *noun* a top line of the screen that displays the menu names

action bar pull-down /'ækʃən bɑː pʊl/ *noun* (*in a SAA CUA front end*) a feature whereby the full menu is displayed below the menu name when a user moves the cursor to a particular menu name on the action bar

action code /'ækʃən kəʊd/ *noun* (*in a SAA CUA front end*) a single letter associated with a particular menu option to speed up selection. When the letter action code is pressed, the menu option is selected.

action cycle /,ækʃən 'saɪk(ə)l/ *noun* the series of steps required to carry out a process or operation on data, e.g. reading, processing, output and storage

action list /'ækʃən lɪst/ *noun* (*in a SAA CUA front end*) a list of choices

ActionMedia /,ækʃən'miːdiə/ a trade name for a digital video system developed by Intel that uses its i750 video processor chip to allow a computer to record, play back and manipulate digital video

action message /,ækʃən 'mesɪdʒ/ *noun* a message displayed to inform the user that an action or input is required

action-object /,ækʃən əb'dʒekt/ *noun* (*in a SAA CUA front end*) an object to which a user specifies an action should be applied

activate /'æktɪ,veɪt/ *verb* **1.** to start a process or to make a device start working ○ *Pressing CR activates the printer.* **2.** (*in an authoring tool or programming language*) to make a button or menu option or field on a screen layout available to a user ○ *If the button or field is not activated, it is normally displayed greyed out and does not respond if a user selects it.* (NOTE: activates – activating – activated)

active /'æktɪv/ *adjective* busy, working or being used

active application /,æktɪv ,æplɪ 'keɪʃ(ə)n/ *noun* (*in a multitasking operating system*) an application currently being used by a user

active area /,æktɪv 'eəriə/ *noun* **1.** (*in a spreadsheet program*) the area that contains data bounded by the top left hand corner and the bottom right hand cell **2.** (*in a graphical window*) an area that will start or select a function if the user moves the pointer into it with a mouse

active cell /'æktɪv sel/ *noun* the spreadsheet cell that is currently selected with a cursor or pointer

active code page /,æktɪv 'kəʊd ,peɪdʒ/ *noun* a code page currently in use by the system

active database /,æktɪv 'deɪtəbeɪs/ *noun* a database file currently being accessed by a database management program

active device /,æktɪv dɪ'vaɪs/ *noun* an electronic component that requires electrical power to operate and provides gain or a logical function

Active Document /,æktɪv 'dɒkjʊmənt/ *noun* a standard Windows application that is accessed from within a web browser and controlled by special commands in the webpage

active file /,æktɪv 'faɪl/ *noun* a file that is currently being worked on

active gateway /ˌæktɪv ˈgeɪtweɪ/ *noun* (*in a network*) a gateway that exchanges routing information

active high /ˈæktɪv haɪ/ *noun* an electronic signal that is valid when it is high or logical one or at five volts

active hub /ˌæktɪv ˈhʌb/ *noun* a hub that selectively directs packets of data according to their address or content

active line /ˌæktɪv ˈlaɪn/ *noun* a line in a communications link or port that is being used to transfer data or carry control signals

active link /ˌæktɪv ˈlɪŋk/ *noun* a link currently being used to transfer information

active low /ˌæktɪv ˈləʊ/ *noun* an electronic signal that is valid when it is low or logical zero or at zero volts

active menu /ˌæktɪv ˈmenjuː/ *noun* a menu selection currently displayed below a menu bar

active node /ˌæktɪv ˈnəʊd/ *noun* a node on a network connected to or available to connect to another node

active pixel region /ˌæktɪv ˈpɪks(ə)l ˌriːdʒən/ *noun* an area of a computer screen that can display graphic image information

active printer /ˌæktɪv ˈprɪntə/ *noun* a printer that is currently connected to the computer's printer port

active program /ˌæktɪv ˈprəʊɡræm/ *noun* (*in a multitasking system*) a program that is currently in control of the processor

active record /ˌæktɪv ˈrekɔːd/ *noun* a record that is being updated or accessed

active region /ˌæktɪv ˈriːdʒ(ə)n/ *noun* an area on a screen that will start an action or has been defined as a hotspot

Active Server Page /ˌæktɪv ˈsɜːvə peɪdʒ/ *noun* a webpage that is created only when accessed by a visitor, allowing the website to display up-to-date information or information from a database ○ *The database search results page is implemented as an Active Server Page.* Abbr **ASP**

active star /ˈæktɪv stɑː/ *noun* a network consisting of a central point with nodes branching out, in which a central processor controls and routes all messages between devices

active state /ˌæktɪv ˈsteɪt/ *noun* an electronic state in which an action occurs

active storage /ˌæktɪv ˈstɔːrɪdʒ/ *noun* a main storage, fast access RAM whose locations can be directly and immediately addressed by the CPU

active streaming format /ˌæktɪv ˈstriːmɪŋ ˌfɔːmæt/ *noun* full form of **ASF**

active video /ˌæktɪv ˈvɪdiəʊ ˌsɪgn(ə)l/, **active video signal** *noun* a part of a video signal that contains picture information

ActiveVRML /ˌæktɪv viː ɑː em ˈel/ *noun* ♦ **VRML**

active window /ˌæktɪv ˈwɪndəʊ/ *noun* **1.** an area of the display screen where the operator is currently working **2.** (*in a GUI or SAA CUA front end*) the window that is currently the focus of cursor movements and screen displays. ◊ **window**

ActiveX /ˌæktɪv ˈeks/ a trade name for a programming language and program definition used to create small applications designed to enhance the functionality of a webpage. ◊ **Java, VBScript**

COMMENT: ActiveX applications, called applets, are often used to add database or multimedia effects to a website that cannot be supported with basic HTML commands. When a user visits the web page that uses the ActiveX applet, the program is automatically downloaded by the user's browser and run on the user's computer.

activities /ækˈtɪvɪtiz/ *plural noun* jobs or tasks which are being performed on a computer

activity level /ækˌtɪvəti ˈlev(ə)l/ *noun* the maximum number of jobs that can run in a multitasking system

activity light /ækˈtɪvɪti laɪt/ *noun* small light or LED on the front of a disk drive or computer that indicates when the disk drive is reading or writing data to disk

activity loading /ækˌtɪvɪti ˈləʊdɪŋ/ *noun* a method of organising disk contents so that the most often accessed files or programs can be loaded quickly

activity ratio /ækˌtɪvɪti ˈreɪʃiəʊ/ *noun* the number of files currently in use compared to the total stored

activity trail /ækˈtɪvɪti treɪl/ *noun* a record of activities carried out

actual address /ˌæktʃuəl əˈdres/ *noun* same as **absolute address**

actual code /ˈæktʃuəl kəʊd/ *noun* same as **absolute code**

actual data transfer rate /ˌæktʃuəl ˌdeɪtə ˈtrænsfɜː ˌreɪt/ *noun* the average number of data bits transferred in a period of time

actual instruction /ˌæktʃuəl ɪn
'strʌkʃən/ *noun* the resulting instruction
executed after the modification of an original instruction

actuator /ˈæktʃʊeɪtə/ *noun* a mechanical device that can be controlled by an external signal, e.g. the read/write head in a
disk drive

ACU /ˌeɪ siː ˈjuː/ *noun* a device that allows a computer to call stations or dial telephone numbers automatically. Full form
automatic calling unit

ad *abbr* Andorra (NOTE: used in email
and website addresses)

A/D *abbr* analog to digital

ADA /ˌeɪ diː ˈeɪ/ *noun* a high-level programming language that is used mainly in
military, industrial and scientific fields of
computing

adapt /əˈdæpt/ *verb* to change, adjust or
modify something so that it fits ○ *Can this
computer be adapted to take 5.25 inch
disks?*

adaptation /ˌædæpˈteɪʃ(ə)n/ *noun* the
ability of a device to adjust its sensitivity
range according to various situations

adapter /əˈdæptə/, **adaptor** *noun* a device that allows two or more incompatible
devices to be connected together

adapter card /əˈdæptə kɑːd/ *noun* a
card that plugs into an expansion bus in a
PC and adds a new function to the computer or allows it to communicate with another device (NOTE: A sound card is a type of
adapter card that plugs into an expansion connector and allows sound to be
played back or recorded.)

adapter plug /əˈdæptə plʌg/ *noun* a
plug that allows plugs with different numbers or shapes of pins to be fitted into the
same socket

adaptive channel allocation /ə
ˌdæptɪv ˈtʃæn(ə)l æləˌkeɪʃ(ə)n/ *noun*
provision of communications channels according to demand rather than a fixed allocation

adaptive compression /əˌdæptɪv
kəmˈpreʃ(ə)n/ *noun* a data compression
system that continuously monitors the data
it is compressing and adjusts its own algorithm to provide the most efficient compression

**adaptive differential pulse code
modulation** /əˌdæptɪv dɪfəˌrenʃ(ə)l
ˈpʌls kəʊd mɒdjuˌleɪʃ(ə)n/ *noun* full
form of **ADPCM**

adaptive packet assembly /ə
ˌdæptɪv ˈpækɪt əˌsembli/ *noun* a method
used by the MNP error correcting protocol
to adjust the size of data packets according
to the quality of the telephone line. The
better the line, the bigger the packet size.

adaptive routing /əˌdæptɪv ˈruːtɪŋ/
noun the ability of a system to change its
communications routes in response to various events or situations such as line failure (NOTE: The messages are normally
sent along the most cost-effective path
unless there is a problem with that route,
in which case they are automatically re-
routed.)

adaptive system /əˌdæptɪv ˈsɪstəm/
noun a system that is able to alter its responses and processes according to inputs
or situations

adaptor /əˈdæptə/ *noun* another spelling of **adapter**

ADB *abbr* Apple Desktop Bus

ADC /ˌeɪ diː ˈsiː/ *noun* an electronic device that converts an analog input signal to
a digital form, which can be processed by
a computer. Full form **analog to digital
converter**

add /æd/ *verb* 1. to put figures together to
make a total 2. to put things together to
form a larger group ○ *The software house
has added a new management package to
its range of products.*

addend /ˈædend/ *noun* the number added to the augend in an addition

adder /ˈædə/ *noun* a device or routine
that provides the sum of two or more inputs, either digital or analog

COMMENT: A parallel adder takes one clock cycle to add two words, a serial adder takes a
time equal to the number of bits in a word to
add.

adder-subtractor /ˌædə səbˈtræktə/
noun a device that can either add or subtract

add file /ˈæd faɪl/ *noun* a file in which
new records are stored prior to updating
the main database

add-in /ˈæd ɪn/ *noun, adjective* something that is added to something else ■ *adjective* that is added to something else

addition /əˈdɪʃ(ə)n/ *noun* an arithmetic
operation that produces the sum of an addend and augend

additional /əˈdɪʃ(ə)nəl/ *adjective* which
is added or extra ○ *Can we link three additional workstations to the network?*

addition record /ə,dɪʃ(ə)n 'rekɔːd/ *noun* a record with changes used to update a master record or file

addition time /ə'dɪʃ(ə)n taɪm/ *noun* the time an adder takes to carry out an addition operation

addition without carry /ə,dɪʃ(ə)n wɪð,aʊt 'kæri/ *noun* an addition operation without any carry bits or words

additive colour /,ædətɪv 'kʌlə/ *noun* a colour produced by mixing two or three colours from red, green and blue

add-on /'æd ɒn/ *adjective* added to a computer system to improve its performance ○ *The add-on hard disk will boost the computer's storage capabilities.* Opposite **built-in** ■ *noun* a piece of software or hardware that is added to a computer system to improve its performance

add on board /'æd ɒn bɔːd/ *noun* same as **expansion board**

add register /æd 'redʒɪstə/ *noun* a register that is an adder

address /ə'dres/ *noun* **1.** a number allowing a central processing unit to reference a physical location in a storage medium in a computer system ○ *Each separate memory word has its own unique address.* **2.** a unique number that identifies a device on a network ○ *This is the address at which the data starts.* ■ *verb* to put the location data onto an address bus to identify which word in memory or storage device is to be accessed ○ *A larger address word increases the amount of memory a computer can address.*

addressability /ə,dresə'bɪlɪti/ *noun* the control available over pixels on screen

addressable /ə'dresəb(ə)l/ *adjective* which can be addressed ○ *With the new operating system, all of the 5MB of installed RAM is addressable.*

addressable cursor /ə,dresəb(ə)l 'kɜːsə/ *noun* a cursor which can be programmed to be placed in a certain position

addressable point /ə,dresəb(ə)l 'pɔɪnt/ *noun* a point or pixel in a graphics system that can be directly addressed

addressable terminal /ə,dresəb(ə)l 'tɜːmɪn(ə)l/ *noun* a terminal that will only accept data if it has the correct address and identification number in the message header

address access time /ə,dres 'ækses taɪm/ *noun* the total time which a storage device takes between the moment the data is requested and the return of the data

address base /ə'dres beɪs/ *noun* the part of an address that defines the origin to which the logical address is added

address book /ə'dres bʊk/ *noun* **1.** (*in a network*) a list of node addresses **2.** (*in electronic mail*) a list of the network addresses of other users to which electronic mail can be sent

address bus /ə'dres bʌs/ *noun* a physical connection that carries the address data in parallel form from the central processing unit to external devices

address code /ə'dres kəʊd/ *noun* a special code that identifies the part of a document that is an address

address computation /ə,dres ,kɒmpjʊ'teɪʃ(ə)n/ *noun* an operation on address data in an instruction

address decoder /ə'dres diː,kəʊdə/ *noun* a logical circuit that will produce a signal when a certain address or range is placed on the address bus

address field /ə'dres fiːld/ *noun* **1.** (*in a network*) the part of a packet that contains the address of the destination node **2.** (*in programming*) the part of a computer instruction that contains the location of the operand

address format /ə'dres ,fɔːmæt/ *noun* the set of rules defining the way the operands, data and addresses are arranged in an instruction

address harvester /ə'dres ,hɑːvɪstə/ *noun* a computer program that collects email addresses from the Internet

address highway /ə'dres ,haɪweɪ/ *noun* the set of physical connections that carry the address data in a parallel form between the central processing unit and memory or external devices

addressing /ə'dresɪŋ/ *noun* the process of accessing a location in memory

addressing capacity /ə'dresɪŋ kə ,pæsɪti/ *noun* the largest location that a certain program or CPU can directly address, without special features, e.g. virtual memory or memory banks

addressing level /ə'dresɪŋ ,lev(ə)l/ *noun* zero-level: operand is the address part of the instruction; first-level: operand stored at the address of the instruction; second-level: operand stored at the address given in the instruction

addressing method /ə'dresɪŋ ,meθəd/ *noun* the manner in which a section of memory is located

addressing mode /əˈdresɪŋ məʊd/ *noun* a way in which a location is addressed, e.g. sequential, indexed or direct

address mapping /əˈdres ˌmæpɪŋ/ *noun* the translation of a virtual address to an absolute real address

address mark /əˈdres mɑːk/ *noun* a special code on a disk that indicates the start of sector location data

address mask /əˈdres mɑːsk/ *noun* a pattern of binary data bits that is used to block out parts of an address data word. It is normally used to separate the network and subnet parts of an address within a long Internet or IP address. ○ *The address mask '111000' will block off the last three bits of any address data.*

address modification /əˌdres ˌmɒdɪfɪˈkeɪʃ(ə)n/ *noun* the changing of the address field, so that it can refer to a different location

address register /əˈdres ˌredʒɪstə/ *noun* register in a computer that is able to store all the bits that make up an address ,which can then be processed as a single unit

address resolution /əˈdres ˌrezəluːʃ(ə)n/ *noun* the converting pf an Internet address into the correct physical network address that corresponds to the distant computer or resource

address resolution protocol /əˈdres ˌrezəˈluːʃ(ə)n ˌprəʊtəkɒl/ *noun* full form of **ARP**

address space /əˈdres speɪs/ *noun* the total number of possible locations that can be directly addressed by the program or CPU

address strobe /əˈdres strəʊb/ *noun* a signal in the form of a pulse that indicates that a valid address is on the address bus

address track /əˈdres træk/ *noun* track on a magnetic disk containing the addresses of files or other data stored on other tracks

address translation /əˌdres trænsˈleɪʃ(ə)n/ *noun* an address produced by calculating an expression

address word /əˈdres wɜːd/ *noun* a computer word that contains the address data. In a small micro it is usually made up of two data words.

add time /ˈæd taɪm/ *noun* a period of time taken either by a CPU or adder to perform one addition operation

adjacent domains /əˌdʒeɪs(ə)nt dəʊ ˈmeɪnz/ *plural noun* two domains linked by two adjacent nodes

adjacent nodes /əˈdʒeɪs(ə)nt nəʊdz/ *plural noun* two nodes connected by a path that does not connect any other node

adjunct register /ˌædʒʌŋkt ˈredʒɪstə/ *noun* a 32-bit register in which the top 16 bits are used for control information and only the bottom 16 bits are available for use by a program

adjustment /əˈdʒʌstmənt/ *noun* the making of a slight change made to something so that it works better, or a change made ○ *The brightness needs adjustment.*

AdLib /ædˈlɪb/ *noun* a type of sound card for a PC with basic sound playback and MIDI functions

administrator /ədˈmɪnɪstreɪtə/ *noun* a person who is responsible for looking after a network, including installing, configuring and maintaining it

Adobe Acrobat /əˌdəʊbi ˈækrəbæt/ a trade name for a piece of software that converts documents and formatted pages into a file format that can be viewed on almost any computer platform or using a web browser on the Internet (NOTE: For example, if you publish a newsletter, you could lay out the pages using a desktop publish system, print the pages for a paper version and convert the files to Acrobat format allowing you to distribute the same formatted pages on CD-ROM or over the Internet.)

Adobe Systems /əˌdəʊbi ˈsɪstəmz/ a software company that developed products including Acrobat, ATM, and PostScript

Adobe Type Manager /əˌdəʊbi taɪp ˈmænɪdʒə/ a trade name for a standard for describing scalable fonts, used with Apple System 7 and Microsoft Windows to provide fonts that can be scaled to almost any point size, and printed on almost any printer. Abbr **ATM**

ADP /ˌeɪ diː ˈpiː/ *noun* data processing done by a computer. Full form **automatic data processing**

ADPCM /ˌeɪ diː piː siː ˈem/ *noun* a CCITT standard that defines a method of converting a voice or analog signal into a compressed digital signal. Full form **adaptive differential pulse code modulation**

ADSL /ˌeɪ diː es ˈel/ *noun* high-speed transmission standard that uses the same copper telephone wires as a normal telephone service, but is much faster than a standard modem or a digital system such as ISDN. Full form **Asymmetric Digital Subscriber Line** (NOTE: As well as the speed, ADSL provides a user with an 'always on' connection to the Internet – there is no need to dial an access number and no delay. Typically, companies provide ADSL for a fixed monthly rental; data is usually transferred from the Internet to the user's computer at 2Mbps but transferred from the user's computer to the Internet at a slower rate of 256Kbps.)

advanced configuration and power interface /əd,vɑːnst kən,fɪgjə ,reɪʃ(ə)n ən ,paʊə 'ɪntəfeɪs/ noun full form of **ACPI**

Advanced Micro Devices /əd ,vɑːnst 'maɪkrəʊ dɪ,vaɪsɪz/ full form of **AMD**

advanced peer-to-peer networking /əd,vɑːnst ,pɪə tə ,pɪə 'netwɜːkɪŋ/ noun full form of **APPN**

advanced power management /əd ,vɑːnst ,paʊə 'mænɪdʒmənt/ noun full form of **APM**

advanced program to program communications /əd,vɑːnst ,prəʊgræm tə ,prəʊgræm kə,mjuːnɪ 'keɪʃ(ə)nz/ noun full form of **APPC**

Advanced Research Projects Agency Network /əd,vɑːnst ,riːsɜːtʃ ,prɒdʒekts ,eɪdʒ(ə)nsi 'netwɜːk/ noun full form of **ARPANET**

advanced run-length limited /əd ,vɑːnst 'rʌn leŋθ ,lɪmɪtɪd/ noun a method of storing data onto a hard disk that is faster and more efficient than RLL. Abbr **ARLL**

advanced technology attachment /əd,vɑːnst tek,nɒlədʒi ə'tætʃmənt/ noun full form of **ATA**

advanced technology attachment packet interface /əd,vɑːnst tek ,nɒlədʒi ə,tætʃmənt ,pækɪt 'ɪntəfeɪs/ noun a type of standard interface that is used for CD-ROMs. Abbr **ATAPI**. Also called **ATA packet interface**

Advanced Television Systems Committee /əd,vɑːnst 'telɪvɪʒ(ə)n ,sɪstəmz kə,mɪti/ noun full form of **ATSC**

advanced version /əd,vɑːnst 'vɜːʃ(ə)n/ noun a program with more complex features for use by an experienced user

advanced wave modulation /əd ,vɑːnst 'weɪv ,mɒdjʊleɪʃ(ə)n/ noun full form of **AWM**

advisory lock /əd'vaɪz(ə)ri lɒk/ noun (in a multitasking system) a lock placed on a region of a file by one process to prevent any other process accessing the same data

advisory system /əd,vaɪz(ə)ri 'sɪstəm/ noun an expert system that provides advice to a user

aerial perspective /,eəriəl pə 'spektɪv/ noun a view of a three-dimensional landscape as if the viewer is above the scene

AFAIK abbr as far as I know (NOTE: used in emails and text messages)

affiliate marketing /ə'fɪliət ,mɑːkɪtɪŋ/ noun a type of marketing that uses a central website to advertise and sell products and services from other sites

affirmative /ə'fɜːmətɪv/ adjective meaning 'yes' □ **the answer was in the affirmative** the answer was 'yes'

affirmative acknowledgement /ə ,fɜːmətɪv ək'nɒlɪdʒmənt/ noun an ACK from the receiver that it has accepted the message and is ready for the next one

AFIPS abbr American Federation of Information Processing Societies

AFP /,eɪ ef 'piː/ noun a protocol used to communicate between workstations and servers in a network of Apple Macintosh computers. Full form **Appletalk Filing Protocol**

afterglow /'ɑːftəɡləʊ/ noun ♦ persistence

after-image /,ɑːftə 'ɪmɪdʒ/ noun a copy of a block of data that has been modified

AGC /,eɪ dʒiː 'siː/ noun an electronic circuit that adjusts the level of an incoming signal so that it is suitable for the next part of the circuit. Full form **automatic gain control**

agent /'eɪdʒənt/ noun **1.** a program or piece of software that runs on a workstation in a network and sends performance and statistical information about the workstation to a central network management console **2.** a series of commands or actions that are carried out automatically on a particular file or data

aggregate /'æɡrɪɡət/ noun a collection of data objects

aggregate bandwidth /,æɡrɪɡət 'bændwɪdθ/ noun the total bandwidth of a channel carrying a multiplexed data stream

aggregate function /ˌægrɪgət ˈfʌŋkʃən/ *noun* a mathematical database function performed on a selected field in every record in a selected database

aggregate line speed /ˌægrɪgət ˈlaɪn ˌspiːd/ *noun* the maximum speed at which data can be transmitted through a particular channel

aggregate operator /ˌægrɪgət ˈɒpəreɪtə/ *noun* a command in a database management program that starts an aggregate function

AGP /ˌeɪ dʒiː ˈpiː/ *noun* a dedicated bus between a graphics controller and main memory that allows data to be transferred very quickly without using the main processor. Full form **accelerated graphics port** (NOTE: It is used with the Intel Pentium II processor to provide very high-speed three-dimensional graphics and video processing. This port does not replace a PCI bus but works with it.)

AI /ˌeɪ ˈaɪ/ *noun* the design and development of computer programs that attempt to imitate human intelligence and decision-making functions, providing basic reasoning and other human characteristics. Full form **artificial intelligence**. ◊ **IKBS**

aiming symbol /ˈeɪmɪŋ ˌsɪmb(ə)l/, **aiming field** *noun* a symbol displayed on screen which defines the area in which a light-pen can be detected

airbrush /ˈeəˌbrʌʃ/ *noun* (*in graphics software*) a painting tool that creates a diffuse pattern of dots, like an mechanical airbrush ○ *We used the airbrush to create the cloud effects in this image.*

air gap /ˈeə gæp/ *noun* a narrow gap between a recording or playback head and the magnetic medium

AIX /ˌeɪ aɪ ˈeks/ a trade name for a version of UNIX produced by IBM to run on its range of PCs, minicomputers and mainframes. Full form **advanced interactive executive**

A law /ˈə lɔː/ *noun* a method of encoding digital audio data so that an 8-bit data word can contain a 13-bit audio sample

alert /əˈlɜːt/ *noun* a warning message sent from software to warn a person or application that an error or problem has occurred

alert box /əˈlɜːt bɒks/ *noun* a warning panel displayed on screen to warn a user

about something ○ *The alert box warned me that I was about to delete all my files.*

alert condition /əˌlɜːt kənˈdɪʃ(ə)n/ *noun* a status of a particular object or device that triggers an alarm

algebra /ˈældʒɪbrə/ *noun* the use of letters in certain mathematical operations to represent unknown numbers or a range of possible numbers

algebraic language /ˌældʒɪbreɪɪk ˈlæŋgwɪdʒ/ *noun* a context-free language

ALGOL /ˈælgɒl/ *noun* a high-level programming language using algorithmic methods for mathematical and technical applications. Full form **algorithmic language**

algorithm /ˈælgərɪð(ə)m/ *noun* a set of rules used to define or perform a specific task or to solve a specific problem

'…image processing algorithms are step by step procedures for performing image processing operations' [*Byte*]

'…the steps are: acquiring a digitized image, developing an algorithm to process it, processing the image, modifying the algorithm until you are satisfied with the result' [*Byte*]

algorithmic /ˌælgəˈrɪðmɪk/ *adjective* expressed using algorithms

algorithmic language /ˌælgərɪðmɪk ˈlæŋgwɪdʒ/ *noun* full form of **ALGOL**

alias /ˈeɪliəs/ *noun* a representative name given to a file, port, device or spreadsheet cell or range of cells ○ *The operating system uses the alias COM1 to represent the serial port address 3FCh.*

aliasing /ˈeɪliəsɪŋ/ *noun* jagged edges that appear along diagonal or curved lines displayed on a computer screen caused by the size of each pixel

alias name /ˈeɪliəs neɪm/ *noun* another name that is used on a network instead of the user name

alien /ˈeɪliən/ *adjective* not fitting the usual system

alien disk /ˈeɪliən dɪsk/ *noun* a disk formatted on another system or containing data in a format that cannot be read or understood ○ *When you have an alien disk select the multi-disk option to allow you to turn the disk drive into an alien disk reader.*

alien disk reader /ˌeɪliən ˈdɪsk ˌriːdə/ *noun* an add-on device that allows a computer to access data on disks from other computers or systems

align /əˈlaɪn/ *verb* **1.** to make sure that the characters to be printed are spaced and levelled correctly, either vertically or horizontally **2.** to arrange numbers into a column with all figured lines up against the right hand side (right-aligned) or the left-hand side (left-aligned) **3.** to ensure that a read/write head is correctly positioned over the recording medium

aligner /ə'laɪnə/ *noun* a device used to make sure that the paper is straight in a printer

aligning edge /ə'laɪnɪŋ edʒ/ *noun* an edge of an optical character recognition system used to position a document

alignment /ə'laɪnmənt/ *noun* the correct spacing and levelling of printed characters □ **in alignment** correctly aligned

alignment pin /ə'laɪnmənt pɪn/ *noun* a peg that fits in a hole to ensure that two devices are correctly aligned

allocate /'ælə,keɪt/ *verb* to divide a period of time or a piece of work in various ways and share it out between users ○ *The operating system allocated most of main memory to the spreadsheet program.* (NOTE: allocates – allocating – allocated)

allocation /,ælə'keɪʃ(ə)n/ *noun* the dividing of something such as memory, disk space, printer use, operating system time, or a program or device in various ways

allocation routine /,ælə'keɪʃ(ə)n ruː ,tiːn/ *noun* a short program that divides the memory resources of a system between the software and peripherals that use it

allocation unit /,ælə'keɪʃ(ə)n ,juːnɪt/ *noun* a sector or set of sectors on a hard disk that is used to store a file or part of a file

all points addressable mode /,ɔːl ,pɔɪnts ə'dresəb(ə)l ,məʊd/ *noun* a graphics mode in which each pixel can be individually addressed and its colour and attributes defined. Also called **APA mode**

alpha /'ælfə/ *noun* **1.** same as **alpha test** ○ *The new software is still in an alpha product stage.* **2.** an item of data that defines the properties of a pixel or part of an image

ALPHA /'ælfə/ *noun* a 64-bit RISC processor chip developed by Digital Equipment Corporation

alpha beta technique /,ælfə 'biːtə tek,niːk/ *noun* a free structure technique used in artificial intelligence for solving game and strategy problems

alphabetic character set /,ælfəbetɪk 'kærɪktə ,set/ *noun* the set of characters, both capitals and small letters, that make up the alphabet

alphabetic string /,ælfəbetɪk 'strɪŋ/ *noun* a string that only contains alphabetic characters

alphabetise /'ælfəbetaɪz/, **alphabetize** *verb* to put items into alphabetical order ○ *Enter the bibliographical information and alphabetise it.* (NOTE: alphabetises – alphabetising – alphabetised)

alpha blending /'ælfə ,blendɪŋ/ *noun* control over the transparency of a graphical object, normally used to display complex graphical objects such as glass and water

alpha channel /'ælfə ,tʃæn(ə)l/ *noun* (*in 32-bit graphics systems*) the top eight bits that define the properties of a pixel (NOTE: The lower 24 bits define the pixel's colour.)

alphageometric /,ælfədʒiːəʊ'metrɪk/ *adjective* referring to a set of codes that instruct a teletext terminal to display various graphics patterns or characters

alphameric /,ælfə'merɪk/ *adjective US* same as **alphanumeric**

alphamosaic /,ælfəməʊ'zeɪɪk/ *adjective* (character set) used in teletext to provide alphanumeric and graphics characters

alphanumeric /,ælfənjʊ'merɪk/ *adjective* using the letters of the alphabet, the Arabic numerals and punctuation marks (NOTE: The US term is **alphameric**.)

alphanumeric array /,ælfənjʊmerɪk ə'reɪ/ *noun* an array whose elements are letters and numbers

alphanumeric characters /,ælfənjʊmerɪk 'kærɪktəz/ *plural noun* Roman letters and Arabic numerals and other signs such as punctuation marks. Also called **alphanumerics**

alphanumeric data /,ælfənjʊmerɪk 'deɪtə/ *noun* data that represents the letters of the alphabet and the Arabic numerals

alphanumeric display /,ælfənjʊmerɪk dɪ'spleɪ/ *noun* a display device able to show characters as well as numbers

alphanumeric key /,ælfənjʊmerɪk 'kiː/ *noun* a keyboard key which produces a letter, symbol or figure

alphanumeric keyboard /,ælfənjʊmerɪk 'kiːbɔːd/ *noun* a keyboard containing character keys as well as numerical keys

alphanumeric operand /,ælfənjʊmerɪk 'ɒpərænd/ *noun* an operand which can contain alphanumeric characters, e.g. a string

alphanumerics /ˌælfənjʊ'merɪks/ *plural noun* same as **alphanumeric characters**

alphanumeric string /ˌælfənjʊmerɪk 'strɪŋ/ *noun* a series of alphanumeric characters that are manipulated and treated as a single unit

alpha-particle /'ælfə ˌpɑːtɪk(ə)l/ *noun* an emitted alpha radiation particle

alpha-particle sensitivity /ˌælfə ˌpɑːtɪk(ə)l ˌsensə'tɪvəti/ *noun* a problem experienced by certain MOS memory devices exposed to alpha radiation, causing loss of stored charge and so of data

alphaphotographic /ˌælfəfəʊtəʊ 'græfɪk/ *adjective* which represents pictures using predefined graphics characters, for teletext services

alphasort /ˌælfə'sɔːt/ *verb* to sort data into alphabetical order

alpha test /'ælfə test/ *noun* the first working attempt of a computer product. Also called **alpha**. ◊ **beta test**

alt /ɔːlt/ *noun* a type of newsgroup on the Internet that contains discussions about alternative subjects. ◊ **newsgroup** (NOTE: These are not official newsgroups and are not supported or monitored by any company, and any user can write just about anything that he or she wants to say. Some online service providers do not allow their subscribers to view all of the alt newsgroups because they may contain offensive and pornographic material.)

alternate /'ɔːltəneɪt/ *verb* to change from one state to another and back, over and over again (NOTE: alternates – alternating – alternated)

alternate character set /ɔːlˌtɜːnət 'kærɪktə ˌset/ *noun* a second set of special characters that can be accessed from a keyboard ○ *We can print Greek characters by selecting the alternate character set.*

alternate key /ɔːl'tɜːnət kiː/ *noun* a key in a database file that is not the primary key

alternate mode /ɔːl'tɜːnət məʊd/ *noun* an application for multi-user use, in which two operators can access and share a single file at the same time

alternate route /ɔːl'tɜːnət ruːt/ *noun* a backup path in a communications system, used in case of a fault or breakdown

alternating current¹ /ˌɔːltəneɪtɪŋ 'kʌrənt/ *noun* an electrical current whose value varies with time in a regular sinusoidal way, changing direction of flow each half cycle. Abbr **AC**

COMMENT: The mains electricity supply uses alternating current to minimise transmission power loss, with a frequency of 50 Hz in the UK, 60 Hz in the USA.

alternating current² /ˌɔːltəneɪtɪŋ 'kʌrənt/ *noun* full form of **AC**

alternation /ˌɔːltə'neɪʃ(ə)n/ *noun* a logical function that produces a true output if any input is true

alternative denial /ɔːlˌtɜːnətɪv dɪ 'naɪəl/ *noun* a logical function whose output is false if all inputs are true and true if any input is false

Alt key /'ɔːlt kiː/ *noun* a special key on a PC's keyboard used to activate special functions in an application ○ *Press Alt and P at the same time to print your document.*

COMMENT: The Alt key has become the standard method of activating a menu bar in any software running on a PC. For example, Alt-F normally displays the File menu of a program, Alt-X normally exits the program.

ALU /ˌeɪ el 'juː/ *noun* a section of the CPU that performs all arithmetic and logical functions. Full form **arithmetic logic unit**. Also called **arithmetic unit**. ◊ **CPU**

always on /'ɔːlweɪz ɒn/ *adjective* referring to a feature of high-speed broadband communications devices such as cable modems and ADSL that link your computer to the Internet whereby your computer appears to be permanently connected to the net and you do not need to dial up a special number

AM *abbr* amplitude modulation

ambience /'æmbiəns/ *noun* the sum of acoustic properties of a room that gives the listener a sense of space, creating echoes due to the size of the room

ambient /'æmbiənt/ *adjective* referring to normal background conditions

ambient noise /ˌæmbiənt 'nɔɪz/ *noun* normal background noise that is present all the time, usually given a reference pressure level of 0.00002 pascal in SI units

ambient temperature /ˌæmbiənt 'temprɪtʃə/ *noun* the normal average temperature of the air around a device

ambiguity /ˌæmbɪ'gjuːɪti/ *noun* something which is not clearly defined

ambiguity error /ˌæmbɪ'gjuːɪti ˌerə/ *noun* an error due to incorrect selection of ambiguous data

ambiguous /æmˈbɪgjuəs/ *adjective* which has two or more possible meanings

ambiguous filename /æmˌbɪgjuəs ˈfaɪlneɪm/ *noun* a filename which is not unique to a single file, making it difficult to locate the file

AMD a company that develops and produces processor components including a range of processors that are compatible with Intel processors and are used in many PCs. Full form **Advanced Micro Devices**

amendment record /əˌmen(d)mənt ˈrekɔːd/ *noun* a record containing new information used to update a master record or file

American National Standards Institute /əˌmerɪkən ˌnæʃ(ə)nəl ˈstændədz ˌɪnstɪtjuːt/ *noun* full form of **ANSI**

American Standard Code for Information Interchange /əˌmerɪkən ˌstændəd kəud fər ˌɪnfəmeɪʃ(ə)n ˈɪntətʃeɪndʒ/ *noun* full form of **ASCII**

America Online /əˌmerɪkə ˈɒnlaɪn/ a company that is the largest Internet service provider in the world. Abbr **AOL**

amount /əˈmaunt/ *verb* □ **to amount to** to make a total of ○ *The total keyboarded characters amount to ten million.*

amp /æmp/ *noun* same as **ampere** (NOTE: used with figures: **a 13-amp fuse**)

ampere /ˈæmpeə/ *noun* the base SI unit of electrical current, defined as the current flowing through an impedance of one ohm which has a voltage of one volt across it. Abbr **A**

amplification /ˌæmplɪfɪˈkeɪʃ(ə)n/ *noun* the output-to-input signal strength ratio ○ *Increase the amplification of the input signal.*

amplifier /ˈæmplɪˌfaɪə/ *noun* an electronic circuit that magnifies the power of a signal

amplify /ˈæmplɪˌfaɪ/ *verb* to magnify a signal power or amplitude ○ *The received signal needs to be amplified before it can be processed.* (NOTE: amplifies – amplifying – amplified)

amplitude /ˈæmplɪˌtjuːd/ *noun* the strength or size of a signal

amplitude modulation /ˈæmplɪtjuːd mɒdjuˌleɪʃ(ə)n/ *noun* a method of carrying data by varying the size of a carrier signal of fixed frequency according to the data

amplitude quantisation /ˌæmplɪtjuːd ˌkwɒntaɪˈzeɪʃ(ə)n/ *noun* conversion of an analog signal to a numerical representation

analog /ˈænəlɒg/, **analogue** /ˈæn(ə)lɒg/ *noun* the representation and measurement of numerical data by continuously variable physical quantities, as for the size of electrical voltages. Compare **digital**

analog channel /ˌænəlɒg ˈtʃæn(ə)l/ *noun* a communications line that carries analog signals such as speech

analog computer /ˌænəlɒg kəmˈpjuːtə/ *noun* a computer which processes data in analog form, represented by a continuously varying signal

analog data /ˌænəlɒg ˈdeɪtə/ *noun* data that is represented as a continuously variable signal. Speech is a form of analog data.

analog display /ˌænəlɒg dɪˈspleɪ/ *noun* a display or monitor that can display an infinite range of colours or shades of grey, unlike a digital display that can only display a finite range of colours. VGA monitors are a form of analog display.

analog gate /ˈænəlɒg geɪt/ *noun* a logic gate whose output is proportional to an input signal

analog input card /ˌænəlɒg ˈɪnput ˌkɑːd/ *noun* all circuitry on one PCB required for amplifying and converting analog input signals to a digital form

analog line /ˌænəlɒg ˈlaɪn/ *noun* a communications line that carries analog signals, e.g. a telephone line

analog loopback /ˌænəlɒg ˈluːpbæk/ *noun* a test mode on a modem used to test the serial port of the local computer or terminal □ **analog loopback with selftest** a test mode on a modem used to test the serial port of the modem

analog monitor /ˌænəlɒg ˈmɒnɪtə/ *noun* a display screen that uses a continuously variable input signal to control the colours display so that it can display a near infinite range of colours

analog output card /ˌænəlɒg ˌaut ˈput ˌkɑːd/ *noun* all circuitry on one PCB required to convert digital output data from a computer to an analog form

analog recording /ˌænəlɒg rɪˈkɔːdɪŋ/ *noun* the storing of signals in their natural form without conversion to digital form

analog representation /ˌænəlɒg ˌreprɪzenˈteɪʃ(ə)n/ *noun* a value or variable in analog form

analog signal /ˌænəlɒg ˈsɪgn(ə)l/ *noun* a continuously varying signal

analog to digital /ˌænəlɒg tə ˈdɪdʒɪt(ə)l/ *adjective* referring to changing a signal from an analog form to a digitally coded form. Abbr **A/D, A to D**

analog to digital converter /ˌænəlɒg tə ˌdɪdʒɪt(ə)l kənˈvɜːtə/ *noun* full form of **ADC**

analog transmission /ˌænəlɒg trænzˈmɪʃ(ə)n/ *noun* data transmission in which the data is sent as a series of changes in a continuously varying signal

analyser /ˈænəlaɪzə/ *noun* a piece of electronic test equipment that displays various features of a signal (NOTE: The US spelling is **analyzer**.)

analyst /ˈænəlɪst/ *noun* a person who carries out an analysis of a problem

analytical engine /ˌænəlɪtɪk(ə)l ˈendʒɪn/ *noun* a mechanical calculating machine developed by Charles Babbage in 1833 that is generally considered the first general-purpose digital computer

anamorphic /ˌænəˈmɔːfɪk/ *adjective* referring to an image that has unequal vertical and horizontal scaling, making it appear squashed or taller than the original

ancestral file /æn ˌsestrəl ˈfaɪl/ *noun* a system of backing up files based on a son to father to grandfather file, where the son is the current working file

anchor cell /ˈæŋkə sel/ *noun* a cell in a spreadsheet program that defines the start of a range of cells

ancillary equipment /ænˌsɪləri ɪˈkwɪpmənt/ *noun* equipment which is used to make a task easier but which is not absolutely necessary

AND /ænd/ *noun* an operator, often used in searches, that matches text that contains both search words. Compare **OR** (NOTE: For example, searching for 'cat AND dog' finds all entries that contain both the words 'cat' and 'dog')

AND circuit, AND element *noun* same as **AND gate**

AND function /ˈænd ˌfʌŋkʃən/ *noun* a logical function whose output is true if both its inputs are true. Also called **coincidence function**

COMMENT: If both inputs are 1, results of the AND will be 1. If one of the input digits is 0, then AND will produce a 0.

AND gate /ˈænd geɪt/ *noun* electronic gate that performs a logical AND function on electrical signals. Also called **AND circuit, AND element**. Compare **coincidence gate**

AND operation /ˈænd ˌɒpəreɪʃ(ə)n/ *noun* the processing of two or more input signals, outputting their AND function

anechoic chamber /ˌænekəʊɪk ˈtʃeɪmbə/ *noun* a perfectly quiet room in which sound or radio waves do not reflect off the walls

angle /ˈæŋgəl/ *noun* a measure of the change in direction, usually as the distance turned from a reference line

angled line /ˌæŋgləd ˈlaɪn/ *noun* a line with three or more points, e.g. a zig-zag

angstrom /ˈæŋstrɒm/ *noun* a unit of measurement equal to one thousand millionth of a metre. Abbr **Å**

ANI /ˌeɪ en ˈaɪ/ *noun* a telephone system which displays the telephone number of the caller. Full form **automatic number identification**

animated GIF /ˌænɪˌmeɪtɪd ˌdʒiː aɪ ˈef/ *noun* a simple animation effect created by saving several small graphic images within one file so that they can be repeatedly displayed in sequence giving an impression of animation. It is often used to create animated buttons or other effects on a webpage. ◊ **transparent GIF**

animation /ˌænɪˈmeɪʃ(ə)n/ *noun* the creation of the illusion of movement by displaying a series of slightly different images on screen very rapidly to give the effect of smooth movement. Also called **computer animation**

animation software /ˌænɪˈmeɪʃ(ə)n ˌsɒftweə/ *noun* software that allows you to draw several separate frames, each slightly different, and then display them one after another in rapid succession to give the impression of movement. Each frame is called a cel and the objects that move are normally called actors.

animatronics /ˌænɪməˈtrɒnɪks/ *noun* a technology that uses computers and a form of radio control to make puppets or other models appear to move in a lifelike way, e.g. in films

annotation /ˌænəˈteɪʃ(ə)n/ *noun* a comment or note in a program which explains how the program is to be used

annotation symbol /ˌænəʊˈteɪʃ(ə)n ˌsɪmb(ə)l/ *noun* a symbol used when making flowcharts, to allow comments to be added

announce /ə'naʊns/ *verb* to publicise a new or updated website by registering the domain name with the main search engines; (NOTE: announces – announcing – announced)

COMMENT: Each search engine allows a person to add a new website and enter a description and category. Because there are now several hundred search engines, special software utilities are available to automatically register the website with each engine.

annunciator /ə'nʌnsieɪtə/ *noun* a signal which can be heard or seen in order to attract attention

anode /'ænəʊd/ *noun* a positive electrical terminal of a device

anonymiser /ə'nɒnɪmaɪzə/, **anonymizer** *noun* a website that allows a person to browse the World Wide Web without leaving any traces of his or her identity

anonymous FTP /ə,nɒnɪməs ef tiː 'piː/ *noun* a method commonly used on the Internet that allows a user to connect to a remote computer using the FTP protocol and log in as a guest to download publicly accessible files. ◊ **FTP** (NOTE: If you are using the FTP protocol to connect to a remote computer and you are asked for a login name and password, you can normally gain access to the remote computer's public areas by entering 'anonymous' as the login user name and your full email address as the password.)

ANSI /'ænsi/ a US organisation which specifies computer and software standards, including those of high-level programming languages (*US*) Full form **American National Standards Institute**

ANSI C /,ænsi 'siː/ *noun* a standard version of the C programming language

ANSI driver /'ænsi ,draɪvə/ *noun* a small resident software program in a PC that interprets ANSI screen control codes and controls the screen appropriately

ANSI escape sequence /,ænsi ɪ 'skeɪp ,siːkwəns/ *noun* a sequence of ANSI screen control characters that controls the colours and attributes of text on screen (NOTE: The sequence must begin with the ASCII character Esc (ASCII 27) and the character [(ASCII 91).)

ANSI keyboard /,ænsi 'kiːbɔːd/ *noun* a standard for a keyboard that provides either uppercase or upper and lowercase characters on a typewriter-style keyboard

ANSI screen control /,ænsi 'skriːn kən,trəʊl/ *noun* a set of standard codes developed by ANSI that control how colours and simple graphics are displayed on a computer screen

answer /'ɑːnsə/ *verb* to reply to a signal and set up a communications link ○ *The first modem originates the call and the second answers it.*

answer back /'ɑːnsə bæk/ *noun* a signal sent by a receiving computer to identify itself

answering machine /'ɑːns(ə)rɪŋ mə ,ʃiːn/ *noun* an application software that runs on a PC and controls a modem that has voice-mail functionality

answer mode /'ɑːnsə məʊd/ *noun* the state of a modem that is waiting to receive a telephone call and establish a connection

answer modem /'ɑːnsə ,məʊdem/ *noun* the state of a modem that emits an answertone before establishing a connection with an originate modem

answer/originate, **answer/originate device** *noun* a communications device, e.g. a modem, that can receive or send data

answer time /'ɑːnsə taɪm/ *noun* the time taken for a receiving device to respond to a signal

answertone /'ɑːnsətəʊn/ *noun* a tone an answering modem emits before the carrier is exchanged

anthropomorphic software /,ænθrəpəmɔːfɪk 'sɒftweə/ *noun* artificial intelligence software that appears to react to what a user says

anti-aliasing /,ænti 'eɪliəsɪŋ/ *noun* **1.** a method of reducing the effects of jagged edges in graphics by using shades of grey to blend in along edges. Also called **dejagging 2.** a method of adding sound signals between the sound samples to create a smoother sound

anticoincidence circuit /,æntikəʊ 'ɪnsɪdəns ,sɜːkɪt/, **anticoincidence function** *noun* a logical function whose output is true if either of two inputs is true, and false if both inputs are the same

anti-static mat /,ænti ,stætɪk 'mæt/ *noun* a special rubberised mat which dissipates static electricity charge through an electrical earth connection (NOTE: An operator touches the mat before handling sensitive electronic components that could be damaged by static electricity.)

anti-tinkle suppression /,ænti 'tɪŋk(ə)l sə,preʃ(ə)n/ *noun* a switch that prevents other telephones on a line ringing when a modem dials out

anti-virus program /ˌænti ˈvaɪrəs ˌprəʊɡræm/ *noun* a software program that looks for virus software on a computer and destroys it before it can damage data or files

anti-virus software /ˌænti ˈvaɪrəs ˌsɒftweə/ *noun* software that removes a virus from a file

anycast /ˈenikɑːst/ *noun* a type of communication in which a single computer user sends data across a network to the nearest of a group of receivers

AOL *abbr* America Online

APA *abbr* all points addressable

Apache HTTPD /əˌpætʃi ˌeɪtʃ tiː tiː piː ˈdiː/ *noun* a popular piece of web server software that provides the basic functions required to operate a web server on a computer

aperture /ˈæpətʃə/ *noun* an opening in a device that allows a certain amount of light or a signal to pass through it

aperture mask /ˈæpətʃə mɑːsk/ *noun* a mask used in colour monitors to keep the red, green and blue beams separate

API /ˌeɪ piː ˈaɪ/ *noun* a set of standard program functions and commands that allow any programmer to interface a program with another application ○ *If I follow the published API for this system, my program will work properly.* Full form **application programming interface**

APL /ˌeɪ piː ˈel/ *noun* a high-level programming language used in scientific and mathematical work. Full form **A programming language**

APM /ˌeɪ piː ˈem/ *noun* a specification that allows an operating system such as older Windows to control the power management features of a computer. Full form **advanced power management**. ◊ **ACPI** (NOTE: This standard has been replaced by the ACPI standard in Windows 98 and Windows NT 5.0.)

APPC /ˌeɪ piː piː ˈsiː/ *noun* a set of protocols developed by IBM that allows peer-to-peer communication between workstations connected to an SNA network. Full form **advanced program to program communication**. Also called **LU 6.2 protocols**

append /əˈpend/ *verb* **1.** to add data to an existing file or record ○ *If you enter the DOS command COPY A+B, the file B will*

be appended to the end of file A. **2.** to add a file or data to the end of an existing file

Apple Computer Corporation /ˌæp(ə)l kəmˈpjuːtə ˌkɔːpəreɪʃ(ə)n/ a company, formed in 1975, that has developed a range of personal computers including the Apple II, Apple Lisa and, more recently, the Apple Mac

'Apple Computer has fleshed out details of a migration path to the PowerPC RISC architecture for its 7 million Apple Macintosh users. Developments in the pipeline include PowerPC versions of the AppleTalk Remote Access networking protocol.' [*Computing*]

Apple Desktop Bus /ˌæp(ə)l ˌdesktɒp ˈbʌs/ a trade name for a serial bus built into Apple Macs that allows low-speed devices, e.g. the keyboard and mouse, to communicate with the processor. Abbr **ADB**

Apple file exchange /ˌæp(ə)l ˈfaɪl ɪksˌtʃeɪndʒ/ a trade name for a software program that runs on an Apple Mac allowing it to read disks from a PC

Apple filing protocol /ˌæp(ə)l ˈfaɪlɪŋ ˌprəʊtəkɒl/ a trade name for a method of storing files on a network server so that they can be accessed from an Apple Mac. Abbr **AFP**

Apple Key /ˈæp(ə)l kiː/ a trade name for a special key on the keyboard of an Apple Mac that, when pressed with another key, provides a short-cut to a menu selection

Apple Mac /ˈæp(ə)l mæk/ , **Apple Macintosh computer** a trade name for any of a range of personal computers developed by Apple Computer Corporation that has a graphical user interface and uses the 68000 family of processors

AppleScript /ˈæp(ə)lskrɪpt/ a trade name for a script language built into the operation system of an Apple Mac that allows a user to automate simple tasks

Appleshare /ˈæp(ə)lʃeə/ a trade name for software that allows Apple Macs to share files and printers using a file server

Apple System /ˌæp(ə)l ˈsɪstəm/ a trade name for a version of the operating system for the Apple Mac that introduces multitasking, virtual memory and peer-to-peer file sharing

applet /ˈæplət/ *noun* **1.** a small utility within Microsoft Windows, originally any of the icons in the Control Panel window, but now any piece of software that is used to configure the computer ○ *There are applets to help format your disk and configure your keyboard.* **2.** a small applications on the Internet designed to enhance the functionality of a webpage. ◊ **ActiveX, Java, VBScript** (NOTE: For example, if you want to add multimedia effects to your webpage, you cannot carry out these functions with standard HTML commands, but you could write a small ActiveX program, called an applet, that is automatically downloaded by the user's browser and run on the user's computer.)

AppleTalk /ˈæp(ə)ltɑːk/ a trade name for a communications protocol developed by the Apple Computer Corporation that carries data over network hardware between two or more Apple Macs and peripherals (NOTE: AppleTalk is similar to the seven-layer OSI protocol model. It can link up to 32 devices, uses a CSMA/CA design and transmits data at 230 Kbps.)

AppleTalk Filing Protocol /ˌæp(ə)l tɔːk ˈfaɪlɪŋ ˌprəʊtəkɒl/ full form of **AFP**

appliance computer /əˌplaɪəns kəm ˈpjuːtə/ noun a ready-to-run computer system that can be bought in a shop, taken home and used immediately for a particular purpose. ◊ **turnkey system**

application /ˌæplɪˈkeɪʃ(ə)n/ noun a task which a computer performs or a problem which a computer solves

application configuration access protocol /ˌæplɪkeɪʃ(ə)n kənˌfɪɡjʊ reɪʃ(ə)n ˈækses ˌprəʊtəkɒl/ full form of **ACAP**

application developer /ˌæplɪkeɪʃ(ə)n dɪˈveləpə/ noun a programmer who designs the look of an application and defines its functions

application file /ˌæplɪˈkeɪʃ(ə)n faɪl/ noun a binary file stored on disk that contains the machine code instructions of a program

application form /æplɪˈkeɪʃ(ə)n fɔːm/ noun a form to be filled in when applying for something ○ to fill in an application form for an account on the system

application generator /ˌæplɪ ˈkeɪʃ(ə)n ˌdʒenəreɪtə/ noun a piece of special software that allows a programmer to define the main functions and look of an application. The generator then automatically creates the instructions to carry out the defined application.

application icon /ˌæplɪˈkeɪʃ(ə)n ˌaɪkɒn/ noun a small image or graphical symbol that represents an application program in a graphical user interface

application layer /ˌæplɪˈkeɪʃ(ə)n ˌleɪə/ noun the seventh and top layer in an ISO/OSI network, which allows a user to requests functions such as transfer files, send mail and use resources. The other layers are not normally accessed by users.

application orientated language /ˌæplɪkeɪʃ(ə)n ˌɔːriənteɪtɪd ˈlæŋɡwɪdʒ/ noun a programming language that provides functions which allow the user to solve certain application problems

application package /ˌæplɪˈkeɪʃ(ə)n ˌpækɪdʒ/ noun a set of computer programs and manuals that cover all aspects of a particular task, e.g. payroll, stock control or tax. Also called **applications package**

application program /ˌæplɪˈkeɪʃ(ə)n ˌprəʊɡræm/ noun a piece of application software ○ The multi-window editor is used to create and edit applications programs.

application programming interface /ˌæplɪkeɪʃ(ə)n ˈprəʊɡræmɪŋ ˌɪntəfeɪs/ noun full form of **API**

application service element /ˌæplɪkeɪʃ(ə)n ˈsɜːvɪs ˌelɪmənt/ noun a part of a program in the application layer of an OSI environment that interacts with the layers beneath it

application service provider /ˌæplɪkeɪʃ(ə)n ˈsɜːvɪs prəˌvaɪdə/ noun a specialist company that installs, configures and manages software on its own server and then allows any business to use the software via the Internet or a private network. Abbr **ASP** (NOTE: The user does not realise that the software is located on a distant server, and the business does not need to buy or support the software, just rent it.)

application software /ˌæplɪkeɪʃ(ə)n ˈsɒftweə/ noun software designed to make the computer do what is required and perform particular tasks. Also called **applications software**

applications package /ˌæplɪ ˈkeɪʃ(ə)nz ˌpækɪdʒ/ noun same as **application package**

application specific integrated circuits /ˌæplɪkeɪʃ(ə)n spəˌsɪfɪk ˌɪntɪɡreɪtɪd ˈsɜːkɪts/ noun full form of **ASIC**

applications programmer /ˌæplɪ ˈkeɪʃ(ə)nz ˌprəʊɡræmə/ noun a programmer who writes application software

applications software /ˌæplɪ
ˈkeɪʃ(ə)nz ˌsɒftweə/ *noun* same as **application software**

application terminal /ˌæplɪˈkeɪʃ(ə)n
ˌtɜːmɪn(ə)l/, **applications terminal**
/ˌæplɪˈkeɪʃ(ə)nz ˌtɜːmɪn(ə)l/ *noun* a terminal, e.g. at a sales desk, which is specially configured to carry out certain tasks

application window /ˌæplɪˈkeɪʃ(ə)n
ˌwɪndəʊ/ *noun* an application program
running in a window displayed in a graphical user interface such as Microsoft's
Windows

APPN /ˌeɪ piː piː ˈen/ *noun* an extension
to the IBM SNA protocol that allows
workstations to share information on a
peer-to-peer basis without the need for a
central mainframe. Full form **advanced
peer-to-peer networking** (NOTE: It is often used to route information around a
network and dynamically adjusts the
route if part of the network is damaged.)

approximation error /əˌprɒksɪ
ˈmeɪʃ(ə)n ˌerə/ *noun* an error caused by
rounding off a real number

A programming language /ˌeɪ
ˈprəʊɡræmɪŋ ˌlæŋɡwɪdʒ/ *noun* full form
of **APL**

APT /ˌeɪ piː ˈtiː/ *noun* a programming
language used to control numerically controlled machines. Full form **automatically programmed tools**

Arabic figures /ˌærəbɪk ˈfɪɡəz/ *noun*
same as **Arabic numbers**

Arabic numbers /ˌærəbɪk ˈnʌmbəz/,
Arabic figures /ˌærəbɪk ˈfɪɡəz/, **Arabic
numerals** /ˌærəbɪk ˈnjuːmərəl/ *noun*
figures such as 1, 2, 3, 4, etc. (as opposed
to the Roman numerals I, II, III. IV, etc.) ○
*The page numbers are written in Arabic
figures.*

arbitration software /ˌɑːbɪˈtreɪʃ(ə)n
ˌsɒftweə/ *noun* software that is responsible for allocating resources to devices, often used to manage the way Plug and Play
adapters use other resources in a computer

Archie /ˈɑːtʃiː/ *noun* a system of servers
on the Internet that catalogue the public
files available on the Internet

architecture /ˈɑːkɪtektʃə/ *noun* the
layout and interconnection of a computer's
internal hardware and the logical relationships between CPU, memory and I/O devices

'Software giant Microsoft is also interested in using
Xerox' Glyph technology as part of its Microsoft At
Work architecture that seeks to unite office comput-
ers with fax machines and copiers.' [*Computing*]

archival quality /ˈɑːkaɪv(ə)l ˌkwɒləti/
noun the length of time that a copy can be
stored before it becomes illegible

archive /ˈɑːkaɪv/ *noun* storage of data
over a long period ■ *verb* to put data in
storage (NOTE: archives – archiving – archived)

archive attribute /ˈɑːkaɪv əˈtrɪbjuːt/,
archive bit *noun* a special attribute attached to a file that indicates if the file has
been archived since it was last changed.
Also called **archive flag**

archived copy /ˈɑːkaɪvd ˈkɒpi/ *noun* a
copy kept in storage

archive file /ˈɑːkaɪv faɪl/ *noun* a file
containing data which is out of date but
which is kept for future reference

archive flag /ˈɑːkaɪv flæɡ/ *noun* same
as **archive attribute**

archive site /ˈɑːkaɪv saɪt/ *noun* one
computer on the Internet that provides a
vast collection of public-domain files and
programs, copied from other computers
around the Internet, that a user can download

archive storage /ˈɑːkaɪv ˈstɔːrɪdʒ/
noun storage of data for a long period of
time

area /ˈeəriə/ *noun* a section of memory or
code that is reserved for a certain purpose

area fill /ˈeəriə fɪl/ *noun* (*in graphics*) an
instruction to fill an area of the screen or
an enclosed pattern with a colour or pattern

area graph /ˈeəriə ɡrɑːf/ *noun* a line
graph in which the area below the line is
filled with a pattern or colour

area search /ˈeəriə sɜːtʃ/ *noun* a
search for specific data within a certain
section of memory or files

arg /ɑːɡ/ *noun* same as **argument**

argument /ˈɑːɡjʊmənt/ *noun* a variable
acted upon by an operator or function ○ *If
you enter the words 'MULTIPLY A, B', the
processor will recognise the operator,
MULTIPLY, and use it with the two arguments, A and B.* ◊ **operand**. Abbr **arg**

argument separator /ˈɑːɡjʊmənt
ˌsepəreɪtə/ *noun* a punctuation mark or
symbol that separates several arguments
on one line ○ *The command 'MULTIPLY
A, B' uses a comma as the argument separator.*

arithmetic capability /ˌærɪθmetɪk
ˌkeɪpəˈbɪlɪti/ *noun* the ability of a device
to perform mathematical functions

arithmetic check /ə'rɪθmətɪk tʃek/ *noun* a further arithmetic operation carried out to ensure that a result is correct

arithmetic functions /ə,rɪθmətɪk 'fʌŋkʃənz/ *plural noun* calculations carried out on numbers, e.g. addition, subtraction, multiplication and division

arithmetic instruction /,ærɪθmetɪk ɪn'strʌkʃən/ *noun* an instruction to perform an arithmetic operation on data rather than a logical function

arithmetic logic unit /,ærɪθmetɪk 'lɒdʒɪk ,juːnɪt/ *noun* full form of **ALU**

arithmetic operation /,ærɪθmetɪk ,ɒpə'reɪʃ(ə)n/ *noun* a mathematical function carried out on data

arithmetic operator /,ærɪθmetɪk 'ɒpəreɪtə/ *noun* a symbol which indicates an arithmetic function, e.g. + for addition, x for multiplication

arithmetic register /,ærɪθmetɪk 'redʒɪstə/ *noun* a memory location which stores operands

arithmetic shift /,ærɪθmetɪk 'ʃɪft/ *noun* a word or data moved one bit to the left or right inside a register, losing the bit shifted off the end

arithmetic unit /,ærɪθmetɪk 'juːnɪt/ *noun* same as **ALU**

arm /ɑːm/ *verb* 1. to prepare a device or machine or routine for action or inputs 2. to define which interrupt lines are active

armed interrupt /ɑːmd 'ɪntərʌpt/ *noun* an interrupt line which has been made active, using an interrupt mask

ARP /,eɪ ɑː 'piː/ *noun* a protocol within the TCP/IP standard that is used to determine whether the source and destination address in a packet are in the data-link control or Internet protocol format. Full form **address resolution protocol** (NOTE: Once the format of the address is known, the packet can be correctly routed over a network.)

ARPANET /'ɑːpənet/ *noun* the original network of interconnected computers, linked by leased lines, that formed the first prototype for the current Internet. It was developed by the US Department of Defense. Full form **advanced research projects agency network**

ARQ /,eɪ ɑː 'kjuː/ *noun* an error correction system, used in some modems, which asks for data to be re-transmitted if it contains errors. Full form **automatic repeat request**

array /ə'reɪ/ *noun* an ordered structure containing individually accessible elements referenced by numbers, used to store tables or sets of related data

array bounds /ə'reɪ baʊndz/ *plural noun* limits to the number of elements which can be given in an array

array dimension /ə'reɪ daɪ,menʃ(ə)n/ *noun* the number of elements in an array, given as rows and columns

array element /ə'reɪ ,elɪmənt/ *noun* one individual piece of data within an array

array processor /ə'reɪ ,prəʊsesə/ *noun* a computer that can act upon several arrays of data simultaneously, for very fast mathematical applications ○ *The array processor allows the array that contains the screen image to be rotated with one simple command.*

arrow key /'ærəʊ kiː/ *noun* each of a set of four keys on a keyboard that move the cursor or pointer around the screen, controlling movement up, down, left and right

arrow pointer /,ærəʊ 'pɔɪntə/ *noun* a small arrow on-screen that you can move using the mouse

artefact /'ɑːtɪfækt/, **artifact** *noun* 1. a very small error in a video signal 2. a very small error in a digital version of an analog signal

article /'ɑːtɪk(ə)l/ *noun* one message in a newsgroup

artifact /'ɑːtɪfækt/ *noun* another spelling of **artefact**

artificial intelligence /,ɑːtɪfɪʃ(ə)l ɪn 'telɪdʒ(ə)ns/ *noun* full form of **AI**

artificial life /,ɑːtɪfɪʃ(ə)l 'laɪf/ *noun* the use of computer systems to imitate aspects of natural human behaviour such as learning and reproduction

artificial neural network /,ɑːtɪfɪʃ(ə)l 'njʊərəl ,netwɜːk/ *noun* a system for processing information that is made up of interconnected elements that behave in a similar way to the neurons in the human nervous system and have the ability to learn through experience

artwork /'ɑːt,wɜːk/ *noun* graphical work or images

ascend /ə'send/ *verb* to increase

ascender /ə'sendə/ *noun* a part of a character that rises above the main line of printed characters, e.g. the upward line of a 'b' or 'd'

ascending order /əˌsendɪŋ ˈɔːdə/ *noun* an arrangement of data with the smallest value or date first in the list

ASCII /ˈæskiː/ *noun* a code which represents alphanumeric characters in binary code. Full form **American Standard Code for Information Interchange**

ASCII character /ˈæski ˌkærɪktə/ *noun* a character which is in the ASCII list of codes

ASCII file /ˈæski faɪl/ *noun* a stored file containing only ASCII coded character data ○ *Use a word processor or other program that generates a standard ASCII file.*

ASCII keyboard /ˌæski ˈkiːbɔːd/ *noun* a keyboard that provides a key for every ASCII code

ASCII text /ˈæski tekst/ *noun* the set of letter and number characters with an ASCII code between 0 and 127

ASCIIZ string /ˌæskiː ˈzed ˌstrɪŋ/ *noun* a sequence of ASCII characters followed by the ASCII code zero that indicates the end of the sequence in programming

ASF /ˌeɪ es ˈef/ *noun* a multimedia delivery format developed by Microsoft for delivery over the Internet and used in its NetShow product. Full form **active streaming format**

ASIC /ˌeɪ es aɪ ˈsiː/ *plural noun* specially designed ICs for one particular function or to special specifications. Full form **application specific integrated circuits**

ASP *abbr* **1.** Active Server Page **2.** application service provider

aspect ratio /ˌæspekt ˈreɪʃiəʊ/ *noun* the ratio of the width to the height of pixel shapes

aspect system /ˌæspekt ˈsɪstəm/ *noun* a method of storing and indexing documents in a retrieval system

ASR /ˌeɪ es ˈɑː/ *noun* a device or terminal that can transmit and receive information. Full form **automatic send/receive**. Compare **KSR**

COMMENT: An ASR terminal can input information via a keyboard or via a tape cassette or paper tape. It can receive information and store it in internal memory or on tape.

ASR keyboard /ˌeɪ es ɑː ˈkiːbɔːd/ *noun* a communications console keyboard that has all the characters and punctuation keys and special control, send and receive keys

assemble /əˈsemb(ə)l/ *verb* **1.** to put a hardware or software product together from various smaller parts ○ *The parts for*

the disk drive are made in Japan and assembled in France. (NOTE: assembles – assembling – assembled) **2.** to translate assembly code into machine code ○ *There is a short wait during which time the program is assembled into object code.* **3.** to insert specific library routines or macros or parameters into a program

assembler /əˈsemblə/ *noun* a program which converts a program written in assembly language into machine code. Also called **assembler program**

assembler error messages /əˌsemblə ˈerə ˌmesɪdʒ/ *plural noun* messages produced by an assembler that indicate that errors have been found in the source code

assembler language /əˈsemblə ˌlæŋgwɪdʒ/ *noun* same as **assembly language**

assembler mnemonic /əˌsemblə nɪ ˈmɒnɪk/ *noun* a standard word abbreviation used when writing a program for a particular CPU in assembly language, e.g. LDA for load register A

assembler program /əˈsemblə ˌprəʊɡræm/ *noun* same as **assembler**

assembly /əˈsemblɪ/ *noun* the process of putting an item together from various parts ○ *There are no assembly instructions to show you how to put the computer together.*

assembly code /əˈsembli kəʊd/ *noun* a set of mnemonics which are used to represent machine code instructions in an assembler program

assembly language /əˈsembli ˌlæŋgwɪdʒ/ *noun* a programming language using mnemonics to code instructions which will then be converted to machine code. Also called **assembler language, base language**

assembly listing /əˈsembli ˌlɪstɪŋ/ *noun* a display of an assembler ordered according to memory location

assembly plant /əˈsembli plɑːnt/ *noun* a factory where units are put together from parts made in other factories

assembly routine /əˈsembli ruːˌtiːn/, **assembly system** /əˈsemblɪ ˌsɪstəm/ *noun* a part of a computer program that translates assembly code into machine code

assembly system /əˈsemblɪ ˌsɪstəm/ *noun* same as **assembly routine**

assembly time /ə'sembli taɪm/ *noun* the time taken by an assembler to translate a program

assertion /ə'sɜːʃ(ə)n/ *noun* a program statement of a fact or rule

assets /'æsets/ *plural noun* separate data elements such as video, audio and image that are used in a multimedia application

assign /ə'saɪn/ *verb* **1.** to give a computer or person something to do ○ *He was assigned the job of checking the sales figures.* **2.** to set a variable equal to a string of characters or numbers **3.** to keep part of a computer system for use while a program is running

assigned numbers /ə,saɪnd 'nʌmbəz/ *plural noun* unique numbers that are each assigned to an Internet or network manufacturer's device, protocol or other resource (NOTE: Manufacturers apply for a unique ID number from the IANA organisation.)

assignment /ə'saɪnmənt/ *noun* the process of setting a variable equal to a value or string or character

assignment compatible /ə ,saɪnmənt kəm'pætəb(ə)l/ *adjective* (*in the Pascal programming language*) referring to a value whose type is established by a check to be allowed

assignment conversion /ə ,saɪnmənt kən'vɜːʃ(ə)n/ *noun* (*in the C and Fortran programming languages*) an operation to change the type of a value

assignment statement /ə,saɪnmənt 'steɪtmənt/ *noun* a basic programming command that sets a variable equal to a value or string or character

associated document /faɪl/, **associated file** *noun* a document or file that is linked to its originating application (NOTE: When you select the file, the operating system automatically starts the originating application.)

associative addressing /ə,səʊsiətɪv ə'dresɪŋ/ *noun* the identification of a location by its contents rather than its address. Also called **content-addressable addressing**

associative memory /ə,səʊsiətɪv 'mem(ə)ri/ *noun* a method of data retrieval that uses part of the data rather than an address to locate the data. Also called **associative storage**

associative processor /ə,səʊsiətɪv 'prəʊsesə/ *noun* a processor that uses associative memory

associative storage /ə,səʊsiətɪv 'stɔːrɪdʒ/ *noun* same as **associative memory**

associative storage register /ə ,səʊsiətɪv 'stɔːrɪdʒ ,redʒɪstə/ *noun* a register that is located by its contents rather than a name or address

asterisk /'æstərɪsk/ *noun* **1.** a graphical symbol (*) used in programming as a sign for multiplication **2.** a graphical symbol (*) used as a wildcard in many operating systems, including DOS, to mean any characters

asterisk fill /'æst(ə)rɪsk fɪl/ *noun* the filling of unused decimal places with the asterisk symbol

asymmetric compression /,æsɪ ,metrɪk kəm'preʃ(ə)n/ *noun* a method of reducing the space taken by data

Asymmetric Digital Subscriber Line /,æsɪ,metrɪk ,dɪdʒɪt(ə)l səb 'skraɪbə ,laɪn/ *noun* full form of **ADSL**

asymmetric transmission /eɪsɪ ,metrɪk trænz'mɪʃ(ə)n/ *noun* a method of data transmission which has two different speeds for data received by the computer and data transmitted by the computer

asymmetric video compression /eɪsɪ,metrɪk 'vɪdiəʊ kəm,preʃ(ə)n/ *noun* the use of a powerful computer to compress video, allowing it to be played back on a less powerful computer

async /eɪ'sɪŋk/ *adjective* same as **asynchronous** (*informal*)

asynchronous /ə'sɪŋkrənəs/ *adjective* referring to serial data or equipment which does not depend on being synchronised with another piece of equipment

asynchronous access /eɪ,sɪŋkrənəs 'ækses/ *noun* communication using handshaking to synchronise data transmission

asynchronous cache /eɪ,sɪŋkrənəs 'kæʃ/ *noun* a type of cache memory that provides the slowest performance and uses a type of SDRAM that is cheap but slow

asynchronous communication /eɪ ,sɪŋkrənəs kə,mjuːnɪ'keɪʃ(ə)n/ *noun* data transmission between devices that is not synchronized to a clock, but is transmitted when ready

asynchronous communication server /eɪ,sɪŋkrənəs kə,mjuːnɪ 'keɪʃ(ə)n ,sɜːvə/ *noun* full form of **ACS**

asynchronous communications interface adapter /əˌsɪŋkrənəs kə ˌmjuːnɪkeɪʃ(ə)nz ˈɪntəfeɪs əˌdæptə/ noun full form of **ACIA**

asynchronous computer /eɪ ˌsɪŋkrənəs kəmˈpjuːtə/ noun **1.** a computer that changes from one operation to the next according to signals received when the process is finished **2.** a computer in which a process starts on the arrival of signals or data rather than on a clock pulse

asynchronous data transfer /eɪ ˌsɪŋkrənəs ˌdeɪtə ˈtrænsfɜː/ noun transfer of data between two devices that takes place without any regular or predictable timing signal

asynchronous mode /eɪˈsɪŋkrənəs məʊd/ noun the state of a terminal linked to another piece of equipment in a way in which the two need not be synchronised

asynchronous port /eɪˌsɪŋkrənəs ˈpɔːt/ noun a connection to a computer allowing asynchronous data access ○ Since asynchronous ports are used no special hardware is required.

asynchronous procedure call /eɪ ˌsɪŋkrənəs prəˈsiːdʒə ˌkɔːl/ noun a program function that runs separately from the main program and will execute when a particular set of conditions exist. Abbr **APC**

asynchronous transfer mode /eɪ ˌsɪŋkrənəs ˈtrænsfɜː ˌməʊd/ noun full form of **ATM**

asynchronous transmission /eɪ ˌsɪŋkrənəs trænzˈmɪʃ(ə)n/ noun data transmission that uses handshaking signals rather than clock signals to synchronize data pulses

AT /ˌeɪ ˈtiː/ noun a trade name for a standard of PC originally developed by IBM that uses a 16-bit 80286 processor

COMMENT: AT originally meant IBM's Advanced Technology personal computer, but is now used to describe any IBM PC compatible that uses a 16-bit processor.

ATA /ˌeɪ tiː ˈeɪ/ noun hard disk drive technology in which the controller is part of the disk drive rather than being part of the main computer or located on the motherboard. Full form **advanced technology attachment**. Also called **AT attachment**

ATA Fast /ˌeɪ tiː ˌeɪ ˈfɑːst/ noun a proprietary standard interface developed by Seagate and based on ATA that improves the transfer rate and has three modes of operation that provide either 11.1 MBps, 13.3 MBps or 16.6 MBps transfer rates

ATA packet interface /ˌeɪ tiː ˌeɪ ˈpækɪt ˌɪntəfeɪs/ noun same as **advanced technology attachment packet interface**

ATAPI abbr advanced technology attachment packet interface

AT attachment /eɪ tiː əˌtætʃmənt/ noun same as **ATA**

ATA Ultra /ˌeɪ tiː ˌeɪ ˈʌltrə/ noun a proprietary extension to ATA-2, developed by Quantum Corp., that provides a high-speed standard interface that provides data transfer at up to 33 MBps.

AT-bus /ət bʌs/ noun an expansion bus standard developed by IBM that uses an edge connector to carry 16-bits of data and address information

ATC /ˌeɪ tiː ˈsiː/ noun permission granted by the software publisher to the user to make a certain number of copies of a program. Full form **authorization to copy** (NOTE: Some companies have introduced ATC schemes that allow users of certain software to make duplicates of the companies' programs for a fee.)

AT command set /ˌeɪ tiː kəˈmɑːnd set/ noun a standard set of commands to control a modem, developed by Hayes Corporation

ATD /ˌeɪ tiː ˈdiː/ noun a standard command for compatible modems used to dial a telephone number; defined by Hayes Corporation. Full form **attention, dial**

ATE /ˌeɪ tiː ˈiː/ noun computer controlled testing facilities that can check a complex circuit or PCB for faults or problems. Full form **automatic test equipment**

Athlon XP /ˈæθlɒn eks ˌpiː/ a trade name for a 32-bit processor, developed by AMD, that can run the same software as an Intel Pentium processor

AT-keyboard /ət ˈkiːˌbɔːd/ noun a standard keyboard layout for IBM AT personal computers, with 102 keys with a row of 12 function keys along the top

ATM¹ /ˌeɪ tiː ˈem/ abbr Adobe Type Manager

ATM² /ˌeɪ tiː ˈem/ noun **1.** method of transferring data very rapidly, at up to 155 Mbps, across an ISDN link or network **2.** a CCITT and ANSI standard defining cell relay transmission ▶ full form **asynchronous transfer mode**

ATM adaptation layer /ˌeɪ tiː ˌem ˌædæpˈteɪʃ(ə)n ˌleɪə/ noun part of the ATM system that translates a user's data to the standard ATM cell format. Abbr **AAL**

ATM cell format /ˌeɪ tiː 'em sel/ *noun* data sent over an ATM network in a 53-octet packet that includes a header and address information

ATM layers /ˌeɪ tiː ˌem 'leɪəs/ *noun* a method of dividing the functions of an ATM network system into hierarchical layers

AT mode /ˌeɪ 'tiː ˌməʊd/ *noun* a state of a modem that is ready to accept commands using the Hayes AT command set

ATM payload /ˌeɪ tiː ˌem ˌpeɪ'ləʊd/ *noun* a section of an ATM cell that contains the data. It contains 48 octets of data within the 53-octet cell.

A to D *adjective* same as **analog to digital**

A to D converter /'ə tə, tʊ diː/ *noun* same as **ADC** ○ *The speech signal was first passed through an A to D converter before being analysed.*

atom /'ætəm/ *noun* **1.** the smallest particle of an element that has the same properties as the element **2.** a value or string that cannot be reduced to a simpler form

atomic /ə'tɒmɪk/ *adjective* an referring to an operation that returns data to its original state if it is stopped during processing

ATSC /ˌeɪ tiː es 'siː/ *noun* a committee that defines the SDTV and HDTV standards for use in the USA. Full form **Advanced Television Systems Committee**

attach /ə'tætʃ/ *verb* to connect a node or login to a server on a network

attached processor /əˌtætʃt 'prəʊsesə/ *noun* a separate microprocessor in a system that performs certain functions under the control of a central processor

attachment /ə'tætʃmənt/ *noun* a named file which is transferred together with an electronic mail message ○ *There is an attachment with my last mail message – it contains the sales report.*

attack /ə'tæk/ *noun* the shape of the start of a sound signal over time

attended operation /əˌtendɪd ˌɒpə'reɪʃ(ə)n/ *noun* a process which has an operator standing by in case of problems

attention, dial /əˌtenʃən 'daɪəl/ *noun* full form of **ATD**

attention code /ə'tenʃən kəʊd/ *noun* the two characters 'AT' that are used to preface a command to a Hayes-compatible modem (NOTE: For example, 'ATD123' tells the modem to dial the number '123')

attention interruption /əˌtenʃ(ə)n ˌɪntə'rʌpʃən/ *noun* an interrupt signal that requests the attention of the processor

attention key /ə'tenʃ(ə)n kiː/ *noun* a key on a terminal that sends an interrupt signal to the processor

attenuation /əˌtenjuˈeɪʃ(ə)n/ *noun* **1.** reduction or loss of signal strength **2.** the difference between transmitted and received power measured in decibels ○ *If the cable is too long, the signal attenuation will start to cause data errors.* Opposite **gain**

attribute /'ætrɪbjuːt/ *noun* **1.** a field entry in a file ○ *This attribute controls the colour of the screen.* **2.** a piece of information concerning the display or presentation of information **3.** a set of control data stored with and controlling particular functions or aspects of the file in some operating systems such as DOS and OS/2

auctioneering device /ˌɔːkʃəˈnɪərɪŋ dɪˌvaɪs/ *noun* a device that will select the maximum or minimum signal from a number of input signals

audible /'ɔːdɪb(ə)l/ *adjective* which can be heard ○ *The printer makes an audible signal when it runs out of paper.*

audio /'ɔːdiəʊ/ *adjective* referring to sound or to things which can be heard

audio board /'ɔːdiəʊ bɔːd/ *noun* same as **sound card**

audio file /'ɔːdiəʊ faɪl/ *noun* a digital sound sample stored on disk

audio range /'ɔːdiəʊ reɪndʒ/ *noun* the frequency range between 50–20,000 Hz that can be detected by a human ear

audio response unit /ˌɔːdiəʊ rɪ 'spɒns ˌjuːnɪt/ *noun* a speech synthesiser that allows a computer to speak responses to requests

audiotex /'ɔːdiəʊteks/ *noun* an interactive voice response over the telephone in which a computer asks the caller questions and the caller responds by pressing numbers on his telephone

audio/video interleaved /ˌɔːdiəʊ ˌvɪdiəʊ ˌɪntə'liːvd/ *noun* full form of **AVI**

audio-video support system /ˌɔːdiəʊ ˌvɪdiəʊ sə'pɔːt/ *noun* full form of **AVSS**

audit /'ɔːdɪt/ *noun* the process of noting tasks carried out by a computer ■ *verb* to examine the state of a system and check that it is still secure or working properly

audit trail /'ɔːdɪt treɪl/ *noun* a record of details of the use made of a system by noting transactions carried out, used for checking on illegal use or malfunction

augend /ˈɔːgend/ *noun* the number to which another number, the addend, is added to produce the sum

augmented addressing /ɔːgˌmentɪd əˈdresɪŋ/ *noun* the producing of a usable address word from two shorter words

augmenter /ˌɔːgˈmentə/ *noun* a value added to another

AUI connector /ˌeɪ juː ˈaɪ kəˌnektə/ *noun* a D-connector used to connect thick Ethernet cable to a network adapter

AUP *abbr* acceptable use policy

authentication of messages /ɔːˌθentɪkeɪʃ(ə)n əv ˈmesɪdʒɪz/ *noun* the use of special codes to identify the sender of messages, so that the messages can be recognised as being genuine

authenticator /ɔːˈθentɪkeɪtə/ *noun* a trustworthy company that provides authentication for digital signatures on the Internet (NOTE: This process is used by secure websites (shopping or payment sites) to prove to a visitor that the website has been created by the authorised publisher.)

author /ˈɔːθə/ *noun* the person who wrote a program ■ *verb* to create a multimedia application by combining sound, video and images

'The authoring system is a software product that integrates text and fractally compressed images, using any wordprocessor line editor, to create an electronic book with hypertext links between different pages.' [*Computing*]

authoring language /ˌɔːθərɪŋ ˈlæŋgwɪdʒ/ *noun* a programming language used to write CAL and training programs

authoring software /ˌɔːθərɪŋ ˈsɪstəm/, **authoring system** *noun* 1. a special application that allows you to create multimedia titles. Authoring software lets you design the pages of the multimedia book and place video clips, images, text and sound on a page. (NOTE: Almost all multimedia developers use some type of authoring software rather than a traditional programming language because it's a much faster and easier way to create multimedia programs.) 2. same as **webpage design software**

authorisation /ˌɔːθəraɪˈzeɪʃ(ə)n/, **authorization** *noun* 1. permission or power to do something 2. the process of giving a user permission to access a system

authorisation code /ˌɔːθəraɪˈzeɪʃ(ə)n kəʊd/ *noun* a code used to restrict access to a computer system to authorised users only

authorisation to copy /ˌɔːθəraɪzeɪʃ(ə)n tə ˈkɒpɪ/ *noun* full form of **ATC**

authorised user /ˌɔːθəˌraɪzd ˈjuːzə/, **authorized user** *noun* person who is allowed to access a system

authority file, **authority list** *noun* a list of special terms used by people compiling a database and also by the users of the database

author level /ˌɔːθə ˈlev(ə)l/ *noun* the mode of an authoring software package that is used by the author to design the application (NOTE: The user uses the finished application at user level.)

auto advance /ˌɔːtəʊ ədˈvɑːns/ *noun* a system by which the paper in a printer is automatically moved forward to the next line at the end of a line

auto-answer /ˌɔːtəʊ ˈɑːnsə/ *noun* a feature of a modem that will automatically answer a telephone when called

auto-baud scanning /ˈɔːtəʊ bɔːd/, **auto-baud sensing** /ˈɔːtəʊ bɔːd/ *noun* a feature of a modem that can automatically sense and select the correct baud rate for a line

auto-boot /ˈɔːtəʊ buːt/ *noun* a feature of a computer system that will initiate a boot-up procedure when it is switched on

auto-dial /ˌɔːtəʊ ˈdaɪəl/ *noun* feature of a modem that dials a number automatically using stored data

AUTOEXEC.BAT /ˌɔːtəʊɪgˈzek bæt/ *noun* (*in an IBM PC running the MS-DOS operating system*) a batch file that contains commands that are executed when the computer is first switched on or reset

autoflow /ˈɔːtəʊfləʊ/ *noun* a feature of DTP or wordprocessing software that automatically flows text around a graphic image or from one page to the next

auto-login /ˌɔːtəʊ ˈlɒgɪn/, **auto-logon** /ˌɔːtəʊ ˈlɒgɒn/ *noun* a phone number, password and user's number transmitted when requested by a remote system to automate logon. Also called **automatic logon**

automated teller machine /ˌɔːtəmeɪtɪd ˈtelə məˌʃiːn/ *noun* full form of **ATM**

automatically programmed tools
/ˌɔːtəmætɪkli ˌprəʊɡræmd ˈtuːlz/ *plural noun* full form of **APT**

automatic backup /ˌɔːtəmætɪk ˈbækʌp/ *noun* same as **auto save**

automatic call distribution /ˌɔːtəmætɪk ˈkɔːl ˌdɪstrɪbjuːʃ(ə)n/ *noun* full form of **ACD**

automatic calling unit /ˌɔːtəmætɪk ˈkɔːlɪŋ ˌjuːnɪt/ *noun* full form of **ACU**

automatic carriage return /ˌɔːtəmætɪk ˈkærɪdʒ rɪˌtɜːn/ *noun* a system in which the cursor automatically returns to the beginning of a new line when it reaches the end of the previous one

automatic checking /ˌɔːtəmætɪk ˈtʃekɪŋ/ *noun* error detection and validation check carried out automatically on received data

automatic data capture /ˌɔːtəmætɪk ˈdeɪtə ˌkæptʃə/ *noun* a system in which data is automatically recorded in a computer system, as it is input

automatic data processing /ˌɔːtəmætɪk ˈdeɪtə ˌprəʊsesɪŋ/ *noun* full form of **ADP**

automatic decimal adjustment /ˌɔːtəmætɪk ˈdesɪm(ə)l əˌdʒʌstmənt/ *noun* the process of lining up all the decimal points in a column of figures

automatic error correction /ˌɔːtəmætɪk ˈerə kəˌrekʃ(ə)n/ *noun* correction of received data, using error detection and correction codes

automatic error detection /ˌɔːtəmætɪk ˈerə dɪˌtekʃ(ə)n/ *noun* use of an alphanumeric code, e.g. a grey code, that will allow any errors to be detected

automatic font downloading /ˌɔːtəmætɪk ˈfɒnt dəʊnˌləʊdɪŋ/ *noun* the process in which special font information is sent to a printer by the application

automatic frequency switching /ˌɔːtəmætɪk ˈfriːkwənsi ˌswɪtʃɪŋ/ *noun* same as **automatic mode**

automatic gain /ˌɔːtəmætɪk ˈɡeɪn/ *noun* an electronic circuit which automatically increases the volume when someone is speaking quietly and drops it when someone is speaking loudly

automatic gain control /ˌɔːtəmætɪk ˌɡeɪn kənˈtrəʊl/ *noun* full form of **AGC**

automatic hyphenation /ˌɔːtəmætɪk ˌhaɪfəˈnaɪʃ(ə)n/ *noun* a feature of a software program that looks up in an electronic dictionary how to correctly split and hyphenate words

automatic letter writing /ˌɔːtəmætɪk ˈletə ˌraɪtɪŋ/ *noun* the writing of form letters using a word-processor

automatic loader /ˌɔːtəmætɪk ˈləʊdə/ *noun* a short program, usually in ROM, that will boot up a system and load a program

automatic log on /ˌɔːtəmætɪk ˈlɒɡ ˌɒn/ *noun* same as **auto-login**

automatic mailing list /ˌɔːtəmætɪk ˈmeɪlɪŋ ˌlɪst/ *noun* ▶ **listserv**

automatic mode /ˌɔːtəˈmætɪk məʊd/ *noun* a feature of a monitor that can adjust its internal circuits to the different frequencies used by different video standards. Also called **automatic frequency switching**

automatic number identification /ˌɔːtəmætɪk ˈnʌmbə aɪˌdentɪfɪkeɪʃ(ə)n/ *noun* full form of **ANI**

automatic power off /ˌɔːtəmætɪk ˌpaʊə ˈɒf/ *noun* a feature of equipment that will switch itself off if it has not been used for a certain time

automatic programming /ˌɔːtəmætɪk ˈprəʊɡræmɪŋ/ *noun* the process of producing an optimum operating system for a particular process

automatic recalculation /ˌɔːtəmætɪk riːˌkælkjuˈleɪʃ(ə)n/ *noun* a spreadsheet mode in which the answers to new formula are calculated every time any value or cell changes

automatic recovery program /ˌɔːtəmætɪk rɪˈkʌv(ə)ri ˌprəʊɡræm/ *noun* a piece of software that is automatically run when a piece of equipment fails, to ensure that the system continues to operate

automatic repeat /ˌɔːtəmætɪk rɪˈpiːt/ *noun* a facility whereby a character is automatically repeated if the key is kept pressed down. Also called **auto repeat**

automatic repeat request /ˌɔːtəmætɪk rɪˈpiːt rɪˌkwest/ *noun* full form of **ARQ**

automatic send/receive /ˌɔːtəmætɪk ˌsend rɪˈsiːv/ *noun* full form of **ASR**

automatic sequencing /ˌɔːtəmætɪk ˈsiːkwənsɪŋ/ *noun* the ability of a computer to execute a number of programs or tasks without extra commands

automatic speed matching /ˌɔːtəmætɪk ˈspiːd ˌmætʃɪŋ/ *noun* the ability of a modem to adjust its data rate to the speed of the remote modem

automatic test equipment /ˌɔːtəmætɪk 'test ɪˌkwɪpmənt/ *noun* full form of **ATE**

automatic volume control /ˌɔːtəmætɪk 'vɒljuːm kənˌtrəʊl/ *noun* full form of **AVC**

auto-redial /ˌɔːtəʊ 'riːdaɪəl/ *noun* a feature of a modem that dials a telephone number again if engaged, until it replies

auto-reliable mode /ˌɔːtəʊ rɪ 'laɪəb(ə)l ˌməʊd/ *noun* a feature of a modem in which the modem will try and establish a reliable connection with another modem using error correction

auto repeat /ˌɔːtəʊ rɪ'piːt/ *noun* same as **automatic repeat**

autoresponder /ˌɔːtəʊrɪ'spɒndə/ *noun* a software application that automatically indicates that a person is unavailable to respond to incoming email

auto restart /ˌɔːtəʊ 'riːstɑːt/ *noun* a feature of a computer that can initialise and reload its operating system if there is a fault or power failure or at switch on

auto save /'ɔːtəʊ seɪv/ *noun* a feature of some application programs, e.g. word-processor or database software, that automatically saves the file being used every few minutes in case of a power failure or system crash. Also called **automatic backup**

auto scan /'ɔːtəʊ skæn/ *noun* the ability of a monitor to maintain the same rectangular image size when changing from one resolution to another

auto start /'ɔːtəʊ stɑːt/ *noun* a facility to load a program automatically when the computer is switched on

auto stop /'ɔːtəʊ stɒp/ *noun* a feature of a tape player which stops when it has reached the end of a tape

autosync /'ɔːtəʊsɪŋk/ *noun* a feature of a modem that allows it to transfer synchronous data signals to and from a computer that can only transfer asynchronous signals

auto trace /'ɔːtəʊ treɪs/ *noun* a feature of some graphics programs that will transform a bit-mapped image into a vector image by automatically locating the edges of the shapes in the image and drawing lines around them

auto verify /ˌɔːtəʊ 'verɪfaɪ/ *noun* a verification procedure carried out automatically, as soon as the data has been saved

AUX /ˌeɪ juː 'eks/ *noun* a serial communications port under the DOS operating system. Full form **auxiliary**

A/UX a trade name for a version of the Unix operating system for the Apple Mac range of computers

auxiliary /ɔːg'zɪliəri/ *noun* full form of **AUX**

auxiliary device /ɔːgˌzɪliəri dɪ'vaɪs/ *noun* a piece of computer hardware that is not part of the central processing unit but is controlled by it, e.g. a printer or scanner. Also called **peripheral**

auxiliary equipment /ɔːgˌzɪliəri ɪ'kwɪpmənt/ *noun* backup or secondary equipment in case of a breakdown

auxiliary memory /ɔːgˌzɪliəri 'mem(ə)ri/ *noun* same as **auxiliary storage**

auxiliary processor /ɔːgˌzɪliəri 'prəʊsesə/ *noun* an extra, specialised processor, e.g. an array or numerical processor, that can work with a main processor to improve performance

auxiliary storage /ɔːgˌzɪliəri 'stɔːrɪdʒ/, **auxiliary store** *noun* any data storage medium that is not the main high speed computer storage (RAM) ○ *Disk drives are auxiliary storage on this machine.* Also called **auxiliary memory**

auxilliary audio device /ɔːgˌzɪliəri 'ɔːdiəʊ dɪˌvaɪs/ *noun* an audio device whose output is mixed with other waveforms

available bit rate /əˌveɪləb(ə)l 'bɪt ˌreɪt/ *noun* full form of **ABR**

available list /ə'veɪləb(ə)l lɪst/ *noun* a list of unallocated memory and resources in a system

available point /ə'veɪləb(ə)l pɔɪnt/ *noun* the smallest single unit or point of a display whose colour and brightness can be controlled

available power /əˌveɪləb(ə)l 'paʊə/ *noun* the maximum electrical or processing power that a system can deliver

available time /ə'veɪləb(ə)l taɪm/ *noun* the time during which a system may be used

avalanche /'ævəlɑːntʃ/ *noun* a sequence of actions in which each action starts another ○ *There was an avalanche of errors after I pressed the wrong key.*

avatar /'ævətɑː/ *noun* **1.** the graphical image that is used to represent a real person in a cyberspace or three-dimensional system, e.g. the image of a person in a three-dimensional adventure game **2.** the name for the superuser account on a UNIX system. Also called **root**

AVC¹ /ˌeɪ viː 'siː/ *noun* an electronic circuit that maintains a constant sound level despite undesired differences in strength of the incoming signal. Full form **automatic volume control**

AVC² /ˌeɪ viː 'siː/ a trade name for multimedia software developed by IBM that works with its Audio Capture and Video Capture boards

average access time /ˌæv(ə)rɪdʒ 'ækses ˌtaɪm/ *noun* the average time taken between a request being sent and data being returned from a memory device

average delay /ˌæv(ə)rɪdʒ dɪ'leɪ/ *noun* the average time that a user must wait when trying to access a communication network ○ *The average delay increases at nine-thirty when everyone tries to log-in.*

AVI /ˌeɪ viː 'aɪ/ *noun* a Windows multimedia video format developed by Microsoft. Full form **audio/video interleaved**

AVSS /ˌeɪ viː es 'es/ *noun* a digital video system, originally for MS-DOS, used to

play back video and audio files on a computer. Full form **audio-video support system**

AWM /ˌeɪ ˌdʌb(ə)l juː 'em/ *noun* a system developed by Yamaha to sample natural sounds and convert them to digital form. Full form **advanced wave modulation**

axis /'æksɪs/ *noun* **1.** a line around which something turns ○ *The CAD package allows an axis to be placed anywhere.* (NOTE: The plural is **axes**.) **2.** a reference line which is the basis for coordinates on a graph

azerty keyboard /əˌzɜːti 'kiːbɔːd/ *noun* a method of arranging the keys on a keyboard where the first line begins AZERTY, used mainly in Continental Europe. Compare **QWERTY keyboard**

azimuth /'æzɪməθ/ *noun* the angle of a tape head to a reference, e.g. a tape plane

azimuth alignment /ˌæzɪməθ ə 'laɪnmənt/ *noun* the correct horizontal angle of a tape head to the magnetic tape ○ *Azimuth alignment is adjusted with this small screw*

B

b *abbr* bit

B¹ *abbr* byte

B² *symbol* the hexadecimal equivalent of the decimal number 11

B: used in personal computers to indicate the second disk drive, normally a floppy disk drive ○ *Copy the files from the hard drive, C:, to the floppy drive, B:.*

B2B /ˌbiː tə 'biː/ *adjective* referring to advertising or marketing that is aimed at other businesses rather than at consumers. Full form **business-to-business**

B2C /ˌbiː tə 'siː/ *adjective* referring to advertising or marketing that is aimed at

consumers rather than at other businesses. Full form **business-to-consumer**

babble /'bæb(ə)l/ *noun* crosstalk or noise from other sources which interferes with a signal

BABT /ˌbiː eɪ biː 'tiː/ *noun* an independent organisation that tests and certifies telecommunications equipment ○ *If you design a new modem, you must have BABT approval before you can sell it.* Full form **British Approvals Board for Telecommunications**

BABT approval /ˌbiː eɪ biː ˌtiː ə 'pruːvəl/ *noun* official approval required before a new modem can be sold and be connected to the UK telephone network (NOTE: The approval does not provide any quality assurance about the modem, but ensures that it is manufactured in such a way that it does not damage the telephone network. A green label is visible on modem equipment that has received BABT approval.)

backbone /ˈbækˌbəʊn/ *noun* a high-speed, high-capacity connection path that links smaller sub-networks, usually used to connect servers on a network ○ *We have linked the servers in each office using a high-speed backbone.* (NOTE: Smaller workgroups or networks are connected to the backbone as segments or ribs.)

backbone ring /ˈbækˌbəʊn rɪŋ/ *noun* a high-speed ring network that connects a number of smaller ring networks

back buffer /bæk ˈbʌfə/ *noun* a section of memory used as a temporary storage for graphics before they are displayed on screen (NOTE: The image is built up in the back buffer memory area then transferred to the main video memory area for display.)

backdoor /ˈbækˌdɔː/ *noun* same as **trapdoor**

backdrop /ˈbækdrɒp/ *noun* a static background image in front of which are displayed actors or scenes

back-end network /ˌbæk end ˈnetwɜːk/ *noun* a connection between a mainframe computer and a high-speed mass storage device or file server

back-end processor /ˌbæk end ˈprəʊsesə/ *noun* a special purpose auxiliary processor

back-end server /ˌbæk end ˈsɜːvə/ *noun* a computer connected to a network that carries out tasks requested by client workstations

background /ˈbækɡraʊnd/ *noun* **1.** the part of a picture which is behind the main object of interest ○ *The new graphics processor chip can handle background, foreground and sprite movement independently.* **2.** a system in a computer where low-priority work can be done in the intervals when very important work is not being done

background colour /ˌbækɡraʊnd ˈkʌlə/ *noun* the colour of a computer screen display, different from that of characters and graphics ○ *White background colour with black characters is less stressful for the eyes.*

background communication /ˌbækɡraʊnd kəˌmjuːnɪˈkeɪʃ(ə)n/ *noun* data communication activity, e.g. downloading a file, carried out as a low-priority task in the background

background image /ˌbækɡraʊnd ˈɪmɪdʒ/ *noun* an image displayed as a backdrop behind a program or windows of a GUI (NOTE: The background image does not move and does not interfere with any programs.)

background job /ˈbækɡraʊnd dʒɒb/ *noun* a low-priority task

background mode /ˈbækɡraʊnd ˌməʊd/ *noun* in a computer system in which two modes for program execution are possible, the mode that is for housekeeping and other necessary system programs. Compare **foreground mode**

background noise /ˌbækɡraʊnd ˈnɔɪz/ *noun* noise which is present along with the required signal ○ *The other machines around this device will produce a lot of background noise.*

background operation /ˌbækɡraʊnd ˌɒpəˈreɪʃ(ə)n/ *noun* a low-priority process that works as and when resources become available from high-priority foreground tasks

background printing /ˌbækɡraʊnd ˈprɪntɪŋ/ *noun* printing from a computer while it is processing another task ○ *Background printing can be carried out whilst you are editing another document.*

background processing /ˌbækɡraʊnd ˈprəʊsesɪŋ/ *noun* the execution of a low-priority job when there are no higher priority activities for the computer to attend to

background program /ˌbækɡraʊnd ˈprəʊɡræm/ *noun* a computer program with a very low priority

background recalculation /ˌbækɡraʊnd riːˌkælkjuˈleɪʃ(ə)n/ *noun* a facility in a spreadsheet program that allows a user to enter new numbers or equations while the program recalculates the solutions in the background

background reflectance /ˌbækɡraʊnd rɪˈflektəns/ *noun* light reflected from a sheet of paper that is being scanned or read by an optical character reader

background task /ˈbækɡraʊnd tɑːsk/ *noun* a process executed at any time by the computer system, not normally noticed by the user

backing memory /ˌbækɪŋ ˈmem(ə)ri/ *noun* same as **backing store**

backing storage /ˈbækɪŋ ˌstɔːrɪdʒ/ *noun* same as **backing store**

backing store /ˈbækɪŋ stɔː/, **backing storage** /ˈbækɪŋ ˌstɔːrɪdʒ/, **backing memory** /ˌbækɪŋ ˈmem(ə)ri/ *noun* a permanent storage medium onto which data can be recorded before being processed by the computer or after processing for later retrieval ○ *By adding another disk drive, I will increase the backing store capabilities.*

back-level /bæk ˈlev(ə)l/ *noun* the earlier release of a product which may not support a current function

backlight /ˈbæklaɪt/ *noun* light behind a liquid crystal display unit that improves the contrast of characters on the screen and allows it to be read in dim light

backlit display /ˌbæklɪt dɪˈspleɪ/ *noun* a liquid crystal display unit that has a backlight fitted to improve the contrast of the display

backlog /ˈbækˌlɒg/ *noun* work or tasks that have yet to be processed ○ *The programmers can't deal with the backlog of programming work.*

back office /ˌbæk ˈɒfɪs/ *noun* a secure area of e-commerce software containing details of a company's store properties and products and tax tables

backout /ˌbækˈaʊt/ *verb* to restore a file to its original condition before any changes were made

back panel /bæk ˈpæn(ə)l/ *noun* a panel at the rear of a computer which normally holds the connectors to peripherals such as keyboard, printer, video display unit and mouse

backplane /ˈbækpleɪn/ *noun* part of the body of a computer which holds the circuit boards, buses and expansion connectors (the backplane does not provide any processing functions) (NOTE: The backplane does not provide any processing functions.)

back pointer /bæk ˈpɔɪntə/ *noun* a pointer in a tree structure that holds the position of the parent node relative to the current node, used in programming to search backwards through a file

back projection /bæk prəˈdʒekʃ(ə)n/ *noun* the projection of an image from behind a screen (NOTE: It is often used in animation where the static scene is displayed with back projection, then the foreground characters are displayed and the composite scene photographed.)

backslash /ˈbækslæʃ/ *noun* ASCII character 92, , the sign which is used in MS-DOS to represent the root directory of a disk, such as C: or to separate subdirectories in a path, such as C:

backspace /ˈbækˌspeɪs/ *noun* a movement of a cursor or printhead left or back by one character

backspace character /ˈbækspeɪs ˌkærɪktə/ *noun* a code that causes a backspace action in a display device. Abbr **BS**

backspace key /ˈbækˌspeɪs kiː/ *noun* the key which moves the cursor left on the screen or back by one character ○ *If you make a mistake entering data, use the backspace key to correct it.*

backtab /ˈbæktæb/ *verb* (*in an SAA CUA front end*) to move the cursor back to the previous field (NOTE: **backtabbing – backtabbed**)

backtrack /ˈbæktræk/ *verb* to carry out list processing in reverse, starting with the goal and working towards the proofs

back up /ˈbæk ʌp/ *verb* **1.** to support something or help someone ○ *He brought along a file of documents to back up his claim.* **2.** to make a copy of a file or data or disk ○ *The company accounts were backed up on disk as a protection against fire damage.*

backup /ˈbækʌp/ *noun* **1.** the providing of help ○ *We offer a free backup service to customers.* **2.** the process of making a copy of a file or data or disk as a security precaution **3.** a copy of a file or data or disk made as a security precaution. Also called **backup copy, backup version**

'…the previous version is retained, but its extension is changed to .BAK indicating that it's a back-up' [*Personal Computer World*]

backup agent /ˈbækʌp ˌeɪdʒənt/ *noun* a software program that will carry out an automatic backup of a set of files or folders for you at a regular time and date each week

backup copy /ˈbækʌp ˌkɒpi/ *noun* same as **backup 3**

backup disk /ˈbækʌp dɪsk/ *noun* a disk which contains a copy of the information from other disks, as a security precaution

backup domain controller /ˌbækʌp dəʊˈmeɪn kənˌtrəʊlə/ *noun* a server in a network that keeps a copy of database of user accounts to validate login requests in case of a fault with the main server

backup file /'bækʌp faɪl/ *noun* a copy of a file, made as a security precaution

backup path /'bækʌp pɑːθ/ *noun* (*in a Token-Ring network*) an alternative path for a signal around a network avoiding a malfunctioning device

backup plan /'bækʌp plæn/ *noun* a set of rules that take effect when normal operation has gone wrong ○ *The normal UPS has gone wrong, so we will have to use our backup plan to try and restore power.*

backup procedure /ˌbækʌp prə'siːdʒə/ *noun* a method of making backup copies of files

backup server /ˌbækʌp 'sɜːvə/ *noun* a second computer on a network that contains duplicate files and up-to-date data in case of a problem with the main server

backup utility /ˌbækʌp juː'tɪlɪti/ *noun* a piece of software that simplifies the process of backing up data (NOTE: Backup utilities often allow a user to back up files automatically at a particular time.)

backup version /ˌbækʌp 'vɜːʃ(ə)n/ *noun* same as **backup 3**

Backus-Naur-Form /ˌbækəs 'nauə ˌfɔːm/ *noun* full form of **BNF**

backward chaining /'bækwəd tʃeɪnɪŋ/ *noun* a method used in artificial intelligence systems to calculate a goal from a set of results

backward channel /ˌbækwəd 'tʃæn(ə)l/ *noun* a channel from the receiver to transmitter allowing the receiver to send control and handshaking signals

backward error correction /ˌbækwəd 'erə kəˌrekʃ(ə)n/ *noun* correction of errors which are detected by the receiver and a signal is sent to the transmitter to request a re-transmission of the data

backward LAN channel /ˌbækwəd 'læn ˌtʃæn(ə)l/ *noun* (*in a broadband network*) a channel from receiver to sender used to carry control signals

backward mode /'bækwəd məʊd/ *noun* negative displacement from an origin

backward recovery /ˌbækwəd rɪ'kʌv(ə)ri/ *noun* data retrieval from a system that has crashed

backwards compatible /ˌbækwədz kəm'pætəb(ə)l/ *adjective* **1.** able to work with older versions or systems **2.** referring to a new piece of software that provides the same functions as the previous version and can read the files created in the previous version

backwards search /ˌbækwədz 'sɜːtʃ/ *noun* a search for data in a word-processor or database that begins at the position of the cursor or end of the file and searches to the beginning of the file

backwards supervision /ˌbækwədz ˌsuːpə'vɪʒ(ə)n/ *noun* data transmission controlled by the receiver

BACS /bæks/ *noun* a system to transfer money between banks using computer linked via a secure network. Full form **Bankers Automated Clearing Services**

bad break /ˌbæd 'breɪk/ *noun* a hyphen inserted in the wrong place within a word, a problem sometimes caused by the automatic hyphenation feature of word-processing software

badge reader /bædʒ 'riːdə/ *noun* a machine that reads data from an identification badge ○ *A badge reader makes sure that only authorised personnel can gain access to a computer room.*

bad sector /bæd 'sektə/ *noun* a disk sector that has been wrongly formatted or which contains an error or fault and is unable to be correctly written to or read from ○ *You will probably receive error messages when you copy files that are stored on bad sectors on a disk.*

baffle /'bæf(ə)l/ *noun* a loudspeaker which is built into a unit

bag /bæg/ *noun* a number of elements in no particular order

BAK file extension /ˌbæk faɪl ɪg 'stenʃ(ə)n/ *noun* a standard three-letter file extension used in MS-DOS systems to signify a backup or copy of another file

balance /'bæləns/ *noun* the placing of text and graphics on a page in an attractive way ○ *The dtp package allows the user to see if the overall page balance is correct.*

balanced circuit /ˌbælənst 'sɜːkɪt/ *noun* an electronic circuit that presents a correct load to a communications line (NOTE: The correct load is usually equal to the impedance of a line element.)

balanced error /ˌbælənst 'erə/ *noun* the probability of any error occurring from a number of errors when it is the same for all errors

balanced line /'bælənst laɪn/ *noun* a communications line that is terminated at each end with a balanced circuit, preventing signal reflections

balanced routing /'bælənst raʊtɪŋ/ *noun* a method of using all possible routes through a network equally

balun /'bælən/ *noun* a transformer that matches two circuits which have different impedances ○ *We have used a balun to connect the coaxial cable to the twisted-pair circuit.*

band /bænd/ *noun* **1.** a range of frequencies between two limits **2.** a group of tracks on a magnetic disk

bandpass filter /'bændpɑːs ˌfɪltə/ *noun* an electronic filter that allows a range of frequencies to pass but attenuates all frequencies outside the specified range

bandwidth /'bændwɪdθ/ *noun* **1.** a range of frequencies **2.** a measure of the amount of data that can be transmitted along a cable or channel or other medium ○ *This fibre-optic cable has a greater bandwidth than the old copper cable and so it can carry data at higher speeds.* **3.** a measure of the range of frequencies that a monitor or CRT will accept and display (NOTE: High resolution monitors display more pixels per area so need high speed data input and so a higher bandwidth.)

bandwidth on demand /ˌbænd.wɪdθ ɒn dɪ'mɑːnd/ *noun* a system used with a switching service, e.g. ISDN, in a wide area network that allows a user to send as much information as he or she wants because the network will adjust to transmit this amount of information

bank /bæŋk/ *noun* a collection of similar devices ○ *A bank of minicomputers process all the raw data.*

COMMENT: Memory banks are used to expand the main memory of a CPU (often above the addressing range of the CPU) by having a number of memory chips arranged into banks. Each bank operates over the same address range but is selected independently by a special code.

Bankers Automated Clearing Services /ˌbæŋkəz ˌɔːtəmeɪtɪd 'klɪərɪŋ ˌsɜːvɪsɪz/ *noun* full form of **BACS**

bank Internet payment system /ˌbæŋk ˌɪntənet 'peɪmənt ˌsɪstəm/ *noun* a protocol that enables bank payments to be made over the Internet and gives each financial institution a unique identification number for the purposes of Internet transactions. Abbr **BIPS**

bank switching /'bæŋk ˌswɪtʃɪŋ/ *noun* selection of a particular memory bank from a group

banner /'bænə/, **banner advertisement, banner ad** *noun* an image that car-ries an advertising slogan, logo or message and is displayed on a web page

COMMENT: A long, narrow strip is now the unofficial standard format for advertisements that appear on almost every commercial website on the Internet. Some banner ads are images, others include animation to attract the viewer's attention. If you click on a banner ad, you will usually jump to the advertiser's own site. If you would rather not see banner advertisements when you surf, you can install special software that blocks them. Websites normally charge advertisers according either to the number of times the banner ad is displayed (called the number of impressions) or the number of times that a user clicks on the ad (called the click-through rate).

banner page /'bænə peɪdʒ/ *noun* a page that is printed out first with the time, date, name of the document and the name of the person who has printed it

bar /bɑː/ *noun* a thick line or block of colour

bar chart /'bɑː tʃɑːt/ *noun* a graph on which values are represented as vertical or horizontal bars. Also called **bar graph**

bar code /'bɑː kəʊd/ *noun* data represented as a series of printed stripes of varying widths (NOTE: The US term is **bar graphics**.)

COMMENT: Bar codes are found on most goods and their packages; the width and position of the stripes is sensed by a light pen or optical wand and provides information about the goods such as price and stock quantities.

bar code reader /'bɑː kəʊd ˌriːdə/ *noun* same as **optical bar reader**

bare board /'beə bɔːd/ *noun* a circuit board with no components on it, especially a memory expansion board that does not yet have any memory chips mounted on it

bar graph /'bɑː grɑːf/ *noun* same as **bar chart**

bar graphics /bɑː 'græfɪks/ *noun* US same as **bar code**

barrel /'bærəl/ *noun* a conducting post in a terminal

base /beɪs/ *noun* **1.** the lowest or first position **2.** a collection of files used as a reference. ♦ **database 3.** an initial or original position **4.** notation referring to a number system **5.** (*in C++ programming language*) a class from which other classes can be derived by inheritance ■ *verb* **1.** to start to calculate something from a position ○ *We based our calculations on the basic keyboarding rate.* **2.** to set up a company or a person in a place ○ *The European manager is based in our London office.* (NOTE: bases – basing – based)

base 2 /'beɪs tuː/ *noun* the binary number system, using the two digits 0 and 1

base 8 /'beɪs eɪt/ *noun* the octal number system, using the eight digits 0 – 7

base 10 /ˌbeɪs 'ten/ *noun* the decimal number system, using the ten digits 0 – 9

base 16 /ˌbeɪs sɪks'tiːn/ *noun* the hexadecimal number system, using the ten digits 0 – 9 and the six letters A – F

base address /beɪs ə'dres/ *noun* an initial address in a program used as a reference for others

base address register /ˌbeɪs ə'dres ˌredʒɪstə/ *noun* a register in a CPU that is used to store the base address

baseband /'beɪsbænd/, **base band** *noun* **1.** the frequency range of a signal before it is processed or transmitted ○ *Voice baseband ranges from 20 Hz to 15 KHz.* **2.** digital signals transmitted without modulation **3.** information modulated with a single carrier frequency

base band local area network /ˌbeɪs bænd ˌləʊk(ə)l ˌeəriə 'netwɜːk/ *noun* a transmission method in which the whole bandwidth of the cable is used and the data signal is not modulated ○ *Base band local area networks can support a maximum cable length of around 300m.* (NOTE: Ethernet is a baseband local area network.)

base band modem /ˌbeɪs bænd 'məʊdem/ *noun* a communications circuit that transmits an unmodulated, baseband signal over a short distance ○ *Do not use a base band modem with a normal phone line.*

baseband signalling /ˌbeɪsbænd 'sɪgnəlɪŋ/ *noun* transmission of data as varying voltage levels across a link

base font /'beɪs fɒnt/ *noun* a default font and point size used by a word-processing program

base hardware /beɪs 'hɑːdˌweə/ *noun* the minimum hardware requirements that a particular software package needs in order to run

base language /beɪs 'læŋgwɪdʒ/ *noun* same as **assembly language**

base level synthesizer /ˌbeɪs ˌlev(ə)l 'sɪnθesaɪzə/ *noun* (*on a sound card*) a synthesiser that supports three melodic instruments and can play six notes simultaneously

base line /'beɪs laɪn/ *noun* **1.** any of the lines, only displayed during the design

stage or author level of an application, which define the size and layout of a page in an application **2.** a horizontal line along which characters are printed or displayed and below which the descenders of a character drop

base memory /beɪs 'mem(ə)ri/, **base RAM** *noun* the first 640Kb of random access memory fitted to an IBM-compatible PC

base register /beɪs 'redʒɪstə/ *noun* a register in a CPU, though not usually in a small computer, that contains the address of the start of a program. Also called **B box**

base station /beɪs 'steɪʃ(ə)n/ *noun* a fixed radio transmitter/receiver that relays radio signals to and from data terminals or radios

BASIC /'beɪsɪk/ *noun* a high-level programming language for developing programs in a conversational way, providing an easy introduction to computer programming. Full form **beginner's all-purpose symbolic instruction code**

basic code /'beɪsɪk kəʊd/ *noun* same as **absolute code**

basic controller /ˌbeɪsɪk kən'trəʊlə/ *noun* a part of a communications controller that carries out arithmetic and logic functions

basic control system satellite /ˌbeɪsɪk kənˌtrəʊl ˌsɪstəm 'sætəlaɪt/ *noun* a system that runs dedicated programs or tasks for a central computer. It is controlled by using interrupt signals. Abbr **BCS**

basic direct access method /ˌbeɪsɪk ˌdaɪrekt 'ækses ˌmeθəd/ *noun* a method of directly updating or retrieving a particular block of data stored on a direct access device. Abbr **BDAM**

basic encoding rules /ˌbeɪsɪk ɪn 'kəʊdɪŋ ˌruːlz/ *plural noun* full form of **BER**

basic exchange format /ˌbeɪsɪk ɪks 'tʃeɪndʒ ˌfɔːmæt/ *noun* a standard method of storing data on a disk so that it may be accessed by another type of computer

basic input/output operating system /ˌbeɪsɪk ˌɪnpʊt ˌaʊtpʊt 'ɒpəreɪtɪŋ ˌsɪstəm/ *noun* full form of **BIOS**

basic instruction /ˌbeɪsɪk ɪn 'strʌkʃən/ *noun* an unmodified program instruction which is processed to obtain the instruction to be executed

basic mode link control /ˌbeɪsɪk məʊd 'lɪŋk kənˌtrəʊl/ *noun* a standardised control of transmission links using special codes

basic product /ˌbeɪsɪk 'prɒdʌkt/ *noun* the main product made from a raw material

basic rate access /ˌbeɪsɪk reɪt 'ækses/ *noun* full form of **BRA**

basic rate interface /ˌbeɪsɪk reɪt 'ɪntəfeɪs/ *noun* full form of **BRI**

basic sequential access method /ˌbeɪsɪk sɪˌkwenʃ(ə)l ˌækses 'meθəd/ *noun* a method of storing or retrieving blocks of data in a continuous sequence. Abbr **BSAM**

basic telecommunications access method /ˌbeɪsɪk ˌtelikəmjuːnɪkeɪʃ(ə)nz 'ækses ˌmeθəd/ *noun* full form of **BTAM**

BAT /bæt/ *noun* a three-letter file extension used in MS-DOS systems to signify a batch file

batch /bætʃ/ *noun* **1.** a group of documents which are processed at the same time ○ *today's batch of orders* **2.** a group of tasks or amount of data to be processed as a single unit ○ *We deal with the orders in batches of fifty.* ■ *verb* to put data or tasks together in groups

batched communication /ˌbætʃ kəˌmjuːnɪ'keɪʃ(ə)n/ *noun* high-speed transmission of large blocks of data without requiring an acknowledgement from the receiver for each data item

batch file /'bætʃ faɪl/ *noun* a file stored on disk that contains a sequence of system commands. When the batch file is run, the commands are executed, saving a user typing them in. ○ *This batch file is used to save time and effort when carrying out a routine task.*

batch processing /'bætʃ ˌprəʊsesɪŋ/ *noun* **1.** computer system able to process groups of tasks **2.** a system of data processing where information is collected into batches before being processed by the computer in one machine run

COMMENT: Batch processing is the opposite of interactive processing, where the user gives instructions and receives an immediate response.

batch processor /'bætʃ ˌprəʊsesə/ *noun* a computer system able to process groups of tasks

batch region /bætʃ 'riːdʒ(ə)n/ *noun* a memory area where the operating system executes batch programs

batch system /bætʃ 'sɪstəm/ *noun* a system that executes batch files

batch total /bætʃ 'təʊt(ə)l/ *noun* the sum of a number of batches of data, used for error checking, validation or to provide useful information

BAT file extension /ˌbæt faɪl ɪk 'stenʃən/ *noun* a standard three-letter file extension used in MS-DOS systems to signify a batch file

battery-backed /'bæt(ə)ri bækd/ *noun* referring to a volatile storage device that has a battery backup

battery backup /ˌbæt(ə)ri 'bækʌp/ *noun* a battery to provide power to volatile storage devices to retain data after a computer has been switched off

battery charging /'bæt(ə)ri ˌtʃɑːdʒɪŋ/ *noun* the replenishing of the charge stored in a re-chargeable battery

battery meter /ˌbæt(ə)ri 'miːtə/ *noun* a utility in a laptop computer that tells you how much life or working time you have left in your batteries (NOTE: In Windows 95, a tiny icon appears in the bottom right-hand corner of the screen and this shows you when you are about to run out of battery power and need to recharge.)

baud /bɔːd/ *noun* a unit of data compression speed equal to one unit element per second

baud rate /'bɔːd reɪt/ *noun* a measure of the number of signal changes transmitted per second ○ *The baud rate of the binary signal was 300 bits per second.*

COMMENT: Baud rate is often considered the same as bits per second, but in fact it depends on the protocol used and the error checking (300 baud is roughly equivalent to 30 characters per second using standard error checking).

baud rate generator /ˌbɔːd reɪt 'dʒenəreɪtə/ *noun* a device that produces various timing signals to synchronise data at different baud rates

bay /beɪ/ *noun* a space within a computer's casing where a disk drive is fitted. Also called **drive bay**

B box /'biː bɒks/ *noun* same as **base register**

BBS /ˌbiː biː 'es/ *noun* an information and message database accessible by modem and computer link. Full form **bulletin board system**

BCC /ˌbiː siː ˈsiː/ *noun* an error detection method for blocks of transmitted data. Full form **block character check**

BCD /ˌbiː siː ˈdiː/ *noun* a representation of single decimal digits as a pattern of four binary digits ○ *The BCD representation of decimal 8 is 1000.* Full form **binary coded decimal**

BCD adder /ˌbiː siː ˌdiː ˈædə/ *noun* a full adder able to add two four-bit BCD words

BCH code /ˌbiː siː ˌsiːˈeɪt ʃ kəʊd/ *noun* an error correcting code. Full form **Bose-Chandhuri-Hocquenghem code**

BCNF /ˌbiː siː en ˈef/ *noun* ♦ **normal form**

BCPL /ˌbiː siː piː ˈel/ *noun* a high level programming language

BCS *abbr* **1.** British Computer Society **2.** basic control system satellite

beacon /ˈbiːkən/ *verb* a signal transmitted repeatedly by a device that is malfunctioning on a network

beacon frame /ˈbiːkən freɪm/ *noun* a special frame within the FDDI protocol that is sent after a network break has occurred

bead /biːd/ *noun* a small section of a program that is used for a single task

beam /biːm/ *noun* a narrow set of light or electron rays ○ *A beam of laser light is used in this printer to produce high-resolution graphics.*

beam deflection /biːm dɪˈflekʃ(ə)n/ *noun* to move a CRT's electron beam with the CRT across the screen

BEC *abbr* bus extension card

beginner's all-purpose symbolic instruction code /bɪˌɡɪnəz ɔːl ˌpɜːpəs sɪmˌbɒlɪk ɪnˈstrʌkʃən ˌkəʊd/ *noun* full form of **BASIC**

beginning of file /bɪˌɡɪnɪŋ əv ˈfaɪl/ *noun* a character or symbol that shows the start of a valid section of data. Abbr **bof**

beginning of information mark /bɪˌɡɪnɪŋ əv ˌɪnfəˈmeɪʃ(ə)n ˌmɑːk/ *noun* full form of **BIM**

beginning of tape marker /bɪˌɡɪnɪŋ əv ˈteɪp ˌmɑːkə/ *noun* a section of material that marks the start of the recording area of a reel of magnetic tape. Also called **bot marker**

bell character /bel ˈkærɪktə/, **BEL** *noun* a control code that causes a machine to produce an audible signal, equivalent to ASCII code 7

Bell-compatible modem /ˌbel kəm ˌpætɪb(ə)l ˈməʊdem/ *noun* a modem that operates according to standards set down by AT&T

bells and whistles /ˌbelz ənd ˈwɪs(ə)lz/ *plural noun* advanced features or added extras to an application or peripheral ○ *This word-processor has all the bells and whistles you would expect – including page preview.*

below-the-fold /bɪˌləʊ ðə ˈfəʊld/ *adjective* referring to the lower part of a webpage that is seen only by a user who scrolls down the page and that is therefore less commercially valuable. Compare **above-the-fold**

benchmark /ˈbentʃmɑːk/ *noun* **1.** a point in an index which is important, and can be used to compare with other figures **2.** a program used to test the performance of software or hardware or a system ○ *The magazine gave the new program's benchmark test results.*

benchmarking /ˈbentʃmɑːkɪŋ/ *noun* the testing of a system or program with a benchmark

benchmark problem /ˌbentʃmɑːk ˈprɒbləm/ *noun* a task or problem used to test and evaluate the performance of hardware or software

COMMENT: The same task or program is given to different systems and their results and speeds of working are compared.

BER /ˌbiː iː ˈɑː/ *noun* a standard method of encoding data that is stored in the ASN language, often used in libraries and other Internet data sites. Full form **basic encoding rules**

Berkeley UNIX /ˌbɜːkli ˈjuːnɪks/ *noun* a version of the UNIX operating system developed by the University of California, Berkeley

bespoke software /bɪˌspəʊk ˈsɒftweə/ *noun* software that has been written especially for a customer's particular requirements

best fit /best ˈfɪt/ *noun* a function that selects the smallest free space in main memory for a requested virtual page

beta site /ˈbiːtə saɪt/ *noun* a company or person that tests new software before it is released in a real environment to make sure it works correctly

beta software /ˈbiːtə ˌsɒf(t)weə/ *noun* software that has not finished all its testing before release and so may still contain bugs

beta test /'biːtə ˌtest/ *noun* a second stage of tests performed on new software just before it is due to be released ○ *The application has passed the alpha tests and is just entering the beta test phase.*

'The client was so eager to get his hands on the product that the managing director bypassed internal testing and decided to let it go straight out to beta test.' [*Computing*]

beta version /'biːtə ˌvɜːʒn/ *noun* a version of a software application that is almost ready to be released ○ *We'll try out the beta test software on as many different PCs as possible to try and find all the bugs.*

betaware /'biːtəweə/ *noun* of computer software in a version that is given to a few customers before the final version is put on sale

bezel /'bez(ə)l/ *noun* the front cover of a computer's casing or disk drive unit

Bézier curve /'beziei kɜːv/ *noun* a geometric curve with the overall shape defined by two midpoints, called control handles

COMMENT: Bézier curves are a feature of many high-end design software packages. They allow a designer to create smooth curves by defining a number of points. The PostScript page description language uses Bézier curves to define the shapes of characters during printing.

BGP /ˌbiː dʒiː 'piː/ *noun* a protocol that allows routers to share routing information to allow each router to calculate the most efficient path for information. Full form **border gateway protocol** (NOTE: This protocol is most often used between routers installed at Internet Service Providers (ISPs).)

biased exponent /ˌbaɪəst ɪk'spəʊnənt/ *noun* the value of the exponent in a floating point number

bid /bɪd/ *verb* (*of a computer*) to gain control of a network in order to transmit data ○ *The terminal had to bid three times before there was a gap in transmissions on the network.*

bi-directional bus /ˌbaɪ daɪˌrekʃ(ə)n(ə)l 'bʌs/ *noun* data or control lines that can carry signals travelling in two directions

bi-directional printer /ˌbaɪ daɪˌrekʃ(ə)n(ə)l 'printə/ *noun* a printer that is able to print characters from left to right and from right to left as the head is moving forwards or backwards across the paper, speeding up the printing operation

bi-directional transmission /ˌbaɪ daɪˌrekʃ(ə)n(ə)l trænz'mɪʃ(ə)n/ *noun* data transfer that can occur to and from a device along a particular channel

Big Blue /bɪg 'bluː/ *noun* same as **IBM** (*informal*)

bilinear filtering /baɪˌlɪniə 'fɪltərɪŋ/ *noun* a method of removing unwanted image defects, particularly on a texture-mapped object, by looking at the four adjacent pixels that surround each pixel to check that there is no sudden change in colour

billion /'bɪljən/ *noun* a number equal to one thousand million. Abbr **bn**

BIM /ˌbiː aɪ 'em/ *noun* a symbol indicating the start of a data stream stored on a disk drive. Full form **beginning of information mark**

bin /bɪn/ *noun* a tray used to hold a supply of paper ready to be fed into a printer

binary /'baɪnəri/ *adjective* referring to the number notation system which uses only the digits 0 and 1

binary adder /ˌbaɪnəri 'ædə/ *noun* a device that provides the sum of two or more binary digits

binary arithmetic /ˌbaɪnəri ə'rɪθmətɪk/ *noun* the rules and functions governing arithmetic operations in the binary system

binary bit /'baɪnəri bɪt/ *noun* same as **binary digit**

binary cell /'baɪnəri sel/ *noun* a storage element for one bit

binary chop /'baɪnəri tʃɒp/ *noun* same as **binary search**

binary code /'baɪnəri kəʊd/ *noun* code using different patterns of binary digits to represent various symbols and elements

binary coded characters /ˌbaɪnəri ˌkəʊdɪd 'kærɪktəz/ *plural noun* alphanumeric characters represented as patterns of binary digits

binary coded decimal /ˌbaɪnəri ˌkəʊdɪd 'desɪm(ə)l/ *noun* full form of **BCD**

binary counter /ˌbaɪnəri 'kaʊntə/ *noun* a circuit that will divide a binary input signal by two, producing one output pulse for two input pulses

binary digit /ˌbaɪnəri 'dɪdʒɪt/ *noun* smallest single unit in binary notation, either a 0 or a 1. Also called **binary, binary bit, binary number, bit**

binary dump /'baɪnəri dʌmp/ *noun* a section of memory dumped onto another medium or printed out in binary form

binary encoding /ˌbaɪnəri ɪnˈkəʊdɪŋ/ *noun* representation of each character or element with a unique combination or pattern of bits in a word

binary exponent /ˌbaɪnəri ɪk ˈspəʊnənt/ *noun* one word that contains the sign and exponent of a binary digit, expressed in exponent and mantissa form

binary field /ˈbaɪnəri fiːld/ *noun* a field in a database record that contains binary digits, often one capable of holding any information, including data, text, graphics images, voice and video

binary file /ˈbaɪnəri faɪl/ *noun* a file that contains data rather than alphanumeric characters. A binary file can include any character code and cannot always be displayed or edited. ○ *The program instructions are stored in the binary file.*

binary fraction /ˌbaɪnəri ˈfrækʃən/ *noun* a representation of a decimal fraction in binary form ○ *The binary fraction 0.011 is equal to one quarter plus one eighth (i.e. three eighths).*

binary half adder /ˌbaɪnəri ˈhɑːf ˌædə/ *noun* a binary adder that can produce the sum of two inputs, producing a carry output if necessary, but cannot accept a carry input

binary large object /ˌbaɪnəri lɑːdʒ ˈɒbdʒekt/ *noun* a field in a database record that can contain a large quantity of binary data, normally a bitmap image. Abbr **blob**

binary loader /ˌbaɪnəri ˈləʊdə/ *noun* a short section of program code that allows programs in binary form, e.g. object code from a linker or assembler, to be loaded into memory

binary look-up /ˈbaɪnəri lʊk/ *noun* same as **binary search**

binary mantissa /ˌbaɪnəri mænˈtɪsə/ *noun* a fractional part of a number, in binary form

binary notation /ˌbaɪnəri nəʊ ˈteɪʃ(ə)n/ *noun* the numerical system using only the digits 0 and 1. Also called **base 2, binary representation**

binary operation /ˌbaɪnəri ˌɒpə ˈreɪʃ(ə)n/ *noun* **1.** an operation on two operands **2.** an operation on an operand in binary form

binary point /ˈbaɪnəri pɔɪnt/ *noun* a dot that indicates the division between the bits for the numbers' whole units and the fractional part of the binary number

binary representation /ˌbaɪnəri ˌreprɪzenˈteɪʃ(ə)n/ *noun* same as **binary notation**

binary scale /ˈbaɪnəri skeɪl/ *noun* a power of two associated with each bit position in a word ○ *In a four bit word, the binary scale is 1,2,4,8.*

binary search /ˈbaɪnəri sɜːtʃ/ *noun* a search method for use on ordered lists of data. Also called **binary chop, binary look-up** (NOTE: The search key is compared with the data in the middle of the list and one half is discarded. This is repeated with the remaining half until only the required data item is left.)

binary sequence /ˌbaɪnəri ˈsiːkwəns/ *noun* a series of binary digits

binary signalling /ˌbaɪnəri ˈsɪgnəlɪŋ/ *noun* transmission using positive and zero voltage levels to represent binary data

binary split /ˈbaɪnəri splɪt/ *noun* a method of iteration in which the existing number is compared to a new value calculated as the mid-point between the high and low limits

binary synchronous communications /ˌbaɪnəri ˌsɪŋkrənəs kəˌmjuːnɪ ˈkeɪʃ(ə)nz/ *noun* full form of **BSC**

binary system /ˈbaɪnəri ˌsɪstəm/ *noun* the use of binary digits, or the data system that operates with binary digits

binary-to-decimal conversion /ˌbaɪnəri tə, tʊ ˈdesɪm(ə)l/ *noun* the process to convert a binary digit into its equivalent decimal value

binary tree /ˈbaɪnəri triː/ *noun* a data system where each item of data or node has only two branches. Also called **btree**

binary variable /ˌbaɪnəri ˈveəriəb(ə)l/ *noun* a variable that can contain either a one or zero

binaural sound /baɪnˈɔːrl saʊnd/ *noun* a method of recording sound so that it gives the impression of stereophony when played back. ◊ **Dolby Digital**

bind /baɪnd/ *verb* to link and convert one or more object code programs into a form that can be executed

BIND /ˌbiː aɪ en ˈdiː/ *noun* software that provides the functions of a Domain Name Server for server computers running BSD UNIX

binder /ˈbaɪndə/ *noun* a program that converts object code into a form that can be executed

Bindery /ˈbaɪndəri/ *noun* a special database used in a Novell NetWare network operating system to store user account, access and security details

binding offset /ˌbaɪndɪŋ ˈɒfset/ *noun* an extra wide margin on the inside of a printed page to prevent text being hidden during binding (NOTE: It is the left margin on a right hand page, the right margin on a left hand page.)

binding time /ˈbaɪndɪŋ taɪm/ *noun* the time taken to produce actual addresses from an object code program

BinHex /bɪnˈheks/ *noun* a method encoding binary data into ASCII characters. ◊ **Uuencoding**

> COMMENT: Software programs and data files are stored as binary data (using all eight bits of information within one byte of storage space), whereas ASCII characters can be stored in just the first seven of the eight bits of storage space within one byte. Email and many communication systems originally only supported the transfer of text (ASCII characters), so if you wanted to attach a data file to your email message, the data had to be encoded before it could be transferred. Now almost all email software and links between computers support full eight-bit transfer, so data does not have to be encoded.

biochip /ˈbaɪəʊtʃɪp/ *noun* a computer chip that uses organic molecules to store and process information

biocomputer /ˈbaɪəʊkəmˌpjuːtə/ *noun* a very fast computer that operates using biological processes instead of semiconductor technology

BIOS /ˈbaɪɒs/ *noun* a set of system routines that interface between high-level program instructions and the system peripherals to control the input and output to various standard devices. Full form **basic input/output system** (NOTE: This often includes controlling the screen, keyboard and disk drives.)

bipolar /baɪˈpəʊlə/ *adjective* with two levels

bipolar coding /ˌbaɪpəʊlə ˈkɒdɪŋ/ *noun* a transmission method that uses alternate positive and negative voltage levels to represent a binary one, with binary zero represented by zero level

bipolar signal /ˌbaɪpəʊlə ˈsɪgn(ə)l/ *noun* the use of positive and negative voltage levels to represent the binary digits

bipolar transistor /ˌbaɪpəʊlə træn ˈzɪstə/ *noun* a transistor constructed of three layers of alternating types of doped semiconductor, p-n-p or n-p-n

BIPS *abbr* bank Internet payment system

biquinary code /baɪˌkwɪnəri ˈkəʊd/ *noun* code in which decimal digits are represented as two digits added together (NOTE: Decimal digits smaller than 5 are represented as 0 + the digit; decimal digits greater than 4 are represented as 5 + the digit minus 5.)

B-ISDN /biː ˌaɪ es diː ˈen/ *abbr* broadband ISDN

bistable /baɪˈsteɪb(ə)l/ *adjective* referring to a device or circuit that has two possible states, on and off

bit /bɪt/ *noun* **1.** same as **binary digit 2.** the smallest unit of data that a system can handle

bit addressing /bɪt əˈdresɪŋ/ *noun* selection of a register or word and examining one bit of it

bit blit /ˈbɪt blɪt/ *noun* same as **blit**

bit block /ˈbɪt blɒk/ *noun* (*in computer graphics*) a group of bits treated as one unit

bit block transfer /ˌbɪt blɒk ˈtrænsfɜː/ *noun* full form of **blit**

bit bucket /bɪt ˈbʌkɪt/ *noun* an area of memory into which data can be discarded

BITC *abbr* burned-in time code

bit density /bɪt ˈdensəti/ *noun* the number of bits that can be recorded per unit of storage medium

bit depth /ˈbɪt depθ/ *noun* the number of bits used to represent the number of colours that can be displayed on a screen or printer at one time (NOTE: The bit depth of each pixel is represented by a number of bits associated with the pixel that describe the number of colours that can be displayed.)

bit error rate /ˌbɪt ˈerə ˌreɪt/ *noun* the ratio of the number of bits received compared to the number of errors in a transmission, especially in fibre optics. Abbr **BER**

bit flipping /bɪt ˈflɪpɪŋ/ *noun* inversion of the state of bits from 0 to 1 and 1 to 0

bitFTP /ˌbɪt ef tiː ˈpiː/ *noun* a type of server that allows a user to retrieve a file using only an email link (NOTE: The user sends an email to the bitFTP server, containing a series of FTP commands that ask it to fetch the file from a remote server. When it has done this, the bitFTP server sends an email back to the user as an email attachment or encoded mail message. If you want to retrieve a file, send a message that contains just 'help' to 'ftpmail@doc.ic.ac.uk' to find out how the system works.)

bit handling /bɪt ˈhændlɪŋ/ *noun* the use of CPU commands and processes that allow bit manipulation and changing

bit image /bɪt ˈɪmɪdʒ/ *noun* a collection of bits that represent the pixels that make up an image on screen or on a printer

bit interleaving /ˈbɪt ɪntəˌliːvɪŋ/ *noun* a form of time domain multiplexing used in some synchronous transmission protocols such as HDLC and X.25.

bit manipulation /bɪt məˌnɪpjʊ ˈleɪʃ(ə)n/ *noun* the use of various instructions that provide functions such as examine a bit, change or set or move a bit within a word

bit-map /ˈbɪtmæp/, **bitmap** *verb* to define events or data using an array of single bits, which can be, e.g., an image or graphics or a table of devices in us (NOTE: bit-mapping – bitmapped)

'…the expansion cards fit into the PC's expansion slot and convert bit-mapped screen images to video signals' [*Publish*]

bit-mapped font /ˌbɪt mæpt ˈfɒnt/ *noun* a font whose characters are made up of patterns of pixels

bit-mapped graphics /ˌbɪt mæpt ˈɡræfɪks/ *plural noun* images whose individual pixels can be controlled by changing the value of stored bits (NOTE: One is on, zero is off. In colour displays, more than one bit is used to provide control for the three colours red, green and blue.)

bit-mapped register /ˌbɪt mæpt ˈredʒɪstə/ *noun* a memory location that holds configuration information in a processor in which each separate bit within the location has a different use or meaning (NOTE: For example, a register that refers to a mouse might be one byte (eight bits) wide and each bit could indicate whether a mouse button is up or down.)

bitmp /ˈbɪtmæp/ *abbr* bit-map

BitNet /ˈbɪtnet/ *noun* a network used to connect mostly academic sites and computers and allows transfer of electronic mail and listserver application (NOTE: Bit-Net is similar to the Internet and is connected to allow the transfer of electronic mail to and from academic users to other users on the Internet.)

bit parallel /bɪt ˈpærəlel/ *noun* the transmission of a collection of bits simultaneously over a number of lines. The parallel printer port uses bit parallel transmis-

sion to transfer eight bits at a time to a printer.

bit pattern /bɪt ˈpæt(ə)nⁿ/ *noun* an arrangement of bits within a word, that represents a particular character or action

bit plane /ˈbɪt pleɪn/ *noun* (*in computer graphics*) one layer of a multiple-layer image in which each layer defines one colour of each pixel

bit position /bɪt pəˈzɪʃ(ə)n/ *noun* the place of a bit of data in a computer word

bit rate /ˈbɪt reɪt/ *noun* a measure of the number of bits transmitted per second

bit rotation /bɪt rəʊˈteɪʃ(ə)n/ *noun* a shifting a pattern of bits in a word to the left or right, the old last bit moving to the new first bit position

bit-significant /ˌbɪt sɪɡˈnɪfɪkənt/ *adjective* using the bits within a byte to describe something ○ *Testing bit six of a byte containing an ASCII character is bit significant and determines if the ASCII character is upper* or *lower case.*

bit-slice architecture /ˌbɪt slaɪs ˈɑːkɪtektʃə/, **bit-slice design** /ˌbɪt slaɪs dɪˈzaɪn/ *noun* the construction of a large word size CPU by joining a number of smaller word size blocks ○ *The bit-slice design uses four four-bit word processors to make a sixteen-bit processor.*

bit-slice microprocessor /ˌbɪt slaɪs ˈmaɪkrəʊprəʊsesə/, **bit-slice processor** /ˌbɪt slaɪs ˈprəʊsesə/ *noun* a large word size CPU constructed by joining a number of smaller word size blocks ○ *The bit-slice microprocessor uses four 4-bit processors to make a 16-bit word processor.*

bits per inch /ˌbɪts pɜː ˈɪntʃ/ *noun* full form of **BPI**

bits per pixel /ˌbɪts pɜː ˈpɪks(ə)l/ *noun* full form of **BPP**

bits per second /ˌbɪts pɜː ˈsekənd/ *noun* a measure of the number of binary digits transmitted every second. Abbr **bps**

bit stream /ˈbɪt striːm/ *noun* a binary data sequence that does not consist of separate, distinct character codes or groups

bit stuffing /bɪt ˈstʌfɪŋ/ *noun* the addition of extra bits to a group of data to make up the length required for transmission

bit track /ˈbɪt træk/ *noun* a track on a magnetic disk along which bits can be recorded or read back

bitwise /ˈbɪtwaɪz/ *adverb* carried out on each bit in a byte, one bit at a time

BIX /ˌbiː aɪ 'eks/ *noun* a commercial on-line system founded by Byte magazine

biz /bɪz/ *noun* a type of newsgroup that contains business discussions and opportunities (NOTE: For example, 'biz.opportunities' contains messages from users that are offering ways of making money. Only the biz series of newsgroups are supposed to discuss commercial aspects: the rest of the newsgroups are for technical or academic discussion.)

black and white /ˌblæk ən 'waɪt/ *noun* **1.** the use of shades of grey to represent colours on a monitor or display **2.** an image in which each pixel is either black or white with no shades of grey

black box /blæk 'bɒks/ *noun* a device that performs a function without the user knowing how

black level /blæk 'lev(ə)l/ *noun* a level of a video signal that represents absolutely no light: total blackness

black matrix /blæk 'meɪtrɪks/ *noun* a CRT monitor tube in which the colour phosphor dots are surrounded by black for increased contrast

black writer /blæk 'raɪtə/ *noun* a printer in which toner sticks to the points hit by the laser beam when the image drum is scanned ○ *A black writer produces sharp edges and graphics, but large areas of black are muddy.*

blank cell /blæŋk 'sel/ *noun* an empty cell in a spreadsheet

blank character /blæŋk 'kærɪktə/ *noun* a character code that prints a space

blank disk /blæŋk 'dɪsk/ *noun* a disk that does not have data stored on it

blanking interval /'blæŋkɪŋ ˌɪntəvəl/ *noun* the period during which a screen displays nothing, in between two images or during the picture beam flyback

blank instruction /blæŋk ɪn 'strʌkʃən/ *noun* an instruction in a program that is only there to satisfy language syntax or to make up a block length

blank string /blæŋk 'strɪŋ/ *noun* same as **null string**

blank tape /blæŋk 'teɪp/ *noun* a tape that does not have data stored on it

blast /blɑːst/ *verb* **1.** to write data into a programmable ROM device **2.** to free sections of previously allocated memory or resources

blast-through alphanumerics /ˌblɑːst θruː ˌælfənjuːˈmerɪks/ *plural noun* characters that can be displayed on a

videotext terminal when it is in graphics mode

bleed /bliːd/ *noun* **1.** a line of printing that runs off the edge of the paper **2.** a badly adjusted colour monitor in which colours of adjoining pixels blend

bleeding edge /ˌbliːdɪŋ 'edʒ/ *adjective* referring to technology that is very new and has not yet fully tested to see whether it works correctly

blessed folder /ˌblesɪd 'fəʊldə/ *noun* the Apple Mac System Folder that contains files loaded automatically when the Mac is switched on

blind /blaɪnd/ *adjective* which will not respond to certain codes

blind certificate /ˌblaɪnd sə'tɪfɪkət/ *noun* a means of tracking visitors to websites that identifies the user's system but not his or her name

blind dialling /ˌblaɪnd 'daɪəlɪŋ/ *noun* the ability of a modem to dial out even if the line appears dead, used on certain private lines

blind keyboard /ˌblaɪnd 'kiːbɔːd/ *noun* a keyboard whose output is not displayed but is stored directly on disk

B-line counter /ˌbiː laɪn 'kaʊntə/ *noun* an address register that is added to a reference address to provide the location to be accessed

blinking /'blɪŋkɪŋ/ *noun* a flashing effect caused by varying the intensity of a displayed character

blit /blɪt/ *noun* (*in computer graphics*) the act of moving a block of bits from one memory location to another. Full form **bit block transfer**. Also called **bit blit**

blitter /'blɪtə/ *noun* an electronic component designed to process or move a bit-mapped image from one area of memory to another ○ *The new blitter chip speeds up the graphics display.*

bloatware /'bləʊtweə/ *noun* a computer program that has many, often unnecessary features, which take up so much memory that the computer does not work as well as it should

blob /blɒb/ *noun* a field in a database record that can contain a large quantity of binary data, usually a bitmap image. Full form **binary large object**

block /blɒk/ *noun* **1.** a number of stored records treated as a single unit **2.** a wide printed bar

block capitals /ˌblɒk 'kæpɪt(ə)lz/ *plural noun* capital letters, e.g. A,B,C ○ *Write*

your name and address in block letters.
Also called **block letter**

block character check /ˌblɒk
ˈkærɪktə tʃek/ *noun* full form of **BCC**

block code /blɒk ˈkəʊd/ *noun* an error
detection and correction code for block
data transmission

block-copy /ˌblɒk ˈkɒpi/ *verb* **1.** to duplicate a block of data to another section of
memory **2.** to copy a selected area of
word-processed text from one part of a
document to another

block cursor /blɒk ˈkɜːsə/ *noun* a cursor in the shape of a solid rectangle that
fills a character position

block-delete /ˌblɒk dɪˈliːt/ *verb* to delete a selected area of word-processed text

block device /blɒk dɪˈvaɪs/ *noun* a device that manipulates many bytes of data at
once ○ *The disk drive is a block device that
can transfer 256bytes of data at a time.*

block diagram /blɒk ˈdaɪəˌɡræm/
noun a graphical representation of a system or program operation

block error rate /blɒk ˈerə reɪt/ *noun*
the number of blocks of data that contain
errors compared with the total number
transmitted

block gap /blɒk ˈɡæp/ *noun* a stretch of
blank magnetic tape between the end of
one block of data and the start of the next
in backing store

block header /blɒk ˈhedə/ *noun* a section of information at the start of a file describing content organisation or characteristics

block ignore character /ˌblɒk ɪɡˈnɔː
ˌkærɪktə/ *noun* a symbol at the start of a
block indicating that it contains corrupt
data

blocking factor /blɒkɪŋ ˈfæktə/ *noun*
the number of records in a block

block input processing /ˌblɒk
ˈɪnpʊt ˌprəʊsesɪŋ/ *noun* an input system
that requires a whole error-free block to be
received before it is processed

block length /blɒk ˈleŋθ/ *noun* the
number of records or fields or characters in
a block of data

block letters /ˌblɒk ˈletəz/ *plural noun*
same as **block capitals**

block list /ˈblɒk lɪst/ *noun* a list of the
blocks and records as they are organised in
a file

block mark /ˈblɒk mɑːk/ *noun* a code
that indicates the end of a block

block marker /ˈblɒk ˌmɑːkə/ *plural
noun* each of two markers inserted at the
start and finish of a section of data or text
to indicate a special block which can then
be moved or deleted or copied as a single
unit

block move /ˈblɒk muːv/ *verb* **1.** to
move selected word-processed text from
one area of a document to another **2.** to
move the contents of an area of memory to
another area of memory

block operation /blɒk ˌɒpəˈreɪʃ(ə)n/
noun a process carried out on a block of
data

block parity /blɒk ˈpærəti/ *noun* a parity error check on a block of data

block protection /blɒk prəˈtekʃən/
noun prevention of the splitting of a selected block of word-processed text by an
automatic page break

block retrieval /blɒk rɪˈtriːv(ə)l/ *noun*
the accessing of blocks of data stored in
memory

block synchronisation /ˌblɒk
ˌsɪŋkrənaɪˈzeɪʃ(ə)n/ *noun* the correct
timing of start, stop and message bits according to a predefined protocol

block transfer /blɒk ˈtrænsfɜː/ *noun*
the moving of large numbers of records
around in memory

blog /blɒɡ/ *verb* to create or run a weblog
(NOTE: **blogging – blogged**)

blogosphere /ˈblɒɡəˌsfɪə/ *noun* the
area of the World Wide Web in which
bloggers communicate with each other
(*informal*)

blogware /ˈblɒɡweə/ *noun* computer
software tools for creating a weblog

bloop /bluːp/ *verb* to pass a magnet over
a tape to erase signals which are not needed

blow /bləʊ/ *verb* to program a PROM device with data. Also called **burn** (NOTE:
blew – blown)

Blue Book Ethernet /ˌbluː bʊk
ˈiːθənet/ *noun* a version of Ethernet developed by DEC, Intel and Xerox

blueprint /ˈbluːˌprɪnt/ *noun* a copy of
an original set of specifications or design
in graphical form

blue-ribbon program /ˌbluː ˈrɪbən
ˌprəʊɡræm/ *noun* a perfect program that
runs first time, with no errors or bugs

Bluetooth /ˈbluːtuːθ/ a trade name for a
short-range radio communications system
that is designed to provide a simple way

r computer, Internet and input devices to communicate (NOTE: For example, a palm-top computer could transfer information to a mobile phone using a Bluetooth link. The technology was developed by a group of computer and telecommunications companies that included Ericsson, IBM, Intel, Nokia and Toshiba.)

blur /blɜː/ *noun* an image in which the edges or colours are not clear ■ *verb* to make the edges or colours of an image fuzzy ○ *The image becomes blurred when you turn the focus knob.* (NOTE: blurring – blurred)

BMP /ˌbiː em ˈpiː/ *noun* a three-letter extension to a filename that indicates that the file contains a bitmapped graphics image ○ *This paint package lets you import BMP files.* ◊ **GIF, JPEG, TIFF**

bn *abbr* billion

BNC connector /ˌbiː en ˈsiː kəˌnektə/ *noun* a cylindrical metal connector with a copper core that is at the end of coaxial cable and is used to connect cables together (NOTE: It attaches by pushing and twisting the outer cylinder onto two locking pins.)

BNC T-piece connector /ˌbiː en ˌsiː ˈtiː piːs kəˌnektə/ *noun* a T-shaped metal connector used to connect an adapter card to the ends of two sections of RG-58 'thin' coaxial cable, used in many Ethernet network installations

BNF /ˌbiː en ˈef/ *noun* a system of writing and expressing the syntax of a programming language. Full form **Backus-Naur-Form**

board /bɔːd/ *noun* a flat insulation material on which electronic components are mounted and connected

body /ˈbɒdi/ *noun* **1.** the main section of text in a document **2.** the main part of a program

body type /ˈbɒdi taɪp/ *noun* a default font and point size that is used for the main section of text in a document

bof, BOF *abbr* beginning of file

boilerplate /ˈbɔɪləpleɪt/ *noun* a final document that has been put together using standard sections of text held in a word-processor

boilerplating /ˈbɔɪləpleɪtɪŋ/ *noun* the putting together of a final document out of various standard sections of text

bold face /ˈbəʊld feɪs/ *noun* a thicker and darker form of a typeface

bomb /bɒm/ *noun* a routine in a program designed to crash the system or destroy data at a particular time ■ *verb* (*of software*) to fail (*informal*) ○ *The program bombed, and we lost all the data.*

book /bʊk/ *noun* a multimedia title. ◊ **ebook** (NOTE: The name comes from the fact that most multimedia titles are arranged as a series of different pages, which together form a book.)

bookmark /ˈbʊkmɑːk/ *noun* a code inserted at a particular point in a document that allows the user to move straight to that point at a later date

book palette /ˈbʊk ˌpælət/ *noun* a set of colours that is used in a particular multimedia application (NOTE: Two different applications could use different palettes, and each must load its own palette otherwise the colours will appear corrupted.)

Boolean algebra /ˌbuːliən ˈældʒɪbrə/ *noun* a set of rules that define, simplify and manipulate logical functions, based on statements which are true or false. ♦ **AND, NOT function, OR**. Also called **Boolean logic**

Boolean connective /ˌbuːliən kəˈnektɪv/ *noun* a symbol or character in a Boolean operation that describes the action to be performed on the operands

Boolean data type /ˌbuːliən ˈdeɪtə ˌtaɪp/ *noun* same as **Boolean variable**

Boolean logic /ˌbuːliən ˈlɒdʒɪk/ *noun* same as **Boolean algebra**

Boolean operation /ˌbuːliən ˌɒpəˈreɪʃ(ə)n/ *noun* a logical operation on a number of operands, conforming to Boolean algebra rules

Boolean operation table /ˌbuːliən ˌɒpəˈreɪʃ(ə)n ˌteɪb(ə)l/ *noun* a table showing two binary words, or operands, the operation and the result

Boolean operator /ˌbuːliən ˈɒpəreɪtə/ *noun* a logical operator such as AND, NOT and OR

Boolean search /ˌbuːliən ˈsɜːtʃ/ *noun* a search that uses the AND and OR functions

Boolean value /ˌbuːliən ˈvæljuː/ *noun* each of two values, either true or false

Boolean variable /ˌbuːliən ˈveəriəb(ə)l/ *noun* a binary word in which each bit represents true or false, using the digits 1 or 0. Also called **Boolean data type**

boot /buːt/ *verb* to execute a set of instructions automatically in order to reach a required state

bootable /ˈbuːtəb(ə)l/ *adjective* referring to a storage device that holds the commands to boot up a computer and load the operating system (NOTE: The main hard disk normally is a bootable device as is the floppy disk drive A:.)

boot block /ˈbuːt blɒk/ *noun* the first track, track 0, on a boot disk of an IBM-compatible floppy disk. Also called **boot record**

boot disk /ˈbuːt dɪsk/ *noun* a special disk that contains a bootstrap program and the operating system software ○ *After you switch on the computer, insert the boot disk.*

booting /ˈbuːtɪŋ/ *noun* same as **boot up**

bootleg /ˈbuːtˌleg/ *noun* an illegal copy of recorded material

BOOTP /ˌbiː əʊ əʊ tiː ˈpiː/ *noun* an Internet protocol used by a diskless workstation to find out its IP address, then load its operating system from a central server. Full form **bootstrap protocol**. ♢ **IP** (NOTE: This protocol allows a workstation to start up and load all its software over the network: a normal workstation would load its operating system software stored on an internal floppy or hard disk drive.)

boot partition /buːt pɑːˈtɪʃ(ə)n/ *noun* a partition on a hard disk that contains the bootstrap and operating system

boot record /ˈbuːt ˌrekɔːd/ *noun* same as **boot block**

boot sector /buːt ˈsektə/ *noun* a part of a disk that contains instructions that are read by the computer when it is first switched on or reset (NOTE: The instructions tell the computer how to load the operating system from the disk.)

bootstrap, bootstrap loader *noun* a set of instructions that are executed by the computer before a program is loaded, usually to load the operating system once the computer is switched on. Compare **loader**

bootstrap memory /ˈbuːtstræp ˌmem(ə)ri/ *noun* permanent memory within a terminal or microcomputer, that allows a user to customise the attributes, booting the system and loading programs

bootstrap protocol /ˌbuːtstræp ˈprəʊtəkɒl/ *noun* full form of **BOOTP**

boot up /buːt ˈʌp/ *noun* automatic execution of a set of instructions usually held in ROM when a computer is switched on. Also called **booting**

border /ˈbɔːdə/ *noun* **1.** an area around printed or displayed text **2.** a thin boundary line around a button or field or a graphic image

border style /ˈbɔːdə ˌstaɪl/ *noun* an attribute that determines the type of border around a button or field, e.g. a single line, a shadow or a double line

borrow /ˈbɒrəʊ/ *noun* an operation in certain arithmetic processes such as subtraction from a smaller number

Bose-Chandhuri-Hocquenghem code *noun* full form of **BCH code**

bot[1] /bɒt/, **BOT** *abbr* beginning of tape

bot[2] /bɒt/ *noun* a robot utility program that helps a user or another application carry out a particular task – e.g. a search bot will help a user search the Internet by submitting the query to several engines at once; a link bot will check that all the hyperlinks on a website are correct

BOT marker /ˈbɒt ˌmɑːkə/ *noun* a section of material that marks the start of the recording area of magnetic tape

bottom up method /ˈprəʊgræmɪŋ/, **bottom up programming** *noun* a method in which low-level instructions are combined to form a high-level instruction, which can then be further combined

bounce /baʊns/ *noun* **1.** a multiple key contact caused by a faulty switch **2.** an electronic mail message that could not be correctly delivered and is returned to the sender

boundary /ˈbaʊnd(ə)ri/ *noun* a line or marker that indicates the limits of something

boundary protection /ˌbaʊnd(ə)ri prəˈtekʃən/ *noun* a function designed to prevent any program writing into a reserved area of memory

boundary punctuation /ˌbaʊnd(ə)ri ˌpʌŋktʃuˈeɪʃ(ə)n/ *noun* punctuation that marks the beginning or end of a file

boundary register /ˌbaʊnd(ə)ri ˈredʒɪstə/ *noun* a register in a multi-user system that contains the addresses for the limits of one user's memory allocation

bounding box /ˈbaʊndɪŋ bɒks/ *noun* a rectangle that determines the shape and position of an image that has been placed in a document or on screen

Boyce-Codd normal form /ˌbɔɪs kɒd ˈnɔːməl ˌfɔːm/ *noun* ♦ **normal form**. Abbr **BCNF**

ɔozo bit /'bəʊzəʊ bɪt/ *noun* (*in an Apple Macintosh system*) an attribute bit that prevents a file being copied or moved

BPI, bpi *noun* the number of bits that can be recorded per inch of recording medium. Full form **bits per inch**

BPP /ˌbiː piː 'piː/ *noun* the number of bits assigned to store the colour of each pixel. One bit provides black or white, four bits give 16 colour combinations, eight bits give 256 colour combinations. Full form **bits per pixel**

bps /ˌbiː piː 'es/ *noun* the number of bits that can be transmitted per second ○ *Their transmission rate is 60,000 bits per second (bps) through a parallel connection.* Full form **bits per second**

Bps /ˌbiː piː 'es/ *noun* the number of bytes that can be transmitted per second. Full form **bytes per second**

bps rate /ˌbiː piː 'es reɪt/ *noun* the rate at which information is sent, equal to the number of bits transmitted or received per second

bps rate adjust /ˌbiː piː ˌes reɪt ə 'dʒʌst/ *noun* the ability of a modem to adjust the speed of its serial port automatically so as to match the communications speed

BRA /ˌbiː ɑː 'eɪ/ *noun* a basic ISDN service that provides two data channels capable of carrying data at a rate of 64Kbps together with a signalling channel used to carry control signals at 16Kbps. Full form **basic rate access**

braces /'breɪsɪz/ *plural noun* curly bracket characters ({ }) used in some programming languages to enclose a routine

bracket /'brækɪt/ *noun* a printing sign to show that an instruction or operation is to be processed separately ■ *verb* □ **to bracket together** to print brackets round several items to show that they are treated in the same way and separated from the rest of the text

branch /brɑːntʃ/ *noun* **1.** a possible path or jump from one instruction to another **2.** a line linking one or more devices to the main network ○ *The faulty station is on this branch.* ■ *verb* to jump from one section of a program to another, often using a test or decision with two or more possible results that lead to two different points in the program

COMMENT: In BASIC, the instruction GOTO makes the system jump to the line indicated; this is an unconditional branch. The instruction IF…THEN is a conditional branch, because the jump will only take place if the condition is met.

branch cable /brɑːntʃ 'keɪb(ə)l/ *noun* a cable that runs from a main cable to a node

branch instruction /brɑːntʃ ɪn 'strʌkʃən/ *noun* a conditional program instruction that provides the location of the next instruction in the program, if a condition is met

branchpoint /'brɑːntʃpɔɪnt/ *noun* a point in a program where a branch can take place

branch table /'brɑːntʃ ˌteɪb(ə)l/ *noun* a table that defines where to jump to in a program depending on the result of a test

breach /briːtʃ/ *noun* a failure to carry out the terms of an agreement □ **breach of warranty** the supplying of goods which do not meet the standards of the warranty applied to them

breadboard /'bredbɔːd/ *noun* a device that allows prototype electronic circuits to be constructed easily without permanent connections or soldering

break /breɪk/ *noun* an action performed, or a key pressed, to stop the execution of a program

Break key /'breɪk kiː/ *noun* a special key on an IBM-compatible keyboard that halts the execution of a program when it is pressed at the same time as the Control key ○ *I stopped the problem by pressing Ctrl-Break.*

breakout box /'breɪkaʊt bɒks/ *noun* a device that displays the status of lines within an interface, cable or connector ○ *The serial interface doesn't seem to be working – use the breakout box to see which signals are present.*

breakpoint /'breɪkpɔɪnt/ *noun* a symbol inserted into a program which stops its execution at that point to allow registers, variables and memory locations to be examined (NOTE: Breakpoints are often used when debugging a program.)

breakpoint halt /'breɪkpɔɪnt ˌhɔːlt/ *noun* same as **breakpoint instruction**

breakpoint instruction /'breɪkpɔɪnt ɪnˌstrʌkʃən/ *noun* a halt command inserted in a program to stop its execution temporarily. This allows the programmer to examine data and registers while debugging a program.

breakpoint symbol /'breɪkpɔɪnt ˌsɪmb(ə)l/ *noun* a special character used to provide a breakpoint in a debugging program. The program allows breakpoint symbols to be inserted, then executes the program until it reaches one, then halts.

breakup /'breɪkʌp/ *noun* (*in video*) loss or distortion of a signal

B register /biː 'redʒɪstə/ *noun* **1.** an address register that is added to a reference address to provide the location to be accessed **2.** a register used to extend the accumulator in multiplication and division operations

BRI /ˌbiː ɑː 'aɪ/ *noun* one part of the ISDN service that provides two data transfer channels, also called bearer channels, that can transmit data at 64Kbit/second and one control channel that can transfer extra control information at 16Kbit/second. Full form **basic rate interface**

bricks-and-mortar /ˌbrɪks ən 'mɔːtə/ *adjective* referring to businesses that operate using buildings such as shops and warehouses, as opposed to operating only or mainly via the Internet. Compare **clicks-and-mortar**

bridge /brɪdʒ/ *verb* to use bridgeware to help transfer programs and data files to another system (NOTE: A bridging product is available for companies with both generations of machines.) ■ *noun* **1.** a device that connects two networks together and allow information to flow between them. ◊ **router, brouter** (NOTE: Bridges function at the data link layer of the OSI network model.) **2.** a process of ensuring that pieces of computer equipment match, so that power losses between them are kept to a minimum **3.** hardware or software that allows parts of an old system to be used on a new system

'Lotus Development and IMRS are jointly developing a bridge linking their respective spreadsheet and client server reporting tools. It will allow users of IMRS' Hyperion reporting tool to manipulate live data from Lotus Improv.' [*Computing*]

bridgeware /'brɪdʒweə/ *noun* hardware or software used to make the transfer from one computer system to another easier, by changing e.g. file format and translation

bridging /'brɪdʒɪŋ/ *noun* the use of bridgeware to help transfer programs and data files to another system

COMMENT: A bridge connects two similar networks: a gateway connects two different networks. To connect two Ethernet networks, use a bridge.

bridging product /'brɪdʒɪŋ ˌprɒdʌkt/ *noun* same as **bridge**

Briefcase utility /'briːfkeɪs juːˌtɪlɪtɪ *noun* (*in Windows*) a special utility that allows you to keep files stored on a laptop and a desktop PC up to date

brightness /'braɪtnəs/ *noun* the intensity of the light emitted by an image on a screen ○ *A control knob allows you to adjust brightness and contrast.*

brightness range /'braɪtnəs reɪndʒ/ *noun* the variation in the intensity of the light emitted by something

brilliant /'brɪljənt/ *adjective* (*of light or colour*) very bright and shining

bring up /ˌbrɪŋ 'ʌp/ *verb* to start a computer system

British Approvals Board for Telecommunications /ˌbrɪtɪʃ əˌpruːvəlz bɔːd fɔː ˌtelikəmjuːnɪ'keɪʃ(ə)nz/ *noun* full form of **BABT**

British Standards Institute /ˌbrɪtɪʃ 'stændədz ˌɪnstɪtjuːt/ *noun* full form of **BSI** (*UK*)

broadband /'brɔːdbænd/ *noun* (*in local area networks or communications*) a transmission method that combines several channels of data onto a carrier signal and can carry the data over long distances. Compare **baseband**. Also called **wideband**

COMMENT: The three most popular broadband communication devices are ISDN, cable modems and ADSL, which is part of the wider DSL standard. Each country has different prevalent standards and pricing models. For example, ISDN provides a digital link that can transfer data at the rate of 64Kbps; it dials an access number and provides a link when required. ADSL, in contrast, provides a direct connection that appears to be 'always on' using a network adapter to link the computer to the Internet provider. ADSL normally supports a transfer speed of up to 2Mbps.

broadband communication device /ˌbrɔːdbænd kəˌmjuːnɪ'keɪʃ(ə)n dɪˌvaɪs/ *noun* a communication channel and device that allow a computer to connect to the Internet at a very high speed, often several thousand times faster than a dial-up modem connected to a telephone line

broadband ISDN /ˌbrɔːdbænd ˌaɪ es diː 'en/ *noun* a high-speed data transfer service that allows data and voice to be transmitted over a wide area network. Abbr **B-ISDN**

broadcast /'brɔːdkɑːst/ *noun* (*in a network*) a message or data sent to a group of users ■ *verb* to distribute information over a wide area or to a large audience ○ *He*

broadcast the latest news over the WAN.
(NOTE: broadcasts – broadcasting – broadcast)

broadcast message /ˌbrɔːdkɑːst ˈmesɪdʒ/ *noun* a message sent to everyone on a network ○ *Five minutes before we shut down the LAN, we send a broadcast message to all users.*

broadcast network /ˌbrɔːdkɑːst ˈnetwɜːk/ *noun* a network for sending data to a number of receivers

broadcast quality /ˌbrɔːdkɑːst ˈkwɒlɪti/ *noun* a quality of video image or signal that is the same as that used by professional television stations ○ *We can use your multimedia presentation as the advert on TV if it's of broadcast quality.*

brochure site /ˈbrəʊʃə saɪt/ *noun* a simple, often one-page, website that advertises a company's products and gives its contact details

brouter /ˈbruːtə/ *noun* a device that combines the functions of a router and bridge to connect networks together ○ *The brouter provides dynamic routing and can bridge two local area networks.* ◊ **bridge, router**

brown-out /ˈbraʊn aʊt/ *noun* a power failure caused by a low voltage level rather than no voltage level

browse /braʊz/ *verb* **1.** to view data in a database or online system **2.** to search through and access database material without permission

browser /ˈbraʊzə/ *noun* a software program that is used to navigate through webpages stored on the Internet. A browser program asks the Internet server to send it a page of information, stores, decodes and displays the page, and will jump to other pages if you click on hyperlinks. ◊ **HTML, NetScape, IE**

COMMENT: A browser program asks the Internet server (called the HTTP server) to send it a page of information; this page is stored in the HTML layout language that is decoded by the browser and displayed on screen. The browser displays any hotspots and will jump to another page if the user clicks on a hyperlink.

browsing /ˈbraʊzɪŋ/ *noun* the activity of moving through sites on the Internet, a list of files or a multimedia title in no particular order. You control which page you move to next and what you view.

brush /brʌʃ/ *noun* a tool in paint package software that draws pixels on screen ○ *The paint package lets you vary the width of the brush (in pixels) and the colour it produces.*

brush style /ˈbrʌʃ staɪl/ *noun* the width and shape of the brush tool in a paint package ○ *To fill in a big area, I select a wide, square brush style.*

brute force method /ˌbruːt fɔːs ˈmeθəd/ *noun* a problem-solving method which depends on computer power rather than elegant programming techniques

BS *abbr* backspace

BSAM *abbr* basic sequential access method

BSC /ˌbiː es ˈsiː/ *noun* an old standard for medium/high speed data communication links. Full form **binary synchronous communications**

BSI /ˌbiː es ˈaɪ/ *noun* an organisation that monitors design and safety standards in the UK. Full form **British Standards Institute**

BTAM /ˌbiː tiː eɪ ˈem/ *noun* a method of providing access for read or write operations to a remote device. Full form **basic telecommunications access method**

btree /ˈbiː triː/ *noun* same as **binary tree**

bubble-help /ˈbʌb(ə)l help/ *noun* a single line that appears on screen to describe what you are pointing at

bubble jet printer /ˌbʌb(ə)l dʒet ˈprɪntə/ *noun* ▸ **ink-jet printer**

bubble memory /ˌbʌb(ə)l ˈmem(ə)ri/ *noun* a method of storing binary data using the magnetic properties of certain materials, allowing very large amounts of data to be stored in primary memory

bubble memory cassette /ˌbʌb(ə)l ˈmem(ə)ri kəˌset/ *noun* a bubble memory device on a removable cartridge similar to an audio cassette that can be inserted into a controller card to provide removable memory

bubble sort /ˈbʌb(ə)l sɔːt/ *noun* a sorting method which repeatedly exchanges various pairs of data items until they are in order

bucket /ˈbʌkɪt/ *noun* a storage area containing data for an application

buffer /ˈbʌfə/ *noun* **1.** a circuit that isolates and protects a system from damaging inputs from driven circuits or peripherals. ◊ **driver 2.** a temporary storage area for data waiting to be processed ■ *verb* to use a temporary storage area to hold data until the processor or device is ready to deal with it

COMMENT: Buffers allow two parts of a computer system to work at different speeds, e.g. a high-speed central processing unit and a slower line printer.

buffered input/output /ˌbʌfəd ˌɪnpʊt ˈaʊtpʊt/ *noun* the use of a temporary storage area on input or output ports to allow slow peripherals to operate with a fast CPU

buffered memory /ˌbʌfəd ˈmem(ə)ri/ *noun* a type of memory that allows instructions or data to be entered before the processor has finished processing the ones it is currently dealing with

buffering /ˈbʌfərɪŋ/ *noun* using buffers to provide a link between slow and fast devices

buffer length /ˈbʌfə leŋθ/ *noun* the number of data item that can be stored in a buffer while waiting for the processor to attend to them

buffer register /ˌbʌfə ˈredʒɪstə/ *noun* temporary storage for data read from or being written to main memory

buffer size /ˈbʌfə saɪz/ *noun* the total number of characters that can be held in a buffer

bug /bʌg/ *noun* an error in a computer program which makes it run incorrectly (*informal*)

buggy /ˈbʌgi/ *noun* a small computer-controlled vehicle (NOTE: The plural is **buggies**.)

bug patch /ˈbʌg pætʃ/ *noun* **1.** a temporary correction made to a program **2.** a small correction made to software by a user on the instructions of the software publisher

build /bɪld/ *noun* a particular version of a program ○ *This is the latest build of the new software.*

building block /ˈbɪldɪŋ blɒk/ *noun* a self-contained unit that can be joined to others to form a system

built-in /ˈbɪlt ɪn/ *adjective* already included in a system ○ *The built-in adapter card makes it fully IBM compatible.* Opposite **add-on**

built-in check /ˌbɪlt ɪn ˈtʃek/ *noun* an error detection and validation check carried out automatically on received data

built-in font /ˌbɪlt ɪn ˈfɒnt/ *noun* a font stored permanently within a peripheral, normally a printer

built-in function /ˌbɪlt ɪn ˈfʌŋkʃ(ə)n/ *noun* a special function already implemented in a program

built-in message /ˌbɪlt ɪn ˈmesɪdʒ/ *noun* a message generated by a system or authoring language in response to an action such as a mouse click

bulk erase /bʌlk ɪˈreɪz/ *verb* to erase a complete disk in one action

bulk storage medium /ˌbʌlk ˈstɔːrɪdʒ ˌmiːdiəm/ *noun* a medium that is able to store large amounts of data in a convenient size and form

bulk update terminal /ˌbʌlk ˈʌpdeɪt ˌtɜːmɪn(ə)l/ *noun* a device used by an information provider to prepare videotext pages off-line, then transmit them rapidly to the main computer

bullet /ˈbʊlɪt/ *noun* a symbol, often a filled circle ● or square ■, placed in front of a line of text and used to draw attention to a particular line in a list

'For a bullet chart use four to six bullet points and no more than six to eight words each' [*Computing*]

bulleted *adjective* marked with a bullet in front of the line of text ○ *a bulleted list*

bulletin board /ˈbʊlɪtɪn bɔːd/, **bulletin board system** *noun* an online forum used to exchange e-mails, chat and access software. Abbr **BBS**

bundle /ˈbʌnd(ə)l/ *noun* **1.** a number of optic fibres gathered together **2.** a package containing a computer together with software or accessories offered at a special price ○ *The bundle now includes a PC with CD-rewriter, digital camera and scanner for just £599.* ■ *verb* to market at a special price a package that contains a computer together with a range of software or accessories

bundled software /ˌbʌnd(ə)ld ˈsɒftweə/ *noun* software included in the price of a computer system

bureau /ˈbjʊərəʊ/ *noun* an office that specialises in keyboarding data or processing batches of data for other small companies ○ *The company offers a number of bureau services, such as printing and data collection.*

'IMC has a colour output bureau that puts images onto the uncommon CD-ROM XA format.' [*Computing*]

burn /bɜːn/ *verb* **1.** same as **blow 2.** to copy data onto a CD-ROM or DVD-ROM

burned-in time code /ˌbɜːnd ɪn ˈtaɪm ˌkəʊd/ *noun* time code information included in the video signal as an image that is visible on any TV or monitor. Abbr **BITC**

burner /ˈbɜːnə/ *noun* a device which burns in programs onto PROM chips

burn in /bɜːn ˈɪn/ *verb* **1.** to mark a television or monitor screen after displaying a high-brightness image for too long **2.** to write data into a PROM chip

burn-in /ˈbɜːn ɪn/ *noun* a heat test for electronic components

burn out /ˌbɜːn ˈaʊt/ *noun* excess heat or incorrect use that causes an electronic circuit or device to fail

burst /bɜːst/ *noun* a short isolated sequence of transmitted signals

burster /ˈbɜːstə/ *noun* a machine used to separate the sheets of continuous fanfold paper

burst mode /ˈbɜːst məʊd/ *noun* data transmission using intermittent bursts of data

bursty /ˈbɜːsti/ *adjective* transmitted in short uneven bursts, rather than a smooth continuous stream

bus /bʌs/ *noun* **1.** a communication link consisting of a set of leads or wires which connects different parts of a computer hardware system, and over which data is transmitted and received by various circuits in the system. Also called **highway** **2.** a central source of information that supplies several devices

bus address lines /ˌbʌs əˈdres ˌlaɪnz/ *plural noun* wires, each of which carries one bit of an address word

bus arbitration /bʌs ˌɑːbɪˈtreɪʃ(ə)n/ *noun* the protocol and control of transmission over a bus that ensures fair usage by several users

'The slot controller detects when a new board is inserted, it activates power up and assigns a bus arbitration and card slot ID to the board.' [*Computing*]

bus bar /ˈbʌs bɑː/ *noun* an electrical conductor or group of electrical conductors used as a connector in a circuit, especially as a bus in a computer system

bus board /ˈbʌs bɔːd/ *noun* a PCB containing conducting paths for all the computer signals for the address, data and control buses

bus clock /ˈbʌs klɒk/ *noun* the speed at which data is transferred along the main bus in a computer (NOTE: This is not always the same speed as the processor speed.)

bus clock speed /ˌbʌs klɒk ˈspiːd/ *noun* the frequency of the clock that governs the main bus in a computer

bus control lines /ˌbʌs kənˈtrəʊl ˌlaɪnz/ *plural noun* wires, each of which carries one bit of a control word

bus data lines /ˌbʌs ˈdeɪtə ˌlaɪnz/ *plural noun* wires, each of which carries one bit of a data word

bus driver /bʌs ˈdraɪvə/ *noun* high power transistors or an amplifier that can provide enough power to transmit signals to a number of devices

bus extender /ˌbʌs iksˈtendə/, **bus extension card** /bʌs ɪkˈstenʃən kɑːd/ *noun* **1.** device that extends an 8-bit bus to accommodate 16-bit add-in cards **2.** special board (used by repair engineers) that moves an add-in board up to a position that is easier to work on

business computer /ˈbɪznɪs kəmˌpjuːtə/ *noun* a powerful small computer which is programmed for special business tasks

business package /ˈbɪznɪs ˌpækɪdʒ/ *noun* same as **business system**

business system /ˈbɪznɪs ˌsɪstəm/ *noun* a set of programs adapted for business use, comprising e.g. payroll, invoicing and customers file

bus master /bʌs ˈmɑːstə/ *noun* a device that controls the bus whilst transmitting (NOTE: Bus master status can move between sending stations.)

bus master adapter /ˌbʌs ˌmɑːstə ə ˈdæptə/ *noun* an adapter card that fits in a EISA or MCA expansion slot in a PC, and that can take control of the main bus and transfer data to the computer's main memory independently of the main processor ○ *The bus master network adapter provides much faster data throughput than the old adapter.*

bus network /bʌs ˈnetwɜːk/ *noun* a network of computers where the machines are connected to a central bus unit which transmits the messages it receives

bus slave /ˈbʌs sleɪv/ *noun* a data sink that receives data from a bus master

bus structure /bʌs ˈstrʌktʃə/ *noun* the way in which buses are organised, i.e. whether serial, parallel or bidirectional

bus topology /ˌbʌs təˈpɒlədʒi/ *noun* a network topology in which all devices are connected to a single cable which has terminators at each end ○ *Ethernet is a network that uses the bus topology.*

bus unit /bʌs ˈjuːnɪt/ *noun* (*within a microprocessor*) the place where instructions flow between the main memory and the processor

busy /'bɪzi/ *adjective* (*of a signal*) indicating that a device is not ready to receive data

button /'bʌt(ə)n/ *noun* **1.** a switch on a mouse or joystick that carries out an action ○ *Use the mouse to move the cursor to the icon and start the application by pressing the mouse button.* **2.** a square shape displayed that will carry out a particular action if selected with a pointer or keyboard ○ *There are two buttons at the bottom of the status window, select the left button to cancel the operation or the right to continue.*

button bar /'bʌt(ə)n bɑː/ *noun* a line of small buttons along the top of the screen, just below the menu bar, in many applications such as Microsoft Word, Works and Excel. Each button on the bar contains an icon that helps describe its function and is equipped with bubble-help.

BYAM *abbr* between you and me

BYKT *abbr* but you know/knew that

bypass /'baɪpɑːs/ *noun* an alternative route around a component or device, usually a faulty one, so that it is not used ○ *There is an automatic bypass around any faulty equipment.*

byte /baɪt/ *noun* a group of usually eight bits or binary digits that a computer operates on as a single unit

byte address /'baɪt ə,dres/ *plural noun* the location of data bytes in memory

bytecode /'baɪtkəʊd/ *noun* a form of Java instructions that can be executed in a Java Virtual Machine. When a programmer develops a program written in Java, the Java compiler converts the instructions into a bytecode form that can then be run on any computer that supports the Virtual Machine software. ♢ **Java, virtual machine**

byte machine /baɪt mə'ʃiːn/ *noun* a variable word length computer

byte manipulation /baɪt mə,nɪpjʊ 'leɪʃ(ə)n/ *noun* the process of moving, editing and changing the contents of a byte

byte mode /'baɪt məʊd/ *noun* a way of transmitting data one byte at a time

byte-orientated protocol /,baɪt ,ɔːriənteɪtɪd 'prəʊtəkɒl/ *noun* a communications protocol that transmits data as characters rather than as a bit-stream

byte serial mode /,baɪt 'sɪəriəl ,məʊd/ *noun* same as **byte serial transmission**

byte serial transmission /,baɪt ,sɪəriəl trænz'mɪʃ(ə)n/ *noun* the transmission of bytes of data sequentially, during which individual bits can be sent in a serial or parallel way

bytes-per-inch /baɪtz pə/ *noun* a measure of the data storage capacity of magnetic tape

bytes per second /,baɪts pɜː 'sekənd/ *noun* full form of **Bps**

C

C¹ *symbol* the hexadecimal number equivalent to decimal 12

C² *noun* a high level programming language developed mainly for writing structured systems programs (NOTE: The C language was originally developed for and with the UNIX operating system.)

C++ /ˌsiː plʌs 'plʌs/ *noun* a high-level programming language based on its predecessor, C, but providing object-oriented programming functions

CA *abbr* certificate authority

CAAT *abbr* certificate authority administration tool

cable /'keɪb(ə)l/ *noun* a flexible conducting electrical or optical link ○ *The cable has the wrong connector for this printer.*

cable connector /ˌkeɪb(ə)l kə'nektə/ *noun* a connector at either end of a cable

cable matcher /'keɪb(ə)l ˌmætʃə/ *noun* an impedance matching device that allows non-standard cable to be used with a particular device

cable modem /ˌkeɪb(ə)l 'məʊdem/ *noun* a device that links a computer to the Internet via an existing cable television line. This system provides high speed access to the Internet by sharing the coaxial cable that is used to distribute cable television signals.

cable plant /'keɪb(ə)l plɑːnt/ *noun* all the cables, connectors and patch panels within a building or office

cable tester /ˌkeɪb(ə)l 'testə/ *noun* test equipment used to find breaks or faults or cracks in cabling

cabling /'keɪblɪŋ/ *noun* cable as a material ○ *Using high-quality cabling will allow the user to achieve very high data transfer rates.*

'It has won a £500,000 contract to supply a structured voice and data cabling system to the bank and its stockbrocking subsidiary.' [*Computing*]

cabling diagram /'keɪb(ə)lɪŋ ˌdaɪəgræm/ *noun* a drawing showing where the main cable runs through an office, and where the connection points to it are

cache /kæʃ/ *noun* a section of memory used to store a temporary copy of selected data for faster access. Also called **cache memory** ■ *verb* to file or store in a cache ○ *This CPU caches instructions so improves performance by 15 percent.*

cache controller /kæʃ kən'trəʊlə/ *noun* a set of logic circuits that determines when to store data in the high-speed cache memory, when to access data in the cache and when to access data stored in the slower storage device

cache hit /'kæʃ hɪt/ *noun* data retrieved from cache memory rather than from the storage device

cache memory /'kæʃ ˌmem(ə)ri/ *noun* same as **cache**

CAD /kæd/ *noun* the use of a computer and graphics terminal to help a designer in his work ○ *All our engineers design on CAD workstations.* Full form **computer-aided design, computer-assisted design**

'John Smith of CAD supplier CAD/CAM Limited has moved into sales with responsibilities for the North of England. He was previously a technical support specialist.' [*Computing*]

CAD/CAM *noun* interaction between computers used for designing and those for manufacturing a product

caddy /'kædi/ *noun* ♦ **CD caddy**

CAE /ˌsiː eɪ 'iː/ *noun* the use of a computer to help an engineer solve problems or calculate design or product specifications. Full form **computer-aided engineering, computer-assisted engineering**

CAI /ˌsiː eɪ 'aɪ/ *noun* the use of a computer to assist in teaching a subject. Full form **computer-aided instruction, computer-assisted instruction**

CAL /ˌsiː eɪ 'el/ *noun* the use of a computer to assist pupils to learn a subject. Full form **computer-aided learning, computer-assisted learning**

calculated field /'kælkjʊˌleɪtɪd fiːlⁿd/ *noun* a field within a database record that contains the results of calculations performed on other fields

Calculator /'kælkjʊˌleɪtə/ a software utility that is supplied with Windows, works just like a normal calculator and is started by double-clicking on the Calculator icon in the Accessories group

calendar program /ˌkælɪndə 'prəʊɡræm/ *noun* a software diary utility that allows a user to enter and keep track of appointments

calibrate /'kælɪbreɪt/ *verb* to adjust a monitor or joystick so that it is responding correctly and accurately to the signals or movements

calibration /ˌkælə'breɪʃ(ə)n/ *noun* the process of comparing the signal from an input with a known scale to provide a standardised reading

call /kɔːl/ *verb* to transfer control from a main program to a separate program or routine

call accepted signal /kɔːl ək'septɪd/, **call accept signal** /kɔːl ək'sept/ *noun* a signal sent by a device showing that it is willing to accept a caller's data

callback /'kɔːlbæk/ *noun* a security system that is used to reduce the risk of any unauthorised user connecting to your computer if you have installed dial-in networking . With callback, you use your communications software and modem to dial the remote computer and enter your name and password. The remote computer then hangs up the telephone line and calls you back on a preset telephone number.

call back modem /'kɔːl bæk ˌməʊdem/ *noun* a modem that, on answering a call, immediately hangs up and calls the user back to establish a connection. It is used to provide better security than a normal dial-up modem.

call control signal /'kɔːl kənˌtrəʊl ˌsɪɡn(ə)l/ *noun* the signal necessary to establish and end a call

call discrimination /kɔːl dɪˌskrɪmɪ'neɪʃ(ə)n/ *noun* a feature of a modem that allows it to check if an incoming telephone call is from a fax machine, another computer with a modem or from a person

call duration /kɔːl djʊ'reɪʃ(ə)n/ *noun* the length of time spent between starting and ending a call ○ *Call duration depends on the complexity of the transaction.*

called party /kɔːld 'pɑːti/ *noun* the person or station to which a call is made

caller /'kɔːlə/ *noun* a person who telephones or requests a call

call handler /kɔːl 'hændlə/ *noun* ♦ **handler**

calling /'kɔːlɪŋ/ *noun* a signal to request attention, sent from a terminal or device to the main computer

calling sequence /ˌkɔːlɪŋ 'siːkwəns/ *noun* a series of program commands required to direct execution to or back from a subroutine

call instruction /kɔːl ɪn'strʌkʃən/ *noun* a programming instruction that directs control to a routine (NOTE: Before the call, the program counter contents are saved to show the return instruction where to return to in the main program, and control is passed back once the routine has finished.)

call logger /kɔːl 'lɒɡə/ *noun* a device which keeps a record of telephone calls

call scheduling /'kɔːl ˌʃedjuːlɪŋ/ *noun* (*in a fax server*) the process of arranging calls so that long-distance calls are made at off-peak times

call up /ˌkɔːl 'ʌp/ *verb* to ask for information from a backing store to be displayed ○ *All the customers addresses were called up.*

CAM /ˌsiː eɪ 'em/ *noun* the use of a computer to control machinery or assist in a manufacturing process. Full form **computer-aided manufacture, computer-assisted manufacturing** ■ *abbr* content addressable memory

Cambridge ring /ˌkeɪmbrɪdʒ 'rɪŋ/ *noun* a local area networking standard used for connecting several devices and computers together in a ring with simple cable links

campus environment /ˌkæmpəs ɪn'vaɪrənmənt/ *noun* a large area or location that has lots of users connected by several networks, such as a university or hospital

campus network /ˌkæmpəs 'netwɜːk/ *noun* a network that connects together the smaller local area networks in each department within a building or university site

cancel /'kænsəl/ *verb* to stop a process or instruction before it has been fully executed

cancelbot /'kæns(ə)lbɒt/ *noun* a computer program that cancels unwanted articles sent to an Internet newsgroup by a particular user

cancel character /ˌkæns(ə)l 'kærɪktə/ *noun* a control code used to indicate that the last data transmitted was incorrect

cancellation /ˌkænsə'leɪʃ(ə)n/ *noun* the action of stopping a process which has been started

canonical schema /kəˌnɒnɪkl 'skiːmə/ *noun* a model of a database that is independent of hardware or software available

capability list /ˌkeɪpə'bɪləti lɪst/ *noun* a list of operations that can be carried out

capacitance /kæ'pæsɪtəns/ *noun* the ability of a component to store electrical charge

capacitative /kə'pæsɪtətɪv/, **capacitive** *adjective* that has capacitance

capacitor /kə'pæsɪtə/ *noun* an electronic component that can store charge

capacitor storage /kəˌpæsɪtə 'stɔːrɪdʒ/ *noun* a device that uses the capacitative properties of a material to store data

capacity /kə'pæsɪti/ *noun* the amount of storage space available in a system or on a disk

capitalisation /ˌkæpɪt(ə)laɪ'zeɪʃ(ə)n/, **capitalization** *noun* function of a word-processor to convert a line or block of text into capitals

capitals /'kæpɪt(ə)lz/, **caps** *plural noun* letters in their large form, A,B,C,D, etc., as opposed to lower-case letters, a,b,c,d, etc. ○ *The word BASIC is always written in caps.*

caps lock /'kæps lɒk/ *noun* a key on a keyboard that allows all characters to be entered as capitals ○ *The LED lights up when caps lock is pressed.*

capstan /'kæpstən/ *noun* a spindle of a tape player or tape backup unit that keeps the tape pressed against the magnetic read/write head or pinch roller

caption /'kæpʃən/ *noun* a descriptive text that appears at the top of a window, in white text on a blue background

caption generator /'kæpʃən ˌdʒenəreɪtə/ *noun* a computer or electronic device that allows a user to add titles or captions to a video sequence

capture /'kæptʃə/ *verb* **1.** to take data into a computer system ○ *The software allows captured images to be edited.* □ **capture a printer port** to redirect data intended for a local printer port over a network to a shared printer □ **capture a screen** to store the image that is currently displayed on the screen in a file ○ *In Windows, you can capture the current screen as a graphics image by pressing the PrintScreen key on the keyboard.* **2.** (*in a Token-Ring network*) to remove a token from the network in order to transmit data across the network

carbon copy /ˌkɑːbən 'kɒpi/ *noun* full form of **cc**

carbon ribbon /ˌkɑːbən 'rɪbən/ *noun* a thin plastic ribbon, coated with black ink, used in printers. Compare **fibre ribbon**

card /kɑːd/ *noun* a sheet of insulating material on which electronic components can be mounted

'A smart card carries an encryption chip, which codifies your ID and password prior to their being transmitted across a network.' [*Computing*]

CardBus /'kɑːdbʌs/ a high-speed, up to 33MHz, version of the original PCMCIA PC Card standard that allows 32-bits of data to be transferred in one operation compared to the 16-bit capability of the original PC Card standard

card cage /'kɑːd keɪdʒ/ *noun* a metal supporting frame for circuit boards

card chassis /kɑːd 'ʃæsi/ *noun* same as **card frame**

card edge connector /ˌkɑːd edʒ kə'nektə/ *noun* a series of metal tracks ending at the edge and on the surface of a circuit board, allowing it to be plugged into an edge connector to provide an electrical path for data transmission

card extender /'kɑːd ikˌstendə/ *noun* a card containing only conducting tracks, inserted between a motherboard connector and an expansion board, allowing the expansion board to be worked on and examined easily, outside the card cage

card frame /'kɑːd freɪm/ *noun* a frame containing a motherboard into which printed circuit boards can be plugged to provide a flexible system

cardinal number /ˌkɑːdɪn(ə)l 'nʌmbə/ *noun* a positive whole number ○ *13, 19 and 27 are cardinal numbers, −2.3 and 7.45 are not.*

cardioid microphone /ˌkɑːdiɔɪd 'maɪkrəfəʊn/ *noun* a highly sensitive microphone that is used to pick up sound in a specific area, not used for general noise recording

cardioid response /ˌkɑːdiɔɪd rɪ 'spɒns/ *noun* the heart-shaped response curve of an antenna or microphone when a signal source is moved around it

card reader /kɑːd 'riːdə/ *noun* a device which reads data from the magnetic strip on the back of a identity or credit card

caret /'kærət/ *noun* symbol '^' that is often used to mean the Control key

carpal tunnel syndrome /ˌkɑːp(ə)l 'tʌn(ə)l ˌsɪndrəʊm/ *noun* same as **repetitive strain injury**

carriage /'kærɪdʒ/ *noun* the mechanical section of a printer that correctly feeds or moves the paper that is being printed

carriage control /'kærɪdʒ kənˌtrəʊl/ *noun* a set of codes that control the movements of a printer carriage ○ *Carriage control codes can be used to move the paper forward two lines between each line of text.*

carriage return /ˌkærɪdʒ rɪ'tɜːn/ *noun* a code or key to indicate the end of an input line and to move the cursor to the start of the next line. Abbr **CR**

carriage return key /ˌkærɪdʒ rɪ'tɜːn ˌkiː/ *noun* a key that moves a cursor or printhead to the beginning of the next line on screen or in printing

carrier /'kæriə/ *noun* a continuous high-frequency waveform that can be modulated by a signal

carrier detect /ˌkæriə dɪ'tekt/ *noun* a signal generated by a modem to inform the local computer that it has detected a carrier from a remote modem. Abbr **CD**

carrier frequency /ˌkæriə 'friːkwənsi/ *noun* the frequency of the carrier signal before it is modulated

carrier sense multiple access-collision avoidance /ˌkæriə sens ˌmʌltip(ə)lˌækses kə'lɪʒ(ə)n əˌvɔɪdəns/ *noun* full form of **CSMA-CA**

carrier sense multiple access-collision detection /ˌkæriə sens ˌmʌltip(ə)l ˌækses kə'lɪʒ(ə)n dɪ ˌtek∫(ə)n/ *noun* full form of **CSMA-CD**

carrier signal /ˌkæriə 'sɪgn(ə)l/ *noun* a continuous high-frequency waveform that can be modulated by a signal ○ *He's not using a modem – there's no carrier signal on the line.*

carrier signalling /'kæriə ˌsɪgnəlɪŋ/ *noun* a simple form of data transmission in which a carrier signal is switched on and off according to binary data

carrier system /ˌkæriə 'sɪstəm/ *noun* a method of transmitting several different signals on one channel by using different carrier frequencies

carrier wave /'kæriə weɪv/ *noun* a waveform used as a carrier

carry /'kæri/ *noun* an extra digit due to an addition result being greater than the number base used ○ *When 5 and 7 are added, there is an answer of 2 and a carry which is put in the next column, giving 12.*

carry bit /'kæri bɪt/ *noun* an indicator that a carry has occurred

carry complete signal /ˌkæri kəm 'pliːt ˌsɪgn(ə)l/ *noun* a signal from an adder circuit indicating that all carry operations have been completed

carry flag /'kæri flæg/ *noun* same as **carry bit**

carry look ahead /ˌkæri lʊk ə'hed/ *noun* a high-speed adder that can predict if a carry will be generated by a sum and add it in, removing the delay found in an adder with ripple-through carry

carry time /'kæri taɪm/ *noun* the period of time taken to transfer a carry digit to the next higher digit position

cartesian coordinates /kɑːˌtiːziən kəʊ'ɔːdɪnəts/ *plural noun* a positional system that uses two axes at right angles and represents a point within these axes by means of two numbers that give the point's position on each axis. Compare **axis, polar coordinates**

cartesian structure /kɑːˌtiːziən 'strʌkt∫ə/ *noun* a data structure whose size is fixed and the elements are in a linear order

cartridge /'kɑːtrɪdʒ/ *noun* a removable cassette, containing a disk or tape or program or data, usually stored in ROM

cartridge drive /'kɑːtrɪdʒ draɪv/ *noun* a drive which uses a disk or tape in a cartridge

cartridge fonts /'kɑːtrɪdʒ fɒntz/ *plural noun* fonts contained in a ROM cartridge which can be plugged into a printer, providing a choice of new typefaces

cartridge ribbon /ˌkɑːtrɪdʒ 'rɪbən/ *noun* a printer ribbon in a closed cartridge

CAS /ˌsiː eɪ 'es/ *noun* a standard developed by Intel and DCA to allow communication software to control a fax modems.

Full form **communicating applications specification**

cascade carry /kæ,skeɪd 'kæri/ *noun* a carry generated in an adder from an input carry signal

cascade connection /kæ,skeɪd kə 'nekʃ(ə)n/ *noun* a number of devices or circuits arranged in series, the output of one driving the input of the next

cascade control /kæ,skeɪd kən'trəʊl/ *noun* a set of several control units, each controlling the next

cascaded star /kæ'skeɪdd stɑː/ *noun* a setup in which the nodes in a star topology network are connected to more than one hub to provide a backup in case of a problem

cascading menu /kæ,skeɪdɪŋ 'menjuː/ *noun* a secondary menu that is displayed to the side of the main pull-down menu

cascading style sheet /kæ,skeɪdɪŋ 'staɪl ,ʃiːt/ *noun* a method of describing the font, spacing and colour of text within a webpage and storing this information in a style sheet that can be applied to any text within the page. Abbr **CSS**

cascading windows /kæ,skeɪdɪŋ 'wɪndəʊz/ *plural noun* (*in a GUI*) multiple windows that are displayed overlapping so that only the title bar at the top of each window is showing

case /keɪs/ *noun* **1.** □ **upper case** capital letters ○ *He corrected the word 'coMputer', replacing the upper case M with a lower case letter.* **2.** a programming command that jumps to various points in a program depending on the result of a test

case branch /'keɪs brɑːntʃ/ *noun* a branch to a part of a program that is dependent upon the result of a test

case change /'keɪs tʃeɪndʒ/ *noun* a key used to change from upper to lower case on a keyboard

case sensitive /keɪs 'sensətɪv/ *adjective* referring to a command or operation that will only work when the characters are entered in a particular case ○ *The password is case sensitive.*

case sensitive search /,keɪs ,sensətɪv 'sɜːtʃ/ *noun* a search function that succeeds only if both the search word and the case of the characters in the search word match

cassette /kə'set/ *noun* a hard container used to store and protect magnetic tape

cassette recorder /kə'set rɪ,kɔːdə/ *noun* a machine to transfer audio signals onto magnetic tape

cassette tape /kə'set teɪp/ *noun* narrow reel of magnetic tape housed in a solid case for protection (NOTE: Using cassette tape allows data to be stored for future retrieval. It is used instead of a disk system on small computers or as a slow, serial access, high-capacity back-up medium for large systems.)

cast /kɑːst/ *noun* **1.** (*in a programming language*) an instruction that converts data from one type to another ○ *To convert the variable from an integer to a character type, use the cast command.* **2.** (*in a multimedia presentation or animation*) each individual part of a multimedia presentation or animation. The members of a cast can be individual images, sound clips or text.

cast-based animation /,kɑːst beɪs ,ænɪ'meɪʃ(ə)n/ *noun* a type of animation in which everything is an object and has its defined movement, colour and shape, and the actions of each object are controlled by a script

cast member /kɑːst 'membə/ *noun* a single object, e.g. text, an image or an animated object, within a cast used in a presentation

CAT /kæt/ *noun* **1.** the use of a computer to demonstrate to and assist pupils in learning a skill. Full form **computer-aided training, computer-assisted training 2.** the use of a computer to test equipment or programs to find any faults. Full form **computer-aided testing, computer-assisted testing**

catalogue /'kæt(ə)lɒg/ *noun* a list of contents or items in order □ **disk catalogue, directory** list of files stored on a magnetic disk ○ *The entry in the disk catalogue is removed when the file is deleted.* ■ *verb* to make a catalogue of items stored ○ *All the terminals were catalogued, with their location, call sign and attribute table.*

catastrophe /kə'tæstrəfi/ *noun* a serious fault, error or breakdown of equipment, usually leading to serious damage and shutdown of a system

catastrophic error /,kætəstrɒfɪk 'erə/ *noun* an error that causes a program to crash or files to be accidentally erased

catastrophic failure /ˌkætəstrɒfɪk 'feɪljə/ *noun* a complete system failure or crash

Category 1 /ˌkætəg(ə)ri 'wʌn/ *noun* (part of the EIA/TIA 568 specification) a standard that defines an older-style unshielded twisted-pair cable, unsuitable for data transmission, that is formed by loosely twisting two insulated wires together to reduce noise and interference

Category 2 /ˌkætəg(ə)ri 'tuː/ *noun* (part of the EIA/TIA 568 specification) a standard that defines a type of unshielded twisted-pair cable that can be used to transmit data at rates up to 4MHz

Category 3 /ˌkætəg(ə)ri 'θriː/ *noun* (part of the EIA/TIA 568 specification) a standard that defines a type of unshielded twisted-pair cable that can be used to transmit data at rates up to 10MHz. This type of cable is the minimum standard of cable required for a 10BaseT network (NOTE: The standard suggests that the cable should have three twists per foot of cable.).

Category 4 /ˌkætəg(ə)ri 'fɔː/ *noun* (part of the EIA/TIA 568 specification) a standard that defines a type of unshielded twisted-pair cable that is the minimum standard of cable required for data transmission rates up to 16Mbit/second on a Token Ring network

Category 5 /ˌkætəg(ə)ri 'faɪv/ *noun* (part of the EIA/TIA 568 specification) a standard that defines a type of cable that can carry data transmitted at up to 100MHz and is suitable for FDDI over copper wire, 100BaseT or other high-speed networks

category wiring /ˌkætəg(ə)ri 'waɪərɪŋ/ *noun* one of five levels of standards defined by the Electronics Industry Association/Telecommunications Industry Association (EIA/TIA) that defines the type of cable or wire used in a network

catena /kə'tiːnə/ *noun* **1.** a chained list consisting of a number of items **2.** a series of characters in a word

catenate /'kætəneɪt/ *verb* to join together two or more sets of data

cathode ray tube /ˌkæθəʊd 'reɪ tjuːb/ *noun* full form of **CRT**

COMMENT: Cathode ray tubes are used in traditional-style television sets, computer monitors and VDUs. A CRT consists of a vacuum tube, one end of which is flat and coated with phosphor, while the other end contains an electron beam source. Characters or graphics are visible when the controllable electron beam strikes the phosphor, causing it to glow.

cathode ray tube storage /ˌkæθəʊd reɪ ˌtjuːb 'stɔːrɪdʒ/ *noun* a cathode ray tube with a long-persistence phosphor screen coating that retains an image for a long time

CAV /ˌsiː eɪ 'viː/ *noun* a CD-ROM that spins at a constant speed. The size of each data frame on the disc varies so as to maintain a regular data throughput of one frame per second. Full form **constant angular velocity**

CB *abbr* call back

CBI /n/ *abbr* computer-based instruction

CBL /ˌsiː biː 'el/ *noun* education or learning using special programs running on a computer. Full form **computer-based learning**

CBMS /ˌsiː biː em 'es/ *noun* the use of a computer system to allow users to send and receive messages from other users, usually in-house. Full form **computer-based message system**. ◊ BBS

CBT /ˌsiː biː 'tiː/ *noun* the use of a computer system to train students. Full form **computer-based training**

cc /ˌsiː 'siː/ *noun* a feature of electronic mail software that allows you to send a copy of a message to another user (*see*) Full form **carbon copy**

CCA *abbr* cardholder certificate authority

CCD *abbr* charge-coupled device

CCD memory /ˌsiː siː diː 'mem(ə)ri/ *noun* capacitors used with MOS transistors to store data, allowing either serial or random access

CCIR 601 /ˌsiː siː aɪ ɑː ˌsɪks əʊ 'wʌn/ *noun* a recommended standard for defining digital video

CCITT /ˌsiː siː aɪ tiː 'tiː/ *noun* an international committee that defines communications protocols and standards. Full form **Comité Consultatif International Téléphonique et Télégraphique**

CCP /ˌsiː siː 'piː/ *noun* software which interfaces between a user's terminal and system BIOS. Full form **command console processor**

CD¹ /siː'diː/ *noun* a system instruction in MS-DOS and UNIX that moves you around a directory structure ○ *Type in CD DOCS to move into the DOCS subdirectory.* Also called **CHDIR**. Full form **change directory**

CD² /siː'diː/ *abbr* compact disc

CD32 /ˌsiː diː ˌθɜːti 'tuː/ *noun* a unit with a processor and CD-ROM drive developed by Commodore that uses its Amiga computer

CD-audio /ˌsiː ˌdiː 'ɔːdiəʊ/ *noun* a standard that defines how music can be stored in digital form, i.e. as a series of numbers, on a compact disc

CD-bridge /ˌsiː 'diː brɪdʒ/ *noun* an extension to the CD-ROM XA standard that allows extra data to be added so that the disc can be read on a CD-i player

CD caddy /ˌsiː 'diː ˌkædi/ *noun* a flat plastic container that is used to hold a compact disc

CD-DA *abbr* compact disc digital audio (NOTE: also called **Red Book audio**)

CD-E /ˌsiː 'diː iː/ *noun* a format that allows data to be saved to and erased from a compact disc

CD+G /ˌsiː diː plʌs 'dʒiː/, **CD+Graphics** /ˌsiː diː plʌs 'græfɪks/ *noun* CD format that adds a text track to an audio disc – used to store song title information

CD-i /ˌsiː diː 'aɪ/ *noun* hardware and software standards that combine sound, data, video and text onto a compact disc and allow a user to interact with the software stored on a CD-ROM. The standard defines encoding, compression and display functions.

CD-I /ˌsiː 'diː aɪ/ *noun* set of enhancements to the normal CD-ROM standard, developed by Philips, and aimed for home use. The system uses its own special hardware console with speakers, joystick and a connection to a television screen to display the images. The special feature of CD-I is that it allows you to interact with what you see on the television screen and choose options or respond to questions or a game.

CD-i digital audio /ˌsiː diː aɪ ˌdɪdʒɪt(ə)l 'ɔːdiəʊ/ *noun* a format that enables a CD-i disc to record audio in digital format in one of four ways, either mono or stereo and at two different sample rates

CD-i digital imaging /ˌsiː diː aɪ ˌdɪdʒɪt(ə)l 'ɪmɪdʒɪŋ/ *plural noun* the compression method used to store images and video frames on a CD-i disc

CD-i sector /ˌsiː diː 'aɪ ˌsektə/ *noun* a unit of storage on a CD-i disc that can store 2352 bytes

CD Player /ˌsiː 'diː ˌpleɪə/ *noun* a utility supplied with Windows that allows a user to play back audio CDs in the PC's CD-ROM drive

CD quality /ˌsiː 'diː ˌkwɒlɪti/ *adjective* able to provide recording quality similar to a compact disc. The term normally refers to equipment that can store 16-bit samples at a sample rate of over 44,000 samples per second. ○ *A sound card in a computer might have several modes of operation: low-quality for general use that does not use up too much memory and CD quality recording mode for final recordings.*

CD-R /ˌsiː diː 'aː/ *noun* technology that allows a user to write data to and read from a CD-R disc ○ *A CD-R disc can be played in any standard CD-ROM drive but needs a special CD-R drive to write data to the disc.* Full form **recordable CD**

C: drive /ˈsiː draɪv/ *noun* the main hard disk drive, denoted by the letter C in many operating systems, including DOS, Windows and OS/2. ◊ **floppy disk, hard disk**

COMMENT: Normally, a PC has two or three disk drives within its casing. The convention is to provide one floppy disk, called 'A:' and one hard disk called 'C:'. If you have a second floppy disk, this is called 'B:' and a CD-ROM drive is normally 'D:'. When talking about the different disk drives, you say 'Drive A' for the floppy drive, but normally write 'A:'. If you are using DOS, when your PC starts up it will normally show what's called the C-prompt (which looks like 'C:\ your screen); this means you are currently looking at the hard drive. If you want to change to drive A to read data from a floppy disk, enter 'A:' and press return.

CD-ROM /ˌsiː diː 'rɒm/ *noun* a small plastic disc that is used as a high capacity ROM storage device that can store 650Mb of data; data is stored in binary form as holes etched on the surface which are then read by a laser

"Customers' images will be captured, digitised, and stored on optical disk or CD-ROM, and produced if queries arise about responsibility for ATM transactions." [*Computing*]

CD-ROM drive /ˌsiː diː 'rɒm/ *noun* a mechanical device that spins a compact disc and reads data stored on the surface of the disc using a tiny laser beam

CD-ROM Extended Architecture /ˌsiː ˌdiː rɒm ɪkˌstendɪd 'aːkɪtektʃə/ *noun* an extended CD-ROM format that defines how audio, images and data are stored on a CD-ROM disc. Abbr **CD-ROM/XA**

CD-ROM Extensions /ˌsiː 'diː rɒm/ *plural noun* the software required to allow an operating system to access a CD-ROM drive

CD-ROM mode 1 /ˌsiː 'diː rɒm məʊd/ *noun* the standard, original method of storing data in the High Sierra file format

CD-ROM mode 2 /ˌsiː 'diː rɒm məʊd/ *noun* the higher-capacity storage format that stores data in the space used in mode 1 for error correction (NOTE: Neither mode 1 nor mode 2 can play audio and simultaneously read data, hence the XA extension.)

CD-ROM player /ˌsiː 'diː rɒm/ *noun* a disc drive that allows a computer to read data stored on a CD-ROM; the player uses a laser beam to read etched patterns on the surface of the CD-ROM that represent data bits

CD-ROM Re-Writable /ˌsiː 'diː rɒm reɪ/ *noun* a disc technology that can read a standard CD-ROM, write to a CD-R or write data many times to the same CD-R

CD-ROM/XA *abbr* CD-ROM Extended Architecture

CDRTOS /ˌsiː diː ɑː tiː əʊ 'es/ *noun* an operating system used to run a CD-i hardware platform

CD-RW /ˌsiː diː ɑː 'dʌb(ə)ljuː/ *noun* a compact disc that can have its contents erased and something else recorded onto it many times

CDTV /ˌsiː diː tiː 'viː/ *noun* a CD-ROM standard developed by Commodore that combines audio, graphics and text. This standard is mainly intended as an interactive system for home use, with the player connected to a television and also able to play music CDs.

CD-V /ˌsiː 'diː viː/ *noun* a format, now no longer used, for storing 5 minutes of video data on a 3-inch disc in analog form

CD-video /ˌsiː diː 'vɪdiəʊ/ *noun* a compact disc used to store and play back video images

CD-WO /ˌsiː 'diː ˌdʌb(ə)l juː 'əʊ/ *noun* a CD-ROM disc and drive technology that allows a user to write data to the disc once only. It is useful for storing archived documents or for testing a CD-ROM before it is duplicated.

cel /sel/ *noun* a single frame in an animation sequence

cell /sel/ *noun* **1.** a single function or number in a spreadsheet program **2.** a single memory location, capable of storing a data word, accessed by an individual address **3.** (*in a transmission system such as ATM*) a fixed-length packet of data, e.g. a cell in the ATM system contains 53

cell address /sel ə'dres/ *noun* (*in a spreadsheet*) a code that identifies the position of a cell by row and column. The

rows are normally numbered and the columns use the letters of the alphabet.

cellar /'selə/ *noun* a temporary storage for data or registers or tasks, in which items are added and retrieved from the same end of the list in a LIFO order

cell definition /sel ˌdefə'nɪʃ(ə)n/ *noun* (*in a spreadsheet*) a formula that is contained in a cell

cell format /sel 'fɔːmæt/ *noun* (*in a spreadsheet*) the way in which the result or data in a cell is displayed ○ *The cell format is right-aligned and emboldened.*

Cello /'tʃeləʊ/ *noun* a web browser application. ◊ **browser**

cell protection /sel prə'tekʃən/ *noun* a function that prevents the contents of a particular cell or range of cells from being changed

cell reference variable /ˌsel ˌref(ə)rəns 'veəriəb(ə)l/ *noun* a register that contains the reference locating a certain cell that is being operated on

cell relay /sel 'riːˌleɪ/ *noun* a way of transmitting packets of information over a broadband network, such as Broadband ISDN. The ATM system, e.g., transfers data by moving cells of data between nodes in a wide area network.

cellular phone /ˌseljʊlə 'fəʊn/ *noun* same as **mobile phone**

central computer /ˌsentrəl kəm'pjuːtə/ *noun* same as **host computer**

centralised computer network /ˌsentrəˌlaɪzd kəm'pjuːtə/, **centralized computer network** *noun* a network with processing power provided by a central computer

centralised data processing /ˌsentrəˌlaɪzd 'deɪtə/, **centralized data processing** *noun* data processing facilities located in a centralised place that can be accessed by other users

central memory /ˌsentrəl 'mem(ə)ri/ *noun* full form of **CM**

central processing element /ˌsentrəl 'prəʊsesɪŋ ˌelɪmənt/ *noun* a short, i.e. 2, 4 or 8 bit, word length module that can be used to produce large word CPU's using bit slice techniques. Abbr **CPE**

central processing unit, central processor *noun* full form of **CPU**

central terminal /ˌsentrəl 'tɜːmɪn(ə)l/ *noun* a terminal which controls communications between a central or host computer and remote terminals

:ntre /ˈsentə/ *verb* **1.** to align the :ead/write head correctly on a magnetic :lisk or tape **2.** to place a piece of text in the centre of the paper or display screen ○ *Which key do you press to centre the heading?*

centre channel /ˌsentə ˈtʃæn(ə)l/ *noun* (*in a multichannel sound system*) the audio channel that carries sound information that will be played back by a loudspeaker placed in the centre of a room, in front of the listener

centre operator /ˌsentə ˈɒpəreɪtə/ *noun* a person who looks after central computer operations

centre text /ˌsentə ˈtekst/ *noun* an option in a word-processing or DTP package that changes the formatting of a line of text so that is in the centre of the page or frame

Centronics interface /senˈtrɒnɪks ˌɪntəfeɪs/ *noun* a parallel printer interface devised by Centronics Inc

Centronics port /senˈtrɒnɪks ˌpɔːt/ *noun* a standard that defines the way in which a parallel printer port on a PC operates

CERN /sɜːn/ *noun* the research laboratory in Switzerland where the world wide web was originally invented. Full form **Conseil Européen pour la Recherche Nucléaire**

CERT /sɜːt/ *abbr* computer emergency response team

certificate /səˈtɪfɪkət/ *noun* a unique set of numbers that identifies a person or company and is used to prove the person's identity

COMMENT: A certificate is normally used to provide security over the Internet for secure e-mail or secure website transactions. A trusted company, such as VeriSign (www.verisign.com) or Thawte (www.thawte.com) issues the certificate once it is satisfied that the person or company is legitimate, authentic and who they claim to be. The company can now use this certificate to prove its identity, create secure messages or setup a secure website to accept payments online.

certificate authority /səˈtɪfɪkət ɔːˌθɒrɪti/ *noun* an independent server or company on the Internet that supplies or validates a special digital certificate to prove that another company is genuine (NOTE: The certificate authority issues a special encrypted number that complies with the X.509 standard and is encrypted with a public-key encryption system.)

certificate database /səˈtɪfɪkət ˌdeɪtəbeɪs/ *noun* a database in which all the certificates issued and used by a certificate authority are stored

certificate of approval /səˌtɪfɪkət əv əˈpruːv(ə)l/ *noun* a document showing that an item has been approved officially

certificate walker /səˈtɪfɪkət ˌwɔːkə/ *noun* a software program that reads digital certificates and displays their contents

CGI /ˌsiː dʒiː ˈaɪ/ *noun* a standard that defines how a webpage can call programs or scripts stored on an Internet server to carry out functions and exchange information with the program, e.g., to provide a search function. Full form **common gateway interface.** ◊ Perl

CGM /ˌsiː dʒiː ˈem/ *noun* a device-independent file format that provides one method of storing an image as objects. Full form **computer graphics metafile**

chain /tʃeɪn/ *noun* **1.** a series of files or data items linked sequentially **2.** a series of instructions to be executed sequentially ■ *verb* to link files or data items in series by storing a pointer to the next file or item at each entry ○ *More than 1,000 articles or chapters can be chained together when printing.* ◊ catena

chain code /ˈtʃeɪn kəʊd/ *noun* a series of words, each word being derived from the previous word, usually by being shifted one bit

chained file /ˌtʃeɪnd ˈfaɪl/ *noun* a file in which an entry will contain data and an address to the next entry that has the same data content . It allows rapid retrieval of all identical data records.

chained list /ˈtʃeɪnd lɪst/ *noun* a list in which each element contains data and an address to the next element in the list

chained record /tʃeɪnd ˈrekɔːd/ *noun* a data record in a chained file

chaining /ˈtʃeɪnɪŋ/ *noun* the execution of a very large program by executing small segments of it at a time. This allows programs larger than memory capacity to be run.

chaining search /ˈtʃeɪnɪŋ sɜːtʃ/ *noun* a search of a file of elements arranged in a chained list

chain list /ˈtʃeɪn lɪst/ *noun* a list of data with each piece of information providing an address for the next consecutive item in the list

chain printer /tʃeɪn ˈprɪntə/ *noun* a printer whose characters are located on a continuous belt

change directory /'tʃeɪndʒ daɪ ˌrekt(ə)ri/ *noun* full form of **CD, CHDIR**

change dump /'tʃeɪndʒ dʌmp/ *noun* a printout of all the locations whose contents have been changed during a program run

change file /'tʃeɪndʒ faɪl/ *noun* a file containing records that are to be used to update a master file

change over /ˌtʃeɪndʒ 'əʊvə/ *verb* to switch from one computer system to another

changer /'tʃeɪndʒə/ *noun* a device which changes one thing for another

change record /tʃeɪndʒ 'rekɔːd/ *noun* a record containing new data which is to be used to update a master record

change tape /ˌtʃeɪndʒ 'teɪp/ *noun* a magnetic tape containing recent changes or transactions to records which is used to update a master file

channel /'tʃæn(ə)l/ *noun* a physical connection between two points that allows data to be transmitted, e.g. a link between a CPU and a peripheral ■ *verb* to send signals or data via a particular path

channel adapter /'tʃæn(ə)l əˌdæptə/ *noun* an interfacing device allowing different channels to be interconnected

channel bank /'tʃæn(ə)l bæŋk/ *noun* a collection of a number of channels, and circuits to switch between them

channel capacity /'tʃæn(ə)l kəˌpæsɪti/ *noun* the maximum rate for data transmission over a channel

channel command /'tʃæn(ə)l kəˌmɑːnd/ *noun* an instruction to a channel or control unit, providing control information such as data selection or routes

channel isolation /ˌtʃæn(ə)l ˌaɪsə 'leɪʃ(ə)n/ *noun* the separation of channels measured as the amount of crosstalk between two channels (NOTE: Low crosstalk is due to good channel isolation.)

channelling /'tʃænəlɪŋ/ *noun* a protective pipe containing cables or wires

channel map /'tʃæn(ə)l mæp/ *noun* (*in the Windows MIDI Mapper utility*) a list that shows if a MIDI channel is being redirected to another channel

channel overload /'tʃæn(ə)l ˌəʊvələʊd/ *noun* the transmission of data at a rate greater than the channel capacity

channel queue /'tʃæn(ə)l kjuː/ *noun* **1.** a queue of requests to use a channel **2.** a queue of data that has yet to be sent over a channel

channel synchroniser /'tʃæn(ə)ˌsɪŋkrənaɪzə/, **channel synchronizer** *noun* an interface between a central computer and peripherals, providing a channel, channel command interpretation and status signals from the peripherals

channel-to-channel connection /ˌtʃæn(ə)l tə ˌtʃæn(ə)l kə'nekʃ(ə)n/ *noun* a direct link between the main I/O channels of two computers, allowing high speed data transfer

chapter /'tʃæptə/ *noun* a section of a main program that can be executed in its own right, without the rest of the main program being required

char /tʃɑː/ *noun* (*in programming*) a data type which defines a variable as containing data that represents a character using the ASCII code

character /'kærɪktə/ *noun* a graphical symbol which appears as a printed or displayed mark such as one of the letters of the alphabet, a number or a punctuation mark

character assembly /'kærɪktə əˌsembli/ *noun* a method of designing characters with pixels on a computer screen

character-based /'kærɪktə ˌbeɪst/ *adjective* referring to a screen design that is drawn using ASCII characters rather than graphical windows

character blink /'kærɪktə blɪŋk/ *noun* a character whose intensity is switched on and off as an indicator

character block /'kærɪktə blɒk/ *noun* the pattern of dots that will make up a character on a screen or printer

character byte /'kærɪktə baɪt/ *noun* a byte of data containing the character code and any error check bits

character check /'kærɪktə tʃek/ *noun* a check to ensure that a character code protocol and format are correct

character code /'kærɪktə kəʊd/ *noun* a system where each character is represented by a unique number ○ *The ASCII code is the most frequently used character coding system.*

character density /'kærɪktə ˌdensɪti/ *noun* the number of characters that can be stored or displayed per unit area

character display /'kærɪktə dɪˌspleɪ/ *noun* a device that displays data in alphanumeric form

character fill /'kærɪktə fɪl/ *noun* the writing of one character to every location within an area of memory, a process used for clearing and resetting the memory

character generator /'kærɪktə ˌdʒenəreɪtə/ *noun* a ROM that provides the display circuits with a pattern of dots which represent the character block ○ *The ROM used as a character generator can be changed to provide different fonts.*

character interleaving /ˌkærɪktə ˌɪntə'liːvɪŋ/ *noun* a form of time division multiplexing for asynchronous protocols

characteristic /ˌkærɪktə'rɪstɪk/ *noun* **1.** the value of exponent in a floating point number ○ *The floating point number 1.345 x 10^3, has a characteristic of 3.* **2.** a measurement or property of a component

characteristic overflow /ˌkærɪktərɪstɪk 'əʊvəfləʊ/ *noun* an exponent value of a floating point number that is greater than the maximum allowable

character key /'kærɪktə kiː/ *noun* same as **alphanumeric key**

character machine /'kærɪktə mə ˌʃiːn/ *noun* a computer in which the number of bits which make up a word is variable, and varies according to the type of data

Character Map /'kærɪktə mæp/ *noun* a utility that is provided with Windows to allow you access the full range of 256 characters that make up every font rather than the limited range that you can access from the keyboard

character matrix /'kærɪktə ˌmeɪtrɪks/ *noun* the pattern of dots that makes up a displayed character

character mode /'kærɪktə məʊd/ *noun* (*of a display adapter*) a mode that can only display the characters defined in the built-in character set

character-orientated /'kærɪktə ˌɔːriənteɪtɪd/ *adjective* referring to a computer that addresses character locations rather than words

character printer /'kærɪktə ˌprɪntə/ *noun* a device, e.g. a daisy wheel printer, that prints characters one at a time

character recognition /ˌkærɪktə ˌrekəg'nɪʃ(ə)n/ *noun* a system that optically reads written or printed characters into a computer, using various algorithms to ensure that characters are correctly recognised

character repertoire /ˌkærɪktə ˌrepə 'twɑː/ *noun* a list of all the characters that can be displayed or printed

character representation /ˌkærɪktə ˌreprɪzen'teɪʃ(ə)n/ *noun* the combination of bits used for each character code

character rounding /'kærɪktə ˌraʊndɪŋ/ *noun* the process of making a displayed character more pleasant to look at, within the limits of pixel size, by making sharp corners and edges smooth

character set /'kærɪktə set/ *noun* a list of all the characters that can be displayed or printed

characters per inch /ˌkærɪktəz pɜːr 'ɪntʃ/ *plural noun* the number of printed characters that fit within the space of one inch ○ *You can select 10 or 12 cpi with the green button.* Abbr **cpi**

characters per second /ˌkærɪktəz pə 'sekənd/ *noun* the number of characters that are transmitted or printed per second

character string /'kærɪktə strɪŋ/ *noun* same as **alphanumeric string**

'This explains a multitude of the database's problems – three-letter months are treated like character strings instead of as dates.' [*Computing*]

character stuffing /'kærɪktə ˌstʌfɪŋ/ *noun* the addition of blank characters to a file to increase its length to a preset size

charge /tʃɑːdʒ/ *noun* **1.** a quantity of electricity **2.** the number of, excess of or lack of electrons in a material or component ■ *verb* to supply a device with an electric charge

charge-coupled device /ˌtʃɑːdʒ ˌkʌp(ə)ld dɪ'vaɪs/ *noun* an electronic device operated by charge. Abbr **CCD**

charge-coupled device memory /tʃɑːdʒ ˌkʌp(ə)ld dɪ'vaɪs/ *noun* a set of capacitors used, with MOS transistors, to store data, allowing serial and random access

chart /tʃɑːt/ *noun* a diagram showing information as a series of lines or blocks

chassis /'ʃæsi/ *noun* a metal frame that houses the circuit boards together with the wiring and sockets required in a computer system or other equipment. ◊ **rack**

chat /tʃæt/ *verb* to send and receive messages, in real time, with other users on the Internet

chat group /'tʃæt gruːp/ *noun* a group of people, often with a common interest, who exchange messages online

chat room /'tʃæt ruːm/ *noun* an area of a website where visitors can exchange messages with other visitors in real time. Special software displays the name of the visitor as he or she types in a message to all the other visitors, allowing them to 'talk' to each other.

CHCP /ˌsiː aɪtʃ siː ˈpiː/ *noun* (*in MS-DOS and OS/2 operating systems*) a system command that selects which code page to use

CHDIR /ˌsiː aɪtʃ diː aɪ ˈɑː/ *abbr* change directory. ♦ **CD**

cheapernet /ˈtʃiːpənet/ *noun* same as **thin-Ethernet** (*informal*)

check bit /ˈtʃek bɪt/ *noun* one bit of a binary word that is used to provide a parity check

check box /ˈtʃek bɒks/ *noun* a small box displayed with a cross inside it if the option has been selected, or empty if the option is not selected ○ *Select the option by moving the cursor to the check box and pressing the mouse button.*

check character /ˈtʃek ˈkærɪktə/ *noun* an additional character inserted into transmitted data to serve as an error detection check, its value being dependent on the text

check digit /ˈtʃek ˈdɪdʒɪt/ *noun* an additional digit inserted into transmitted text to monitor and correct errors

checkerboarding /ˈtʃekəˌbɔːdɪŋ/ *noun* (*on a virtual page*) a form of memory organisation that results in only odd pages, spread-out pages or segments of memory being filled, leaving unusable gaps in between and wasting memory

check indicator /ˈtʃek ˈɪndɪˌkeɪtə/ *noun* a hardware or software device that shows that received text is not correct and a check has failed

checking program /ˈtʃekɪŋ ˈprəʊɡræm/ *noun* software that finds errors in program or data syntax, format and coding

check key /ˈtʃek kiː/ *noun* a series of characters derived from a text used to check for and correct errors

check mark /ˈtʃek mɑːk/ *noun* an indicator in a check box that shows if the check box has been selected; often a cross or tick

check number /ˈtʃek ˈnʌmbə/ *noun* same as **check digit**

check point /ˈtʃek pɔɪnt/ *noun* a point in a program where data and program status can be recorded or displayed

check point dump /ˈtʃek pɔɪnt ˈdʌmp/ *noun* a printout of data and program status at a check point

check register /ˈtʃek ˈredʒɪstə/ *noun* a temporary storage for received data before it is checked against the same data received via another path or method

checksum /ˈtʃek ˈtaʊt(ə)l/, **check total** *noun* a program that checks that data retrieved from memory is correct, summing it and comparing the sum with a stored value ○ *The data must be corrupted if the checksum is different.*

child process, child program *noun* a routine or program called by another program which remains active while the second program runs

child window /ˈtʃaɪld ˈwɪndəʊ/ *noun* a window within a main window. The smaller window cannot be moved outside the boundary of the main window and is closed when the main window is closed.

chip /tʃɪp/ *noun* a device consisting of a small piece of a crystal of a semiconductor onto which are etched or manufactured a number of components such as transistors, resistors and capacitors, which together perform a function

chip architecture /tʃɪp ˈɑːkɪˌtektʃə/ *noun* the design and layout of components on a chip

chip card /ˌtʃɪp ˈkɑːd/ *noun* a plastic card with a memory and microprocessor device embedded in it, so that it can be used for electronic funds transfer or identification of a user

chip count /ˌtʃɪp ˈkaʊnt/ *noun* number of chips on a PCB or in a device

'Where the display is provided by an LCD system, high levels of performance must be achieved with the lowest cost, smallest chip count and lowest power consumption.' [*Computing*]

chip select /ˌtʃɪp sɪˈlekt/ *noun* a single line on a chip that will enable it to function when a signal is present. Abbr **CS** (NOTE: ICs often do not function, even when power is applied, until a CS signal is provided.)

chip select line /ˌtʃɪp sɪˈlekt ˌlaɪn/ *noun* a connection to a chip that will enable it to function when a signal is present ○ *The data strobe line is connected to the latch chip select line.*

chip set /ˌtʃɪp ˈset/ *noun* a set of chips that together will carry out a function

CHKDSK /ˈtʃekdɪsk/ *noun* (*in MS-DOS*) a system command that runs a check on the status of a disk drive and installed RAM

ɴoiceboard /'tʃɔɪsbɔːd/ *noun* a program used on the Internet that allows consumers and online companies to communicate in real time

choke /tʃəʊk/ *noun* ♦ **inductor**

Chooser /'tʃuːzə/ an operating system utility supplied with the Apple Macintosh that allows a user to select the type of printer, network and other peripherals that are connected

chop /tʃɒp/ ♦ **binary search**

chord keying /'kɔːd kiːɪŋ/ *noun* the action of pressing two or more keys at the same time to perform a function

  COMMENT: As an example, to access a second window, you may need to press control and F2; pressing shift and character delete keys at the same time will delete a line of text.

chroma /'krəʊmə/ *noun* a measure of colour hue and saturation. Also called **chrominance**

chroma key /'krəʊmə kiː/ *noun* (*in video*) a special effect in which an object is photographed against a normally blue background, which is then replaced with another image to give the impression that the object appears against the image. To give the appearance of flying, e.g., record a video sequence of a person against a blue background, then electronically replace this blue colour, the chroma key with footage of sky. ◊ **colour key**

chrominance /'krəʊmɪnəns/ *noun* same as **chroma**

chrominance signal /'krəʊmɪnəns ˌsɪɡn(ə)l/ *noun* the section of a colour monitor signal containing colour hue and saturation information

chunk /tʃʌŋk/ *noun* a basic part of a RIFF file that consists of an identifier (chunk ID) and data

CIDR /ˌsiː aɪ diː 'ɑː/ *noun* a system of organising IP addresses that is more compact and efficient than the older system, adding a slash and a new IP Prefix number that represents a number of individual addresses. For example, the old system used an IP address such as '194.124.0.0' whereas CIDR would replace this with '194.124.0.0/12'. The IP Prefix number 12 represents 4,096 unique addresses, and the lower the number the more addresses are represented.

CIE /ˌsiː aɪ 'iː/ *noun* the international group that defines colour and illumination standards. Full form **Commission International de l'Éclairage**

CIF /ˌsiː aɪ 'ef/ *abbr* common intermediate format

CIF videophone /ˌsiː aɪ ef 'vɪdiəʊfəʊn/ *noun* an ISDN standard for video image transmission over a telephone link which displays colour images at a resolution of 352x288 pixels. This standard uses two ISDN B channels.

CIM /ˌsiː aɪ 'em/ *noun* **1.** the coordinated use of microfilm for computer data storage and the method of reading the data. Full form **computer input microfilm 2.** the coordinated use of computers in every aspect of design and manufacturing. Full form **computer-integrated manufacturing**

cine-oriented /'sɪni ˌɔːrientɪd/ *adjective* (*in a film or video clip*) referring to an image that is oriented parallel to the outside edge of the medium

cipher /'saɪfə/ *noun* a system that transforms a message into an unreadable form with a secret key ○ *Always use a secure cipher when sending data over a telephone line.* (NOTE: The message can be read normally after it has passed through the cipher a second time to decrypt it.)

cipher key /'saɪfə kiː/ *noun* a secret sequence of characters used with a cipher system to provide a unique ciphertext

cipher system /'saɪfə ˌsɪstəm/ *noun* a formula used to transform text into a secret form

ciphertext /'saɪfətekst/ *noun* data output from a cipher. Opposite **plaintext**

CIR /ˌsiː aɪ 'ɑː/ *noun* a CPU register that stores the instruction that is currently being executed. Full form **current instruction register**

circuit /'sɜːkɪt/ *noun* a connection between the electronic components that perform a function

circuit analyser /'sɜːkɪt ˌænəlaɪzə/ *noun* a device that measures voltage or current or impedance or signal in a circuit

circuit board /'sɜːkɪt bɔːd/ *noun* an insulating board used to hold components which are then connected together electrically to form a circuit

  'The biggest shock was to open up the PC and find the motherboard smothered in patch wires (usually a sign that a design fault in the printed circuit board was rectified at the last minute).' [*Computing*]

circuit breaker /'sɜːkɪt ˌbreɪkə/ *noun* a device which protects equipment by cutting off the electrical supply when conditions are abnormal

circuit capacity /'sɜːkɪt kə,pæsɪti/ *noun* the information-carrying capacity of a particular circuit

circuit card /'sɜːkɪt kɑːd/ *noun* same as **circuit board**

circuit design /'sɜːkɪt dɪ,zaɪn/ *noun* the layout of components and interconnections in a circuit

circuit diagram /'sɜːkɪt ,daɪəgræm/ *noun* a graphical description of a circuit ○ *The CAD program will plot the circuit diagram rapidly.*

circuit switching /'sɜːkɪt ,swɪtʃɪŋ/ *noun* a method of describing a type of communication system in which a path from sender to receiver is created when required rather than using a permanent, fixed line. The normal telephone system is an example of a circuit switching network.

circular buffer /,sɜːkjʊlə 'bʌfə/ *noun* a computer-based queue that uses two markers, for top and bottom of the line of stored items. The markers move as items are read from or written to the stack.

circular file /'sɜːkjʊlə faɪl/ *noun* a data file that has no visible beginning or end, each item points to the location of the next item with the last pointing back to the first

circularity /,sɜːkjʊ'lærɪti/ *noun* a fault that makes reasoning illogical, because the arguments that are supposed to lead to a conclusion are only valid if the conclusion itself is true

circular list /'sɜːkjʊlə lɪst/ *noun* a list in which each element contains data and an address to the next element in the list ·with the last item pointing back to the first

circular reference /,sɜːkjʊlə 'ref(ə)rəns/ *noun* (*in a spreadsheet*) an error condition that occurs when two equations in two cells reference each other

circular shift /'sɜːkjʊlə ʃɪft/ *noun* the rotation of bits in a word with the previous last bit inserted in the first bit position

circulate /'sɜːkjʊ,leɪt/ *verb* to go round in a circle, and return to the first point

circulating register /,sɜːkjuleɪtɪŋ 'redʒɪstə/ *noun* a shift register whose output is fed back into its input to form a closed loop

circulating storage /,sɜːkjuleɪtɪŋ 'stɔːrɪdʒ/ *noun* a storage device that maintains stored data as a series of pulses that move along the length of the medium, being regenerated and re-input when they reach the end

CIS /,si: aɪ 'es/ *noun* a scanner in whic the detectors, a flat bar of light-sensitiv diodes, touch the original, without any lens that might distort the image. Full form **contact image sensor**

CISC /,si: aɪ es 'si:/ *noun* a type of CPU design whose instruction set contains a number of long, complex instructions that make program writing easier, but reduce execution speed. Full form **complex instruction set computer**. Compare **RISC**

CIT *abbr* computer-integrated telephony

CIX *abbr* commercial Internet exchange

cladding /'klædɪŋ/ *noun* protective material surrounding a conducting core ○ *If the cladding is chipped, the fibre-optic cable will not function well.*

claim frame /'kleɪm freɪm/ *noun* (*in an FDDI protocol network*) a special frame that is used to determine which station will initialise the network

clamper /'klæmpə/ *noun* a circuit which limits the level of a signal from a scanning head or other input device to a maximum before this is converted to a digital value. Clampers are used to cut out noise and spikes.

clapper /'klæpə/ *noun* the mechanical part of a dot matrix printer that drives the printing needles onto the ribbon to print a character on the paper

class /klɑːs/ *noun* (*in programming language*) a definition of what a particular software routine will do or what sort of data a variable can hold

Class 1 /,klɑːs 'wʌn/, **Class 2** /,klɑːs 'tu:/ *noun* a set of standards that define how a to control a fax modem using software, using extensions to the Hayes AT command set used for data modems. Class 2 expects the modem to carry out more work in managing fax communications. Class 1 units can often be upgraded through software.

class interval /klɑːs 'ɪntəv(ə)l/ *noun* the range of values that can be contained in a class

clean /kliːn/ *adjective* containing no errors ○ *I'll have to start again – I just erased the only clean copy.*

clean copy /kliːn 'kɒpi/ *noun* a copy which is ready for keyboarding and does not have many changes to it

clean machine /kliːn mə'ʃiːn/ *noun* a computer that contains only the minimum of ROM-based code to boot its system from disk, any languages required must be loaded separately

clean page /ˈkliːn peɪdʒ/ *noun* a page of memory that has not been changed since it was read

clean room /ˈkliːn ruːm/ *noun* an area where hard disks, wafers and chips are manufactured. The air inside a clean room has been filtered to ensure that no dust or particles are present that could damage a chip.

clear /klɪə/ *verb* **1.** to wipe out or erase or set to zero a computer file or variable or section of memory ○ *Type CLS to clear the screen.* **2.** to release a communications link when transmissions have finished

clearance /ˈklɪərəns/ *noun* authority to access a file ○ *You do not have the required clearance for this processor.*

Clearing House Interbank Payment System /ˌklɪərɪŋ haʊs ˌɪntəbæŋk ˈpeɪmənts ˌsɪstəm/ *noun* an electronic system for international dollar payments and currency exchanges

clear to send /ˌklɪə tə ˈsend/ *noun* full form of **CTS**

click /klɪk/ *noun* the act of pressing a mouse button or a key on a keyboard ○ *You move through text and graphics with a click of the button.* ■ *verb* to press and release a key or a button on a keyboard or the mouse ○ *Use the mouse to enlarge a frame by clicking inside its border.*

click rate /ˈklɪk reɪt/ *noun* a figure representing the number of times that a particular site in an Internet advertisement is visited, and calculated as a percentage of the number of times that the advertisement is viewed

clicks-and-mortar /ˌklɪks ən ˈmɔːtə/ *noun* referring to businesses that use both the Internet and physical shops to sell their products. Compare **bricks-and-mortar**

clickstream /ˈklɪkstriːm/ *noun* a record of how often and for what purpose a user clicks on something with the mouse while navigating the Internet

'…the only way of achieving it would be to monitor the clickstreams of every single UK user of the net.' [*The Guardian*]

click through /ˈklɪk θruː/ *noun* the act of clicking on a banner advertisement and jumping to the advertiser's website

click through rate /ˈklɪk θruː ˌreɪt/ *noun* full form of **CTR**

client /ˈklaɪənt/ *noun* (*in a network*) a workstation or PC or terminal connected to a network that can send instructions to a server and display results

client application /ˌklaɪənt ˌæplɪˈkeɪʃ(ə)n/ *noun* an application that can accept linked or embedded objects from a server application or an application that is used in a client-server system

client area /ˈklaɪənt ˌeəriə/ *noun* (*in a GUI*) an area inside a window that can be used to display graphics or text

client-server architecture /ˌklaɪənt ˌsɜːvə ˈɑːkɪtektʃə/ *noun* a distribution of processing power in which a central server computer carries out the main tasks in response to instructions from terminals or workstations, the results being sent back across the network to be displayed on the terminal that sent the instruction. The client, i.e. the terminal or workstation, does not need to be able to directly access the data stored on the server. nor does it need to carry out a lot of processing.

client-server network /ˌklaɪənt ˈsɜːvə ˌnetwɜːk/ *noun* a method of organising a network in which one central dedicated computer, the server, looks after tasks such as security, user accounts, printing and file sharing, while clients, the terminals or workstations connected to the server, run standard applications

client-side /ˈklaɪənt saɪd/ *adjective* referring to data or a program that runs on the client's computer rather than on the server, e.g. a JavaScript program runs on the user's web browser and is a client side application

clip /klɪp/ *verb* to select an area of an image that is smaller than the original

clip-art /klɪp ɑːt/ *noun* a set of predrawn images or drawings that a user can incorporate into a presentation or graphic ○ *We have used some clip-art to enhance our presentation.*

clipboard /ˈklɪpˌbɔːd/ *noun* a temporary storage area for data ○ *Copy the text to the clipboard, then paste it back into a new document.*

Clipper chip /ˈklɪpə tʃɪp/ *noun* an electronic component, e.g. an integrated circuit, or chip, that was designed in accordance with the instructions of the US Government to provide a data encryption feature for computers, Internet traffic, telephones, and television programmes. In the original scheme the US Government held the master key to the chip and so could decrypt and read any encrypted messages. This angered many groups concerned with freedom of speech and the US Government has since redesigned the original scheme and suggested an alternative.

clock /klɒk/ *noun* a circuit that generates pulses used to synchronise equipment ■ *verb* to synchronise signals or circuits with a clock pulse

clock cycle /klɒk 'saɪk(ə)l/ *noun* the period of time between two consecutive clock pulses

clock doubler /'klɒk ˌdʌb(ə)lə/ *noun* a component that doubles the speed of the main system clock ○ *The new CPU from Intel has an optional clock doubler that will double performance.*

clocked signals /klɒkd 'sɪgn(ə)lz/ *plural noun* signals that are synchronised with a clock pulse

clock frequency /klɒk 'friːkwənsi/ *noun* the frequency of the main clock that synchronises a computer system ○ *The main clock frequency is 10MHz.*

clock pulse /'klɒk pʌls/ *noun* a regular pulse used for timing or synchronising purposes

clock rate /'klɒk reɪt/ *noun* the number of pulses that a clock generates every second

clock speed /'klɒk spiːd/ *noun* same as **clock rate**

clock track /'klɒk træk/ *noun* a line of marks on a disk or tape, which provides data about the read head location

clone /kləʊn/ *noun* a computer or circuit that behaves in the same way as the original it was copied from ○ *They have copied our new personal computer and brought out a cheaper clone.*

'On the desktop, the IBM/Motorola/Apple triumvirate is planning to energise a worldwide clone industry based on the PowerPC chip.' [*Computing*]

close /kləʊz/ *verb* to shut down access to a file or disk drive

CLOSE /kləʊz/ *noun* (*in a programming language*) a command that means the program has finished accessing a particular file or device

closed bus system /ˌkləʊzd 'bʌs ˌsɪstəm/ *noun* a computer with no expansion bus, which makes it very difficult for a user to upgrade

closed captioning /ˌkləʊzd 'kæpʃənɪŋ/ *noun* a system that transfers text information with a video signal, so that the text data can be decoded and dis-

played at the bottom of the television screen

closed loop /ˌkləʊzd 'luːp/ *noun* a computer control operation in which data is fed back from the output of the controlled device to the controlling loop

closed routine /kləʊzd ruːˈtiːn/ *noun* one section of code at a location, that is used by all calls to the routine

closed subroutine /kləʊzd 'sʌbruːˌtiːn/ *noun* same as **closed routine**

closed user group /ˌkləʊzd ˌjuːzə 'gruːp/ *noun* full form of **CUG**

close file /'kləʊs faɪl/ *noun* to execute a computer instruction to shut down access to a stored file

close menu option /ˌkləʊz 'menjuː ˌɒpʃ(ə)n/ *noun* a menu option, normally under the File menu, that will shut the document that is currently open, but will not exit the application. If you have not saved the document, the application will warn you before it closes the document and give you the chance to save any changes.

cloud /klaʊd/ *noun* a part of a computer network, which data passes through, that is either unknown or behaves unpredictably

CLS /ˌsiː el 'es/ *noun* (*in MS-DOS*) a system command to clear the screen, leaving the system prompt and cursor at the top, left-hand corner of the screen

cluster /'klʌstə/ *noun* **1.** one or more sectors on a hard disk that are used to store a file or part of a file **2.** a number of terminals, stations, devices or memory locations, grouped together in one place and controlled by a cluster controller

cluster controller /'klʌstə kənˌtrəʊlə/ *noun* a central computer that controls communications to a cluster of devices or memory locations

clustering /'klʌstərɪŋ/ *noun* a series of elements, occurring in a sequential line within a hash table

'...these include IBM networking and clustering hardware and software' [*Personal Computer World*]

CLUT /ˌsiː el juː 'tiː/ *noun* a table of numbers used in Windows and graphics programs to store the range of colours used in an image. Full form **colour lookup table**. ◊ **palette**

CLV /ˌsiː el 'viː/ *noun* a disk technology in which the disk spins at different speeds according to the track that is being accessed. Full form **constant linear velocity**

CM /ˌsiː ˈem/ *noun* an area of memory whose locations can be directly and immediately addressed by the CPU. Full form **central memory**

CMI *abbr* computer-managed instruction

CMIP /ˌsiː em aɪ ˈpiː/ *noun* a protocol officially adopted by the ISO that is used to carry network management information across a network. Full form **common management information protocol**

CMIP over TCP, CMIS over TCP full form of **CMOT**

CMIS /ˌsiː em aɪ ˈes/ *noun* a powerful network management system. Full form **common management information specification**

CML *abbr* computer-managed learning

CMOS /ˌsiː em əʊ ˈpiː/ *noun* an integrated circuit design and construction method that uses a pair of complementary p- and n-type transistors. Full form **complementary metal oxide semiconductor**

'Similarly, customers who do not rush to acquire CMOS companion processors for their mainframes will be rewarded with lower prices when they finally do migrate.' [*Computergram*]

COMMENT: The CMOS package uses very low power but is relatively slow and sensitive to static electricity as compared to TTL integrated circuits. Its main use is in portable computers where battery power is being used.

CMOT /ˌsiː em əʊ ˈtiː/ *noun* the use of CMIP and CMIS network management protocols to manage gateways in a TCP/IP network. Full form **CMIP over TCP, CMIS over TCP**

CMYK /ˌsiː em waɪ ˈkeɪ/ *noun* (*in graphics or DTP*) a method of describing a colour by its four component colours. Full form **cyan-magenta-yellow-black**

CNC /ˌsiː en ˈsiː/ *noun* automatic operation of a machine by computer. Full form **computer numeric control.** ◊ **numerical control**

coalesce /ˌkəʊəˈles/ *verb* to merge two or more files

co-axial cable /kəʊks/, **coax** *noun* a cable made up of a central core, surrounded by an insulating layer then a second shielding conductor. Compare **twisted-pair cable** (NOTE: Co-axial cable is used for high frequency, low loss applications including thin Ethernet network cabling and Arcnet network cabling.)

COBOL /ˈkəʊbɒl/ *noun* a programming language mainly used in business applications. Full form **common ordinary business-oriented language**

cobweb site /ˈkɒbweb saɪt/ *noun* a website that has not been updated for a long time

code /kəʊd/ *noun* a sequence of computer instructions ■ *verb* to write a program in a programming language

code area /kəʊd ˈeəriə/ *noun* a section of main memory in which program instructions are stored

code bit /ˈkəʊd bɪt/ *noun* the smallest signalling element used by the physical layer of an OSI model network for transmission

CODEC /ˈkəʊdek/ *noun* a device which encodes a signal being sent or decodes a signal received. Full form **coder/decoder**

code conversion /kəʊd kənˈvɜːʃ(ə)n/ *noun* rules used to change characters coded in one form to another

code element /kəʊd ˈelɪmənt/ *noun* a voltage or signal used to represent binary digits

code group /ˈkəʊd gruːp/ *noun* a special sequence of five code bits that represent an FDDI symbol

code line /ˈkəʊd laɪn/ *noun* one written or displayed computer program instruction

code page /ˈkəʊd peɪdʒ/ *noun* (*in MS-DOS*) a table that defines the characters that are produced from each key ○ *In order to enter Swedish characters from an English keyboard, you have to change the system code page.*

coder /ˈkəʊdə/ *noun* a device which encodes a signal

coder/decoder /ˌkəʊdə diːˈkəʊdə/ *noun* full form of **CODEC**

code segment /kəʊd ˈsegmənt/ *noun* (*in an IBM-compatible PC*) an area of memory assigned to hold the instructions that form a program

coding /ˈkəʊdɪŋ/ *noun* the act of putting a code on something

coding form /ˈkəʊdɪŋ fɔːm/ *noun* same as **coding sheet**

coding sheet /ˈkəʊdɪŋ ʃiːt/ *noun* a special printed sheet used by programmers to write instructions for coding a certain type of program

coincidence circuit /ˈelɪmənt/, **coincidence element** *noun* same as **coincidence gate**

coincidence function /kəʊ ˈɪnsɪd(ə)ns ˌfʌŋkʃən/ *noun* same as **AND function**

coincidence gate /kəʊˈɪnsɪd(ə)ns ɡeɪt/, **coincidence circuit, coincidence element** *noun* a gate that produces a logical output depending on various input coincidences. An AND gate requires the coincidence in time of all logically true inputs. ◊ **AND**

coincidence operation /kəʊ ˈɪnsɪd(ə)ns ˌɒpəreɪʃ(ə)n/ *noun* same as **AND operation**

COL *abbr* computer-oriented language

cold boot /ˌkəʊld ˈbuːt/ *noun* the act of switching on a computer, or the act of re-starting a computer by switching it off and then on again. Compare **warm boot**

cold fault /ˈkəʊld fɔːlt/ *noun* a computer fault or error that occurs as soon as it is switched on

cold standby /kəʊld ˈstændbaɪ/ *noun* a backup system that will allow the equipment to continue running but with the loss of any volatile data. Compare **hot standby, warm standby**

cold start /kəʊld ˈstɑːt/ *noun* the act of switching on a computer or to run a program from its original start point

collating sequence /kəˈleɪtɪŋ ˌsiːkwəns/ *noun* a sequence of characters ordered according to their codes

collator /kəˈleɪtə/ *noun* **1.** a piece of software that collates data **2.** a device that collates punched cards

collect /kəˈlekt/ *verb* to receive or capture data

collect transfer /kəˌlekt trænsˈfɜː/ *verb* to load a register with bits from a number of different locations

collision /kəˈlɪʒ(ə)n/ *noun* an event that occurs when two electrical signals meet and interfere with each other over a network, normally causing an error

collision detection /kəˈlɪʒ(ə)n dɪ ˌtekʃ(ə)n/ *noun* the detecting and reporting of the coincidence of two actions or events

co-location /kəʊ ləʊˈkeɪʃ(ə)n/ *noun* an arrangement whereby a computer used as an Internet server is located at a specialist site that is designed to support and maintain servers on behalf of their customers

COMMENT: If you want to set up a website, you might start by renting web space from your ISP or web hosting provider. If your website grows in popularity or requires complex or secure e-commerce facilities, you might find it effective to rent or purchase a server computer dedicated to serving your website – you could locate this server computer anywhere,

for example, in your office, but you would need to install a high-speed link to the Internet and maintain the computer and its software. A more cost-effective solution is co-location: moving the server to a specialist site, often provided by an ISP, who takes on the job of supporting the high-speed link and the computer.

colour balance /ˈkʌlə ˌbæləns/ *noun* the adjustment of the red, green and blue primary colours to produce a pure white colour. When a colour monitor is configured, a colour sensor is placed on the screen and the red, green and blue electron gun settings are adjusted to produce a pure white colour.

colour bits /ˈkʌlə bɪts/ *plural noun* the number of data bits assigned to a pixel to describe its colour. One bit provides two colours, two bits give four colours and eight bits allow 256 colour combinations.

colour cell /ˈkʌlə sel/ *noun* the smallest area on a CRT screen that can display colour information

colour cycling /ˈkʌlə ˌsaɪklɪŋ/ *noun* a process that changes the colours in a palette over a period of time, normally used to create a special effect or animation

colour depth /ˈkʌlə depθ/ *noun* the number of different colours that can be displayed by any single pixel in a display, which is determined by the number of colour bits in each pixel

colour display /ˌkʌlə dɪˈspleɪ/ *noun* a display device able to represent characters or graphics in colour

colour key /ˈkʌlə kiː/ *noun* an image manipulation technique used to superimpose one image on another. It is often used with two video sources to create special effects. One image is photographed against a coloured background, the matte, when then has another image superimposed on it to produce a combined picture. ◊ **chroma key**

colour look-up table /ˌkʌlə ˈlʊk ʌp ˌteɪb(ə)l/ *noun* full form of **CLUT**

colour monitor /ˌkʌlə ˈmɒnɪtə/ *noun* a screen that has a demodulator that shows information in colour ○ *The colour monitor is great for games.*

colour palette /ˌkʌlə ˈpælət/ *noun* the selection of colours that are currently being used in an image

colour printer /ˌkʌlə ˈprɪntə/ *noun* a printer that can produce hard copy in colour

colour saturation /ˌkʌlə ˌsætʃə ˈreɪʃ(ə)n/ *noun* the purity of a colour signal

colour separation /ˌkʌlə ˌsepə ˈreɪʃ(ə)n/ *noun* the process of separating a colour image into its constituent colours in order to produce printing plates for colour printing. Full colour printing needs four-colour separation to produce four printing plates for the cyan, magenta, yellow and black inks that together create a colour image.

colour standard /ˈkʌlə ˌstændəd/ *noun* one of three international standards, NTSC, PAL and SECAM, used to describe how colour TV and video images are displayed and transmitted

colour temperature /ˈkʌlə ˌtemprɪtʃə/ *noun* the hue or shade of the colour white seen if pure carbon is heated to a particular temperature measured in Kelvin. The standard for many TV and video systems is a colour temperature of 6500K, known as Illuminant D65.

colour tool /ˈkʌlə tuːl/ *noun* a utility or icon in a graphics or DTP application that allows the user to create custom colours by specifying the CMYK or RGB values and then draw or fill an area with this colour

column /ˈkɒləm/ *noun* a series of characters, numbers or lines of text printed one under the other ○ *to add up a column of figures*

columnar graph /kəˌlʌmnə ˈgrɑːf/ *noun* a graph on which values are shown as vertical or horizontal bars

columnar working /kəˌlʌmnə ˈwɜːkɪŋ/ *noun* a method of working that shows information in columns

column balance /ˈkɒləm ˌbæləns/ *noun* (*in a word-processor or DTP system*) a method of making sure that the ends of two columns of text are level

column guide /ˈkɒləm gaɪd/ *noun* (*in a DTP application*) a vertical line that indicates the position and width of a column

column indicator /ˈkɒləm ˌɪndɪkeɪtə/ *noun* (*in word-processing software*) the status bar at the bottom of the screen that displays in which column the cursor is positioned

column parity /ˌkɒləm ˈpærɪti/ *noun* a parity check on every punched card or tape column

column report /ˈkɒləm rɪˌpɔːt/ *noun* a method of viewing data in columns, in which each column is one field of a record and each row a separate record

com /kɒm/ *suffix* a suffix that means that the Internet domain name is a company, usually one based in the USA ○ *www.amazon.com is the website address of the US version of the Amazon Internet bookshop.*

COM /ˌsiː əʊ ˈem/ *noun* **1.** a standard defined by Microsoft to standardise the way an application can access an object. Full form **component object model** (NOTE: This is a rival standard to CORBA.) **2.** the process of recording the output from a computer directly onto microfilm. Full form **computer output on microfilm**

COM1 /ˌkɒm ˈwʌn/ *noun* a name used in PCs to represent the first serial port on the computer. There are normally two serial ports, COM1 and COM2, in a PC, although it can support four. Some PCs have a mouse plugged into the first serial port and the modem plugged into the second port. ◊ **AUX**. Also called **COM port, COM device**

COMAL /ˈkəʊbæl/ *noun* a structured programming language similar to BASIC. Full form **common algorithmic language**

comb filter /kəʊm ˈfɪltə/ *noun* an electronic device used to separate the luma, Y, and chroma, C, signals from a composite video signal. ◊ **S-Video, Y/C**

combinational circuit /ˌkɒmbɪneɪʃ(ə)l ˈsɜːkɪt/ *noun* an electronic circuit consisting of a number of connected components

combinational logic /ˌkɒmbɪneɪʃ(ə)l ˈlɒdʒɪk/ *noun* a logic function made up from a number of separate logic gates

combined head /kəmˈbaɪnd hed/ *noun* a transducer that can read or write data from the surface of a magnetic storage medium such as a floppy disk

combined station /kəmˌbaɪnd ˈsteɪʃ(ə)n/ *noun* a high-level data link control station that processes commands and responses

combined symbol matching /kəmˌbaɪnd ˈsɪmbəl ˌmætʃɪŋ/ *noun* full form of **CSM**

combi player /ˈkɒmbi ˌpleɪə/ *noun* a hardware drive that can read two or more different CD-ROM formats

combo box /ˈkɒmbəʊ bɒks/ *noun* a box that displays a number of different input and output objects

COM device /ˈkɒm dɪˌvaɪs/ *noun* same as **COM1**

COM file /ˈkɒm faɪl/ *noun* (*in operating systems for the PC*) a file with the three-letter extension .com to its name that indicates that the file contains a machine code in binary format and so can be executed by the operating system.

comic-strip oriented /ˌkɒmɪk strɪp ˈɔːrientɪd/ *adjective* referring to a film image that is oriented at right angles to the outer edge of the film. Compare **cine-oriented**

Comité Consultatif Internationale de Télégraphie et Téléphonie *noun* full form of **CCITT**

comma /ˈkɒmə/ *noun* a symbol (,) that is often used to separate data or variables or arguments

comma-delimited file /ˌkɒmə diː ˌlɪmɪtd ˈfaɪl/ *noun* data file in which each data item is separated by a comma ○ *All databases can import and export to a comma-delimited file format.*

command /kəˈmɑːnd/ *noun* **1.** an electrical pulse or signal that will start or stop a process **2.** a word or phrase which is recognised by a computer system and starts or terminates an action ○ *interrupt command*

command chain /kəˈmɑːnd tʃeɪn/ *noun* list of commands (in a file) executed sequentially by a batch mode system

command code /kəˈmɑːnd kəʊd/ *noun* a binary code that starts or stops an instruction or action in a CPU

COMMAND.COM /kəˈmɑːnd kɒm/ *noun* (*in MS-DOS*) a program file that contains the command interpreter for the operating system. This program is always resident in memory and recognises and translates system commands into actions. ○ *MS-DOS will not work because you deleted the COMMAND.COM file by mistake.*

command console processor /kə ˈmɑːnd ˌkɒnsəʊl ˌprəʊsesə/ *noun* full form of **CCP**

command control language /kə ˌmɑːnd kənˈtrəʊl ˌlæŋgwɪdʒ/ *noun* a programming language that allows equipment to be easily controlled

command-driven program /kə ˌmɑːnd ˌdrɪv(ə)n ˈprəʊgræm/ *noun* a program which requires the user to enter instructions at every stage

command file /kəˈmɑːnd faɪl/ *noun* a sequence of frequently used commands stored in a file

command file processor /kəˈmɑːnd faɪl ˌprəʊsesə/ *noun* a device that executes a user's command file, allowing the user to create a customised simple operating environment or to carry out a series of frequently used commands

command interface /kəˈmɑːnd ˌɪntəfeɪs/ *noun* the cue and prompts used by a program to inform and accept from user-required inputs. This can be user-friendly, like a WIMP environment, or not so friendly, like a question mark.

command interpreter /kəˈmɑːnd ɪn ˌtɜːprɪtə/ *noun* a program within an operating system that recognises a set of system commands and controls the processor, screen and storage devices accordingly ○ *When you type in the command 'DIR', the command interpreter asks the disk drive for a list of files and instructs the monitor to display the list.*

command key /kəˈmɑːnd kiː/ *noun* (*on an Apple Macintosh*) a special key that gives access to various special functions, similar in effect to the Control key on an IBM PC

command language /kəˈmɑːnd ˌlæŋgwɪdʒ/ *noun* a programming language made up of procedures for various tasks, that can be called up by a series of commands

command line /kəˈmɑːnd laɪn/ *noun* **1.** a program line that contains a command instruction **2.** a command prompt and system command

'This gives Unix a friendly face instead of the terrifyingly complex command-line prompts that make most users reach for their manuals.' [*Computing*]

command line argument /kəˌmɑːnd laɪn ˈɑːgjʊmənt/ *noun* additional items entered following a command ○ *Use the command 'DIR' to view the files on disk, add the command line argument 'A:' to view the files on drive A:.*

command line interface /kəˌmɑːnd laɪn ˈɪntəfeɪs/ *noun* a user interface in which the user controls the operating system or program by typing in commands; e.g., DOS is a command line interface

command line operating system /kəˌmɑːnd laɪn ˈɒpəreɪtɪŋ ˌsɪstəm/ *noun* a computer system software that is controlled by a user typing in commands, as in MS-DOS, rather than allowing a user to control the system through images

command message /kə'mɑːnd ˌmesɪdʒ/ *noun* (*in MCI*) a character or symbol that represents an MCI command

command mode /kə'mɑːnd məʊd/ *noun* the operating mode of a modem in which the user or communications software can send instructions to the modem that it will then try and execute. The standard method of switching a modem to command mode is to type or send it the three characters '+++'. The modem will reply with an 'OK' message and is ready to execute configuration or other commands.

command prompt /kə'mɑːnd prɒmpt/ *noun* a symbol displayed by the operating system to indicate that a command is expected

command register /kə'mɑːnd ˌredʒɪstə/ *noun* a register that stores the instruction that is to be carried out or that is being processed

command state /kə'mɑːnd steɪt/ *noun* the state of a modem in which it is ready to accept commands

command string /kə'mɑːnd strɪŋ/ *noun* (*in MCI*) a character string that contains all the information to carry out an MCI command. The string ends with a null character and is split by MCI into the command message and data structure.

command window /kə'mɑːnd ˌwɪndəʊ/ *noun* an area of the screen that always displays the range of commands available ○ *The command window is a single line at the bottom of the screen.*

command window history /kə ˌmɑːnd ˌwɪndəʊ 'hɪst(ə)ri/ *noun* a list of previous commands entered in the command window ○ *The user can define the size of the command window.*

comment /'kɒment/ *noun* a helpful note in a program to guide the user ○ *The lack of comments is annoying.*

comment field /'kɒment fiːld/ *noun* a section of a command line in an assembly language program that is not executed, but provides notes and comments

comment out /'kɒment aʊt/ *noun* a method of temporarily disabling a command by enclosing it in a comment field

commerce /'kɒmɜːs/ ♦ **e-commerce**

commerce server /'kɒmɜːs ˌsɜːvə/ *noun* web software that supports the main functions of an online shop including managing the shopping cart and dealing with the credit card payment processing

commercial Internet exchange /kə ˌmɜːʃ(ə)l 'ɪntənet ɪks,tʃeɪndʒ/ *noun* a connection point for commercial Internet service providers

Commission International de l'Eclairage full form of **CIE**

common algorithmic language /ˌkɒmən ˌælgərɪðmɪk 'læŋgwɪdʒ/ *noun* full form of **COMAL**

common business orientated language /ˌkɒmən ˌbɪznɪs ˌɔːriənteɪtɪd 'læŋgwɪdʒ/ *noun* a programming language mainly used in business applications. Abbr **COBOL**

common carrier /ˌkɒmən 'kæriə/ *noun* a private company that supplies data and voice communications services for a fee to anybody

common channel signalling /ˌkɒmən 'tʃæn(ə)l ˌsɪgn(ə)lɪŋ/ *noun* the use of one channel as a communications link to a number of devices or circuits

common gateway interface /ˌkɒmən 'geɪtweɪ ˌɪntəfeɪs/ *noun* full form of **CGI**

common hardware /ˌkɒmən 'hɑːdweə/ *noun* hardware items that can be used for a variety of tasks

common intermediate format /ˌkɒmən ˌɪntəmiːdiət 'fɔːmæt/ *noun* a standard for video images that displays an image 352 pixels wide and 288 pixels high. Abbr **CIF**

common language /ˌkɒmən 'læŋgwɪdʒ/ *noun* a set of data or program instructions in a standardised form that can be understood by other processors or compilers/interpreters

common management information protocol /ˌkɒmən ˌmænɪdʒmənt ˌɪnfə'meɪʃ(ə)n ˌprəʊtəkɒl/ *noun* full form of **CMIP**

common management information specification /ˌkɒmən ˌmænɪdʒmənt ˌɪnfə'meɪʃ(ə)n ˌspesɪfɪkeɪʃ(ə)n/ full form of **CMIS**

common object request broker architecture /ˌkɒmən əb,dʒekt rɪ,kwest ˌbrəʊkə 'ɑːkɪtektʃə/ *noun* a standard defined by the Object Management Group to standardise the way an application can access an object. Abbr **CORBA**. Compare **COM**

common ordinary business-oriented language /ˌkɒmən ˌɔːd(ə)n(ə)ri ˌbɪznɪs ˌɔːriəntɪd 'læŋgwɪdʒ/ *noun* full form of **COBOL**

common real-time applications language /ˌkɒmən ˌrɪəl taɪm ˌæplɪ'keɪʃ(ə)nz ˌlæŋgwɪdʒ/ *noun* full form of **CORAL**

common software /ˌkɒmən 'sɒftweə/ *noun* useful routines that can be used by any program

common storage area /ˌkɒmən 'stɔːrɪdʒ ˌeərɪə/ *noun* a memory or storage area used by more than one program ○ *The file server memory is mainly common storage area, with a section reserved for the operating system.*

communicating applications specification /kəˌmjuːnɪkeɪtɪŋ ˌæplɪkeɪʃ(ə)n spə'sɪfɪk/ *noun* full form of **CAS**

communicating word processor /kəˌmjuːnɪkeɪtɪŋ 'wɜːd ˌprəʊsesə/ *noun* a word processor workstation which is able to transmit and receive data

communications buffer /kəˌmjuːnɪ'keɪʃ(ə)nz ˌbʌfə/ *noun* a terminal or modem that is able to store transmitted data

communications channel /kəˌmjuːnɪ'keɪʃ(ə)nz ˌtʃæn(ə)l/ *noun* a physical link over which data can be transmitted

communications computer /kəˌmjuːnɪ'keɪʃ(ə)nz kəm,pjuːtə/ *noun* a computer used to control data transmission in a network

communications control unit /kəˌmjuːnɪkeɪʃ(ə)nz kən'trəʊl ˌjuːnɪt/ *noun* an electronic device that controls data transmission and routes in a network

communications executive /kəˌmjuːnɪ'keɪʃ(ə)nz ɪg,zekjʊtɪv/ *noun* the main set of programs that ensure that protocol, format and device and line handlers are correct for the type of device or line in use

communications interface adapter /kəˌmjuːnɪkeɪʃ(ə)nz 'ɪntəfeɪs ə ,dæptə/ *noun* an electronic circuit that allows a computer to communicate with a modem

communications link /kəˌmjuːnɪ'keɪʃ(ə)nz lɪŋk/ *noun* the physical path that joins a transmitter to a receiver

communications link control /kəˌmjuːnɪkeɪʃ(ə)nz lɪŋk kən'trəʊl/ *noun* a processor that provides various handshaking and error detection functions for a number of links between devices

communications network /kəˌmjuːnɪ'keɪʃ(ə)nz ˌnetwɜːk/ *noun* a group of devices such as terminals and printers that are interconnected with a central computer, allowing the rapid and simple transfer of data

communications network processor /kəˌmjuːnɪkeɪʃ(ə)nz ˌnetwɜːk 'prəʊsesə/ *noun* a processor that provides various types of interfacing and management, e.g. buffering or code conversion, between a computer and communications link control

communications package /kəˌmjuːnɪ'keɪʃ(ə)nz ˌpækɪdʒ/ *noun* a package of software that allows a user to control a modem and use an online service

communications port /kəˌmjuːnɪ'keɪʃ(ə)nz pɔːt/ *noun* a socket or physical connection allowing a device to communicate

communications protocol /kəˌmjuːnɪ'keɪʃ(ə)nz ˌprəʊtəʊkɒl/ *noun* the parameters that define how the transfer of information will be controlled ○ *The communications protocol for most dial-up online services is eight-bit words, no stop bit and even parity.*

communications scanner /kəˌmjuːnɪ'keɪʃ(ə)nz ˌskænə/ *noun* a piece of line-monitoring equipment that checks for data request signals

communications server /kəˌmjuːnɪ'keɪʃ(ə)nz ˌsɜːvə/ *noun* a computer with a modem or fax card attached that allows users on a network to share the use of the modem

communications software /kəˌmjuːnɪ'keɪʃ(ə)nz ˌsɒftweə/ *noun* software that allows a user to control a modem and use an online service

community /kə'mjuːnɪti/ *noun* same as **virtual community**

comp /kɒmp/ *noun* a type of newsgroup that provides discussion about computers and computer programming

compact code /'kɒmpækt kəʊd/ *noun* the minimum number of program instructions required for a task

compact disc /ˌkɒmpækt 'dɪsk/ *noun* a small plastic disc that contains audio signals in digital form etched onto the surface. Abbr **CD**

compact disc-digital audio /ˌkɒmpækt ˌdɪsk ˌdɪdʒɪt(ə)l 'ɔːdiəʊ/ *noun* a standard that defines how music can be stored in digital form, i.e. as a series of numbers, on a compact disc. Abbr **CD-DA**. Also called **CD-audio**

compact disc erasable /ˌkɒmpækt ˌdɪsk ɪ'reɪzəb(ə)l/ *noun* a format that allows data to be saved to and erased from a compact disc. Abbr **CD-E**

compact   disc-interactive /ˌkɒmpækt dɪsk ˌɪntər'æktɪv/ *noun* full form of **CD-I**

compact disc player /ˌkɒmpækt 'dɪsk ˌpleɪə/ *noun* a machine that reads the digital data from a CD and converts it back to its original form

compact disc ROM /ˌkɒmpækt ˌdɪsk 'rɒm/ *noun* same as **CD-ROM** ○ *The compact disc ROM can store as much data as a dozen hard disks.*

compact disc write once /ˌkɒmpækt dɪsk ˌraɪt 'wʌns/ *noun* CD-ROM disc and drive technology that allows a user to write data to the disc once only. Full form **CD-WO**

compact Flash /kəmˌpækt 'flæʃ/ *noun* a tiny memory expansion device that uses Flash-ROM to store up to 512Mb of data, often used in MP3 music players and digital cameras. Abbr **CF**

compacting algorithm /ˌkɒmpæktɪŋ 'ælgəˌrɪð(ə)m/ *noun* a formula for reducing the amount of space required by text

compact model /'kɒmpækt ˌmɒd(ə)l/ *noun* a memory model in the Intel 80x86 family of CPUs that allows only 64Kb of space for the code of a program, but 1Mb of space for the program's data

companding /kɒm'pændɪŋ/ *noun* two processes which reduce or compact data before transmission or storage then restore packed data to its original form. Full form **compressing and expanding**

COMPAQ /'kɒmpæk/ a US personal computer company, founded in 1983, that was the first manufacturer to produce a clone to the IBM PC

comparator /kəm'pærətə/ *noun* a logical device whose output is true if there is a difference between two inputs

compatibility /kəmˌpætɪ'bɪlɪti/ *noun* the ability of two hardware or software devices to function together (NOTE: Compatibility of hardware and software, which means that those of one manufacturer or organisation conform to the standards of another, allows programs and hardware to be interchanged without modification.)

'The manufacturer claims that this card does not require special drivers on the host machine… and therefore has fewer compatibility problems.' [*Computing*]

compatibility box /kəmˌpætə'bɪlɪti bɒks/ *noun* **caret mark, caret sign** a window or session in an operating system that can execute programs written for a different, but related, operating system ○ *OS/2 has a compatibility box to allow it to run DOS applications.*

compatible /kəm'pætɪb(ə)l/ *adjective* used to describe two hardware or software devices that function correctly together ■ *noun* a hardware or software device that functions correctly with other equipment ○ *Buy an IBM PC or a compatible.*

'…this was the only piece of software I found that wouldn't work, but it does show that there is no such thing as a totally compatible PC clone' [*Personal Computer World*]

compilation /ˌkɒmpɪ'leɪʃ(ə)n/ *noun* the translation of an encoded source program into machine readable code

'This utility divides the compilation of software into pieces and performs the compile in parallel across available machines on the network.' [*Computergram*]

compilation error /ˌkɒmpɪ'leɪʃ(ə)n ˌerə/ *noun* an error occurring during program compilation time

compilation time /ˌkɒmpɪ'leɪʃ(ə)n taɪm/ *noun* the length of time it takes for a computer to compile a program

compile /kəm'paɪl/ *verb* to convert a high-level language program into a machine code program that can be executed by itself

compile and go /kəmˌpaɪl ən 'gəʊ/ *noun* a computer program not requiring operator interaction that will load, compile and execute a high-level language program

compile phase /kəm'paɪl feɪz/ *noun* the time during a program run, when the instructions are compiled

compiler, compiler program *noun* a piece of software that converts an encoded program into a machine code program ○ *The new compiler has an in-built editor.* Compare **interpreter**

compiler diagnostics /kəmˌpaɪlə ˌdaɪəg'nɒstɪks/ *plural noun* a function in a compiler that helps a programmer find faults in the program code ○ *Thorough compiler diagnostics make debugging easy.*

compiler language /kəm'paɪlə ˌlæŋgwɪdʒ/ *noun* a high-level language such as C or pascal that will convert a source program that follows the language syntax into a machine code version, then run it

complement /'kɒmplɪment/ *noun* **1.** an inversion of a binary digit ○ *The complement is found by changing the 1s to 0s and 0s to 1s.* **2.** the result after subtracting a number from one less than the radix ■ *verb* to invert a binary digit

complementary metal oxide semiconductor /ˌkɒmplɪment(ə)ri ˌmet(ə)l ˌɒksaɪd 'semikən,dʌktə/ *noun* full form of **CMOS**

complementary operation /ˌkɒmplɪment(ə)ri ˌɒpə'reɪʃ(ə)n/ *noun* a logical operation that results in the logical NOT of a function

complementation /ˌkɒmplɪmən'teɪʃ(ə)n/ *noun* a number system used to represent positive and negative numbers

complemented /'kɒmplɪməntɪd/ *adjective* referring to a binary digit that has had a complement performed

complete operation /kəm,pliːt ,ɒpə 'reɪʃ(ə)n/ *noun* an operation that retrieves the necessary operands from memory, performs the operation and returns the results and operands to memory, then reads the next instruction to be processed

completion /kəm'pliːʃ(ə)n/ *noun* the point at which something is complete ○ *Completion date for the new software package is November 15th.*

complex instruction set computer /ˌkɒmpleks ɪn,strʌkʃən ,set kəm 'pjuːtə/ *noun* full form of **CISC**

complexity measure /kəm'pleksɪti ,meʒə/ *noun* a measure of the system resources used in an operation or job

compliant /kəm'plaɪənt/ *adjective* that conforms to a particular set of standards ○ *If you want to read PhotoCD compact discs in your computer you must be sure that the CD-ROM drive is PhotoCD or CD-ROM XA compliant.*

component density /kəm,pəʊnənt 'densɪti/ *noun* number of electronic components per unit area on a PCB ○ *Component density increases with production expertise.*

component error /kəm'pəʊnənt ,erə/ *noun* error introduced by a malfunctioning device or component rather than by incorrect programming

Component Object Model /kəm ,pəʊnənt 'ɒbdʒekt ,mɒd(ə)l/ *noun* full form of **COM**

component video /kəm'pəʊnənt ,vɪdiəʊ/ *noun* a method of transmitting video information, used in professional video systems, that has separate signals for the luminance and two chrominance channels to avoid interference

COM port /'kɒm pɔːt/ *noun* same as **COM1**

composite circuit /ˌkɒmpəzɪt 'sɜːkɪt/ *noun* an electronic circuit made up of a number of smaller circuits and components

composite display /ˌkɒmpəzɪt dɪ 'spleɪ/ *noun* a video display unit that accepts a single composite video signal and can display an infinite number of colours or shades of grey

composite monitor /ˌkɒmpəzɪt 'mɒnɪtə/ *noun* a colour monitor that receives one video signal from a graphics display adapter, which must then be electronically separated inside the monitor into the red, green and blue colour signals

composite video /ˌkɒmpəzɪt 'vɪdiəʊ/ *noun* a video signal that combines the colour signals and the monochrome signal into one single signal ○ *Most TV set and video players expect a composite video feed.*

compound device /ˌkɒmpaʊnd dɪ 'vaɪs/ *noun* a Windows MCI multimedia device that requires a data file

compound document /'kɒmpaʊnd ,dɒkjʊmənt/ *noun* a document that contains information created by several other applications

compound file /'kɒmpaʊnd faɪl/ *noun* a number of individual files grouped together in one file

compound logical element /ˌkɒmpaʊnd ,lɒdʒɪk(ə)l 'elɪmənt/ *noun* a logical circuit or function that produces an output from a number of inputs

compound statement /ˌkɒmpaʊnd 'steɪtmənt/ *noun* a number of program instructions in one line of program ○ *The debugger cannot handle compound statements.*

compressed video /ˌkɒmprest 'vɪdiəʊ/ *noun* video signals that have been compressed to reduce the data rate required to transmit the information. Whereas a normal television picture is transmitted at around 5090Mbits/second, a compressed video signal can be transmitted at around one tenth of the data rate.

compression /kəm'preʃ(ə)n/ *noun* the process of reducing the size of a file by encoding the data in a more efficient form. For example, if the file contains five letter 'A's in line, which take up five bytes of space, the compression software could encode this to 5A which takes two byes of space.

compression ratio /kəm'preʃ(ə)n ˌreɪʃiəʊ/ *noun* a ratio of the size of an original, uncompressed file to the final, compressed file that has been more efficiently encoded

CompuServe /'kɒmpjuːsɜːv/ an online service provider and information service

computer /kəm'pjuːtə/ *noun* a machine that receives or stores or processes data very quickly using a program kept in its memory

computer-aided /kəmˌpjuːtə 'eɪdɪd/ *adjective* that uses a computer to make the work easier. Also called **computer-assisted**

computer-aided design /kəm ˌpjuːtər ˌeɪdɪd dɪ'zaɪn/ *noun* full form of **CAD**

computer-aided engineering /kəm ˌpjuːtər ˌeɪdɪd ˌendʒɪ'nɪərɪŋ/ *noun* full form of **CAE**

computer-aided instruction /kəm ˌpjuːtər ˌeɪdɪd ɪn'strʌkʃən/ *noun* full form of **CAI**

computer-aided learning /kəm ˌpjuːtər ˌeɪdɪd 'lɔːnɪŋ/ *noun* full form of **CAL**

computer-aided manufacture /kəm ˌpjuːtər ˌeɪdɪd ˌmænjʊ'fæktʃə/ *noun* full form of **CAM**

computer-aided testing /kəm ˌpjuːtər ˌeɪdɪd 'testɪŋ/ *noun* full form of **CAT**

computer-aided training /kəm ˌpjuːtər ˌeɪdɪd 'treɪnɪŋ/ *noun* full form of **CAT**

computer animation /kəmˌpjuːtə ˌænɪ'meɪʃ(ə)n/ *noun* same as **animation**

computer applications /kəmˌpjuːtə ˌæplɪ'keɪʃ(ə)nz/ *plural noun* the tasks and uses that a computer can carry out in a particular field or job

computer architecture /kəmˌpjuːtə 'ɑːkɪtektʃə/ *noun* **1.** the layout and interconnection of a computer's internal hardware and the logical relationships between CPU, memory and I/O devices **2.** the way

in which the CPU, terminals, printers and network connections are arranged

computer-assisted /kəmˌpjuːtər ə 'sɪstɪd/ *adjective* same as **computer-aided**

computer-assisted design /kəm ˌpjuːtər əˌsɪstɪd dɪ'zaɪn/ *noun* full form of **CAD**

computer-assisted engineering /kəmˌpjuːtər əˌsɪstɪd ˌendʒɪ'nɪərɪŋ/ *noun* full form of **CAE**

computer-assisted instruction /kəmˌpjuːtər əˌsɪstɪd ɪn'strʌkʃən/ *noun* full form of **CAI**

computer-assisted learning /kəm ˌpjuːtər əˌsɪstɪd 'lɜːnɪŋ/ *noun* full form of **CAL**

computer-assisted manufacture /kəmˌpjuːtər əˌsɪstɪd ˌmænjʊ'fæktʃə/ *noun* full form of **CAM**

computer-assisted testing /kəm ˌpjuːtər əˌsɪstɪd 'testɪŋ/ *noun* full form of **CAT**

computer-assisted training /kəm ˌpjuːtər əˌsɪstɪd 'treɪnɪŋ/ *noun* full form of **CAT**

computer-based learning /kəm ˌpjuːtə beɪst 'lɜːnɪŋ/ *noun* full form of **CBL**

computer-based message system /kəmˌpjuːtə beɪst 'mesɪdʒ ˌsɪstəm/ *noun* full form of **CBMS**

computer-based training /kəm ˌpjuːtə beɪst 'treɪnɪŋ/ *noun* full form of **CBT**

computer bureau /kəm'pjuːtə ˌbjʊərəʊ/ *noun* an office that offers to do work on its computers for companies which do not have their own

computer code /kəm'pjuːtə kəʊd/ *noun* a programming language that consists of commands in binary code that can be directly understood by the central processing unit, without the need for translation

computer conferencing /kəm ˌpjuːtə 'kɒnf(ə)rənsɪŋ/ *noun* the use of a number of computers or terminals connected together to allow a group of users to communicate

computer crime /kəm'pjuːtə kraɪm/ *noun* theft, fraud or other crimes involving computers

computer dating /kəmˌpjuːtə 'deɪtɪŋ/ *noun* the use of a computer to match single people who may want to get married

computer department /kəm'pju:tə dɪ,pɑ:tmənt/ *noun* a department in a company that manages the company's computers

computer engineer /kəm,pju:tə ,endʒɪ'nɪə/ *noun* a person who maintains, programs or designs computer equipment

computer error /kəm,pju:tər 'erə/ *noun* a mistake made by a computer

computer file /kəm'pju:tə faɪl/ *noun* a section of information on a computer, e.g. the payroll, list of addresses or customer accounts

computer fraud /kəm'pju:tə frɔ:d/ *noun* the theft of data, dishonest use of data or other crimes involving computers

computer game /kəm'pju:tə geɪm/ *noun* a game played on a computer, using special software

computer-generated /kəm,pju:tə 'dʒenəreɪtɪd/ *adjective* produced using a computer ○ *They analysed the computer-generated image.*

computer generation /kəm,pju:tə ,dʒenə'reɪʃ(ə)n/ *noun* any one in a series of classifications used to define the advances in the field of computing

COMMENT: The development of computers has been divided into a series of 'generations'. The first generation consisted of computers constructed using valves and having limited storage. The second generation of computers were constricted using transistors. The third generation used integrated circuits. The fourth generation, which includes the computers most often used at present, uses low-cost memory and IC packages. The fifth generation comprises future computers using very fast processors, large memory and allowing human input/output.

computer graphics /kəm,pju:tə 'græfɪks/ *plural noun* information represented graphically on a computer display

computer graphics metafile /kəm ,pju:tə ,græfɪks 'metəfaɪl/ *noun* full form of **CGM**

computer illiterate /kəm,pju:tə ɪ 'lɪtərət/ *adjective* unable to understand computer-related expressions or operations

computer image processing /kəm ,pju:tə 'ɪmɪdʒ ,prəʊsesɪŋ/ *noun* the analysis of information in an image, usually by electronic means or using a computer, also used for recognition of objects in an image

computer-independent language /kəm,pju:tə ,ɪndɪpendənt 'læŋgwɪdʒ/ *noun* a programming language that will operate on any computer that has a correct compiler or interpreter

computer indexing /kəm,pju:tə 'ɪndeksɪŋ/ *noun* the use of a computer to compile an index for a book by selecting relevant words or items from the text

computer input microfilm /kəm ,pju:tə ,ɪnpʊt 'maɪkrəʊfɪlm/ *noun* full form of **CIM**

computer-integrated manufacturing /kəm,pju:tə ,ɪntɪgreɪtɪd ,mænjʊ 'fæktʃərɪŋ/ *noun* full form of **CIM**

computer-integrated system /kəm ,pju:tə ,ɪntɪgreɪtɪd 'sɪstəm/ *plural noun* a system designed to allow the coordinated use of computers and other related equipment in a process ○ *This firm is a very well-known supplier of computer-integrated systems which allow both batch pagination of very long documents with alteration of individual pages.*

computer-integrated telephony /kəm,pju:tə ,ɪntɪgreɪtɪd tə'lefəni/ *noun* same as **CTI**

computerisation /kəm,pjʊtəraɪ 'zeɪʃ(ə)n/, **computerization** *noun* the process of introducing a computer system or of changing from a manual to a computer system ○ *Computerisation of the financial sector is proceeding very fast.*

computerise /kəm'pju:təraɪz/, **computerize** *verb* to change from a manual system to one using computers ○ *Our stock control has been completely computerised.*

computer language /kəm'pju:tə ,læŋgwɪdʒ/ *noun* a language, formed of figures or characters, used to communicate with a computer

computer listing /kəm,pju:tə 'lɪstɪŋ/ *noun* a printout of a list of items taken from data stored in a computer

computer literacy /kəm,pju:tə 'lɪt(ə)rəsi/ *noun* understanding of the basic principles of computers, related expressions and concepts, and the ability to use computers for programming or applications

computer-literate /kəm,pju:tə 'lɪt(ə)rət/ *adjective* able to understand expressions relating to computers and how to use a computer

computer logic /kəm,pju:tə 'lɒdʒɪk/ *noun* (*in hardware*) the way in which the various sections of the CPU, memory and I/O are arranged

computer-managed instruction /kəm‚pju:tə ‚mænɪdʒd ɪn'strʌkʃən/ *noun* the use of a computer to assist students in learning a subject. Abbr **CMI**

computer-managed learning /kəm ‚pju:tə ‚mænɪdʒd 'lɜ:nɪŋ/ *noun* the use of a computer to teach students and assess their progress. Abbr **CML**

computer manager /kəm'pju:tə ‚mænɪdʒə/ *noun* the person in charge of a computer department

computer name /kəm'pju:tə neɪm/ *plural noun* (*in Windows 95 and later versions of Windows*) a series of words that identify a computer on a network and distinguish it from all other computers on a network (NOTE: If you are linked to an office network, you will see an icon on your Desktop called Network Neighborhood. Double-click on this and it will display a list of the other computers on the network, and their computer name.)

computer network /kəm‚pju:tə 'netwɜ:k/ *noun* the shared use of a series of interconnected computers, peripherals and terminals

computer numerical control /kəm ‚pju:tə nju:‚merɪk(ə)l kən'trəʊl/ *noun* same as **numerical control**

computer numeric control /kəm ‚pju:tə nju:‚merɪk kən'trəʊl/ *noun* full form of **CNC**

computer office system /kəm ‚pju:tər 'ɒfɪs ‚sɪstəm/ *noun* a computer and related peripherals used for office tasks such as filing and word processing

computer operator /kəm'pju:tər ‚ɒpəreɪtə/ *noun* a person who operates a computer

computer organisation /kəm 'pju:tər ‚ɔ:gənaɪzeɪʃ(ə)n/, **computer organization** *noun* ♦ **computer architecture**

computer output /kəm‚pju:tər 'aʊtpʊt/ *noun* the data or information produced after processing by a computer

computer output on microfilm /kəm‚pju:tər ‚aʊtpʊt ɒn 'maɪkrəʊfɪlm/ *noun* full form of **COM**

computer power /kəm'pju:tə ‚paʊə/ *noun* a measure of the speed and capacity of a computer (NOTE: Several tests for computer power exist, e.g. FLOPS or benchmark timings.)

computer printer /kəm‚pju:tə 'prɪntə/ *noun* a machine which prints information from a computer

computer printout /kəm‚pju:tə 'prɪntaʊt/ *noun* a printed copy of information from a computer ○ *The sales director asked for a printout of the agents' commissions.*

computer program /kəm'pju:tə ‚prəʊgræm/ *noun* a series of instructions to a computer, telling it to do a particular piece of work ○ *The user cannot write a computer program with this system.*

computer programmer /kəm‚pju:tə 'prəʊgræmə/ *noun* a person who writes computer programs

computer-readable /kəm‚pju:tə 'ri:dəb(ə)l/ *adjective* which can be read and understood by a computer ○ *computer-readable codes*

computer run /kəm'pju:tə rʌn/ *noun* the action of processing instructions in a program by a computer

computer science /kəm‚pju:tə 'saɪəns/ *noun* the scientific study of computers, the organisation of hardware and the development of software

computer services /kəm‚pju:tə 'sɜ:vɪsɪz/ *plural noun* work using a computer, done by a computer bureau

computer stationery /kəm‚pju:tə 'steɪʃ(ə)n(ə)ri/ *noun* paper specially made for use in a computer printer

computer system /kəm'pju:tə ‚sɪstəm/ *noun* a central processor with storage and associated peripherals that make up a working computer

computer-telephony integration /kəm‚pju:tə tə‚lefəni ‚ɪntɪ'greɪʃ(ə)n/ *noun* full form of **CTI**

computer time /kəm'pju:tə taɪm/ *noun* the time when a computer is being used, which is paid for at an hourly rate ○ *Running all those sales reports costs a lot in computer time.*

computer virus /kəm'pju:tə ‚vaɪrəs/ *noun* a program which adds itself to an executable file and copies or spreads itself to other executable files each time an infected file is run. A virus can corrupt data, display a message or do nothing.

computer word /kəm'pju:tə wɜ:d/ *noun* a number of bits, usually 8, 16 or 32, that make up a standard word within a CPU

computing /kəm'pjuːtɪŋ/ *adjective, noun* referring to computers ■ *noun* work done on computers

computing power /kəm'pjuːtɪŋ ˌpaʊə/ *noun* a measure of the speed of a computer and its ability to perform calculations

computing speed /kəm'pjuːtɪŋ spiːd/ *noun* the speed at which a computer calculates

CON /kɒn/ *noun* (*in IBM-PC compatible systems*) a name used to identify the console, i.e. the keyboard and monitor

concatenate /kən'kætəneɪt/ *verb* to join together two or more sets of data

concatenated data set /kən ˌkætəneɪtɪd 'deɪtə ˌset/ *noun* more than one file or set of data joined together to produce one set

concatenation operator /kənˌkætə 'neɪʃ(ə)n ˌɒpəreɪtə/ *noun* an instruction that joins two pieces of data or variables together

conceal /kən'siːl/ *verb* to hide information or graphics from a user, or not to display them ○ *The hidden lines are concealed from view with this algorithm.*

concentrate /'kɒnsəntreɪt/ *verb* to combine a number of lines or circuits or data to take up less space ○ *The concentrated data was transmitted cheaply.*

concentrator /'kɒnsəntreɪtə/ *noun* **1.** (*in a Token-Ring network*) a device at the centre of a Token-Ring network, which provides a logical star topology in which nodes are connected to the concentrator, but which connects each arm of the star as a physical ring within the device **2.** (*in an FDDI network*) a node which provides access for one or more stations to the network **3.** (*in an 10Base-T Ethernet network*) the device at the centre of a star-topology 10Base-T Ethernet network that receives signals from one port and regenerates them before sending them out to the other ports **4.** (*in general networking*) a device in which all the cables from nodes are interconnected

conceptual model /kənˌseptʃuəl 'mɒd(ə)l/ *noun* a description of a database or program in terms of the data it contains and its relationships

concertina fold /ˌkɒnsə'tiːnə fəʊld/ *noun* a method of folding continuous paper, one sheet in one direction, the next sheet in the opposite direction, allowing the paper to be fed into a printer continuously with no action on the part of the user. Also called **accordion fold**

concurrency /kən'kʌrənsi/ *noun* data or a resource that is accessed by more than one user or application at a time

concurrent operating system /kən ˌkʌrənt 'ɒpəreɪtɪŋ ˌsɪstəm/ *noun* operating system software that allows several programs or activities to be processed at the same time

concurrent processing /kənˌkʌrənt 'prəʊsesɪŋ/ *noun* ♦ **multitasking**

concurrent programming /kən ˌkʌrənt 'prəʊɡræmɪŋ/ *noun* the act of running several programs apparently simultaneously, achieved by executing small sections from each program in turn

condition /kən'dɪʃ(ə)n/ *noun* **1.** the state of a circuit or device or register **2.** a series of requirements that have to be met before an action can occur ■ *verb* to modify data that is to be transmitted so as to meet set parameters ○ *Condition the raw data to a standard format.*

conditional /kən'dɪʃ(ə)n(ə)l/ *adjective* **1.** provided that certain things take place **2.** referring to a process that is dependent on the result of another

conditional branch /kənˌdɪʃ(ə)n(ə)l 'brɑːntʃ/ *noun* same as **conditional jump**

conditional breakpoint /kən ˌdɪʃ(ə)nəl 'breɪkpɔɪnt/ *noun* an inserted breakpoint, after which the programmer can jump to one of a number of sections, depending on data or program status

conditional jump /kən'dɪʃ(ə)nəl dʒʌmp/ *noun* a programming instruction that provides a jump to a section of a program if a certain condition is met ○ *The conditional branch will select routine one if the response is yes and routine two if no.*

conditional statement /kən ˌdɪʃ(ə)nəl 'steɪtmənt/ *noun* a program instruction which will redirect program control according to the outcome of an event

conditional transfer /kənˌdɪʃ(ə)nəl 'trænsfɜː/ *noun* same as **conditional jump**

condition code /kən'dɪʃ(ə)n kəʊd/ *noun* a number, or another type of signal, that indicates the status of an arithmetic, logic or input/output operation carried out previously

condition code register /kən ˌdɪʃ(ə)n 'kəʊd ˌredʒɪstə/ *noun* a register that contains the state of the CPU after the execution of the last instruction

conduct /kən'dʌkt/ *verb* to allow an electrical current to flow through a material ○ *to conduct electricity*

conduction /kən'dʌkʃən/ *noun* the ability of a material to conduct ○ *The conduction of electricity by gold contacts.*

conductive /kən'dʌktɪv/ *adjective* referring to the ability of a material to conduct

conductor /kən'dʌktə/ *noun* a substance such as a metal that conducts electricity ○ *Copper is a good conductor of electricity.* ◊ **semiconductor**

conduit /'kɒndjuɪt/ *noun* a protective pipe or channel for wires or cables ○ *The cables from each terminal are channelled to the computer centre by metal conduit.*

conferencing /'kɒnf(ə)rənsɪŋ/ *noun* discussion between remote users using computers linked by a modem or a network

'Small organisations and individuals find it convenient to use online services, offering email, conferencing and information services.' [*Computing*]

confidence level /'kɒnfɪd(ə)ns ˌlev(ə)l/ *noun* the likelihood that a particular number will lie within a range of values

CONFIG.SYS /kən'fɪg sɪs/ *noun* (*in MS-DOS*) a configuration text file that contains commands to set parameters and load driver software. This file is read automatically once the PC is switched on and the operating system has loaded. ○ *If you add a new adapter card to your PC you will have to add a new command to your CONFIG.SYS file.*

configuration /kənˌfɪgjə'reɪʃ(ə)n/ *noun* the way in which the hardware and software of a computer system are planned and set up

'He said only Banyan Vines had the network configuration and administration capabilities required for implementing an international business plan based on client-server computing.' [*Computing*]

configuration file /kənˌfɪgjə'reɪʃ(ə)n faɪl/ *noun* a file that contains data that describes how a particular software program or device has been configured ○ *The main Windows configuration file is stored in a file called the Registry.*

configuration state /kənˌfɪgjə 'reɪʃ(ə)n steɪt/ *noun* the state of a computer that allows it or the system or a program to be configured

configure /kən'fɪgə/ *verb* to select hardware, software and interconnections to make up a special system ○ *This terminal has been configured to display graphics.*

configured-in /kən'fɪgəd ɪn/ *adjective* referring to a device whose configuration state indicates that it is ready and available for use

configured-off, configured-out *adjective* referring to a device whose configuration state indicates that it is not available for use

congestion /kən'dʒestʃən/ *noun* a state that occurs when communication or processing demands are greater than the capacity of a system

conjunct /'kɒndʒʌŋkt/ *noun* one of the variables in a logical AND function

conjunction /kən'dʒʌŋkʃən/ *noun* a logical function whose output is true if all inputs are true

connect /kə'nekt/ *verb* to link together two points in a circuit or communications network

connect charge /kə'nekt tʃɑːdʒ/ *noun* (*in a commercial on-line system*) the cost per minute of time when you are connected to the remote system

connectionless /kə'nekʃənləs/ *adjective* data transfer that occurs between two devices that do not have a fixed or permanent link and so can take different routes between the two devices. ◊ **circuit switching**

connectionless network protocol /kəˌnekʃənləs 'netwɜːk ˌprəʊtəkɒl/ *noun* an OSI transport protocol that provides an efficient way of routing information around a local area network using a datagram to carry the information. Abbr **CLNP**

connection-oriented /kə'nekʃ(ə)n ˌɔːrientɪd/ *adjective* referring to data transfer that occurs according to a series of fixed, pre-defined steps that will create a known and reliable path between the two devices. For example, TCP/IP is a connection-oriented protocol that uses a known modem or network adapter to contact another known computer and establish a link via TCP/IP commands.

connection-oriented network services /kəˌnekʃən ˌɔːrientɪd 'netwɜːk ˌsɜːvɪsɪz/ *plural noun* an OSI transport protocol that provides an efficient way of routing information around a wide area network. Abbr **CONS**

connective /kə'nektɪv/ *noun* a symbol between two operands that describes the operation to be performed

connectivity /ˌkɒnek'tɪvɪti/ *noun* the ability of a device to connect with other devices and transfer information

connector /kə'nektə/ *noun* a physical device with a number of metal contacts that allow devices to be easily linked together ○ *The connector at the end of the cable will fit any standard serial port.*

connector plug /kə'nektə plʌg/ *noun* (*in an FDDI network*) a device at the end of a fibre-optic or copper cable that connects to a receptacle

connector receptacle /kə'nektə rɪˌseptək(ə)l/ *noun* (*in an FDDI network*) a device mounted on a panel that connects to a plug

connect state /kə'nekt steɪt/ *noun* the state of a modem in which it is transferring data across a communications line

connect time /kə'nekt taɪm/ *noun* the length of time that a user is logged onto an interactive system

conscious error /ˌkɒnʃəs 'erə/ *noun* an operator error that is immediately spotted, but cannot be prevented in time

consistency check /kən'sɪstənsi tʃek/ *noun* a check to make sure that objects, data or items conform to their expected formats

console /'kɒnsəʊl/ *noun* a unit consisting of a keyboard, VDU, and usually a printer, which allows an operator to communicate with a computer system ○ *The console consists of input device such as a keyboard, and an output device such as a printer or CRT.* ◊ **CON**

constant /'kɒnstənt/ *noun* an item of data whose value does not change. Opposite **variable** ■ *adjective* which does not change ○ *The disk drive motor spins at a constant velocity.*

constant angular velocity /ˌkɒnstənt ˌæŋgjʊlə və'lɒsɪti/ *noun* full form of **CAV**

constant bit rate /ˌkɒnstənt 'bɪt ˌreɪt/ *noun* a data transfer service that is part of ATM and is used to guarantee a certain data transmission rate over a network even if there is a lot traffic. Abbr **CBR**

constant length field /ˌkɒnstənt leŋθ 'fiːld/ *noun* a data field that always contains the same number of characters

constant linear velocity /ˌkɒnstənt ˌlɪniə və'lɒsɪti/ *noun* full form of **CLV**

constant ratio code /ˌkɒnstənt 'reɪʃiəʊ ˌkəʊd/ *noun* a character representation code that has a constant number of binary ones per word length

constrain /kən'streɪn/ *verb* to set limits that define the maximum movement of an object on screen

consumables /kən'sjuːməb(ə)lz/ *plural noun* small cheap extra items required in the day-to-day running of a computer system, e.g. paper and printer ribbons ○ *Put all the printer leads and paper with the other consumables.*

contact /'kɒntækt/ *noun* the section of a switch or connector that provides an electrical path when it touches another conductor ○ *The circuit is not working because the contact is dirty.* ■ *verb* to try to call a user or device in a network

contact bounce /'kɒntækt baʊns/ *noun* ♦ **bounce, de-bounce**

contact card /'kɒntækt kɑːd/ *noun* a smart card with a chip that can be read when it is touched by a reading machine

contact image sensor /ˌkɒntækt 'ɪmɪdʒ ˌsensə/ *noun* full form of **CIS**

container /kən'teɪnə/ *noun* something that can be set to a value ○ *The programmer uses this variable as a container, storing the object's colour.*

content /'kɒntent/ *noun* information, ideas, text, images or data that form a letter, document, web page, database or book

content-addressable addressing /ˌkɒntent əˌdresəb(ə)l ə'dresɪŋ/ *noun* same as **associative addressing**

content-addressable file /ˌkɒntent əˌdresəb(ə)l 'faɪl/ *noun* a file for storing data in which each item may be individually accessed

content-addressable location /ˌkɒntent əˌdresəb(ə)l ləʊ'keɪʃ(ə)n/ *noun* same as **content-addressable file**

content-addressable memory /ˌkɒntent əˌdresəb(ə)l 'mem(ə)ri/, **content-addressable storage** /əˌsəʊsiətɪv 'stɔːrɪdʒ/ *noun* abbr **CAM**. same as **associative memory**

contention /kən'tenʃən/ *noun* a situation that occurs when two or more devices are trying to communicate with the same piece of equipment

contention bus /kən'tenʃ(ə)n bʌs/ *noun* a communication control system in which a device must wait for a free moment before transmitting data

contention delay /kən'tenʃ(ə)n dɪ ˌleɪ/ *noun* the length of time spent waiting for equipment to become free for use

content provider /'kɒntent prə ˌvaɪdə/ *noun* a company that supplies information, e.g. text, news stories, images, video, software, for a publication in a website or other medium

content-rich /kən'tent rɪtʃ/ *adjective* containing a lot of useful information

contents /'kɒntents/ *plural noun* a list of items in a file

context /'kɒntekst/ *noun* a particular way of organising data that is used when transferring it into and out of a business management system

context-sensitive /ˌkɒntekst 'sensɪtɪv/ *adjective* that relates to the particular context

context-sensitive help /ˌkɒntekst ˌsensɪtɪv 'help/ *noun* a help message that gives useful information about the particular function or part of the program you are in rather than general information about the whole program

context-switching /'kɒntekst ˌswɪtʃɪŋ/ *noun* a process in which several programs are loaded in memory, but only one at a time can be executed

COMMENT: Unlike a true multitasking system which can load several programs into memory and run several programs at once, context-switching only allows one program to be run at a time.

contiguous file /kənˌtɪgjʊəs 'faɪl/ *noun* a file stored in a series of adjacent disk sectors

contiguous graphics /kənˌtɪgjʊəs 'græfɪks/ *plural noun* graphic cells or characters which touch each other ○ *Most display units do not provide contiguous graphics: their characters have a small space on each side to improve legibility.*

contingency plan /kən'tɪndʒənsi plæn/ *noun* a secondary plan that will be used if the first fails to work

continuation page /kənˌtɪnjʊ 'eɪʃ(ə)n peɪdʒ/ *noun* a page or screen of text that follows on from a main page

continuity /ˌkɒntɪ'njuːɪti/ *noun* a clear conduction path between two points

continuous data stream /kən ˌtɪnjʊəs 'deɪtə ˌstriːm/ *noun* high-speed serial data transmission, in which data

words are not synchronised, but follow on immediately one after the other

continuous feed /kənˌtɪnjuəs 'fiːd/ *noun* a device which feeds continuous stationery into a printer

continuous labels /kənˌtɪnjuəs 'leɪb(ə)lz/ *plural noun* removable adhesive labels attached to a backing sheet that can be fed into a printer

continuous loop /kənˌtɪnjuəs 'luːp/ *noun* an endless piece of recording or projection tape

continuous signal /kənˌtɪnjuəs 'sɪgn(ə)l/ *noun* a continuously variable analog signal

continuous stationery /kənˌtɪnjuəs 'steɪʃ(ə)n(ə)ri/ *noun* printer stationery which takes the form of a single long sheet

continuous tone /kən'tɪnjuəs təʊn/ *noun* an image such as a photograph that uses all possible values of grey or colours,

contouring /'kɒntʊərɪŋ/ *noun* **1.** (*in a graphics application*) a process that converts a wire-frame drawing into a solid-looking object by adding shadows and texture **2.** (*in a graphics application*) a function that creates realistic-looking ground, e.g. in a virtual-reality system, or a surface

contrast /'kɒntrɑːst/ *noun* **1.** the difference between black and white or between colours ○ *The control allows you to adjust brightness and contrast.* **2.** a control knob on a display that alters the difference between black and white tones or between colours

contrast enhancement filter /ˌkɒntrɑːst ɪn'hɑːnsmənt ˌfɪltə/ *noun* a special filter put over a monitor to increase contrast and prevent eye-strain

control /kən'trəʊl/ *noun* **1.** a section of a computer or device that carries out instructions and processes signals **2.** conditional program statements **3.** a key on a computer keyboard which sends a control character **4.** data or a key that controls something

control block /kən'trəʊl blɒk/ *noun* a reserved area of computer memory that contains control data

control bus /kən'trəʊl bʌs/ *noun* a set of connections to a microcomputer that carry the control signals between CPU, memory and input/output devices

control change /kən'trəʊl tʃeɪndʒ/ *noun* (*in MIDI*) a message sent to a synthesiser to instruct it to change a setting, e.g. to change the volume of a MIDI channel

control character /kən'trəʊl ˌkærɪktə/ *noun* a special character that provides a control sequence

'…there are seven print control characters which can be placed in a document' [*Personal Computer World*]

control computer /kən'trəʊl kəm ˌpjuːtə/ *noun* a dedicated computer used to control a process or piece of equipment

control cycle /kən'trəʊl ˌsaɪk(ə)l/ *noun* the events required to retrieve, decode and execute an instruction stored in memory

control data /kən'trəʊl ˌdeɪtə/ *noun* data that controls the actions of a device

control-driven /kən'trəʊl ˌdrɪv(ə)n/ *adjective* referring to computer architecture where instructions are executed once a control sequence has been received

control field /kən'trəʊl fiːld/ *noun* a storage area for control instructions

control group /kən'trəʊl gruːp/ *noun* a small group which is used to check a sample group

control instruction /kən'trəʊl ɪn ˌstrʌkʃən/ *noun* a program instruction that controls the actions of a device ○ *The next control instruction will switch to italics.*

control key /kən'trəʊl kiː/ *noun* (*on IBM-PC compatible systems*) a special key, usually in the lower left corner of the keyboard, that provides a secondary function when pressed with another key ○ *To halt a program, press Ctrl-C – the control key and letter C – at the same time.* Abbr **Ctrl**

control language /kən'trəʊl ˌlæŋgwɪdʒ/ *noun* commands that identify and describe the resources required by a job that a computer has to perform

controlled vocabulary /kənˌtrəʊld vəʊ'kæbjʊləri/ *noun* a set of terms or words used in an indexing language

controller /kən'trəʊlə/ *noun* a hardware or software device that controls a peripheral such as a printer, or that monitors and directs the data transmission over a local area network

'…a printer's controller is the brains of the machine. It translates the signals coming from your computer into printing instructions that result in a hard copy of your electronic document' [*Publish*]

control memory /kən'trəʊl ˌmem(ə)ri/ *noun* memory which decodes control instructions into microinstructions that operate the computer or microcontroller

control menu /kən'trəʊl ˌmenjuː/ *noun* (*in Microsoft Windows*) a menu that allows you to move, resize or close the current window, and that is accessed by pressing Alt-Space

control mode /kən'trəʊl məʊd/ *noun* the state of a device in which control signals can be received to select options or functions

control panel /kən'trəʊl ˌpæn(ə)l/ *noun* **1.** a panel with indicators and switches that allows an operator to monitor and control the actions of a computer or peripheral **2.** a utility that displays the user-definable options such as keyboard, country-code and type of mouse

control register /kən'trəʊl ˌredʒɪstə/ *noun* a storage location for control data

control ROM /kənˌtrəʊl 'rɒm/ *noun* same as **control memory**

control sequence /kən'trəʊl ˌsiːkwəns/ *noun* a series of codes containing a control character and various arguments, used to carry out a process or change mode in a device

control signals /kən'trəʊl ˌsɪgn(ə)lz/ *plural noun* electrical signals transmitted to control the actions of a circuit

control statement /kən'trəʊl ˌsteɪtmənt/ *noun* **1.** a program instruction that directs a CPU to provide controlling actions or controls the operation of the CPU **2.** a program instruction which directs a program, e.g. to another branch

control structure /kən'trəʊl ˌstrʌktʃə/ *noun* a set of instructions that are run in a particular circumstance. An IF.THEN statement selects a particular control structure depending on the value of a variable.

control systems /kən'trəʊl ˌsɪstəmz/ *plural noun* systems used to check that a computer system is working correctly

control token /kən'trəʊl ˌtəʊkən/ *noun* a special sequence of bits transmitted over a LAN to provide control actions

control total /kən'trəʊl ˌtəʊt(ə)l/ *noun* the result of summing certain fields in a computer file to provide error detection

control transfer /kən'trəʊl ˌtrænsfɜː/ *noun* the redirection of the CPU when a jump or call instruction is encountered

control unit /kən'trəʊl ˌjuːnɪt/ *noun* the section of the CPU which selects and executes instructions

control word /kən'trəʊl wɜːd/ *noun* a word that defines the actions that are to be followed in a particular process

convention /kən'venʃən/ *noun* a set of well-known standards or rules that have to be followed so as to produce hardware or software compatibility

conventional memory /kənˌvenʃ(ə)n(ə)l 'mem(ə)ri/ *noun* (*in an IBM-PC compatible system*) the random access memory region installed in a PC from 0 up to 640Kb. This area of memory can be directly controlled by MS-DOS. Compare **high memory, expanded memory**. Also called **RAM**

convergence /kən'vɜːdʒəns/ *noun* **1.** the combination of two or more different technologies producing a new technology. For example, fax machines are the product of the convergence of telephone, scanning and printing technologies. **2.** (*in a colour monitor*) the accuracy with which the picture beam strikes the three colour dots that form each colour pixel ▶ ◊ **picture beam, pixel**

conversation /ˌkɒnvə'seɪʃ(ə)n/ *noun* a form of communication between a computer and its user in which the computer responds immediately to instructions and questions put to it as if taking part in a dialogue

conversational mode /ˌkɒnvə'seɪʃ(ə)n(ə)l məʊd/ *noun* a method of operating that provides immediate responses to a user's input. ◊ **interactive mode**

converse /kən'vɜːs/ *verb* to engage in a conversation with a computer

conversion /kən'vɜːʃ(ə)n/ *noun* a change from one system to another

conversion equipment /kən 'vɜːʃ(ə)n ɪˌkwɪpmənt/ *noun* a device that will convert data from one format to another, which is suitable for another system, without changing the content

conversion program /kən'vɜːʃ(ə)n ˌprəʊɡræm/ *noun* **1.** a program that converts programs written for one computer into a suitable form for another **2.** a program that converts data format, coding, etc. for use in another program

conversion tables /kən'vɜːʃ(ə)n ˌteɪb(ə)lz/ *plural noun* a list of source codes or statements and their equivalent in another language or form ◊ *Conversion tables may be created and used in conjunction with the customer's data to con-*

vert it to our system codes. Also called **translation tables**

converter /kən'vɜːtə/ *noun* a device or program that translates data from one form to another ◊ *The converter allowed the old data to be used on the new system.*

convertibility /kənˌvɜːtə'bɪləti/ *noun* ability to be changed

convertible /kən'vɜːtəb(ə)l/ *adjective* that can be converted

convertor /kən'vɜːtə/ *noun* another spelling of **converter**

cookie /'kʊki/ *noun* a tiny file that is stored on your computer when you connect to a remote Internet site using a browser. The cookie is used by the remote site to store information about your options which can then be read when you next visit the site.

cookie file /'kʊki faɪl/ *noun* a file that contains the cookie data supplied by the remote Internet site

cooperative processing /kəʊ ˌɒp(ə)rətɪv 'prəʊsesɪŋ/ *noun* a system in which two or more computers in a distributed network can each execute a part of a program or work on a particular set of data

coordinate graph /kəʊ'ɔːdɪnət ɡrɑːf/ *noun* a means of displaying one point on a graph, using two values referring to axes which are usually at right angles to each other

coordinates /kəʊ'ɔːdɪnəts/ *plural noun* values used to locate a point on a graph or map

coordination /kəʊˌɔːdɪ'neɪʃ(ə)n/ *noun* the process of organising complex tasks

coprocessor /kəʊ'prəʊsesə/ *noun* an extra, specialised processor, e.g. an array or numerical processor, that can work with a main CPU to increase execution speed

'Inmos is hiring designers to create highly integrated transputers and co-processors for diverse computer and telecoms systems.' [*Computing*]

copy /'kɒpi/ *verb* to make a second document which is like the first, or to duplicate original data ◊ *He copied all the personnel files at night and took them home.*

COPY /'kɒpi/ *noun* an operating system command that copies the contents of one file to another file on a storage device ◊ *Make a copy of your data using the COPY command before you edit it.*

copy protect /ˌkɒpi prə'tekt/ *noun* a switch that prevents copies of a disk being made ■ *verb* to move a switch to prevent copies of a disk being made ○ *The program is not copy protected.*

copy protection /'kɒpi prə,tekʃən/ *noun* the act of preventing copies from being made ○ *A hard disk may crash because of copy protection.*

CORAL /'kɒpi/ *noun* a computer programming language used in a real-time system. Full form **common real-time applications language**

CORBA /'kɔːbə/ *abbr* common object request broker architecture

core /kɔː/ *noun* the central conducting section of a cable

core dump /'kɔː dʌmp/ *noun* a transfer of data from the main memory of a computer, usually to an external storage medium

core memory /kɔː 'mem(ə)ri/ *noun* a central fast-access memory which stores the programs and data currently in use

core program /kɔː 'prəʊɡræm/ *noun* a computer program stored in core memory

coresident /kəʊ'rezɪd(ə)nt/ *adjective* referring to two or more programs that are stored in the main memory at the same time

core store /'kɔː stɔː/ *noun* a non-volatile magnetic storage method used in old computers

corona /kə'rəʊnə/ *noun* an electric discharge that is used to charge the toner within a laser printer

corona wire /kə'rəʊnə ,waɪə/ *noun* a thin wire that charges the powdered toner particles in a laser printer as they pass across it ○ *If your printouts are smudged, you may have to clean the corona wire.*

coroutine /'kəʊruː,tiːn/ *noun* a section of a program or procedure that can pass data and control to another coroutine then halt itself

corrective maintenance /kə,rektɪv 'meɪntənəns/ *noun* actions to trace, find and repair a fault after it has occurred

corrupt /kə'rʌpt/ *adjective* that contains errors ■ *verb* to introduce errors into data or a program ○ *Power loss during disk access can corrupt the data.*

cost analysis /'kɒst ə,næləsɪs/ *noun* an examination in advance of the costs of a new product

cost per action /,kɒst pɜː 'ækʃən/ full form of **CPA**

co.uk a domain name suffix that indicates a business based in the UK ○ *The Peter*

Collin Publishing domain name is '*pcp.co.uk*' ◊ **domain**

counter /'kaʊntə/ *noun* a register or variable whose contents are increased or decreased by a set amount every time an action occurs

counter-rotating ring /,kaʊntə rəʊ ,eɪtɪŋ 'rɪŋ/ *noun* two signal paths transmitted in opposite directions around a ring network

country file /'kʌntri faɪl/ *noun* a file within an operating system that defines the parameters, e.g. character set and keyboard layout, for different countries

coupler /'kʌplə/ *noun* a mechanical device that is used to connect three or more conductors

Courier /'kʊriə/ *noun* a fixed-space or monospace typeface

courseware /'kɔːsweə/ *noun* the software, manuals and video that make up a training package or CAL product

CPA /,siː piː 'eɪ/ *noun* the cost of displaying a banner advertisement once to one visitor to a website. Full form **cost per action**. ◊ **banner**

cpi /,siː piː 'aɪ/ *noun* the number of printed characters which fit within the space of one inch. Full form **characters per inch**

CPM *abbr* critical path method

cps /,siː piː 'es/ *noun* the number of characters printed or processed every second. Full form **characters per second**

CPU /,siː piː 'juː/ *noun* a group of circuits that performs the basic functions of a computer. The CPU is made up of three parts, the control unit, the arithmetic and logic unit and the input/output unit. Full form **central processing unit**

CPU bound /,siː piː 'juː baʊnd/ *adjective* referring to the performance of a computer insofar as it is limited by the number of instructions the CPU can carry out. Effectively, the memory and I/O devices can transfer data faster than the CPU can produce it.

CPU clock /,siː piː 'juː klɒk/ *noun* a clock inside a processor device that generates a regular signal millions of times every second to control operations and data transfer within the processor

CPU clock speed /,siː piː 'juː klɒk/ *noun* the frequency of the CPU clock that controls the operations within the processor

CPU cycle /,siː piː 'juː ,saɪk(ə)l/ *noun* the period of time taken to fetch and execute an instruction, usually a simple ADD instruction, used as a measure of computer speed

CPU elements /ˌsiː piː ˌjuː ˈelɪmənts/ *plural noun* the main sections that make up a CPU, including the ALU, control unit, I/O bus, memory and various registers

CPU handshaking /ˌsiː piː juː ˈhændʃeɪkɪŋ/ *noun* the process of interfacing signals between a CPU and a peripheral or I/O device

CPU time /ˌsiː piː ˈjuː taɪm/ *noun* the total period of time that a CPU is used to actually process instructions (NOTE: In a file handling program, CPU time might be minimal, since data retrieval from disk would account for a large part of the program run. In a mathematical program, the CPU time could be much higher in proportion to the total run time.)

CR *abbr* card reader

crash /kræʃ/ *noun* a failure of a component or a bug in a program during a run, which halts and prevents further use of the system

COMMENT: It is sometimes possible to recover data from a crashed hard disk before reformatting, if the crash was caused by a bad sector on the disk rather than contact between the r/w head and disk surface.

crash-protected /kræʃ prəˈtektɪd/ *adjective* that uses a head protection or data corruption protection system ○ *If the disk is crash-protected, you will never lose your data.*

crawler /ˈkrɔːlə/ *noun* a computer program that collects online documents and reference links

CRC *abbr* cyclic redundancy check

crippled leapfrog test /ˌkrɪp(ə)ld ˈliːpfrɒg ˌtest/ *noun* a standard leapfrog test that uses a single memory location rather than a changing location

critical error /ˌkrɪtɪk(ə)l ˈerə/ *noun* an error that stops processing or crashes the computer

critical fusion frequency /ˌkrɪtɪk(ə)l ˈfjuːʒ(ə)n ˌfriːkwənsi/ *noun* (*on a video, computer or film screen*) the rate of display of frames of graphics or text that makes them appear flicker-free

critical path analysis /ˌkrɪtɪk(ə)l ˈpɑːθ əˌnæləsɪs/ *noun* the definition of tasks or jobs and the time each requires arranged in order to achieve certain goals. Also called PERT – Program Evaluation and Review Techniques.

'Surprisingly, critical path analysis and project management, frequently the next career step for engineers, did not seem to warrant a mention.' [*Computing*]

critical path method /ˌkrɪtɪk(ə)l ˈpɑːθ ˌmeθəd/ *noun* the use of analysis and the projection of each critical step in a large project to help a management team. Abbr **CPM**

critical resource /ˌkrɪtɪk(ə)l rɪˈzɔːs/ *noun* a resource that can only be used by one process at a time

crop /krɒp/ *verb* to reduce the size or margins of an image

crop mark /ˈkrɒp mɑːk/ *noun* (*in DTP software*) one of the printed marks that show the edge of a page or image and allow it to be cut accurately

cross-assembler /krɒs əˈsemblə/ *noun* an assembler that produces machine-code code for one computer while running on another

cross-compiler /krɒs kəmˈpaɪlə/ *noun* an assembler or compiler that compiles programs for one computer while running on another

COMMENT: Cross-compilers and assemblers are used to compile programs for micros, but are run on larger computers to make the operation faster.

crosshair /ˈkrɒsheə/ *noun* (*in a drawing or paint program*) a cursor shape that looks like a cross

cross-linked files /ˌkrɒs lɪŋkt ˈfaɪlz/ *noun* an error in MS-DOS in which two files claim to be using the same cluster on disk

crossover /ˈkrɒsˌəʊvə/ *noun* a change from one system to another ○ *The crossover to computerised file indexing was difficult.*

crossover circuit /ˈkrɒsəʊvə ˌsɜːkɪt/ *noun* an electronic circuit which splits an audio signal into different frequency ranges and assigns these to different size loudspeakers in a loudspeaker system

cross-platform /ˌkrɒs ˈplætfɔːm/ *adjective* available for more than one type of computer or operating system

cross-post /ˌkrɒs ˈpəʊst/ *verb* to send a single electronic message or article to many different newsgroups at the same time

cross-reference generator /ˌkrɒs ˈref(ə)rəns ˌdʒenəreɪtə/ *noun* a section of an assembler or compiler or interpreter that provides a list of program labels, variables or constants with their location within the program

crosstalk /'krɒstɑːk/ *noun* interference between two communication cables or channels

CRT /ˌsiː ɑː 'tiː/ *noun* a device used for displaying characters, figures or graphical information, similar to a TV set. Full form **cathode ray tube**

COMMENT: Cathode ray tubes are used in television sets, computer monitors and VDUs. A CRT consists of a vacuum tube, one end of which is flat and coated with phosphor, the other end containing an electron beam source. Characters or graphics are visible when the controllable electron beam strikes the phosphor, causing it to glow.

crunch /krʌntʃ/ *verb* to process data or numbers at high speed

cruncher, crunching *noun* ♦ **number cruncher, number crunching**

cryogenic memory /ˌkraɪəʊdʒenɪk 'mem(ə)ri/ *noun* a storage medium operating at very low temperatures of around 4°K to use the superconductive properties of a material

cryptanalysis /ˌkrɪptə'næləsɪs/ *noun* the study and methods of breaking ciphers

cryptographic /ˌkrɪptə'græfɪk/ *adjective* referring to cryptography

cryptographic algorithm /ˌkrɪptəgræfɪk 'ælɡərɪð(ə)m/ *noun* a set of rules used to encipher and decipher data

cryptographic key /ˌkrɪptəgræfɪk 'kiː/ *noun* a number or code that is used with a cipher algorithm to personalise the encryption and decryption of data

cryptography /ˌkrɪp'tɒɡrəfi/ *noun* the study of encryption and decryption methods and techniques

crystal /'krɪstəl/ *noun* a small slice of quartz crystal which vibrates at a certain frequency, used as a very accurate clock signal for computer or other high precision timing applications

crystal shutter printer /ˌkrɪst(ə)l ˌʃʌtə 'prɪntə/ *noun* a page printer that uses a powerful light controlled by a liquid crystal display to produce an image on a photo-sensitive drum

CSLIP *noun* a version of the SLIP protocol that compresses data before it is transmitted, resulting in greater data transfer rate

CSM /ˌsiː es 'em/ *noun* an efficient optical character recognition system. Full form **combined symbol matching**

CSMA-CA /ˌsiː es em siː 'eɪ/ *noun* a method of controlling access to a network not covered by OSI standards, but used in AppleTalk networks. Full form **carrier sense multiple access-collision avoidance**

CSMA-CD /ˌsiː es em siː 'diː/ *noun* a network communications protocol that prevents two sources transmitting at the same time by waiting for a quiet moment, then attempting to transmit. It is used to control data transmission over an Ethernet network. Full form **carrier sense multiple access-collision detection**

CSS *abbr* cascading style sheet

CTI /ˌsiː tiː 'aɪ/ *noun* a system that allows normal audio telephone conversations to be transmitted over a computer data network and controlled by a computer. Full form **computer-telephony integration**

CTM /ˌsiː tiː 'em/ *noun* a method of charging an advertiser for the display of a banner advertisement, where the price covers one thousand visitors clicking on the advertisement and jumping to the advertiser's own website. Full form **click through per thousand**

CTR¹ /kən'trəʊl/ *noun* the number of visitors who click on a banner advertisement on a website and jump to the advertiser's own website. Full form **click through rate**. ◊ **CTM** (NOTE: A click through rate of just a few percent is common, and most advertisers have to pay per thousand impressions of their banner ad.)

CTR² /kən'trəʊl/, **CTRL, Ctrl** *noun* the control key, or a key on a computer terminal that sends a control character to the computer when pressed

Ctrl-Alt-Del /kənˌtrəʊl ɔːlt dɪ'liːt/ *noun* a combination of three keys that, when pressed at once, will cause a PC to carry out a soft reset

CTS /ˌsiː tiː 'es/ *noun* an RS232C indicating that a line or device is ready for data transmission. Full form **clear to send**

CU *abbr* control unit

cue /kjuː/ *noun* a prompt or message displayed on a screen to remind the user that an input is expected

CUG /ˌsiː juː 'dʒiː/ *noun* entry to a database or bulletin board system that is restricted to certain known and registered users, usually by means of a password. Full form **closed user group**

cull /kʌl/ *verb* to remove hidden or distant objects from a three-dimensional scene or storage space and reduce processing time

cumulative trauma disorder /ˌkjuːmjʊlətɪv ˈtrɔːmə dɪsˌɔːdə/ *noun* same as **repetitive strain injury**

curly brackets /ˈkɜːli ˈbrækɪtz/, **curly braces** *plural noun* the pair of characters {} used in some programming languages to enclose a routine

current address /ˌkʌrənt əˈdres/ *noun* the address being accessed at this time

current address register /ˌkʌrənt ə ˈdres ˌredʒɪstə/ *noun* a CPU register that stores the address that is currently being accessed. Abbr **CAR**

current directory /ˌkʌrənt daɪ ˈrekt(ə)ri/ *noun* a directory within the directory tree which is currently being used

current drive /ˌkʌrənt ˈdraɪv/ *noun* a disk drive that is currently being used or has been selected

current instruction register /ˌkʌrənt ɪnˈstrʌkʃən ˌredʒɪstə/ *noun* full form of **CIR**

cursor /ˈkɜːsə/ *noun* a marker on a display device which shows where the next character will appear

'Probably the most exciting technology demonstrated was ScreenCam, which allows users to combine voice, cursor movement and on-screen activities into a movie which can be replayed.' [*Computing*]

'…further quick cursor movements are available for editing by combining one of the arrow keys with the control function' [*Personal Computer World*]

COMMENT: Cursors can take several forms, including a square of bright light, a bright underline or a flashing light.

cursor control keys /ˈkɜːsə kən ˌtrəʊl kiːz/ *plural noun* keys on a keyboard that allow the cursor to be moved in different directions

cursor home /ˈkɜːsə həʊm/ *noun* the movement of the cursor to the top left hand corner of the screen

cursor pad /ˈkɜːsə pæd/ *noun* a group of four arrowed cursor control keys, used to move the cursor up and down or to the right or left

cursor resource /ˈkɜːsə rɪˌzɔːs/ *noun* an image that is displayed as a cursor (NOTE: Programming languages and authoring tools normally provide a range of different cursor images that a developer can use, for example an egg-timer cursor when waiting or an arrow when pointing.)

custom-built /ˈkʌstəm bɪlt/ *adjective* made specially for one customer

custom colours /ˌkʌstəm ˈkʌləs/ *plural noun* a range of colours in a palette that are used by an image or application. ◊ **system palette**

customer engineering /ˌkʌstəmə ˌendʒɪˈnɪərɪŋ/ *noun* maintenance and repair of a customer's equipment

customer service department /ˌkʌstəmə ˈsɜːvɪs dɪˌpɑːtmənt/ *noun* a department which deals with customers and their complaints and orders

customise /ˈkʌstəmaɪz/, **customize** *verb* to modify a system to the customer's requirements ○ *We used customised computer terminals.* (NOTE: customises – customising – customised)

custom ROM /ˌkʌstəm ˈrɒm/ *noun* a ROM produced, usually in small numbers, by a manufacturer to suit a customer's requirements

cut /kʌt/ *noun* **1.** the process of removing a piece from a file **2.** a piece removed from a file ■ *verb* to remove sections of text from a file to make it shorter (NOTE: cutting – cut)

cut and paste /ˌkʌt ən ˈpeɪst/ *noun* the action of taking a section of text or data from one point and inserting it at another, often used in word-processors and DTP packages for easy page editing

cut over /ˌkʌt ˈəʊvə/ *verb* to organise the transfer of data, functions or users from an old computer system to a new one in such a way that all the transfer operations take place at the same time and there is minimum disruption

CUTS *abbr* Computer Users' Tape System

cut sheet feeder /ˌkʌt ˈʃiːt ˌfiːdə/ *noun* a mechanism that automatically feeds single sheets of paper into a printer

CWP *abbr* communicating word processor

cXML /ˌsiː eks em ˈel/ *noun* a feature of the XML webpage markup language that provides a standard way of producing pages about products for sale on an online shop (NOTE: The new features allow designers to include information about the product being displayed and how it can be purchased by the viewer.)

cyan-magenta-yellow-black /ˌsaɪən məˌdʒentə ˈjeləʊ/ *noun* full form of **CMYK**

cyber- /ˈsaɪbə/ *prefix* computers and information systems

cyber age /ˈsaɪbə eɪdʒ/ *noun* the present age, considered as a period in which computer technology and electronic communications have become more important and more widely used

cybercafé /ˈsaɪbəˌkæfeɪ/ *noun* a place that provides a shop with terminals connected to the Internet as well as coffee and pastries

cybercast /ˈsaɪbəkɑːst/ *noun* a broadcast of an event transmitted via the Internet, in either sound or vision or in both

cyberlaw /ˈsaɪbəlɔː/ *noun* the set of laws that relate to computers, information systems and networks, considered as a body

cybermediary /ˌsaɪbəˈmiːdiəri/ *noun* an organisation that makes it easier for customers and businesses to buy and sell online, but that does not own the products or services that are being sold

cybernate /ˈsaɪbəneɪt/ *verb* to use computers to control manufacturing processes (NOTE: **cybernates – cybernating – cybernated**)

cybernetics /ˌsaɪbəˈnetɪks/ *noun* the study of the mechanics of human or electronic machine movements, and the way in which electronic devices can be made to work and imitate human actions

cybershopping /ˈsaɪbəˌʃɒpɪŋ/ *noun* shopping for goods and services on the Internet

cyberspace /ˈsaɪbəspeɪs/ *noun* the world in which computers and people interact, normally via the Internet

cybersquatting /ˈsaɪbəˌskwɒtɪŋ/ *noun* act by which someone registers a website address, normally a trademark or brand name, then tries to sell the name to the rightful owner (NOTE: Although not yet illegal in most countries, court cases almost always find in favour of the company trying to recover its name. For example, if you registered the domain name 'windows.com' then tried to sell this back to Microsoft Corp. you would be guilty of cybersquatting.)

cyberterrorism /ˈsaɪbəˌterərɪz(ə)m/ *noun* terrorist activities that use the Internet to damage complex electronic systems or the data they contain

'There were some instances of war-related hacking over the past few weeks, but nothing that would be considered cyberterrorism.' [*The Guardian*]

cyberwoozling /ˈsaɪbəˌwuːz(ə)lɪŋ/ *noun* the practice of gathering data from the computer of a visitor to a website without his or her knowledge or authorisation

cycle /ˈsaɪk(ə)l/ *noun* one completed operation in a repeated process

cycle availability /ˌsaɪk(ə)l əˌveɪlə ˈbɪlɪti/ *noun* a period of time in a cycle during which data can be accessed or transmitted

cycle count /ˈsaɪk(ə)l kaʊnt/ *noun* the number of times a cycle has been repeated

cycle index /ˈsaɪk(ə)l ˌɪndeks/ *noun* the number of times a series of instructions has been or has to be repeated

cycle shift /ˈsaɪk(ə)l ʃɪft/ *verb* to shift a pattern of bits within a word, with the bit or bits shifted off the end being inserted at the beginning of the word

cycle stealing /ˈsaɪk(ə)l ˌstiːlɪŋ/ *noun* a memory access operation by a peripheral that halts a CPU for one or more clock cycles while data is being transferred from memory to the device

cycle time /ˈsaɪk(ə)l taɪm/ *noun* the time between start and stop of an operation, especially between addressing a memory location and receiving the data

cyclic /ˈsɪklɪk, ˈsaɪklɪk/ *adjective* that is repeated regularly

cyclic access /ˌsaɪklɪk ˈækses/ *noun* access to stored information that can only occur at a certain point in a cycle

cyclic check /ˌsaɪklɪk ˈtʃek/ *noun* an error detection method that uses or examines a bit of data every n bits, one bit examined then n bits transmitted, then another bit examined and so on

cyclic code /ˌsaɪklɪk ˈkəʊd/ *noun* a coding system in which the binary representation of decimal numbers changes by only one bit at a time from one number to the next

cyclic decimal code /ˌsaɪklɪk ˈdesɪm(ə)l kəʊd/ *noun* a cyclic code that refers to decimal digits

cyclic redundancy check /ˌsɪklɪk rɪ ˈdʌndənsi ˌtʃek/ *noun* an error detection check used in modem communications and many file transfer protocols that looks at one bit in every n bits and compares this with the original to see if an error has occurred in the last n bits. Abbr **CRC**

cyclic shift /ˌsaɪklɪk ˈʃɪft/ *noun* the rotation of bits in a word with the previous last bit inserted in the first bit position

cylinder /'sɪlɪndə/ *noun* **1.** a group of tracks on a disk **2.** the tracks in a multi-disk device that can be accessed without moving the read/write head

cypher /'saɪfə/ *noun* another spelling of **cipher**

D

D *symbol* the hexadecimal figure equivalent to decimal number 13

DA *abbr* desk accessory

DAC /ˌdiː eɪ 'siː/ *noun* a circuit that outputs an analog signal that is proportional to the input digital number, and so converts a digital input to an analog form ○ *Speech is output from the computer via a D/A converter.* Full form **digital to analog converter**. Also called **D to A converter, d/a converter**

d/a converter /ˌdiː tʊ eɪ kən'vɜːtə/ *noun* same as **DAC**

daemon /'diːmən/ *noun* (*in a UNIX system*) a utility program that performs its job automatically without the knowledge of the user

daisy chain /'deɪzi tʃeɪn/ *noun* a method of connecting equipment with a single cable passing from one machine or device to the next, rather than separate cables to each device

daisy-chain /'deɪzi tʃeɪn/ *verb* to connect equipment using the daisy chain method

'…you can often daisy-chain cards or plug them into expansion boxes' [*Byte*]

daisy chain bus /ˌdeɪzi tʃeɪn 'bʌs/ *noun* a communications bus that joins one device to the next, each device being able to receive or transmit or modify data as it passes through to the next device in line

daisy-chaining /'deɪzi tʃeɪnɪŋ/ *noun* the process of connecting equipment using the daisy chain method ○ *Daisy-chaining saves a lot of cable.*

daisy chain interrupt /ˌdeɪzi tʃeɪn 'ɪntərʌpt/ *noun* a line joining all the inter-

rupt outputs of a number of devices to a CPU

daisy chain recursion /ˌdeɪzi tʃeɪn rɪ'kɜːʒ(ə)n/ *noun* the use of subroutines in a program that call another in the series, so that the first routine calls the second routine, which calls the third routine, and so on

DAL *abbr* data access language (*see*)

DAMA *abbr* demand assigned multiple access

DAO /ˌdiː eɪ 'əʊ/ *noun* a programming interface provided with many of Microsoft's database applications that allow the developer to access Jet or ODBC compatible data sources. Full form **data access objects**

dark fibre /ˌdɑːk 'faɪbə/ *noun* an optical fibre that is not carrying a signal, often one that has just been installed but has not yet been used

DASD /ˌdiː eɪ es 'diː/ *noun* a storage medium whose memory locations can be directly read or written to. Full form **direct access storage device**

DAT /ˌdiː eɪ 'tiː/ *noun* a compact cassette, smaller than an audio cassette, that provides a system of recording sound as digital information onto magnetic tape with very high-quality reproduction. Full form **digital audio tape** (NOTE: It is also used as a high-capacity tape backup system that can store 1.3 Gb of data; sound is recorded at a sample rate of either 32, 44.1 or 48 KHz to provide up to two hours of CD-quality sound.)

data /'deɪtə/ *noun* a collection of facts made up of numbers, characters and symbols, stored on a computer in such a way that it can be processed by the computer □

data area amount of storage space that contains data (rather than instructions)

COMMENT: Data is different from information in that it is facts stored in machine-readable form. When the facts are processed by the computer into a form that can be understood by people, the data becomes information.

data access language /ˌdeɪtə 'ækses ˌlæŋgwɪdʒ/ noun a language developed by the Apple Computer Corporation and used to query a database, based on SQL. Abbr **DAL**

data access management /ˌdeɪtə 'ækses ˌmænɪdʒmənt/ noun the process of regulating the users who can access stored data

data access objects /ˌdeɪtə 'ækses ˌɒbjekts/ noun full form of **DAO**

data acquisition /'deɪtə ækwɪˌzɪʃ(ə)n/ noun the process of gathering data about a subject

data adapter unit /ˌdeɪtə ə'dæptə ˌjuːnɪt/ noun a device that interfaces a CPU to one or more communications channels

data administrator /ˌdeɪtə əd'mɪnɪstreɪtə/ noun a control section of a database management system

data aggregate /'deɪtə ˌægrɪgət/ noun a collection of items of data that are related

data analysis /ˌdeɪtə ə'næləsɪs/ noun the process of extracting information and results from data

databank /'deɪtəbæŋk/ noun **1.** a large amount of data stored in a structured form **2.** a store of personal records in a computer

database /'deɪtəbeɪs/ noun an integrated collection of files of data stored in a structured form in a large memory, which can be accessed by one or more users at different terminals

'This information could include hypertext references to information held within a computer database, or spreadsheet formulae.' [*Computing*]

database administrator /ˌdeɪtəbeɪs əd'mɪnɪstreɪtə/ noun full form of **DBA**

database engine /'deɪtəbeɪs ˌendʒɪn/ noun a program that provides an interface between a program written to access the functions of a DBMS and the DBMS

database language /'deɪtəbeɪs ˌlæŋgwɪdʒ/ noun any one of a series of languages, e.g. data description language, that makes up a database management system

database machine /ˌdeɪtəbeɪs mə'ʃiːn/ noun a hardware and software combination designed for the rapid processing of database information

database management system /ˌdeɪtəbeɪs 'mænɪdʒmənt ˌsɪstəm/, **database manager** /ˌdeɪtəbeɪs 'mænɪdʒə/ noun full form of **DBMS**

database mapping /'deɪtəbeɪs ˌmæpɪŋ/ noun a description of the way in which the records and fields in a database are related

database schema /ˌdeɪtəbeɪs 'skiːmə/ noun a way in which a database is organised and structured

database server /ˌdeɪtəbeɪs 'sɜːvə/ noun a piece of database management software that runs on a server computer on a network and is used in a client-server system (NOTE: The user works with client software that formats and displays data that is retrieved by the server software.)

database system /'deɪtəbeɪs ˌsɪstəm/ noun a series of programs that allows the user to create, modify, manage and use a database and that often includes features such as a report writer or graphical output of data

data block /'deɪtə blɒk/ noun the set of all the data required for or from a process

data break /'deɪtə breɪk/ noun a memory access operation by a peripheral that halts a CPU for one or more cycles while data is being transferred from memory to the device

data buffer /'deɪtə ˌbʌfə/ noun a temporary storage location for data received by a device that is not yet ready to process it

data bus /'deɪtə bʌs/ noun a bus carrying data between a CPU and memory and peripheral devices

data capture /'deɪtə ˌkæptʃə/ noun the act of obtaining data, either by keyboarding or scanning, or often automatically from a recording device or peripheral ○ *In July this year it signed a two-year outsourcing and disaster-recovery deal ... for the operation and management of its Birmingham-based data-capture facility.* [*Computing*]

data carrier /'deɪtə ˌkæriə/ noun **1.** a device or medium capable of storing data **2.** a waveform used as a carrier for data signals

data carrier detect /ˌdeɪtə ˌkæriə dɪ'tekt/ noun full form of **DCD**

data cartridge /'deɪtə ˌkɑːtrɪdʒ/ *noun* a cartridge that contains stored data

data cassette /'deɪtə kəˌset/ *noun* a special high-quality tape for storing data

data chaining /'deɪtə ˌtʃeɪnɪŋ/ *noun* the process of storing one record that holds the address of the next in the list

data channel /'deɪtə ˌtʃæn(ə)l/ *noun* a communications link able to carry data signals

data check /'deɪtə tʃek/ *noun* an error in reading data due to a fault with the magnetic medium

data circuit /'deɪtə ˌsɜːkɪt/ *noun* a circuit which allows bi-directional data communications

data cleaning /'deɪtə ˌkliːnɪŋ/ *noun* the process of removing errors from data

data collection /'deɪtə kəˌlekʃən/ *noun* the act of receiving data from various sources, either directly from a data capture device or from a cartridge, and inserting it correctly in order into a database

data collection platform /ˌdeɪtə kə 'lekʃən ˌplætfɔːm/ *noun* a station that transmits collected data to a central point, usually via satellite

data communications /ˌdeɪtə kə ˌmjuːnɪ'keɪʃ(ə)nz/ *noun* the transmission and reception of data rather than speech or images

data communications buffer /ˌdeɪtə kəˌmjuːnɪ'keɪʃ(ə)nz ˌbʌfə/ *noun* a buffer on a receiver that allows a slow peripheral to accept data from a fast peripheral, without slowing either down

data communications equipment /ˌdeɪtə kəˌmjuːnɪ'keɪʃ(ə)nz ˌkwɪpmənt/ *noun* equipment, e.g. a modem, that receives or transmits data. Abbr **DCE**

data communications network /ˌdeɪtə kəˌmjuːnɪ'keɪʃ(ə)nz ˌnetwɜːk/ *noun* a number of computers, terminals, operators and storage units connected together to allow data transmission between devices or files or users

data compacting /'deɪtə ˌkɒmpæktɪŋ/ *noun* the process of reducing the storage space taken by data by coding it in a more efficient way

data compression /ˌdeɪtə kəm 'preʃ(ə)n/ *noun* a means of reducing the size of blocks of data by removing spaces, empty sections and unused material

data concentrator /'deɪtə ˌkɒns(ə)ntreɪtə/ *noun* a means of combining intermittent data from various lines and sending it along a single line in one go

data connection /ˌdeɪtə kə'nekʃ(ə)n/ *noun* a link which joins two devices and allows data transmission

data control /'deɪtə kənˌtrəʊl/ *noun* data management to and from a database or processing system

data corruption /'deɪtə kəˌrʌpʃ(ə)n/ *noun* the introduction of errors into data through noise or faulty equipment ○ *Data corruption occurs each time the motor is switched on.*

data delimiter /'deɪtə diːˌlɪmɪtə/ *noun* a special symbol or character that marks the end of a file or data item

data description language /ˌdeɪtə dɪ'skrɪpʃən ˌlæŋgwɪdʒ/ *noun* full form of **DDL**

data dictionary/directory /ˌdeɪtə ˌdɪkʃən(ə)ri daɪ'rekt(ə)ri/ *noun* full form of **DD/D**

data division /'deɪtə dɪˌvɪʒ(ə)n/ *noun* a part of a COBOL program giving full definitions of the data types and structures

data-driven /'deɪtə ˌdrɪv(ə)n/ *adjective* referring to computer architecture in which instructions are executed, once the relevant data has been received

data element /'deɪtə ˌelɪmənt/ *noun* same as **data item**

data element chain /ˌdeɪtə 'elɪmənt ˌtʃeɪn/ *noun* a group of data elements treated as a single element

data encryption /'deɪtə ɪnˌkrɪpʃ(ə)n/ *noun* the process of encrypting data using a cipher system

data encryption standard /ˌdeɪtə ɪn 'krɪpʃən ˌstændəd/ *noun* full form of **DES**

data entry /ˌdeɪtə 'entri/ *noun* a method of entering data into a system, usually using a keyboard but also direct from disks after data preparation

data error /'deɪtə ˌerə/ *noun* an error due to incorrect or illegal data

data field /'deɪtə fiːld/ *noun* a part of a computer instruction that contains the location of the data

data file /'deɪtə faɪl/ *noun* a file containing data, as opposed to a program file ○ *Programs act upon data files.*

data flow /'deɪtə fləʊ/ *noun* the movement of data through a system

data flowchart /ˌdeɪtə ˈfləʊtʃɑːt/ *noun* a diagram used to describe a computer or data processing system structure

data flow diagram /ˈdeɪtə fləʊ ˌdaɪəgræm/ *noun* full form of **DFD**

data format /ˈdeɪtə ˌfɔːmæt/ *noun* the set of rules defining the way in which data is stored or transmitted

data glove /ˈdeɪtə glʌv/ *noun* an electronic glove that fits over a user's hand and contains sensors that transmit the position of the user's hand and fingers to a computer; used in virtual reality systems

datagram /ˈdeɪtəgræm/ *noun* a packet of information in a packet switching system that contains its destination address and route

data hierarchy /ˌdeɪtə ˈhaɪərɑːki/ *noun* a data structure organised hierarchically

data highway /ˌdeɪtə ˈhaɪweɪ/ *noun* a bus carrying the data signals in parallel form between the central processing unit and memory or external devices

data independence /ˌdeɪtə ˌɪndɪˈpendəns/ *noun* a structure of a database which can be changed without affecting what the user sees

data input /ˌdeɪtə ˈɪnpʊt/ *noun* data transferred into a computer, from an I/O port or peripheral

data input bus /ˌdeɪtə ˈɪnpʊt ˌbʌs/ *noun* full form of **DIB 1**

data integrity /ˌdeɪtə ɪnˈtegrɪti/ *noun* the state of data which has not been corrupted by damage or errors

data interchange format /ˌdeɪtə ˈɪntətʃeɪndʒ ˌfɔːmæt/ *noun* a de facto standard method of storing spreadsheet formula and data in a file. Abbr **DIF**

data item /ˈdeɪtə ˌaɪtəm/ *noun* one unit of data, e.g. the quantity of items in stock, a person's name, age or occupation. Also called **data element**

data jack /ˈdeɪtə dʒæk/ *noun* a plug that allows a modem to be connected directly to the telephone system

data level /ˈdeɪtə ˌlev(ə)l/ *noun* a position of a data item within a database structure

data link /ˈdeɪtə lɪŋk/ *noun* a connection between two devices to allow the transmission of data

data link control /ˌdeɪtə lɪŋk kənˈtrəʊl/ *noun* a protocol and rules used to define the way in which data is transmitted or received

data link layer /ˈdeɪtə lɪŋk ˌleɪə/ *noun* the second layer in the ISO/OSI defined network that sends transmits packets of data to the next link and deals with error correction (NOTE: This layer is normally split into two further sub-layers, medium access control and logical link control.)

data logging /ˈdeɪtə ˌlɒgɪŋ/ *noun* automatic data collection

data management /ˈdeɪtə ˌmænɪdʒmənt/ *noun* maintenance and upkeep of a database

data manipulation language /ˌdeɪtə məˌnɪpjʊˈleɪʃ(ə)n ˌlæŋgwɪdʒ/ *noun* a piece of database software that allows the user to access, store and change data. Abbr **DML**

data medium /ˈdeɪtə ˌmiːdiəm/ *noun* a medium which allows data to be stored or displayed, e.g. a VDU, magnetic disk or screen

data migration /ˌdeɪtə maɪˈgreɪʃ(ə)n/ *noun* the process of moving data between a high priority or on-line device to a low-priority or off-line device

data mining /ˈdeɪtə ˌmaɪnɪŋ/ *noun* the task of searching a database in order to find previously unknown patterns and relationships within the data it contains, e.g. searching a retailer's database to find customers who share an interest in a particular activity

'Both companies specialise in decision support, statistical analysis and data mining.' [*The Guardian*]

data name /ˈdeɪtə neɪm/ *noun* a group of characters used to identify one item of data ○ *Problems occur if an ambiguous data name is chosen.*

data network /ˈdeɪtə ˌnetwɜːk/ *noun* a networking system which transmits data

data origination /ˈdeɪtə əˌrɪdʒɪneɪʃ(ə)n/ *noun* the conversion of data from its original form to one which can be read by a computer

data path /ˈdeɪtə pɑːθ/ *noun* a bus or set of connections over which data is transmitted

dataplex /ˈdeɪtəpleks/ *noun* multiplexing of data signals

data pointer /ˈdeɪtə ˌpɔɪntə/ *noun* a register containing the location of the next item of data

dataport /ˈdeɪtəpɔːt/ *noun* a socket for connecting a laptop computer to the Internet

data preparation /ˌdeɪtə ˌprepəˈreɪʃ(ə)n/ *noun* the conversion of data into a machine-readable form, usually by keyboarding, before data entry

data processing /ˌdeɪtə ˈprəʊsesɪŋ/ *noun* the process of selecting and examining data in a computer to produce information in a special form. Abbr **dp, DP**

data processing manager /ˌdeɪtə ˈprəʊsesɪŋ ˌmænɪdʒə/ *noun* a person who runs a computer department

data projector /ˈdeɪtə prəˌdʒektə/ *noun* a device that uses three large coloured lights, red, green and blue, to project a colour image output from a computer onto a large screen

data protection /ˈdeɪtə prəˌtekʃən/ *noun* the procedure of making sure that data is not copied by an unauthorised user

Data Protection Act /ˌdeɪtə prə ˈtekʃən ˌækt/ *noun* a piece of legislation passed in 1984 in the UK that requires any owner of a database that contains personal details to register

data rate /ˈdeɪtə reɪt/ *noun* the maximum rate at which data is processed or transmitted in a synchronous system, usually equal to the system clock rate

data record /ˈdeɪtə ˌrekɔːd/ *noun* one record containing data for use with a program

data reduction /ˌdeɪtə rɪˈdʌkʃən/ *noun* the production of compact, useful data from raw data

data register /ˈdeɪtə ˌredʒɪstə/ *noun* an area within a CPU used to store data temporarily before it is processed

data reliability /ˈdeɪtə rɪˌlaɪəbɪlɪti/ *noun* a measure of the number of data words with errors compared to the total number of words

data retrieval /ˌdeɪtə rɪˈtriːv(ə)l/ *noun* the process of searching, selecting and reading data from a stored file

data routing /ˈdeɪtə ˌruːtɪŋ/ *noun* the process of defining the path to be taken by a message in a network

data security /ˈdeɪtə sɪˌkjʊərɪti/ *noun* protection of data against corruption or unauthorised use

dataset /ˈdeɪtəset/ *noun US* same as **modem** (*US*)

data set ready /ˌdeɪtə set ˈredi/ *noun* full form of **DSR**

data sharing /ˈdeɪtə ˌʃeərɪŋ/ *noun* a facility allowing one file or set of data to be accessed by several users

data signalling rate /ˌdeɪtə ˈsɪgn(ə)lɪŋ ˌreɪt/ *noun* the total amount of data that is transmitted through a system per second

data signals /ˈdeɪtə ˌsɪgn(ə)lz/ *plural noun* electrical or optical pulses or waveforms that represent binary data

data sink /ˈdeɪtə sɪŋk/ *noun* a device in a data terminal which receives data

data source /ˈdeɪtə sɔːs/ *noun* a device in a data terminal which sends data

data space transfer protocol /ˌdeɪtə speɪs ˈtrænsfɜː ˌprəʊtəkɒl/ *noun* full form of **DSTP**

data station /ˈdeɪtə ˌsteɪʃ(ə)n/ *noun* a point that contains a data terminal and a data circuit

data storage /ˈdeɪtə ˌstɔːrɪdʒ/ *noun* a medium able to store data, especially in large quantities

data stream /ˈdeɪtə striːm/ *noun* a set of data transmitted serially one bit or character at a time

data strobe /ˈdeɪtə strəʊb/ *noun* a signal indicating that valid data is on the data bus

data structure /ˈdeɪtə ˌstrʌktʃə/ *noun* a number of related items that are treated as one by the computer (NOTE: For example, in an address book record, the name, address and telephone number form separate entries that would be processed as one by the computer.)

data switching exchange /ˌdeɪtə ˈswɪtʃɪŋ ɪksˌtʃeɪndʒ/ *noun* a device used to direct and switch data between lines

data tablet /ˈdeɪtə ˌtæblət/ *noun* ♦ **graphics tablet**

data terminal /ˈdeɪtə ˌtɜːmɪn(ə)l/ *noun* a device that is able to display and transmit or receive data ○ *A printer is a data terminal for computer output.*

data terminal equipment /ˈdeɪtə ˌtɜːmɪn(ə)l ɪˌkwɪpmənt/ *noun* full form of **DTE**

data terminal ready /ˌdeɪtə ˌtɜːmɪn(ə)l ˈredi/ *noun* full form of **DTR**

data transaction /ˈdeɪtə trænˌzækʃən/ *noun* one complete operation on data

data transfer rate /ˌdeɪtə ˈtrænsfɜː ˌreɪt/ *noun* the rate at which data is moved from one point to another

data translation /'deɪtə træns
ˌleɪʃ(ə)n/ *noun* the conversion of data
from one system format to another

data transmission /'deɪtə trænz
ˌmɪʃ(ə)n/ *noun* the process of sending
data from one location to another over a
data link

data type /'deɪtə taɪp/ *noun* a category
of data which can be stored in a register,
e.g. a string or number

data validation /'deɪtə ˌvælɪdeɪʃ(ə)n/
noun the process of checking data for errors and relevance in a situation

data vetting /'deɪtə ˌvetɪŋ/ *noun* the
process of checking data as it is input, for
errors and validity

data warehouse /'deɪtə ˌweəhaʊs/
noun a database used for analysing the
overall strategy of a business rather than its
routine operations

data word /'deɪtə wɜːd/ *noun* a piece of
data stored as a single word

data word length /ˌdeɪtə 'wɜːd ˌleŋθ/
noun the number of bits that make up a
word in a computer

DAT drive /'dæt draɪv/ *noun* a mechanical drive that records data onto a DAT and
retrieves data from a tape ○ *We use a DAT
drive as the backup device for our network.*

date /deɪt/ *noun* the current day, month
and year stored on your computer □ **to
keep something up to date** to keep adding
information to something so that it is always up to date ○ *We spend a lot of time
keeping our files up to date.*

date-time /ˌdeɪt 'taɪm/ *noun* the current
time and date stored on your computer
(NOTE: Each PC has a tiny battery inside
it that allows one area of memory to store
the current time and date. If you need to
change the time or date in Windows, use
the Control Panel feature.)

daughter board /'dɔːtə bɔːd/ *noun* an
add-on board that connects to a system
motherboard

daylight saving time /ˌdeɪlaɪt 'seɪvɪŋ
ˌtaɪm/ *noun* a scheme that defines changes
in time over the course of a year, which in
the UK involves moving the clocks forward by one hour at a particular date in
spring and backward by one hour at a particular date in the autumn (NOTE: Windows
will automatically detect if the system
time and date needs to be adjusted and
either effect it or warn you.)

dB *abbr* decibel

DBA /ˌdiː biː 'eɪ/ *noun* a person in charge
of running and maintaining a database system. Full form **database administrator**

DB connector /ˌdiː biː kə'nektə/ *noun*
a D-shape connector normally with two
rows of pins used to connect devices that
transfer data ○ *The most common DB connectors are DB-9, DB-25 and DB-50 with
9, 25 and 50 connections respectively.* Full
form **data bus connector**

DBMS /ˌdiː biː em 'es/ *noun* a series of
programs that allow the user to create and
modify databases easily. Full form **database management system**. Also called
database manager

DC *abbr* direct current

DCA /ˌdiː siː 'eɪ/ *noun* a document format defined by IBM that allows documents to be exchanged between computer
systems. Full form **document content
architecture**

DCC /ˌdiː siː 'siː/ *noun* a magnetic tape in
a compact cassette box that is used to store
computer data or audio signals in a digital
format. Full form **digital compact cassette**

DCD /ˌdiː siː 'diː/ *noun* an RS232C signal from a modem to a computer indicating a carrier is being received ○ *The call is
stopped if the software does not receive a
DCD signal from the modem.* Full form
data carrier detect

DCE *abbr* data communications equipment

DCE rate /ˌdiː siː 'iː reɪt/ *plural noun*
the number of bits of information that a
modem can transmit per second over a telephone line, e.g. 36,600 bps (NOTE: This is
not the same as the DTE rate which
measures how fast a modem can exchange data with another PC and takes
into account data compression.)

DCOM /'diː kɒm/ *noun* an enhanced version of the COM specification that allows
applications to access objects over a network or over the Internet. Full form **distributed component object model**

DC signalling /ˌdiː siː 'sɪgn(ə)lɪŋ/
noun a method of communications using
pulses of current over a wire circuit, like a
telegraph system

DCT *abbr* discrete cosine transform

DD *abbr* double density

DDC /ˌdiː diː 'siː/ *noun* a machine operated automatically by machine. Full form
direct digital control

DD/D /ˌdiː diː 'diː/ *noun* a piece of software which gives a list of types and forms of data contained in a database. Full form **data dictionary/directory**

DDE /ˌdiː diː 'iː/ *noun* **1.** the keying in of data directly onto disk. Full form **direct data entry 2.** a method in which two active programs can exchange data, one program asking the operating system to create a link between the two programs. Full form **dynamic data exchange**

DDL /ˌdiː diː 'el/ *noun* a part of database system software which describes the structure of the system and data ○ *Many of DDL's advantages come from the fact that it is a second generation language.* Full form **data description language**

DDP /ˌdiː diː 'piː/ *noun* the process of deriving information from data which is kept in different places. Full form **distributed data processing**

DDR memory /ˌdiː diː ɑː 'mem(ə)ri/ *noun* the set of electronic memory components used for RAM storage in computers and peripherals. Full form **double data rate memory**

dead /ded/ *adjective* referring to a computer or piece of equipment that does not function

deaden /ˈded(ə)n/ *verb* to make a sound or colour less sharp ○ *Acoustic hoods are used to deaden the noise of printers.*

dead halt /ˈded hɔːlt/ *noun* a program instruction from the user or an error that causes the program to stop without allowing recovery

dead key /ˈded kiː/ *plural noun* any one of the keys on a keyboard that cause a function rather than a character to occur, e.g. the shift key

deadlock /ˈdedˌlɒk/, **deadly embrace** /ˈdedli ɪmˈbreɪs/ *noun* a situation in which two users want to access the same two resources at the same time and one resource is assigned to each user, leaving neither able to use the other

deadstart /ˈdedstɑːt/ *verb* same as **cold boot**

dead time /ˈded taɪm/ *noun* a period of time between two events in which nothing happens, to ensure that they do not interfere with each other ○ *Efficient job management minimises dead time.*

deal /diːl/ *noun* a business agreement or contract ■ *verb* □ **to deal with something** to organise or handle something ○ *Leave it to the DP manager – he'll deal with it.*

deallocate /diːˈæləkeɪt/ *verb* to free resources previously allocated to a job, process or peripheral ○ *When a reset button is pressed all resources are deallocated.* (NOTE: **deallocates – deallocating – deallocated**)

debit /ˈdebɪt/ *noun* a bit transmission rate that is twice the baud rate

deblock /diːˈblɒk/ *verb* to return a stored block of data to its original form of individual records

de-bounce /diː ˈbaʊns/ *noun* the process of preventing a single touch on a key from giving multiple key contact

de-bounce circuit /diː ˈbaʊns ˌsɜːkɪt/ *noun* an electronic circuit that prevents a key contact from producing more than one signal when pressed

debug /diːˈbʌg/ *verb* to test a program and locate and correct any faults or errors ○ *They spent weeks debugging the system.* (NOTE: debugging – debugged)

  'Further questions, such as how you debug an application built from multi-sourced software to run on multisourced hardware, must be resolved at this stage.' [*Computing*]

DEBUG /diːˈbʌg/ *noun* an MS-DOS software utility that allows a user to view the contents of binary files and assemble small assembly-language programs

debugged program /ˌdiːbʌgd ˈprəʊɡræm/ *noun* a piece of software that works correctly and in which all the mistakes have been removed or corrected

debugger /diːˈbʌɡə/ *noun* a piece of software that helps a programmer find faults or errors in a program

decade /ˈdekeɪd/ *noun* a set of ten items or events

decay /dɪˈkeɪ/ *noun* the process of a sound signal fading away ○ *With a short decay, it sounds very sharp.*

deceleration time /diːˌseləˈreɪʃ(ə)n ˌtaɪm/ *noun* the time taken for an access arm to come to a stop after it has moved to the correct location over the surface of a hard disk

decentralised computer network /diːˌsentrəˌlaɪzd kəmˈpjuːtə/, **decentralized computer network** *noun* a network where the control is shared between several computers

decentralised data processing /diːˌsentrəˌlaɪzd ˈdeɪtə/, **decentralized data processing** *noun* data processing and storage carried out at each location rather than in one central location

decibel /'desɪbel/ *noun* a unit for measuring the power of a sound or the strength of a signal. Abbr **dB** (NOTE: The decibel scale is logarithmic.)

deciding factor /dɪˌsaɪdɪŋ 'fæktə/ *noun* the most important factor which influences someone's decision ○ *The deciding factor was the superb graphics.*

decimal tabbing /ˌdesɪm(ə)l 'tæbɪŋ/ *noun* the process of adjusting a column of numbers so that the decimal points are vertically aligned

decimal tab key /ˌdesɪm(ə)l 'tæb ˌkiː/ *noun* a key for entering decimal numbers, using a word-processor, so that the decimal points are automatically vertically aligned

decimal-to-binary conversion /ˌdesɪm(ə)l tə ˌbaɪnəri kən'vɜːʃ(ə)n/ *noun* the process of converting a decimal number into a binary digit, i.e. base 10 into base 2

decipher /dɪ'saɪfə/ *verb* to convert an encrypted or encoded message (**ciphertext**) into the original message (**plaintext**). Opposite **encipher**

decision box /dɪ'sɪʒ(ə)n bɒks/ *noun* a graphical symbol used in a flowchart to indicate that a decision is to be made and a branch or path or action carried out according to the result

decision circuit /dɪ'sɪʒ(ə)n ˌsɜːkɪt/ *noun* a logical circuit that operates on binary inputs, producing an output according to the function set in hardware

decision instruction /dɪ'sɪʒ(ə)n ɪn ˌstrʌkʃən/ *noun* a conditional program instruction that directs control by providing the location of the next instruction to be executed if a condition is met

decision support system /dɪ ˌsɪʒ(ə)n sə'pɔːt ˌsɪstəm/ *noun* a suite of programs that helps a manager reach decisions using previous decisions, information and other databases

decision table /dɪ'sɪʒ(ə)n ˌteɪb(ə)l/ *noun* a chart that shows the relationships between certain variables and actions available when various conditions are met

decision tree /dɪ'sɪʒ(ə)n triː/ *noun* a graphical representation of a decision table showing possible paths and actions if different conditions are met

declaration /ˌdeklə'reɪʃ(ə)n/ *noun* a statement within a program that informs the compiler or interpreter of the form, type and size of a particular element, constant or variable. Also called **declarative statement**

declarative language /dɪˌklærətɪv 'læŋgwɪdʒ/ *noun* a programming language, usually in a database application, in which you enter what you want to achieve, rather than instructions

declare /dɪ'kleə/ *verb* to define a computer program variable or to set a variable equal to a number ○ *He declared at the start of the program that X was equal to nine.* (NOTE: declares – declaring – declared)

decode /diː'kəʊd/ *verb* to translate encoded data back to its original form (NOTE: decodes – decoding – decoded)

decoder /diː'kəʊdə/ *noun* a program or device used to convert data into another form

decode unit /diː'kəʊd ˌjuːnɪt/ *noun* a part of a microprocessor that translates a complex instruction into a simple form that the ALU part of the processor can understand and process

decollate /ˌdiːkə'leɪt/ *verb* to separate continuous stationery into single sheets

decollator /ˌdiːkə'leɪtə/ *noun* a machine used to separate continuous stationery into single sheets or to split 2-part or 3-part stationery into separate parts

decompilation /diːˌkɒmpɪ'leɪʃ(ə)n/ *noun* the conversion of a compiled program in object code into a source language ○ *fast incremental compilation and decompilation*

decompiler /ˌdiːkəm'paɪlə/ *noun* a computer program that translates basic machine code back into high-level source code

decompress /ˌdiːkəm'pres/ *verb* **1.** to take electronic data that has been compressed and expand it to its normal extent **2.** to be expanded to its normal extent again after being compressed ○ *Such files decompress easily.*

decompression /ˌdiːkəm'preʃ(ə)n/ *noun* the process of expanding a compressed image or data file so that it can be viewed

decrement /'dekrɪmənt/ *verb* to subtract a set number from a variable ○ *The register contents were decremented until they reached zero.*

decrypt /diː'krɪpt/ *verb* to convert encrypted data back into its original form

decryption /diː'krɪpʃ(ə)n/ *noun* the converting of encrypted data back into its original form ○ *Decryption is done using hardware to increase speed.*

dedicated /'dedɪkeɪtɪd/ *adjective* referring to a program, procedure or system that is reserved for a particular use ○ *There's only one dedicated graphics workstation in this network.*

'The PBX is changing from a dedicated proprietary hardware product into an open application software development platform.' [*Computing*]

dedicated channel /ˌdedɪkeɪtɪd 'tʃæn(ə)l/ *noun* a communications line reserved for a particular use

dedicated computer /ˌdedɪkeɪtɪd kəm'pjuːtə/ *noun* a computer that is only used for a single special purpose

dedicated line /ˌdedɪkeɪtɪd 'laɪn/ *noun* a telephone line that provides a computer or network with a permanent connection to the Internet

dedicated logic /ˌdedɪkeɪtɪd 'lɒdʒɪk/ *noun* a logical function implemented in hardware design, usually for only one task or circuit ○ *The person appointed should have a knowledge of micro-based hardware and dedicated logic* ○ *The dedicated logic cuts down the chip count.*

dedicated print server /ˌdedɪkeɪtɪd 'prɪnt ˌsɜːvə/ *noun* a computer on a network connected to a printer with the sole task of managing print jobs and print queues of users on the network

dedicated word-processor /ˌdedɪkeɪtɪd 'wɜːd ˌprəʊsesə/ *noun* a computer which has been configured specially for word-processing and which cannot run any other programs

de facto standard /deɪ ˌfæktəʊ 'stændəd/ *noun* a design, method or system which is so widely used that it has become a standard but has not been officially recognised by any committee

default /dɪ'fɔːlt/ *noun* a predefined course of action or value that is assumed unless the operator alters it .

default drive /dɪ'fɔːlt draɪv/ *noun* a disk drive that is accessed first in a multidisk system, to try and load the operating system or a program ○ *The operating system allows the user to select the default drive.*

default option /dɪˌfɔːlt 'ɒpʃən/ *noun* a preset value or option that is to be used if no other value has been specified

default palette /dɪˌfɔːlt 'pælət/ *noun* the range of colours used on a particular system if no other is specified (NOTE: A user or application can often change the default palette to create an individual range of colours.)

default printer /dɪˌfɔːlt 'prɪntə/ *noun* a printer that is used unless another is specified, in systems that allow several printers to be defined

default rate /dɪˌfɔːlt 'reɪt/ *noun* the baud rate in a modem that is used if no other is selected

default response /dɪˌfɔːlt rɪ'spɒns/ *noun* a value that is used if the user does not enter new data

default value /dɪˌfɔːlt 'væljuː/ *noun* a value which is automatically used by the computer if no other value has been specified ○ *Screen width has a default value of 80.*

'The default values of columns cannot be set in the database schema, so different applications can trash the database.' [*Computing*]

defective sector /dɪˌfektɪv 'sektə/ *noun* a fault with a hard disk in which data cannot be correctly read from a particular sector (NOTE: It could be caused by a damaged disk surface or faulty head alignment.)

defect skipping /'diːfekt ˌskɪpɪŋ/ *noun* a means of identifying and labelling defective magnetic tracks during manufacture so that they will not be used, pointing instead to the next good track to be used

defensive computing /dɪˌfensɪv kəm'pjuːtɪŋ/ *noun* a method of programming that takes into account any problems or errors that might occur

deferred addressing /dɪˌfɜːd ə'dresɪŋ/ *noun* indirect addressing, in which the location accessed contains the address of the operand to be processed

deferred mode /dɪ'fɜːd məʊd/ *noun* the process of entering a command as a program line, then executing the program

deferred printing /dɪˌfɜːd 'prɪntɪŋ/ *noun* the process of delaying the printing of a document until a later time

define /dɪ'faɪn/ *verb* **1.** to assign a value to a variable ○ *All the variables were defined at initialisation.* **2.** to assign the characteristics of processes or data to something (NOTE: defines – defining – defined)

definition /ˌdefɪ'nɪʃ(ə)n/ *noun* **1.** the ability of a screen to display fine detail **2.** a value or formula assigned to a variable or label

deflect /dɪ'flekt/ *verb* to change the direction of an object or beam

deflection yokes /dɪˈflekʃ(ə)n jəʊkz/ *plural noun* magnetic coils around a cathode ray tube used to control the position of the picture beam on the screen

DEFRAG /ˈdiːfræg/ *noun* a defragmentation utility supplied with MS-DOS

defragmentation /ˌdiːfrægmenˈteɪʃ(ə)n/ *noun* the reorganisation of files scattered across non-contiguous sectors on a hard disk

COMMENT: When a file is saved to disk, it is not always saved in adjacent sectors. This will increase the retrieval time. Defragmentation moves files back into adjacent sectors so that the read head does not have to move far across the disk, and it increases performance.

defragmentation utility /ˌdiːfrægmenˈteɪʃ(ə)n juːˌtɪlɪti/ *noun* a software utility that carries out the process of defragmentation on a hard disk

degauss /diːˈgaʊs/ *verb* to remove unwanted magnetic fields and effects from magnetic tape, disks or read/write heads ○ *The r/w heads have to be degaussed each week to ensure optimum performance.*

degausser /diːˈgaʊsə/ *noun* a device used to remove unwanted magnetic fields from a disk, tape or recording head

degradation /ˌdegrəˈdeɪʃ(ə)n/ *noun* **1.** the loss of picture or signal quality **2.** the loss of processing capacity because of a malfunction

dejagging /diːˈdʒægɪŋ/ *noun* same as **anti-aliasing**

DEL /del/ *noun* an MS-DOS command to delete a file ○ *To delete all files with the extension BAK, use the command DEL or .BAK.* Full form **delete**

delay line /dɪˈleɪ laɪn/ *noun* a device that causes a signal to take a certain time in crossing it

delay line store /dɪˈleɪ laɪn ˌstɔː/ *noun* an outdated method of storing serial data as sound or pulses in a delay line, the data being constantly read, regenerated and fed back into the input

delay vector /dɪˈleɪ ˌvektə/ *noun* the time that a message will take to pass from one packet switching network node to another

delete /dɪˈliːt/ *verb* **1.** to cut out words in a document **2.** to remove text, data or a file from a storage device ○ *The word-processor allows us to delete the whole file by pressing this key.* Full form of **DEL** (NOTE: deletes – deleting – deleted)

COMMENT: When you delete a file, you are not actually erasing it but making its space on disk available for another file by instructing the operating system to ignore the file by inserting a special code in the file header and deleting the entry from the directory.

delete character /dɪˌliːt ˈkærɪktə/ *noun* a special code used to indicate data or text to be removed

deletion /dɪˈliːʃ(ə)n/ *noun* **1.** the making of a cut in a document ○ *The editors asked the author to make several deletions in the last chapter.* **2.** a piece of text removed from a document

deletion record /dɪˈliːʃ(ə)n ˌrekɔːd/ *noun* a record containing new data which is to be used to update or delete data in a master record

deletion tracking /dɪˈliːʃ(ə)n ˌtrækɪŋ/ *noun* a method of allowing deleted files to be undeleted by monitoring the sectors on disk for a period of time in case the file was deleted by mistake

delimit /diːˈlɪmɪt/ *verb* to set up the size of data using delimiters

delimited-field file /diːˌlɪmɪtd fiːld ˈfaɪl/ *noun* a data file in which each field is separated by a special character, often a tab character or comma, and each record is separated by a carriage return or a second special character

delimiter /diːˈlɪmɪtə/ *noun* **1.** a character or symbol used to indicate to a language or program the start or end of data or a record or information **2.** the boundary between an instruction and its argument

delivery system /dɪˌlɪv(ə)ri ˈsɪstəm/ *noun* the combination of hardware and software required to play a particular multimedia title

DEL key /ˈdel kiː/ *noun* a key on a keyboard that moves the cursor back one character space and deletes any character at that position ○ *To remove a word from the screen, press the DEL key repeatedly.*

Delphi /ˈdelfiː/ a commercial online information provider that provides subscribers with access to its own databases and access to the Internet

delta clock /ˈdeltə klɒk/ *noun* a clock that provides timing pulses to synchronise a system, and will restart a computer or circuit, with an interrupt signal, that has had an error or entered an endless loop or faulty state

delta frame /ˈdeltə ˌfreɪm/ *noun* a video frame that contains only the pixel information that has changed since the last frame of the sequence, used to save space when storing video on disk

delta YUV /ˌdeltə ˌwaɪ juː 'viː/ *noun* full form of **DYUV**

demagnetise, demagnetize *verb* to remove stray or unwanted magnetic fields from a disk, tape or recording head (NOTE: demagnetises – demagnetising – demagnetised)

demagnetiser, demagnetizer *noun* a device which demagnetises a disk, tape or recording head ○ *He used the demagnetiser to degauss the tape heads.*

demand assigned multiple access /dɪˌmɑːnd əˌsaɪnd ˌmʌltɪp(ə)l 'æksɛs/ *noun* a means of switching in circuits as and when they are required. Abbr **DAMA**

demand fetching /dɪ'mɑːnd ˌfetʃɪŋ/ *noun* a virtual page management system in which the pages are selected as required

demand paging /dɪ'mɑːnd ˌpeɪdʒɪŋ/ *noun* system software that retrieves pages in a virtual memory system from backing store when it is required

demand processing /dɪ'mɑːnd ˌprəʊsesɪŋ/ *noun* the processing of data when it appears, rather than waiting

demand protocol architecture /dɪˌmɑːnd ˌprəʊtəkɒl 'ɑːkɪtektʃə/ *noun* full form of **DPA**

demand reading/writing /dɪˌmɑːnd ˌriːdɪŋ 'raɪtɪŋ/ *noun* a direct data transfer between a processor and storage

demand staging /dɪ'mɑːnd ˌsteɪdʒɪŋ/ *noun* the process of moving files or data from a secondary storage device to a fast access device when required by a database program

demarcation /ˌdiːmɑː'keɪʃ(ə)n/ *noun* the process of showing the difference between two areas

democratic network /ˌdeməkrætɪk 'netwɜːk/ *noun* a synchronised network in which each station has equal priority

demodulation /diːˌmɒdju'leɪʃ(ə)n/ *noun* the recovery of the original signal from a received modulated carrier wave

demonstration model /ˌdemən'streɪʃ(ə)n ˌmɒd(ə)l/ *noun* a piece of equipment in a shop, used to show customers how the equipment works

demonstration software /ˌdemənstreɪʃ(ə)n 'sɒftweə/ *noun* software that shows what an application is like to use and what it can do, without implementing all the functions ○ *The company gave away demonstration software that*

lets you do everything except save your data.

demultiplex /diː'mʌltɪpleks/ *verb* to split one channel into the original signals that were combined at source

demultiplexor /diː'mʌltɪpleksə/ *noun* a device that separates out the original multiplexed signals from one channel

denial-of-service attack /dɪˌnaɪəl əv 'sɜːvɪs əˌtæk/ *noun* an illegal action in which a great deal of data is sent to a computer system from many sources at the same in an attempt to overload the system and put it out of action

dense index /dens 'ɪndeks/ *noun* a database index containing an address or entry for every item or entry in the database

dense list /'dens lɪst/ *noun* a list that has no free space for new records

density /'densɪti/ *noun* the amount of data that can be packed into a space

'…diode lasers with shorter wavelengths will make doubling of the bit and track densities possible' [*Byte*]

COMMENT: Scanner software produces various shades of grey by using different densities or arrangements of black and white dots and/or different size dots.

departmental LAN /ˌdiːpɑːt'ment(ə)l læn/ *noun* a small local network used to connect a group of people that are working in the same department or office and allows the users to share files, printers and other resources. ◊ **LAN, peer-to-peer network**

dependent /dɪ'pendənt/ *adjective* which is variable because of a particular factor ○ *A process which is dependent on the result of another process.*

deposit /dɪ'pɒzɪt/ *noun* a printout of the contents of all or a selected area of memory ■ *verb* to write data into a register or storage location

deposition /ˌdepə'zɪʃ(ə)n/ *noun* a process by which a surface of a semiconductor is coated with a thin layer of a substance

depth cueing /'depθ ˌkjuːɪŋ/ *noun* (*in graphics*) a method of changing the hue and colour of an object to reflect its depth in a three-dimensional scene

deque /ˌdiː 'iː ˌkjuː/ *noun* same as **double ended queue**

derivation graph /ˌderɪ'veɪʃ(ə)n grɑːf/ *noun* a structure within a global database that provides information on the rules and paths used to reach any element or item of data

derive /dɪˈraɪv/ *verb* to come from a source ○ *The results are derived from the raw data.* (NOTE: derives – deriving – derived)

DES /ˌdiː iː ˈes/ *noun* a standard developed by the US Government for a high-security block data cipher system. Full form **data encryption standard**. Compare **public key encryption**

descender /dɪˈsendə/ *noun* a part of a printed letter that is below the line

de-scramble /diː ˈskræmb(ə)l/ *verb* to reassemble an original message or signal from its scrambled form

de-scrambler /diː ˈskræmblə/ *noun* a device which changes a scrambled message back to its original, clear form

description list /dɪˈskrɪpʃən lɪst/ *noun* a list of data items and their attributes

descriptor /dɪˈskrɪptə/ *noun* a code used to identify a filename or program name or to pass code to a file

deselect /ˌdiːsɪˈlekt/ *verb* to cancel the selection of an option or of data on a menu or list on a computer screen

design parameters /dɪˈzaɪn pəˌræmɪtəz/ *plural noun* specifications for the design of a product

desk accessory /ˈdesk əkˌsesəri/ *noun* an add-in Apple Mac utility that enhances the system ○ *We have installed several desk accessories that help us manage our fonts.* Abbr **DA**

desk check /ˈdesk tʃek/ *noun* a dry run of a program

desktop /ˈdesktɒp/ *adjective* able to be placed on a desk ■ *noun* a GUI workspace that is a graphical representation of a real-life desktop, with icons for telephone, diary, calculator, filing cabinet

COMMENT: A desktop makes it easier for a new user to operate a computer, since he or she does not have to type in commands but instead can point at icons on the desktop using a mouse.

Desktop background /ˌdesktɒp ˈbækgraʊnd/ *noun* a pattern or image that is displayed by Windows as a backdrop

desktop computer /ˌdesktɒp kəmˈpjuːtə/, **desktop computer system** /ˌdesktɒp kəmˈpjuːtə ˌsɪstəm/ *noun* a small microcomputer system that can be placed on a desk

Desktop file /ˌdesktɒp ˈfaɪl/ *noun* an Apple Mac system file used to store information about all the files on a disk or volume, e.g. version, date, size and author

Desktop icons /ˌdesktɒp ˈaɪkɒnz/ *plural noun* icons that are displayed on the Desktop

desktop media /ˌdesktɒp ˈmiːdiə/ *plural noun* a combination of presentation graphics, desktop publishing and multimedia (NOTE: The term was originally used by Apple.)

desktop presentations /ˌdesktɒp ˌprez(ə)nˈteɪʃ(ə)nz/ *plural noun* presentation graphics, text and charts produced and designed on a desktop personal computer

desktop publishing /ˌdesktɒp ˈpʌblɪʃɪŋ/ *noun* full form of **DTP**

'…desktop publishing or the ability to produce high-quality publications using a minicomputer, essentially boils down to combining words and images on pages' [*Byte*]

Desktop taskbar /ˌdesktɒp ˈtɑːskbɑː/ *noun* a status bar that is normally displayed along the bottom of the screen in Windows 95

desktop unit /ˌdesktɒp ˈjuːnɪt/ *noun* a computer or machine that will fit onto a desk

desktop video /ˌdesktɒp ˈvɪdiəʊ/ *noun* full form of **DTV**

despatch /dɪˈspætʃ/ *noun* another spelling of **dispatch**

despool /diːˈspuːl/ *verb* to print out spooled files

despotic network /dɪˌspɒtɪk ˈnetwɜːk/ *noun* a network synchronised and controlled by one single clock

destination address /ˌdestɪneɪʃ(ə)n əˈdres/ *noun* the address of the node to which data is being transferred or sent

destination object /ˌdestɪneɪʃ(ə)n ˈɒbdʒekt/ *noun* the object or icon onto which you drop an object in a drag and drop operation

destination page /ˌdestɪˈneɪʃ(ə)n peɪdʒ/ *noun* a target page within a hyperlink ○ *When a user clicks on the active object in a hyperlink, the software displays the destination page.*

destructive addition /dɪˌstrʌktɪv əˈdɪʃ(ə)n/ *noun* an addition operation in which the result is stored in the location of one of the operands used in the sum, so overwriting it

destructive cursor /dɪˌstrʌktɪv ˈkɜːsə/ *noun* a cursor that erases the text as it moves over it ○ *Reading the screen becomes difficult without a destructive cursor.*

destructive read /dɪ'strʌktɪv riːd/ *noun* a read operation in which the stored data is erased as it is retrieved

destructive readout /dɪ,strʌktɪv 'riːdaʊt/ *noun* full form of **DRO**

detail file /'diːteɪl faɪl/ *noun* a file containing records that are to be used to update a master file

detail paper /'diːteɪl ,peɪpə/ *noun* a thin transparent paper used for layouts and tracing

detected error /dɪ,tektɪd 'erə/ *noun* an error noticed during a program run but not corrected

deterministic /dɪ,tɜːmɪ'nɪstɪk/ *adjective* referring to a result that depends on the initial state and inputs of a process

Deutsche Industrienorm /,dɔɪtʃə 'ɪndʊstriː,nɔːm/ *noun* full form of **DIN**

development software /dɪ'veləpmənt ,sɒftweə/ *noun* a suite of programs that helps a programmer write, edit, compile and debug new software

development time /dɪ'veləpmənt taɪm/ *noun* the amount of time required to develop a new product

device /dɪ'vaɪs/ *noun* a small useful machine or piece of equipment

'Users in remote locations can share ideas on the Liveboard through the use of a wireless pen-input device and network connections.' [*Computing*]

device address /dɪ'vaɪs ə,dres/ *noun* a location within the memory area that is used by a particular device (NOTE: The CPU can control the device by placing instructions at this address.)

device character control /dɪ,vaɪs ,kærɪktə kən'trəʊl/ *noun* a device control using various characters or special combinations to instruct the device

device code /dɪ'vaɪs kəʊd/ *noun* a unique identification and selection code for each peripheral

device control character /dɪ,vaɪs kən'trəʊl ,kærɪktə/ *noun* a special code sent in a transmission to a device to instruct it to perform a special function

device-dependent /dɪ,vaɪs dɪ'pendənt/ *adjective* referring to a software program that will only work on a certain type of computer or with a certain type of device

device driver /dɪ'vaɪs ,draɪvə/ *noun* same as **driver**

device element /dɪ'vaɪs ,elɪmənt/ *noun* data required for an MCI compound

device, usually a data file, e.g. a WAVE file that is played back through a sound card

device flag /dɪ'vaɪs flæg/ *noun* one bit in a device status word, used to show the state of a device

device handler /dɪ,vaɪs 'hændlə/ *noun* same as **driver**

device-independent /dɪ,vaɪs ,ɪndɪ'pendənt/ *adjective* referring to a programming technique that results in a program that is able to run with any peripheral hardware

device independent bitmap /dɪ ,vaɪs ,ɪndɪpendənt 'bɪtmæp/ *noun* full form of **DIB 2**

device manager /dɪ'vaɪs ,mænɪdʒə/ *noun* a piece of software, usually part of the operating system, that lets you change the settings or configure a device such as a printer or monitor (NOTE: In Windows 95 and later, right-click on the My Computer icon on the Desktop and click on the Device Manager page tab – you can now see and manage all the devices connected to your computer.)

device name /dɪ'vaɪs neɪm/ *noun* an abbreviation that denotes a port or I/O device, e.g. COM for serial port, PRN for printer port or CON for keyboard and monitor

device priority /dɪ'vaɪs praɪ,ɒrɪti/ *noun* the importance of a peripheral device assigned by the user or central computer which dictates the order in which the CPU will serve an interrupt signal from it ○ *The master console has a higher device priority than the printers and other terminals.*

device queue /dɪ'vaɪs kjuː/ *noun* a list of requests from users or programs to use a device

device status word /dɪ,vaɪs 'steɪtəs ,wɜːd/ *noun* full form of **DSW** ○ *This routine checks the device status word and will not transmit data if the busy bit is set.*

devise /dɪ'vaɪz/ *verb* to plan or build a system ○ *They devised a cheap method to avoid the problem.* (NOTE: **devises – devising – devised**)

DFD /,diː ef 'diː/ *noun* a diagram used to describe the movement of data through a system. Full form **data flow diagram**

DGIS /,diː dʒiː aɪ 'es/ *noun* a standard graphics interface for video adapters, primarily used with the 340x0 range of graphics chips. Full form **direct graphics interface standard**

DHCP /ˌdiː siː eɪtʃ 'piː/ *noun* an TCP/IP protocol that is used to assign an Internet address to workstations and servers that are nodes in a network. Full form **dynamic host configuration protocol** (NOTE: A special server running DHCP software manages the process of assigning addresses. A client computer can then ask this server for the address of another node on the network.)

Dhrystone benchmark /ˌdraɪstəʊn 'bentʃmɑːk/ *noun* a benchmarking system developed to try and measure and compare the performance of computers

DIA/DCA /ˌdiː aɪ eɪ ˌdiː siː 'eɪ/ *noun* a standard method for the transmission and storage of documents, text and video over networks. It is part of the IBM SNA range of standards. Full form **document interchange architecture/document content architecture**

diagnose /'daɪəgnəʊz/ *verb* to find the cause and effect of a fault in hardware or an error in software (NOTE: diagnoses – diagnosing – diagnosed)

diagnosis /ˌdaɪəg'nəʊsɪs/ *noun* the process of finding of a fault or discovering the cause of a fault

diagnostic aid /ˌdaɪəgnɒstɪk 'eɪd/ *noun* a hardware or software device that helps to find faults

diagnostic chip /ˌdaɪəgnɒstɪk 'tʃɪp/ *noun* a chip that contains circuits to carry out tests on other circuits or chips

diagnostic error message /ˌdaɪəgnɒstɪk 'erə ˌmesɪdʒ/ *noun* an explanatory line of text displayed when an error has been found

diagnostic message /ˌdaɪəgnɒstɪk 'mesɪdʒ/ *noun* a message that appears to explain the type, location and probable cause of a software error or hardware failure

diagnostic program /ˌdaɪəgnɒstɪk 'prəʊgræm/ *noun* a piece of software that helps find faults in a computer system

diagnostic routine /ˌdaɪəgnɒstɪk ruː'tiːn/ *noun* a routine in a program that helps to find faults in a computer system

diagnostics /ˌdaɪəg'nɒstɪks/ *plural noun* functions or tests that help a user find faults in hardware or software

diagnostic test /ˌdaɪəgnɒstɪk 'test/ *noun* a means of locating faults in hardware and software by testing circuits or programs

dialect /'daɪəlekt/ *noun* a slight variant of a standard language ○ *This manufacturer's dialect of BASIC is a little different to the one I'm used to.*

Dialer /'daɪələ/ a Windows 95 utility that, if you have a modem connected to your PC, will dial telephone numbers for you. Also called **Phone Dialer**

dial-in modem /ˌdaɪəl ɪn 'məʊdem/ *noun* an auto-answer modem that can be called at any time to access a system

dial modifier /'daɪəl ˌmɒdɪfaɪə/ *noun* any one of a set of extra commands sent to a Hayes-compatible modem that instruct the modem to use a particular system when dialling a telephone number. ◊ **AT command set** (NOTE: For example, the command 'ATDT123' tells the modem to use tone-dialling to dial the number '123')

dialog box /'daɪəlɒg bɒks/ *noun* an on-screen message from a program to the user

dialogue /'daɪəlɒg/, **dialog** *noun* conversation between people, or an instance of this

dialup *noun* an online information service that is accessed by dialling into the central computer. Also called **dial-up service**

dial-up access /ˌdaɪəl ʌp 'ækses/ *noun* a connection to the Internet that is not permanent but requires a modem or ISDN adapter to dial a telephone access number to connect to the Internet, as in making a normal telephone call

dial-up connection /ˌdaɪəl ʌp kə'nekʃ(ə)n/ *noun* a connection that uses a standard telephone line or ISDN link to connect a computer to an ISP or another computer

Dial-up Networking /ˌdaɪəl ʌp 'netwɜːkɪŋ/ *noun* the part of the Windows operating system that supports and manages a dial-up connection to a remote computer

dial-up service /ˌdaɪəl ʌp 'sɜːvɪs/ *noun* same as **dialup**

diaphragm /'daɪəfræm/ *noun* a thin flexible sheet that vibrates in response to sound waves to create an electrical signal, as in a microphone, or in response to electrical signals to create sound waves, as in a speaker

DIB /ˌdiː aɪ 'biː/ *noun* **1.** a bus used when transferring data from one section of a computer to another, as between memory and CPU. Full form **data input bus 2.** a file format for a Windows graphics image that consists of a header, colour table and bitmap data. Full form **device independent bitmap** (NOTE: It can be in 1–, 4–, 8– or 24-bit colour resolution.)

dibit /'dɪbɪt/ *noun* a digit made up of two binary bits

dichotomising   search /daɪ 'kɒtəmaɪzɪŋ ˌsɜːtʃ/, **dichotomizing search** *noun* same as **binary search**

dichroic /daɪ'krəʊɪk/ *adjective* referring to a chemical coating on the surface of a lens that reflects selectively different colours of light

dichroic filter /daɪˌkrəʊɪk 'fɪltə/ *noun* a filter that allows certain wavelengths of light to pass and reflects back those that are not transmitted

dichroic head /daɪˌkrəʊɪk 'hed/ *noun* a coloured light source that is based on adjustable dichroic filters, generally used with rostrum cameras and enlargers

dictionary /'dɪkʃən(ə)ri/ *noun* **1.** a data management structure that allows files to be referenced and sorted **2.** a part of a spelling checker program consisting of a list of correctly spelt words against which the program checks a text (NOTE: The plural is **dictionaries**.)

differential pulse coded modulation /ˌdɪfərenʃəl ˌpʌls ˌkəʊdɪd ˌmɒdjʊ 'leɪʃ(ə)n/ *noun* full form of **DPCM**

DIF file /'dɪf faɪl/ *noun* a file in a de facto standard that defines the way a spreadsheet, its formula and data are stored in a file

diffusion /dɪ'fjuːʒ(ə)n/ *noun* a means of transferring doping materials into an integrated circuit substrate

digit /'dɪdʒɪt/ *noun* a symbol or character that represents an integer that is smaller than the radix of the number base used ○ *a phone number with eight digits* or *an eight-digit phone number*

digital /'dɪdʒɪt(ə)l/ *adjective* which represents data or physical quantities in numerical form, especially using a binary system in computer related devices

'Xerox Parc's LCD breakthrough promises the digital equivalent of paper, by producing thin, low-cost flat displays with a 600dpi resolution.' [*Computing*]

digital audio tape /ˌdɪdʒɪt(ə)l 'ɔːdiəʊ ˌteɪp/ *noun* full form of **DAT**

digital camera /ˌdɪdʒɪt(ə)l 'kæm(ə)rə/ *noun* a camera that uses a bank of CCD units to capture an image and store it digitally onto a miniature disk or in RAM in the camera's body

digital cash /ˌdɪdʒɪt(ə)l 'kæʃ/ *noun* a method of paying for goods over the Internet (NOTE: There are several payment systems that use different models including a new bank account for each customer and an electronic purse that carries electronic tokens paid for by a customer.)

digital cassette /ˌdɪdʒɪt(ə)l kə'set/ *noun* a high quality magnetic tape housed in a standard size cassette with write protect tabs and a standard format leader

digital certificate /ˌdɪdʒɪt(ə)l sə 'tɪfɪkət/ *noun* ♦ **certificate**

digital channel /ˌdɪdʒɪt(ə)l 'tʃæn(ə)l/ *noun* a communications path that can only transmit data as digital signals. ◊ **ADC** (NOTE: Voice, image or video signals have to be converted from analog to digital form before they can be transmitted over a digital channel.)

digital circuit /ˌdɪdʒɪt(ə)l 'sɜːkɪt/ *noun* an electronic circuit that operates on digital information providing logical functions or switching

digital clock /ˌdɪdʒɪt(ə)l 'klɒk/ *noun* a clock THAT shows the time as a series of digits, e.g. 12:22:04

digital   compact   cassette /ˌdɪdʒɪt(ə)l ˌkɒmpækt kə'set/ *noun* full form of **DCC**

digital computer /ˌdɪdʒɪt(ə)l kəm 'pjuːtə/ *noun* a computer that processes data represented in discrete digital form

digital data /ˌdɪdʒɪt(ə)l 'deɪtə/ *noun* data represented in numerical, especially binary, form

digital display /ˌdɪdʒɪt(ə)l dɪ'spleɪ/ *noun* a video display unit that can only show a fixed number of colours or shades of grey

digital divide /ˌdɪdʒɪt(ə)l dɪ'vaɪd/ *noun* the state of inequality that exists between people who have access to modern information technology and those who do not, since the former have many more opportunities open to them than the latter

digital   encryption   standard /ˌdɪdʒɪt(ə)l ɪn'krɪpʃən ˌstændəd/ *noun* the standard for encrypting private key data, which uses 56-bit encryption

digital light processing /ˌdɪdʒɪt(ə)l 'laɪt ˌprəʊsesɪŋ/ *noun* full form of **DLP**

digital logic /ˌdɪdʒɪt(ə)l 'lɒdʒɪk/ *noun* the process of applying Boolean algebra to hardware circuits

digital monitor /ˌdɪdʒɪt(ə)l ˈmɒnɪtə/ *noun* a monitor that can only show a fixed number of colours or shades of grey

digital nonlinear editing /ˌdɪdʒɪt(ə)l nɒnˌlɪniə ˈedɪtɪŋ/ *noun* same as **nonlinear video editing**

digital optical recording /ˌdɪdʒɪt(ə)l ˌɒptɪk(ə)l rɪˈkɔːdɪŋ/ *noun* full form of **DOR**

digital output /ˌdɪdʒɪt(ə)l ˈaʊtpʊt/ *noun* computer output in digital form

digital plotter /ˌdɪdʒɪt(ə)l ˈplɒtə/ *noun* a plotter whose pen position is controllable in discrete steps, so that drawings in the computer can be output graphically

digital read-out /ˌdɪdʒɪt(ə)l ˈriːdaʊt/ *noun* data displayed in numerical form, e.g. numbers on an LCD in a calculator

digital representation /ˌdɪdʒɪt(ə)l ˌreprɪzenˈteɪʃ(ə)n/ *noun* data or quantities represented using digits

digital resolution /ˌdɪdʒɪt(ə)l ˌrezəˈluːʃ(ə)n/ *noun* the smallest number that can be represented with one digit

digital signal /ˌdɪdʒɪt(ə)l ˈsɪgn(ə)l/ *noun* an electrical signal that has only a number of possible states, as opposed to an analog signal, which is continuously variable

digital signal level one /ˌdɪdʒɪt(ə)l ˌsɪgn(ə)l ˌlev(ə)l ˈwʌn/ *noun* full form of **DS-1**

digital signal level zero /ˌdɪdʒɪt(ə)l ˌsɪgn(ə)l ˌlev(ə)l ˈzɪərəʊ/ *noun* full form of **DS-0**

digital signalling /ˌdɪdʒɪt(ə)l ˈsɪgnəlɪŋ/ *noun* control and dialling codes sent down a telephone line in digital form

digital signal processing /ˌdɪdʒɪt(ə)l ˈsɪgn(ə)l ˌprəʊsesɪŋ/ *noun* full form of **DSP**

digital signature /ˌdɪdʒɪt(ə)l ˈsɪgnətʃə/ *noun* a unique identification code sent by a terminal or device in digital form

digital speech /ˌdɪdʒɪt(ə)l ˈspiːtʃ/ *noun* ♦ **speech synthesis**

digital subscriber line /ˌdɪdʒɪt(ə)l səbˈskraɪbə ˌlaɪn/ *noun* full form of **DSL**

digital switching /ˌdɪdʒɪt(ə)l ˈswɪtʃɪŋ/ *noun* the process of operating communications connections and switches only by use of digital signals

digital system /ˌdɪdʒɪt(ə)l ˈsɪstəm/ *noun* a system that deals with digital signals

digital theatre system /ˌdɪdʒɪt(ə)l ˈθɪətə ˌsɪstəm/ *noun* full form of **DTS**

digital to analog converter /ˌdɪdʒɪt(ə)l tə ˌænəlɒg kənˈvɜːtə/ *noun* full form of **DAC**

digital transmission system /ˌdɪdʒɪt(ə)l trænzˈmɪʃ(ə)n ˌsɪstəm/ *noun* communication achieved by converting analog signals to a digital form then modulating and transmitting this and finally converting the signal back to analog form at the receiver

digital TV /ˌdɪdʒɪt(ə)l tiːˈviː/ *noun* a television that can receive and decode television images and audio sent as digital data, then displayed on a standard screen

digital versatile disc /ˌdɪdʒɪt(ə)l ˌvɜːsətaɪl ˈdɪsk/ *noun* full form of **DVD**

digital video /ˌdɪdʒɪt(ə)l ˈvɪdiəʊ/ *noun* a video recorded in digital form (NOTE: The output from a video camera is converted to digital form using either a digital camera or a frame grabber. The digital output is then usually compressed before being processed or transmitted or stored on videotape.)

digital video effects /ˌdɪdʒɪt(ə)l ˈvɪdiəʊ ɪˌfekts/ *plural noun* full form of **DVE**

digital video interactive /ˌdɪdʒɪt(ə)l ˌvɪdiəʊ ˌɪntərˈæktɪv/ *noun* full form of **DV-I**

digital wallet /ˌdɪdʒɪt(ə)l ˈwɒlɪt/ *noun* a feature of web browsers that contains a unique personal digital signature and allows the user to pay for goods at online shops in many different ways, including credit card or digital cash (NOTE: A digital wallet makes it simpler and more secure to buy goods from online shops.)

digitise /ˈdɪdʒɪˌtaɪz/, **digitize** *verb* to change analog movement or signals into a digital form that can be processed by computers ○ *We can digitise your signature to allow it to be printed with any laser printer.* (NOTE: digitises – digitising – digitised)

'The contract covers fibre optic cable and Synchronous Digital Hierarchy transmission equipment to be used to digitize the telecommunications network.' [*Computergram*]

digitised photograph /ˌdɪdʒɪˌtaɪzd ˌfəʊtəˈɡrɑːf/, **digitized photograph** *noun* an image or photograph that has been scanned to produce an analog signal which is then converted to digital form and stored or displayed on a computer

digitiser, digitizer *noun* same as **ADC**

digitising pad /ˈdɪdʒɪtaɪzɪŋ ˌpæd/, **digitising tablet, digitizing pad, digitizing tablet** *noun* a sensitive surface that translates the position of a pen into numerical form, so that drawings can be entered into a computer

digit place /ˈdɪdʒɪt pleɪs/, **digit position** *noun* the position of a digit within a number

DIL /ˌdiː aɪ ˈel/ *noun* full form **dual-in-line package**. same as **DIP**

DIM /ˌdiː aɪ ˈem/ *noun* software that allows a user to capture, store and index printed text in a digital form. Full form **document image management** (NOTE: It usually works in conjunction with a scanner and a storage medium such as a recordable CD-ROM.)

dimension /daɪˈmenʃən/ *noun* a measurement of size ○ *The dimensions of the computer are small enough for it to fit into a case.*

dimensioning /daɪˈmenʃənɪŋ/ *noun* the definition of the size of something, especially an array or matrix ○ *Array dimensioning occurs at this line.*

diminished radix complement /dɪˌmɪnɪʃt ˈreɪdɪks ˌkɒmpleks/ *noun* a number representation in which each digit of the number is subtracted from one less than the radix. ◊ **one's complement, nine's complement**

DIMM /ˌdiː aɪ em ˈem/ *noun* a system of arranging RAM memory chips on two sides of a tiny expansion card that can be inserted into a slot on the computer's motherboard to upgrade the main memory ○ *DIMM cards are used to expand the memory in high-performance computers.* Full form **dual in-line memory module**

DIN /ˌdiː aɪ ˈen/ *noun* a German industry standards organisation known particularly for specifications for plugs and sockets. Full form **Deutsche Industrienorm**

Dingbat /ˈdɪŋbæt/ *noun* a font that contains stars, bullets, symbols, images and drawings in place of characters ○ *To insert a copyright symbol, use the Dingbat font.*

diode /ˈdaɪəʊd/ *noun* an electronic component that allows an electrical current to pass in one direction and not the other

DIP /ˌdiː aɪ ˈpiː/ *noun* **1.** a standard layout for integrated circuit packages using two parallel rows of connecting pins along each side. Full form **dual-in-line package 2.** software that allows a user to capture, store and index printed text in a digital form

DIP switch /ˈdɪp swɪtʃ/ *noun* a small bank of switches that are used to configure a device. Full form **dual-in-line package switch**

DIR /ˌdiː aɪ ˈɑː/ *noun* a MS-DOS system command that displays a list of files stored on a disk. Full form **directory**

direct /daɪˈrekt/ *adjective, adverb* straight

direct access /ˌdaɪrekt ˈækses/ *noun* storage and retrieval of data without the need to read other data first

direct access storage device /daɪ ˌrekt ˌækses ˈstɔːrɪdʒ dɪˌvaɪs/ *noun* full form of **DASD**

direct addressing /ˌdaɪrekt əˈdresɪŋ/ *noun* a method of addressing in which the storage location address given in the instruction is the location to be used

direct cable connection /ˌdaɪrekt ˈkeɪb(ə)l kəˌneks(ə)n/ *noun* a utility supplied with Windows 95 that allows you to link two computers together using a serial cable plugged into each serial port

direct change-over /daɪˈrekt tʃeɪndʒ/ *noun* the process of switching from one computer to another in one go

direct code /daɪˈrekt kəʊd/ *noun* a binary code which directly operates the central processing unit, using only absolute addresses and values (NOTE: This is the final form of a program after a compiler or assembler pass.)

direct coding /daɪˈrekt kɒdɪŋ/ *noun* program instructions written in absolute code

direct connect /ˌdaɪrekt kəˈnekt/ *adjective* referring to a modem which plugs straight into the standard square telephone socket

direct connection /daɪˌrekt kəˈnekʃən/ *noun* a fast permanent connection linking a computer or system to a network such as the Internet

direct current /dɪˌrekt ˈkʌrənt/ *noun* a constant value electric current that flows in one direction. Abbr **DC**

direct data entry /daɪˌrekt ˌdeɪtə ˈentri/ *noun* full form of **DDE 1**

direct digital control /daɪˌrekt ˌdɪdʒɪt(ə)l kənˈtrəʊl/ *noun* full form of **DDC**

directed scan /daɪˈrektd skæn/ *noun* a file or array search method in which a starting point and a direction of scan is provided, either up or down from the starting point, an address or record number

direct graphics interface standard /daɪˌrekt ˌgræfɪks 'ɪntəfeɪs ˌstændəd/ *noun* full form of **DGIS**

direct image /ˌdaɪrekt 'ɪmɪdʒ/ *noun* an image that is composed directly onto the screen rather than being composed off screen in memory before it is displayed

direct information access network for Europe /daɪˌrekt ˌɪnfəmeɪʃ(ə)n ˌækses ˌnetwɜːk fə 'jʊərəp/ *noun* a package of services offered over the Euronet network. Abbr **DIANE**

direct-insert routine /ˌdaɪrekt ɪn 'sɜːt ruːˌtiːn/ *noun* a routine which can be directly copied into a larger routine or program without the need for a call instruction

direct instruction /ˌdaɪrekt ɪn 'strʌkʃən/ *noun* a program command that contains an operand and the code for the operation to be carried out

directive /daɪ'rektɪv/ *noun* a programming instruction used to control the language translator or compiler

'…directives are very useful for selecting parts of the code for particular purposes' [*Personal Computer World*]

directive statement /daɪˌrektɪv 'steɪtmənt/ *noun* a program instruction used to control the language translator or compiler

direct memory access /daɪˌrekt 'mem(ə)ri ˌækses/ *noun* full form of **DMA** ○ *direct memory access transfer between the main memory and the second processor*

direct memory access channel /daɪˌrekt ˌmem(ə)ri 'ækses ˌtʃæn(ə)l/ *noun* a high-speed data transfer link

direct mode /daɪ'rekt məʊd/ *noun* the process of typing in a command which is executed once carriage return has been pressed

Director /daɪ'rektə/ a trade name for multimedia authoring software developed by Macromedia that uses a grid to allow a user to control elements over time

directory /daɪ'rekt(ə)ri/ *noun* **1.** a method of organising the files stored on a disk, into groups of files or further sub-directories ○ *The disk directory shows file name, date and time of creation.* **2.** full

form **DIR** (NOTE: The plural is **directories**.)

COMMENT: A directory is best imagined as a folder within a drawer of a filing cabinet: the folder can contain files or other folders.

directory services /daɪ'rekt(ə)ri ˌsɜːvɪsɪz/ *noun* a method of listing all the users and resources linked to a network in a simple and easy-to-access way so that a user can locate another user by name rather than by a complex network address ○ *With directory services installed, it's much easier for our users to find and connect to the shared printers.*

directory synchronisation /daɪ 'rekt(ə)ri ˌsɪŋkrənaɪ'zeɪʃ(ə)n/ *noun* a way of ensuring that the files stored in similar directories on two computers contain the same, up-to-date information

directory website /də,rekt(ə)ri 'websaɪt/ *noun* a website that contains a list of other websites, usually organised into sections and often with a search feature (NOTE: Yahoo! (www.yahoo.com) is one of the best-known directories and lists over half a million websites.)

direct page register /daɪˌrekt 'peɪdʒ ˌredʒɪstə/ *noun* a register that provides memory page access data when a CPU is carrying out a direct memory access, to allow access to any part of memory

direct reference address /ˌdaɪrekt ˌref(ə)rəns ə'dres/ *noun* a virtual address that can only be altered by indexing

DirectSound /ˌdaɪrekt'saʊnd/ a trade name for a standard within Microsoft Windows for a programming interface used to allow games software to control sound hardware

direct transfer /ˌdaɪrekt 'trænsfɜː/ *noun* a bit-for-bit copy of the contents of one register into another register, including any status bits

dirty bit /'dɜːti bɪt/ *noun* a flag bit set by memory-resident programs to indicate that they have already been loaded into main memory

disable interrupt /dɪsˌeɪb(ə)l 'ɪntərʌpt/ *noun* a command to the CPU to ignore any interrupt signals

disarm /dɪs'ɑːm/ *verb* to prevent an interrupt having any effect

disarmed state /dɪs'ɑːmd steɪt/ *noun* the state of an interrupt that has been disabled and cannot accept a signal

disassemble /ˌdɪsə'semb(ə)l/ *verb* to translate machine code instructions back into assembly language mnemonics (NOTE: disassembles – disassembling – disassembled)

disassembler /ˌdɪsəˈsemblə/ *noun* a piece of software that translates a machine code program back into an assembly language form

disaster dump /dɪˈzɑːstə dʌmp/ *noun* a program and data dump just before or caused by a fatal error or system crash

disc /dɪsk/ *noun* a disc refers only to compact disc, magnetic media uses the spelling 'disk.' Another spelling of **disk** (NOTE: used only in the context of the **compact disc** and **videodisc**. Magnetic media use the spelling **disk**.)

disconnect /ˌdɪskəˈnekt/ *verb* to unplug or break a connection between two devices ○ *Do not forget to disconnect the cable before moving the printer.*

discrete /dɪˈskriːt/ *adjective* referring to values, events, energy or datawhich occur in small individual units ○ *The data word is made up of discrete bits.*

discrete cosine transform /dɪˌskriːt ˈkəʊsaɪn trænsˌfɔːm/ *noun* an algorithm used to encode and compress images. Abbr **DCT**

discrete multi-tone /dɪˌskriːt ˈmʌlti ˌtəʊn/ *noun* full form of **DMT**

discrimination instruction /dɪ ˌskrɪmɪˌneɪʃ(ə)n ɪnˈstrʌkʃən/ *noun* a conditional program instruction that directs control by providing the location of the next instruction to be executed, if a condition is met

discussion group /dɪˈskʌʃ(ə)n gruːp/ *noun* a feature of a website that lets any visitor write and post a message on a particular subject, which is displayed to any other visitors, who can then add their comments in reply to the message

disjunction /dɪsˈdʒʌŋkʃ(ə)n/ *noun* a logical function that produces a true output if any input is true

disjunctive search /dɪsˌdʒʌŋktɪv ˈsɜːtʃ/ *noun* a search for data items that match at least one of a number of keys

disk /dɪsk/ *noun* a flat circular plate coated with a substance that is capable of being magnetised. Data is stored on this by magnetising selective sections to represent binary digits. (NOTE: The alternative spelling **disc** is used only in the context of the **compact disc** and **videodisc**.)

COMMENT: The disk surface is divided into tracks that can be accessed individually; magnetic tapes cannot be accessed in this way.

disk access /dɪsk ˈækses/ *noun* the set of operations required to read from or write to a magnetic disk, including device selection, sector and track address, movement of read/write head to the correct location and access the location on disk

disk access management /ˌdɪsk ˌækses ˈmænɪdʒmənt/ *noun* the process of regulating the users who can access stored data

disk-based /ˈdɪsk beɪsd/ *adjective* referring to an operating system held on floppy or hard disk

disk cache /ˈdɪsk kæʃ/ *noun* a high speed section of memory that is used to temporarily store frequently used data that has been read from the disk (NOTE: The computer checks the cache to see if the data is there before it accesses the (much slower) disk and by using special controller software, this system can dramatically improve apparent disk performance.)

disk cartridge /dɪsk ˈkɑːtrɪdʒ/ *noun* a protective case containing a removable hard disk

disk compression /dɪsk kəmˈpreʃ(ə)n/ *noun* a method of increasing the apparent capacity of a disk to store data by using a special piece of software that compresses the data as it is being saved to disk and then decompresses the data when it is read back

disk compression software /ˌdɪsk kəmˈpreʃ(ə)n ˌsɒftweə/ *noun* a resident software that compresses data as it is written to disk and decompresses it as it is read back

disk controller /dɪsk kənˈtrəʊlə/ *noun* an IC or set of circuits used to translate a request for data by the CPU into control signals for the disk drive, including motor control and access arm movement

disk-controller card /ˈdɪsk kənˌtrəʊlə ˌkɑːd/ *noun* an add-on card that contains all the electronics and connectors to interface a disk drive to a CPU

disk crash /ˈdɪsk kræʃ/ *noun* a fault caused by the read/write head touching the surface of the disk

disk doctor /dɪsk ˈdɒktə/ *noun* a utility that can sometimes repair corrupted data stored on a disk

disk drive /'dɪsk draɪv/ *noun* a device that spins a magnetic disk and controls the position of the read/write head. Also called **disk unit**

disk duplexing /'dɪsk ˌdjuːpleksɪŋ/ *noun* same as **disk mirroring**

diskette /dɪˈsket/ *noun* a light, flexible disk that can store data in a magnetic form, used in most personal computers

disk file /'dɪsk faɪl/ *noun* a number of related records or data items stored under one name on disk

disk formatting /'dɪsk ˌfɔːmætɪŋ/ *noun* the initial setting up of a blank disk with track and sector markers and other control information

disk head /'dɪsk hed/ *noun* a head which reads or writes on a floppy disk

disk index holes /ˌdɪsk 'ɪndeks ˌhəʊlz/ *plural noun* holes around the hub of a disk that provide rotational information to a disk controller, or a number of holes providing sector location indicators on a hard-sectored disk

diskless /'dɪskləs/ *adjective* referring to a workstation which does not have any disk drives for data storage

disk map /'dɪsk mæp/ *noun* a display of the organisation of data on a disk

disk memory /dɪsk 'mem(ə)ri/ *noun* memory held on disk

disk mirroring /'dɪsk ˌmɪrərɪŋ/ *noun* a data protection system in which all or part of a hard disk is duplicated onto another, separate, disk drive. Also called **disk duplexing** (NOTE: Any changes made to the a data on the original drive are duplicated on the mirrored drive.)

disk operating system /ˌdɪsk 'ɒpəreɪtɪŋ ˌsɪstəm/ *noun* full form of **DOS**

disk pack /'dɪsk pæk/ *noun* a number of disks on a single hub, each with its own read/write head

disk partition /dɪsk pɑːˈtɪʃ(ə)n/ *noun* ♦ partition

disk sector /dɪsk 'sektə/ *noun* the smallest area on a magnetic disk that can be addressed by a computer

disk sector formatting /ˌdɪsk ˌsektə 'fɔːmætɪŋ/ *noun* the process of dividing a disk into a series of addressable sectors (NOTE: A table of their addresses is also formed, allowing each sector to be accessed.)

disk storage /dɪsk 'stɔːrɪdʒ/ *noun* the process of using disks as a backing store

disk tools /'dɪsk tuːlz/ *plural noun* software programs that help monitor the performance of a disk drive, maintain it and ensure that it is storing data efficiently

disk track /'dɪsk træk/ *noun* one of a series of thin concentric rings on a magnetic disk, which the read/write head accesses and along which data is stored in separate sectors

disk unit /dɪsk 'juːnɪt/ *noun* same as **disk drive**

disorderly close-down /dɪsˈɔːdəli kləʊs/ *noun* a system crash that did not provide enough warning to carry out an orderly close-down

dispatch /dɪˈspætʃ/, **despatch** /dɪˈspætʃ/ *noun* the action of sending material, information or messages to a location

dispersion /dɪˈspɜːʃ(ə)n/ *noun* a logical function whose output is false if all inputs are true, and true if any input is false

displacement /dɪsˈpleɪsmənt/ *noun* an offset used in an indexed address

display /dɪˈspleɪ/ *noun* a device on which information or images can be presented visually

display adapter /dɪˈspleɪ əˌdæptə/ *noun* a device which allows information in a computer to be displayed on a CRT, interfacing with both the computer and CRT

display attribute /dɪˈspleɪ ˌætrɪbjuːt/ *noun* a variable which defines the shape, size or colour of text or graphics displayed

display character /dɪˈspleɪ ˌkærɪktə/ *noun* a graphical symbol which appears as a printed or displayed item, e.g. one of the letters of the alphabet or a number

display character generator /dɪˈspleɪ ˌkærɪktə ˌdʒenəreɪtə/ *noun* ROM that provides the display circuits with a pattern of dots which form the character

display colour /dɪˈspleɪ ˌkʌlə/ *noun* the colour of characters in a videotext display system

display controller /dɪˈspleɪ kənˌtrəʊlə/ *noun* a device that accepts character or graphics codes and instructions, and converts them into dot-matrix patterns that are displayed on a screen

display cycle /dɪˈspleɪ ˌsaɪk(ə)l/ *noun* the set of operations required to display an image on screen

display element /dɪˈspleɪ ˌelɪmənt/ *noun* 1. (*in graphics*) a basic graphic component such as a background, foreground, text or graphics image **2.** (*in computer graphics*) any component of an image

display format /dɪˈspleɪ ˌfɔːmæt/ *noun* the number of characters that can be displayed on a screen, given as row and column lengths

display highlights /dɪˈspleɪ ˌhaɪlaɪts/ *plural noun* emphasis of certain words or paragraphs by changing character display colour

display line /dɪˈspleɪ laɪn/ *noun* a horizontal printing position for characters in a line of text

display mode /dɪˈspleɪ məʊd/ *noun* a way of referring to the character set to be used, usually graphics or alphanumerics

Display PostScript /dɪˌspleɪ ˈpəʊstskrɪpt/ a trade name for an extension of PostScript that allows PostScript commands to be interpreted and displayed on screen so that a user can see exactly what will appear on the printout

display processor /dɪˈspleɪ ˌprəʊsesə/ *noun* a processor that changes data to a format suitable for a display controller

display register /dɪˈspleɪ ˌredʒɪstə/ *noun* a register that contains character, control or graphical data that is to be displayed

display resolution /dɪˌspleɪ ˌrezəˈluːʃ(ə)n/ *noun* the number of pixels per unit area that a display can clearly show

display screen /dɪˈspleɪ skriːn/ *noun* the physical part of a VDU, terminal or monitor, which allows the user to see characters or graphics (NOTE: It is usually a cathode ray tube, but sometimes LCD or LED displays are used.)

display scrolling /dɪˈspleɪ ˌskrəʊlɪŋ/ *noun* the movement of a screenful of information up or down one line or pixel at a time

display space /dɪˈspleɪ speɪs/ *noun* memory or the amount of screen available to show graphics or text

display unit /dɪˈspleɪ ˌjuːnɪt/ *noun* a computer terminal or piece of equipment that is capable of showing data or information, usually by means of CRT

dissolve /dɪˈzɒlv/ *noun* a special effect that is used in presentation graphics software or multimedia to fade out one image and fade in the next

distance vector protocols /ˌdɪstəns ˈvektə ˌprəʊtəkɒlz/ *plural noun* informa-tion about the different routes over a wide area network that can be used by a router to find the shortest and fastest route to send information

distort /dɪˈstɔːt/ *verb* to introduce unwanted differences between a signal input and output from a device

distortion /dɪˈstɔːʃ(ə)n/ *noun* unwant-ed differences in a signal before and after it has passed through a piece of equipment

distribute /dɪˈstrɪbjuːt/ *verb* to send out data or information to users in a net-work or system (NOTE: distributes – dis-tributing – distributed)

distributed adaptive routing /dɪˌstrɪbjʊtɪd əˌdæptɪv ˈruːtɪŋ/ *noun* the process of directing messages in a packet network switching system by an exchange of information between nodes

distributed component object model /dɪˌstrɪbjʊtɪd kəmˌpəʊnənt ˈɒbdʒekt ˌmɒd(ə)l/ *noun* full form of **DCOM**

distributed database system /dɪˌstrɪbjʊtɪd ˈdeɪtəbeɪs ˌsɪstəm/ *noun* a database system in which the data is stored on several different computers but can be searched as if it is one single location

distributed data processing /dɪˌstrɪbjʊtɪd ˈdeɪtə ˌprəʊsesɪŋ/ *noun* full form of **DDP**

distributed file system /dɪˌstrɪbjʊtɪd ˈfaɪl ˌsɪstəm/ *noun* a system that uses files stored in more than one lo-cation or backing store but processed at a central point

distributed intelligence /dɪˌstrɪbjʊtɪd ɪnˈtelɪdʒ(ə)ns/ *noun* a decen-tralised system in which a number of small micros or mini-computers carry out a set of fixed tasks, rather than one large com-puter

distributed network /dɪˌstrɪbjʊtɪd ˈnetwɜːk/ *noun* a network in which each node can operate as a server storing files or working as a print server

distributed processing /dɪˌstrɪbjʊtɪd ˈprəʊsesɪŋ/ *noun* a technique to enable processors or computers to share tasks amongst themselves most effective-ly, in which each processor completes al-located sub-tasks independently and the results are then recombined

distributed processor /dɪˌstrɪbjʊtɪd ˈprəʊsesə/ *noun* a computer system using many small computers at different work-stations instead of one central computer

distributed system /dɪˌstrɪbˈjʊtɪd
ˈsɪstəm/ *noun* a computer system which
uses more than one processor in different
locations, all connected to a central computer

distribution /ˌdɪstrɪˈbjuːʃ(ə)n/ *noun*
the act of sending information out, especially via a network

distribution network /ˌdɪstrɪ
ˈbjuːʃ(ə)n ˌnetwɜːk/ *noun* ⬧ **LAN, WAN**

dither /ˈdɪðə/ *verb* to create a curve or
line that looks smoother by adding shaded
pixels beside the pixels that make up the
image

dithered colour /ˌdɪðəd ˈkʌlə/ *noun* a
colour that is made up of a pattern of different coloured pixels

divide /dɪˈvaɪd/ *verb* to find out how
many times one number can be contained
in another number ○ *Twenty-one divided
by three is seven.*

dividend /ˈdɪvɪdend/ *noun* an operand
that is divided by a divisor in a division operation

COMMENT: The dividend is divided by the divisor to form the quotient and a remainder.

division /dɪˈvɪʒ(ə)n/ *noun* the act of dividing numbers

divisor /dɪˈvaɪzə/ *noun* an operand used
to divide a dividend in a division operation

DL *abbr* download

DLL /ˌdiː el ˈel/ *noun* a library of utility
programs that can be called from a main
program. Full form **dynamic link library**

DLL file /ˌdiː el ˈel ˌfaɪl/ *noun* a file containing a library of routines that can be
used by another program

DLP /ˌdiː el ˈpiː/ *noun* a method of pro-
jecting an image using an electronic chip
that contains thousands of tiny mirrors.
Full form **digital light processing**

DMA /ˌdiː em ˈeɪ/ *noun* a direct rapid link
between a peripheral and a computer's
main memory, which avoids accessing
routines for each item of data read. Full
form **direct memory access**

'A 32-bit DMA controller, 16-bit video I/O ports and
I/O filters complete the chip.' [*Computing*]

DMA controller /ˌdiː em ˈeɪ kən
ˌtrəʊlə/ *noun* an interface IC that controls
high-speed data transfer between a high-
speed peripheral and main memory, and
will usually also halt or cycle steal from
the CPU

DMA cycle stealing /ˌdiː em eɪ
ˈsaɪk(ə)l ˌstiːlɪŋ/ *noun* a CPU allowing
the DMA controller to send data over the

bus during clock cycles when it performs
internal or NOP instructions

DML *abbr* data manipulation language

DMS *abbr* data management system

DMT /ˌdiː em ˈtiː/ *noun* technology that
uses digital signal processors to create
sound signals that carry digital video,
sound, image and data over cable at high
speed. Full form **discrete multi-tone**

DNS /ˌdiː en ˈes/ *noun* a distributed database used in an Internet system to map
names to addresses. Full form **domain
name system** (NOTE: For example, you
can use the name
'www.bloomsbury.com' to locate the
Bloomsbury Publishing website rather
than a complex network address (called
the IP address).)

dock /dɒk/ *verb* to connect a laptop computer to a special docking station on a desk
to give it the same resources as a normal
desktop

docking station¹ /ˈdɒkɪŋ ˌsteɪʃ(ə)n/
noun a piece of hardware with an opening
into which a portable computer can be inserted when it is recharged or used in expanded operations

docking station² /ˈdɒkɪŋ ˌsteɪʃ(ə)n/,
docking unit /ˈdɒkɪŋ ˌjuːnɪt/ *noun* a
special base unit that allows a laptop computer to be inserted into it and provide the
same resources as a normal desktop, e.g.
mains power, a network adapter, connection to a full-size monitor and extra expansion ports

document *noun* /ˈdɒkjʊmənt/ a file
containing text created with a word-processor ■ *verb* /ˈdɒkjʊˌment/ to write a description of a process

document assembly /ˈdɒkjʊmənt ə
ˌsembli/ *noun* the process of creating a
new file by combining two or more sections or complete documents. Also called
document merge

documentation /ˌdɒkjʊmenˈteɪʃ(ə)n/
noun the set of information, notes and diagrams that describe the function, use and
operation of a piece of hardware or software

document content architecture
/ˌdɒkjʊmənt ˈkɒntent ˌɑːkɪtektʃə/
noun full form of **DCA**

document image management
/ˌdɒkjʊmənt ˌɪmɪdʒ ˈmænɪdʒmənt/
noun full form of **DIM**

document image processing
/ˌdɒkjʊmənt ˈɪmɪdʒ ˌprəʊsesɪŋ/ *noun*

the process of scanning paper documents, performing OCR on the contents and storing this on disk so that it can be searched for. Abbr **DIP**

document interchange architecture/document content architecture /ˌdɒkjʊmənt ˌɪntətʃeɪndʒ ˌɑːkɪtektʃə ˌdɒkjʊmənt ˈkɒntent ˌɑːkɪtektʃə/ *noun* full form of **DIA/DCA**

document merge /ˈdɒkjʊmənt mɜːdʒ/ *noun* same as **document assembly**

document object model /ˌdɒkjʊmənt ˌɒbdʒekt ˈmʊd(ə)l/ *noun* full form of **DOM**

document processing /ˌdɒkjʊmənt ˈprəʊsesɪŋ/ *noun* the processing of documents, e.g. invoices, by a computer

document reader /ˈdɒkjʊmənt ˌriːdə/ *noun* a device which converts written or typed information to a form that a computer can understand and process

document recovery /ˌdɒkjʊmənt rɪˈkʌv(ə)ri/ *noun* a program which allows a document which has been accidentally deleted to be recovered

Dolby /ˈdɒlbi/ a research laboratory that provides ways to improve the quality of recorded sound

Dolby AC-3 /ˌdɒlbi eɪ esiː ˈθriː/ an algorithm used to provide sound-sound effects (NOTE: This system has been adopted by computer and entertainment industries as a standard for audio on movies and digital recordings.)

Dolby Digital /ˌdɒlbi ˈdɪdʒɪt(ə)l/ a trade name for a multichannel audio compression and transmission system that uses 5.1 channels

Dolby system /ˈdɒlbi ˌsɪstəm/ a trade name for a system for reducing background noise for recordings

dollar sign /ˈdɒlə saɪn/ *noun* a printed or written character ($) used in some programming languages to identify a variable as a string type

DOM /ˌdiː əʊ ˈem/ *noun* a scheme that describes how the different parts of a webpage, the text, images and hyperlinks, are represented. Full form **document object model**

COMMENT: Each item is an object and has a set of attributes that defines how it is displayed and managed by a web browser Dynamic HTML (DHTML) uses DOM to change how a webpage is displayed by a user's web browser – currently, the Microsoft and Net-scape web browsers use different DOM specifications.

domain /dəʊˈmeɪn/ *noun* an area or group of nodes in a network □ **in the public domain** (information or program) which belongs to and is available to the public

domain name /dəʊˈmeɪn neɪm/ *noun* a unique name that identifies the location of an Internet server or computer on the Internet

COMMENT: The domain name 'bloomsbury.com' is registered to the Bloomsbury Publishing website. The domain name is in a convenient text format, but refers to a physical address that locates the computer that stores the website for the domain name. This physical address is called the IP address and is in the format '194.33.322.22' – the domain name system (DNS) is used to translate the domain name into its correct IP address. The domain name is made up of two or three parts, separated by a 'dot'. There are some global thematic suffixes such as .com (company) and .net (network) which are not restricted by country. For example, 'bloomsbury.com' has the company name 'bloomsbury' followed by the domain type 'com' (for company). There are also country suffixes such as '.au' for Australia, '.cn' for China, '.uk' for the UK and '.de' for Germany, within which each country can have its own private system of domain names. Some of these might look the same as the global thematic suffixes (.net.uk, .org.uk, etc.), but are restricted to the UK, e.g. co.uk, .nhs.uk, .plc.uk and .ltd.uk.

domain name registration /dəʊ ˌmeɪn neɪm ˌredʒɪˈstreɪʃ(ə)n/ *noun* the registration of a domain name with the relevant local registration office. ◊ **DNS, IP address**

COMMENT: Before you can use a domain name, you must check that it is available and then fill in an application form with your country's local registration office (your ISP will also be able to help). Domain name registration is centred in the USA at the InterNIC organisation; you can also register a domain name directly with the InterNIC using its online order form (www.internic.net). Once the domain name has been approved, it will be assigned a unique IP address that will be used by your ISP to modify the DNS to allow your website to be located by other users.

domain name server /dəʊˌmeɪn neɪm ˈsɜːvə/ *noun* a computer on the Internet that stores part or all of the domain name system database

domain name system /dəʊˈmeɪn neɪm ˌsɪstəm/ *noun* full form of **DNS**

dongle /ˈdɒŋgl/ *noun* a coded circuit or chip that has to be present in a system before a piece of copyright software will run

do-nothing instruction /ˌduː ˈnʌθɪŋ ɪnˌstrʌkʃən/ noun a programming instruction that does not carry out any action other than increasing the program counter to the next instruction address

dopant /ˈdəʊpənt/ noun a chemical substance that is diffused or implanted onto the substrate of a chip during manufacture, to provide it with n- or p-type properties

dope /dəʊp/ verb to introduce a dopant into a substance (NOTE: dopes – doping – doped)

doped /ˈdəʊpt/ adjective referring to a chip which has had a dopant added

DOR /ˌdiː əʊ ˈɑː/ noun the recording of signals in binary form as small holes in the surface of an optical or compact disk which can then be read by laser. Full form **digital optical recording**

DOS /dɒs/ noun a section of the operating system software, that controls the disk and file access. Full form **disk operating system**

DOS prompt /ˈdɒs prɒmpt/ noun an indicator that shows that DOS is ready to accept a command typed in at the keyboard

dot address /ˈdɒt əˌdres/ noun the common method of writing Internet addresses in the form of symbols, A.B.C.D., where each letter represents one byte of a four-byte address

dot addressable /ˈdɒt əˌdresəb(ə)l/ adjective referring to a display adapter that allows software to control each pixel on the display

dot command /dɒt kəˈmɑːnd/ noun a method of writing instructions with a full stop followed by the command, used mainly for embedded commands in word-processor systems

dot matrix /ˌdɒt ˈmeɪtrɪks/ noun a method of forming characters by use of dots inside a rectangular matrix

dot-matrix printer /ˌdɒt ˈmeɪtrɪks ˌprɪntə/ noun a printer in which the characters are made up by a series of closely spaced dots (NOTE: The printer produces a page line by line. Dot-matrix printers can be used either for printing using a ribbon or for thermal or electrostatic printing.)

dot pitch /ˈdɒt pɪtʃ/ noun the spacing between two adjacent pixels displayed on a monitor ○ The smaller the dot pitch, the sharper the image displayed.

dot prompt /ˈdɒt prɒmpt/ noun (in dBASE programming language) a command prompt displayed as a single dot on screen

dots per inch /ˌdɒtz pɜːr ˈɪntʃ/ plural noun a standard method used to describe the resolution capabilities of a page printer or scanner ○ Some laser printers offer high resolution printing: 400 dots per inch. Abbr **dpi, d.p.i.**

dotted-decimal-notation /ˌdɒtɪd ˈdesɪm(ə)l/ noun a method of writing a domain name, email address or other IP network address using a decimal point, or full stop, to separate the numeric parts of the address (NOTE: For example 'www.bloomsbury.com' is the domain name that can be written in dotted-decimal-notation as '133.223.33.22')

double buffering /ˌdʌb(ə)l ˈbʌfərɪŋ/ noun the use of two buffers together so that one can be read while the other is accepting data

double-click /ˌdʌb(ə)l ˈklɪk/ noun two rapid press-release actions on a mouse button; normally to start a program or select an option

double data rate memory /ˌdʌb(ə)l ˌdeɪtə reɪt ˈmem(ə)ri/ noun full form of **DDR memory**

double density /ˌdʌb(ə)l ˈdensəti/ noun a system to double the storage capacity of a disk drive by doubling the number of bits which can be put on the disk surface. Abbr **DD**

double density disk /ˌdʌb(ə)l ˌdensɪti ˈdɪsk/ noun a disk that can store two bits of data per unit area, compared to a standard disk

double ended queue /ˌdʌb(ə)l ˌendɪd ˈkjuː/ noun a queue in which new items can be added to either end. Also called **deque**

double frequency scanning /ˌdʌb(ə)l ˌfriːkwənsi ˈskænɪŋ/ noun (in CD-i) method of doubling the vertical resolution of a monitor by scanning at twice the normal rate

double-length arithmetic /ˌdʌb(ə)l ˌleŋθ əˈrɪθmətɪk/ noun the use of two data words to store a number, providing greater precision. Also called **double-precision arithmetic**

double precision /ˌdʌb(ə)l prɪˈsɪʒ(ə)n/ noun the process of using two data words to store a number, providing greater precision

double-precision   arithmetic
/ˌdʌb(ə)l prɪˌsɪʒ(ə)n əˈrɪθmətɪk/ *noun*
same as **double-length arithmetic**

double-precision integer /ˌdʌb(ə)l
prɪˌsɪʒ(ə)n ˈɪntɪdʒə/ *noun* a unit of two
computer words used to store an integer

double-sided disk /ˌdʌb(ə)l ˌsaɪdɪd
ˈdɪsk/ *noun* a disk which can store information on both sides

double-sided disk drive /ˌdʌb(ə)l
ˌsaɪdɪd ˈdɪsk ˌdraɪv/ *noun* a disk drive
which can access data on double-sided
disks

**double-sided   printed   circuit
board** /ˌdʌb(ə)l ˌsaɪdɪd ˌprɪntɪd ˈsɜːkɪt
ˌbɔːd/ *noun* a circuit board with conducting tracks on both sides

DoubleSpace /ˌdʌb(ə)lˈspeɪs/ software program that is part of MS-DOS 6
and is used to provide disk compression

double speed /ˌdʌb(ə)l ˈspiːd/ *noun*
the high speed at which a CD-ROM disc is
spun by a drive, normally 460 rpm

double-speed drive /ˌdʌb(ə)l spiːd
ˈdraɪv/ *noun* a CD-ROM drive that spins
the disc at twice the speed of a normal
drive

double strike /ˈdʌb(ə)l straɪk/ *noun*
the process of printing a character twice in
order to make it appear bolder

doublet /ˈdʌblət/ *noun* a word made up
of two bits. Also called **dyad**

double word /ˈdʌb(ə)l wɜːd/ *noun* a
unit of two bytes of data handled as one
word, often used for address data

down /daʊn/ *adjective, adverb* referring
to computers or programs that are temporarily not working ○ *The computer system
went down twice during the afternoon.*
Opposite **up**

download /ˌdaʊnˈləʊd/ *verb* **1.** to load a
program or section of data from a remote
computer via a telephone line ○ *There is
no charge for downloading public domain
software from the BBS.* Opposite **upload**
2. to load data from a CPU to a small computer. Opposite **upload** **3.** to send printer
font data stored on a disk to a printer,
where it will be stored in temporary memory or RAM

'The cards will also download the latest version of
the network drivers from the server.' [*Computing*]

downloadable font /ˌdaʊnləʊdəb(ə)l
ˈfɒnt/ *noun* a font or typeface which is
stored on a disk and can be downloaded to
a printer and stored in temporary memory.
Also called **resident font**

downsize /ˈdaʊnsaɪz/ *verb* to move a
company from a computer system based
around a central mainframe computer to a
networked environment, usually using
PCs as workstations, in which the workstations are intelligent ○ *Downsizing is more
cost effective and gives more processing
power to the end-user.* (NOTE: downsizes –
downsizing – downsized)

downstream /ˈdaʊnstriːm/ *noun* the
transmission of data on a network away
from a central distribution point

downtime /ˈdaʊntaɪm/, **down time**
noun a period of time during which a computer system is not working or usable. Opposite **uptime**

downward compatibility /ˌdaʊnwəd
kəmˌpætəˈbɪlɪti/ *noun* the ability of a
complex computer system to work with a
simple computer

dp, DP *abbr* data processing

DPA /ˌdiː piː ˈeɪ/ *noun* a technique of
loading protocol stacks in memory only if
they are required for a particular session.
Full form **demand protocol architecture**

DPCM /ˌdiː piː siː ˈem/ *noun* a method of
encoding an analog signal into a digital
form in which the value recorded is equal
to the difference between the current and
previous samples. Full form **differential
pulse coded modulation**

d.p.i. /ˌdiː piː ˈaɪ/, **dpi** *abbr* dots per inch
○ *a 300 d.p i. black and white A4 monitor*
COMMENT: 300 d.p.i. is the normal industry
standard for a laser printer.

DPM *abbr* data processing manager

draft printing /drɑːft ˈprɪntɪŋ/ *noun*
low quality, high speed printing

draft quality /drɑːft ˈkwɒlɪti/ *noun* the
state of a printed output that is formatted
and readable but might not have all the illustrations in place or uses ragged typeface, which are both faster to print

drag /dræg/ *verb* to move a mouse while
holding the button down, so moving an image or icon on screen ○ *You can enlarge a
frame by clicking inside its border and
dragging to the position wanted.* (NOTE:
dragging – dragged)

'…press the mouse button and drag the mouse: this
produces a dotted rectangle on the screen; you can
easily enlarge the frame by dragging from any of the
eight black rectangles round the border, showing that
it is selected' [*Desktop Publishing*]

drag and click /ˌdræg ən ˈklɪk/ *verb* to
hold down a mouse button while moving
the mouse, so moving the object selected

drag and drop /ˌdræg ən ˈdrɒp/ *verb* to drag a section of text or icon or object onto another program icon which starts this program and inserts the data ○ *Drag and drop the document icon onto the word-processor icon and the system will start the program and load the document.*

drag image /dræg ˈɪmɪdʒ/ *noun* the cursor, icon or outline image that is displayed when you drag an object across the screen

DRAM /ˈdiː ræm/ *abbr* dynamic random access memory

draw direct /ˌdrɔː daɪˈrekt/ *noun* the process of drawing an object directly to the screen rather than to an off-screen memory buffer

drawing program /ˈdrɔːɪŋ ˌprəʊgræm/ *noun* a piece of software that allows the user to draw and design on screen

drawing tool /ˈdrɔːɪŋ tuːl/ *noun* any one of a range of functions in a paint program that allows the user to draw (NOTE: Normally displayed as icons in a toolbar, the drawing tools might include a circle-draw, line-draw and freehand drawing tool.)

drive /draɪv/ *noun* a part of a computer which operates a disk

drive array /draɪv əˈreɪ/ *noun* a system of multiple hard disk drives linked together with an intelligent controller that uses the drives to store multiple copies of the data on each drive for reliability or parts of each data on each drive for speed

drive bay /ˈdraɪv beɪ/ *noun* same as **bay**

drive designator /ˈdraɪv ˌdezɪɡneɪtə/ *noun* same as **drive letter**

drive letter /draɪv ˈletə/, **drive designator** /ˈdraɪv ˌdezɪɡneɪtə/ *noun* a letter that denotes the disk drive currently being used, e.g. C, which is usually the hard disk in a personal computer

driver /ˈdraɪvə/ *noun* a piece of software that sits between Windows and a peripheral and translates the instructions from Windows into a form that the peripheral can understand. Also called **device driver, device handler**

DRO /ˌdiː ɑːr ˈəʊ/ *noun* a form of storage medium that loses its data after it has been read. Full form **destructive readout**

drop cable /drɒp ˈkeɪb(ə)l/ *noun* a section of cable that links an adapter fitted in a workstation to the main network cable, or sometimes to a transceiver or T-connector in the main network cable

drop dead halt /ˌdrɒp ded ˈhɔːlt/ *noun* a program instruction from the user or an error that causes the program to stop without allowing recovery

drop-down list box /ˌdrɒp daʊn ˈlɪst/ *noun* a list of options for an entry that appears when you move the cursor to the entry field

drop-down menu /ˌdrɒp daʊn ˈmenjuː/ *noun* a menu that appears below a menu title when it is selected

drop in /ˌdrɒp ˈɪn/ *noun* a small piece of dirt on a disk or tape surface, which does not allow data to be recorded on that section

drop out /ˌdrɒp ˈaʊt/ *noun* the failure of a small piece of tape or disk to be correctly magnetised for the accurate storage of data

drum /drʌm/ *noun* an early type of magnetic computer storage

drum plotter /ˈdrʌm ˌplɒtə/ *noun* a computer output device that consists of a movable pen and a piece of paper around a drum that can be rotated, creating patterns and text when both are moved in various ways

dry contact /draɪ ˈkɒntækt/ *noun* a faulty electrical connection, often causing an intermittent fault

dry run /draɪ ˈrʌn/ *noun* an act of running a program with test data to check that everything works

DS-0 /ˌdiː es ˈzɪərəʊ/ *noun* one single circuit in a high-speed T-1 data transmission line, capable of transmitting information in 8-bit frames at a rate of 8,000 frames per second, equal to 64 Kbits/second. Full form **digital signal level zero**

DS-1 /ˌdiː es ˈwʌn/ *noun* a standard that defines the way data is formatted and transmitted over a T-1 line. Full form **digital signal level one**

DSL /ˌdiː es ˈel/ *noun* a system of transmitting data at high speed over standard telephone copper wire. Full form **digital subscriber line**

COMMENT: One of the most popular DSL implementations is the ADSL (asymmetric digital subscriber line) scheme that provides a permanent, high-speed connection to the Internet over standard telephone lines.

DSP /ˌdiː es ˈpiː/ *noun* a special integrated circuit used to manipulate digital signals. Full form **digital signal processing**

DSR /ˌdiː es ˈɑː/ *noun* a signal from a device that it is ready to accept data, occurring after a DTR signal is received. Full form **data set ready**

DSTP /ˌdiː es tiː ˈpiː/ *noun* a scheme used to store and retrieve web-based data using the XML page markup system. Full form **data space transfer protocol**

D-SUB connector /ˌdiː sʌb kəˈnektə/ *noun* a video connector commonly used on PC monitors to carry all the video signals in one cable

DSW /ˌdiː es ˈdʌb(ə)l juː/ *noun* a data word transmitted from a device that contains information about its current status. Full form **device status word**

DTE /ˌdiː tiː ˈiː/ *noun* a device at which a communications path starts or finishes. Full form **data terminal equipment**

DTE rate /ˌdiː tiː ˈiː reɪt/ *noun* a measure of how fast a device, especially a modem, can exchange data with another PC taking into account data compression and coding systems (NOTE: The DTE rate is normally much higher than the DCE rate.)

DTMF /ˌdiː tiː em ˈef/ *noun* a method of dialling in a telephone system in which each number on the telephone handset generates two tones. Each row and column of the telephone number grid generates a different tone, so each number will send one tone for the corresponding column and another for the row. Full form **dual tone multi-frequency**. Compare **pulse-dialling** (NOTE: If you press number '5' it will send the tone for row two and for column two.)

D to A converter /ˌdiː tʊ ˌeɪ kən ˈvɜːtə/ *noun* full form **digital to analog converter**. ♦ DAC

DTP /ˌdiː tiː ˈpiː/ *noun* the design, layout and printing of documents using special software, a desktop computer and a printer. Full form **desktop publishing**

DTR /ˌdiː tiː ˈɑː/ *noun* a signal from a device that indicates that it is ready to send data. Full form **data terminal ready**

DTS /ˌdiː tiː ˈes/ *noun* a multichannel audio system. Full form **digital theatre system**

DTV /ˌdiː tiː ˈviː/ *noun* a combination of special software and extra hardware that allows a user to edit video on a PC. Full form **desktop video** (NOTE: The hardware connects the PC to a video recorder or camera and captures the video

frames. The software can then be used to cut individual frames and rearrange the sequence.)

D-type connector /ˌdiː taɪp kəˈnektə/ *noun* a connector that is shaped like an elongated letter D, which prevents the connector from being plugged in upside down ○ *The serial port on a PC uses a 9-pin D-type connector.*

dual /ˈdjuːəl/ *adjective* using two or a pair

dual attachment /ˈdjuːəl ə ˈtætʃmənt/, **dual attached station** /ˌdjuːəl əˌtætʃt ˈsteɪʃ(ə)n/ *noun* a station that connects to both rings in an FDDI network, normally used for fault tolerance

dual bus system /ˌdjuːəl ˈbʌs ˌsɪstəm/ *noun* a way of linking different parts of a system which keeps the memory bus separate from the input/output bus

dual channel /ˌdjuːəl ˈtʃæn(ə)l/ *noun* the use of two separate audio recording paths, as found in stereo equipment

dual clocking /ˈdjuːəl klɒkɪŋ/ *noun* multiplexed data, in which each set of data is available and valid on a different clock pulse or edge

dual column /ˌdjuːəl ˈkɒləm/ *noun* a unit of two separate parallel lists of information

dual homing /ˌdjuːəl ˈhəʊmɪŋ/ *noun* (*in an FDDI system*) a method of arranging cables so that there are two separate routes between servers in case of a fault

dual in-line memory module /ˌdjuːəl ˌɪn laɪn ˈmem(ə)ri ˌmɒdjuːl/ *noun* full form of **DIMM**

dual-in-line package /ˌdjuːəl ɪn laɪn ˈpækɪdʒ/ *noun* full form of **DIL, DIP**

dual port memory /ˌdjuːəl pɔːt ˈmem(ə)ri/ *noun* memory with two sets of data and memory lines to allow communications between CPUs

dual processor /ˌdjuːəl ˈprəʊsesə/ *noun* a computer system with two processors for faster program execution

dual-scan display /ˌdjuːəl skæn dɪ ˈspleɪ/ *noun* a colour LCD screen that updates the image on screen in two passes

dual systems /ˌdjuːəl ˈsɪstəmz/ *plural noun* two computer systems, working in parallel on the same data, with the same instructions, to ensure high reliability

dual tone multi-frequency /ˌdjuːəl təʊn ˌmʌlti ˈfriːkwənsi/ *noun* full form of **DTMF**

dub /dʌb/ *verb* to add sound effects to an animation, multimedia presentation, film or video (NOTE: dubbing – dubbed)

duct /dʌkt/ *noun* a pipe containing cables, providing a tidy and protective surrounding for a group of cables

dumb /dʌm/ *adjective* referring to a device such as a computer terminal that is only able to transmit information to a computer or receive information from it, but cannot process data itself

dumb terminal /dʌm 'tɜːmɪn(ə)l/ *noun* a peripheral that can only transmit and receive data from a computer, but is not capable of processing data. Compare **smart terminal**

dummy /'dʌmi/ *noun* an imitation product used to test the reaction of potential customers to its design

dummy instruction /'dʌmi ɪn ˌstrʌkʃən/ *noun* same as **blank instruction**

dummy variable /ˌdʌmi 'veəriəb(ə)l/ *noun* a variable set up to satisfy the syntax of a language but replaced when the program is executed

dump /dʌmp/ *noun* **1.** data which has been copied from one device to another for storage **2.** the transferring of data to a disk for storage **3.** *US* a printout of the contents of all or selected data in memory ■ *verb* to move data from one device or storage area to another ○ *The account results were dumped to the backup disk.*

dump and restart /ˌdʌmp ən 'riːstɑːt/ *noun* software that will stop a program execution, dump any relevant data or program status then restart the program

dump point /'dʌmp pɔɪnt/ *noun* a point in a program where the program and its data are saved onto backing store to minimise the effects of any future faults

duodecimal number system /djuːəʊˌdesɪm(ə)l 'nʌmbə ˌsɪstəm/ *noun* a number system with a radix of 12

duplex /'djuːpleks/ *noun* the simultaneous transmission of two signals on one line

duplex circuit /'djuːpleks ˌsɜːkɪt/ *noun* an electronic circuit used to transmit data in two directions simultaneously

duplex computer /'djuːpleks kəm ˌpjuːtə/ *noun* a unit of two identical computer systems used in an on-line application, with one used as a backup in case of failure of the other

duplexing /'djuːpleksɪŋ/ *noun* a technique to increase the fault tolerance of net-works by using two identical controllers and disk drives (NOTE: Data is written to both via a separate controller. If one goes wrong, the second device is switched in under software control with no effect to the user. This is a more fault-tolerant system than disk mirroring.)

duplex operation /ˌdjuːpleks ˌɒpə 'reɪʃ(ə)n/ *noun* the transmission of data in two directions simultaneously

duty-rated /'djuːti rætd/ *adjective* referring to the maximum number of operations that a device can perform in a set time to a certain specification

DVD /ˌdiː viː 'diː/ *noun* a way of storing over 17Gb of data on a CD-ROM type disc. Full form **digital versatile disc, digital videodisc**

DVD-A /ˌdiː viː 'diː eɪ/ *noun* an audio DVD

DVD-RAM /ˌdiː viː 'diː ræm/ *noun* a DVD disc drive that allows a user to write, erase and rewrite data onto a DVD disc

DVD-Recordable /ˌdiː viː diː rɪ 'kɔːdəb(ə)l/ *noun* a DVD disc drive that allows a user to write data once onto a DVD disc. Abbr **DVD-R**

DVD-ROM /ˌdiː viː 'diː rɒm/ *noun* a DVD disc drive that can read a DVD disc and provides data transfer rates equal to a standard nine-times CD-ROM

DVD+RW /ˌdiː viː diː plʌs ɑː 'dʌb(ə)l juː/ *noun* a type of rewritable DVD disc that allows a user to store data on the disc (NOTE: The DVD disc offers much greater storage capacity than a standard compact disc in a similar-sized disc. This standard was developed by Hewlett-Packard, Philips and Sony and has a capacity of 3GB per side.)

DVD-video /ˌdiː viː 'diː 'vɪdiəʊ/ *noun* a standard that defines how full-length films can be compressed and stored on a DVD disc and played back on a dedicated player attached to a television set or viewed on a computer fitted with a DVD drive

DVE /ˌdiː viː 'iː/ *noun* special effects carried out by a PC on a video sequence; e.g., a fade between two sequences or a dissolve. Full form **digital video effects**

DV-I /ˌdiː viː 'aɪ/ *noun* a system that defines how video and audio signals should be compressed and displayed on a computer. Full form **digital video interactive**

DVI connector /ˌdiː viː 'aɪ kəˌnektə/ *noun* a connector on a monitor or graphics equipment for video signals (NOTE: DVI-D supports digital video signals, DVI-I supports both analog and digital signals.)

Dvorak keyboard /ˌdvɔːræk 'kiːbɔːd/ *noun* a keyboard layout that is more efficient to use than a normal QWERTY keyboard layout

DX /ˌdiː/ 'eks/ *suffix* used after an Intel processor model number to signify that the processor has a floating-point arithmetic unit, a 32-bit data path and a built-in cache

dyad /'daɪæd/ *noun* same as **doublet**

dyadic Boolean operation /daɪ ˌædɪk ˌbuːliən ˌɒpə'reɪʃ(ə)n/ *noun* a logical operation that produces an output from two inputs

dyadic operation /daɪˌædɪk ˌɒpə 'reɪʃ(ə)n/ *noun* a binary operation using two binary operands

dye-polymer recording /ˌdaɪ 'pɒlɪmə rɪˌkɔːdɪŋ/ *noun* (*in optical disks*) recording method which creates minute changes in a thin layer of dye embedded in the plastic optical disk (NOTE: Dye-polymer recording has one big advantage – that the data stored on the optical disk using this method can be erased.)

dye-sublimation printer /daɪ sʌblɪ ˌmeɪʃ(ə)n 'prɪntə/ *noun* a high-quality colour printer that produces images by squirting tiny drops of coloured ink onto paper ○ *The new dye-sublimation printer can produce colour images at a resolution of 300dpi.*

dynamic /daɪ'næmɪk/ *adjective* referring to data which can change with time

dynamic allocation /daɪˌnæmɪk ˌælə 'keɪʃ(ə)n/ *noun* a system in which resources are allocated during a program run, rather than being determined in advance

dynamically redefinable character set /daɪˌnæmɪkli riːdɪˌfaɪnəb(ə)l 'kærɪktə ˌset/ *noun* a computer or videotext character set that can be changed when required

dynamic buffer /daɪˌnæmɪk 'bʌfə/ *noun* a buffer whose size varies with demand

dynamic data exchange /daɪ ˌnæmɪk 'deɪtə ɪksˌtʃeɪndʒ/ *noun* full form of **DDE**

dynamic data structure /daɪˌnæmɪk 'deɪtə ˌstrʌktʃə/ *noun* a structure of a data management system which can be changed or adapted

dynamic dump /daɪˌnæmɪk 'dʌmp/ *noun* a dump that is carried out periodically during a program run

dynamic host configuration protocol /daɪˌnæmɪk həʊst kənˌfɪgjʊ 'reɪʃ(ə)n ˌprəʊtəkɒl/ *noun* full form of **DHCP**

dynamic link library /daɪˌnæmɪk 'lɪŋk ˌlaɪbrəri/ *noun* full form of **DLL**

dynamic memory /daɪˌnæmɪk 'mem(ə)ri/ *noun* same as **dynamic storage**

dynamic multiplexing /daɪˌnæmɪk 'mʌltɪpleksɪŋ/ *noun* a multiplexing method which allocates time segments to signals according to demand

dynamic RAM /daɪˌnæmɪk 'ræm/ *noun* same as **dynamic storage**

dynamic random access memory /daɪˌnæmɪk ˌrændəm ˌækses 'mem(ə)ri/ *noun* same as **dynamic storage**

dynamic relocation /daɪˌnæmɪk ˌriːləʊ'keɪʃ(ə)n/ *noun* the process of moving data or coding or assigning absolute locations during a program execution

dynamic relocation program /daɪ ˌnæmɪk ˌriːləʊ'keɪʃ(ə)n ˌprəʊgræm/ *noun* a program that is moved from one section of memory to another during its run-time without affecting it or its data

dynamic routing /daɪˌnæmɪk 'ruːtɪŋ/ *noun* the process of selecting the shortest or most reliable path for data through exchanges at the time of the connection

dynamic stop /daɪˌnæmɪk 'stɒp/ *noun* a stop in a process where the system tells the user that some action must be taken before the processing will continue

dynamic storage /daɪˌnæmɪk 'stɔːrɪdʒ/ *noun* RAM that requires its contents to be updated regularly. Also called **dynamic memory, dynamic random access memory**

dynamic storage allocation /daɪ ˌnæmɪk 'stɔːrɪdʒ ˌæləkeɪʃ(ə)n/ *noun* the process of allocating memory to a program when it needs it rather than reserving a block before it has run

dynamic subroutine /daɪˌnæmɪk 'sʌbruːtiːn/ *noun* a subroutine whose function must be defined each time it is called

dynamic update /daɪ'næmɪk ˌʌpdeɪt/ *noun* a display, e.g. a graph, updated in real time as new data arrives

DYUV /ˌdiː waɪ juː 'viː/ *noun* a digital video encoding technique in which luminance of a pixel is calculated by the RGB input signal, Y0.6G + 0.3R + O.1B=. Full form **delta YUV** (NOTE: From the value of Y it is possible to calculate the values of U and V as UR – Y; VB – Y.)

E

E *symbol* the hexadecimal number equivalent to decimal number 14

E-1 /i: wʌn/ *noun* a European high-speed telecommunications line that can carry data at 2.048 Mbits/second and is normally divided into hundreds of channels that carry information at a lower transmission rate but are more convenient for customers (NOTE: The US equivalent is **T-1**.)

EAPROM /ˌi: eɪ 'pi: ˌrɒm/ *noun* a version of EAROM which can be programmed. Full form **electrically alterable programmable read-only memory**

early token release /ˌɜːli 'təʊkən rɪ ˌliːs/ *noun* (*in a Token-Ring or FDDI network*) system that allows two tokens to be present on a ring network, useful when traffic is very busy

EAROM /ˌi: 'eɪ ˌrɒm/ *noun* a read-only memory chip whose contents can be programmed by applying a certain voltage to a write pin, and can be erased by light or a reverse voltage. Full form **electrically alterable read-only memory**

earth /ɜːθ/ *noun* a connection in a circuit representing zero potential ○ *All loose wires should be tied to earth.* ■ *verb* to connect an electrical device to the earth ○ *All appliances must be earthed.* (NOTE: US English is **ground**)

earth wire /ɜːθ 'waɪə/ *noun* a connecting wire between an electrical device and the earth, representing zero potential

EBCDIC /ˌi: bi: si: di: aɪ 'si:/ *noun* an 8-bit binary character coding system used mainly on IBM computers, in which each number represents a different character or symbol. It is similar to the ASCII system.

Full form **extended binary coded decimal interchange code**

EBNF /ˌi: bi: en 'ef/ *noun* a more flexible way of defining the syntax of a language. Full form **extended Backus-Naur Form**. ◊ **BNF**

ebook /'i:bʊk/ *noun* an electronic version of a book, in which the text and any pictures are stored in a file format that can then be displayed using special software on a PC or laptop screen or on a dedicated portable or hand-held device or PDA. Also called **electronic book**

EBR /ˌi: bi: 'ɑ:/ *noun* the process of recording the output from a computer directly onto microfilm using an electron beam. Full form **electron beam recording**

e-business /'i: ˌbɪznəs/ *noun* **1.** a company that does business on the Internet **2.** business activity that is carried out using the Internet

echo /'ekəʊ/ *noun* the return of a signal back to the source from which it was transmitted (NOTE: The plural is **echoes**.) ■ *verb* to return a received signal along the same transmission path (NOTE: echoes - echoing – echoed)

echo cancellation /'ekəʊ ˌkænsəleɪʃ(ə)n/ *noun* a technique used in high speed modems to remove echo signals from the line

echo check /'ekəʊ tʃek/ *noun* a procedure in which each character received at a terminal is returned to the transmitter and checked to ensure accurate data transmission

ECL /ˌi: si: 'el/ *noun* a high-speed logic circuit design using the emitters of the transistors as output connections to other stages. Full form **emitter coupled logic**

ECMA *abbr* European Computer Manufacturers Association

ECMA symbol /ˌi: si: em 'eɪ ˌsɪmbəl/ *noun* any one of a standard set of symbols used to draw flowcharts

ECML /ˌi: si: em 'el/ *abbr* electronic commerce modelling language

e-commerce /'i: ˌkɒmɜːs/ *noun* a the process of buying and selling products on the Internet. Also called **electronic commerce**

ECP /ˌi: si: 'pi:/ *noun* a system developed by Microsoft to improve the performance and functionality of the parallel printer port. Full form **enhanced communication port**

EDAC /ˌi: di: eɪ 'si:/ *noun* a forward error correction system for data communications. Full form **error detection and correction**

EDC /ˌi: di: 'si:/ *abbr* electronic data capture

edge /edʒ/ *noun* a side of a flat object

edge board /'edʒ bɔːd/ *noun* a printed circuit board that has a series of contact strips along one edge allowing it to be inserted into an edge connector

edge card /'edʒ kɑːd/ *noun* same as **edge board**

edge connector /edʒ kə'nektə/ *noun* a long connector with a slot containing metal contacts to allow it to make electrical contact with an edge board

'Connections to the target board are made via IC test clips or the edge connector.' [*Electronics Today*]

edge detection /edʒ dɪ'tekʃ(ə)n/ *noun* an algorithm and routines used in image recognition to define the edges of an object

edge notched card /ˌedʒ nɒtʃt 'kɑːd/ *noun* a paper card which has punched holes along an edge to represent data

edge-triggered /edʒ 'trɪgəd/ *adjective* referring to a process or circuit which is clocked or synchronised by the changing level of a clock signal rather than the level itself

EDI /ˌi: di: 'aɪ/ *noun* a system of sending orders, paying invoices or transferring company information over a network or telephone line using an email system. Full form **electronic data interchange** (NOTE: EDI is often used to send instructions to pay money direct from one com-

pany to another, or from one bank to a company.)

edit /'edɪt/ *verb* to change, correct and modify text or programs

edit command /'edɪt kəˌmɑːnd/ *plural noun* a sequence of characters or keys that must be pressed to accomplish a function in an editor

edit decision list /ˌedɪt dɪ'sɪʒ(ə)n ˌlɪst/ *noun* a method of editing video in which the operator defines the points where he or she would like the video to be edited and then this list of actions is used in an on-line edit suite to carry out the edits automatically. Abbr **EDL**

editing run /'edɪtɪŋ rʌn/ *noun* processing carried out to check that new data meets certain requirements before actually analysing the data and its information content

editing term /'edɪtɪŋ tɜːm/ *plural noun* a command word or instruction sequence used when editing

edit key /'edɪt kiː/ *noun* a key which starts a function that makes an editor easier to use ○ *There are several special edit keys – this one will re-format the text.*

editor program /'edɪtə ˌprəʊgræm/ *noun* a piece of software that allows the user to select sections of a file and alter, delete or add to them

edit window /'edɪt ˌwɪndəʊ/ *noun* the area of the screen in which the user can display and edit text or graphics

EDLIN /ˌi: di: el aɪ 'en/ *noun* an MS-DOS system utility that allows a user to make changes to a file on a line-by-line basis

EDO memory /ˌi: di: əʊ 'mem(ə)ri/ *noun* memory technology that provides better performance by being able to find and read data from a memory location in one operation. Full form **extended data output memory** (NOTE: It can also store the last piece of data that was saved to memory in a cache ready to be read back from memory.)

EDP /ˌi: di: 'pi:/ *noun* data processing using computers and electronic devices. Full form **electronic data processing**

EDP capability /ˌi: di: pi: ˌkeɪpə'bɪlɪti/ *noun* the capacity of a word-processor to carry out certain data processing functions

EDS /ˌi: di: 'es/ *noun* a disk drive using a removable disk pack as opposed to a fixed disk. Full form **exchangeable disk storage**

EDT *abbr* electronic depository transfer

EDTV /ˌiː diː tiː ˈviː/ *noun* an enhancement to the NTSC standard for television transmission that offers higher definition and a wide aspect ratio. Full form **extended-definition television** (NOTE: EDTV normally has an aspect ratio of 4:3; if greater than this it is called EDTV-wide.)

edu *suffix* used at the end of an Internet domain name to indicate that the organisation is an educational institution rather than a commercial company

edutainment /ˌedjʊˈteɪnmənt/ *noun* software that is a cross between entertainment or games software and educational products

EEMS /ˌiː iː iː em ˈes/ *noun* a development of EMS that is a standard method of expanding the main memory fitted into an IBM PC. Full form **enhanced expanded memory system.** ◊ **EMS**

EEPROM *abbr* electrically erasable programmable read-only memory

EEROM *abbr* electrically erasable read-only memory

effective address /ɪˌfektɪv əˈdres/ *noun* the address resulting from the modification of an address

effective instruction /ɪˌfektɪv ɪnˈstrʌkʃən/ *noun* the resulting instruction executed after the modification of an original instruction

effective search speed /ɪˌfektɪv ˈsɜːtʃ ˌspiːd/ *noun* the rate of finding a particular section of information from a storage device

effective throughput /ɪˌfektɪv ˈθruːpʊt/ *noun* the average throughput of a processor

EFT /ˌiː ef ˈtiː/ *noun* a system in which computers are used to transmit money to and from banks. Full form **electronic funds transfer**

EFTPOS /ˌiː ef ˌtiː piː əʊ ˈes/ *noun* a terminal at a POS that is linked to a central computer which automatically transfers money from the customer's account to the shop's. Full form **electronic funds transfer point-of-sale**

'Alphameric has extended its range specifically for the hospitality market and has developed an eftpos package which allows most credit and debit cards to be processed.' [*Computing*]

egg timer /ˈeg ˌtaɪmə/ *noun* a computer icon shaped like an hourglass that appears

on the screen to show that a task is being performed but is not yet completed

EIA *abbr* Electronics Industry Association

EIA interface /ˌiː aɪ ˌeɪ ˌɪntəˈfeɪs/ *noun* a standard defining interface signals, transmission rate and power usually used to connect terminals to modems

EIDE /ˌiː aɪ diː ˈiː/ *noun* an enhanced IDE specification that improves the performance and data transfer rates to and from a hard disk drive. Full form **extended integrated drive electronics**

eight-bit /eɪt bɪt/, **8-bit** *adjective* referring to an outdated small, low cost, low power home computer in which the CPU can process eight-bit words

eight-bit byte /eɪt bɪt/, **eight-bit octet** /ˌeɪt bɪt ɒkˈtet/ *noun* a byte made up of eight binary digits

eight-bit octet /ˌeɪt bɪt ɒkˈtet/ *noun* same as **eight-bit byte**

8-bit sample /ˌeɪt bɪt ˈstændəd/ *noun* single sample of an analogue signal which is stored as an 8-bit number, meaning that it can detect 256 possible levels. ◊ **16-bit sample, 24-bit sample**

eight-inch disk, 8-inch disk *noun* a high-capacity floppy disk which is eight inches in diameter

eight-inch drive, 8-inch drive *noun* a disk drive for a eight-inch disk

eighty-column screen, 80-column screen *noun* a screen that can display eighty characters horizontally

eighty-track disk, 80-track disk *noun* a disk formatted to contain eighty tracks

EIS /ˌiː aɪ ˈes/ *noun* easy-to-use software providing information to a manager or executive about his or her company. Full form **executive information system**

EISA /ˌiː aɪ es ˈeɪ/ *noun* a group of PC manufacturers who formed an association to promote a 32-bit expansion bus standard as a rival to the MCA bus standard from IBM. Full form **Electronics Industry Standards Association**

COMMENT: The EISA expansion bus standard is backwards compatible with the older ISA standard of expansion cards, but also features 32-bit data path and allows bus mastering.

either-or operation /ˌaɪðə ˈɔː ˌɒpəreɪʃ(ə)n/ *noun* a logical function that produces a true output if any input is true

either-way operation /ˌaɪðə ˈweɪ ˌɒpəreɪʃ(ə)n/ *noun* data transmission in one direction at a time over a bidirectional channel

elapsed time /ɪˌlæpst 'taɪm/ *noun* the time taken by the user to carry out a task on a computer

elastic banding /ɪ'læstɪk bændɪŋ/ *noun* a method of defining the limits of an image on a computer screen by stretching a boundary around it

elastic buffer /ɪˌlæstɪk 'bʌfə/ *noun* a buffer size that changes according to demand

electrically alterable programmable read-only memory /ɪˌlektrɪkli ˌɔːltərəʊ(ə)l ˌprəʊɡræməb(ə)l ˌriːd ˌəʊnli 'mem(ə)ri/ *noun* full form of **EAPROM**

electrically alterable read-only memory /ɪˌlektrɪkli ˌɔːltərəʊ(ə)l ˌriːd ˌəʊnli 'mem(ə)ri/ *noun* full form of **EAROM**

electrically erasable programmable read-only memory /ɪˌlektrɪkli ɪ ˌreɪzəb(ə)l ˌprəʊɡræməb(ə)l ˌriːd ˌəʊnli 'mem(ə)ri/ *noun* a ROM storage chip which can be programmed and erased using an electrical signal. Abbr **EEPROM**

electrically erasable read-only memory /ɪˌlektrɪkli ɪˌreɪzəb(ə)l ˌriːd ˌəʊnli 'mem(ə)ri/ *noun* an EAROM memory chip whose contents can be programmed by applying a certain voltage to a write pin, and can be erased by light or a reverse voltage. Abbr **EEROM**

electrical polarity /ɪˌlektrɪk(ə)l pəʊ 'lærɪti/ *noun* the definition of whether an electrical signal is positive or negative, indicating whether a point is a source or collector of electrical current (NOTE: Positive polarity terminals are usually marked red, negative are black.)

electric charge /ɪ'lektrɪk tʃɑːdʒ/ *noun* the presence of a number of atoms that are charged, because of an excess or deficiency of electrons

electric current /ɪˌlektrɪk 'kʌrənt/ *noun* the mass movement of electric charge in a conductor

electricity /ɪˌlek'trɪsɪti/ *noun* an electric current used to provide light or heat or power ○ *The electricity was cut off, and the computers crashed.*

electrographic printer /ɪ ˌlektrəʊɡræfɪk 'prɪntə/ *noun* same as **electrostatic printer**

electroluminescence /ˌelektrəʊ ˌluːmɪ'nes(ə)ns/ *noun* light emitted from a phosphor dot when it is struck by an electron or charged particle

electroluminescent /ˌelektrəʊˌluːmɪ 'nes(ə)nt/ *adjective* capable of emitting light due to electroluminescence ○ *The screen coating is electroluminescent.*

electroluminescent display /ɪ ˌlektrəʊluːmɪnesənt dɪ'spleɪ/ *noun* a flat, lightweight display screen made up of two pieces of glass covered with a grid of conductors, separated by a thin layer of gas which luminesces when a point of the grid is selected by two electric signals

electroluminescing /ˌelektrəʊˌluːmɪ 'nesɪŋ/ *adjective* emitting light due to electroluminescence

electromagnetic /ɪˌlektrəʊmæɡ 'netɪk/ *adjective* generating a magnetic field or magnetic effect when supplied with electrical power

electromagnetic interference /ɪ ˌlektrəʊmæɡnetɪk ˌɪntə'fɪərəns/ *noun* full form of **EMI**

electron beam /ɪ'lek,trɒn biːm/ *noun* a narrow, focused stream of electrons moving at high speed in the same direction, often in a vacuum ○ *The electron beam draws the image on the inside of a CRT screen.*

electron beam recording /ɪˌlektrɒn ˌbiːm rɪ'kɔːdɪŋ/ *noun* full form of **EBR**

electron gun /ɪ'lek,trɒn ɡʌn/ *noun* a part of a CRT that produces a beam of electrons. Also called **gun**

electronic agenda /ˌelektrɒnɪk ə 'dʒendə/ *noun* software that allows a user to record appointments for each day

electronic blackboard /ˌelektrɒnɪk 'blækbɔːd/ *noun* a means of transmitting handwritten text and diagrams over a telephone line

electronic book /ˌelektrɒnɪk 'bʊk/ *noun* same as **ebook**

electronic commerce /ˌelektrɒnɪk 'kɒmɜːs/ *noun* same as **e-commerce**

electronic data interchange /ˌelektrɒnɪk 'deɪtə ˌɪntətʃeɪndʒ/ *noun* full form of **EDI**

electronic data processing /ˌelektrɒnɪk 'deɪtə ˌprəʊsesɪŋ/ *noun* full form of **EDP**

electronic data processing capability /ˌelektrɒnɪk ˌdeɪtə ˌprəʊsesɪŋ ˌkeɪpə'bɪlɪti/ *noun* the ability of a word-processor to carry out certain data processing functions

electronic digital computer
/ɪˌelektrɒnɪk ˌdɪdʒɪt(ə)l kəmˈpjuːtə/
noun a digital computer constructed with
electronic components (NOTE: The basic
form uses a CPU, main memory, backing
storage and input/output devices. these
are all implemented with electronic components and integrated circuits.)

electronic filing /ɪˌelektrɒnɪk ˈfaɪlɪŋ/
noun a system of storage of documents
which can be easily retrieved

electronic funds transfer
/ɪˌelektrɒnɪk ˈfʌndz ˌtrænsfɜː/ *noun* full
form of **EFT**

**electronic funds transfer point-of-
sale** /ɪˌelektrɒnɪk ˌfʌndz ˌtrænsfɜː
ˌpɔɪnt əv ˈseɪl/ *noun* full form of **EFT-
POS**

electronic mail /ɪˌelɪktrɒnɪk ˈmeɪl/
noun same as **email**

electronic mailbox /ɪˌelektrɒnɪk
ˈmeɪlbɒks/ *noun* a system for storing
messages sent by email until the person to
whom they were sent is ready to read them
○ *When I log onto the network, I always
check my electronic mailbox for new messages.*

electronic pen /ɪˌelektrɒnɪk ˈpen/
noun a light pen or wand. Also called
electronic stylus

electronic point-of-sale
/ɪˌelektrɒnɪk ˌpɔɪnt əv ˈseɪl/ *noun* full
form of **EPOS**

electronic publishing /ɪˌelektrɒnɪk
ˈpʌblɪʃɪŋ/ *noun* **1.** the use of desktop publishing packages and laser printers to produce printed matter **2.** the process of using
computers to write and display information, as in viewdata

electronic pulse /ɪˌelektrɒnɪk ˈpʌls/
noun a short voltage pulse

electronics /ɪˌelekˈtrɒnɪks/ *noun* the
application of knowledge of electrons and
their properties to manufactured products
such as computers and telephones ○ *the
electronics industry*

electronic shopping /ɪˌelektrɒnɪk
ˈʃɒpɪŋ/ *noun* a system of shopping from
the home, using computerised catalogues
and paying by credit card, by means of a
home computer terminal

electronic signature /ɪˌelektrɒnɪk
ˈsɪɡnɪtʃə/ *noun* a piece of text in code, attached to an email, that confirms the identity of its sender

**electronics industry association
interface** /ɪˌelektrɒnɪks ˌɪndəstri ə

ˌsəʊsieɪʃ(ə)n ˈɪntəfeɪs/ *noun* a standard
defining interface signals, transmission
rate and power usually used to connect terminals to modems. Abbr **EIA**

**Electronics Industry Standards
Association** /elekˌtrɒnɪks ˌɪndəstri
ˈstændədz əˌsəʊsieɪʃ(ə)n/ *noun* full
form of **EISA**

electronic smog /ɪˌelektrɒnɪk ˈsmɒɡ/
noun excessive stray electromagnetic
fields and static electricity generated by
large numbers of electronic equipment
(NOTE: This can damage equipment or a
person's health.)

electronic stylus /ɪˌelektrɒnɪk
ˈstaɪləs/ *noun* same as **electronic pen**

electronic traffic /ɪˌelektrɒnɪk
ˈtræfɪk/ *noun* data transmitted in the form
of electronic pulses

electronic wand /ɪˌelektrɒnɪk ˈwɒnd/
noun same as **electronic pen**

electrophotographic /ɪˌelektrəʊ
ˌfəʊtəˈɡræfɪk/ *adjective* referring to a
printing technique used in many laser
printers in which a laser beam creates an
image on a charged drum (NOTE: The
drum then attracts particles of fine black
toner to the charged areas and transfers
the image to paper which is then passed
near a heater to melt the toner onto the
paper.)

electrosensitive paper /ɪ
ˌlektrəʊsensɪtɪv ˈpeɪpə/ *noun* metal-
coated printing paper which can display
characters using localised heating with a
special dot-matrix print head

electrosensitive printing /ɪ
ˌlektrəʊsensɪtɪv ˈprɪntɪŋ/ *noun* printing
using electrosensitive paper

electrostatic /ɪˌlektrəʊˈstætɪk/ *adjective* referring to devices using the properties of static electrical charge

electrostatic printer /ɪˌlektrəʊstætɪk
ˈprɪntə/ *noun* a type of printer which
forms an image on the paper by charging
certain regions to provide character shapes
and other images and using ink with an opposite charge which sticks to the paper
where required. Also called **electrographic printer**

electrostatic screen /ɪ
ˌlektrəʊstætɪk ˈskriːn/ *noun* a metal
cage surrounding sensitive equipment and
connected to ground to protect it from interference

electrostatic storage /ɪ
ˌlektrəʊstætɪk ˈstɔːrɪdʒ/ *noun* storage of

data in the form of small electrically charged regions on a dielectric material

electrothermal printer /ɪˌlektrəʊθɜːməl 'prɪntə/ *noun* a printer that uses a printing head with a dot matrix of heating elements to form characters on electrosensitive paper

elegant programming /ˌelɪgənt ˌprəʊ'græmɪŋ/ *noun* the writing of well-structured programs using the minimum number of instructions

element /'elɪmənt/ *noun* **1.** a small part of an object which is made up of many similar parts **2.** one number or cell of a matrix or array

elementary /ˌelɪ'ment(ə)ri/ *adjective* made of many similar small sections or objects

elevator /'elɪveɪtə/ *noun* a small, square indicator displayed within a scroll bar that indicates where you are within a long document or image ○ *The user can scroll through the image or text by dragging the elevator up or down the scroll bar.*

elimination factor /ɪˌlɪmɪ'neɪʃ(ə)n ˌfæktə/ *noun* the section of data that is not used during a search

else rule /'els ruːl/ *noun* a program logical rule used with an IF-THEN instruction to provide an alternative if the IF-THEN condition is not met

em /em/ *noun* a measure equal to the width of the letter 'm' in a particular font

EM /ˌiː 'em/ *abbr* end of medium

email /'iː meɪl/, **e-mail** *noun* a system of sending messages to and receiving messages from other users on a network. Also called **electronic mail**

email-enabled application /ˌiːmeɪl ɪnˌeɪb(ə)ld ˌæplɪkeɪʃ(ə)n/ *noun* a software application, e.g. a word-processor or spreadsheet, that includes a direct link to an email application to allow a user to send the current document as an email (NOTE: In Microsoft applications, there is a Send option under the File menu that allows a user to send the document using email.)

embedded code /ɪmˌbedɪd 'kəʊd/ *noun* sections or routines written in machine code, inserted into a high-level program to speed up or perform a special function

embedded command /ɪmˌbedɪd kə 'mɑːnd/ *noun* a printer control command, e.g. one indicating that text should be in italics, inserted into text and used by a word-processor when text formatting

embedded computer /ɪmˌbedɪd kəm 'pjuːtə/ *noun* a dedicated computer controlling a machine

embedded object /ɪmˌbedɪd əb 'dʒekt/ *noun* a feature of Windows OLE that allows a file or object, e.g. an image, to be included within another document or file

embedded system /ɪmˌbedɪd 'sɪstəm/ *noun* same as **embedded computer**

embedding /ɪm'bedɪŋ/ *noun* (*in Windows*) the act of dragging an object and dropping it into a document or file so that is included within the document

EMI /ˌiː em 'aɪ/ *noun* corruption of data due to nearby electrically generated magnetic fields. Full form **electromagnetic interference**

emitter-coupled logic /ɪˌmɪtə ˌkʌp(ə)ld 'lɒdʒɪk/ *noun* full form of **ECL**

EMM /ˌiː em 'em/ *noun* a utility that manages the extra expanded memory fitted in an IBM PC and makes it available for programs to use. Full form **expanded memory manager**

emoticon /ɪ'məʊtɪkɒn/ *noun* an arrangement of letters and symbols that represents a particular emotion, e.g. :- for happiness

'Smileys, or emoticons, have been around for a long time: the simplest ones, such as :-), can indicate in a tense-sounding email or text message that you are not feeling as angry as you may appear.' [*The Guardian*]

emphasis /'emfəsɪs/ *noun* **1.** a filter that helps cut down the background noise and so boost a signal **2.** a special effects function in a paint program that will increase the value of a range of colours so that they appear brighter (NOTE: The plural is **emphases**.)

empty medium /ˌempti 'miːdiəm/ *noun* a blank but formatted storage medium that is ready to accept data

empty slot /'empti slɒt/ *noun* **1.** a packet of data in a packet-switching LAN that is carrying no information **2.** an unused expansion edge connector on a motherboard

EMS /ˌiː em 'es/ *noun* a standard in an IBM PC that defines extra memory added above the 640 Kb limit of conventional memory. Full form **expanded memory system** (NOTE: This memory can only be used by specially written programs.)

emulate /'emjʊˌleɪt/ *verb* to copy or behave like something else ○ *Some laser* *printers are able to emulate the more popular office printers.* (NOTE: emulates – emulating – emulated)

'...some application programs do not have the right drivers for a laser printer, so look out for laser printers which are able to emulate the more popular office printers' [*Publish*]

emulation /ˌemjʊ'leɪʃ(ə)n/ *noun* behaviour by one computer or printer which is exactly the same as another and which allows the same programs to be run and the same data to be processed

emulation facility /ˌemjʊ'leɪʃ(ə)n fə ˌsɪlɪti/ *noun* a feature of hardware or software which emulates another system

'...full communications error checking built into the software ensures reliable file transfers and a terminal emulation facility enables a user's terminal to be used as if it were a terminal to the remote computer' [*Byte*]

emulator /'emjʊleɪtə/ *noun* a piece of software or hardware that allows a machine to behave like another

'...for an authentic retro coding experience, download an emulator and turn your computer into a virtual BBC Micro.' [*The Guardian*]

emulsion laser storage /ɪˌmʌlʃ(ə)n 'leɪzə ˌstɔːrɪdʒ/ *noun* a digital storage technique using a laser to expose light-sensitive material

en /en/ *noun* a unit of measure equal to half the width of an em

enable /ɪn'eɪb(ə)l/ *verb* to use an electronic signal to start a process or access a function on a chip or circuit (NOTE: enables – enabling – enabled)

enabled /ɪn'eɪb(ə)ld/ *adjective* referring to a function or menu item that is available to the user ○ *If an option on a menu appears in grey text rather than black, this indicates that these are not enabled and that you cannot use the option.*

enabling signal /ɪn'eɪblɪŋ ˌsɪgn(ə)l/ *noun* a signal that starts a process or allows one to take place

encapsulated /ɪn'kæpsjʊleɪtɪd/ *adjective* referring to something contained within another thing

encapsulated PostScript /ɪn ˌkæpsjʊleɪtɪd 'pəʊstskrɪpt/ *noun* a PostScript facility providing commands that describe an image or page contained within a file that can be placed within a graphics or DTP program. Abbr **EPS**

encapsulated PostScript file /ɪn ˌkæpsjʊleɪtɪd 'pəʊstskrɪpt ˌfaɪl/ *noun* a file that contains encapsulated PostScript instructions. Abbr **EPSF**

encapsulation /ɪn'kæpsjʊleɪʃ(ə)n/ *noun* (*in a network*) a system of sending a frame of data in one format within a frame of another format

encipher /ɪn'saɪfə/ *verb* to convert plaintext into a secure coded form by means of a cipher system ○ *Our competitors cannot understand our files – they have all been enciphered.* Opposite **decipher**

enclosed object /ɪnˌkləʊzd əb'dʒekt/ *noun* a graphic object that is closed on all sides and so can be filled with a colour or pattern

encode /ɪn'kəʊd/ *verb* to apply the rules of a code to a program or data (NOTE: encodes – encoding – encoded)

encoder /ɪn'kəʊdə/ *noun* a device that can translate data from one format to another

encoding /ɪn'kəʊdɪŋ/ *noun* the translation of a message or text according to a coding system

encoding format /ɪn'kəʊdɪŋ ˌfɔːmæt/ *noun* a method of coding data stored on a magnetic disk to avoid a series of similar bits

encrypt /ɪn'krɪpt/ *verb* to convert plaintext to a secure coded form, using a cipher system ○ *The encrypted text can be sent along ordinary telephone lines, and no one will be able to understand it.*

encryption /ɪn'krɪpʃən/ *noun* the conversion of plaintext to a secure coded form by means of a cipher system

end /end/ *noun* a statement or character to indicate the last word of a source file

end about carry /ˌend ə'baʊt ˌkæri/ *noun* (*in BCD arithmetic*) the most significant digit added into the least significant place. Also called **end around carry**

end about shift /ˌend ə'baʊt ˌʃɪft/ *noun* data movement to the left or right in a word, in which the bits falling outside the word boundary are discarded and replaced with zeros

end around carry /ˌend ə'raʊnd ˌkæri/ *noun* same as **end about carry**

end key /'end kiː/ *noun* (a key on an IBM PC keyboard that moves the cursor to the end of the current line

endless loop /'endləs luːp/ *noun* a continuous piece of recording tape or number of computer instructions that are continuously repeated

end of address /ˌend əv əˈdres/ *noun* a transmitted code which indicates that address data has been sent. Abbr **EOA**

end of block /ˌend əv ˈblɒk/ *noun* a code which shows that the last byte of a block of data has been sent through a communications link. Abbr **EOB**

end of data /ˌend əv ˈdeɪtə/ *noun* a code which shows that the end of a stored data file has been reached. Abbr **EOD**

end of document /ˌend əv ˈdɒkjʊmənt/ *noun* same as **end of file**

end of file /ˌend əv ˈfaɪl/ *noun* a marker after the last record in a file. Also called **end of document**. Abbr **EOF**

end of job /ˌend əv ˈdʒɒb/ *noun* a code used in batch processing to show that a job has been finished. Abbr **EOJ**

end of line /ˌend əv ˈlaɪn/ *noun* a code to indicate the end of a line, usually either a CR or LF character. Abbr **EOL**

end of medium /ˌend əv ˈmiːdiəm/ *noun* a code that indicates the end of usable physical medium. Abbr **EM**

end of message /ˌend əv ˈmesɪdʒ/ *noun* a code used to separate the last character of one message from the first of another message. Abbr **EOM**

end of record /ˌend əv ˈrekɔːd/ *noun* a code used to show the end of a record. Abbr **EOR**

end of run routines /ˌend əv ˈrʌn ˌruːˌtiːnz/ *plural noun* routines carried out before a program run finishes to perform certain system housekeeping functions

end of tape /ˌend əv ˈteɪp/ *noun* a code used to indicate the end of a magnetic tape

end of text /ˌend əv ˈtekst/ *noun* a code sent after last character of text. Abbr **EOT, ETX**

end of transmission /ˌend əv trænz ˈmɪʃ(ə)n/ *noun* a sequence of characters indicating that all the data from a terminal or peripheral has been transmitted. Abbr **EOT**

end product /end ˈprɒdʌkt/ *noun* a product made at the end of a production process

end system /end ˈsɪstəm/ *noun* a server or host computer connected to the Internet

end system to intermediate system /ˌend ˌsɪstəm tə ˌɪntəˈmiːdiət ˌsɪstəm/ *noun* an OSI protocol standard that allows host computers to locate a router. Abbr **ES-IS** (NOTE: The host computers constitute the end system and the router is the intermediate system.)

end user /end ˈjuːzə/ *noun* a person who will use the device, program or product ○ *The company is creating a computer with a specific end user in mind.*

Energy Star /ˈenədʒi stɑː/ *noun* a standard and logo on a monitor, computer or other electrical device indicating that the product has been specially designed to save electricity

engine /ˈendʒɪn/ *noun* a part of a software package that carries out a particular function ○ *A search engine is the part of a multimedia title that lets a user search for text in a multimedia book.*

enhanced communication port /ɪn ˌhɑːnst kəˌmjuːnɪˈkeɪʃ(ə)n pɔːt/ *noun* full form of **ECP**

enhanced-definition television /ɪn ˌhɑːnst ˌdefɪnɪʃ(ə)n ˌtelɪˈvɪʒ(ə)n/ *noun* full form of **EDTV**

enhanced dot matrix /ɪnˌhɑːnst ˌdɒt ˈmeɪtrɪks/ *noun* a clearer character or graphics printout using smaller dots and more dots per inch than standard dot matrix

enhanced expanded memory specification /ɪnˌhɑːnst ɪkˌspændɪd ˈmem(ə)ri ˌspesɪfɪkeɪʃ(ə)n/ *noun* full form of **EEMS**

enhanced keyboard /ɪnˌhɑːnst ˈkiːbɔːd/ *noun* an IBM PC keyboard with 101 or 102 keys and a row of 12 function keys arranged along the top of the keyboard, with a separate numeric keypad on the right

enhanced parallel port /ɪnˌhɑːnst ˈpærəlel ˌpɔːt/ *noun* full form of **EPP**

enhanced small device interface /ɪnˌhɑːnst smɔːl dɪˈvaɪs ˌɪntəfeɪs/ *noun* full form of **ESDI**

enhancement /ɪnˈhɑːnsmənt/ *noun* an add-on facility which improves the output or performance of equipment

enhancer /ɪnˈhɑːnsə/ *noun* a device or software which enhances a process or product

ENQ *abbr* enquiry

enquiry /ɪnˈkwaɪri/ *noun* a request for data or information from a device or database

enquiry character /ɪnˈkwaɪri ˌkærɪktə/ *noun* a special control code that is a request for identification or status or data from a device

enter /'entə/ *verb* to type in information on a terminal or keyboard

entering /'entərɪŋ/ *noun* the act of typing in data or writing items in a record

enter key /'entə ki:/ *noun* a key pressed to indicate the end of an input or line of text

enterprise network /'entəpraɪz ˌnetwɜːk/ *noun* a network which connects all the workstations or terminals or computers in a company (NOTE: It can be within one building or link several buildings in different countries.)

enterprise software /'entəpraɪz ˌsɒftweə/ *noun* computer software that is designed to integrate and automate all of a company's functions

entity /'entɪti/ *noun* a subject to which the data stored in a file or database refers (NOTE: The plural is **entities**.)

entry /'entri/ *noun* a single record or data about one action or object in a database or library (NOTE: The plural is **entries**.)

entry condition /'entri kənˌdɪʃ(ə)n/ *noun* a condition that must be satisfied before a routine can be entered

entry instruction /ˌentri ɪn'strʌkʃən/ *noun* the first instruction executed in a called subroutine

entry point /'entri pɔɪnt/ *noun* the address from which a program or subroutine is to be executed

entry time /'entri taɪm/ *noun* a point in time when a program or job or batch will be executed by the operating system scheduler

enumerated type /ɪ'njuːməreɪtd taɪp/ *noun* data storage or classification using numbers to represent chosen convenient labels

COMMENT: If 'man', 'horse', 'dog', 'cat' are the items of data, stored by the machine simply as 0, 1, 2, 3, they can still be referred to in the program as man, horse etc. to make it easier for the user to recognise them.

enumeration /ɪˌnjuːmə'reɪʃ(ə)n/ *noun* a method of identifying resources or objects using a unique number

envelope /'envələʊp/ *noun* **1.** a transmitted packet of data containing error-detection and control information **2.** (*in multimedia*) the shape of the decay curve of a sound **3.** (*in email*) the data which contains a mail message with the destination address information

envelope feeder /'envələʊp ˌfiːdə/ *noun* a special add-on to a printer used to

print on an envelope instead of a sheet of paper

envelope printer /'envələʊp ˌprɪntə/ *noun* a special printer used to print the address on an envelope

environment /ɪn'vaɪrənmənt/ *noun* **1.** the condition in a computer system of all the registers and memory locations **2.** the imaginary space in which a user works when using a computer. This can be changed to suit the user's needs – by defining its characteristics such as colour or wallpaper and by setting up a printer, keyboard and fonts.

environment space /ɪn'vaɪrənmənt speɪs/ *noun* the amount of memory free to be used by a program

environment variable /ɪn'vaɪrənmənt ˌveəriəb(ə)l/ *noun* a variable set by the system or by a user at the system command line which can be used by any program

EOA *abbr* end of address

EOB *abbr* end of block

EOD *abbr* end of data

EOF *abbr* end of file

EOJ *abbr* end of job

EOL *abbr* end of line

EOM *abbr* end of message

EOR *abbr* end of record

EOT *abbr* end of text

EPOS /'iːpɒs/ *noun* a system that uses a computer terminal at a point-of-sale site for electronic funds transfer or stock control as well as matters such as product identification. Full form **electronic point-of-sale**

EPP /ˌiː piː 'piː/ *noun* a standard that defines the way data can be transferred at high speed through a parallel port connector. Full form **enhanced parallel port**

EPROM /ˌiː 'piː ˌrɒm/ *abbr* erasable programmable read-only memory

EPS *abbr* encapsulated PostScript

EPSF *abbr* encapsulated PostScript file

equality /ɪ'kwɒlɪti/ *noun* a logical function whose output is true if either of two inputs is true, and false if both inputs are the same (NOTE: The plural is **equalities**.)

equipment failure /ɪ'kwɪpmənt ˌfeɪljə/ *noun* a hardware fault, rather than a software fault

equivalence /ɪ'kwɪvələns/ *noun* a logical operation that is true if all the inputs are the same

COMMENT: Output is 1 if both inputs are 1 or if both are 0; if the two inputs are different, the output is 0.

equivalence function /ɪˈkwɪvələns ˈfʌŋkʃən/ *noun* **1.** an AND function **2.** a logical function whose output is true if both inputs are the same ▶ also called **equivalence operation**

equivalence gate /ɪˈkwɪvələns geɪt/ *noun* a gate which performs an equivalence function

erasable memory /ɪˌreɪzəb(ə)l ˈmem(ə)ri/ *noun* same as **erasable storage**

erasable programmable read-only memory /ɪˌreɪzəb(ə)l ˌprəʊgræməb(ə)l ˌriːd ˌəʊnli ˈmem(ə)ri/ *noun* a read-only memory chip which can be programmed by a voltage applied to a write pin and data applied to its output pins, usually erasable with ultraviolet light. Abbr **EPROM**

erasable read-only memory /ɪ ˌreɪzəb(ə)l ˌriːd ˌəʊnli ˈmem(ə)ri/ *noun* full form of **EROM**

erasable storage /ɪˌreɪzəb(ə)l ˈstɔːrɪdʒ/ *noun* **1.** a storage medium which can be reused **2.** temporary storage ▶ also called **erasable memory**

erase /ɪˈreɪz/ *verb* **1.** to set all the digits in a storage area to zero **2.** to remove any signal from a magnetic medium (NOTE: erases – erasing – erased) ■ *noun* same as **eraser tool**

erase character /ɪˈreɪz ˌkærɪktə/ *noun* a character which means 'do nothing'

erase head /ɪˈreɪz hed/ *noun* a small magnet that clears a magnetic tape or disk of recorded signals

eraser /ɪˈreɪzə/ *noun* a device that erases the contents of something, e.g. a device using UV light to erase an EPROM

eraser tool /ɪˈreɪzə tuːl/ *noun* (*in a graphics program*) function that allows areas of an image to be erased, or set to the background colour. Also called **erase**

EROM /ˈiː rɒm/ *noun* full form **erasable read-only memory**. same as **EAROM**

error /ˈerə/ *noun* a mistake due to a human operator ○ *He made an error in calculating the total.* □ **in error, by error** by mistake

'…syntax errors, like omitting a bracket, will produce an error message from the compiler' [*Personal Computer World*]

error ambiguity /ˌerə ˌæmbɪˈgjuːɪti/ *noun* an error due to an incorrect selection from ambiguous data

error box /ˈerə bɒks/ *noun* a dialog box displayed with a message alerting the user that an error has occurred

error burst /ˈerə bɜːst/ *noun* a group of several consecutive errors in a transmission

error checking code /ˈerə ˌtʃekɪŋ ˌkəʊd/ *noun* a code that detects or corrects errors

error code /ˈerə kəʊd/ *noun* a code that indicates that a particular type of error has occurred

error condition /ˈerə kənˌdɪʃ(ə)n/ *noun* a state that is entered if an attempt is made to operate on data containing errors

error control /ˈerə kənˌtrəʊl/ *noun* the use of routines which ensure that errors are minimised and any errors that occur are detected and dealt with rapidly

error correcting code /ˈerə kə ˌrektɪŋ ˌkəʊd/ *noun* a coding system that allows bit errors occurring during transmission to be rapidly corrected by logical deduction methods rather than retransmission

error correction /ˈerə kəˌrekʃ(ə)n/ *noun* hardware or software that can detect and correct an error in a transmission

error detecting code /ˈerə dɪˌtektɪŋ ˌkəʊd/ *noun* a coding system that allows bit errors occurring during transmission to be detected, but is not complex enough to correct them

error detection /ˈerə dɪˌtekʃ(ə)n/ *noun* the process of using special hardware or software to detect errors in a data entry or transmission, then usually to ask for retransmission

error detection and correction /ˌerə dɪˌtekʃən ən kəˈrekʃən/ *noun* full form of **EDAC**

error diagnosis /ˈerə ˌdaɪəgnəʊsɪs/ *noun* the process of finding the cause of an error

error diagnostics /ˈerə ˌdaɪəgnɒstɪks/ *noun* information and system messages displayed when an error is detected to help a user debug and correct it

error handler /ˈerə ˌhændlə/ *noun* a software routine that controls and reports on an error when it occurs

error handling /ˈerə ˌhændlɪŋ/ *noun* same as **exception handling**

error interrupt /'erə ˌɪntərʌpt/ *plural noun* an interrupt signal sent because of an error in hardware or software

error logging /'erə ˌlɒgɪŋ/ *noun* the process of recording errors that have occurred ○ *Features of the program include error logging.*

error management /'erə ˌmænɪdʒmənt/ *noun* same as **exception handling**

error message /'erə ˌmesɪdʒ/ *noun* a report displayed to the user saying that an error has occurred

error propagation /'erə ˌprɒpəgeɪʃ(ə)n/ *noun* a situation in which one error causes another

error rate /'erə reɪt/ *noun* **1.** the number of errors that occur within a certain time **2.** the number of corrupt bits of data in relation to the total transmission length

error recovery /'erə rɪˌkʌv(ə)ri/ *noun* software or hardware which can continue to run after an error has occurred

error routine /'erə ruːˌtiːn/ *noun* a short routine within a main program that handles any errors when they occur

error trapping /'erə ˌtræpɪŋ/ *noun* the process of detecting and correcting errors before they cause any problems

ESC /ɪˈskeɪp/ *noun* same as **escape character**

escape character /ɪˈskeɪp ˌkærɪktə/ *noun* a character used to represent an escape code. Also called **ESC**

escape code /ɪˈskeɪp kəʊd/ *noun* a transmitted code sequence which informs the receiver that all following characters represent control actions. Also called **ESC**

escape key /ɪˈskeɪp kiː/ *noun* a key on a keyboard which allows the user to enter escape codes to control the computer's basic modes or actions. Also called **ESC, Esc key**

escapement /ɪˈskeɪpmənt/ *noun* a preset vertical movement of a sheet of paper in a printer

escape sequence /ɪˈskeɪp ˌsiːkwəns/ *noun* a method of switching a Hayes-compatible modem into command mode by sending the three characters '+++' allowing a user to enter new commands while still online

Esc key /ɪˈskeɪp kiː/ *noun* same as **escape key**

ESDI /ˌiː es diː ˈaɪ/ *noun* an interface standard between a CPU and peripherals such as disk drives. Full form **enhanced small device interface**. ◊ SCSI

ES-IS *abbr* end system to intermediate system

Ethernet /'iːθənet/ *noun* a standard, IEEE 802.3, defining the protocol and signalling method of a local area network

COMMENT: Ethernet has several implementations: 10Base5 (the most common) is a bus-based topology running over coaxial cable; 10BaseT uses unshielded-twisted-pair cable in a star-based topology; Ethernet normally has a data transmission rate of 10Mbps.

EtherTalk /'iːθətɑːk/ (*in Apple Mac systems*) a trade name for a variation of the standard Ethernet network developed to connect Macs together as an alternative to the slower AppleTalk

ETX *abbr* end of text

Eudora /juːˈdɔːrə/ a common commercial software program used to send, receive and manage email messages sent via the Internet

evaluation copy /ɪˌvæljuˈeɪʃ(ə)n ˌkɒpi/ *noun* a demonstration version of a software product that allows a user to try the main functions of a software product before buying it

even parity /ˌiːv(ə)n ˈpærɪti/, **even parity check** /ˌiːv(ə)n ˈpærɪti tʃek/ *noun* an error checking system in which any series of bits transmitted must have an even number of binary ones

event /ɪˈvent/ *noun* an action or activity

event-driven /ɪˈvent ˌdrɪv(ə)n/ *adjective* referring to a computer program or process in which each step of the execution relies on external actions

'Forthcoming language extensions will include object-oriented features, including classes with full inheritance, as well as event-driven programming.' [*Computing*]

event focus /ɪˈvent ˌfəʊkəs/ *noun* an object that is currently receiving messages from an action or event

event handler /ɪˈvent ˌhændlə/ *noun* a routine that responds to an event or message within an object-oriented programming environment ○ *If a user clicks the mouse button this generates a message which can be acted upon by the event handler.*

ewallet /'iːˌwɒlət/, **e-wallet** *noun* a feature of web browsers that allows a user to store personal details about his or her credit card, bank account or other ways of paying for goods on the Internet

except gate /ɪk'sept geɪt/ *noun* a logical function whose output is true if either of two inputs is true, and false if both inputs are the same

exception /ɪk'sepʃən/ *noun* something which is different from all others in the same category

exception dictionary /ɪk'sepʃ(ə)n ˌdɪkʃən(ə)ri/ *noun* a store of words and their special word-break requirements, for word-processing and photocomposition

exception handling /ɪk'sepʃ(ə)n ˌhændlɪŋ/ *noun* routines and procedures that diagnose and correct errors or minimise the effects of errors, so that a system will run when an error is detected. Also called **error handling, error management**

excess-3 code /ˌekses 'θriː kəʊd/ *noun* a code in which decimal digits are represented by the binary equivalent of three greater than the number ○ *The excess-3 code representation of 6 is 1001.*

exchange /ɪks'tʃeɪndʒ/ *verb* **1.** □ **to exchange one article for another** to give one thing in place of something else **2.** to swap data between two locations (NOTE: exchanges – exchanging – exchanged)

Exchange /ɪks'tʃeɪndʒ/ an application supplied with Windows 95 that provides features that allow you to manage your communications including email and fax

exchangeable /ɪks'tʃeɪndʒəb(ə)l/ *adjective* which can be exchanged

exchangeable disk storage /ɪks ˌtʃeɪndʒəb(ə)l dɪsk 'stɔːrɪdʒ/ *noun* full form of **EDS**

exchange selection /ɪks'tʃeɪndʒ sɪ ˌlekʃən/ *noun* a sorting method which repeatedly exchanges various pairs of data items until they are in order

exclusion /ɪk'skluːʒ(ə)n/ *noun* restriction of access to a system

exclusive NOR /ɪkˌskluːsɪv 'nɔː/ *noun* full form of **EXNOR**

exclusive OR /ɪkˌskluːsɪv 'ɔː/ *noun* full form of **EXOR**

exe /'eksi/ *noun* an extension to a filename which indicates that the file is a program and can be executed directly by the operating system ○ *In DOS, to start a program type in its EXE file name.*

executable file /'eksɪˌkjuːtəb(ə)l faɪl/ *noun* a file that contains a program rather than data

executable form /'eksɪˌkjuːtəb(ə)l fɔːm/ *noun* a program translated or compiled into a machine code form that a processor can execute

execute /'eksɪˌkjuːt/ *verb* to run or carry out a computer program or process (NOTE: executes – executing – executed)

execute cycle /'eksɪkjuːt ˌsaɪk(ə)l/ *noun* events required to fetch, decode and carry out an instruction stored in memory. Also called **execution cycle**

execute mode /'eksɪkjuːt məʊd/ *noun* the process of entering a command in direct mode to start a program run

execute phase /'eksɪkjuːt feɪz/ *noun* a section of the execute cycle when the instruction is carried out. Also called **execution phase**

execute signal /'cksɪkjuːt ˌsɪgn(ə)l/ *noun* a signal that steps the CPU through the execute cycle

execute statement /'eksɪkjuːt ˌsteɪtmənt/ *noun* a basic operating system command to start a program run

execute time /'eksɪkjuːt taɪm/ *noun* same as **execution time**

execution /ˌeksɪ'kjuːʃ(ə)n/ *noun* the process of carrying out a computer program or process

execution address /ˌeksɪ'kjuːʃ(ə)n ə ˌdres/ *noun* a location in memory at which the first instruction in a program is stored

execution cycle /ˌeksɪ'kjuːʃ(ə)n ˌsaɪk(ə)l/ *noun* same as **execute cycle**

execution error /ˌeksɪ'kjuːʃ(ə)n ˌerə/ *noun* an error occurring during program execution, due to bad inputs or a faulty program

execution phase /ˌeksɪ'kjuːʃ(ə)n ˌfeɪz/ *noun* same as **execute phase**

execution time /ˌeksɪ'kjuːʃ(ə)n ˌtaɪm/ *noun* **1.** the time taken to run or carry out a program or series of instructions **2.** the time taken for one execution cycle

executive /ɪg'zekjʊtɪv/ *adjective* normally refers to the operating system of a computer

executive control program /ɪg ˌzekjʊtɪv kən'trəʊl ˌprəʊgræm/ *noun* same as **OS**

executive information system /ɪg ˌzekjʊtɪv ɪnfə'meɪʃ(ə)n ˌsɪstəm/ *noun* full form of **EIS**

executive instruction /ɪgˌzekjʊtɪv ɪn'strʌkʃən/ *noun* an instruction used to control and execute programs under the control of an operating system

executive program /ɪg,zekjʊtɪv 'prəʊgræm/ *noun* same as **supervisory program**

exerciser /'eksəsaɪzə/ *noun* a tester for a device

exhaustive search /ɪg'zɔːstɪv sɜːtʃ/ *noun* a search through every record in a database

exit /'egzɪt/ *verb* to stop program execution or to leave a program and return control to the operating system or interpreter ○ *You have to exit to another editing system to add headlines.*

EXIT /'eksɪt/ *noun* an MS-DOS system command to stop and leave a child process and return to the parent process

exit point /'eksɪt pɔɪnt/ *noun* a point in a subroutine at which control is returned to the main program

exjunction /'ɛks,dʒʌŋkʃən/ *noun* a logical function whose output is true if either of two inputs is true, and false if both inputs are the same

EXNOR /,eks 'nɔː/ *noun* a logical function whose output is true if all inputs are the same level, false if any are different. Full form **exclusive nor**

EXNOR gate /,eks 'nɔː ,geɪt/ *noun* an electronic implementation of the EXNOR function

EXOR /,eks 'ɔː/ *noun* a logical function whose output is true if any input is true, and false if all the inputs are the same. Full form **exclusive or**

EXOR gate /,eks 'ɔː ,geɪt/ *noun* an electronic implementation of the EXOR function

expandable system /ɪk,spændəb(ə)l 'sɪstəm/ *noun* a computer system that is designed to be able to grow in power or memory by hardware or software additions

expanded memory /ɪk,spændɪd 'mem(ə)ri/ *noun* an extra RAM memory fitted to a computer that is located at an address above 1 Mb

expanded memory board /ɪk ,spændɪd 'mem(ə)ri ,bɔːd/ *noun* an expansion board used to add extra memory to an IBM PC (NOTE: The memory follows the EMS standard.)

expanded memory manager /ɪk ,spændɪd 'mem(ə)ri ,mænɪdʒə/ *noun* full form of **EMM**

expanded memory system /ɪk ,spændɪd 'mem(ə)ri ,sɪstəm/ *noun* full form of **EMS**

expansion /ɪk'spænʃən/ *noun* an increase in computing power or storage size

expansion board /ɪk'spænʃən bɔːd/ *noun* a printed circuit board connected to a system to increase its functions or performance. Also called **expansion card**

expansion box /ɪk'spænʃ(ə)n bɒks/ *noun* a device that plugs into an expansion bus and provides several more free expansion slots

'…it can be attached to most kinds of printer, and, if that is not enough, an expansion box can be fitted to the bus connector' [*Personal Computer World*]

expansion bus /ɪk'spænʃ(ə)n bʌs/ *noun* data and address lines leading to a connector and allowing expansion cards to control and access the data in main memory

expansion card /ɪk'spænʃ(ə)n kɑːd/ *noun* same as **expansion board**

expansion slot /ɪk'spænʃ(ə)n slɒt/ *noun* a connector inside a computer into which an expansion board can be plugged ○ *Insert the board in the expansion slot.*

expert system /'ekspɜːt ,sɪstəm/ *noun* ♦ IKBS

explicit address /ɪk,splɪsɪt ə'dres/ *noun* an address provided in two parts, a reference point and a displacement or index value

explicit reference /ɪk,splɪsɪt 'ref(ə)rəns/ *noun* (*within a program or script*) a way of identifying a particular object, e.g. a field or button, by a unique name

Explorer /ɪk'splɔːrə/ a program supplied with Windows 95 that lets you manage all the files stored on a disk

exponentiation /,ekspə,nenʃi 'eɪʃ(ə)n/ *noun* the raising of a base number to a certain power

export /ɪk'spɔːt/ *verb* to save data in a different file format from the default

expression /ɪk'spreʃ(ə)n/ *noun* **1.** a mathematical formula or relationship **2.** the definition of a value or variable in a program

extended arithmetic element /ɪk ,stendɪd ,ærɪθmetɪk 'elɪmənt/ *noun* a section of a CPU that provides hardware implementations of various mathematical functions

extended Backus-Naur-Form, **extended BNF** *noun* full form of **EBNF**

extended binary coded decimal interchange code /ɪk,stendɪd ,baɪnəri ,kəʊdɪd ,desɪm(ə)l 'ıntətʃeɪndʒ ˌkəʊd/ *noun* full form of **EBCDIC**

extended character set /ɪkˌstendɪd 'kærɪktə ˌset/ *noun* a set of 128 special characters that includes accents, graphics and symbols

extended data output memory /ɪk ˌstendɪd ˌdeɪtə 'aʊtpʊt ˌmem(ə)ri/ *noun* full form of **EDO memory**

extended-definition television /ɪk ˌstendɪd ˌdefɪnɪʃ(ə)n ˌtelɪ'vɪʒ(ə)n/ *noun* full form of **EDTV**

extended graphics array /ɪk ˌstendɪd 'græfɪks əˌreɪ/ *noun* a high resolution graphics standard developed by IBM that is capable of displaying resolutions of up to 1024x768 pixels. Abbr **XGA**

extended integrated drive electronics /ɪkˌstendɪd ˌɪntɪˌgreɪtɪd 'draɪv ˌelektrɒnɪks/ *noun* full form of **EIDE**

extended memory /ɪkˌstendɪd 'mem(ə)ri/ *noun* (*in an IBM PC*) the most popular standard method of adding extra memory above 1 Mb which can be used directly by many operating systems or programs

extended memory manager /ɪk ˌstendɪd 'mem(ə)ri ˌmænɪdʒə/ *noun* a software utility that configures extra memory fitted in a PC to conform to the EMS standard

extended memory specification /ɪkˌstendɪd 'mem(ə)ri ˌspesɪfɪkeɪʃ(ə)n/ *noun* full form of **XMS**

extending serial file /ɪkˌstendɪŋ 'sɪərɪəl ˌfaɪl/ *noun* a file which can be added to or which has no maximum size

extensible hypertext markup language /ɪkˌstensɪb(ə)l ˌhaɪpətekst 'mɑːkʌp ˌlæŋgwɪdʒ/ *noun* full form of **XHTML**

extensible language /ɪkˌstensɪb(ə)l 'læŋgwɪdʒ/ *noun* a computer programming language that allows the user to add his or her own data types and commands

extensible markup language /ɪk ˌstensɪb(ə)l 'mɑːkʌp ˌlæŋgwɪdʒ/ *noun* full form of **XML**

extension memory /ɪk'stenʃən ˌmem(ə)ri/ *noun* storage which is located outside the main computer system but which can be accessed by the CPU

external arithmetic /ɪkˌstɜːn(ə)l ə 'rɪθmətɪk/ *noun* arithmetic performed by a coprocessor

external clock /ɪk'stɜːn(ə)l klɒk/ *noun* a clock or synchronising signal supplied from outside a device

external data file /ɪkˌstɜːn(ə)l 'deɪtə ˌfaɪl/ *noun* a file containing data for a program but stored separately from it

external device /ɪkˌstɜːn(ə)l dɪ'vaɪs/ *noun* **1.** an item of hardware, e.g. a terminal or printer, which is attached to a main computer **2.** any device that allows communications between the computer and itself but which is not directly operated by the main computer

external disk drive /ɪkˌstɜːn(ə)l 'dɪsk ˌdraɪv/ *noun* a device not built into the computer but added to increase its storage capabilities

external interrupt /ɪkˌstɜːn(ə)l 'ɪntərʌpt/ *plural noun* an interrupt signal from a peripheral device indicating that attention is required

external label /ɪkˌstɜːn(ə)l 'leɪb(ə)l/ *noun* an identifying piece of paper stuck to the outside of a device or disk

external memory /ɪkˌstɜːn(ə)l 'mem(ə)ri/ *noun* memory which is located outside the main computer system confines but which can be accessed by the CPU

external modem /ɪkˌstɜːn(ə)l 'məʊdem/ *noun* a modem which is self-contained with its own power supply unit that connects to a serial port of a computer

external register /ɪkˌstɜːn(ə)l 'redʒɪstə/ *plural noun* any one of a user's registers located in main memory rather than within the CPU

external schema /ɪkˌstɜːn(ə)l 'skiːmə/ *noun* a user's view of the structure of data or a program

external sort /ɪkˌstɜːn(ə)l 'sɔːt/ *noun* a method of sorting which uses a file stored in secondary memory, e.g. a disk, as its data source and uses the disk as temporary memory during sorting

external storage /ɪkˌstɜːn(ə)l 'stɔːrɪdʒ/, **external store** /ɪkˌstɜːn(ə)l 'stɔː/ *noun* a storage device which is located outside the main computer system but which can be accessed by the CPU

extracode /'ekstrəkəʊd/ *noun* a set of short routines within the operating system that emulate a hardware function

extract /ɪk'strækt/ *verb* to remove required data or information from a database ○ *We can extract the files required for typesetting.*

extract instruction /ek'strækt ɪn ˌstrʌkʃən/ *noun* an instruction to select and read required data from a database or file

extractor /ɪk'stræktə/ *noun* same as **mask**

extranet /'ekstrənet/ *noun* an intranet that has a connection to the public Internet and allows users to gain access via the Internet (NOTE: It is often used to provide access to people in the company who are working away from the office. Most intranets do not allow access via the public Internet and include security measures that protect against hackers and unauthorised users.)

eyeball /'aɪbɔːl/ *noun* a user of the Internet who visits a particular website or uses a particular product (*slang*)

eye candy /'aɪ ˌkændi/ *noun* the decorative elements on a computer screen or a web page that are intended to make it attractive to look at (*informal*)

eye-dropper /aɪ 'drɒpə/ *noun* a tool in a graphics software application that allows a user to click on a pixel in an image and select the colour of the pixel

e-zine /'iː ziːn/ *noun* a website that models its contents and layout a printed magazine

F

f *symbol* femto-

F *symbol* the hexadecimal number equivalent to decimal number 15

face /feɪs/ *noun* same as **typeface**

faceted code /'fæsɪtd kəʊd/ *noun* a code which indicates various details of an item by assigning each one a value. Also called **significant digit code**

facility /fə'sɪlɪti/ *noun* a mechanism or means allowing something to being done, especially easily ○ *We offer facilities for processing a customer's own disks.* (NOTE: The plural is **facilities**.)

facsimile character generator /fæk ˌsɪmɪli 'kærɪktə ˌdʒenəreɪtə/ *noun* a means of displaying characters on a computer screen by copying preprogrammed images from memory

facsimile copy /fæk,sɪmɪli 'kɒpi/ *noun* an exact copy of a document

facsimile transmission /fæk'sɪmɪli trænz,mɪʃ(ə)n/ *noun* full form of **fax**

factor /'fæktə/ *noun* any number in a multiplication that is the operand

factorial /fæk'tɔːriəl/ *noun* the product of all the numbers below a number ○ *example: 4 factorial (written 4!) = 1x2x3x4 = 24*

factorise /'fæktəraɪz/, **factorize** *verb* to break down a number into two whole numbers which when multiplied will give the original number ○ *When factorised, 15 gives the factors 1, 15 or 3, 5.* (NOTE: factorises – factorising – factorised)

fade /feɪd/ *verb* to become less strong (*of radio or electrical signal*) (NOTE: fades – fading – faded)

fade in /ˌfeɪd 'ɪn/ *noun* **1.** an image that starts with a blank screen that gradually shows the image **2.** a sound that starts inaudibly and gradually increases in volume

fade out /ˌfeɪd 'aʊt/ *noun* **1.** an image that gradually changes to a blank screen **2.** a sound that gradually decreases in volume until it is inaudible

fail /feɪl/ *verb* not to do something which should be done ○ *The company failed to carry out routine maintenance of its equipment.*

fail safe system /f'eɪl seɪf ˌsɪstəm/ *noun* a system which has a predetermined state it will go to if a main program or device fails, so avoiding the total catastrophe that a complete system shutdown would produce

'The DTI is publishing a new code of best practice which covers hardware reliability and fail-safe software systems.' [*Computing*]

fail soft system /ˈfeɪl sɒft ˌsɪstəm/ *noun* a system that will still be partly operational even after a part of the system has failed

failure logging /ˈfeɪljə ˌlɒɡɪŋ/ *noun* a section of an operating system that automatically saves the present system states and relevant data when an error or fault is detected

failure rate /ˈfeɪljə reɪt/ *noun* the number of occurrences of a particular type of failure within a specified period of time

failure recovery /ˈfeɪljə rɪˌkʌv(ə)ri/ *noun* the process of resuming a process or program after a failure has occurred and has been corrected

fall back /ˌfɔːl ˈbæk/ *noun* a special or temporary set of instructions, procedures or data used in the event of a fault or failure

fall back recovery /ˌfɔːl bæk rɪˈkʌv(ə)ri/ *noun* the process of resuming a program after a fault has been fixed, from the point at which fall back routines were called

fall back routines /ˈfɔːl bæk ruːˌtiːnz/ *plural noun* routines that are called or procedures which are executed by a user when a machine or system has failed

false /fɔːls/ *adjective* referring to a logical term equal to binary 0, the opposite of true

false code /ˌfɔːls ˈkəʊd/ *noun* a code that contains values not within specified limits

false drop /ˌfɔːls ˈdrɒp/ *noun* a batch of unwanted files retrieved from a database through the use of incorrect search codes. Also called **false retrieval**

false error /fɔːls ˈerə/ *noun* an error warning given when no error has occurred

false retrieval /ˌfɔːls rɪˈtriːv(ə)l/ *noun* same as **false drop**

FAM *abbr* fast access memory

family /ˈfæm(ə)li/ *noun* **1.** a range of different designs of a particular typeface **2.** a range of machines from one manufacturer that are compatible with other products in the same line from the same manufacturer

fanfold /ˈfænfəʊld/ *noun* same as **accordion fold**

fan-in /fæn ɪn/ *noun* the maximum number of inputs that a circuit or chip can deal with

fanning strip /ˈfænɪŋ strɪp/ *noun* a cable supporting insulated strip

fan-out /ˈfæn aʊt/ *noun* the maximum number of outputs that a circuit or chip can drive without exceeding its power dissipation limit

FAQ /fæk, ˌef eɪ ˈkjuː/ *noun* a webpage or help file that contains common questions and their answers related to a particular subject

Faraday cage /ˈfærədeɪ keɪdʒ/ *noun* a wire or metal screen, connected to ground, that completely encloses sensitive equipment to prevent any interference from stray electromagnetic radiation

fast access memory /ˌfɑːst ˌækses ˈmem(ə)ri/ *noun* abbr **FAM**. same as **rapid access memory**

fast core /ˈfɑːst kɔː/ *noun* a high speed, low access time working memory for a CPU ○ *The fast core is used as a scratchpad for all calculations in this system.*

fast line /ˈfɑːst laɪn/ *noun* a special telecommunications line which allows data to be transmitted at 48 K or 96 K baud rates

fast packet /fɑːst ˈpækɪt/ *noun* an asynchronous method of transferring data over a network

fast page RAM /ˌfɑːst peɪdʒ ˈræm/ *noun* an older type of memory component that seeks and reads data from a memory location in two separate operations. Abbr **FPM RAM** (NOTE: This component has now been replaced by EDO memory.)

fast peripheral /fɑːst pəˈrɪf(ə)rəl/ *noun* a peripheral that communicates with the computer at very high speeds, limited only by the speed of the electronic circuits

Fast-SCSI /fɑːst ˈskʌzi/ *noun* a development that allows data to be transferred at a higher rate than with the original SCSI specification

fast time-scale /ˈfɑːst taɪm/ *noun* an operation in which the time-scale factor is less than one

FAT /ˌef eɪ ˈtiː/ *noun* (*in a PC operating system*) a data file stored on disk that contains the names of each file stored on the disk, together with its starting sector position, date and size. Full form **file allocation table**

fatal error /ˌfeɪt(ə)l ˈerə/ *noun* a fault in a program or device that causes the system to crash

FatBits /ˈfætbɪts/ a MacPaint option which allows a user to edit an image one pixel at a time

father file /ˈfɑːðə faɪl/ *noun* a backup of the previous version of a file. ◊ **grandfather file, son file**

fault /fɔːlt/ *noun* a situation in which something has gone wrong with software or hardware, causing it to malfunction ○ *The technical staff are trying to correct a programming fault.* ◊ **bug, error**

fault detection /fɔːlt dɪˈtekʃ(ə)n/ *noun* an automatic process which logically or mathematically determines that a fault exists in a circuit

fault diagnosis /fɔːlt ˌdaɪəɡˈnəʊsɪs/ *noun* a process by which the cause of a fault is located

fault location program /ˌfɔːlt ləʊˈkeɪʃ(ə)n ˌprəʊɡræm/ *noun* a routine that is part of a diagnostic program that identifies the cause of faulty data or equipment

fault management /fɔːlt ˈmænɪdʒmənt/ *noun* one of the five categories of network management specified by the ISO that will detect, isolate and correct network faults

fault time /ˌfɔːlt ˈtaɪm/ *noun* a period of time during which a computer system is not working or usable due to a fault

fault tolerance /fɔːlt ˈtɒlərəns/ *noun* the ability of a system to continue functioning even when a fault has occurred

fault-tolerant /fɔːlt ˈtɒlərənt/ *adjective* referring to a system or device that is able to continue functioning even when a fault occurs ○ *They market a highly successful range of fault-tolerant minis.*

fault trace /ˌfɔːlt ˈtreɪs/ *noun* a program that checks and records the occurrences of faults in a system

faulty sector /ˌfɔːlti ˈsektə/ *noun* a sector of a magnetic disk that cannot be written to or read from correctly

fax /fæks/, **FAX** *noun* a method of sending and receiving images in digital form over a telephone or radio link (*informal*) ○ *We will send a fax of the design plan.* Full form **facsimile transmission**

fax card /fæks kɑːd/, **fax adapter, fax board** *noun* an adapter card which plugs into an expansion slot and allows a computer to send or receive fax data

fax gateway /fæks ˈɡeɪtweɪ/ *noun* a computer or piece of software that allows users to send information as a fax transmission instead of as a file stored on a disk

fax group /ˈfæks ɡruːp/ *noun* a method of defining the basic features of a fax machine or modem: (NOTE: Groups 1 and 2 are old and rarely used now. Group 3 is the most common standard used today. Groups 3 and 4 provide higher speed and better resolution of transmission.)

fax modem /fæks ˈməʊˌdem/ *noun* a modem that can be used to send and receive faxes to and from a standard fax machine as well as being used as a modem to connect to other computers

fax server /fæks ˈsɜːvə/ *noun* a computer connected to a network and fitted with a fax card that is shared by all users on the network

fd, FD *abbr* **1.** full duplex **2.** floppy disk

FDC /ˌef diː ˈsiː/ *noun* a combination of hardware and software devices that control and manage the read/write operations of a disk drive from a computer. Full form **floppy disk controller**

FDD *abbr* floppy disk drive

FDDI /ˌef diː diː ˈaɪ/ *noun* an ANSI standard for high-speed networks which use fibre optic cable in a dual ring topology, transmitting data at 100 Mbps. Full form **fibre distributed data interface**

FDDI II /ˌef diː diː aɪ ˈtuː/ *noun* an enhanced ANSI standard for high-speed networks that uses fibre optic cable and transmits data at 100 Mbps but can also allocate part of the bandwidth to a 64 Kbits/second analog channel for audio or video data. Full form **fibre distributed data interface II**

FDISK /ˈef dɪsk/ *noun* an MS-DOS system utility that configures the partitions on a hard disk

FDM /ˌef diː ˈem/ *noun* a system used to assign a number of different signals to different frequencies to allow many signals to be sent along one channel ○ *Using FDM we can transmit 100 telephone calls along one main cable.* Full form **frequency division multiplexing**

fdx, FDX *abbr* full duplex

feasibility /ˌfiːzəˈbɪlɪti/ *noun* the likelihood that something will or can be done ○ *He has been asked to report on the feasibility of a project.*

feasibility study /ˌfiːzəˈbɪlɪti ˌstʌdi/ *noun* an examination and report into the usefulness and cost of a new product that is being considered for purchase

FED *abbr* field emission display

FEDS /ˌef iː diː 'es/ *noun* a magnetic disk storage system that contains some removable disks such as floppy disks and some fixed or hard disk drives. Full form **fixed and exchangeable disk storage**

feed /fiːd/ *noun* a device which puts something such as paper into and through a machine such as a printer or photocopier

feedback /'fiːdbæk/ *noun* information from one source which can be used to modify something or provide a constructive criticism of something ○ *We are getting customer feedback on the new system.*

feedback control /'fiːdbæk kənˌtrəʊl/ *noun* information about the effects of a controlling signal on a machine or device, returned to the controlling computer

feeder /'fiːdə/ *noun* **1.** a channel that carries signals from one point to another **2.** a mechanism that automatically inserts the paper into a printer

feed hole /'fiːd həʊl/ *noun* a any one of the punched sprocket holes along the edge of continuous paper

female connector /ˌfiːmeɪl kə'nektə/ *noun* a connector with female sockets

female socket /ˌfiːmeɪl 'sɒkɪt/ *noun* a hole into which a pin or plug can be inserted to make an electrical connection

femto- /femtəʊ/ *prefix* equal to ten exponent minus fifteen (10⁻¹⁵). Abbr **f**

femtosecond /'femtəʊˌsekənd/ *noun* a thousandth of a picosecond

FEP /ˌef iː 'piː/ *noun* a processor placed between an input source and the central computer, whose function is to preprocess received data to relieve the workload of the main computer. Full form **front end processor**

ferric oxide /ˌferɪk 'ɒksaɪd/, **ferrite** /'feraɪt/ *noun* iron oxide used as a tape or disk coating that can be magnetised to store data or signals

ferromagnetic material /ˌferəʊmægnetɪk mə'tɪəriəl/ *noun* any ferrite material that can be magnetised

FET /ˌef iː 'tiː/ *noun* an electronic device that can act as a variable current flow control. Full form **field effect transistor** (NOTE: An external signal varies the resistance of the device and current flow by changing the width of a conducting channel by means of a field. It has three terminals: source, gate and drain.)

fetch /fetʃ/ *noun* a command that retrieves the next instruction from memory

fetch cycle /fetʃ 'saɪk(ə)l/ *noun* the series of events that retrieve the next instruction to be executed from memory by placing the program counter contents on the address bus

fetch-execute cycle /ˌfetʃ 'eksɪkjuːt ˌsaɪk(ə)l/ *noun* the series of events required to retrieve, decode and carry out an instruction stored in memory

fetch instruction /fetʃ ɪn'strʌkʃən/ *noun* a computer instruction to select and read the next instruction or data to be processed

fetch phase /'fetʃ feɪz/ *noun* a section of the fetch-execute cycle that retrieves and decodes the instructions from memory

fetch-protect /ˌfetʃ prə'tekt/ *verb* to restrict access to a section of memory

fetch signal /fetʃ 'sɪgn(ə)l/ *noun* a signal that steps the CPU through the fetch cycle

FF *abbr* **1.** flip-flop **2.** form feed

fibre /'faɪbə/ *noun* a very thin glass or plastic strand that can carry data in the form of light signals (NOTE: The US spelling is **fiber**.)

fibre channel /'faɪbə ˌtʃæn(ə)l/ *noun* an ANSI standard that defines a high-speed serial interface that can transfer data at up to 1.06 Gbps and is often used as a backbone technology to link servers or high-speed devices (NOTE: The technology is normally used over optic fibre, but will work over twisted-pair cable or coax cable.)

fibre connector /'faɪbə kəˌnektə/ *noun* a connector that can be used to connect two fibre optic cables together

fibre distributed data interface /ˌfaɪbə dɪˌstrɪbjʊtɪd 'deɪtə ˌɪntəfeɪs/ *noun* full form of **FDDI**

fibre distributed data interface II /ˌfaɪbə dɪˌstrɪbjʊtɪd ˌdeɪtə ˌɪntəfeɪs 'tuː/ *noun* full form of **FDDI II**

fibre Ethernet /ˌfaɪbə 'iːθənet/ *noun* a high-speed network that uses optical fibre to link one node to another in a point-to-point topology

fibre optic cable /'faɪbə 'ɒptɪk/, **fibre optic connection** *noun* a bundle of fine strands of glass or plastic protected by a surrounding material, used for transmission of light signals that carry data at very high speeds

fibre optics /ˌfaɪbə ˈɒptɪks/ *plural noun* the use of thin strands of glass or plastic that can transmit light signals at the speed of light (NOTE: The light or laser signal is pulsed or modulated to represent data being transmitted.)

fibre over Ethernet /ˌfaɪbə ˈəʊvə ˌiːθənet/ *noun* an enhanced version of the 802.3 Ethernet network protocol standard that allows data to be transferred at 10 Mbits/second (10 BaseFX) or 100 Mbits/second (100Base FX)

fibre ribbon /ˌfaɪbə ˈrɪbən/ *noun* a fabric-based ribbon used in printers

field /fiːld/ *noun* **1.** an area of force and energy distribution, caused by magnetic or electric energy sources **2.** a section containing particular data items in a record ○ *The employee record has a field for age.* **3.** □ **in the field** outside an office or factory

field effect transistor /ˌfiːld ɪˌfekt trænˈzɪstə/ *noun* full form of **FET**

field emission display /ˌfiːld ɪˈmɪʃ(ə)n dɪˌspleɪ/ *noun* a method of producing thin, flat displays for laptop computers in which a miniature colour CRT is located at each pixel point. Abbr **FED**

field engineer /ˈfiːld ˌendʒɪˈnɪə/ *noun* an engineer who does not work at one single company, but travels between customers carrying out maintenance on their computers

fielding /ˈfiːldɪŋ/ *noun* the arrangement of field allocations inside a record and file

field label /fiːld ˈleɪb(ə)l/ *noun* a series of characters used to identify a field or its location. Also called **field name**

field length /ˈfiːld leŋθ/ *noun* the number of characters that a field can contain

field marker /fiːld ˈmɑːkə/ *noun* a code used to indicate the end of one field and the start of the next. Also called **field separator**

field name /ˈfiːld neɪm/ *noun* same as **field label**

field programmable device /ˌfiːld ˌprəʊgræməb(ə)l dɪˈvaɪs/ *noun* same as **PLA**

field programming /ˈfiːld ˈprəʊˌgræmɪŋ/ *noun* the writing of data into a PROM

field separator /ˈfiːld ˌsepəreɪtə/ *noun* same as **field marker**

field-tested /ˈfiːld ˌtestɪd/ *adjective* referring to a product tested outside a company or research laboratory, in a real situation

FIF /ˌef aɪ ˈef/ *noun* a file format used to store graphics images which have been highly compressed using fractals. Full form **fractal image format**

FIFO /ˈfaɪfəʊ/ *noun* a storage read/write method in which the first item stored is the first read. Full form **first in first out**

FIFO memory /ˌfaɪfəʊ ˈmem(ə)ri/ *noun* memory using a FIFO access scheme

FIFO queue /ˈfaɪfəʊ kjuː/ *noun* temporary queue storage in which the first item written to the queue is the first to be read

fifth generation computer /ˌfɪfθ ˌdʒenəreɪʃ(ə)n kəmˈpjuːtə/ *noun* a computer belonging to the next stage of computer system design using fast VLSI circuits and powerful programming languages to allow human interaction

figures shift /ˈfɪgəs ʃɪft/ *noun* **1.** a transmitted code which indicates to the receiver that all following characters should be read as uppercase **2.** a mechanical switch which allows a keyboard to produce special characters and symbols located on the same keys as the numbers

file /faɪl/ *noun* a section of data on a computer, e.g. payroll, address list or customer accounts, in the form of individual records which may contain data, characters, digits or graphics ■ *verb* to put documents in order so that they can be found easily ○ *The correspondence is filed under 'complaints'.* (NOTE: files – filing – filed)

'The first problem was solved by configuring a Windows swap file, which I hadn't done before because my 4Mb 486 had never been overloaded.' [*Computing*]

'...the lost file, while inaccessible without a file-recovery utility, remains on disk until new information writes over it' [*Publish*]

file activity ratio /ˌfaɪl ækˈtɪvɪti ˌreɪʃiəʊ/ *noun* the ratio of the number of different records accessed within a file compared to the total number in store

file allocation table /ˌfaɪl ˌælə ˈkeɪʃ(ə)n ˌteɪb(ə)l/ *noun* full form of **FAT**

file attribute /ˈfaɪl ˌætrɪbjuːt/ *plural noun* a set of data stored with each file which controls particular functions or aspects of the file such as read-only, archived or system file

file cleanup /ˈfaɪl ˌkliːnʌp/ *noun* the process of tidying and removing out-of-date or unnecessary data from a file

file collating /'faɪl kə,leɪtɪŋ/ *noun* the process of putting the contents of a file into order

file conversion /'faɪl kən,vɜːʃ(ə)n/ *noun* the changing of the format or structure of a file system, usually when using a new program or file handling routine

file copy /'faɪl ,kɒpi/ *noun* a copy of a document which is filed in an office for reference

file creation /'faɪl kri,eɪʃ(ə)n/ *noun* the writing of file header information onto a disk and the writing of an entry into the directory

file defragmentation /'faɪl ,diːfrægmenteɪʃ(ə)n/ *noun* ♦ **defragmentation**

file deletion /'faɪl dɪ,liːʃ(ə)n/ *noun* the process of erasing a file from storage

file descriptor /'faɪl dɪ,skrɪptə/ *noun* a code or series of characters used to identify a file

file directory /'faɪl daɪ,rekt(ə)ri/ *noun* a list of names and information about files in a backing storage device

file element /'faɪl ,elɪmənt/ *noun* a complete file contained within a RIFF compound file

file extent /'faɪl ɪk,stent/ *noun* the actual area or number of tracks required to store a file

file format /'faɪl ,fɔːmæt/ *noun* a way in which data is stored in a file

file fragmentation /'faɪl ,frægmənteɪʃ(ə)n/ *noun* a storage of a file in noncontiguous sectors on a disk

file gap /'faɪl gæp/ *noun* a section of blank tape or disk that indicates the end of a file

file handle /'faɪl ,hænd(ə)l/ *noun* a number by which an open file is identified within a program ○ *The new data is written to the file identified by file handle 1.*

file handling routine /'faɪl ,hændlɪŋ ruː,tiːn/ *noun* a short computer program that manages the reading/writing and organisation of stored files

file header /'faɪl ,hedə/ *noun* a section of information about the file stored at the beginning of the file ○ *The file header in the database file shows the total number of records and lists the index fields.*

file identification /'faɪl aɪ,dentɪfɪkeɪʃ(ə)n/ *noun* a unique label or name used to identify and locate a file stored on backing store

file index /'faɪl ,ɪndeks/ *noun* a sorted table of the main entries in a file, with their address, allowing the rapid location of entries

file interrogation /'faɪl ɪn,terəgeɪʃ(ə)n/ *noun* questions asked to select various records or data items from a file

file label /'faɪl ,leɪb(ə)l/ *noun* a character or set of characters used to identify a file

file layout /'faɪl ,leɪaʊt/ *noun* a set of rules defining internal file structure. Also called **file organisation**

file length /'faɪl leŋθ/ *noun* the number of characters or bytes in a stored file

file locking /'faɪl ,lɒkɪŋ/ *noun* a software mechanism that prevents data in a file from being updated by two different users at the same time

file maintenance /'faɪl ,meɪntənəns/ *noun* the process of updating a file by changing, adding or deleting entries

file management /'faɪl ,mænɪdʒmənt/, **file management system** /'faɪl ,mænɪdʒmənt ,sɪstəm/ *noun* a section of a DOS that allocates disk space to files, keeping track of the sections and their sector addresses

file manager /'faɪl ,mænɪdʒə/ *noun* a section of a disk operating system that allocates disk space to files, keeping track of the file sections if it has to be split and their sector addresses

file merger /'faɪl ,mɜːdʒə/ *noun* **1.** the process of combining two data files while retaining an overall structure **2.** one file created from two or more files written one after the other and with no order preserved

filename /'faɪlneɪm/ *noun* a unique identification code allocated to a program

'…when the filename is entered at the prompt, the operating system looks in the file and executes any instructions stored there' [*PC User*]

filename extension /'faɪlneɪm ɪk,stenʃ(ə)n/ *noun* an additional three-character name that is used together with a filename, indicating the type or use of the file

file organisation /'faɪl ,ɔːgənaɪzeɪʃ(ə)n/ *noun* ♦ **file layout**

file processing /'faɪl ,prəʊsesɪŋ/ *noun* the applying of a set of rules or search limits to a file, in order to update or find information

file property /'faɪl ,prɒpəti/ *plural noun* (*in Windows*) any one of the attributes that are assigned to a particular file, including its name, the date that it was created and its owner, which are all stored in the file's properties page (NOTE: To view these properties, highlight the file with a single click from within Windows Explorer and click on the right-hand mouse button – now choose the Properties menu option to view the file's properties page.)

file protection /ˌfaɪl prəˈtekʃən/ *noun* a software or physical device used to prevent any accidental deletion or modification of a file or its records

file protect tab /ˌfaɪl prəˈtekt ˌtæb/ *noun* a plastic tab on a disk which prevents accidental erasure of a file

file purge /ˈfaɪl pɜːdʒ/ *noun* the process of erasing the contents of a file

file queue /ˈfaɪl kjuː/ *noun* a number of files temporarily stored in order before being processed ○ *Output devices such as laser printers are connected on-line with an automatic file queue.*

file-recovery utility /ˌfaɪl rɪˈkʌv(ə)ri juːˌtɪlɪti/ *noun* a piece of software which allows files that have been accidentally deleted or damaged to be read again ○ *A lost file cannot be found without a file-recovery utility.*

file security /ˈfaɪl sɪˌkjʊərɪti/ *noun* hardware or software organisation of a computer system to protect users' files from unauthorised access

file server /ˈfaɪl ˌsɜːvə/ *noun* a computer connected to a network which runs a network operating system software to manage user accounts, file sharing and printer sharing

file set /ˈfaɪl set/ *noun* a number of related files treated as one unit

file sharing /ˈfaɪl ˌʃeərɪŋ/ *noun* a facility allowing one file to be used by two or more users or programs in a network, often using file locking

file size /ˈfaɪl saɪz/ *noun* the number of bytes a file occupies on disk

file sort /ˈfaɪl sɔːt/ *verb* to put the contents of a file into order

file storage /ˈfaɪl ˌstɔːrɪdʒ/ *noun* a physical means of preserving data in a file, e.g. a disk drive

file store /ˈfaɪl stɔː/ *noun* the set of files that are available in main memory at any time

file structure /ˈfaɪl ˌstrʌktʃə/ *noun* a way in which a data file is organised

file transfer /ˈfaɪl ˌtrænsfɜː/ *noun* the process of moving a file from one area of

memory to another or to another storage device or between computers

file transfer access and management /ˌfaɪl ˌtrænsfɜː ˌækses ən ˈmænɪdʒmənt/ *noun* full form of **FTAM**

file transfer protocol /ˌfaɪl ˈtrænsfɜː ˌprəʊtəkɒl/ *noun* full form of **FTP**

file transfer utility /ˌfaɪl ˈtrænsfɜː juːˌtɪlɪti/ *noun* a software utility that links two computers together, usually via a physical serial cable, and allows files to be transferred between the computers

file type /ˈfaɪl taɪp/ *noun* a method of classifying what a file contains ○ *Files with the extension exe are file types that contain program code.*

file update /ˈfaɪl ˌʌpdeɪt/ *noun* **1.** the recent changes or transactions to a file **2.** a new version of software which is sent to users of an existing version

file validation /ˈfaɪl ˌvælɪdeɪʃ(ə)n/ *noun* the process of checking that a file is correct

filing system /ˈfaɪlɪŋ ˌsɪstəm/ *noun* **1.** a way of putting documents in order for reference **2.** a piece of software which organises files

fill /fɪl/ *verb* **1.** to put characters into gaps in a field so that there are no spaces left **2.** to draw an enclosed area in one colour or shading

fill character /fɪl ˈkærɪktə/ *noun* a character added to a string of characters to make up a required length

film optical scanning device for input into computers /ˌfɪlm ˌɒptɪk(ə)l ˌskænɪŋ dɪˌvaɪs fə ˌɪnpʊt ˌɪntə kəmˈpjuːtəz/ *noun* full form of **FOSDIC**

film recorder /ˈfɪlm rɪˈkɔːdə/ *noun* a device that produces a 35 mm slide from a computer image (NOTE: A film recorder can produce slides at very high resolution, normally around 3,000 lines, by regenerating the image on an internal screen.)

filter /ˈfɪltə/ *noun* **1.** an electronic circuit that allows certain frequencies to pass while stopping others **2.** a pattern of binary digits used to select various bits from a binary word. A one in the filter retains that bit in the source word. ■ *verb* **1.** to remove unwanted elements from a signal or file **2.** to select various bits from a word ○ *Filter the top three bits of the video attribute word.* **3.** to select various records from a database file ○ *We filtered the data to select those customers based in New York.*

final product /ˌfaɪn(ə)l ˈprɒdʌkt/ *noun* same as **end product**

find /faɪnd/ *noun* a command to locate a piece of information

Find /faɪnd/ a utility program supplied with Windows 95 that will search through any disk for a particular file, folder or computer ○ *To use the Find function, select the Start/Find menu option.*

find and replace /ˌfaɪnd ən rɪˈpleɪs/ *noun* a feature on a word-processor that allows certain words or sections of text to be located and replaced with others

Finder /ˈfaɪndə/ a trade name for a graphical user interface to an Apple Mac allowing a user to view files and folders and start applications using a mouse

fine-tune /ˌfaɪn ˈtjuːn/ *verb* to adjust by small amounts the features or parameters of hardware or software to improve performance ○ *Fine-tuning improved the speed by ten per cent.*

finger /ˈfɪŋɡə/ *noun* a software program on the Internet that will retrieve information about a user based on his or her email address

finite-precision numbers /ˌfaɪnaɪt prɪˌsɪʒ(ə)n ˈnʌmbəz/ *noun* the use of a fixed number of bits to represent numbers

firewall /ˈfaɪəwɔːl/ *noun* a hardware or software security system between a server or intranet and the public Internet that allows information to pass out to the Internet but checks any incoming data before passing it on to the private server ○ *We have installed a firewall in our intranet to prevent hackers accessing company data via the Internet link.*

Firewire /ˈfaɪəwaɪə/ a trade name for a high-speed serial interface developed by the Apple Computer Corporation and used to link devices such as a digital camera with the computer. ◊ **USB**

firmware /ˈfɜːmweə/ *noun* a computer program or data that is permanently stored in a hardware memory chip, e.g. a ROM or EPROM. Compare **hardware, software**

firmware monitor /ˈfɜːmweə ˌmɒnɪtə/ *noun* a monitor program that is resident in a ROM device, used to load in the operating system when a machine is switched on

first fit /ˈfɜːst fɪt/ *noun* a routine or algorithm that selects the first, largest section

of free memory in which to store a virtual page

first generation /ˌfɜːst dʒenə ˈreɪʃ(ə)n/ *noun* the earliest type of technology

first generation computer /ˌfɜːst ˌdʒenəreɪʃ(ə)n kəmˈpjuːtə/ *noun* an original computer made with valve-based electronic technology, started around 1951

first generation image /ˌfɜːst ˌdʒenəreɪʃ(ə)n ˈɪmɪdʒ/ *noun* a master copy of an original image, text or document

first in first out /ˌfɜːst ɪn ˌfɜːst ˈaʊt/ *noun* full form of **FIFO**

first-level address /ˌfɜːst ˌlev(ə)l ə ˈdres/ *noun* a computer storage address that directly, without any modification, accesses a location or device

fit /fɪt/ *verb* to plot or calculate a curve that most closely approximates a number of points or data (NOTE: fitting – fitted)

fixed and exchangeable disk storage /ˌfɪkst ən ɪksˌtʃeɪndʒəb(ə)l ˈdɪsk ˌstɔːrɪdʒ/ *noun* full form of **FEDS**

fixed cycle operation /ˌfɪkst ˌsaɪk(ə)l ˌɒprəˈreɪʃ(ə)n/ *noun* **1.** a process in which each operation is allocated a fixed time limit **2.** a series of actions within a process that are synchronised to a clock

fixed data /fɪkst ˈdeɪtə/ *noun* data written to a file or screen for information or identification purposes and which cannot be altered by the user

fixed disk /ˌfɪkst ˈdɪsk/ *noun* a magnetic disk which cannot be removed from the disk drive

fixed disk storage /ˌfɪkst dɪsk ˈstɔːrɪdʒ/ *noun* a hard disk or magnetic disk which cannot be removed from the disk drive

fixed field /ˌfɪkst ˈfiːld/ *noun* an area in a stored record that can only contain a certain amount of data

fixed-field file /ˌfɪkst fiːld ˈfaɪl/ *noun* a data file in which each field consists of a predefined and fixed number of characters and in which spaces are used to pad out each field to the correct length

fixed-frequency monitor /ˌfɪkst ˌfriːkwənsi ˈmɒnɪtə/ *noun* a monitor that can only accept one frequency and type of video signal

fixed head disk /ˌfɪkst hed ˈdɪsk/, **fixed head disk drive** /ˌfɪkst hed ˈdɪsk ˌdraɪv/ *noun* a separate immovable read/write head over each disk track that makes access time very short

fixed-length field /ˌfɪkst leŋθ 'fiːld/ *noun* a field whose size cannot be changed

fixed-length record /ˌfɪkst leŋθ 'rekɔːd/ *noun* a record whose size cannot be changed

fixed-length word /ˌfɪkst leŋθ 'wɜːd/ *noun* a preset number of bits that make up a computer word

fixed-point arithmetic /ˌfɪkst pɔint ə 'rɪθmətɪk/ *noun* arithmetic rules and methods using fixed-point notation

fixed-point notation /ˌfɪkst pɔint nəʊ'teɪʃ(ə)n/ *noun* a number representation that retains the position of the digits and decimal points in the computer, so limiting the maximum manageable numbers

fixed program computer /ˌfɪkst ˌprəʊɡræm kəʊ'pjuːtə/ *noun* a hard-wired computer program that cannot be altered and is run automatically

fixed routing /ˌfɪkst 'raʊtɪŋ/ *noun* communications direction routing that does not consider traffic or efficient paths

fixed word length /ˌfɪkst 'wɜːd ˌleŋθ/ *noun* a computer word size in bits that cannot be changed

flag /flæɡ/ *noun* **1.** a way of showing the end of field or of indicating something special in a database ○ *If the result is zero, the zero flag is set.* **2.** a method of reporting the status of a register after a mathematical or logical operation ■ *verb* to attract the attention of a program while it is running to provide a result, report an action or indicate something special (NOTE: flagging – flagged)

flag bit /'flæɡ bɪt/ *noun* a single bit of a word used as a flag for certain operations

flag code /'flæɡ kəʊd/ *noun* a code sequence which informs the receiver that following characters represent control actions

flag event /flæɡ ɪ'vent/ *noun* a process or condition that sets a flag

flagging /'flæɡɪŋ/ *noun* the process of putting an indicator against an item so that it can be found later

flag register /flæɡ 'redʒɪstə/ *noun* a register that contains the status and flag bits of a CPU

flag sequence /flæɡ 'siːkwəns/ *noun* a sequence of codes sent on a packet switching network as identification of the start and finish of a frame of data

flame /fleɪm/ *verb* send a rude or angry Internet message to a user (NOTE: flames – flaming – flamed)

flash /flæʃ/ *verb* to switch a light on and off

flash A/D /ˌflæʃ eɪ 'diː/ *noun* a parallel high speed A/D converter

flashing character /flæʃɪŋ 'kærɪktə/ *noun* a character intensity that is switched on and off as an indicator

flash memory /flæʃ 'mem(ə)ri/ *noun* nonvolatile memory similar to an EEP-ROM device but operating with blocks of data rather than single bytes (NOTE: Flash memory is most often used as an alternative to a disk drive.)

flash ROM /'flæʃ rɒm/ *noun* an electronic memory component that contains data that can normally only be read, but that does allow new data to be stored in the memory using a special electrical signal

flat address space /ˌflæt ə'dres ˌspeɪs/ *noun* an area of memory in which each location has a unique address

flatbed /'flæt ˌbed/ *adjective* referring to a printing or scanning machine that holds the paper or image on a flat surface while processing ○ *Scanners are either flatbed models or platen type, paper-fed models.*

flatbed plotter /ˌflætbed 'plɒtə/ *noun* a movable pen that draws diagrams under the control of a computer onto a flat piece of paper

flatbed scanner /ˌflætbed 'skænə/ *noun* a device with a flat sheet of glass on which artwork is placed and a scan head that moves below the glass and converts the image into a graphics file

flat file /'flæt faɪl/ *noun* a two-dimensional file of data items

flat file database /ˌflæt faɪl 'deɪtəbeɪs/ *noun* a database program that can only access data stored in one file at a time, not allowing relational data

flat pack /'flæt pæk/ *noun* an integrated circuit package whose leads extend horizontally, allowing the device to be mounted directly onto a PCB without the need for holes

flat panel /ˌflæt 'pæn(ə)l/ *noun* a very thin computer screen with a flat viewing surface (NOTE: Flat panels use liquid-crystal display technology and are commonly found in portable personal computers.)

flat rate /flæt 'reɪt/ *noun* a set pricing rate that covers all the uses of a facility

flat screen /ˈflæt skriːn/ *noun* a display monitor that has been manufactured with a flat, square-edged front to the monitor

flexible array /ˌfleksəb(ə)l əˈreɪ/ *noun* an array whose size and limits can be altered

flexible machining system /ˌfleksɪb(ə)l məˈʃiːnɪŋ ˌsɪstəm/ *noun* full form of **FMS 1**

flexible manufacturing system /ˌfleksɪb(ə)l ˌmænjʊˈfæktʃərɪŋ ˌsɪstəm/ *noun* full form of **FMS 2**

flicker /ˈflɪkə/ *noun* a computer graphic image whose brightness varies rapidly at a visible rate because of a low image refresh rate or signal corruption

flicker-free /ˈflɪkə friː/ *adjective* referring to a display that does not flicker

'A CRT (cathode ray tube) monitor paints the screen from top to bottom, and is usually considered 'flicker free' if it refreshes the image 75 times a second, or more' [*The Guardian*]

flight simulator /ˈflaɪt ˌsɪmjʊleɪtə/ *noun* a computer program which allows a user to pilot a plane, showing a realistic control panel and moving scenes, used either as a training programme or a computer game

flip-flop /ˈflɪp flɒp/ *noun* an electronic circuit or chip whose output can be one of two states determined by one or two inputs, and which can be used to store one bit of digital data. Abbr **FF**

flippy /ˈflɪpi/ *noun* a disk that is double sided but for use in a single-sided drive, so that it has to be turned over to read the other side (NOTE: The plural is **flippies**.)

float /fləʊt/ *noun* the addition of the origin address to all indexed or relative addresses to check the amount of memory a program will require

float factor /fləʊt ˈfæktə/ *noun* a location in memory at which the first instruction of a program is stored

floating /ˈfləʊtɪŋ/ *adjective* referring to a character which is separate from the character it should be attached to

floating address /ˌfləʊtɪŋ əˈdres/ *noun* a location specified in relation to a reference address

floating point arithmetic /ˌfləʊtɪŋ pɔɪnt əˈrɪθmətɪk/ *noun* arithmetical operations on floating point numbers ○ *The fixed number 56.47 in floating-point arithmetic would be 0.5647 and a power of 2.*

floating point notation /ˌfləʊtɪŋ pɔɪnt nəʊˈteɪʃ(ə)n/ *noun* a numerical no-

tation in which a fractional number is represented with a point after the first digit and a power, so that any number can be stored in a standard form

floating point number /ˌfləʊtɪŋ pɔɪnt ˈnʌmbə/ *noun* a number represented using floating point notation

floating point operation /ˌfləʊtɪŋ pɔɪnt ˌɒpəˈreɪʃ(ə)n/ *noun* a mathematical operation carried out on a floating point number. Abbr **FLOP**

floating point processor /ˌfləʊtɪŋ pɔɪnt ˈprəʊsesə/ *noun* same as **floating point unit**

floating point routine /ˌfləʊtɪŋ pɔɪnt ruːˈtiːn/ *plural noun* a set of routines that allow floating-point numbers to be handled and processed

floating point unit /ˌfləʊtɪŋ pɔɪnt ˈjuːnɪt/ *noun* a specialised CPU that can process floating point numbers very rapidly ○ *The floating point unit speeds up the processing of the graphics software.* Abbr **FPU**. Also called **floating point processor**

floating symbolic address /ˌfləʊtɪŋ sɪmˌbɒlɪk əˈdres/ *noun* a symbol or label that identifies a particular instruction or word, regardless of its location

floating window /ˌfləʊtɪŋ ˈwɪndəʊ/ *noun* a window that can be moved anywhere on screen

float relocate /fləʊt ˌriːləʊˈkeɪt/ *noun* the process of converting floating addresses to absolute addresses

FLOP /flɒp/ *abbr* floating point operation

floppy disk /ˌflɒpi ˈdɪsk/, **floppy** /ˈflɒpi/ *noun* a secondary storage device in the form of a flat, circular flexible disk onto which data can be stored in a magnetic form. Abbr **FD** (NOTE: The plural of **floppy** is **floppies**.)

COMMENT: Floppy disks are available in various sizes: the commonest are 3.5 inch, 5.25 inch and 8 inch. The size refers to the diameter of the disk inside the sleeve.

floppy disk controller /ˌflɒpi ˈdɪsk kənˌtrəʊlə/ *noun* full form of **FDC**

floppy disk drive /ˌflɒpi ˈdɪsk ˌdraɪv/ *noun* a disk drive for floppy disks. Abbr **FDD**. Also called **floppy disk unit**

floppy disk sector /ˌflɒpi ˈdɪsk ˌsektə/ *noun* the smallest area on a magnetic disk that can be individually addressed by a computer

floppy disk unit /ˌflɒpi 'dɪsk ˌjuːnɪt/ *noun* same as **floppy disk drive**

FLOPs per second /ˌflɒps pɜː 'sekənd/ *noun* a measure of computing power as the number of floating point operations that a computer can execute every second

flowchart /'fləʊtʃɑːt/ *noun* a chart which shows the arrangement of the steps in a process or program ■ *verb* to describe a process, its control and routes graphically. Also called **flow diagram**

flowchart stencil /'fləʊtʃɑːt ˌstens(ə)l/ *noun* a plastic sheet with template symbols cut out, to allow flowcharts to be quickly and clearly drawn. Also called **flowchart template**

flowchart symbol /'fləʊtʃɑːt ˌsɪmb(ə)l/ *plural noun* any one of the special symbols used to represent devices, decisions and operations in a flowchart

flowchart template /'fləʊtʃɑːt ˌtempleɪt/ *noun* same as **flowchart stencil**

flow control /fləʊ kən'trəʊl/ *noun* management of the flow of data into queues and buffers, to prevent heavy traffic

flow diagram /'fləʊ ˌdaɪəgræm/ *noun* same as **flowchart**

flow direction /fləʊ daɪ'rekʃən/ *noun* the order in which events occur in a flowchart

flowline /'fləʊlaɪn/ *noun* a line connecting flowchart symbols, showing the direction of flow within a flowchart

flow text /ˌfləʊ 'tekst/ *verb* to insert text into a page format in a DTP system (NOTE: The text fills all the space around pictures, and between set margins.)

flush /flʌʃ/ *verb* to clear or erase all the contents of a queue, buffer, file or section of memory ■ *adjective* level or in line with something

flush buffers /flʌʃ 'bʌfəz/ *noun* erasure of any data remaining in a buffer, ready for a new job or after a job has been aborted

flutter /'flʌtə/ *noun* the occurrence of fluctuations of tape speed due to mechanical or circuit problems, causing signal distortion ○ *Wow and flutter and common faults on cheap tape recorders.*

flyback /'flaɪbæk/ *noun* an electron picture beam return from the end of a scan to the beginning of the next. Also called **line flyback**

flying head /'flaɪɪŋ hed/ *noun* a hard disk read/write head that is wing-shaped to fly just above the surface of the spinning disk

flying mouse /ˌflaɪɪŋ 'maʊs/ *noun* a computer mouse that can be lifted and used as a pointer

FM /ˌef 'em/ *verb* a method of changing the frequency of one signal according to another. Full form **frequency modulation**

COMMENT: FM is often used as a method of representing data through changes in the frequency of a signal (the carrier), and as a method of carrying data over fibre-optic or telephone cables (e.g., many modem standards use FM to transmit data).

FMS /ˌef em 'es/ *noun* 1. CNC or control of a machine by a computer. Full form **flexible machining system 2.** the use of CNC machines, robots and other automated devices in manufacturing. Full form **flexible manufacturing system**

FM synthesiser /ˌef em 'sɪnθəˌsaɪzə/ *noun* a device or other means for creating sounds by combining base signals of different frequencies (NOTE: Sound cards using an FM synthesiser create sounds of a piano, drum or guitar by combining different frequencies at different levels to recreate the complex sound of a musical instrument.)

focus /'fəʊkəs/ *noun* a particular window or field that is currently ready to accept a user's command ○ *In Windows, the object that currently has the user's focus has a dotted line around it.* ■ *verb* to adjust a monitor so that the image that is displayed on the screen is sharp and clear

focus window /'fəʊkəs ˌwɪndəʊ/ *noun* a window in a GUI that is currently active and accepting user input or is being controlled by a program and accepting commands from the program

fogging /'fɒgɪŋ/ *noun* a graphic effect that is used to simulate atmospheric fog or haze, used to make a three-dimensional scene more realistic. Also called **haze**

folder /'fəʊldə/ *noun* a group of files stored together under a name. ◊ **directory**

folding /'fəʊldɪŋ/ *noun* a hashing method for generating an address by splitting the key into parts and adding them together

font /fɒnt/ *noun* a set of characters all of the same style, size and typeface. Also called **fount**

'Word Assistant is designed to help wordprocessing users produce better- looking documents. It has style templates and forms providing 25 TrueType fonts, 100 clip-art images and two font utility programs.' [*Computing*]

'…laser printers store fonts in several ways: as resident, cartridge and downloadable fonts' [*Desktop Publishing Today*]

font card /'fɒnt kɑːd/ *noun* a ROM device that fits into a socket on a printer and adds another resident font

font change /'fɒnt tʃeɪndʒ/ *noun* a function on a computer to change the style of characters used on a display screen

Font/DA Mover /ˌfɒnt ˌdiː eɪ 'muːvə/ *noun* (*in an Apple Mac system*) a former system utility that allowed a user to add fonts and DA files to the system environment

font disk /'fɒnt dɪsk/ *noun* a magnetic disk that contains the data to drive a character generator to make up the various fonts on a computer display

Fonts Folder /'fɒnts ˌfəʊldə/ *noun* a Windows location for all the fonts that are currently installed on your PC

foobar /'fuːbɑː/ *noun* a term used by programmers to refer to whatever is being discussed ○ *If a programmer is explaining how a graphic program works, he might refer to an example graphic file that stores the image as 'foobar.gif' – it does not really exist but is just an example.*

foot /fʊt/ *noun* the bottom part of something ○ *He signed his name at the foot of the letter.*

footer /'fʊtə/, **footing** /'fʊtɪŋ/ *noun* a message at the bottom of all the pages in a printed document, e.g. the page number

footnote /'fʊtˌnəʊt/ *noun* a note at the bottom of a page, referring to the text above it, usually using a superior number as a reference

footprint /'fʊtˌprɪnt/ *noun* **1.** the area covered by a transmitting device such as a satellite or antenna **2.** the area that a computer takes up on a desk

'…signals from satellites in orbit 36,000km above the earth don't care very much whether you are close to an exchange or not….as long as you have a dish within their footprint.' [*The Guardian*]

forbidden character /fə'bɪd(ə)n 'kærɪktə/, **forbidden combination** *noun* a bit combination in a computer word that is not allowed according to the rules defined by the programmer or system designer

forced page break /ˌfɔːst 'peɪdʒ ˌbreɪk/ *noun* an embedded code which indicates a new page start

foreground /'fɔːɡraʊnd/ *noun* **1.** the front part of an illustration, as opposed to the background **2.** a high-priority task done by a computer

'This brighter – but still anti-glare – type of screen is especially useful for people using colourful graphic applications, where both the background and foreground are visually important.' [*Computing*]

foreground colour /ˌfɔːɡraʊnd 'kʌlə/ *noun* the colour of characters and text displayed on a screen

foregrounding /'fɔːɡraʊndɪŋ/ *noun* the execution of high-priority jobs or programs in a multitasking operating system

foreground mode /'fɔːɡraʊnd məʊd/ *plural noun* in a computer system in which two modes for program execution are possible, the mode that is for interactive user programs. Compare **background mode**

foreground processing memory /ˌfɔːɡraʊnd 'prəʊsesɪŋ ˌmem(ə)ri/ *noun* a region of a multitasking operating system in which high-priority jobs or programs are executed

foreground program /ˌfɔːɡraʊnd 'prəʊɡræm/ *noun* a high-priority program in a multitasking system, whose results are usually visible to the user

forest /'fɒrɪst/ *noun* a number of interconnected data structure trees

fork /fɔːk/ *noun* (*in an Apple Mac*) a folder that contains system files and information about a file or application

form /fɔːm/ *noun* **1.** a preprinted document with blank spaces where information can be entered **2.** a graphical display that looks like an existing printed form and is used to enter data into a database **3.** a page of computer stationery

formal methods /'fɔːm(ə)l ˌmeθədz/ *plural noun* methods developed from mathematics and logic that are used when giving the specifications of computer systems or evaluating them

format /'fɔːmæt/ *noun* **1.** a specific method of arranging text or data **2.** the precise syntax of instructions and arguments ■ *verb* to arrange text as it will appear in printed form on paper ○ *Style sheets are used to format documents.*

'As an increasing amount of information within businesses is generated in wordprocessed format, text retrieval tools are becoming a highly attractive pragmatic solution.' [*Computing*]

format mode /'fɔːmæt məʊd/ *noun* the use of protected display fields on a screen to show a blank form or page which cannot be altered, but into which a user can enter information

formatted dump /ˌfɔːmætɪd 'dʌmp/ *noun* a batch of text or data printed in a certain format

formatter /'fɔːmætə/ *noun* a piece of hardware or software that arranges text or data according to certain rules

form factor /fɔːm 'fæktə/ *noun* the size and shape of a device, especially a computer's motherboard or other printed circuit board (NOTE: For example, the motherboard tends to be the size of the first IBM desktop PC computer (full form factor) or smaller.)

form feed /'fɔːm fiːd/ *verb* to the process of advancing the paper in a printer to the top of the next page or sheet. Abbr **FF** (NOTE: If you are using a laser or inkjet printer this has the effect of ejecting the current piece of paper.)

form flash /ˌfɔːm 'flæʃ/ *noun* a text heading held in store and printed out at the same time as the text

form handling equipment /ˌfɔːm 'hændlɪŋ ɪˌkwɪpmənt/ *noun* peripherals, e.g. a decollator,which deal with output from a printer

form letter /fɔːm 'letə/ *noun* a standard letter into which personal details of each addressee are inserted

form mode /'fɔːm məʊd/ *noun* a display method on a data entry terminal in which the form is displayed on the screen and the operator enters relevant details

form overlay /fɔːm ˌəʊvə'leɪ/ *noun* a heading or other matter held in store and printed out at the same time as the text

form stop /ˌfɔːm 'stɒp/ *noun* a sensor on a printer which indicates when the paper has run out

form type /'fɔːm taɪp/ *noun* a four-character code that identifies the type of data chunk within a RIFF file

formula /'fɔːmjʊlə/ *noun* a set of mathematical rules applied to solve a problem (NOTE: The plural is **formulae**.)

formula portability /ˌfɔːmjʊlə ˌpɔːtə'bɪlɪti/ *noun* a feature in a spreadsheet program to find a value in a single cell from data in others, with the possibility of using the same formula in other cells

formula translator /'fɔːmjələ træns ˌleɪtə/ *noun* full form of **FORTRAN**

for-next loop /ˌfɔː 'nekst ˌluːp/ *noun* a loop or routine that is repeated until a condition no longer occurs

FORTH /fɔːθ/ *noun* a programming language mainly used in control applications

FORTRAN /'fɔːtræn/ *noun* a programming language developed in the first place for scientific use. Full form **formula translator**

forum /'fɔːrəm/ *noun* an Internet discussion group for people who share a special interest in something

forward /'fɔːwəd/ *verb* **1.** to send an email message that you have received on to another user ○ *I did not know the answer to the question, so I have forwarded your message to my colleague.* **2.** (*of a bridge in a network*) to copy a packet of data from one segment to another

forward error correction /ˌfɔːwəd 'erə kəˌrekʃ(ə)n/ *noun* an error detection and correction method that is applied to received data to correct errors rather than requesting another transmission

forward mode /'fɔːwəd məʊd/ *noun* positive displacement to an origin

forward pointer /ˌfɔːwəd 'pɔɪntə/ *noun* a pointer that contains the address of the next item in a linked list

for your information /fə ˌjɔːɪ ˌinfə 'meɪʃ(ə)n/ *noun* full form of **FYI**

FOSDIC /ˌef əʊ es diː aɪ 'siː/ *noun* a storage device for computer data using microfilm. Full form **film optical scanning device for input into computers**

four-address instruction /ˌfɔː ə ˌdres ɪn'strʌkʃən/ *noun* a program instruction which contains four addresses within its address field, usually the location of the two operands, the result and the location of the next instruction

fourcc /ˌfɔː si: 'siː/, **four-character code** /ˌfɔː ˌkærɪktə 'kəʊd/ *noun* a method of identifying the type of data within a RIFF file

4GL *abbr* fourth-generation language

four-plus-one address /'fɔː plʌs ˌwʌn/ *noun* an instruction that contains the locations of four registers and the location of the next instruction

fourth generation computer /ˌfɔːθ ˌdʒenəreɪʃ(ə)n kəm'pjuːtə/ *noun* a computer using technology using LSI circuits, developed around 1970 and still in current use

fourth generation language /ˌfɔːθ ˌdʒenəreɪʃ(ə)n 'læŋgwɪdʒ/ *noun* a computer language that is user-friendly and has been designed with the nonexpert in mind. Abbr **4GL**

fps *noun* the number of individual frames of a video sequence that can be displayed each second to give the impression of movement. Full form **frames per second**. ◊ **MPEG**

COMMENT: To give the impression of smooth, continuous video (also called full-motion video), a computer needs to display at least 25 separate frames each second. If the frames are small, there is less data to update; however if the frame is large – e.g. a large window display – then the computer has to update the hundreds of thousands of pixels that make up each image 25 times per second. To do this needs a fast graphics adapter or special video display hardware

FPU *abbr* floating point unit

FQDN /ˌef kjuː diː 'en/ *noun* a complete domain name that can be used to identify a server as well as the host;, e.g. bloomsbury.com. Full form **fully qualified domain name**

fractal /'frækt(ə)l/ *noun* a geometric shape that repeats itself within itself and always appears the same, however much you magnify the image

fractal compression /ˌfrækt(ə)l kəm'preʃ(ə)n/ *noun* a technique used to compress images

fractal image format /ˌfrækt(ə)l 'ɪmɪdʒ ˌfɔːmæt/ *noun* full form of **FIF**

fraction /'frækʃən/ *noun* **1.** a part of a whole unit, expressed as one figure above another, e.g. 1/4, 1/2, or a figure after a decimal point. e.g. 25. **2.** a mantissa of a floating point number. Also called **fractional part**

fractional part /'frækʃənəl pɑːt/ *noun* same as **fraction 2**

fractional services /ˌfrækʃənəl 'sɜːvɪsɪz/ *plural noun* parts of a bandwidth allocated to different signals or customers ○ *The commercial carrier will sell you fractional services that provide 64Kbps data transmission.*

fractional T-1 /'frækʃənəl tiː/ *noun* a method of dividing the capacity of a 1.544 Mbits/second T-1 communications line into smaller 64 Kbits/second channels that are more convenient and cheaper for a customer to use

fragment /'frægmənt/ *noun* a piece of information that has had to be split up into several smaller units of information before being sent over the Internet. The receiver

will re-assemble these units into the correct order.

fragmentation /ˌfrægmən'teɪʃ(ə)n/ *noun* **1.** (*in main memory*) memory allocation to a number of files, which has resulted in many small, free sections or fragments that are too small to be of any use, but waste a lot of space **2.** (*on a disk drive*) a situation with files stored scattered across non-contiguous sectors on a hard disk

COMMENT: When a file is saved to disk, it is not always saved in adjacent sectors. This will increase the retrieval time. Defragmentation moves files back into adjacent sectors so that the read head does not have to move far across the disk, so it increases performance.

frame /freɪm/ *noun* **1.** a space on magnetic tape for one character code **2.** a packet of transmitted data including control and route information **3.** (*in animation, film or video*) one single image within a sequence of different images that together show movement or animation. Each frame is normally slightly different from the previous one to give the impression of movement. **4.** (*in an HTML webpage*) a set of commands that allow the main window of a browser to be split into separate sections, each of which can be scrolled independently. This allows lots of information to be presented clearly. ◊ **HTML 5.** (*in communications*) a standard unit of information that contains a header with the destination address and sender's address followed by the information and a trailer that contains error detection information

frame-based animation % /freɪm beɪsd ˌænɪ'meɪʃ(ə)n/ *noun* a series of screens displayed in quick succession, each one slightly different, that gives the impression of movement

frame buffer /freɪm 'bʌfə/ *noun* a section of memory used to store an image before it is displayed on screen

frame error /freɪm 'erə/ *noun* an error due to a faulty bit within a frame on magnetic tape

frame grabber /'freɪm ˌgræbə/ *noun* a high speed digital sampling circuit that stores a TV picture in memory so that it can then be processed by a computer. Also called **grabber**

'…the frame grabber is distinguished by its ability to acquire a TV image in a single frame interval' [*Electronics & Wireless World*]

frame index /freɪm 'ɪndeks/ *noun* a counter used by the Microsoft Movie Player software that identifies the current frame of the video

frame rate /'freɪm reɪt/ *noun* the speed at which frames in a video sequence are displayed; measured in frames displayed per second (NOTE: PAL is 25fps, NTSC is 30 fps and film is 24 fps.)

frame relay /freɪm rɪ'leɪ/ *noun* a communications protocol, similar to but more efficient to X.25, that operates at OSI level 2.

> COMMENT: The system is used in wide area networks and is a subset of the HDLC (high level data-link control) called LAP-D (link access procedure-D) that allows data to be sent in packets over a shared high-speed channel such as a T-1 line.

frames per second /ˌfreɪmz pə 'sekənd/ *noun* full form of **fps**

frame window /freɪm 'wɪndəʊ/ *noun* the set of controls, including the minimise and maximise buttons, scroll bar and window title, and border that surround a window area

framework /'freɪmwɜːk/ *noun* the basic structure of a database, process or program ○ *The program framework was designed first.*

free /friː/ *adjective* available for use or not currently being used; ■ *verb* to erase, remove or back up programs or files to provide space in memory

freedom of information /ˌfriːdəm əv ɪnfə'meɪʃ(ə)n/ *noun* the opportunity and ability to examine computer records, either(referring to government activities or about individuals)

free form database /ˌfriː fɔːm 'deɪtəbeɪs/ *noun* a database that can store any type of data and does not have a fixed record structure

free running mode /ˌfriː 'rʌnɪŋ ˌməʊd/ *noun* an interactive computer mode that allows more than one user to have simultaneous use of a program

free WAIS /ˌfriː ˌdʌb(ə)l juː eɪ aɪ 'es/ *noun* a non-commercial version of the WAIS search index server

freeware /'friːweə/ *noun* software that is in the public domain and can be used by anyone without having to pay

free wheeling /'friː wiːlɪŋ/ *noun* a transmission protocol in which the computer transmitting receives no status signals from the receiver

freeze /friːz/ *verb* same as **hang.** ➧ **crash**

freeze frame /'friːz freɪm/ *verb* a video sequence stopped so that only one frame is displayed

frequency /'friːkwənsi/ *noun* a number of cycles or periods of a regular waveform that are repeated per second (NOTE: The plural is **frequencies**.)

frequency division multiplexing /ˌfriːkwənsi dɪˌvɪʒ(ə)n 'mʌltɪˌpleksɪŋ/ *noun* full form of **FDM** ○ *Using FDM we can transmit 100 telephone calls along one main cable.*

frequency modulation /ˌfriːkwənsi mɒdjuˈleɪʃ(ə)n/ *noun* full form of **FM**

frequently asked questions /ˌfriːkwənt(ə)li ɑːskd 'kwestʃənz/ *plural noun* common questions and their answers relating to a particular subject that are contained in a document. Abbr **FAQ**

friendly front end /ˌfrendli ˌfrʌnt 'end/ *noun* the design of the display of a program that is easy to use and understand

FROM /'ef rɒm/ *abbr* fusible read only memory

front end /ˌfrʌnt 'end/ *adjective* the visible part of an application that is seen by a user and is used to view and work with information ○ *The program is very easy to use thanks to the uncomplicated front-end.*

front-end processor /ˌfrʌnt end 'prəʊsesə/ *noun* full form of **FEP**

front panel /frʌnt 'pæn(ə)l/ *noun* main computer system control switches and status indicators

FTAM /ˌef tiː eɪ 'em/ *noun* an OSI standard method of transferring files between different computer systems. Full form **file transfer, file access and management**

FTP /ˌef tiː 'piː/ *noun* an TCP/IP standard for transferring files between computers; it is a file sharing protocol that operates at layers 5, 6 and 7 of an OSI model network. Full form **file transfer protocol**

ftp mail /ˌef tiː 'piː ˌmeɪl/ *noun* ➧ **bitFTP**

full adder /ˌfʊl 'ædə/ *noun* a binary addition circuit which can produce the sum of two inputs, and can also accept a carry input, producing a carry output if necessary

full duplex /ˌfʊl 'djuːpleks/ *noun* data transmission down a channel in two directions simultaneously. Abbr **fd, FD, fdx**

full handshaking /ˌfʊl 'hændʃeɪkɪŋ/ *noun* signals transmitted between two communicating devices indicating states and events such as ready to transmit, ready to receive, received and transmitted

full-motion video adapter /ˌful ˌməʊʃ(ə)n ˈvɪdiəʊ əˌdæptə/ *noun* a computer fitted with a digitising card that is fast enough to capture and display moving video images, at a rate of 25 or 30 frames per second

full path /ˌful ˈpɑːθ/ *noun* a description of the position of a directory, in relation to the root directory, in which a file is stored

full scene anti-aliasing /ˌful siːn ˌænti ˈeɪliəsɪŋ/ *noun* a method of anti-aliasing a complete frame of a video or animation rather than just one object, which requires powerful graphics hardware. Abbr **FSAA**

full-screen /ful skriːn/ *adjective* referring to a program display that uses all the available screen, and is not displayed within a window

full-size display /ˌful saɪz dɪsˈpleɪ/ *noun* a large screen VDU which can display a whole page of text

full subtractor /ˌful səbˈtræktə/ *noun* a binary subtractor circuit that can produce the difference of two inputs and can also accept a carry input, producing a carry output if necessary

full-text search /ˌful tekst ˈsɜːtʃ/ *noun* a search for something carried out through all the text in a file or database rather than limited to an area or block

fully formed character /ˌfuli fɔːmd ˈkærɪktə/ *plural noun* a character produced by a printer in a single action

fully-populated /ˌfuli ˈpɒpjʊˌleɪtɪd/ *adjective* 1. referring to a computer with all the options or memory fitted 2. referring to a printed circuit board that has components in all free sockets

fully qualified domain name /ˌfuli ˌkwɒlɪfaɪd dəʊˈmeɪn ˌneɪm/ *noun* full form of **FQDN**

function /ˈfʌŋkʃən/ *noun* 1. a mathematical formula in which a result is dependent upon several other numbers 2. a sequence of computer program instructions in a main program that perform a certain task 3. a special feature available on a computer or word-processor ○ *The word-processor had a spelling-checker function but no built-in text-editing function.*

functional diagram /ˌfʌŋkʃ(ə)nəl ˈdaɪəgræm/ *noun* a drawing of the internal workings and processes of a machine or piece of software

functional specification /ˌfʌŋkʃ(ə)nəl ˌspesɪfɪˈkeɪʃ(ə)n/ *noun* a specification which defines the results which a program is expected to produce

functional unit /ˌfʌŋkʃən(ə)l ˈjuːnɪt/ *noun* a piece of hardware or software that works as it should

function call /ˈfʌŋkʃən kɔːl/ *noun* a program instruction that moves execution to a predefined function or named sequence of instructions

function code /ˈfʌŋkʃən kəʊd/ *noun* a printing code that controls an action rather than representing a character

function digit /ˈfʌŋkʃən ˌdɪdʒɪt/ *noun* a code used to instruct a computer as to which function or branch in a program to follow

function key /ˈfʌŋkʃən kiː/ *noun* one of several special keys placed along the top of a PC keyboard that have different uses according to different applications

COMMENT: Function keys often form a separate group of keys on the keyboard, and have specific functions attached to them. They may be labelled F1, F2 and so on. Most applications use the F1 key to display help information and Alt-F4 to quit an application

function library /ˈfʌŋkʃən ˌlaɪbrəri/ *noun* the collection of functions that can be used by a program

function overloading /ˈfʌŋkʃ(ə)n ˌəʊvələʊdɪŋ/ *noun* a programming system in which several different functions can have the same name, but are differentiated because they operate on different data types

function table /ˈfʌŋkʃən ˌteɪb(ə)l/ *noun* a list that gives the relationship between two sets of instructions or data

fusible link /ˌfjuːzɪb(ə)l ˈlɪŋk/ *noun* a small link in a PLA that can be blown to program the device permanently

fusible read only memory /ˌfjuːzɪb(ə)l riːd ˌəʊnli ˈmem(ə)ri/ *noun* PROM that is made up of a matrix of fusible links which are selectively blown to program it. Abbr **FROM**

fuzzy logic, fuzzy theory *noun* a type of logic applied to computer programming, which tries to replicate the reasoning methods of the human brain

FYI /ˌef waɪ ˈaɪ/ *noun* a document file that contains general background information related to the Internet or the TCP/IP protocols. Full form **for your information**. ◊ **RFC** (NOTE: Specific technical information is normally contained in RFC documents.)

G

G *abbr* giga-

COMMENT: In computing G refers to 2^{30}, equal to 1,073,741,824.

G.711 /ˌdʒiː ˌsev(ə)n ɪˈlev(ə)n/ *noun* a standard used in multimedia and telephony to define an audio signal with a 3.4 KHz bandwidth transferred over a 64 Kbits/second data channel

gain /geɪn/ *noun* **1.** an increase or enlargement **2.** an amount by which a signal amplitude is changed as it passes through a circuit, usually given as a ratio of output to input amplitude. Opposite **attenuation**

gallium arsenide /ˌgæliəm ˈɑːs(ə)naɪd/ *noun* a semiconductor compound, a material used for chip construction, that allows faster operation than silicon chips

game cartridge /ˈgeɪm ˌkɑːtrɪdʒ/ *noun* a ROM device that contains the program code for a computer game, and which is plugged into a game console

game console /ˈgeɪm ˌkɒnsəʊl/ *noun* a dedicated computer that is used primarily to play games, designed to connect to a television set rather than a monitor and usually controlled using a gamepad rather than a keyboard and mouse. Also called **games console**

gamepad /ˈgeɪmpæd/ *noun* a device held in the hand to control a computer game

game port /ˈgeɪm pɔːt/ *noun* a connection that allows a joystick to be plugged into a computer

gaming gear /ˈgeɪmɪŋ gɪə/ *noun* accessories for a computer that are designed to increase the enjoyment of playing a computer game, e.g. a joystick for action games or a steering wheel and foot pedals for a driving game

ganged /gæŋd/ *adjective* referring to mechanically linked devices that are operated by a single action

ganged switch /ˌgæŋd ˈswɪtʃ/ *noun* a series of switches that operate on different parts of a circuit but which are all switched by a single action ○ *A ganged switch is used to select which data bus a printer will respond to.*

gap /gæp/ *noun* **1.** a space between recorded data **2.** a space between a read head and the magnetic medium

gap character /gæp ˈkærɪktə/ *noun* an extra character added to a group of characters for parity or another purpose, but not as data or an instruction

gap digit /gæp ˈdɪdʒɪt/ *noun* an extra digit added to a group of data for parity or another purpose, but not as data or an instruction

gap loss /ˌgæp ˈlɒs/ *noun* a signal attenuation due to incorrect alignment of the read/write head with the storage medium

garbage /ˈgɑːbɪdʒ/ *noun* **1.** a radio interference from adjacent channels **2.** data or information that is no longer required because it is out of date or contains errors

garbage collection /ˈgɑːbɪdʒ kəˌlekʃən/ *noun* the reorganisation and removal of unwanted or out-of-date files and records

garbage in garbage out /ˌgɑːbɪdʒ ɪn ˌgɑːbɪdʒ ˈaʊt/ *noun* full form of **GIGO**

gas discharge display, gas plasma display *noun* a flat, lightweight display screen that is made of two flat pieces of glass covered with a grid of conductors, separated by a thin layer of a gas which luminesces when one point of the grid is selected by two electric signals. Also called **plasma display**

COMMENT: Mainly used in modern portable computer displays, but the definition is not as good as in cathode ray tube displays.

gate /geɪt/ *noun* **1.** a logical electronic switch whose output depends on the states of the inputs and the type of logical function implemented **2.** a connection pin of a FET device

gate array /geɪt ə'reɪ/ *noun* a number of interconnected logic gates built into an integrated circuit to perform a complex function

gate circuit /geɪt 'sɜːkɪt/ *noun* an electronic component that implements a logical function

gated /ˌgeɪt 'diː/ *noun* software that redirects network traffic, usually Internet traffic, according to a set of rules, and can also be used to limit access to a site or to route traffic to another site. Full form **gate daemon**. ◊ **routed**

gate delay /geɪt dɪ'leɪ/ *noun* the time taken for a gate to produce an output after it has received inputs

gateway /'geɪtweɪ/ *noun* **1.** a device that links two dissimilar networks ○ *We use a gateway to link the LAN to WAN.* **2.** a software protocol translation device that allows users working in one network to access another **3.** a piece of software that allows email messages to be sent via a different route or to another network

gateway interface /'geɪtweɪ ˌɪntəfeɪs/ *noun* ♦ **CGI**

gateway page /'geɪtweɪ peɪdʒ/ *noun* the first webpage that a visitor to a website sees and the one that contains the key words and phrases that enable a search engine to find it

gather /'gæðə/ *verb* to receive data from various sources, either directly from a data capture device or from a cartridge, and sort and insert it in correct order into a database

gather write /'gæðə raɪt/ *verb* to write a group of separate records as one block of data

Gb *abbr* gigabyte

GDI *abbr* graphics device interface

gender changer /'dʒendə ˌtʃeɪndʒə/ *noun* a device for changing a female connection to a male or vice versa (*informal*)

General MIDI /ˌdʒen(ə)rəl 'mɪdi/ *noun* a set of standards for a synthesiser that set out the first 128 different instrument sounds in a synthesiser and the number that refers to it. For example, 40 is always a violin.

general packet radio service /ˌdʒen(ə)rəl ˌpækɪt 'reɪdiəʊ ˌsɜːvɪs/ *noun* full form of **GPRS**

general protection fault /ˌdʒen(ə)rəl prə'tekʃən ˌfɔːlt/ *noun* full form of **GPF**

general purpose computer /ˌdʒen(ə)rəl ˌpɜːpəs kəm'pjuːtə/ *noun* a computer whose processing power may be applied to many different sorts of applications, depending on its hardware or software instructions

general purpose interface adapter /ˌdʒen(ə)rəl ˌpɜːpəs 'ɪntəfeɪs əˌdæptə/ *noun* an adapter usually used to interface a processing unit to a IEEE-488 bus. Abbr **GPIA**

general purpose interface bus /ˌdʒen(ə)rəl ˌpɜːpəs 'ɪntəfeɪs ˌbʌs/ *noun* full form of **GPIB**

general purpose program /ˌdʒen(ə)rəl ˌpɜːpəs 'prəʊgræm/ *noun* a program or device able to perform many different jobs or applications

generate /'dʒenəˌreɪt/ *verb* to use software or a device to produce codes or a program automatically ○ *to generate an image from digitally recorded data*

generated address /ˌdʒenəreɪtɪd ə'dres/ *noun* a location used by a program that has been produced by instructions within the program

generated error /ˌdʒenəreɪtɪd 'erə/ *noun* an error occurring due to inaccuracies in data used, e.g. a sum total error due to a series of numbers which are rounded up

generation /ˌdʒenə'reɪʃ(ə)n/ *noun* **1.** the process of producing data or software or programs using a computer ○ *The computer is used in the generation of graphic images.* **2.** the state or age of the technology used in the design of a system **3.** the distance between a file and the original version, used when making backups ○ *The father file is a first generation backup.*

generation loss /ˌdʒenə'reɪʃ(ə)n lɒs/ *noun* degradation of signal quality with each successive recording of a video or audio signal

generator /'dʒenəˌreɪtə/ *noun* a program that generates new programs according to rules or specifications set out by the user

generator lock /'dʒenəˌreɪtə lɒk/ *noun* a device that synchronises the timing signals of two video signals from different sources so that they can be successfully combined or mixed. Also called **genlock** (NOTE: It is often used to synchronise the output of a computer's display adapter with an external video source when using the computer to create overlays or titling.)

generic /dʒə'nerɪk/ *adjective* that is compatible with a whole family of hardware or software devices from one manufacturer

genlock /'dʒenlɒk/ *noun* same as **generator lock**

geometry /dʒi'ɒmətri/ *noun* the first of the two stages used to create and display a three-dimensional object. The second is rendering.

geometry processing /dʒi:'ɒmətri ˌprəʊsesɪŋ/ *noun* a process required to calculate the x, y and z coordinates of a three-dimensional object that is to be displayed on screen ○ *Geometry processing is usually carried out by the CPU or by a specialised graphics processor.*

geotargeting /ˌdʒi:əʊ'tɑːɡɪtɪŋ/ *noun* a method of analysing what a visitor to your website is viewing or doing and deducing his or her location, then displaying custom content or advertisements accordingly ○ *If a website visitor searches for the weather in Seattle, the intelligent geotargeting software displays banner advertisements from taxi companies in Seattle.*

get /get/ *noun* an instruction to obtain a record from a file or database

GET method /'get ˌmeθəd/ *noun* (*in HTML for CGI access*) a method of transferring information between a webpage, which uses the HTML form GET command, and a server-based application

ghost /ɡəʊst/ *noun* 1. a menu item displayed in grey and not currently available 2. an effect on a television image in which a weaker copy of the picture is displayed to one side of the main image, caused by signal reflections

ghost cursor /ɡəʊst 'kɜːsə/ *noun* a second cursor which can be used in some programs

GHz *abbr* gigahertz

GIF /ɡɪf/ a trade name for a graphics file format of a file containing a bit-mapped image. Full form **graphics interface format**

GIF file /ˌdʒi: aɪ 'ef faɪl/ *noun* graphics file format of a file containing a bit-mapped image

giga- /ɡɪɡə/ *prefix* one thousand million. Abbr **G**

COMMENT: In computing giga refers to 2^{30}, which is equal to 1,073,741,824.

gigabit /'ɡɪɡəbɪt/ *noun* a unit of capacity of a computer local area network, equal to one megabyte of computer information or 1,073,741,824 bits

gigabyte /'ɡɪɡəbaɪt/ *noun* 10^9 bytes. Abbr **Gb**

gigaflop /'ɡɪɡəflɒp/ *noun* one thousand million floating-point operations per second

gigahertz /'ɡɪɡəhɜːts/ *noun* a frequency of one thousand million cycles per second. Abbr **GHz**

GIGO /'ɡaɪɡəʊ/ *noun* the principle that the accuracy and quality of information that is output depends on the quality of the input. Full form **garbage in garbage out**

COMMENT: GIGO is sometimes taken to mean 'garbage in gospel out': i.e. that whatever wrong information is put into a computer, people will always believe that the output results are true.

gigs /ɡɪɡz/ *noun* meaning one thousand million; in computing G refers to 2^{30} equal to 1,073,741,824. Abbr **G**

GINO /ˌdʒi: aɪ en 'əʊ/ *noun* a graphical control routine written in FORTRAN. Full form **graphical input output**

GKS /ˌdʒi: keɪ 'es/ *noun* a standard for software command and functions describing graphical input/output to provide the same functions, etc. on any type of hardware. Full form **graphics kernel system**

glare /ɡleə/ *noun* very bright light reflections, especially on a VDU screen ○ *The glare from the screen makes my eyes hurt.*

glare filter /ɡleə 'fɪltə/ *noun* a coated glass or plastic sheet placed in front of a screen to cut out bright light reflections

glitch /ɡlɪtʃ/ *noun* anything which causes the sudden unexpected failure of a computer or equipment (*informal*)

'The programmer was upgrading a verification system at Visa's UK data centre when his work triggered a software glitch causing hundreds of valid cards to be rejected for several hours.' [*Computing*]

global /'ɡləʊb(ə)l/ *adjective* covering everything

'In an attempt to bring order to an electronic Tower of Babel, pharmaceutical giant Rhone-Poulenc has assembled an X.400-based global messaging network and a patchwork directory system that will be used until a single email system is deployed worldwide.' [*Computing*]

global backup /ˌɡləʊb(ə)l 'bækʌp/ *noun* 1. a backup of all data stored on all nodes or workstations connected to a network 2. a backup of all files on a hard disk or file server

global exchange /ˌɡləʊb(ə)l ɪks'tʃeɪndʒ/ *noun* a replace function which replaces one piece of text, e.g. a word, with another throughout a whole text

global knowledge /ˌgləʊb(ə)l ˈnɒlɪdʒ/ *noun* all the knowledge about one problem or task

global memory /ˌgləʊb(ə)l ˈmem(ə)ri/ *noun* memory available to all Windows applications

global search and replace /ˌgləʊb(ə)l ˌsɜːtʃ ən rɪˈpleɪs/ *noun* a word-processor search and replace function covering a complete file or document

global system for mobile communications /ˌgləʊb(ə)l ˌsɪstəm fə ˌməʊbaɪl kəˌmjuːnɪˈkeɪʃ(ə)nz/ *noun* full form of **GSM**

global variable /ˌgləʊb(ə)l ˈveəriəb(ə)l/ *noun* a variable or number that can be accessed by any routine or structure in a program

glyph /glɪf/ *noun* the symbol, or the set of symbols, that forms a single character in a font

GND /ˌdʒiː en ˈdiː/ *abbr* ground

goal /gəʊl/ *noun* the final state reached when a task has been finished or has produced satisfactory results

go down /ˌgəʊ ˈdaʊn/ *verb* to break down or stop working

gold contact /ˌgəʊld ˈkɒntækt/ *noun* an electrical contact, usually for low-level signals, that is coated with gold to reduce the electrical resistance

gold disc /ˌgəʊld ˈdɪsk/ *noun* the original disc from which other copies of a CD-ROM are made

Google /ˈguːg(ə)l/ a trade name for a popular search engine

Gopher /ˈgəʊfə/ *noun* an Internet system that allows a user to find information and files stored on the Internet using a series of commands

GOSIP /ˈgɒsɪp/ *noun* a set of standards defined by the US Government to ensure that computers and communications systems can interact. Full form **Government Open Systems Interconnect Profile**

gospel /ˈgɒspəl/ *noun* ♦ GIGO

GOSUB /ˈgəʊsʌb/ *noun* a programming command which executes a routine then returns to the following instruction

GOTO /ˈgəʊtuː/ *noun* a programming command which instructs a jump to another point or routine in the program ○ *GOTO 105 instructs a jump to line 105.*

> COMMENT: GOTO statements are frowned upon by software experts since their use discourages set, structured programming techniques.

Gouraud shading /ˈguːrəʊ ˌʃeɪdɪŋ/ *noun* shading within a three-dimensional scene created by a mathematical equation that is applied to each side of each object and produces a gradual change in colour to give the impression of light and shade

Government Open Systems Interconnect Profile /ˌgʌv(ə)nmənt ˌəʊpən ˌsɪstəm ˈɪntəkənekt ˌprəʊfaɪl/ *noun* full form of **GOSIP**

GPF /ˌdʒiː piː ˈef/ *noun* an error condition that occurs in Microsoft Windows and causes an application to crash, usually caused by insufficient memory, by using an incompatible peripheral or device driver or by an error in a software program. Full form **general protection fault**

GPIB /ˌdʒiː piː aɪ ˈbiː/ *noun* a standard for an interface bus between a computer and laboratory equipment. Full form **general purpose interface bus**

gpr /ˌdʒiː piː ˈɑː/ *noun* a data register in a computer processing unit that can store items of a data for many different mathematical or logical operations. Full form **general purpose register**. Also called **general register**

GPRS /ˌdʒiː piː ɑː ˈes/ *noun* a standard system for wireless radio and mobile telephone communications that is due to replace the existing GSM system. Full form **general packet radio service** (NOTE: GPRS supports high-speed data transfer rates of up to 150 Kbps compared to the GSM limit of 9.6 Kbps.)

grabber /ˈgræbə/ *noun* same as **frame grabber**

graceful degradation /ˌgreɪsf(ə)l ˌdegrəˈdeɪʃ(ə)n/ *noun* the process of allowing some parts of a system to continue to function after a part has broken down

gradient /ˈgreɪdiənt/ *noun* (*in a graphic image*) a smooth change of colour from one colour to another or from black to white

grammar /ˈgræmə/ *noun* a set of rules for the correct use of a language

grammar checker /ˈgræmə ˌtʃekə/ *noun* a software utility used to check a document or letter to make sure it is grammatically correct

grammatical error /grəˌmætɪk(ə)l ˈerə/ *noun* an incorrect use of a computer programming language syntax

grandfather cycle /ˈgrænfɑːðə ˌsaɪk(ə)l/ *noun* a period in which the grandfather file is retrieved and updated to produce a new father file, the old father file becoming the new grandfather file

grandfather file /'grænfɑːðə faɪl/ *noun* the third most recent version of a backed up file, after father and son files

granularity /ˌgrænjʊ'lærɪti/ *noun* the size of memory segments in a virtual memory system

graphic /'græfɪk/ *adjective* referring to representation of information in the form of pictures or plots instead of by text

graphical input output /ˌgræfɪkl ˌɪnpʊt 'aʊtpʊt/ *noun* full form of **GINO**

graphical user interface /ˌgræfɪkl ˈjuːzə ˌɪntəfeɪs/ *noun* full form of **GUI**

graphic data /'græfɪk ˌdeɪtə/ *noun* stored data that represents graphical information when displayed on a screen

graphic display /'græfɪk dɪˌpleɪ/ *noun* a computer screen able to present graphical information

graphic display resolution /'græfɪk dɪˌspleɪ ˌrezəluːʃ(ə)n/ *noun* the number of pixels that a computer is able to display on the screen

graphic language /'græfɪk ˌlæŋgwɪdʒ/ *noun* a computer programming language with inbuilt commands that are useful when displaying graphics

graphic object /ˌgræfɪk 'ɒbdʒekt/ *noun* a small graphic image imported from another drawing application and placed on a page (NOTE: in most DTP, paint or drawing packages, the object can be moved, sized and positioned independently from the other elements on the page.)

graphics /'græfɪks/ *noun* pictures or lines which can be drawn on paper or on a screen to represent information ○ *graphics output such as bar charts, pie charts, line drawings, etc.*

graphics accelerator /'græfɪks ək ˌseləreɪtə/ *noun* a card that fits inside a computer and uses a dedicated processor chip to speed up the action of drawing lines and images on the screen

graphics adapter /'græfɪks əˌdæptə/ *noun* an electronic device, usually on an expansion card, in a computer that converts software commands into electrical signals that display graphics on a connected monitor ○ *The new graphics adapter is capable of displaying higher resolution graphics.*

graphics character /'græfɪks ˌkærɪktə/ *noun* a preprogrammed shape that can be displayed on a non-graphical screen instead of a character, used extensively in videotext systems to display simple pictures

graphics coprocessor /'græfɪks kəʊˌprəʊsesə/ *noun* same as **graphics processor**

graphics file /'græfɪks faɪl/ *noun* a binary file which contains data describing an image ○ *There are many standards for graphics files including TIFF, IMG and EPS.*

graphics file format /'græfɪks faɪl ˌfɔːmæt/ *noun* a method in which data describing an image is stored

graphics interface format /ˌgræfɪks 'ɪntəfeɪs ˌfɔːmæt/ *noun* full form of **GIF**

graphics kernel system /ˌgræfɪks 'kɜːn(ə)l ˌsɪstəm/ *noun* full form of **GKS**

graphics library /'græfɪks ˌlaɪbr(ə)ri/ *noun* a number of routines stored in a library file that can be added to any user program to simplify the task of writing graphics programs

graphics light pen /ˌgræfɪks 'laɪt ˌpen/ *noun* a high-accuracy light pen used for drawing onto a graphics display screen

graphics mode /'græfɪks məʊd/ *noun* a videotext terminal whose displayed characters are taken from a range of graphics characters instead of text

graphics overlay card /ˌgræfɪks 'əʊvəleɪ ˌkɑːd/ *noun* an expansion card for a PC or Apple Mac that combines generated text or images with an external video source

graphics pad /'græfɪks pæd/ *noun* same as **graphics tablet**

graphics primitive /ˌgræfɪks 'prɪmɪtɪv/ *noun* a basic shape such as an arc, line or filled square that is used to create other shapes or objects

graphics printer /'græfɪks ˌprɪntə/ *noun* a printer capable of printing bitmapped images

graphics processor /'græfɪks ˌprəʊsesə/ *noun* a secondary processor used to speed up the display of graphics ○ *This graphics adapter has a graphics coprocessor fitted and is much faster.* Also called **graphics coprocessor** (NOTE: It calculates the position of pixels that form a line or shape and display graphic lines or shapes.)

graphics software /'græfɪks ˌsɒftweə/ *noun* prewritten routines which perform standard graphics commands such as line drawing and plotting that can be called from within a program to simplify program writing

graphics tablet /'græfɪks ˌtæblət/ noun a flat device which allows a user to input graphical information into a computer by drawing on its surface ○ *It is much easier to draw accurately with a graphics tablet than with a mouse.* Also called **graphics pad**

graphics terminal /'græfɪks ˌtɜːmɪn(ə)l/ noun a special terminal with a high-resolution graphic display and graphics tablet or other input device

graphics VDU /ˌgræfɪks ˌviː diː 'juː/ noun a special VDU which can display high-resolution or colour graphics as well as text

graph plotter /'grɑːf ˌplɒtə/ noun same as **x-y plotter**

Gray code /'greɪ kəʊd/ noun a coding system in which the binary representation of decimal numbers changes by only one bit at a time from one number to the next

    COMMENT: It is used in communications systems to provide error detection facilities.

gray scale /'greɪ skeɪl/ noun *US* another spelling of **grey scale**

greeked /griːkd/ adjective (*in a DTP program*) referring to a font with a point size too small to display accurately, shown as a line rather than individual characters

Green Book /griːn 'bʊk/ noun a formal specification for CD-i standard published by Philips

gremlin /'gremlɪn/ noun an unexplained fault in a system (*informal*)

grey scale /'greɪ skeɪl/ noun the shades which are produced from displaying what should be colour information on a monochrome monitor (NOTE: The US spelling is **gray scale**.)

grid /grɪd/ noun a system of numbered squares used to help when drawing

grid snap /'grɪd snæp/ noun (*in a graphics program*) patterns or lines drawn on screen limited to the points of a grid ○ *If you want to draw accurate lines, you'll find it easier with grid snap turned on.*

ground /graʊnd/ noun an electrical circuit connection to earth or to a point with a zero voltage level. Abbr **GND** (NOTE: **ground** is more common in US English; the British English is **earth**)

group /gruːp/ noun **1.** a set of computer records containing related information **2.** a six-character word used in telegraphic communications **3.** (*in a GUI*) a collection of icons, of files or programs displayed together in a window ○ *All the icons in this group are to do with painting.* **4.** (*in a network*) a collection of users conveniently identified by one name ○ *The group ACCOUNTS contains all the users who work in the accounts department.* ■ verb to bring several things together

Group 3 /ˌgruːp 'θriː/ noun ⧫ **fax group**

group icon /gruːp 'aɪkɒn/ noun (*in a GUI*) an icon that represents a window which contains a collection of icons of files or programs

group mark /gruːp mɑːk/, **group marker** noun a code used to identify the start and end of a group of related records or items of data

group poll /'gruːp pəʊl/ noun a poll of a number of devices at once

groupware /'gruːpweə/ noun software specially written to be used by a group of people connected to a network and help them carry out a particular task (NOTE: It provides useful functions such as a diary or email that can be accessed by all users.)

GSM /ˌdʒiː es 'em/ noun a popular system used for wireless cellular telephone communications throughout Europe, Asia and parts of North America. Full form **global system for mobile communications**. ◊ **GPRS**

    COMMENT: The GSM system allows eight calls to share the same radio frequency and carries the digital data that represents voice signals transmitted by each user's telephone. The main drawback of GSM is that it does not offer very fast data transfer rates which has become more important as users want to access the Internet and read email via a mobile telephone connection. GSM provides data transfer at up to 9.6Kbps, but it is due to be replaced by the GPRS system that can support high-speed data transfer at up to 150Kbps.

guard band /'gɑːd bænd/ noun a section of magnetic tape between two channels recorded on the same tape

guard bit /'gɑːd bɪt/ noun one bit within a stored word that indicates to the computer whether it can be altered or if it is protected

GUI /'guːi/ noun an interface between an operating system or program and the user that uses graphics or icons to represent functions or files and allow the software to be controlled more easily. Full form **graphical user interface**. Compare **command line interface**

    COMMENT: GUIs normally use a combination of windows, icons and a mouse to control the operating system. In many GUIs, such as Microsoft Windows and the Apple Mac System, you can control all the functions of the operating system just using the mouse. Icons represent programs and files; instead of entering the file name, you select it by moving a pointer with a mouse.

guide bar /'gaɪd bɑː/ *noun* a special line in a bar code that shows either the start or the finish of the code ○ *The standard guide bars are two thin lines that are a little longer than the coding lines.*

gulp /gʌlp/ *noun* a group of words, usually two bytes. ◊ **byte, nybble**

gun /gʌn/ *noun* same as **electron gun**

COMMENT: Black and white monitors have a single beam gun, while colour monitors contain three, one for each primary colour (red, green and blue) used.

gutter /'gʌtə/ *noun* (*in a DTP system*) a blank space or inner margin between two facing pages

H

H *abbr* hex

H.323, H.324 *noun* standards that define how a video conferencing call is set up and managed over a communications link

hack /hæk/ *verb* **1.** to experiment and explore computer software and hardware **2.** to break into a computer system for criminal purposes

hacker /'hækə/ *noun* a person who hacks

'The two were also charged with offences under the Computer Misuse Act and found guilty of the very actions upon which every hacker is intent.' [*Computing*]

hairline rule /'heə‚laɪn ruːl/ *noun* (*in a DTP system*) a very thin line

half adder /hɑːf 'ædə/ *noun* a binary addition circuit which can produce the sum of two inputs and a carry output if necessary, but will not accept a carry input

half card /‚hɑːf 'kɑːd/ *noun* an expansion card that is half full length

half duplex /hɑːf 'djuːpleks/ *noun* full form of **HD**

half-duplex modem /‚hɑːf ‚djuːpleks 'məʊdem/ *noun* a modem which works in one mode at a time, either transmitting or receiving ○ *Some modems can operate in half-duplex mode if required.*

half-height drive /‚hɑːf haɪt 'draɪv/ *noun* a disk drive whose front is half the height of a standard drive. Half-height drives, usually 5.25 inches, are now the norm on PCs.

half-intensity /hɑːf ɪn'tensɪti/ *adjective* referring to a character or graphics display at half the usual display brightness

halftone /‚hɑːf'təʊn/ *noun* a photograph or image that originally had continuous tones, displayed or printed by a computer using groups of dots to represent the tones

half word /‚hɑːf 'wɜːd/ *noun* a sequence of bits occupying half a standard computer word, but which can be accessed as a single unit

hall effect /hɔːl ɪ'fekt/ *noun* a description of the effect of a magnetic field on electron flow

hall effect switch /‚hɔːl ɪ‚fekt 'swɪtʃ/ *noun* a solid state electronic switch operated by a magnetic field

halt /hɔːlt/ *noun* a computer instruction to stop a CPU carrying out any further instructions until restarted, or until the program is restarted, usually by external means, e.g. a reset button

halt condition /hɔːlt kən'dɪʃ(ə)n/ *noun* the operating state reached when a CPU comes across a fault or faulty instruction or halt instruction in the program that is being run

halt instruction /hɔːlt ɪn'strʌkʃən/ *noun* a program instruction that causes a

CPU to halt, suspending operations, usually until it is reset

Hamming code /'hæmɪŋ kəʊd/ *noun* a coding system that uses check bits and checksums to detect and correct errors in transmitted data, mainly used in teletext systems

Hamming distance /'hæmɪŋ ˌdɪstəns/ *noun* the number of digits that are different in two equal length words

hand-held computer /ˌhænd held kəm'pjuːtə/, **hand-held programmable** /ˌhænd held 'prəʊgræməb(ə)l/ *noun* a very small computer which can be held in the hand, useful for basic information input, when a terminal is not available

hand-held scanner /ˌhænd held 'skænə/ *noun* a device that is held in your hand and contains a row of photo-electric cells which, when moved over an image, convert it into data which can be manipulated by a computer

H & J /ˌeɪtʃ ənd 'dʒeɪ/ *noun* the process of justifying lines to a set width, splitting the long words correctly at the end of each line. Full form **hyphenation and justification**

handle /'hænd(ə)l/ *noun* **1.** (*in programming*) number used to identify an active file within the program that is accessing the file **2.** (*in a GUI*) a small square displayed that can be dragged to change the shape of a window or graphical object ○ *To stretch the box in the DTP program, select it once to display the handles then drag one handle to change its shape.*

handler /'hændlə/ *noun* a part of an operating system software or a special software routine which controls a device or function ○ *The scanner handler routines are supplied on disk.* ◊ **driver**

handshake /'hæn(d)ˌʃeɪk/, **handshaking** *noun* a set of standardised signals between two devices to make sure that the system is working correctly, the equipment is compatible and data transfer is correct (NOTE: Signals would include ready to receive, ready to transmit and data OK.)

handshake I/O control /ˌhæn(d)ʃeɪk aɪ 'əʊ kənˌtrəʊl/ *noun* the use of handshake signals meaning ready-to-send and ready-to-receive, that allow a computer to communicate with a slower peripheral

hands off /ˌhændz 'ɒf/ *noun* referring to a working system in which the operator

does not control the operation, which is automatic

hands on /ˌhændz 'ɒn/ *adjective* referring to a working system in which the operator controls the operations by keying instructions on the keyboard ○ *The sales representatives have received hands-on experience of the new computer.*

handwriting recognition /'hændraɪtɪŋ ˌrekəgnɪʃ(ə)n/ *noun* software that is capable of recognising handwritten text and converting it into ASCII characters ○ *The new PDA has excellent handwriting recognition.*

hang /hæŋ/ *verb* to enter an endless loop and not respond to further instruction (NOTE: hung)

hangover /'hæŋəʊvə/ *noun* a sudden tone change on a document that is transmitted over a fax machine as a gradual change, caused by equipment faults

hangup /'hæŋʌp/ *noun* a sudden stop of a working program, often caused by the CPU executing an illegal instruction or entering an endless loop

hard /hɑːd/ *adjective* referring to parts of a computer system that cannot be programmed or altered

hard card /ˌhɑːd 'kɑːd/ *noun* a board containing a hard disk drive and the required interfacing electronics, which can be slotted into a system's expansion connector

hard copy /ˌhɑːd 'kɒpi/ *noun* a printed document or copy of information contained in a computer or system, in a form that is readable. Also called **soft copy**

hard copy interface /ˌhɑːd 'kɒpi ˌɪntəfeɪs/ *noun* a serial or parallel interface used to transmit data between a computer and a printer

hard disk /ˌhɑːd 'dɪsk/ *noun* a rigid magnetic disk that is able to store many times more data than a floppy disk, and usually cannot be removed from the disk drive

hard disk drive /ˌhɑːd 'dɪsk ˌdraɪv/ *noun* a unit used to store and retrieve data from a spinning hard disk on the commands of a computer. Abbr **HDD**. Also called **hard drive**

hard drive /'hɑːd draɪv/ *noun* same as **hard disk drive**

hard error /ˌhɑːd 'erə/ *noun* an error which is permanent in a system

hard failure /ˌhɑːd 'feɪljə/ *noun* a fault in hardware that must be mended before a device will function correctly ○ *The hard failure was due to a burnt-out chip.*

hard reset /hɑːd ˌriːˈset/ *noun* a switch that generates an electrical signal to reset the CPU and all devices, equivalent to turning a computer off and back on again

hard return /hɑːd rɪˈtɜːn/ *noun* a code in a word-processing document that indicates the end of a paragraph or its characteristics

hardware /ˈhɑːdˌweə/ *noun* the physical units, components, integrated circuits, disks and mechanisms that make up a computer or its peripherals

'Seuqent's Platform division will focus on hardware and software manufacture, procurement and marketing, with the Enterprise division concentrating on services and client-server implementation.' [*Computing*]

hardware compatibility /ˌhɑːdweə kəmˌpætəˈbɪlɪti/ *noun* architecture of two different computers that allows one to run the programs of the other without changing any device drivers or memory locations, or the ability of one to use the add-on boards of the other

hardware configuration /ˌhɑːdweə kənˌfɪɡjəˈreɪʃ(ə)n/ *noun* a way in which the hardware of a computer system is connected together

hardware dependent /ˌhɑːdweə dɪ ˈpendənt/ *adjective* which will only work with a particular model or brand of hardware ○ *The communications software is hardware dependent and will only work with Hayes-compatible modems.*

hardware failure /ˈhɑːdweə ˌfeɪljə/ *noun* a fault with a hardware device or hardware that has stopped working properly

hardware graphics cursor /ˌhɑːdweə ˈɡræfɪks ˌkɜːsə/ *noun* an electronic component that is used to calculate the position on screen of a pointer, according to the movement of a mouse, and display the pointer

hardware interrupt /ˈhɑːdweə ˌɪntərʌpt/ *noun* an interrupt signal generated by a piece of hardware rather than by software

hardware platform /ˈhɑːdweə ˌplætfɔːm/ *noun* the standard of a particular computer such as IBM PC or Apple Mac

hardware reliability /ˌhɑːdweə rɪˌlaɪə ˈbɪlɪti/ *noun* the ability of a piece of hard-

ware to function normally over a period of time

hardware reset /ˌhɑːdweə ˈriːset/ *noun* a switch that generates an electrical signal to reset the CPU and all devices, equivalent to turning a computer off and back on again

hardware security /ˌhɑːdweə sɪ ˈkjʊərɪti/ *noun* the use of hardware such as keys or cards to make a system secure

hardwired connection /ˌhɑːdwaɪəd kəˈnekʃ(ə)n/ *noun* a permanent phone line connection, rather than a plug and socket

hardwired logic /ˌhɑːdwaɪəd ˈlɒdʒɪk/ *noun* a logical function or software program built using electronic hardware, using electronic devices such as logic components, rather than written in software

hardwired program /ˌhɑːdwaɪəd ˈprəʊɡræm/ *noun* a computer program built into the hardware, and unable to be changed

harmonics /hɑːˈmɒnɪks/ *noun* the integer multiple of a given sound frequency

hartley /ˈhɑːtli/ *noun* a unit of information equal to 3.32 bits, or the probability of one state out of ten equally probable states

hash /hæʃ/ *noun* same as **hashmark** ■ *verb* to produce a unique number derived from the entry itself, for each entry in a database

hash code /ˌhæʃ ˈkəʊd/ *noun* a coding system derived from the ASCII codes, in which the code numbers for the first three letters are added up, giving a new number used as a hash code

hash-code system /ˈhæʃ kəʊd ˌsɪstəm/ *noun* a coding system using hash codes

hash index /hæʃ ˈɪndeks/ *noun* a list of entries according to their hashed numbers

hashing function /hæʃɪŋ ˈfʌŋkʃən/ *noun* an algorithm used to produce a hash code for an entry and ensure that it is different from every other entry

hashmark /ˈhæʃmɑːk/, **hash mark** /ˈhæʃ mɑːk/ *noun* a printed sign (#) used as a hard copy marker or as an indicator. Also called **hash**

COMMENT: The US term is **pound sign**. In US usage # means number; #32 = number 32 (e.g. apartment number in a postal address, paragraph number in a text).

hash table /hæʃ ˈteɪb(ə)l/ *noun* a list of all entries in a file with their hashed key address

hash total /hæʃ 'təʊt(ə)l/ *noun* a total of a number of hashed entries, used for error detection

hash value /hæʃ 'vælju:/ *noun* a number arrived at after a key is hashed

Hayes AT command set /ˌheɪz eɪ ti: kə'mɑːnd set/ *noun* a set of commands to control a modem prefixed with the letters AT

Hayes-compatible /ˌheɪz kəm'pætɪb(ə)l/ *adjective* referring to a modem that is compatible with the Hayes AT command set

Hayes Corporation /'heɪz ˌkɔːpəreɪʃ(ə)n/ a modem manufacturer that developed standard control language for modems

hazard /'hæzəd/ *noun* a fault in hardware due to incorrect signal timing

hazard-free implementation /ˌhæzəd fri: ˌɪmplɪmen'teɪʃ(ə)n/ *noun* a logical function design that has taken into account any hazards that could occur, and solved them

haze /heɪz/ *noun* same as **fogging**

HCI *abbr* host controller interface

HD /ˌeɪtʃ 'di:/ *noun* data transmission in one direction only, over a bidirectional channel. Full form **half duplex**

HDD *abbr* hard disk drive

HDLC *abbr* high-level data link control

HDTV *abbr* high definition television

HDX *abbr* half duplex

head /hed/ *noun* **1.** data that indicates the start address of a list of items stored in memory **2.** a top edge of a book or of a page **3.** the start of a reel of recording tape **4.** the top part of a device, network or body ■ *verb* to be the first item of data in a list ○ *The queue was headed by my file.*

head alignment /hed ə'laɪnmənt/ *noun* **1.** the correct position of a tape or disk head in relation to the magnetic surface, to give the best performance and correct track location **2.** the location of the read head in the same position as the write head was, in relation to the magnetic medium

head cleaning disk /'hed ˌkliːnɪŋ dɪsk/ *noun* a special disk which is used to clean the disk read/write heads

head crash /'hed kræʃ/ *noun* a component failure in a disk drive, in which the head is allowed to hit the surface of the spinning disk, causing disk surface damage and data corruption

head demagnetiser /'hed di: ˌmægnətaɪzə/ *noun* a device used to remove any stray magnetic effects that might have built up on the tape head

head end /'hed end/ *noun* interconnection equipment between an antenna and a cable television network

header /'hedə/ *noun* **1.** (*in a local area network*) a packet of data that is sent before a transmission to provide information on destination and routing **2.** information at the beginning of a list of data relating to the rest of the data **3.** a section of words at the top of a page of a document, giving e.g. the title, author's name or page number. Also called **heading**. ◊ **footer**

header block /'hedə blɒk/ *noun* a block of data at the beginning of a file containing data about file characteristics

header card /'hedə kɑːd/ *noun* a punched card containing information about the rest of the cards in the set

header label /'hedə ˌleɪb(ə)l/ *noun* a section of data at the beginning of a magnetic tape, that contains identification, format and control information

head gap /'hed gæp/ *noun* same as **air gap**

heading /'hedɪŋ/ *noun* **1.** the title or name of a document or file **2.** a header or section of words at the top of each page of a document. Also called **headline**

headlife /'hedlaɪf/ *noun* the length of time that a video or tape head can work before being serviced or replaced

headline /'hedlaɪn/ *noun* same as **heading**

head of form /ˌhed əv 'fɔːm/ *noun* the first line on a form or sheet of paper that can be printed on

head park /'hed pɑːk/ *noun* the process of moving the read/write head in a hard disk drive to a safe position, not over the disk, so that if the unit is knocked or jarred the head will not damage the disk surface

head positioning /hed pə'zɪʃ(ə)nɪŋ/ *noun* the process of moving the read/write head to the correct track on a disk

head wheel /'hed wiːl/ *noun* a wheel that keeps video tape in contact with the head

heap /hiːp/ *noun* **1.** a temporary data storage area that allows random access. Compare **stack 2.** a binary tree

heat-sensitive paper /ˌhiːt ˌsensɪtɪv 'peɪpə/ *noun* ♦ **electrostatic printer**

heat-sink /hiːt sɪŋk/ *noun* a metal device used to conduct heat away from an electronic component to prevent damage

helical scan /ˌhelɪk(ə)l 'skæn/ *noun* a method of storing data on magnetic tape in which the write head stores data in diagonal strips rather than parallel with the tape edge so using the tape area more efficiently and allowing more data to be recorded. It is used most often in video tape recorders.

help /help/ *noun* a function in a program or system that provides useful information about the program in use ○ *Hit the HELP key if you want information about what to do next.*

COMMENT: Most software applications for IBM PCs have standardised the use of the F1 function key to display help text explaining how something can be done.

help desk /'help desk/ *noun* a service that provides technical help and support for people using a computer package or network

helper application /'helpə ˌæplɪkeɪʃ(ə)n/ *noun* software which works with a web browser to increase the functionality of the browser ○ *To view Adobe Acrobat pages in your web browser you will need to get the Adobe helper application.*

help key /'help kiː/ *noun* a key that displays help information, on an Apple Mac a special key, on an IBM PC the F1 function key

help screen /'help skriːn/ *noun* a display of information about a program or function

hertz /hɜːts/ *noun* an SI unit of frequency, defined as the number of cycles per second of time. Abbr **Hz**

COMMENT: Hertz rate is the frequency at which mains electricity is supplied to the consumer. The hertz rate in the USA and Canada is 60; in Europe it is 50.

heterogeneous multiplexing /ˌhetərəʊdʒiːniəs 'mʌltɪˌpleksɪŋ/ *noun* a communications multiplexing system that can deal with channels with different transmission rates and protocols

heterogeneous network /ˌhetərəʊdʒiːniəs 'netwɜːk/ *noun* a computer network joining computers of many different types and makes

heuristic /hjʊə'rɪstɪk/ *adjective* which learns from past experiences ○ *A heuristic program learns from its previous actions and decisions.*

Hewlett Packard /ˌhewlət 'pækɑːd/ manufacturer of computers, test equipment and printers. Abbr **HP**

Hewlett Packard Graphics Language /ˌhewlət ˌpækɑːd 'græfɪks ˌlæŋgwɪdʒ/ a standard set of commands used to describe graphics. Abbr **HPGL**

Hewlett Packard Interface Bus /ˌhewlət ˌpækɑːd 'ɪntəfeɪs bʌs/ a standard method of interfacing peripheral devices or test equipment and computers. Abbr **HPIB**

Hewlett Packard LaserJet /ˌhewlət ˌpækɑːd 'leɪzədʒet/ a trade name for a laser printer manufactured by Hewlett Packard that uses its PCL language to describe a page. Also called **LaserJet**

Hewlett Packard Printer Control Language /ˌhewlət ˌpækɑːd ˌprɪntə kən'trəʊl ˌlæŋgwɪdʒ/ a standard set of commands developed by Hewlett Packard to allow a software application to control a laser printer's functions. Abbr **HP-PCL**

hex /heksəˌdesɪm(ə)l nəʊ'teɪʃ(ə)n/, **hexadecimal notation** *noun* a number system using base 16 and the digits 0–9 and A-F. Abbr **H**

hex dump /'heks dʌmp/ *noun* the display of a section of memory in hexadecimal form

hex keypad /heks 'kiːˌpæd/ *noun* a keypad with 16 keys, 0–9 and A-F, for all the hexadecimal digits

HFS /ˌeɪtʃ ef 'es/ *noun* (*in an Apple Mac system*) a method used to store and organise files on a disk. Full form **hierarchical filing system**

hidden files /'hɪd(ə)n faɪlz/ *plural noun* important system files which are not displayed in a directory listing and cannot normally be read by a user ○ *It allows users to backup or restore hidden files independently.*

hidden line algorithm /ˌhɪd(ə)n laɪn 'ælgərɪð(ə)m/ *noun* a mathematical formula that removes hidden lines from a two-dimensional computer image of a 3-D object

hidden line removal /ˌhɪd(ə)n 'laɪn rɪˌmuːvəl/ *noun* the erasure of lines which should not be visible when looking at a two-dimensional image of a three-dimensional object

hidden lines /'hɪd(ə)n laɪnz/ *plural noun* lines which make up a three-dimensional object, but are obscured when displayed as a two-dimensional image

hierarchical /haɪəˈrɑːkɪk(ə)l/ *adjective* referring to a way of organising data or objects or structures with the most important or highest priority item at the top, then working down a tree structure

hierarchical communications system /ˌhaɪərɑːkɪk(ə)l kəˌmjuːnɪˈkeɪʃ(ə)nz ˌsɪstəm/ *noun* a network in which each branch has a number of separate minor branches dividing from it

hierarchical computer network /ˌhaɪərɑːkɪk(ə)l kəmˈpjuːtə ˌnetwɜːk/ *noun* a method of allocating control and processing functions in a network to the computers which are most suited to the task

hierarchical database /ˌhaɪərɑːkɪk(ə)l ˈdeɪtəbeɪs/ *noun* a database in which records can be related to each other in a defined structure

hierarchical directory /ˌhaɪərɑːkɪk(ə)l daɪˈrekt(ə)ri/ *noun* a directory listing of files on a disk, showing the main directory and its files, branches and any sub-directories

hierarchical filing system /ˌhaɪərɑːkɪk(ə)l ˈfaɪlɪŋ ˌsɪstəm/ *noun* full form of **HFS**

hierarchical routing /ˌhaɪərɑːkɪk(ə)l ˈruːtɪŋ/ *noun* a method of directing network traffic over a complex network by breaking down the structure of the network into separate levels, each level being responsible for directing traffic within its area ○ *The Internet has a three-level hierarchical routing system in which the backbones can direct traffic from one Mid-level to another, the mid-levels can direct traffic from one server site to another and each server site can direct traffic internally.*

hierarchical vector quantisation /ˌhaɪərɑːkɪk(ə)l ˈvektə ˌkwɒntaɪzeɪʃ(ə)n/ *noun* full form of **HVQ**

hierarchy /ˈhaɪərɑːki/ *noun* a way in which objects or data or structures are organised, usually with the most important or highest priority or most general item at the top, then working down a tree structure

high definition television /ˌhaɪ ˌdefɪnɪʃ(ə)n ˈtelɪˌvɪʒ(ə)n/ *noun* a broadcast television standard that displays images at a different aspect ratio and with much better definition than existing television sets. Abbr **HDTV** (NOTE: There are six standards: all display 16:9 aspect ratio images, three support a resolution of 1920x1080 pixels, three support 1280x720.)

high density storage /ˌhaɪ ˌdensɪ ˈstɔːrɪdʒti/ *noun* a very large number of bits stored per area of storage medium

high-end /ˈhaɪ end/ *adjective* referring to expensive or high-performance devices

high fidelity /ˌhaɪ fɪˈdeləti/ *noun* very good quality sound, usually stereo sound recorded in 16 bits at a sample rate of 44.1 KHz

high-level data link control /ˌhaɪ ˌlev(ə)l ˌdeɪtə lɪŋk kənˈtrəʊl/ *noun* an ISO standard that provides a link-layer protocol and defines how data is formatted before being transmitted over a synchronous network. Abbr **HLDLC**

high-level data link control station /ˌhaɪ ˌlev(ə)l ˌdeɪtə lɪŋk kənˈtrəʊl ˌsteɪʃ(ə)n/ *noun* equipment and programs which correctly receive and transmit standard HLDLC data frames

high-level language /ˌhaɪ ˈlev(ə)l/, **high-level programming language** *noun* a computer programming language which is easy to learn and allows the user to write programs using words and commands that are easy to understand and look like English words. Abbr **HLL** (NOTE: The program is then translated into machine code, with one HLL instruction often representing more than one machine code instruction.)

highlight /ˈhaɪlaɪt/ *noun* a character or set of symbols treated so as to stand out from the rest of the text, often by using bold type ■ *verb* to make part of the text stand out from the rest ○ *The headings are highlighted in bold.*

highlight bar /ˈhaɪˌlaɪt bɑː/ *noun* (*in a display*) a line that can be moved up and down by a user that indicates which option is selected from a menu or list of options ○ *Move the highlight bar down to the third menu option and press Return.*

high memory /ˌhaɪ ˈmem(ə)ri/ *noun* (*in an IBM PC*) a memory area between 640 Kb and 1 Mb

high memory area /ˌhaɪ ˈmem(ə)ri ˌeəriə/ *noun* (*in an IBM PC*) the first 64 Kb of extended memory above 1 Mb that can be used by MS-DOS programs. Abbr **HMA**

high order /ˌhaɪ ˈɔːdə/ *noun* a digit with the greatest weighting within a number

high performance filing system /ˌhaɪ pəˌfɔːməns ˈfaɪlɪŋ ˌsɪstəm/ *noun* full form of **HPFS**

high priority program /ˌhaɪ praɪ ˌɒrɪti ˈprəʊɡræm/ *noun* a program that is important or urgent and is processed before others

high-resolution /haɪ ˌrezəˈluːʃ(ə)n/, **high-res** *noun* the ability to display or detect a very large number of pixels per unit area. Also called **hi-res**

high resolution graphics /ˌhaɪ ˌrezəluːʃ(ə)n ˈɡræfɪks/ *noun* full form of **HRG**

High Sierra /ˌhaɪ siˈerə/ *noun* an early CD-ROM standard that then became the ISO 9660 standard (NOTE: It was named after an area near Lake Tahoe, USA.)

high-spec /haɪ spek/ *plural noun* having a high specification ○ *High-spec cabling needs to be very carefully handled.*

high specification /haɪ ˌspesɪfɪ ˈkeɪʃ(ə)n/ *noun* a high degree of accuracy or a large number of features

high-speed /ˈhaɪ spiːd/ *adjective* which operates faster than normal data transmission or processing

high-speed carry /ˌhaɪ spiːd ˈkæri/ *noun* a single operation in which a carry into an adder results in a carry out

high-speed serial interface /haɪ spiːd ˌsɪəriəl ˈɪntəfeɪs/ *noun* full form of **HSSI**

high-speed skip /ˌhaɪ spiːd ˈskɪp/ *noun* a rapid movement of paper in a printer, ignoring the normal line advance

high-tech /haɪ ˈtek/ *adjective* technologically advanced

highway /ˈhaɪweɪ/ *noun* same as **bus**

hill climbing /hɪl ˈklaɪmɪŋ/ *noun* a method of achieving a goal in an IKBS

hi-res /haɪ reɪz/ *noun* same as **high-resolution**

histogram /ˈhɪstəɡræm/ *noun* a graph on which values are represented as vertical or horizontal bars

history /ˈhɪst(ə)ri/ *noun* a feature of some applications that keeps a log of the actions a user has carried out, the places within a hypertext document visited or the sites on the Internet explored

hit /hɪt/ *noun* a successful match or search of a database ○ *There was a hit after just a few seconds.* □ **hit on the line** a short period of noise on a communications line, causing data corruption ■ *verb* to

press a key ○ *To save the text, hit ESCAPE S.* (NOTE: hitting – hit)

hit point /ˈhɪt pɔɪnt/ *noun* an important action or piece of information displayed in a presentation

HLDLC *abbr* high-level data link control

HLL *abbr* high-level language

HLS *abbr* hue, lightness, saturation

HMA *abbr* high memory area

HMI *abbr* human-machine interface

HOF *abbr* head of form

hold /həʊld/ *noun* synchronisation timing pulse for a television time base signal ■ *verb* to retain or keep a value or communications line or section of memory (NOTE: held)

COMMENT: The hold feature keeps the picture steady and central on the screen. Some televisions have horizontal and vertical hold controls to allow the picture to be moved and set up according to various conditions.

holding loop /ˈhəʊldɪŋ luːp/ *noun* a section of program that loops until it is broken by some action, most often used when waiting for a response from the keyboard or a device

holding time /ˈhəʊldɪŋ taɪm/ *noun* the time spent by a communications circuit on call

holdup /ˈhɒldʌp/ *noun* **1.** a time period over which power will be supplied by a UPS **2.** a pause in a program or device due to a malfunction

hologram /ˈhɒləˌɡræm/ *noun* an imaginary three-dimensional image produced by the interference pattern when a part of a coherent light source, e.g. a laser, is reflected from an object and mixed with the main beam

holographic image /ˌhɒləɡræfɪk ˈɪmɪdʒ/ *noun* a hologram of a three-dimensional object

holographic storage /ˌhɒləɡræfɪk ˈstɔːrɪdʒ/ *noun* storage of data as a holographic image which is then read by a bank of photocells and a laser (NOTE: This is a storage medium with massive storage potential.)

home /həʊm/ *noun* a starting point or the initial point

home banking /həʊm ˈbæŋkɪŋ/ *noun* a method of examining and carrying out bank transactions in the user's home via a terminal and modem

home computer /həʊm kəmˈpjuːtə/ *noun* a microcomputer designed for home use, whose applications might include teaching, games, personal finance and word-processing

home key /'həʊm kiː/ *noun* a key on an IBM PC keyboard that moves the cursor to the beginning of a line of text

home page /'həʊm peɪdʒ/ *noun* the opening page of a website ○ *The home page is formatted using HTML and stored in a file called index.html.*

home record /həʊm 'rekɔːd/ *noun* the first or initial data record in a file

homogeneous computer network /ˌhəʊməʊdʒiːniəs kəm'pjuːtə ˌnetwɜːk/ *noun* a network made up of similar machines that are compatible or from the same manufacturer

homogeneous multiplexing /ˌhəʊməʊdʒiːniəs 'mʌltɪˌpleksɪŋ/ *noun* a switching multiplexer system in which all the channels contain data using the same protocol and transmission rate

hood /hʊd/ *noun* a cover which protects something

hook /hʊk/ *noun* a point in a program at which a programmer can insert test code or debugging code

hop /hɒp/ *noun* the path taken by a packet of data as it moves from one server or router to another

hop count /'hɒp kaʊnt/ *noun* the number of hops required to send information from one computer to another over the Internet

hopper /'hɒpə/ *noun* a device which holds punched cards and feeds them into the reader

horizontal axis /ˌhɒrɪzɒnt(ə)l 'æksɪs/ *noun* a reference line used for horizontal coordinates on a graph

horizontal blanking period /ˌhɒrɪzɒnt(ə)l 'blæŋkɪŋ ˌpɪəriəd/ *noun* the time taken for the picture beam in a monitor to return to the start of the next line from the end of the previous line

horizontal check /ˌhɒrɪzɒnt(ə)l 'tʃek/ *noun* an error detection method for transmitted data

horizontal scan frequency /ˌhɒrɪzɒnt(ə)l 'skæn ˌfriːkwənsi/ *noun* the number of lines on a video display that are refreshed each second

horizontal scrollbar /ˌhɒrɪzɒnt(ə)l 'skrəʊlbɑː/ *noun* (*in a GUI*) a bar along the bottom of a window that indicates that the page is wider than the window (NOTE: A user can move horizontally across the

page by dragging the indicator bar on the scrollbar.)

horizontal scrolling /ˌhɒrɪzɒnt(ə)l 'skrəʊlɪŋ/ *noun* the process of moving across a page, horizontally

horizontal wraparound /ˌhɒrɪzɒnt(ə)l 'ræpəˌraʊnd/ *noun* the movement of a cursor on a computer display from the end of one line to the beginning of the next

host /həʊst/ *noun, adjective* to provide storage space on a server computer where a user can store files or data, often used to store the files required for a website ○ *We chose this company to host our website because it has reliable server computers and high-speed connection to the Internet.*

'…you select fonts manually or through commands sent from the host computer along with the text' [*Byte*]

host adapter /həʊst ə'dæptə/ *noun* an adapter which connects to a host computer ○ *The cable to connect the scanner to the host adapter is included.*

host address /'həʊst əˌdres/ *noun* same as **Internet address**

host computer /həʊst kəm'pjuːtə/ *noun* **1.** the main controlling computer in a multi-user *or* distributed system **2.** a computer used to write and debug software for another computer, often using a cross compiler **3.** a computer in a network that provides special services *or* programming languages to all users

'…you select fonts manually or through commands sent from the host computer along with the text' [*Byte*]

hosting service provider /'həʊstɪŋ ˌsɜːvɪs prəˌvaɪdə/ *noun* same as **host service**

host name /'həʊst ˌneɪm/ *noun* a name given to a website on the Internet

host number /'həʊst ˌnʌmbə/ *noun* same as **Internet address**

host service /'həʊst ˌsɜːvɪs/ *noun* a company that provides connections to the Internet and storage space on its computers which can store the files for a user's website ○ *We rent storage space on this host service provider's server for our company website.* ◊ **ISP**. Also called **hosting service provider**

hot chassis /hɒt 'ʃæsi/ *noun* a metal framework or case around a computer that is connected to a voltage supply rather than being earthed

hot fix /ˌhɒt 'fɪks/ *noun* the process of detecting and repairing a fault, usually a corrupt sector on a hard disk, without affecting normal operations

hot key /ˈhɒt kiː/ *noun* a special key or key combination which starts a process or activates a program

hot link /ˌhɒt ˈlɪŋk/ *noun* a command within a hypertext program that links a hotspot or hotword on one page with a second destination page which is displayed if the user selects the hotspot

hot plugging /ˈhɒt ˌplʌɡɪŋ/ *noun* a feature of a computer that allows a device or peripheral to be plugged in or connected while the computer is working ○ *This server support hot plugging so I can plug in this network card and the operating system software will automatically detect and alter its configuration.* Also called **hot swapping**

hotspot /ˈhɒtspɒt/ *noun* a special area on an image or display that does something when the cursor is moved onto it ○ *The image of the trumpet is a hotspot and will play a sound when you move the pointer over it.*

hot standby /hɒt ˈstændbaɪ/ *noun* a piece of hardware that is kept operational at all times and is used as backup in case of system failure. Compare **cold standby, warm standby**

hot swapping /ˈhɒt ˌswɒpɪŋ/ *noun* same as **hot plugging**

hotword /ˈhɒtwɜːd/ *noun* a word within displayed text that does something when the cursor is moved onto it or it is selected

hot zone /ˈhɒt zəʊn/ *noun* a text area to the left of the right margin in a word-processed document where, if a word does not fit completely into the line, a hyphen is automatically inserted

housekeeping /ˈhaʊsˌkiːpɪŋ/ *noun* tasks that have to be regularly carried out to maintain a computer system, e.g. checking backups and deleting unwanted files

housekeeping routine /ˈhaʊskiːpɪŋ ruːˌtiːn/ *noun* a set of instructions executed once, at the start of a new program, to carry out system actions such as clear memory, configure function keys or change screen display mode

housing /ˈhaʊzɪŋ/ *noun* a solid case ○ *The computer housing was damaged when it fell on the floor.*

howler /ˈhaʊlə/ *noun* a buzzer which indicates to a telephone exchange operator that a user's telephone handset is not on the receiver

HP *abbr* Hewlett Packard

HPFS /ˌeɪtʃ piː ef ˈes/ *noun* (*in an OS/2 operating system*) a method of storing file information that is faster and more flexible than MS-DOS FAT. Full form **high performance filing system**

HPGL *abbr* Hewlett Packard Graphics Language

HPIB *abbr* Hewlett Packard Interface Bus

HP-PCL *abbr* Hewlett Packard Printer Control Language

HRG /ˌeɪtʃ ɑː ˈdʒiː/ *noun* the ability to display a large number of pixels per unit area. Full form **high resolution graphics**

HSB *abbr* hue, saturation and brightness

HSI *abbr* hue, saturation and intensity

HSSI /ˌeɪtʃ es es ˈaɪ/ *noun* a serial link that can transfer data at data rates up to 52 Mbits/second, used in some wide area network systems. Full form **high-speed serial interface.** ◊ **USB**

HSV *abbr* hue, saturation and value

HTML /ˌeɪtʃ tiː em ˈel/ *noun* a series of special codes that define the typeface and style that should be used when displaying the text and also allow hypertext links to other parts of the document or to other documents ○ *HTML is used to create documents for the World Wide Web.* Full form **hypertext markup language**

HTTP /ˌeɪtʃ tiː tiː ˈpiː/ *noun* a series of commands used by a browser to ask an Internet web server for information about a webpage. Full form **hypertext transfer protocol**

HTTPd /ˌeɪtʃ tiː tiː piː ˈdiː/ *noun* a server software that carries sends webpage files to a client in response to a request from a user's web browser ○ *When you type a website address into your web browser, this sends a request to the HTTPd server software that replies with the HTML code of a formatted webpage.* Full form **hypertext transfer protocol daemon**

hub /hʌb/ *noun* **1.** the central part of a disk, usually with a hole and ring which the disk drive grips to spin the disk **2.** (*in a star-topology network*) the central ring or wiring cabinet where all circuits meet and form an electrical path for signals

hue /hjuː/ *noun* the colour of an image or pixel

hue, saturation and intensity /ˌhjuː ˌsætʃəreɪʃ(ə)n ənd ɪnˈtensɪti/ *noun* a method of defining a colour through its three properties. Abbr **HSI**. Also called **hue, saturation and brightness, hue saturation and level** (NOTE: Hue is colour defined by its the wavelength; saturation refers to the purity of the colour (where at zero saturation the colour appears white and full saturation is pure colour); and intensity, brightness and level refer to the amount of white.)

hue, saturation and value /ˌhjuː ˌsætʃəreɪʃ(ə)n ənd ˈvæljuː/ *noun* same as **hue, saturation and intensity**. abbr **HSV**

Huffman code /ˈhʌfmən kəʊd/ *noun* a data compression code in which frequent characters occupy less bit space than less frequent ones

human-computer interface *noun* abbr **HMI**

hung ⟶ hang

hunting /ˈhʌntɪŋ/ *noun* the process of searching out a data record in a file

HVQ /ˌeɪtʃ viː ˈkjuː/ *noun* a video compression standard which allows colour video images to be transmitted in a bandwidth of 112 Kbps. Full form **hierarchical vector quantisation**

hybrid circuit /ˌhaɪbrɪd ˈsɜːkɪt/ *noun* the connection of a number of different electronic components such as integrated circuits, transistors, resistors and capacitors in a small package, which since the components are not contained in their own protective packages, requires far less space than the individual discrete components

hybrid computer /ˌhaɪbrɪd kəm ˈpjuːtə/ *noun* a combination of analog and digital circuits in a computer system to achieve a particular goal

hybrid interface /ˌhaɪbrɪd ˈɪntəfeɪs/ *noun* a one-off interface between a computer and a piece of analog equipment

hybrid system /ˌhaɪbrɪd ˈsɪstəm/ *noun* a combination of analog and digital computers and equipment to provide an optimal system for a particular task

HyperCard /ˈhaɪpəkɑːd/ a trade name for a database system controlled by HyperTalk programming language, used to produce hypertext documents

hyperlink /ˈhaɪpəlɪŋk/ *noun* a word or image or button in a webpage or multimedia title that moves the user to another page when clicked

hypermedia /ˈhaɪpəmiːdiə/ *noun* a hypertext system that is capable of displaying images and sound

HyperTalk /ˈhaɪpətɔːk/ a trade name for a programming language used to control a HyperCard database

HyperTerminal /ˈhaɪpəˌtɜːmɪn(ə)l/ *noun* a communications program that is included with Windows 95 and allows a user to call a remote computer via a modem and transfer files

hypertext /ˈhaɪpətekst/ *noun* **1.** a multimedia system of organising information in which certain words in a document link to other documents and display the text when the word is selected ○ *In this hypertext page, click once on the word 'computer' and it will tell you what a computer is.* **2.** a way of linking one word or image on an Internet page to another page in which clicking on certain words or images moves the user directly to the relevant new page

hypertext markup language /ˌhaɪpətekst ˈmɑːkʌp ˌlæŋgwɪdʒ/ *noun* full form of **HTML**

hypertext transfer protocol /ˌhaɪpətekst ˈtrænsfɜː ˌprəʊtəkɒl/ *noun* full form of **HTTP**

hypertext transfer protocol daemon /ˌhaɪpətekst ˈtrænsfɜː ˌprəʊtəkɒl ˌdiːmən/ *noun* full form of **HTTPd**

hyphenated /ˈhaɪfəneɪtɪd/ *adjective* written with a hyphen ○ *The word 'high-level' is usually hyphenated.*

hyphenate justify /ˌhaɪfəneɪt ˈdʒʌstɪfaɪ/ *verb* to break long words correctly where they split at the ends of lines. Some programs will also automatically justify, so as to give a straight right margin. (NOTE: hyphenates – hyphenating – hyphenated)

hyphenation /ˌhaɪfəˈneɪʃ(ə)n/ *noun* the splitting of a word at the end of a line, when the word is too long to fit

hyphenation and justification /ˌhaɪfəˌnaɪʃ(ə)n ən ˌdʒʌstɪfɪˈkeɪʃ(ə)n/ *noun* full form of **H & J** ○ *An American hyphenation and justification program will not work with British English spellings.*

Hz *abbr* hertz

I

I3 /ˌaɪ ˈθriː/ *noun* a signal generated by the pits representing the smallest data word, 3 bits long, from a CD-ROM, defined in Red Book as between 0.3 and 0.7 mV

I11 /ˌaɪ ɪˈlev(ə)n/ *noun* a signal generated by the pits representing the largest data word, 11 bits long, from a CD-ROM, defined in Red Book as greater than 0.6 mV

I750 /ˌaɪ ˌsev(ə)n faɪ ˈəʊ/ *noun* a video processor chip developed by Intel and used to compress and decompress digital video sequences

IAB /ˌaɪ eɪ ˈbiː/ *noun* an independent committee that is responsible for the design, engineering and management of the Internet. Full form **Internet Activities Board**

IAM /ˌaɪ eɪ ˈem/ *noun* memory storage that has an access time between that of main memory and a disk based system. Full form **intermediate access memory**

IANA *abbr* Internet Assigned Numbers Authority

IAR /ˌaɪ eɪ ˈɑː/ *abbr* instruction address register

IAS /ˌaɪ eɪ ˈes/ *noun* a high-speed main memory area in a computer system. Full form **immediate access store**

I-beam /ˈaɪ biːm/ *noun* a cursor shaped like the letter 'I' used in a GUI to edit text or indicate text operations

IBG *abbr* interblock gap

IBM /ˌaɪ biː ˈem/ the largest computer company in the world, which developed the first PC based on the Intel processor. Full form **International Business Machines**

IBM AT /ˌaɪ biː em eɪ ˈtiː/ a trade name for a personal computer based on the Intel 80286 16-bit processor and featured an ISA expansion bus

IBM AT keyboard /ˌaɪ biː em eɪ ˌtiː ˈkiːbɔːd/ a keyboard layout that features 12 function keys in a row along the top of the keyboard, with a separate numeric keypad

IBM-compatible /ˌaɪ biː em kəm ˈpætɪb(ə)l/ *adjective* referring to a personal computer that has hardware and software compatible with the IBM PC regardless of which Intel processor it uses (NOTE: IBM-compatible computers feature an ISA, EISA or MCA expansion bus.)

IBM PC /ˌaɪ biː em piː ˈsiː/ a trade name for a personal computer based on the Intel 8088 8-bit processor

IBM PC keyboard /ˌaɪ biː em piː ˌsiː ˈkiːbɔːd/ a keyboard layout that features 10 function keys arranged to the left of the main keys, with no separate numeric keypad

IBM PS/2, IBM Personal System/2 a trade name for a range of personal computers based on the Intel 8086, 80286 and 80386 processors that feature an MCA expansion bus

IBM XT /ˌaɪ biː em eks ˈtiː/ a trade name for a personal computer based on the IBM PC but with an internal hard disk drive and featuring an ISA expansion bus

IC *abbr* integrated circuit

icand /ˈɪkænd/ *noun* same as **multiplicand**

ICMP /ˌaɪ siː em ˈpiː/ *noun* an extension to the Internet Protocol that provides error detection and control messages ○ *The Internet command 'ping' uses ICMP to test if a named node is working correctly.* Full form **Internet control message protocol**. ◊ IP, PING

icon /ˈaɪkɒn/, **ikon** *noun* a graphic symbol or small picture displayed on screen, used in an interactive computer system to provide an easy way of identifying a function ○ *The icon for the graphics program is a small picture of a palette.*

'Despite (or because of?) the swap file, loading was slow and the hourglass icon of the mouse pointer frequently returned to the arrow symbol well before loading was complete.' [*Computing*]

icon resource /'aɪkɒn rɪˌzɔːs/ *noun* a file that contains the bitmap image of an icon, used by a programmer when writing an application

ICQ a software program developed by Mirabilis that supports instant messaging and allows two or more users to send messages to each other via the Internet that are instantly displayed on the other person's screen (NOTE: pronounced 'I-seek-you')

ID *abbr* identification

ID code /ˌaɪ'diː kəʊd/ *noun* a password or word that identifies a user so that he or she can access a system ○ *After you wake up the system, you have to input your ID code then your password.*

IDE /ˌaɪ diː 'iː/ *noun* a popular standard for a hard disk drive controller unit that allows data transfer rates up to 4.1MBps and can support two hard disk drives on each controller; enhanced versions of the IDE standard provide more flexibility and speed (also known as AT Attachment – ATA – interface) ○ *IDE drives are fitted to most home PCs.* Full form **integrated drive electronics, Intelligent device electronics**. ◊ **ATA, SCSI**

identification /aɪˌdentɪfɪ'keɪʃ(ə)n/ *noun* a procedure used to establish the identity and nature of a computer or user. Abbr **ID**

identification character /aɪˌdentɪfɪ 'keɪʃ(ə)n ˌkærɪktə/ *noun* a single character sent to a host computer to establish the identity and location of a remote computer or terminal

identification division /aɪˌdentɪfɪ 'keɪʃ(ə)n dɪˌvɪʒ(ə)n/ *noun* a section of a COBOL program source code in which the identifiers and formats for data and variables to be used within the program are declared

identifier /aɪ'dentɪfaɪə/ *noun* a set of characters used to distinguish between different blocks of data or files. Abbr **ID**

identifier word /aɪ'dentɪfaɪə wɜːd/ *noun* a word that is used as a block or file identifier

identity burst /aɪ'dentɪti bɜːst/ *noun* a pattern of bits before the first block of data on a magnetic tape that identifies the tape format used

identity gate /aɪ'dentɪti geɪt/, **identity element** /aɪ'dentɪti ˌelɪmənt/ *noun* a logical gate that provides a single output that is true if the inputs are both the same

identity number /aɪ'dentɪti ˌnʌmbə/ *noun* a unique number, used usually with a password to identify a user when logging into a system ○ *Don't forget to log in your identity number.*

identity operation /aɪˌdentɪti ˌɒpə 'reɪʃ(ə)n/ *noun* a logical function whose output is true only if all the operands are of the same value

identity palette /aɪ'dentɪti ˌpælət/ *noun* a 256-colour palette in which the first and last 10 colours are the system colours

idle /'aɪd(ə)l/ *adjective* referring to a machine, telephone line or device which is not being used, but is ready and waiting to be used

idle character /ˌaɪd(ə)l 'kærɪktə/ *noun* a symbol or code that means 'do nothing'

idle time /'aɪd(ə)l taɪm/ *noun* a period of time when a device is switched on but not doing anything

IDP *abbr* integrated data processing

IE *abbr* Internet Explorer

IEC connector /ˌaɪ iː 'siː kəˌnektə/ *noun* a standard for a three-pin connector used on sockets that carry mains electricity to the computer ○ *All PCs have a male IEC connector and use a mains lead with a female IEC connector.*

IEE *abbr* Institution of Electrical Engineers (*UK*)

IEEE *abbr* Institute of Electrical and Electronic Engineers (*US*)

IEEE-488 *noun* an interfacing standard as laid down by the IEEE, in which only data and handshaking signals are used, mainly used in laboratories to connect computers to measuring equipment

IEEE-802.2 *noun* a standard defining data links used with 802.3, 802.4 and 802.5

IEEE-802.3 *noun* a standard defining an Ethernet network system, with CSMA/CD access using a bus-topology

IEEE-802.4 *noun* a standard defining Token Bus

IEEE-802.5 *noun* a standard defining the IBM Token-Ring network system, with access using a token passed around a ring network

IEEE bus *noun* an interface that conforms to IEEE standards

IEN *abbr* Internet experiment note

ier ♦ multiplier

IETF /ˌaɪ iː tiː ˈef/ *noun* a committee that is part of the IAB and determines Internet standards. Full form **Internet Engineering Task Force.** ◊ **IAB**

IFF /ˌaɪ ef ˈef/ *noun* **1.** a standard for compressed files stored on a CD-i. Full form **international file format 2.** a standard that defines how palette data is stored in an Amiga and some graphics programs. Full form **interchange file format**

IF statement /ɪf ˈsteɪtmənt/ *noun* a computer programming statement meaning do an action IF a condition is true, and usually followed by THEN

IF-THEN-ELSE /ɪf ðen/ *noun* a high-level programming language statement, meaning IF something cannot be done, THEN do this or ELSE do that

IGMP /ˌaɪ dʒiː em ˈpiː/ *noun* a standard that helps manage how data is transferred during an IP Multicast operation in which one server computer sends each packet of data to several destinations at the same time. Full form **Internet group management protocol** (NOTE: This is useful when broadcasting a lot of data to several different recipients. The IGMP standard is defined in RFC1112.)

ignore character /ɪgˈnɔː ˌkærɪktə/ *noun* a null or fill character

IGP /ˌaɪ dʒiː ˈpiː/ *noun* a protocol that distributes information to gateways, i.e. routers, within a particular network. Full form **interior gateway protocol**

IH *abbr* interrupt handler

IIL *abbr* integrated injection logic

IIS a piece of web server software developed by Microsoft. Full form **Internet information server**

IKBS /ˌaɪ keɪ biː ˈem/ *noun* software that applies the knowledge, advice and rules defined by an expert in a particular field to a user's data to help solve a problem. Full form **intelligent knowledge-based system.** Also called **expert system**

ikon /ˈaɪkɒn/ *noun* another spelling of **icon**

illegal /ɪˈliːg(ə)l/ *adjective* which is against the law

illegal character /ɪˌliːg(ə)l ˈkærɪktə/ *noun* an invalid combination of bits in a computer word, according to preset rules

illegal instruction /ɪˌliːg(ə)l ɪnˈstrʌkʃən/ *noun* an instruction code not within the repertoire of a language

illegal operation /ɪˌliːg(ə)l ˌɒpəˈreɪʃ(ə)n/ *noun* an instruction or process

that does not follow the computer system's protocol or language syntax

Illuminant D65 /ɪˌluːmɪnənt diː ˌsɪksti ˈfaɪv/ *noun* a colour temperature of 6,500°K

IM *abbr* instant messaging

IMA /ˌaɪ em ˈeɪ/ *noun* a professional organisation that covers subjects including authoring languages, formats and intellectual property. Full form **Interactive Multimedia Association**

iMac /ˌaɪ ˈmæk/ a personal computer developed by Apple Computer Corporation

image /ˈɪmɪdʒ/ *noun* **1.** an exact duplicate of an area of memory **2.** a copy of an original picture or design

image area /ˈɪmɪdʒ ˌeəriə/ *noun* a region of microfilm or display screen on which characters or designs can be displayed

image buffer /ˈɪmɪdʒ ˌbʌfə/ *noun* an area of memory that is used to build up an image before it is transferred to screen

image compression /ˈɪmɪdʒ kəmˌpreʃ(ə)n/ *noun* the process of compressing the data that forms an image

image degradation /ˈɪmɪdʒ ˌdegrədeɪʃ(ə)n/ *noun* the loss of picture contrast and quality due to signal distortion or bad copying of a video signal

image editing /ˈɪmɪdʒ ˌedɪtɪŋ/ *noun* the process of altering or adjusting an image using a paint package or special image editing program

image editor /ˈɪmɪdʒ ˌedɪtə/ *noun* a piece of software that allows a user to edit, change or create a bitmap image

image enhancement /ˈɪmɪdʒ ɪnˌhɑːnsmənt/ *noun* the process of adjusting parts of an image using special image processing software to change the brightness or sharpness of an image

imagemap /ˈɪmɪdʒmæp/ *noun* a graphic image that has areas of the image defined as hyperlink hotspots that link to another webpage

image processing /ˈɪmɪdʒ ˌprəʊsesɪŋ/ *noun* the analysis of information contained in an image, usually by electronic means or using a computer which provides the analysis or recognition of objects in the image

image processing software /ˈɪmɪdʒ ˌprəʊsesɪŋ ˌsɒftweə/ *noun* software that allows a user to adjust contrast, colour or brightness levels or apply special effects to a bitmap image

image processor /ˈɪmɪdʒ ˌprəʊsesə/ *noun* an electronic or computer system used for image processing, and to extract information from the image

'The Max FX also acts as a server to a growing number of printers, including a Varityper 5300 with emerald raster image processor and a Canon CLC 500 colour photocopier.' [*Computing*]

image retention /ˈɪmɪdʒ rɪˌtenʃən/ *noun* the time taken for a TV image to disappear after it has been displayed, caused by long persistence phosphor

image scanner /ˈɪmɪdʒ ˌskænə/ *noun* an input device which converts documents or drawings or photographs into a digitised, machine-readable form

image sensor /ˈɪmɪdʒ ˌsensə/ *noun* a photoelectric device which produces a signal related to the amount of light falling on it

image setter /ˈɪmɪdʒ ˌsetə/ *noun* a typesetting device which can process a PostScript page and produce a high-resolution output

image stability /ˈɪmɪdʒ stəˌbɪlɪti/ *noun* the ability of a display screen to provide a flicker-free picture

image storage space /ˌɪmɪdʒ ˈstɔːrɪdʒ ˌspeɪs/ *noun* a region of memory in which a digitised image is stored

image table /ˈɪmɪdʒ ˌteɪb(ə)l/ *noun* each of two bit-mapped tables used to control input and output devices or processes

imaging /ˈɪmɪdʒɪŋ/ *noun* a technique for creating pictures on a screen, in medicine used to provide pictures of sections of the body, using scanners attached to computers

imaging system /ˌɪmɪdʒɪŋ ˈsɪstəm/ *noun* equipment and software used to capture, digitise and compress video or still images

IMAP /ˈaɪmæp/ *noun* a standard that defines how email messages can be accessed and read over a network. Full form **Internet message access protocol**. ◊ **POP 3, SMTP**

COMMENT: This standard (currently at version four) provides an alternative to the common POP 3 standard. The IMAP standard stores a user's messages on a shared server (e.g. at your ISP) and allows a user to connect from any computer and read, send or manage messages. In contrast, the POP 3 protocol downloads all messages from a shared server onto the user's computer. This makes it very difficult for a user to access messages from a different computer, e.g. if you are travelling. Regardless of whether IMAP or POP 3 is used

to read messages, the SMTP protocol is normally used to send messages.

immediate access store /ɪˌmiːdiət ˌækses ˈstɔː/ *noun* full form of **IAS**

immediate address /ɪˌmiːdiət ə ˈdres/ *noun* same as **zero-level address**

immediate addressing /ɪˌmiːdiət ə ˈdresɪŋ/ *noun* the accessing of data immediately because it is held in the address field of an instruction

immediate instruction /ɪˌmiːdiət ɪn ˈstrʌkʃən/ *noun* a computer instruction in which the operand is included within the instruction, rather than an address of the operand location

immediate mode /ɪˈmiːdiət məʊd/ *noun* a mode in which a computer executes an instruction as soon as it is entered

immediate operand /ɪˈmiːdiət ˌɒpərænd/ *noun* an operand n an immediate addressing operation, which is fetched at the same time as the instruction

immediate processing /ɪˌmiːdiət ˈprəʊsesɪŋ/ *noun* the processing of data when it appears, rather than waiting for a synchronising clock pulse or time. Also called **in-line processing**

impedance /ɪmˈpiːd(ə)ns/ *noun* a measurement of the effect an electrical circuit or cable has on signal current magnitude and phase when a steady voltage is applied. ◊ **ohm**

COMMENT: Network cables need to have the correct impedance for the type of network card installed. 10BaseT unshielded twisted-pair cable normally has an impedance between 100 and 105 ohms, while 10Base2 coaxial cable has an impedance of 50 ohms.

implication /ˌɪmplɪˈkeɪʃ(ə)n/ *noun* a logical operation that uses an IF-THEN structure such that if A is true and if B is true the AND function of A and B will be true

implicit reference /ɪmˌplɪsɪt ˈref(ə)rəns/ *noun* (*in a multimedia programming language*) a reference to an object that does not give its exact page location but assumes that the object is on the current page or is currently visible

implied addressing /ɪmˌplaɪd ə ˈdresɪŋ/ *noun* an assembler instruction that operates on only one register, which is preset at manufacture. The user does not have to specify an address. ○ *Implied addressing for the accumulator is used in the instruction LDA,16.*

import /ɪmˈpɔːt/ *verb* **1.** to bring something in from outside a system ○ *You can* *import images from the CAD package into the DTP program.* **2.** to convert a file stored in one format to the default format used by a program ○ *Select import if you want to open a TIFF graphics file.*

'At the moment, Acrobat supports only the sending and viewing of documents. There are legal implications associated with allowing users to edit documents in the style of the original application, without having the tool itself on their desks, and there is no import facility back into applications.' [*Computing*]

impulse /'ɪmpʌls/ *noun* a voltage pulse which lasts a very short time

impulsive noise /ɪm'pʌlsɪv nɔɪz/ *noun* interference on a signal caused by short periods of noise

IMS *abbr* information management system

inactive window /ɪn,æktɪv 'wɪndəʊ/ *noun* (*in a GUI*) a window still displayed, but not currently being used

in-band signalling /,ɪn bænd 'sɪgn(ə)lɪŋ/ *noun* data transmission in which the signal carrying the data is within the bandwidth of the cable or transmission media

InBox /'ɪnbɒks/ *noun* a feature of the Windows messaging system that can gather together a user's electronic messages including mail sent over the network, fax messages and mail sent over the Internet

inbuilt /'ɪnbɪlt/ *adjective* referring to a feature or device included in a system ○ *This software has inbuilt error correction.*

inches-per-second /,ɪntʃɪz pɜː 'sekənd/ *noun* full form of **ips**

in-circuit emulator /,ɪn ,sɜːkɪt 'emjʊleɪtə/ *noun* a circuit that emulates a device or integrated circuit and is inserted into a new or faulty circuit to test if it is working correctly ○ *This in-circuit emulator is used to test the floppy disk controller by emulating a disk drive.*

inclusion /ɪn'kluːʒ(ə)n/ *noun* a logical operation that uses an IF-THEN structure, such that if A is true and if B is true the AND function of A and B will be true

inclusive OR /ɪn'kluːsɪv ɔː/ *noun* ♦ **OR**

incoming message /,ɪnkʌmɪŋ 'mesɪdʒ/ *noun* a message received in a computer

incoming traffic /,ɪnkʌmɪŋ 'træfɪk/ *noun* the amount of data or number of messages received

incompatible /,ɪnkəm'pætɪb(ə)l/ *adjective* which cannot work together ○ *They tried to link the two systems, but found they were incompatible.*

increment /'ɪŋkrɪmənt/ *noun* **1.** the addition of a set number, usually one, to a register, often for counting purposes ○ *An increment is added to the counter each time a pulse is detected.* **2.** the value of the number added to a register ○ *Increase the increment to three.* ■ *verb* **1.** to add something or to increase a number ○ *The counter is incremented each time an instruction is executed.* **2.** to move forward to the next location

incremental backup /,ɪŋkrɪment(ə)l 'bækʌp/ *noun* a backup procedure that only backs up the files that have changed since the last backup

incremental computer /,ɪŋkrɪment(ə)l kəm'pjuːtə/ *noun* a computer that stores variables as the difference between their actual value and an absolute initial value

incremental data /,ɪŋkrɪment(ə)l 'deɪtə/ *noun* data which represents the difference of a value from an original value

incremental plotter /,ɪŋkrɪment(ə)l 'plɒtə/ *noun* a graphical output device that can only move in small steps, with input data representing the difference between present position and the position required, so drawing lines and curves as a series of short straight lines

indent *noun* /'ɪndent/ a space or series of spaces from the left margin, when starting a line of text ■ *verb* /ɪn'dent/ to start a line of text with a space in from the left margin ○ *The first line of the paragraph is indented two spaces.*

indentation /,ɪnden'teɪʃ(ə)n/ *noun* the process of leaving a space at the beginning of a line of text

Indeo /'ɪndiəʊ/ a trade name for video software technology developed by Intel that allows a computer to store and play back compressed video sequences using software compression techniques

indeterminate system /,ɪndɪtɜːmɪnət 'sɪstəm/ *noun* a system whose logical, output state cannot be predicted

index /'ɪndeks/ *noun* **1.** a list of items in a computer memory, usually arranged alphabetically **2.** the address to be used that is the result of an offset value added to a start location. ♦ **indexed addressing**

index build /'ɪndeks bɪld/ *noun* the creation of an ordered list from the results of a database or file search

indexed address /ˌɪndeksd əˈdres/ *noun* the address of the location to be accessed, which is found in an index register

indexed addressing /ˌɪndeksd əˈdresɪŋ/ *noun* an addressing mode, in which the storage location to be accessed is made up of a start address and an offset value, which is then added to it to give the address to be used

indexed file /ˈɪndeksd faɪl/ *noun* a sequential file with an index of all the entries and their addresses

indexed instruction /ˌɪndeksd ɪnˈstrʌkʃən/ *noun* an instruction that contains an origin and location of an offset that are added together to provide the address to be accessed

indexed sequential access method /ˌɪndeks sɪˌkwensəl ˈækses ˌmeθəd/ *noun* a data retrieval method using a list containing the address of each stored record, where the list is searched, then the record is retrieved from the address in the list. Abbr **ISAM**

indexed sequential storage /ˌɪndeksd sɪˌkwenʃ(ə)l ˈstɔːrɪdʒ/ *noun* a method of storing records in a consecutive order, but in such a way that they can be accessed rapidly

index.html /ˌɪndeks dɒt ˌeɪtʃ tiː em ˈel/ *noun* a filename that is used to store the text and HTML formatting commands for the home page on a website

indexing /ˈɪndeksɪŋ/ *noun* 1. the use of indexed addressing in software or a computer 2. the process of building and sorting a list of records

index key /ˈɪndeks kiː/ *noun* one field which is used to index a record

index letter /ˈɪndeks ˌletə/ *noun* a letter which identifies an item in an index

index number /ˈɪndeks ˌnʌmbə/ *noun* a number which identifies an item in an index

index page /ˈɪndeks peɪdʒ/ *noun* 1. a page of a multimedia book that lists all the other pages within the book and allows a user to locate other pages or areas of interest 2. the initial opening webpage of a site on the Internet or on a company's intranet

index register /ˈɪndeks ˌredʒɪstə/ *noun* a computer address register that is added to a reference address to provide the location to be accessed. Abbr **IR**

index value word /ˌɪndeks ˌvæljuː ˈwɜːd/ *noun* an offset value added to an address to produce a usable address

indicator /ˈɪndɪˌkeɪtə/ *noun* something which shows the state of a process, usually a light or buzzer

indicator chart /ˈɪndɪˌkeɪtə tʃɑːt/ *noun* a graphical representation of the location and use of indicator flags within a program

indicator flag /ˈɪndɪˌkeɪtə flæg/ *noun* a register or single bit that indicates the state of the processor and its registers, e.g. a carry or overflow

indicator light /ˈɪndɪˌkeɪtə laɪt/ *noun* a light used to warn or to indicate the condition of equipment

indirect address /ˌɪndaɪrekt əˈdres/ *noun* same as **relative address**

indirect addressing /ˌɪndaɪrekt əˈdresɪŋ/ *noun* a way of addressing data, in which the first instruction refers to an address which contains a second address

induce /ɪnˈdjuːs/ *verb* 1. to generate an electrical current in a coil of wire by electromagnetic effects 2. to prove something mathematically (NOTE: **induces** – **inducing** – **induced**)

induced failure /ɪnˌdjuːsd ˈfeɪljə/ *noun* the failure of a device due to external effects

induced interference /ɪnˌdjuːsd ˌɪntəˈfɪərəns/ *noun* an electrical noise on a signal due to induced signals from nearby electromagnetic sources

inductance /ɪnˈdʌktəns/ *noun* a measurement of the amount of energy a device can store in its magnetic field

induction /ɪnˈdʌkʃən/ *noun* 1. the generation of an electrical current by electromagnetic effects from a nearby source 2. the process of mathematically proving a formula or fact

inductive coordination /ɪnˌdʌktɪv kəʊˌɔːdɪˈneɪʃ(ə)n/ *noun* agreement between electrical power suppliers and communication providers on methods of reducing induced interference

inductor /ɪnˈdʌktə/ *noun* an electrical component consisting of a coil of wire used to introduce inductance effects into a circuit by storing energy in its magnetic field

Industry Standard Architecture /ˌɪndəstri ˌstændəd ˈɑːkɪˌtektʃə/ *noun* full form of **ISA**

inequality operator /ˌɪnɪˈkwɒlɪti ˌɒpəreɪtə/ *noun* a symbol used to indicate that two variables or quantities are not equal ○ *The C programming language* *uses the symbol '!=' as its inequality operator.*

inequivalence /ˌɪnɪˈkwɪvələns/ *noun* a logical function whose output is true if the inputs are not the same, otherwise the output is false

infect /ɪnˈfekt/ *verb* to contaminate a computer system with a virus that is capable of damaging its programs or data

infected . computer /ɪnˌfektɪd kəmˈpjuːtə/ *noun* a computer that carries a virus program

inference /ˈɪnf(ə)rəns/ *noun* **1.** a deduction of results from data according to certain rules **2.** a method of deducing a result about confidential information concerning an individual by using various data related to groups of people

inference control /ˈɪnf(ə)rəns kənˌtrəʊl/ *noun* the process of determining which information may be released without disclosing personal information about a single individual

inference engine /ˈɪnf(ə)rəns ˈendʒɪn/, **inference machine** *noun* a set of rules used in an IKBS to deduce goals or results from data

inferior figure /ɪnˌfɪəriə ˈfɪɡə/ *noun* any one of the smaller numbers or characters that are printed slightly below normal characters, used in mathematical and chemical formulae. ◊ **subscript, superscript** (NOTE: used with figures and letters: CO_2)

INF file /ˌaɪ en ˈef faɪl/ *noun* a configuration file supplied by a hardware manufacturer to allow Windows to correctly install the device

infinite loop /ˈɪnfɪnət luːp/ *noun* a loop which has no exit other than by ending the running of the program by switching off the machine or resetting

infinity /ɪnˈfɪnɪti/ *noun* **1.** a space or quantity that never ends **2.** the distance of an object from a viewer where beams of light from the object would be seen to be parallel, i.e. very far away

infix notation /ɪnˌfɪks nəʊˈteɪʃ(ə)n/ *noun* a method of computer programming syntax in which operators are embedded inside operands, e.g. C – D or X + Y. Compare **postfix notation, prefix notation**

informatics /ˌɪnfɔːˈmætɪks/ *noun* the science and study of ways and means of information processing and transmission

information /ˌɪnfəˈmeɪʃ(ə)n/ *noun* data that has been processed or arranged to provide facts which have a meaning

information bearer channel /ˌɪnfəmeɪʃ(ə)n ˈbeərə ˌtʃæn(ə)l/ *noun* a communications channel that is able to carry control and message data, usually at a higher rate than a data only channel

information content /ˌɪnfəˈmeɪʃ(ə)n ˌkɒntent/ *noun* a measurement of the amount of information conveyed by the transmission of a symbol or character, often measured in shannons

information flow control /ˌɪnfə ˈmeɪʃ(ə)n fləʊ kənˌtrəʊl/ *noun* the regulation of access to particular information

information input /ˌɪnfəˈmeɪʃ(ə)n ˌɪnpʊt/ *noun* information received from an input device

information line /ˌɪnfəˈmeɪʃ(ə)n laɪn/ *noun* a line running across the screen which gives the user information about the program being executed or the file being edited

information management system /ˌɪnfəmeɪʃ(ə)n ˈmænɪdʒmənt ˌsɪstəm/ *noun* a computer program that allows information to be easily stored, retrieved, searched and updated. Abbr **IMS**

information network /ˌɪnfəˈmeɪʃ(ə)n ˌnetwɜːk/ *noun* a number of databases linked together, usually using telephone lines and modems, allowing a large amount of data to be accessed by a wider number of users

information output /ˌɪnfəmeɪʃ(ə)n ˈaʊtpʊt/ *noun* a display of information on an output device

information processing /ˌɪnfəmeɪʃ(ə)n ˈprəʊsesɪŋ/ *noun* same as **data processing**

information processor /ˌɪnfəmeɪʃ(ə)n ˈprəʊsesə/ *noun* a machine that processes a received signal, according to a program, using stored information, and provides an output (NOTE: This is an example of a computer that is not dealing with mathematical functions.)

information provider /ˌɪnfəˈmeɪʃ(ə)n prəˌvaɪdə/ *noun* a company or user who provides an information source for use in a videotext system, e.g. a company providing weather information or stock market reports. Abbr **ip**

information rate /ˌɪnfəˈmeɪʃ(ə)n reɪt/ *noun* the amount of information content per character multiplied by the number of characters transmitted per second

information retrieval /ˌɪnfəmeɪʃ(ə)n rɪˈtriːv(ə)l/ *noun* the process of locating quantities of data stored in a database and producing useful information from the data. Abbr **IR**

information retrieval centre /ˌɪnfəmeɪʃ(ə)n rɪˈtriːv(ə)l ˌsentə/ *noun* a research system providing specific information from a database for a user

information storage /ˌɪnfəmeɪʃ(ə)n ˈstɔːrɪdʒ/ *noun* the process of storing data in a form which allows it to be processed at a later date

information storage and retrieval /ˌɪnfəmeɪʃ(ə)n ˌstɔːrɪdʒ ən rɪˈtriːv(ə)l/ *noun* techniques involved in storing information and retrieving data from a store. Abbr **ISR**

information structure /ˌɪnfə ˈmeɪʃ(ə)n ˌstrʌktʃə/ *noun* same as **data structure**

information system /ˌɪnfəˈmeɪʃ(ə)n ˌsɪstəm/ *noun* a computer system which provides information according to a user's requests

information technology /ˌɪnfəmeɪʃ(ə)n tekˈnɒlədʒi/ *noun* the technology involved in acquiring, storing, processing, and distributing information by electronic means, including radio, TV, telephone and computers. Abbr **IT**

information theory /ˌɪnfəˈmeɪʃ(ə)n ˌθɪəri/ *noun* the body of formulae and mathematics concerned with data transmission equipment and signals

information transfer channel /ˌɪnfəmeɪʃ(ə)n ˈtrænsfɜː ˌtʃæn(ə)l/ *noun* a connection between a data transmitter and a receiver

infrared /ˌɪnfrəˈred/ *noun* the section of the electromagnetic radiation spectrum extending from visible red to microwaves

infrared controller /ˌɪnfrəred kən ˈtrəʊlə/ *noun* a remote control unit used to control a device from a distance

Infrared Data Association /ˌɪnfrəred ˈdeɪtə əˌsəʊsieɪʃ(ə)n/ *noun* a standard method used to transfer information via an infrared light beam, often used to transfer information from a laptop or PDA to a printer or desktop computer. Abbr **IrDA** (NOTE: To use this feature, your computer or printer needs to have an IrDA port.)

infra-red link /ˌɪnfrə red ˈlɪŋk/ *noun* a system that allows two computers or a computer and a printer to exchange information using an infrared light beam to carry the data

infrastructure /ˈɪnfrəˌstrʌktʃə/ *noun* basic structure or basic services

inherent addressing /ɪnˌhɪərənt ə ˈdresɪŋ/ *noun* an instruction that contains all the data required for the address to be accessed with no further operation

inherit /ɪnˈherɪt/ *verb* (*in object-oriented programming*) to acquire the characteristics of another class or data type

inheritance /ɪnˈherɪt(ə)ns/ *noun* (*in object-oriented programming*) the passing of the characteristics of one class or data type to another, called its descendant

inherited error /ɪnˌherɪtɪd ˈerə/ *noun* an error that is the result of a fault in a previous process or action

inhibit /ɪnˈhɪbɪt/ *verb* to stop a process taking place or to prevent an integrated circuit or gate from operating,, by means of a signal or command

inhibiting input /ɪnˌhɪbɪtɪŋ ˈɪnpʊt/ *noun* an input of a gate which blocks the output signal

INI file /ˌaɪ en ˈaɪ faɪl/ *noun* a configuration file used in Windows 3.x and earlier that tells Windows how to load and run an application. (NOTE: The INI file could contain the working directory, user name and user settings.)

initial address /ɪˌnɪʃ(ə)l əˈdres/ *noun* the address at which the first location of a program is stored

initial condition /ɪˌnɪʃ(ə)l kən ˈdɪʃ(ə)n/ *noun* a condition that must be satisfied before a routine can be entered

initial error /ɪˌnɪʃ(ə)l ˈerə/ *noun* an error in data that is the difference between the value of the data at the start of processing and its present actual value

initial instructions /ɪˌnɪʃ(ə)l ɪn ˈstrʌkʃənz/ *plural noun* routines that act as an initial program loader

initialisation, initialization *noun* the process of initialising values or parameters ○ *Initialisation is often carried out without the user knowing.*

initialisation string /ɪˌnɪʃ(ə)laɪ ˈzeɪʃ(ə)n ˌstrɪŋ/, **initialization string** *noun* a series of AT commands sent to a modem to configure it before it is used

initialise /ɪˈnɪʃəˌlaɪz/, **initialize** *verb* to set values or parameters or control lines to their initial values, to allow a program or process to be restarted (NOTE: initialises – initialising – initialised)

initial program header /ɪˌnɪʃ(ə)l ˈprəʊɡræm ˌhedə/ *noun* a small machine-code program usually stored in a read-only memory device that directs the CPU to load a larger program or operating system from store into main memory (NOTE: An example is a boot up routine that loads the operating system when a computer is switched on.)

initial program loader /ɪˌnɪʃ(ə)l ˈprəʊɡræm ˌləʊdə/ *noun* a short routine that loads the first section of a program, after which it continues the loading process itself. Abbr **IPL**

initial value /ɪˌnɪʃ(ə)l ˈvæljuː/ *noun* the starting point, usually zero, set when initialising variables at the beginning of a program

ink /ɪŋk/ *verb* to draw lines on paper by the use of a plotter device

ink cartridge /ɪŋk ˈkɑːtrɪdʒ/ *noun* a plastic module that contains ink, for use in a bubble-jet or ink-jet printer

ink effect /ˈɪŋk ɪˌfekt/ *noun* features of Windows Movie Player utility that defines how cast members are drawn; e.g., transparent ink effect displays the cast member with the background showing through

ink-jet printer /ˈɪŋk dʒet ˌprɪntə/ *noun* a printer that produces characters by sending a stream of tiny drops of electrically charged ink onto the paper

'…ink-jet printers work by squirting a fine stream of ink onto the paper' [*Personal Computer World*]

inlay card /ˈɪnˌleɪ kɑːd/ *noun* an identification card inside the box of a CD, DVD or similar recording

in-line /ɪn laɪn/ *adjective* referring to connection pins on a chip arranged in one or two rows ■ *noun* referring to a graphical image that is part of a webpage

in-line program /ˌɪn laɪn ˈpiːəʊɡræm/ *noun* a program that contains no loops

inner loop /ˈɪnə luːp/ *noun* a loop contained inside another loop. ◊ **nested loop**

input /ˈɪnpʊt/ *verb* to transfer data or information from outside a computer to its main memory ○ *The data was input via a modem.* ■ *noun* **1.** the action of inputting information **2.** data or information that is transferred into a computer **3.** electrical signals which are applied to relevant circuits to perform the operation ▶ abbr (all senses) **i/p, I/P**

'In fact, the non-Qwerty format of the Maltron keyboard did cause a few gasps when it was first shown to the staff, but within a month all the Maltron users had regained normal input speeds.' [*Computing*]

input area /ˈɪnpʊt ˌeəriə/ *noun* a section of main memory that holds data transferred from backing store until it is processed or distributed to other sections

input block /ˈɪnpʊt blɒk/ *noun* a block of data transferred to an input area

input-bound /ˈɪnpʊt ˌbaʊnd/ *adjective* referring to a program or device that is not running as fast as it could, because it is limited by the input rate from a slower peripheral. Also called **input-limited**

input buffer register /ˌɪnpʊt ˈbʌfə ˌredʒɪstə/ *noun* a temporary store for data from an input device before it is transferred to a main or backing store

input device /ˈɪnpʊt dɪˌvaɪs/ *noun* a device, e.g. a keyboard or bar code reader, that converts actions or information into a form that a computer can understand, and transfers the data to the processor

input lead /ˈɪnpʊt liːd/ *noun* a lead which connects an input device to a computer

input-limited /ˌɪnpʊt ˈlɪmɪtɪd/ *adjective* same as **input-bound**

input mode /ˈɪnpʊt məʊd/ *noun* a mode in which a computer is receiving data

input/output /ˌɪnpʊt ˈaʊtpʊt/ *noun* **1.** full form of **I/O 2.** all the data received or transmitted by a computer. ◊ **input**

input/output buffer /ˌɪnpʊt ˈaʊtpʊt ˌbʌfə/ *noun* a temporary storage area for data waiting to be output or input

input/output bus /ˌɪnpʊt ˈaʊtpʊt bʌs/ *noun* a bus that provides links that allow data and control signals to be transferred between a CPU and memory or peripheral devices. Also called **I/O bus**

input/output channel /ˌɪnpʊt ˈaʊtpʊt ˌtʃæn(ə)l/ *noun* a link between a processor and peripheral allowing data transfer

input/output controller /ˌɪnpʊt ˈaʊtpʊt kənˌtrəʊlə/ *noun* an intelligent device that monitors, directs and controls data flow between a CPU and I/O devices

input/output control program /ˌɪnpʊt ˈaʊtpʊt kənˌtrəʊl/ *noun* a supervisory program or section of the operating system that monitors and controls I/O operations and data flow

input/output device /ˌɪnpʊt ˈaʊtpʊt dɪˌvaɪs/ *noun* a peripheral, e.g. such as a terminal in a workstation, that can be used both for inputting and outputting data to a processor

input/output executive /ˌɪnpʊt ˈaʊtpʊt ɪɡˌzekjʊtɪv/ *noun* a master program that controls all the I/O activities of a computer

input/output instruction /ˌɪnpʊt ˈaʊtpʊt ɪnˌstrʌkʃən/ *noun* a computer programming instruction that allows data to be input or output from a processor

input/output interface /ˌɪnpʊt ˈaʊtpʊt ɪntəˌfeɪs/ *noun* a circuit, consisting usually of an input/output channel, a parallel input/output port and a DMA interface, that allows controlled data input and output from a CPU

input/output interrupt /ˌɪnpʊt ˈaʊtpʊt ɪntəˌrʌpt/ *noun* an interrupt signal that comes from a peripheral device or that indicates that an input or output operation is required

input/output library /ˌɪnpʊt ˈaʊtpʊt ˌlaɪbrəri/ *noun* a set of routines, e.g. printer drivers or port control routines, that can be used by the programmer to help simplify input/output tasks

input/output port /ˌɪnpʊt ˈaʊtpʊt ˌpɔːt/ *noun* a circuit or connector that provides an input/output channel to another device ○ *The joystick can be connected to the input/output port.*

input/output processor /ˌɪnpʊt ˈaʊtpʊt ˌprəʊsesə/ *noun* a processor that carries out input/output transfers for a CPU, including DMA and error correction facilities. Abbr **IOP**

input/output referencing /ˌɪnpʊt ˈaʊtpʊt ˌref(ə)rənsɪŋ/ *noun* the use of labels to refer to specific input/output devices, the actual address of the device being inserted at run time

input/output register /ˌɪnpʊt ˈaʊtpʊt ˌredʒɪstə/ *noun* a temporary storage for data received from memory before being transferred to an I/O device or for data from an I/O device waiting to be stored in main memory or to be processed

input/output request /ˌɪnpʊt ˈaʊtpʊt rɪˌkwest/ *noun* a request signal from the CPU for data input or output. Abbr **IORQ**

input/output status word /ˌɪnpʊt ˈaʊtpʊt ˈsteɪtəs wɜːd/ *noun* a word whose bits describe the state of peripheral devices, e.g. busy or free

input/output unit /ˌɪnpʊt ˈaʊtpʊt ˌjuːnɪt/ *noun* same as **input/output device**

input port /ˈɪnpʊt pɔːt/ *noun* a circuit or connector that allows a computer to receive data from other external devices

input register /ˈɪnpʊt ˌredʒɪstə/ *noun* a temporary store for data received at slow speeds from an I/O device, the data is then transferred at high speed to the main memory

input routine /ˈɪnpʊt ruːˌtiːn/ *noun* a set of instructions which control an I/O device and direct data received from it to the correct storage location

input section /ˈɪnpʊt ˌsekʃ(ə)n/ *noun* **1.** an input routine **2.** an input area

input statement /ˈɪnpʊt ˌsteɪtmənt/ *noun* a computer programming command which waits for data entry from a port or keyboard

input storage /ˈɪnpʊt ˌstɔːrɪdʒ/ *noun* ▶ **input area**

input work queue /ˌɪnpʊt ˈwɜːk ˌkjuː/ *noun* a list of commands to be carried out either in the order in which they were entered or in order of priority

inquiry /ɪnˈkwaɪəri/ *noun* another spelling of **enquiry**

inquiry character /ɪnˈkwaɪəri ˌkærɪktə/ *noun* a code transmitted by a computer to a remote terminal, asking for a response. Abbr **ENQ**

inquiry/response /ɪnˌkwaɪəri rɪˈspɒns/ *noun* an interactive computer mode, in which a user's commands and inquiries are responded to very quickly

inquiry station /ɪnˈkwaɪəri ˌsteɪʃ(ə)n/ *noun* a terminal that is used to access and interrogate files stored on a remote computer

insert /ɪnˈsɜːt/ *verb* to add new text inside a word or sentence

inserted subroutine /ˌɪnsɜːtɪd ˈsʌbruːtiːn/ *noun* a series of instructions that are copied directly into the main program at a point where a call instruction appears or at a point where a user requires

insertion loss /ɪnˈsɜːʃ(ə)n lɒs/ *noun* a weakening of a signal caused by adding a device into an existing channel or circuit

insertion point /ɪnˈsɜːʃ(ə)n pɔɪnt/ *noun* the point in a document, indicated by the position of the cursor, where new text typed by the user will be entered

insert key /ɪn'sɜːt kiː/ *noun* a key that switches a word-processor or editor program from overwrite mode to insert mode. Also called **Ins key**

insert mode /'ɪnsɜːt məʊd/ *noun* an interactive computer mode used for editing and correcting documents (NOTE: This is a standard feature on most word-processing packages. The cursor is placed at the required point in the document and any characters typed will be added, with the existing text moving on as necessary.)

Ins key /'ɪns kiː/ *noun* same as **insert key**

install /ɪn'stɔːl/ *verb* to put a machine into an office or factory ○ *The system is easy to install and simple to use.*

installable device driver /ɪn,stɔːləb(ə)l dɪ'vaɪs ,draɪvə/ *noun* a device driver that is loaded into memory and remains resident, replacing a similar function built into the operating system

installation /,ɪnstə'leɪʃ(ə)n/ *noun* **1.** a computer and equipment used for one type of work and processing ○ *The engineers are still testing the new installation.* **2.** the process of setting up a new computer system ○ *The installation of the equipment took only a few hours.*

installation manual /,ɪnstə'leɪʃ(ə)n ,mænjʊəl/ *noun* a booklet showing how a system should be installed

install program /'ɪnstɔːl ,prəʊɡræm/ *noun* a piece of software that transfers program code from the distribution disks onto a computer's hard disk and configures the program

instance /'ɪnstəns/ *noun* (*in object-oriented programming*) an object or duplicate object that has been created

instantaneous access /,ɪnstənteɪniəs 'ækses/ *noun* an extremely short access time to a random access device

instant jump /'ɪnstənt dʒʌmp/ *noun* (*in a videodisc player*) a hardware feature that allows the player to skip a number of frames, up to 200, in the time it takes to refresh the screen

instant messaging /,ɪnstənt 'mesɪdʒɪŋ/ *noun* a feature that lets a user type in and exchange messages with one or more other people connected via the Internet. Each of the users in the group runs special software that tells them when a friend or colleague has connected to the Internet and is available to receive messag-

es. Any message that he or she types in is then sent instantly to the other user.

instruction /ɪn'strʌkʃən/ *noun* a word used in a programming language that is understood by the computer as a command to carry out a particular action ○ *The instruction PRINT is used in this BASIC dialect as an operand to display the following data.* (NOTE: In a high-level language the instructions are translated by the compiler or interpreter to a form that is understood by the central processing unit.)

'A Taos kernel, typically 15Kb in size, resides at each processing node to 'translate', non-native instructions – on the fly when needed. This kernel contains the only code which has to be written in the processor's native instruction set.' [*Computing*]

instruction address /ɪn'strʌkʃən ə,dres/ *noun* the location of an instruction

instruction address register /ɪn,strʌkʃən ə'dres ,redʒɪstə/ *noun* same as **sequence control register**. abbr **IAR**

instruction area /ɪn'strʌkʃən ,eəriə/ *noun* a section of memory that is used to store instructions

instruction cache /ɪn'strʌkʃən kæʃ/ *noun* an area of high-speed memory which stores the next few instructions to be executed by a processor

instruction character /ɪn'strʌkʃən ,kærɪktə/ *noun* a special character that provides a control sequence rather than an alphanumeric character

instruction codes /ɪn'strʌkʃən kəʊdz/ *plural noun* a set of symbols or codes that a CPU can directly understand and execute

instruction counter /ɪn'strʌkʃən ,kaʊntə/ *noun* same as **sequence control register**

instruction cycle /ɪn'strʌkʃən ,saɪk(ə)l/ *noun* the series of events, taking place in a set order and at specified intervals, that occurs when the processor fetches an instruction from where it is stored in the memory and executes it

instruction cycle time /ɪn,strʌkʃən 'saɪk(ə)l ,taɪm/ *noun* the amount of time taken for one instruction cycle

instruction decoder /ɪn'strʌkʃən diː,kəʊdə/ *noun* hardware that converts a machine-code code instruction in binary form into actions

instruction execution time /ɪn,strʌkʃən ,eksɪ'kjuːʃ(ə)n ,taɪm/ *noun* the time taken to carry out an instruction

instruction format /ɪnˈstrʌkʃən ˌfɔːmæt/ *noun* a set of rules defining the way the operands, data and addresses are arranged in an instruction

instruction manual /ɪnˈstrʌkʃən ˌmænjuəl/ *noun* a document describing how to use a system or software

instruction modification /ɪn ˌstrʌkʃən ˌmɒdɪfɪˈkeɪʃ(ə)n/ *noun* the process of changing part of an instruction, either the data or the operator, so that it carries out a different function the next time that the instruction is executed

instruction pipelining /ɪnˈstrʌkʃən ˌpaɪplaɪnɪŋ/ *noun* the act of beginning to process a second instruction while still processing the present one, which increases the program's speed of execution

instruction pointer /ɪnˈstrʌkʃən ˌpɔɪntə/ *noun* a register in a central processing unit that contains the location of the next instruction to be processed

instruction processor /ɪnˈstrʌkʃən ˌprəʊsesə/ *noun* a section of the central processing unit that decodes instructions and performs the arithmetic and logical functions necessary for carrying them out

instruction register /ɪnˈstrʌkʃən ˌredʒɪstə/ *noun* a register in a central processing unit that stores an instruction during decoding and execution operations. Abbr **IR**

instruction repertoire /ɪnˈstrʌkʃən ˌrepətwɑː/, **instruction set** /set/ *noun* the total number of instructions that a processor can recognise and execute

instruction storage /ɪnˈstrʌkʃən ˌstɔːrɪdʒ/ *noun* a section of memory used to store instructions

instruction time /ɪnˈstrʌkʃən taɪm/ *noun* the amount of time taken for a central processing unit to carry out a complete instruction

instruction word /ɪnˈstrʌkʃən wɜːd/ *noun* a fixed set of characters used to initiate an instruction ○ *The manufacturers of this CPU have decided that JMP will be the instruction word to call the jump function.*

instrument /ˈɪnstrʊmənt/ *noun* an electronic device that can produce a sound in response to a MIDI note or to a keyboard press

integer /ˈɪntɪdʒə/ *noun* a mathematical term to describe a whole number (NOTE: An integer may be positive or negative or zero.)

integral /ˈɪntɪɡrəl, ɪnˈteɡəl/ *adjective* referring to an add-on device or special feature that is already built into a system ○ *The integral disk drives and modem reduced desk space.*

integrated /ˈɪntɪˌɡreɪtɪd/ *adjective* referring to a system containing many peripherals grouped together to provide a neat, complete system

integrated circuit /ˌɪntɪɡreɪtɪd ˈsɜːkɪt/ *noun* a circuit made up of components all of which are formed on one small piece of semiconductor by means of etching and chemical processes. Abbr **IC** (NOTE: Integrated circuits can be classified as follows: Small Scale Integration (SSI): 1 to 10 components per IC; Medium Scale Integration (MSI): 10 to 100 components per IC; Large Scale Integration (LSI): 100 to 5000 components per IC; Very Large Scale Integration (VLSI): 5,000 to 50,000 components per IC; Ultra Large Scale Integration (ULSI): over 100,000 components per IC.)

integrated database /ˌɪntɪɡreɪtɪd ˈdeɪtəbeɪs/ *noun* a database that is able to provide information for varied requirements without any redundant data

integrated data processing /ˌɪntɪɡreɪtɪd ˈdeɪtə ˌprəʊsesɪŋ/ *noun* an organisational method for the entry and retrieval of data that is designed to provide maximum efficiency. Abbr **IDP**

integrated device electronics /ˌɪntɪ ˌɡreɪtɪd dɪ ˌvaɪs ˌelekˈtrɒnɪks/, **integrated drive electronics** *noun* full form of **IDE**

integrated emulator /ˌɪntɪɡreɪtɪd ˈemjʊleɪtə/ *noun* an emulator program run within a multitasking operating system

integrated injection logic /ˌɪntɪɡreɪtɪd ɪnˈdʒekʃən ˌlɒdʒɪk/ *noun* a type of circuit design able to produce very small, low-power components. Abbr **IIL**

integrated modem /ˌɪntɪɡreɪtɪd ˈməʊdem/ *noun* a modem that is an internal part of the system

integrated office /ˌɪntɪɡreɪtɪd ˈɒfɪs/ *noun* an office environment in which all operations are carried out using a central computer

integrated services digital network /ˌɪntɪɡreɪtɪd ˌsɜːvɪsɪz ˌdɪdʒɪt(ə)l ˈnetwɜːk/ *noun* ♦ **ISDN**

integrated software /ˌɪntɪɡreɪtɪd ˈsɒftweə/ *noun* software such as an operating system or word-processor that is stored in the computer system and has been tailored to the requirements of the system

integration /ˌɪntɪ'greɪʃ(ə)n/ noun the process of bringing several operations together ○ small scale integration (SSI)

integrity /ɪn'tegrɪti/ noun the reliability of data which is being processed or stored on disk □ **the data in this file has integrity** the data has not been corrupted □ **integrity of a file** the fact that a file that has been stored on disk is not corrupted or distorted in any way

Intel /'ɪntel/ the company that developed the first commercially available microprocessor, the 4004, and also developed the range of processors that is used in IBM PCs and compatible computers

Intel 8086 a trade name for a microprocessor that uses a 16-bit data bus and can address up to 1Mb of RAM

Intel 8088 a trade name for a microprocessor that uses a 16-bit data bus internally, but uses an 8-bit data bus externally; used in the first IBM PC computers

Intel 80286 a trade name for a microprocessor that uses a 16-bit data bus and can address up to 16Mb of RAM

Intel 80386 a trade name for a microprocessor that uses a 32-bit data bus and can address up to 4Gb of RAM

Intel 80486 a trade name for a microprocessor that uses a 32-bit data bus and can address up to 64Gb of RAM

Intel Indeo /ˌɪntel 'ɪndiəʊ/ a trade name for software technology developed by Intel that allows a computer to store and play back compressed video sequences using software compression techniques

intelligence /ɪn'telɪdʒəns/ noun the ability of a device to carry out processing or run a program

intelligent /ɪn'telɪdʒənt/ adjective referring to a machine, program or device that is capable of limited reasoning facilities, giving it human-like responses

intelligent device /ɪnˌtelɪdʒ(ə)nt dɪ 'vaɪs/ noun a peripheral device that contains a central processing unit allowing it to process data

intelligent knowledge-based system /ɪnˌtelɪdʒ(ə)nt ˌnɒlɪdʒ beɪsd 'sɪstəm/ noun full form of **IKBS**

intelligent spacer /ɪnˌtelɪdʒ(ə)nt 'speɪsə/ noun a facility on a word-processing system used to prevent words

from being hyphenated or separated at the wrong point

intelligent terminal /ɪnˌtelɪdʒ(ə)nt 'tɜːmɪn(ə)l/ noun same as **smart terminal**

intelligent tutoring system /ɪn ˌtelɪdʒ(ə)nt 'tjuːtərɪŋ ˌsɪstəm/ noun a computer-aided learning system that provides responsive and interactive teaching facilities for users

intelligent wiring hub /ɪnˌtelɪdʒ(ə)nt 'waɪərɪŋ hʌb/ noun a wiring hub that can be controlled from a workstation to direct which circuits should be connected to each other

Intel MMX /ˌɪntel em em 'eks/ a trade name for a range of processors that include components that improve their performance when dealing with multimedia and communications

Intel Pentium /ˌɪntel 'pentiəm/ a trade name for a range of advanced microprocessors that use a 32-bit data bus

Intel Pentium Pro /ˌɪntel ˌpentiəm 'prəʊ/ a trade name for a 32-bit processor developed by Intel to replace the Pentium in high-performance PCs and provide features to improve performance. It is suited to multiuser and multitasking environments.

intensity /ɪn'tensɪti/ noun a measure of the strength of a signal or the brightness of a light source

interactive /ˌɪntər'æktɪv/ adjective referring to a system or piece of software that allows communication between the user and the computer in conversational mode

'Oracle today details its interactive information superhighway aims, endorsed by 17 industry partners. The lynchpin to the announcement will be software based on the Oracle Media Server, a multimedia database designed to run on massively parallel computers.' [Computing]

interactive debugging system /ˌɪntəræktɪv diː'bʌgɪŋ ˌsɪstəm/ noun a software development tool that allows the user to run a program under test, set breakpoints, examine source and object code, examine registers and memory contents and trace the instruction execution

interactive graphics /ˌɪntəræktɪv 'græfɪks/ plural noun a display system that is able to react to different inputs from the user

interactive keyboard /ˌɪntəræktɪv 'kiːbɔːd/ noun a keyboard controlled by a program that is designed to help the user by lighting up particular keys on the keyboard to prompt the user to make a particular kind of input

interactive media /ˌɪntəræktɪv ˈmiːdiə/ *plural noun* media that provide two-way communications between users and their machines or systems and enable users to control their systems and obtain responses from them in real time

interactive mode /ˌɪntərˈæktɪv ˌməʊd/ *noun* a computer mode that allows the user to enter commands or programs or data and receive immediate responses

interactive multimedia /ˌɪntəræktɪv ˌmʌltiˈmiːdiə/ *noun* a multimedia system in which users can issue commands to which the program responds, or control actions and control the way the program works ○ *This interactive multimedia title allows a user to make music with a synthesiser program.*

Interactive Multimedia Association /ˌɪntəræktɪv ˌmʌltiˈmiːdiə ə ˌsəʊsieɪʃ(ə)n/ *noun* full form of **IMA**

interactive processing /ˌɪntəræktɪv ˈprəʊsesɪŋ/ *noun* same as **interactive mode**

interactive routine /ˌɪntəræktɪv ruː ˈtiːn/ *noun* a computer program able to accept data from an operator, process it and provide a real-time reaction to it

interactive system /ˌɪntəræktɪv ˈsɪstəm/ *noun* a system which provides an immediate response to the user's commands or programs or data

interactive terminal /ˌɪntəræktɪv ˈtɜːmɪn(ə)l/ *noun* a terminal in an interactive system which sends and receives information

interactive TV /ˌɪntəræktɪv tiː ˈviː/ *noun* a channel that allows two-way communication between the viewer and the broadcasting station. This feature often allows the user to choose which programme to watch or to respond directly to questions displayed on-screen.

interactive video /ˌɪntəræktɪv ˈvɪdiəʊ/ *noun* full form of **IV**

interactive videotext /ˌɪntəræktɪv ˈvɪdiəʊtekst/ *noun* viewdata service that allows the operator to select pages, display them, ask questions, or use a service such as teleshopping

interblock /ˈɪntəblɒk/ *adjective* occurring or located between blocks

interblock gap /ˈɪntəblɒk ɡæp/ *noun* a blank magnetic tape between the end of one block of data and the start of the next in backing store. Abbr **IBG**. Also called **interrecord gap**

interchange file format /ˌɪntətʃeɪndʒ ˈfaɪl ˌfɔːmæt/ *noun* full form of **IFF**

intercharacter spacing /ɪntə ˌkærəktə ˈspeɪsɪŋ/ *noun* a word-processor feature that provides variable spacing between words to create a justified line

interconnection /ˌɪntəkəˈnekʃən/ *noun* a section of connecting material between two devices

interface /ˈɪntəfeɪs/ *noun* **1.** the point at which one computer system ends and another begins **2.** a circuit, device or port that allows two or more incompatible units to be linked together in a standard communication system, allowing data to be transferred between them **3.** a section of a program which allows transmission of data to another program ■ *verb* **1.** to modify a device by adding a circuit or connector to allow it to conform to a standard communications system **2.** to connect two or more incompatible devices together with a circuit, in order to allow them to communicate

'The original release of ODBC only included a driver for Microsoft's own SQL Server database. Microsoft has subsequently published the ODBC application program interface enabling third-party vendors to create drivers for other databases and tools.' [*Computing*]

interface card /ˈɪntəfeɪs kɑːd/ *noun* an add-on board that allows a computer to interface to certain equipment or conform to a certain standard

interface message processor /ˌɪntəfeɪs ˈmesɪdʒ ˌprəʊsesə/ *noun* a computer in a packet switching network that deals with the flow of data, acting as an interface processor

interface processor /ˈɪntəfeɪs ˌprəʊsesə/ *noun* a computer that controls data transfer between a processor and a terminal or network

interface routines /ˈɪntəfeɪs ruː ˌtiːnz/ *plural noun* software that allows programs or data for one system to run on another

interfacing /ˈɪntəfeɪsɪŋ/ *noun* hardware or software used to interface two computers, programs or devices

interference /ˌɪntəˈfɪərəns/ *noun* noise on a radio signal

interframe coding /ˌɪntəfreɪm ˈkəʊdɪŋ/ *noun* a system for compressi‾

video images, in which only the differences between each frame are recorded

interior gateway protocol /ɪnˌtɪəriə ˌgeɪtweɪ ˌprəʊtəʊˈkɒl/ *noun* full form of **IGP**

interior label /ɪnˌtɪəriə ˈleɪb(ə)l/ *noun* identification data that is stored within a storage medium, as opposed to an exterior or physical label stuck to the case

interlace /ˌɪntəˈleɪs/ *verb* to build up an image on a television screen using two passes to create two picture fields. One displays all the odd-numbered lines, the other all the even-numbered lines. The aim is to reduce the flicker effects on the television picture.

interlaced scanning /ˌɪntəleɪsd ˈskænɪŋ/ *noun* a technique for producing an image on a television or computer screen that is clear and correctly aligned in the vertical plane. It involves scanning first all the odd numbered and then all the even numbered lines in the screen image.

interlaced video /ˌɪntəleɪsd ˈvɪdiəʊ/ *noun* a video signal made up of two separate fields. This is the normal display mode for home video.

interleave /ˌɪntərˈliːv/ *noun* a method of storing data on alternate tracks on a hard disk drive to slow down data transfer rates to match a slower processor ○ *Fast computers run the hard disk with no interleave factor, since they can cope with the fast flow of data to and from the hard disk.*

interleaved /ˌɪntərˈliːvd/ *adjective* referring to sections of two programs executed alternately to give the impression that they are running simultaneously

interleaved memory /ˌɪntərliːvd ˈmem(ə)ri/ *noun* memory containing two separate banks of data used together in sequence

interleave factor /ˌɪntərˌliːv ˈfæktə/ *noun* the ratio of sectors skipped between access operations on a hard disk (NOTE: In a hard disk with an interleave of 3, the first sector is read, then three sectors are skipped and the next sector is read. This is used to allow hard disks with slow access time to store more data on the disk.)

interleaving /ˌɪntərˈliːvɪŋ/ *noun* **1.** the technique of dealing with slices or sections of processes alternately, so that they appear to be executed simultaneously **2.** the process of dividing data storage into sections so that each can be accessed separately

interlock /ˌɪntəˈlɒk/ *noun* a security device that is part of the logon prompt and requires a password ■ *verb* to prevent a device from performing another task until the present one has been completed

interlude /ˈɪntəˌluːd/ *noun* a small initial routine at the start of a program that carries out housekeeping tasks

intermediate access memory /ˌɪntəmiːdiət ˌækses ˈmem(ə)ri/ *noun* full form of **IAM**

intermediate code /ˌɪntəmiːdiət ˈkəʊd/ *noun* a code used by a computer or assembler during the translation of a high-level code to machine code

intermediate file /ˌɪntəmiːdiət ˈfaɪl/ *noun* a file containing partially processed data that will be used at a later date to complete a task

intermediate storage /ˌɪntəmiːdiət ˈstɔːrɪdʒ/ *noun* a temporary area of memory for items which are currently being processed

intermediate system /ˌɪntəmiːdiət ˈsɪstəm/ *noun* (*on the Internet*) a router or other device that links a network or user to the Internet. Abbr **IS**

intermediate system to intermediate system /ˌɪntəmiːdiət ˌsɪstəm tə ˌɪntəmiːdiət ˈsɪstəm/ *noun* full form of **IS-IS**

intermittent error /ˌɪntəmɪt(ə)nt ˈerə/ *noun* an error which apparently occurs randomly in a computer or communications system due to a program fault or noise (NOTE: These errors are very difficult to trace and correct due to their apparent random appearance.)

internal arithmetic /ɪnˌtɜːn(ə)l ə ˈrɪθmətɪk/ *noun* arithmetical operations performed by the ALU

internal character code /ɪnˌtɜːn(ə)l ˈkærɪktə ˌkəʊd/ *noun* a representation of characters in a particular operating system

internal command /ɪnˌtɜːn(ə)l kə ˈmɑːnd/ *noun* a command that is part of the operating system, rather than of a separate utility program ○ *In MS-DOS, the internal command DIR is used frequently.*

internal format /ɪnˌtɜːn(ə)l ˈfɔːmæt/ *noun* a format in which data and instructions are represented within a CPU or backing store

internal hard disk /ɪnˌtɜːn(ə)l ˈhɑːd ˌdɪsk/ *noun* a hard disk drive mounted inside the main case of a computer

internal language /ɪn,tɜːn(ə)l
ˈlæŋgwɪdʒ/ *noun* a language used in a
computer system that is not under the direct control of the operator

internally stored program /ɪn
,tɜːn(ə)li stɔːd ˈprəʊgræm/ *noun* a computer program code that is stored in a
ROM device in a computer system and
does not have to be loaded from backing
store

internal memory /ɪn,tɜːn(ə)l
ˈmem(ə)ri/ *noun* storage space that is
available within the main computer and is
under its direct control. Also called **internal store**

internal modem /ɪn,tɜːn(ə)l ,məʊ
ˈdem/ *noun* a modem on an expansion
card that fits into an expansion connector
and transfers information to the processor
through the bus, rather than connecting to
a serial port

internal sort /ɪn'tɜːn(ə)l sɔːt/ *noun* a
sorting program using only the main memory of a system

internal store /ɪn,tɜːn(ə)l ˈstɔː/ *noun*
same as **internal memory**

International Business Machines
/,ɪntənæʃ(ə)nəl ˈbɪznəs mə,ʃiːnz/ full
form of **IBM**

international file format
/,ɪntənæʃ(ə)nəl ˈfaɪl ,fɔːmæt/ *noun* full
form of **IFF**

International MIDI Association
/,ɪntənæʃ(ə)nəl ˈmɪdi ə,səʊsieɪʃ(ə)n/
noun a professional organisation that covers subjects including authoring languages, formats, and intellectual property. Abbr
IMA

**International Standards Organiza-
tion** /,ɪntənæʃ(ə)nəl ˈstændədz
,ɔːgənaɪzeɪʃ(ə)n/ *noun* an organisation
which creates and regulates standards for
many types of computer and networking
products. Abbr **ISO**

**International Standards Organiza-
tion Open System Interconnection** /,ɪntənæʃ(ə)nəl ,stændədz
,ɔːgənaɪzeɪʃ(ə)n ,əʊpən ,sɪstəm
,ɪntəkəˈnekʃ(ə)n/ *noun* a standardised
ISO network design that is constructed in
layered form, with each layer having a
specific task. The design allows different
systems to communicate if they conform
to the standard. Abbr **ISO/OSI**

Internet /ˈɪntənet/ *noun* an international
wide area network that provides file and

data transfer, together with electronic mail
functions for millions of users around the
world. ◊ **HTTP, POP 3, SMTP, World
Wide Web**

Internet Activities Board /,ɪntənet
ækˈtɪvɪtiz ,bɔːd/ *noun* full form of **IAB**

Internet address /ˈɪntənet ə,dres/
noun a unique number that identifies the
precise location of a particular node on the
Internet The address is a 32-bit number
usually written in dotted decimal format,
i.e. in the form '123.33.22.32', and it is
used by the TCP/IP protocol. A domain
name system is used to convert a domain
name, e.g. 'bloomsbury.com', into a full
Internet address. Also called **IP address**

Internet architecture board
/,ɪntənet ˈɑːkɪtektʃə ,bɔːd/ *noun* a
group that monitors and manages the development of the Internet. Abbr **IAB**
(NOTE: Its members include the IETF and
the IRTF.)

**Internet Assigned Numbers Au-
thority** /,ɪntənet ə,saɪnd ˈnʌmbəz ɔː
,θɒrɪti/ *noun* a group that assigns unique
identifying numbers to the different protocols and network products used on the Internet. Abbr **IANA**

Internet banking /,ɪntənet ˈbæŋkɪŋ/
noun a system that allows customers to
check their bank accounts, pay bills and
transfer money by means of the Internet

'…most banks now offer reasonable telephone and
Internet banking facilities.' [*The Guardian*]

Internet café /ˈɪntənet ,kæfeɪ/ *noun*
same as **cybercafé**

Internet control message protocol
/,ɪntənet kən,trəʊl ˈmesɪdʒ ,prəʊtəkɒl/
noun full form of **ICMP**

Internet-draft /ˈɪntənet drɑːft/ *adjective* referring to draft documents produced
by the IETF that often lead to RFCs. Abbr
I-D

**Internet engineering steering
group** /,ɪntənet ,endʒɪnɪərɪŋ ˈstɪərɪŋ
gruːp/ *noun* a group that reviews Internet
standards and manages the IETF. Abbr
IESG

Internet engineering task force
/,ɪntənet ,endʒɪnɪərɪŋ ˈtɑːsk ,fɔːs/ *noun*
full form of **IETF**

Internet Explorer /,ɪntənet ɪk
ˈsplɔːrə/ *noun* a web browser developed
by Microsoft which allows a user to view
formatted HTML information such as
webpages on the Internet. Abbr **IE**

Internet group management protocol /ˌɪntənet gruːp ˈmænɪdʒmənt ˌprəʊtəkɒl/ *noun* full form of **IGMP**

Internet Information Server /ˌɪntənet ˌɪnfəˈmeɪʃ(ə)n ˌsɜːvə/ *noun* full form of **IIS**

Internet merchant account /ˌɪntənet ˈmɜːtʃənt əˌkaʊnt/ *noun* a business bank account that allows the business to accept credit card payments via the Internet. Many businesses have a merchant account, allowing them to accept credit card payments by telephone or mail, but still need a separate IMA to accept payments via the net. Abbr **IMA**

Internet message access protocol /ˌɪntənet ˈmesɪdʒ ˌækses ˌprəʊtəkɒl/ *noun* full form of **IMAP**

Internet number /ˈɪntənet ˌnʌmbə/ *noun* ♦ **Internet address**

Internet protocol /ˌɪntənet ˈprəʊtəkɒl/ *noun* full form of **IP**

Internet protocol address /ˌɪntənet ˌprəʊtəkɒl əˈdres/ *noun* full form of **IP address**. ♦ **Internet address**

Internet relay chat /ˌɪntənet ˌriːleɪ ˈtʃæt/ *noun* a system that allows many users to participate in a chat session in which each user can send messages and sees the text of any other user. Abbr **IRC**

Internet research task force /ˌɪntənet rɪˌsɜːtʃ ˈtɑːsk fɔːs/ *noun* full form of **IRTF**

Internet server application program interface /ˌɪntənet ˌsɜːvə ˌæplɪkeɪʃ(ə)n ˈprəʊgræm ˌɪntəfeɪs/ *noun* full form of **ISAPI**

Internet service provider /ˌɪntənet ˈsɜːvɪs prəˌvaɪdə/ *noun* full form of **ISP**

Internet Society /ˈɪntənet səˌsaɪəti/ *noun* an organisation that has the task of maintaining and enhancing the Internet. It is made up of committees, such as the Internet Advisory Board and the Internet Engineering Task Force, and is not linked to any government or company, so that it provides an independent view of the future of the Internet.

Internet telephony /ˌɪntənet təˈlefəni/ *noun* a system that allows users to make telephone calls using the Internet to carry the voice signals. To make a call, users need a computer with a sound card fitted and a microphone and loudspeaker plugged in, and special software manages the connection and transfers the voice data over the Internet. (NOTE: This system is particularly appealing if you have low-cost dial-up access to the Internet, since it allows you to make long distance calls for the low-price you pay for your Internet connection.)

Internetwork /ˌɪntəˈnetwɜːk/ *noun* a number of networks connected together using bridges or routers to allow users on one network to access any resource on any other of the connected networks

Internetwork Packet Exchange /ˌɪntənetwɜːk ˈpækɪt ɪksˌtʃeɪndʒ/ a trade name for a network protocol developed by Novell that is used to transfer packets of information over a network. Abbr **IPX**

interoperability /ˌɪntəɒpərəˈbɪlɪti/ *noun* the ability of two devices or computers to exchange information

interpolation /ɪnˌtɜːpəˈleɪʃ(ə)n/ *noun* the calculation of intermediate values between two points

interpret /ɪnˈtɜːprɪt/ *verb* to translate what is said in one language into another

interpretative code /ɪnˌtɜːrprɪtətɪv ˈkəʊd/ *noun* a code used with an interpretative program

interpretative program /ɪn ˌtɜːrprɪtətɪv ˈprəʊgræm/ *noun* software that translates high level interpretative code into machine code instructions at run-time

interpreted language /ɪnˌtɜːprɪtd ˈlæŋgwɪdʒ/ *noun* a programming language that is executed by an interpreter

interpreter /ɪnˈtɜːprɪtə/ *noun* a piece of software used to translate a user's high-level program into machine code at the time of execution. Compare **compiler** (NOTE: A compiler translates the high-level language into machine code and then executes it, whereas an interpreter makes a translation in real time.)

interrecord gap /ˌɪntərekɔːd ˈgæp/ *noun* same as **interblock gap**

interrogate /ɪnˈterəgeɪt/ *verb* to send a request for information to a computer device or program

interrupt /ˌɪntəˈrʌpt/ *noun* **1.** the stopping of a transmission as a result of an action at the receiving end of a system **2.** a signal which diverts a central processing unit from one task to another that has higher priority, allowing the CPU to return to the first task later

interrupt disable /ˈɪntərʌpt dɪsˌeɪb(ə)l/ *noun* the process of disabling an interrupt by resetting a bit in the interrupt mask to zero

interrupt-driven /'ɪntərʌpt ˌdrɪv(ə)n/ *adjective* referring to a program that works in response to an interrupt

interrupt enable /'ɪntərʌpt ɪnˌeɪb(ə)l/ *noun* the process of arming an interrupt by setting a bit in the interrupt mask

interrupt handler /'ɪntərʌpt ˌhændlə/ *noun* a piece of software that accepts interrupt signals and acts on them, e.g. by running a special routine or sending data to a peripheral. Abbr **IH**

interrupt level /'ɪntərʌpt ˌlev(ə)l/ *noun* the priority assigned to the interrupt from a peripheral

interrupt line /'ɪntərʌpt laɪn/ *noun* a connection to a central processing unit from outside the system that allows external devices to use the CPU's interrupt facility ○ *This printer port design uses an interrupt line to let the CPU know it is ready to receive data.*

interrupt mask /'ɪntərʌpt mɑːsk/ *noun* a term in computer programming that selects which interrupt lines are to be activated

interrupt priorities /'ɪntərʌpt praɪ ˌɒrɪtiz/ *plural noun* the order in which various interrupts are accepted by a central processing unit

interrupt request /'ɪntərʌpt rɪ ˌkwest/ *noun* a signal from a device that indicates to the CPU that it requires attention. Abbr **IRQ**

interrupt servicing /'ɪntərʌpt ˌsɜːvɪsɪŋ/ *noun* the process of carrying out some action when an interrupt is detected, e.g. running a routine

interrupt signal /'ɪntərʌpt ˌsɪgn(ə)l/ *noun* a voltage pulse from a peripheral sent to the CPU requesting attention

interrupt stacking /'ɪntərʌpt ˌstækɪŋ/ *noun* the process of storing interrupts in a queue and processing them according to interrupt priorities

intersection /'ɪntəˌsekʃən/ *noun* a logical function whose output is only true if both its inputs are true

interval /'ɪntəv(ə)l/ *noun* a short pause between two actions ○ *There was an interval between pressing the key and the starting of the printout.*

interword spacing /ɪntəˌwɜːd 'speɪsɪŋ/ *noun* variable spacing between words in a text, used to justify lines

intimate /'ɪntɪmət/ *adjective* referring to software that operates and interacts closely with hardware in a system

intra /'ɪntrə/, **intra frame** /'ɪntrə freɪm/ *noun* a reference frame used to synchronise video data that has been compressed using the MPEG system

intraframe coding /ˌɪntrəfreɪm 'kəʊdɪŋ/ *noun* a method of compression that works on one video frame at a time, this is less efficient than interframe coding

intranet /'ɪntrənet/ *noun* a private network of computers within a company that provides similar functions to the Internet , e.g. electronic mail, newsgroups and access to the WWW, without the associated security risks of making the information public or linking the company to a public network. ◊ **firewall, Internet, LAN, web server**

intruder /ɪn'truːdə/ *noun* a person who is not authorised to use a computer or connect to a network. ◊ **firewall, hacker**

inverse /ˌɪn'vɜːs/ *noun* a state of a signal or device that is the logical opposite of another ○ *The inverse of true is false.*

inverse video /ˌɪnvɜːs 'vɪdiəʊ/ *noun* a television effect created by swapping the background and foreground text display colours

inversion /ɪn'vɜːʃ(ə)n/ *noun* the process of changing over the numbers in a binary word, one to zero and zero to one ○ *The inversion of a binary digit takes place in one's complement.*

invert /ˌɪn'vɜːt/ *verb* to change all binary ones to zeros and zeros to ones

inverted backbone /ɪnˌvɜːtɪd 'bækbəʊn/ *noun* a network architecture in which the hub is the centre of the network and all sub networks connect to the hub (NOTE: In a traditional backbone network the sub networks connect to the cable that is the main backbone.)

inverted commas /ɪnˌvɜːtɪd 'kɒməz/ *plural noun* a printing sign (") that is usually used to indicate a quotation

inverted file /ɪnˌvɜːtɪd 'faɪl/ *noun* a file with an index entry for every data item

inverter /ɪn'vɜːtə/ *noun* **1.** a logical gate that provides inversion facilities **2.** a circuit used to provide alternating current supply from a DC battery source

invisible /ɪn'vɪzɪb(ə)l/ *adjective* visible on a DTP page or graphics layout during the design phase, but not printed

invitation /ˌɪnvɪ'teɪʃ(ə)n/ *noun* action by a processor to contact another device and allow it to send a message

invitation to send /ˌɪnvɪteɪʃ(ə)n tə 'send/ *noun* a special character transmitted to indicate to a device that the host computer is willing to receive messages. Abbr **ITS**

invoke /ɪn'vəʊk/ *verb* to start or to run a program, often a memory-resident utility

'…when an error is detected, the editor may be invoked and positioned at the statement in error' [*Personal Computer World*]

I/O /ˌaɪ 'əʊ/ *noun* the process of receiving or transmitting data between a computer and its peripherals, and other points outside the system. Full form **input/output**

I/O address /ˌaɪ 'əʊ ə,dres/ *noun* the memory location that is used by an I/O port to transfer data with the CPU

I/O bound /ˌaɪ əʊ 'baʊnd/ *adjective* referring to a processor that is doing very little processing since its time is taken up reading or writing data from a I/O port

I/O buffer /ˌaɪ 'əʊ ˌbʌfə/ *noun* a temporary storage area for data waiting to be input or output

I/O bus /ˌaɪ 'əʊ ˌbʌs/ *noun* a link that allows data and control signals to be transferred between a CPU and memory or peripheral devices

I/O channel /ˌaɪ 'əʊ ˌtʃæn(ə)l/ *noun* a link between a processor and peripheral, allowing data transfer

I/O device /ˌaɪ 'əʊ dɪ,vaɪs/ *noun* a peripheral such as a terminal in a workstation that can be used for both inputting and outputting data to a processor

I/O file /ˌaɪ 'əʊ ˌfaɪl/ *noun* a file whose contents have been or will be transferred from storage to a peripheral

I/O instruction /ˌaɪ 'əʊ ˌɪnstrʌkʃ(ə)n/ *noun* a computer programming instruction that allows data to be input or output from a processor

I/O mapping /ˌaɪ əʊ 'mæpɪŋ/ *noun* a method of assigning a special address to each I/O port in a microcomputer rather than a memory location

ion deposition /'aɪən ˌdepəzɪʃ(ə)n/ *noun* printing technology that uses a printhead that deposits ions to create a charged image which attracts the toner

IOP *abbr* input/output processor

I/O port /ˌaɪ 'əʊ ˌpɔːt/ *noun* a circuit or connector that provides an input/output channel to another device

I/O redirection /ˌaɪ əʊ ˌriːdaɪ'rekʃ(ə)n/ *noun* the process of transferring data to an I/O port rather than to its normal destination ○ *Using I/O redirection, we send all the data from the keyboard to the printer port instead of the monitor.*

IORQ *abbr* input/output request

ip *abbr* information provider

IP /ˌaɪ 'piː/ *noun* one part of the TCP/IP standard that defines how data is transferred over a network. Full form **Internet protocol**

i/p, I/P *abbr* input

IP address /ˌaɪ 'piː ə,dres/ *noun* Internet protocol address

IP Datagram /ˌaɪ piː 'deɪtəgræm/ *noun* a packet of data transferred across a TCP/IP network

IPL *abbr* initial program loader

IP multicast /ˌaɪ piː 'mʌltɪkɑːst/ *noun* a transmission in which one set of data is sent out to several recipients simultaneously

IPng /ˌaɪ piː en 'dʒiː/ *noun* an upgrade of the Internet Protocol that allows more computers to connect to the Internet and supports more data traffic. Full form **Internet Protocol next generation**

ips /ˌaɪ piː 'es/ *noun* a way of showing the speed of tape past the read/write heads. Full form **inches per second**

IPSE *abbr* integrated project support environment

Ipsec, IP Security *noun* a set of security protocols that allows information to be transferred securely over the Internet and is used to set up and support secure virtual private networks. The system works with packets of data at the IP layer and supports two types of public-key data encryption. The first, called Transport mode, encrypts the data within a packet, but does not touch the header information, which contains the destination address, subject and source of a packet. The second mode, Tunnel mode, provides a greater level of security by encrypting all of the packet, including the header information.

IP spoofing /ˌaɪ ˌpiː 'spuːfɪŋ/ *noun* a method of gaining unauthorised access to a computer or network by pretending to be an authorised computer or device (NOTE: Each device on the network has its own unique IP address, and many security systems block or allow access to networks depending on the IP address of the computer that is requesting access. A hacker finds an IP address that is allowed, then modifies the header information in the data packets from his or her own computer to include this IP address. Newer routers and firewalls use a range of techniques to spot this scheme and block the data.)

ip terminal /ˌaɪ ˌpiː ˈtɜːmɪn(ə)l/ *noun* a special visual display unit that allows users to create and edit videotext pages before sending them to the main videotext page database

IPX *abbr* Internetwork Packet Exchange

IR *abbr* **1.** information retrieval **2.** index register **3.** instruction register

IRC *abbr* Internet relay chat

IrDA /ˌaɪ ɑː diː ˈeɪ/ *noun* a standard method used to transfer information via an infrared light beam, often from a laptop or PDA to a printer or desktop computer. Full form **infrared data association**

IRQ /ˌaɪ ɑː ˈkjuː/ *noun* interrupt request. Full form **interrupt request**

irregular polygon /ɪˌreɡjʊlə ˈpɒlɪɡən/ *noun* an enclosed graphic object that has a number of sides of unequal length

IRSG /ˌaɪ ɑː es ˈdʒiː/ *noun* a group that manages the Internet research task force and is part of the Internet Society (*see*) Full form **Internet research steering group**

IRTF /ˌaɪ ɑː tiː ˈef/ *noun* a committee that is part of the IAB and researches new Internet standards before referring them to the IETF for approval. Full form **Internet research task force**

ISA /ˌaɪ es ˈeɪ/ *noun* a standard used for the 16-bit expansion bus in an IBM PC or compatible. Full form **Industry Standard Architecture**. Compare **EISA, MCA**

ISAM *abbr* indexed sequential access method

ISAPI /ˌaɪ es eɪ aɪ ˈpiː/ *noun* (*on a Windows NT server*) a set of commands and procedures that allow web server software to access other applications on the same server running Windows NT. Full form **Internet server application program interface**

ISDN /ˌaɪ es diː ˈen/ *noun* a method of digital data transmission. It utilises the existing telephone network, but omits the digital/analog conversion required by conventional telephonic equipment; the customer therefore has a fully digital connec-

tion. ISDN connections usually provide two 64K bps channels, which can work independently or be combined to achieve transfer speeds of 128K bps. Full form **integrated services digital network**

IS-IS /ˌɪz ɪz/ *noun* an OSI protocol that allows data to be transferred between routers. Full form **intermediate system to intermediate system**

ISO *abbr* International Standards Organization

ISO 9660 *noun* a standard method of storing files on a CD-ROM, used in many formats including PhotoCD

isochronous network /aɪˌsɒkrən(ə)s ˈnetwɜːk/ *noun* a network in which all the components on the network run from a common clock so that their timing is uniform

isochronous transmission /aɪˌsɒkrən(ə)s trænzˈmɪʃ(ə)n/ *noun* the transfer of asynchronous data over a synchronous link

isolate /ˈaɪsəˌleɪt/ *verb* to separate something from a system

isolated location /ˌaɪsəleɪtɪd ləʊ ˈkeɪʃ(ə)n/ *noun* a storage location that cannot be directly accessed by a user's program, so that it is protected against accidental erasure

isolation transformer /ˌaɪsəˌleɪʃ(ə)n trænsˈfɔːmə/ *noun* a transformer used to isolate equipment from direct connection with the mains electricity supply, in case of voltage spikes

isolator /ˈaɪsəleɪtə/ *noun* a device or material which isolates

isometric view /ˌaɪsəʊˈmetrɪk vjuː/ *noun* (*in graphics*) a drawing that shows all three dimensions of an object in equal proportion ○ *An isometric view does not show any perspective.*

ISO/OSI model /ˌaɪ es əʊ əʊ es ˈaɪ ˌmɒd(ə)l/ *noun* a layered architecture that defines how computers and networks should interact

ISP /ˌaɪ es ˈpiː/ *noun* a company that provides one of the permanent links that make up the Internet and sells connections to private users and companies to allow them to access the Internet. Full form **Internet service provider**

ISR *abbr* information storage and retrieval

IT *abbr* information technology

italic /ɪˈtælɪk/ *noun* type of character font in which the characters slope to the right ○ *The headline is printed in italic and underlined.*

item size /'aɪtəm saɪz/ *noun* the number of characters or digits in an item of data

iterate /'ɪtəreɪt/ *noun* a loop or series of instructions in a program which repeat over and over again until the program is completed. Also called **iterative routine**

iteration /ˌɪtə'reɪʃ(ə)n/ *noun* the repeated application of a program to solve a problem

iterative process /ˌɪtərətɪv 'prəʊses/ *noun* a process that is continuously repeated until a condition is met

iterative routine /ˌɪtərətɪv ruː'tiːn/ *noun* same as **iterate**

ITS *abbr* invitation to send

IV /ˌaɪ 'viː/ *noun* a system that uses a computer linked to a video disk player to provide processing power and real images or moving pictures. Full form **interactive video** (NOTE: This system is often used in teaching. A student is asked questions, and if he or she answers correctly, the system responds by providing a filmed sequence from the videodisk.)

J

jabber /'dʒæbə/ *noun* a continuous random signal transmitted by a faulty adapter card or node on a network

jack /dʒæk/, **jack plug** *noun* a plug which consists of a single pin

jaggies /'dʒægiːz/ *plural noun* jagged edges which appear along diagonal or curved lines displayed on a computer screen, caused by the size of each pixel. ◊ **aliasing, anti-aliasing**

Java /'dʒɑːvə/ a trade name for a programming language and program definition developed by Sun Microsystems. Java is used to create small applications designed to enhance the functionality of a webpage. It is similar to object-oriented languages such as C++ and can run on any compatible platform. Compare **JavaScript**

Java Beans /'dʒɑːvə biːnz/ a trade name for a software system, developed by Sun Microsystems, that provides objects within the Java programming language, and is similar to COM and CORBA and can work with both these standards

Java Database Connectivity /ˌdʒɑːvə ˌdeɪtəbeɪs ˌkɒnek'tɪvɪti/ a trade name for a set of standard functions that allow a programmer to access a database from within a Java application. Abbr **JDBC**

JavaScript /'dʒɑːvəskrɪpt/ a trade name for set of programming commands that can be included within a normal webpage written using HTML commands. When the web browser loads the webpage, it runs the JavaScript commands, normally used to create special effects to a webpage. Compare **HTML, Perl, VBScript**

JCL /ˌdʒaɪ si: 'el/ *noun* a set of commands that identify, and describe resources required by, a job that a computer has to process. Full form **job control language**

JDBC *abbr* Java Database Connectivity

jet /dʒet/ ◆ ink-jet printer

jitter /'dʒɪtə/ *noun* **1.** the rapid small up-and-down movement of characters or pixels on a screen displaying image bits in a facsimile transmission ○ *Looking at this screen jitter is giving me a headache.* **2.** a fault in a transmission line that causes some of the data bits being transmitted to be corrupted

JK-flip-flop /ˌdʒeɪ keɪ ˈflɪp flɒp/ *noun* a flip-flop device with two inputs, J and K, and two complementary outputs that are dependent on the inputs

job /dʒɒb/ *noun* a task or a number of tasks to be processed as a single unit ○ *The next job to be processed is to sort all the records.*

job control file /ˈdʒɒb kənˌtrəʊl faɪl/ *noun* a file which contains instructions in a JCL

job control language /ˌdʒɒb kən ˈtrəʊl ˌlæŋgwɪdʒ/ *noun* full form of **JCL**

job control program /ˈdʒɒb kən ˌtrəʊl ˌprəʊgræm/ *noun* a short program of job control instructions loaded before a particular application is run, setting up the system as required by the application

job file /ˈdʒɒb ˌfaɪl/ *noun* a file containing jobs waiting to be processed, or the names of jobs waiting to be processed

job mix /ˈdʒɒb ˌmɪks/ *noun* the jobs being executed at any one time in a system

job number /dʒɒb ˈnʌmbə/ *noun* a number which is given to a job in a queue, waiting to be processed

job orientated language /ˌdʒɒb ˌɔːriənteɪtɪd ˈlæŋgwɪdʒ/ *noun* a computer programming language that provides specialised instructions relating to job control tasks and processing

job orientated terminal /ˌdʒɒb ˌɔːriənteɪtɪd ˈtɜːmɪn(ə)l/ *noun* a computer terminal designed for and used for a particular task

job priority /dʒɒb praɪˈɒrɪti/ *noun* the importance of a particular job compared to others

job processing /dʒɒb ˌprəˈsesɪŋ/ *noun* the process of reading in job control instructions from an input source and executing them

job queue /ˈdʒɒb ˌkjuː/ *noun* a number of tasks arranged in an order waiting to be processed in a multitasking or batch system

job scheduling /ˈdʒɒb ˌʃedjuːlɪŋ/ *noun* the process of arranging the order in which jobs are to be processed

job statement control /ˈdʒɒb ˌsteɪtmənt kənˌtrəʊl/ *noun* the use of instructions and statements to control the actions of the operating system of a computer

job step /ˈdʒɒb ˌstep/ *noun* one unit of processing involved in a task

job stream /ˈdʒɒb ˌstriːm/ *noun* same as **job queue**

jog/shuttle, jog/shuttle control *noun* a manual control on a video player or camera that allows a user to edit a sequence (NOTE: Jog moves the tape one frame a time, shuttle moves the tape more rapidly.)

join /dʒɔɪn/ *verb* to combine two or more pieces of information to produce a single unit of information □ **join files** an instruction to produce a new file consisting of one file added to the end of another ■ *noun* a logical function that produces a true output if any input is true

joint denial /dʒɔɪnt dɪˈnaɪəl/ *noun* a logical function whose output is false if any input is true

Joint Photographic Experts Group /ˌdʒɔɪnt fəʊtəˌgræfɪks ˈekspɜːts gruːp/ *noun* full form of **JPEG**

journal /ˈdʒɜːn(ə)l/ *noun* **1.** a record of all communications to and from a terminal **2.** a list of any changes or updates to a file ○ *The modified records were added to the master file and noted in the journal.*

journal file /ˈdʒɜːn(ə)l faɪl/ *noun* a stored record of every communication between a user and the central computer, used to help retrieve files after a system crash or fault

joystick /ˈdʒɔɪˌstɪk/ *noun* a device that allows a user to move a cursor around the screen by moving an upright rod connected to an I/O port on the computer

joystick port /ˈdʒɔɪˌstɪk pɔːt/ *noun* a socket and interfacing circuit into which a joystick can be plugged

JPEG /ˈdʒeɪ peg/ *noun* a standard that defines a way of storing graphic images in a compressed format in a file on disk. Full form **Joint Photographic Experts Group**

JPEG++ /ˌdʒaɪ peg plʌs ˈplʌs/ *noun* an extension to JPEG that allows parts of an image to be compressed in different ways

JScript /ˈdʒaɪskrɪpt/ a trade name for a version of JavaScript developed by Microsoft

jukebox /ˈdʒuːkˌbɒks/ *noun* a CD-ROM drive that can hold several CD-ROM discs and select the correct disc when required

Julian date /ˈdʒuːliən deɪt/ *noun* a date expressed as the number of days since 1 January of the current year, so that, e.g., 1 February would appear as 032

jumbo chip /ˈdʒʌmbəʊ tʃɪp/ *noun* an integrated circuit made using the whole of a semiconductor wafer. ◊ **wafer scale integration**

jump /dʒʌmp/ *noun* a programming command to end one set of instructions and direct the processor to another section of the program ■ *verb* to direct a CPU to another section of a program

jumper /ˈdʒʌmpə/ *noun* a temporary wire connection on a circuit board

jumper-selectable /ˌdʒʌmpə sɪˈlektəb(ə)l/ *adjective* referring to a circuit or device whose options can be selected by positioning various wire connections ○ *The printer's typeface was jumper-selectable.*

jump on zero /ˌdʒʌmp ɒn ˈzɪərəʊ/ *noun* a conditional jump executed if a flag or register is zero

jump operation /dʒʌmp ˌɒpəˈreɪʃ(ə)n/ *noun* an operation in which the CPU is sent from the instruction it is currently executing to another point in the program

junction /ˈdʒʌŋkʃən/ *noun* a connection between wires or cables

junction box /ˈdʒʌŋkʃən bɒks/ *noun* a small box where a number of wires can be interconnected

junction transistor /ˌdʒʌŋkʃən trænˈzɪstə/ *noun* same as **bipolar transistor**

junk /dʒʌŋk/ *noun* information or hardware which is useless or out of date or non-functional ■ *verb* to make a file or piece of hardware redundant □ **to junk a file** to erase or delete from storage a file that is no longer used

justification /ˌdʒʌstɪfɪˈkeɪʃ(ə)n/ *noun* the process of moving data bits or characters to the left or right so that the lines have straight margins

justify /ˈdʒʌstɪˌfaɪ/ *verb* **1.** to change the spacing between words or characters in a document so that the left and right margins will be straight **2.** to shift the contents of a computer register by a set amount

justify inhibit /ˈdʒʌstɪfaɪ ɪnˌhɪbɪt/ *noun* an instruction to prevent a word processor justifying a document

justify margin /ˌdʒʌstɪfaɪ ˈmɑːdʒɪn/ *noun* ♦ **left justify, right justify**

K

K *symbol* kilo

K6 a trade name for a 64-bit processor developed by AMD Corporation as a rival to the Intel Pentium series of processors

K56flex a trade name for a communications standard developed by Hayes, Pace and other manufacturers for a range of high-speed modems that can transfer data at 56,000 bits per second. ◊ **V series, X2**

Kaleida Labs a company formed as a joint venture between Apple and IBM to produce cross-platform multimedia authoring tools

Karnaugh map /ˈkɑːnəʊ mæp/ *noun* a graphical representation of states and conditions in a logic circuit ○ *The prototype was checked for hazards with a Karnaugh map.*

KB, Kb *abbr* kilobyte

Kbit /ˈkeɪ bɪt/ *abbr* kilobit

Kbps /ˌkeɪ biː piː ˈes/ *noun* a measure of the amount of data that a device can transfer each second ○ *A fast modem can transfer data at a rate of 33.6Kbps, whereas an ISDN adapter can transfer data at a rate of 64Kbps.* Full form **kilo bits per second**

Kbyte /ˈkeɪ baɪt/ *abbr* kilobyte

Kermit /ˈkɜːmɪt/ *noun* a file transfer protocol usually used when downloading data with a modem

kern /kɜːn/ *verb* to adjust the space between pairs of letters so that they are printed closer together

kernel /ˈkɜːn(ə)l/ *noun* the essential instruction routines required as a basis for any operations in a computer system (NOTE: Kernel routines are usually hidden from the user. They are used by the operating system for tasks such as loading a program or displaying text on a screen.)

key /kiː/ *noun* **1.** a button on a keyboard that operates a switch ○ *There are 64 keys on the keyboard.* **2.** an important object or group of characters in a computer system, used to represent an instruction or set of data **3.** a special combination of numbers or characters that are used with a cipher to encrypt or decrypt a message ○ *Type this key into the machine, it will decode the last message.* **4.** an identification code or word used for a stored record or data item ○ *We selected all the records with the word 'disk' in their keys.* ■ *verb* □ **to key in** to enter text or commands via a keyboard ○ *They keyed in the latest data.*

keyboard /ˈkiːbɔːd/ *noun* a number of keys fixed together in some order, used to enter information into a computer ■ *verb* to enter information by using a keyboard ○ *It was cheaper to have the manuscript keyboarded by another company.*

'…the main QWERTY typing area is in the centre of the keyboard with the 10 function keys on the left' [*Personal Computer World*]

keyboard contact bounce /ˌkiːbɔːd ˌkɒntækt ˈbaʊns/ *noun* multiple signals from a key pressed just once, due to a faulty switch and key bounce

keyboard encoder /ˈkiːbɔːd ɪn ˌkəʊdə/ *noun* the way in which each key generates a unique word when pressed

keyboarder /ˈkiːbɔːdə/ *noun* a person who enters data via a keyboard

keyboarding /ˈkiːbɔːdɪŋ/ *noun* the action of entering data using a keyboard ○ *The cost of keyboarding is calculated in keystrokes per hour.*

keyboard layout /ˈkiːbɔːd ˌleɪaʊt/ *noun* the way in which the various function and character keys are arranged on a keyboard

keyboard overlay /ˈkiːbɔːd ˌəʊvəleɪ/ *noun* a strip of paper that is placed above the keys on a keyboard to indicate their function

keyboard send/receive /ˌkiːbɔːd send rɪˈsiːv/ *noun* full form of **KSR**

keyboard to disk entry /ˌkiːbɔːd tə ˈdɪsk ˌentri/ *noun* a system where information entered on a keyboard is stored directly onto disk without any processing

key click /ˈkiː klɪk/ *noun* a sound produced by a computer to allow the operator to know that the key he pressed has been registered

key combination /ˈkiː ˌkɒmbɪneɪʃ(ə)n/ *noun* a combination of two or more keys that carry out a function when pressed at the same time

key database /ˈkiː ˌdeɪtəbeɪs/ *noun* a database that holds all the keys used by a certificate authority

keyed sequential access method /ˌkiːd sɪˌkwenʃəl ˈækses ˌmeθəd/ *noun* full form of **KSAM**

key escrow /ˌkiː ˈeskrəʊ/ *noun* a system in which one person coverts computer data into a secret code but the key that enables this data to be decoded again is held by another person

key feature /ˌkiː ˈfiːtʃə/ *noun* the most important feature ○ *The key features of this system are: 20Mb of formatted storage with an access time of 60ms.*

key field /ˌkiː ˈfiːld/ *noun* a field which identifies entries in a record

key frame /ˌkiː ˈfreɪm/ *noun* **1.** a single picture in an animation that describes the main actions in the sequence **2.** (*in a hypertext document*) a page that gives the user a choice of destination **3.** (*in full motion video*) a frame that is recorded in full rather than being compressed or differentially recorded

key matrix /ˌkiː ˈmeɪtrɪks/ *noun* the way in which the keys of a keyboard are arranged as an array of connections

key number /ˈkiː ˌnʌmbə/ *noun* a numeric code used to identify which key has been pressed

key overlay /ˌkiː ˈəʊvəleɪ/ *noun* a paper placed over the keys on a keyboard describing their functions for a particular application ○ *Without the key overlay, I would never remember which function key does what.*

keypad /ˈkiːˌpæd/ *noun* a group of special keys used for certain applications ○ *You can use the numeric keypad to enter the figures.*

'…it uses a six button keypad to select the devices and functions' [*Byte*]

key punch /'kiː pʌntʃ/ *noun* a machine used for punching data into punched cards by means of a keyboard

key rollover /ˌkiː 'rəʊləʊvə/ *noun* the use of a buffer between the keyboard and computer to provide rapid key stroke storage for fast typists who hit several keys in rapid succession

key shortcut /ˌkiː 'ʃɔːtkʌt/ *noun* same as **key combination**

keystone distortion /ˌkiːstəʊn dɪ'stɔːʃ(ə)n/ *noun* image distortion in which the vertical lines slant out towards the horizontal edges of the monitor. Also called **trapezoidal distortion**

key strip /'kiː strɪp/ *noun* a piece of paper above certain keys used to remind the operator of their special functions

keystroke /'kiːstrəʊk/ *noun* the action of pressing a key ○ *He keyboards at a rate of 3500 keystrokes per hour.*

keystroke count /'kiːstrəʊk ˌkaʊnt/ *noun* a count of each keystroke made, often used to calculate keyboarding costs

keystroke verification /ˌkiːstrəʊk ˌverɪfɪ'keɪʃ(ə)n/ *noun* a check made on each key pressed to make sure it is valid for a particular application

key terminal /ˌkiː 'tɜːmɪn(ə)l/ *noun* the most important terminal in a computer system or the one with the highest priority

key-to-disk /ˌkiː tə 'dɪsk/ *noun* a system where data is keyed in and stored directly on disk without any processing

keyword /'kiːwɜːd/ *noun* a command word used in a programming language to provide a function ○ *The BASIC keyword PRINT will display text on the screen.*

KHz *abbr* kilohertz

kill /kɪl/ *verb* to erase a file or stop a program during execution □ **kill file** a command to erase a stored file completely

kilo /'kɪləʊ/ *prefix* **1.** one thousand **2.** (*used only in computer and electronics applications*) 1,024 units, equal to 2^{10}

kilobaud /'kɪləbɔːd/ *noun* 1,000 bits per second

kilobit /'kɪləbɪt/ *noun* 1,024 bits of data. Abbr **Kbit**

kilo bits per second /ˌkiːləʊ bɪts pɜː 'sekənd/ *noun* a measure of the amount of data that a device can transfer each second. Abbr **Kbps**

kilobyte /'kɪləʊˌbaɪt/ *noun* a unit of measurement for high-capacity storage devices meaning 1,024 bytes of data. Abbr **KB, Kbyte**

kilohertz /'kɪləhɜːts/ *noun* a frequency of one thousand cycles per second. Abbr **KHz**

kilo instructions per second /ˌkɪləʊ ɪnˌstrʌkʃənz pɜː 'sekənd/ *noun* full form of **KIPS**

Kilostream /'kɪləstriːm/ a trade name for a leased line connection supplied by British Telecom that provides data transfer rates of 64Kbit per second

kiloword /'kɪləwɜːd/ *noun* a unit of measurement of 1,024 computer words

kiosk /'kiːɒsk/ *noun* a small booth with a screen, a means of user input and a computer, used to provide information for the general public

KIPS /ˌkeɪ aɪ piː 'es/ *noun* one thousand computer instructions processed every second, used as a measure of computer power. Full form **kilo instructions per second**

Klamath /'klæmæθ/ a trade name for the low-cost version of the Intel Pentium Pro processor

kludge, kluge *noun* (*informal*) **1.** a temporary correction made to a badly written or constructed piece of software or to a keyboarding error **2.** hardware which should be used for demonstration purposes only

kluged /kluːdʒd/ *adjective* temporarily repaired

knob /nɒb/ *noun* a round button (such as on a monitor), which can be turned to control some process ○ *Turn the on/off knob.*

knowledge base /'nɒlɪdʒ beɪs/ *noun* the computerised data in an expert system that can be used to solve a particular type of problem

knowledge-based system /ˌnɒlɪdʒ beɪst 'sɪstəm/ *noun* a computer system that applies the stored reactions, instructions and knowledge of experts in a particular field to a problem

knowledge engineering /'nɒlɪdʒ ˌendʒɪnɪərɪŋ/ *noun* the process of designing and writing expert computer systems

knowledge industry /'nɒlɪdʒ ˌɪndəstri/ *noun* businesses that specialise in data processing or the development and use of information technology

Kodak PhotoCD /ˌkəʊdæk 'fəʊtəʊ siː ˌdiː/ ◆ **PhotoCD**

KSAM /ˌkeɪ es eɪ 'em/ *noun* a file structure that allows data to be accessed using key fields or key field content. Full form **keyed sequential access method**

KSR /ˌkeɪ es 'ɑː/ *noun* a terminal which has a keyboard and monitor, and is linked to a CPU. Full form **keyboard send/receive**. Compare **ASR**

KW *abbr* 1. kilowatt 2. kiloword

KWAC /kwæk/ *noun* a library indexing system that uses keywords from the text and title as indexed entries. Full form **keyword and context**

KWIC /kwɪk/ *noun* a library indexing system that uses keywords from the title or text of a book or document as an indexed entry followed by the text it relates to. Full form **keyword in context**

KWOC /kwɒk/ *noun* a library indexing system that indexes books or document titles under any relevant keywords. Full form **keyword out of context**

L

L1 cache /ˌel 'wʌn ˌkæʃ/ *noun* a small area of high-speed static RAM fitted to a processor chip that stores frequently used data to improve processing speed ○ *The Intel Pentium processor contains 16Kb of L1 cache.* Full form **level one cache.** ◊ **cache**

L2 cache /ˌel 'tuː ˌkæʃ/ *noun* a high-speed cache memory that is fitted to the computer's motherboard and supplies data to the processor faster than the main memory to improve performance. Full form **level two cache.** ◊ **pipeline**

L2TP /ˌel tuː tiː 'piː/ *noun* a network protocol, an extension to the PPP protocol, that allows the data from small Virtual Private Networks to be transferred over a network such as the public Internet. Full form **layer two tunneling protocol.** ◊ **tunnelling, PPP, protocol** (NOTE: L2TP operates enclosing the network packets from the Virtual Private Network within a special packet that can then travel over the Internet, a process called tunneling.)

label /'leɪb(ə)l/ *noun* 1. a word or other symbol used in a computer program to identify a routine or statement ○ *BASIC uses many program labels such as line numbers.* 2. a character or set of characters used to identify a variable or piece of data

or a file ■ *verb* to print an address on a label

label field /'leɪb(ə)l fiːld/ *noun* an item of data in a record that contains a label

labelling /'leɪb(ə)lɪŋ/ *noun* 1. the process of putting a label on something ○ *The word-processor has a special utility allowing simple and rapid labelling.* 2. the process of printing labels

label printer /'leɪb(ə)l ˌprɪntə/ *noun* a special printer used to print addresses onto continuous labels

label record /'leɪb(ə)l ˌrekɔːd/ *noun* a record containing identification for a stored file

lag /læg/ *noun* the time taken for an image to be no longer visible after it has been displayed on a CRT screen (NOTE: Lag is caused by long persistence phosphor.)

lambda calculus /ˌlæmdə 'kælkjʊləs/ *noun* a theory of mathematical functions and the way they combine, used as the basis for some high-level computer programming languages

LAN, lan *noun* a network where the various terminals and equipment are all within a short distance of one another, e.g. in the same building, and can be interconnected by cables. Full form **local area network**

'The opportunities to delete and destroy data are far greater on our LAN than in the days when we had a mainframe. PC people are culturally different from mainframe people. You really don't think about security problems when you can physically lock your system up in a closet.' [*Computing*]

landing zone /'lændɪŋ zəʊn/ *noun* an area of a hard disk which does not carry data. The head can come into contact with the disk in this area without damaging the disk or data. ◊ **park**

landline /'læn(d)laɪn/ *noun* a communications link that uses cable to physically and electrically link two devices

landscape /'lændskeɪp/ *noun* the orientation of a page or piece of paper where the longest edge is horizontal. Compare **portrait**

language /'læŋgwɪdʒ/ *noun* a system of words or symbols which allows communication with computers, especially one that allows computer instructions to be entered as words which are easy to understand, and then translates them into machine code

COMMENT: There are three main types of computer languages: machine code, assembler and high-level language. The more high-level the language is, the easier it is to program and understand, but the slower it is to execute. The following are the commonest high-level languages: ADA, ALGOL, APL, BASIC, C, C++, COBOL, COMAL, CORAL, FORTH, FORTRAN, LISP, LOGO, PASCAL, PL/1, POP-2, PROLOG and Visual Basic. Assembly language uses mnemonics to represent machine code instructions. Machine code is the lowest level of programming language and consists of basic binary patterns that instruct the processor to perform various tasks.

language assembler /'læŋgwɪdʒ ə ˌsemblə/ *noun* a program used to translate and assemble a source code program into a machine-executable binary form

language compiler /'læŋgwɪdʒ kəm ˌpaɪlə/ *noun* a piece of software that converts an encoded source program into another, machine code, form, and then executes it

language interpreter /'læŋgwɪdʒ ɪn ˌtɜːprɪtə/ *noun* any program that takes each consecutive line of a source program and translates it into another, machine code, language at run-time

language processor /ˌlæŋgwɪdʒ ˌprəʊsesə/ *noun* a language translator from source code to machine code (NOTE: There are three types of language processor: assemblers, compilers and interpreters.)

language rules /'læŋgwɪdʒ ruːlz/ *plural noun* the syntax and format for instructions and data items used in a particular language

language support environment /ˌlæŋgwɪdʒ səˈpɔːt ɪnˌveɪərənmənt/ *noun* the hardware and software tools supplied to help the programmer write programs in a particular language

language translation /'læŋgwɪdʒ trænsˌleɪʃ(ə)n/ *noun* the process of using a computer to translate text from one language to another

language translator /'læŋgwɪdʒ trænsˌleɪtə/ *noun* a program that converts code written in one language into equivalent instructions in another language

LAN Manager /'læn ˌmænɪdʒə/ a trade name for a network operating system developed for the PC by Microsoft

LAN segment /læn ˈsegmənt/ *noun* **1.** a part of a network separated from the rest by a bridge **2.** (*in a bus network*) an electrically continuous piece of cable

LAN server /læn ˈsɜːvə/ *noun* a computer which runs a network operating system and controls the basic network operations. All the workstations in a LAN are connected to the central network server and users log onto the network server.

LAN Server /'læn ˌsɜːvə/ a trade name for a network operating system for the PC developed by IBM

lap /læp/ *noun* an overlap of printed colours, which prevents any gaps showing

LAP /ˌel eɪ ˈpiː/ *noun* a CCITT standard protocol used to start and maintain links over an X.25 network. Full form **link access protocol**

LAP-B /læp biː/ *noun* a CCITT standard setup routine to establish a link between a DCE and DTE, e.g. between a computer and a modem

LAP-M /læp em/ *noun* a variation of LAP-B protocol used in V.42 error-correcting modems.

laptop /'læptɒp/, **laptop computer** *noun* a computer that is light enough to carry, but not so small as to fit in a pocket, and that usually consists of a screen, keyboard and disk drive. ◊ **desktop, handheld computer, PDA**

'Michael Business Systems has provided research company BMRB with 240 Toshiba laptop computers in a deal valued at £300,000. The deal includes a three-year maintenance contract.' [*Computing*]

large model /lɑːdʒ ˈmɒd(ə)l/ *noun* (*in an Intel processor*) a memory model in which both code and data can exceed 64Kb in size, but combined size should be less than 1Mb

large-scale /'lɑːdʒ skeɪl/ *adjective* working with large amounts of data. Compare **small-scale**

large-scale computer /ˌlɑːdʒ skeɪl kəm'pjuːtə/ *noun* a high-powered computer system that can access high-capacity memory and backing storage devices as well as multiple users

large-scale integration /ˌlɑːdʒ skeɪl ˌɪntɪ'greɪʃ(ə)n/ *noun* full form of **LSI**

laser /'leɪzə/ *noun* a device that produces coherent light of a single wavelength in a narrow beam, by exciting a material so that it emits photons of light. Full form **light amplification by stimulated emission of radiation**

laser disc /'leɪzə dɪsk/ *noun* same as **compact disc**

laser emulsion storage /ˌleɪzə ɪ ˌmʌlʃ(ə)n 'stɔːrɪdʒ/ *noun* a digital storage technique using a laser to expose light-sensitive material

LaserJet /'leɪzədʒet/ same as **Hewlett Packard LaserJet**

laser printer /'leɪzə ˌprɪntə/ *noun* a high-resolution computer printer that uses a laser source to print high-quality dot matrix character patterns on paper

LaserWriter /'leɪzəraɪtə/ a trade name for a laser printer manufactured by Apple that uses the PostScript page description language

last in first out /ˌlɑːst ɪn ˌfɜːst 'aʊt/ *adjective* full form of **LIFO** ○ *This computer stack uses a last in first out data retrieval method.*

latch /lætʃ/ *verb* to set an output state ○ *The output latched high until we reset the computer.*

latency /'leɪt(ə)nsi/ *noun* a time delay between the moment when an instruction is given to a computer and the execution of the instruction or return of a result, e.g. the delay between a request for data and the data being transferred from memory

launch /lɔːntʃ/ *noun* the process of putting a new product on the market ○ *The launch of the new PC has been put back six months.* ■ *verb* **1.** to put a new product on the market ○ *The new PC was launched at the Computer Show.* **2.** to start or run a program ○ *You launch the word-processor by double-clicking on this icon.*

layer /'leɪə/ *noun* ISO/OSI standards defining the stages a message has to pass through when being transmitted from one

computer to another over a local area network

layered /'leɪəd/ *adjective* that consists of layers ○ *The kernel has a layered structure according to user priority.*

layer two tunneling protocol /ˌleɪə tuː 'tʌnəlɪŋ ˌprəʊtəkɒl/ *noun* full form of **L2TP**

layout /'leɪaʊt/ *noun* **1.** rules governing the data input and output from a computer. ◊ **landscape, portrait 2.** a way of using a sheet of paper

LCD /ˌel si: 'diː/ *noun* a type of display that uses liquid crystals that turn black when a voltage is applied. LCDs are found in many watches, calculators and other small digital devices. Full form **liquid crystal display**

LCD screen /ˌel si: 'diː skriːn/ *noun* a screen that uses LCD technology to create a thin display and is normally found in laptop computers and flat-screen monitors. Full form **liquid crystal display screen**

LCD shutter printer /ˌel si: ˌdiː 'ʃʌtə/ *noun* a page printer that uses an LCD panel in front of a bright light to describe images onto the photosensitive drum. The LCD panel stops the light passing through, except at pixels that describe the image.

LCP /ˌel si: 'piː/ *noun* rules defining the transmission of data over a channel. Full form **link control procedure**

LDAP /'el dæp/ *noun* a new standard that provides directory services over the Internet; derived from the X.500 standard. LDAP is beginning to be included in many Internet applications and provides a way of organising, locating and using resources on the Internet that are listed within its database. Full form **lightweight directory access protocol**

lead /liːd/ *noun* an electrical conducting wire

leader /'liːdə/ *noun* a section of magnetic tape that contains no signal, used at the beginning of the reel for identification and to aid the tape machine to pick up the tape

leader record /'liːdə ˌrekɔːd/ *noun* the initial record containing information, e.g. titles and format, about following records in a file

lead in /'liːd ɪn/ *noun* (*on a CD-ROM*) a section before the data starts, normally used to store the table of contents

leading /'liːdɪŋ/ *noun* space between lines of printed or displayed text

leading edge /'liːdɪŋ edʒ/ *noun* the first edge of a punched card that enters the card reader

leading zero /ˌliːdɪŋ 'zɪərəʊ/ *noun* the zero digit used to pad out the beginning of a stored number

leaf /liːf/ *noun* the final node in a tree structure

leap-frog test /'liːp frɒg ˌtest/ *noun* a memory location test, in which a program skips from one location to another random location, writing data then reading and comparing for faults, until all locations have been tested

learning curve /'lɜːnɪŋ kɜːv/ *noun* a graphical description of how someone can acquire knowledge about a product over time

lease /liːs/ *noun* a written contract for letting or renting a piece of equipment for a period against payment of a fee ■ *verb* **1.** to allow equipment to be used for a period by another person or organisation in return for a fee **2.** to use equipment for a time and pay a fee to its owner ○ *The company leases all its computers.*

leased line /'liːsd ˌlaɪn/ *noun* communications channel, such as a telephone line, which is rented for the exclusive use of the subscriber

least cost design /ˌliːst kɒst dɪ'zaɪn/ *noun* the best money-saving use of space or components ○ *The budget is only £1000, we need the least cost design for the new circuit.*

least recently used algorithm /ˌliːst ˌriːs(ə)ntli juːzd 'ælgəˌrɪð(ə)m/ *noun* an algorithm which finds the page of memory that was last accessed before any other, and erases it to make room for another page. Abbr **LRU**

least significant bit /ˌliːst sɪg ˌnɪfɪkənt 'bɪt/ *noun* full form of **LSB**

least significant digit /ˌliːst sɪg ˌnɪfɪkənt 'dɪdʒɪt/ *noun* full form of **LSD**

LED /ˌel iː 'diː/ *noun* a semiconductor diode that emits light when a current is applied. Full form **light emitting diode** (NOTE: LED displays are used to display small amounts of information, as in pocket calculators, watches, and indicators.)

COMMENT: LED displays are used to display small amounts of information, as in pocket calculators, watches, indicators, etc.

LED printer /ˌel iː ˌdiː 'prɪntə/ *noun* a page printer, similar to a laser printer, that uses an LED light source instead of a laser

left-click /ˌleft klɪk/ *verb* to press and release the left-hand button on a computer mouse

left-handed mouse /ˌeft ˌhændɪd 'maʊs/ *noun* a mouse that has been configured so that the usual functions of the two buttons are reversed

left justification /ˌleft ˌdʒʌstɪfɪ 'keɪʃ(ə)n/ *noun* **1.** the process of shifting a binary number to the left-hand end of the word containing it **2.** the act of making the left-hand margin of the text even

left justify /ˌleft 'dʒʌstɪˌfaɪ/ *verb* to make the left-hand margin of the text even

left shift /ˌleft 'ʃɪft/ *noun* a leftward arithmetic shift by one bit of data in a word (NOTE: A binary number is doubled for each left shift.)

leg /leg/ *noun* one possible path through a routine

legacy /'legəsi/ *noun* an older technology or a previous version of software or hardware that is still supported in new developments to allow existing applications and hardware to continue to be used

legal /'liːg(ə)l/ *adjective* a statement or instruction that is acceptable within language syntax rules

length /leŋθ/ *noun* the number of data items in a variable or list

length of filename /ˌleŋθ əv 'faɪlneɪm/ *noun* the number of characters allowed for identification of a file

letter bomb /'letə bɒm/ *noun* an e-mail message with a destructive code attached to it

level /'lev(ə)l/ *noun* the quantity of bits that make up a digital transmitted signal

Level A /'lev(ə)l eɪ/ *noun* an ADPCM audio quality level with a 20KHz bandwidth, 38.7KHz sample rate and 8-bit samples

Level B /'lev(ə)l biː/ *noun* an ADPCM audio quality level with a 17KHz bandwidth, 38.7KHz sample rate and 8-bit samples

Level C /'lev(ə)l siː/ *noun* an ADPCM audio quality level with an 8.5KHz bandwidth, 18.9KHz sample rate and 4-bit samples

lexical analysis /ˌleksɪk(ə)l ə 'næləsɪs/ *noun* a stage in program translation when the compiling or translating software replaces program keywords with machine code instructions

LF *abbr* line feed

library /'laɪbrəri/ noun a collection of files, documents, books or records, that can be consulted or borrowed by the public, usually kept in a public place

library function /'laɪbrəri ˌfʌŋkʃən/ noun a ready-made software routine that a user can insert into a program of his or her own in order to provide a particular function with no effort

library program /'laɪbrəri ˌprəʊɡræm/ noun 1. a number of specially written or relevant software routines that a user can insert into his or her own program, saving time and effort ○ The square root function is already in the library program. 2. a program containing a group of functions that a computer needs to refer to often, but that are not stored in main memory

library routine /'laɪbrəri ruːˌtiːn/ noun a prewritten routine that can be inserted into a main program and called up when required

library subroutine /ˌlaɪbrəri 'sʌbruːtiːn/ noun a tried and tested subroutine, stored in a library, that can be inserted into a user's program when required

library track /'laɪbrəri træk/ noun one track on a magnetic disk or tape used to store information about the contents (such as titles, format and index data)

licence /'laɪs(ə)ns/ noun a statement of permission that is given by one manufacturer to another and allows the second manufacturer to make copies of the first one's products in return for payment of a fee ○ The software is manufactured in this country under licence.

licence agreement /'laɪs(ə)ns ə ˌɡriːmənt/ noun a legal document that accompanies any commercial software product and defines how you can use the software and, most importantly, how many people can use the software. Unless you buy a network version of a software product, the licence allows one person to use it. Copying the software is illegal. If you want several people to use the software or if you want to use it on a network, then you need to buy a multi-user licence.

lifetime /'laɪftaɪm/ noun the period of time during which a device is useful or not outdated ○ This new computer has a four-year lifetime.

LIFO /'laɪfəʊ/ adjective used to describe a queue system that reads the last item stored, first ○ This computer stack uses a

LIFO data retrieval method. Full form **last in first out.** ◊ FIFO

lifter /'lɪftə/ noun a mechanical device that lifts magnetic tape away from the heads when rewinding the tape

light /laɪt/ noun energy in the form of electromagnetic effects in the frequency range 400 – 750 nm, which allows a person to see ○ The VDU should not be placed under a bright light.

light-emitting diode /ˌlaɪt ɪˌmɪtɪŋ 'daɪəʊd/ noun full form of **LED**

lighting formula /'laɪtɪŋ ˌfɔːmjələ/ noun a mathematical formula that describes the effect of a light source on an object or scene. The formula is used to calculate the position of the highlights and shadows as the position of the light source is moved around the scene. ◊ **shading**

light pen /'laɪt pen/ noun a computer accessory in the shape of a pen that contains a light-sensitive device that can detect pixels on a video screen (NOTE: Light pens are often used with suitable software to draw graphics on a screen or position a cursor.)

lightweight /'laɪtweɪt/ adjective not heavy ○ A lightweight computer which can easily fit into a suitcase.

lightweight directory access protocol /ˌlaɪtweɪt daɪ'rekt(ə)ri ˌækses ˌprəʊtəkɒl/ noun full form of **LDAP**

LILO /'laɪləʊ/ adjective used to describe a data storage method in which the data stored last is retrieved last. Full form **last in last out**

limited distance modem /ˌlɪmɪtɪd ˌdɪstəns 'məʊdem/ noun a data transmission device with a very short range that sends pure digital data rather than data sent on a modulated carrier

limiter /'lɪmɪtə/ noun a device that removes the part of an input signal that is greater than or less than a predefined limit; used with audio and video signals to prevent overloading an amplifier

limiting resolution /ˌlɪmɪtɪŋ ˌrezə 'luːʃ(ə)n/ noun the maximum number of lines that make up an image on a CRT screen

limits /'lɪmɪts/ noun predefined maximum ranges for numbers in a computer

line /laɪn/ noun 1. a physical connection for data transmission, e.g. a cable between parts of a system or a telephone wire 2. single long thin mark drawn by a pen or printed on a surface ○ the printer has dif-

ficulty in reproducing very fine lines **3.** one trace by the electron picture beam on a television screen **4.** row of characters (printed on a page or displayed on a computer screen or printer) ○ *each page has 52 lines of text* **5.** series of characters received as a single input by a computer **6.** one row of commands or arguments in a computer program

'...straight lines are drawn by clicking the points on the screen where you would like the line to start and finish' [*Personal Computer World*]

line adapter /laɪn əˈdæptə/ *noun* an electronic circuit that matches the correct signal voltage and impedance for a particular line

line analyser /ˈlaɪn ˌænəlaɪzə/ *noun* a piece of test equipment that displays the characteristics of a line or the signals carried on the line

linear frame buffer /ˌlɪniə freɪm ˈbʌfə/ *noun* a video memory arranged so that by moving from one address to the next in the buffer you move from one pixel to the one below it on the display

linearity /ˌlɪniˈærɪti/ *noun* the shape of the frequency response curve of a device such as a microphone or A/D converter. If the curve is straight, the device is very accurate, if it is not, the device is introducing frequency distortion.

linear list /ˈlɪniə lɪst/ *noun* a list that has no free space for new records within its structure

linear program /ˌlɪniə ˈprəʊɡræm/ *noun* a computer program that contains no loops or branches

linear programming /ˌlɪniə ˈprəʊɡræmɪŋ/ *noun* a method of mathematically breaking down a problem so that it can be solved by computer

linear search /ˌlɪniə ˈsɜːtʃ/ *noun* a search method which compares each item in a list with the search key, starting with the first item and going through the others in order towards the end, until the correct entry is found

linear video /ˌlɪniə ˈvɪdiəʊ/ *noun* **1.** a continuous playback of a video sequence from videotape **2.** normal video that is played back in a continuous sequence rather than a single frame at a time as in interactive video

linear video editing /ˌlɪniə ˌvɪdiəʊ ˈedɪtɪŋ/ *noun* a video sequence, on videotape, that is edited by inserting or deleting

new frames but without changing the order of the frames

line break *noun* the point at which continuous text is split into separate lines

line busy tone /ˌlaɪn ˈbɪzi ˌtəʊn/ *noun* a signal generated to indicate that a connection or telephone line is already in use

line communications /laɪn kəˌmjuːnɪˈkeɪʃ(ə)ns/ *plural noun* signal transmission using a cable link or telegraph wire

line conditioning /laɪn kənˈdɪʃ(ə)nɪŋ/ *noun* techniques used to keep the quality of data transmissions or signals on a line to a certain standard

line control /laɪn kənˈtrəʊl/ *noun* the use of special codes to control a communications channel

line doubling /ˈlaɪn ˌdʌb(ə)lɪŋ/ *noun* ▶ scan conversion

line drawing /ˈlaɪn ˌdrɔːɪŋ/ *noun* an illustration in which objects are drawn using thin lines, without shading or surface texture

line driver /laɪn ˈdraɪvə/ *noun* a high-power circuit and amplifier used to send signals over a long distance line without too much loss of signal

line editor /laɪn ˈedɪtə/ *noun* a piece of software in which only one line of a source program can be edited at a time

line ending /laɪn ˈendɪŋ/ *noun* a character that shows that a line has ended, inserted by pressing the carriage return key

line feed /ˈlaɪn fiːd/ *noun* a control on a printer or computer terminal that moves the cursor down by one line. Abbr **LF**

line flyback /ˈlaɪn ˌflaɪbæk/ *noun* same as **flyback**

line frequency /laɪn ˈfriːkwənsi/ *noun* (*in a CRT*) the number of times that the picture beam scans a horizontal row of pixels in a monitor

line gremlin /laɪn ˈgremlɪn/ *noun* an unexplained fault when data is lost during transmission

line in /ˈlaɪn ɪn/ *noun* an input connection to audio equipment such as an amplifier that accepts a low voltage audio signal

line input /ˌlaɪn ˈɪnpʊt/ *noun* a command to receive all characters including punctuation entered up to a carriage return code

line length /ˈlaɪn leŋθ/ *noun* the number of characters which can be displayed horizontally on one line of a display (NOTE:

CRT displays often use an 80-character line length.)

line level /laɪn ˈlev(ə)l/ *noun* the amplitude of a signal transmitted over a cable

line noise /ˈlaɪn nɔɪz/ *noun* unwanted interference on a telephone or communications line that causes errors in a data transmission

line number /laɪn ˈnʌmbə/ *noun* a number that refers to a line of program code in a computer program (NOTE: The programming language will sort out the program into order according to line number.)

line out /ˈlaɪn aʊt/ *noun* output connector from audio equipment that provides a low-voltage pre-amplified audio signal; e.g., an amplifier will have a line out connector that can be used to connect to an active loudspeaker or other audio equipment, but cannot be connected to passive loudspeakers

'…while pixel editing is handy for line art, most desktop scanners have trouble producing the shades of grey or half-tones found in black and white photography' [*Publish*]

line printer /ˈlaɪn ˌprɪntə/ *noun* a device for printing draft quality information at high speeds, typical output is 200 to 3000 lines per minute (NOTE: Line printers print a whole line at a time, running from right to left and left to right, and are usually dot matrix printers with not very high quality print. Compare page printers, which print a whole page at a time.)

line spacing /laɪn ˈspeɪsɪŋ/ *noun* the distance between two rows of characters

line speed /ˈlaɪn spiːd/ *noun* the rate at which data is sent along a line

lines per minute /ˌlaɪnz pɜː ˈmɪnət/ *noun* the number of lines printed by a line printer per minute. Abbr **LPM**

line style /ˈlaɪn staɪl/ *noun* the appearance of a line displayed on screen or printed

line width /ˈlaɪn, wɪdθ/ *noun* same as **page width**

Lingo /ˈlɪŋgəʊ/ a trade name for a scripting language used to control the actions in the Macromedia Director authoring software

link /lɪŋk/ *noun* **1.** a communications path or channel between two components or devices ○ *To transmit faster, you can use the direct link with the mainframe.* **2.** a software routine that allows data transfer between incompatible programs ■ *verb* to

join or interface two pieces of software or hardware ○ *The two computers are linked.*
□ **link files** a command to merge together a list of separate files

link access protocol /ˌlɪŋk ˈækses ˌprəʊtəkɒl/ *noun* full form of **LAP**

linkage /ˈlɪŋkɪdʒ/ *noun* the act of linking two things

linkage editing /ˈlɪŋkɪdʒ ˌedɪtɪŋ/ *noun* the process of combining separate programs together, and standardising the calls or references within them

linkage software /ˈlɪŋkɪdʒ ˌsɒftweə/ *noun* a special software which links sections of program code with any library routines or other code ○ *Graphics and text are joined without linkage software.*

link control procedure /ˌlɪŋk kən ˈtrəʊl prəˌsiːdʒə/ *noun* full form of **LCP**

link control protocol /ˌlɪŋk kənˈtrəʊl ˌprəʊtəkɒl/ *noun* a protocol used to create a link between two computers to allow information to be transferred. LCP provides similar functions to the PPP protocol but includes better security and authentication. Abbr **LCP**. ◊ PPP

linked list /ˌlɪŋkd ˈlɪst/ *noun* a list of data where each entry carries the address of the next consecutive entry

linked object /lɪŋkd ˈɒbdʒekt/ *noun* one piece of data that is referred to in another file or application

linked subroutine /ˌlɪŋkd ˌsʌbruːˈtiːn/ *noun* same as **closed routine**

linking /ˈlɪŋkɪŋ/ *noun* the merging of a number of small programs to enable them to run as one unit

linking information /ˈlɪŋkɪŋ ˌɪnfəmeɪʃ(ə)n/ *noun* (*in Windows*) a feature that allows you to insert data from one application into another application using its OLE function

linking loader /ˈlɪŋkɪŋ ˌləʊdə/ *noun* a short software routine that merges sections of programs to allow them to be run as one

link trials /lɪŋk ˈtraɪəlz/ *plural noun* tests on computer programs to see if each module works in conjunction with the others

Linux /ˈlɪnəks/ a trade name for a version of the UNIX operating system originally developed by Linus Torvalds, who then distributed it free of charge over the Internet. Enthusiasts and other developers have extended and enhanced the software, normally also publishing their software free of charge. Linux is one of the most popular operating systems for developers and people running web-based applications. Unlike many other operating systems, such as Microsoft Windows, the Linux software runs on a range of different types of computer hardware including the PC and Macintosh.

LIPS /lɪps/ *noun* a standard for the measurement of processing power of an inference engine. Full form **logical inferences per second**

liquid crystal display /ˌlɪkwɪd ˌkrɪst(ə)l dɪsˈpleɪ/ *noun* full form of **LCD**

liquid crystal display shutter printer /ˌlɪkwɪd ˌkrɪstəl dɪˌspleɪ ˈʃʌtə ˌprɪntə/ *noun* ♦ **LCD shutter printer**

LISP /lɪsp/ *noun* a high-level language used mainly in processing lists of instructions or data and in artificial intelligence work. Full form **list processing**

list /lɪst/ *noun* a series of ordered items of data ■ *verb* to print or display certain items of information □ **to list a program** to display a program line by line in correct order

list box /ˈlɪst ˌbɒks/ *noun* a number of items or options displayed in a list

LIST chunk /ˈlɪst ˌtʃʌŋk/ *noun* (*in a RIFF file*) a four-character code LIST that contains a series of subchunks

listing /ˈlɪstɪŋ/ *noun* a display or printed copy of the lines in a program in order □ **a program listing** a printed copy of the lines of a program

listing paper /ˈlɪstɪŋ ˌpeɪpə/ *noun* continuous stationery used in computer printers

list processing /ˈlɪst ˌprəʊsesɪŋ/ *noun* **1.** the processing of a series of items of data, i.e. such tasks as adding, deleting, sorting or updating entries **2.** full form of **LISP**

listserv /ˈlɪst ˌsɜːv/, **listserver** /ˈlɪstsɜːvə/ *noun* a server on the Internet that sends a newsletter or articles to a list of registered users

listserver /ˈlɪstsɜːvə/ *noun* same as **listserv**

literal /ˈlɪt(ə)rəl/ *noun* **1.** a computer instruction that contains the actual number or address to be used, rather than a label or its location **2.** a printing error when one character is replaced by another or when two characters are transposed

literal operand /ˈlɪt(ə)rəl ˌɒpərænd/ *noun* the actual number or address to be used rather than a label or its location

lithium-Ion battery /ˌlɪθiəm ˈaɪən ˌbæt(ə)ri/ *noun* a type of rechargeable battery that provides high output power in a compact and lightweight unit. This type of battery is often used in mobile telephones, PDAs and lightweight laptop computers.

Live3D /ˌlaɪv θriː ˈdiː/ *noun* same as **VRML** (*see*)

liveware /ˈlaɪvweə/ *noun* the operators and users of a computer system, as opposed to the hardware and software

LLC /ˌel el ˈsiː/ *noun* an IEEE 802.2 standard defining the protocol for datalink-level transmissions. Full form of **logical link control**

LLL *abbr* low-level language

load /ləʊd/ *verb* **1.** to transfer a file or program from disk to main memory **2.** to put something such as a disk into a computer, so that it can be run

'…this windowing system is particularly handy when you want to load or save a file or change directories' [*Byte*]

load and go /ˌləʊd ən ˈɡəʊ/ *noun* same as **load and run**

load and run /ˌləʊd ən ˈrʌn/ *noun* a computer program that is loaded into main memory and then starts to execute itself automatically

loader /ˈləʊdə/ *noun* a program which loads another file or program into computer memory

load high /ˈləʊd ˌhaɪ/ *verb* (*using MS-DOS on a PC*) to transfer a program into high or expanded memory

loading /ˈləʊdɪŋ/ *noun* the action of transferring a file or program from disk to memory ○ *Loading can be a long process.*

load point /ˈləʊd pɔɪnt/ *noun* the start of a recording section in a reel of magnetic tape

load sharing /ˈləʊd ˌʃeərɪŋ/ *noun* the use of more than one computer in a network to even out the work load on each processor

local /ˈləʊk(ə)l/ *adjective* **1.** referring to a device that is physically attached and close to the controlling computer **2.** referring to a variable or argument that is only used in a certain section of a computer program or structure **3.** referring to a system with limited access □ **on local** (*of a terminal*) not working with a CPU, but being used as a stand-alone terminal

local area network /ˌləʊk(ə)l ˌeəriə ˈnetwɜːk/ *noun* full form of **LAN**

local area network server /ˌləʊk(ə)l ˌeəriə ˈnetwɜːk ˌsɜːvə/ *noun* a computer which runs a network operating system and controls the basic network operations. All the workstations in a LAN are connected to the central network server and users log onto it.

local bridge /ˈləʊk(ə)l brɪdʒ/ *noun* a bridge that links two local networks ○ *We use a local bridge to link the two LANs in the office.*

local bus /ˌləʊk(ə)l ˈbʌs/ *noun* a direct link or bus between a device and the processor; with no logic circuits or buffers or decoders in between ○ *The fastest expansion cards fit into this local bus connector.*

local declaration /ˌləʊk(ə)l ˌdeklə ˈreɪʃ(ə)n/ *noun* the assignment of a variable that is only valid in a section of a computer program or structure

local drive /ˈləʊk(ə)l draɪv/ *noun* a disk drive that is physically attached to a computer, as opposed to a resource that is accessed across a network

local format storage /ˌləʊk(ə)l ˌfɔːmæt ˈstɔːrɪdʒ/ *noun* a format stored as an empty form or repeated page in a terminal rather than being repeatedly transmitted

local memory /ˌləʊk(ə)l ˈmem(ə)ri/ *noun* a high speed RAM that is used instead of a hardware device to store bit streams or patterns

local mode /ˈləʊk(ə)l məʊd/ *noun* the operating state of a computer terminal that does not receive messages

local printer /ˌləʊk(ə)l ˈprɪntə/ *noun* a printer physically attached to a computer rather than a shared resource available on a network

LocalTalk /ˈləʊkəltɔːk/ a trade name for a network standard developed by Apple that defines the physical layer, i.e. the cabling system and connectors, used in Apple's AppleTalk network. The network transfers data at 230Kbits/second over unshielded twisted-pair cable.

local variable /ˌləʊk(ə)l ˈveəriəb(ə)l/ *noun* a variable which can only be accessed by certain routines in a certain section of a computer program

locate /ləʊˈkeɪt/ *verb* **1.** to place or to set ○ *The computer is located in the main office building.* **2.** to find ○ *Have you managed to locate the programming fault?*

location /ləʊˈkeɪʃ(ə)n/ *noun* a number or absolute address that specifies the point in memory where a data word can be found and accessed

lock /lɒk/ *verb* to prevent access to a system or file □ **locking a file** the action of preventing any further writing to a file □ **to lock onto** to synchronise an internal clock with a received signal

lockdown /ˈlɒkdaʊn/ *noun* a procedure that prevents users of a computer network or intruders from the Internet from gaining access to files that are essential to the proper functioning of a computer system

lockout /ˈlɒkaʊt/ *noun* the process of preventing a user sending messages over a network by continuously transmitting data

lock up /ˌlɒk ˈʌp/ *noun* a faulty operating state of computer that cannot be recovered from without switching off the power (NOTE: A lock up can be caused by an infinite program loop or a deadly embrace.)

COMMENT: This can be caused by an infinite program loop or a deadly embrace.

log /lɒg/ *noun* a record of computer processing operations ■ *verb* **1.** to record a series of actions □ **to log calls** to note all details of telephone calls made **2.** to make a connection and start using a remote device such as a network server □ **to log in** or **log on** to enter various identification data, e.g. a password, usually by means of a terminal, to the central computer before accessing a program or data □ **to log off** or **log out** to enter a symbol or instruction at the end of a computing session to close all files and break the channel between the user's terminal and the main computer

log file /ˈlɒg faɪl/ *noun* (*see also*) **1.** a file that contains a record of actions **2.** (*on a web server*) a file that contains details of the visitors to a website, recorded automatically with the visitor's DNS address, the time and the name of the webpage that he or she viewed

logger /ˈlɒgə/ *noun* a device which keeps a record of a series of actions

logging /ˈlɒgɪŋ/ *noun* an input of data into a system

logging in /ˈlɒgɪŋ ɪn/ *noun* the process of opening operations with a system

logging off /ˈlɒgɪŋ ɒf/ *noun* the process of ending operations with a system

logging on /ˈlɒgɪŋ ɒn/ *noun* same as **logging in**

logging out /ˈlɒgɪŋ aʊt/ *noun* same as **logging off**

logic /ˈlɒdʒɪk/ *noun* **1.** a mathematical treatment of formal logic operations such as AND, OR, etc., and their transformation into various circuits. ◊ **Boolean algebra** **2.** a system for deducing results from binary data **3.** the components of a computer or digital system

logical /'lɒdʒɪk(ə)l/ *adjective* that uses logic in its operation ○ *Logical reasoning can be simulated by an artificial intelligence machine.*

logical channel /ˌlɒdʒɪk(ə)l 'tʃæn(ə)l/ *noun* an electronic circuit between a terminal and a network node in a packet switching system

logical chart /'lɒdʒɪk(ə)l tʃɑːt/ *noun* a graphical representation of logic elements, steps, decisions and interconnections in a system

logical comparison /ˌlɒdʒɪk(ə)l kəm'pærɪs(ə)n/ *noun* a function to see if two logic signals are the same

logical decision /ˌlɒdʒɪk(ə)l dɪ'sɪʒ(ə)n/ *noun* one of two paths chosen as a result of one of two possible answers to a question

logical drive /'lɒdʒɪk(ə)l draɪv/ *noun* a letter assigned to a disk drive or storage area on a disk drive that can be used as if it were a local drive ○ *The logical drive F: actually stores data on part of the server's disk drive.*

logical error /ˌlɒdʒɪk(ə)l 'erə/ *noun* a fault in a program design causing incorrect branching or operations

logical expression /ˌlɒdʒɪk(ə)l ɪk'spreʃ(ə)n/ *noun* a function made up from a series of logical operators such as AND and OR

logical flowchart /'lɒdʒɪk(ə)l ˌfləʊtʃɑːt/ *noun* a diagram showing where the logical decisions occur in a structure and their effects on program execution

logical high /'lɒdʒɪk(ə)l haɪ/ *adjective* equal to logic TRUE state or 1

logical inferences per second /ˌlɒdʒɪk(ə)l ˌɪnf(ə)rənsɪz pɜː 'sekənd/ *noun* full form of **LIPS**

logical link control /ˌlɒdʒɪk(ə)l 'lɪŋk kənˌtrəʊl/ *noun* full form of **LLC**

logical low /'lɒdʒɪk(ə)l ləʊ/ *adjective* equal to logic false state or 0

logical operator /ˌlɒdʒɪk(ə)l ˌɒpə'reɪtə/ *noun* same as **relational operator**

logical palette /ˌlɒdʒɪk(ə)l 'pælət/ *noun* (*in Windows*) a graphics object that includes the colour palette information it requires

logical record /ˌlɒdʒɪk(ə)l 'rekɔːd/ *noun* a unit of information ready for processing that is not necessarily the same as the original data item in storage, which might contain control data

logical ring /'lɒdʒɪk(ə)l rɪŋ/ *noun* (*in a Token-Ring or FDDI network*) the path a token follows through the layers of each node (NOTE: In FDDI the physical topology does not effect the logical ring.)

logical shift /'lɒdʒɪk(ə)l ʃɪft/ *noun* a data movement to the left or right in a word, in which the bits falling outside the word boundary are discarded, and the free positions are filled with zeros

logical unit /ˌlɒdʒɪk(ə)l 'juːnɪt/ *noun* full form of **LU**

logic board /'lɒdʒɪk bɔːd/ *noun* same as **logic card**

logic bomb /'lɒdʒɪk bɒm/ *noun* a section of code that performs various unpleasant functions such as fraud or system crash when a number of conditions are true ○ *The system programmer installed a logic bomb when they made him redundant.*

logic card /'lɒdʒɪk kɑːd/ *noun* a printed circuit board containing binary logic gates rather than analog components

logic circuit /'lɒdʒɪk ˌsɜːkɪt/ *noun* an electronic circuit made up of various logical gates, such as AND, OR and EXOR

logic element /'lɒdʒɪk ˌelɪmənt/ *noun* a gate or combination of logic gates

logic flowchart /'lɒdʒɪk ˌfləʊtʃɑːt/ *noun* a graphical representation of logic elements, steps and decisions and their interconnections

logic gate /'lɒdʒɪk geɪt/ *noun* an electronic circuit that applies a logical operator to an input signal and produces an output

logic level /'lɒdʒɪk ˌlev(ə)l/ *noun* the voltage used to represent a particular logic state. This is often five volts for a one and zero volts for a zero.

logic map /'lɒdʒɪk mæp/ *noun* a graphical representation of states and conditions in a logic circuit

logic operation /'lɒdʒɪk ˌɒpəreɪʃ(ə)n/ *noun* a computer operation or procedure in which a decision is made

logic-seeking /'lɒdʒɪk ˌsiːkɪŋ/ *adjective* referring to a printer that can print the required information with the minimum head movement, detecting ends of lines, justification commands, etc.

logic state /'lɒdʒɪk steɪt/ *noun* one out of two possible levels in a digital circuit, the levels being 1 and 0 or TRUE and FALSE

logic state analyser /'lɒdʒɪk steɪt ˌænəlaɪzə/ *noun* a piece of test equipment that displays the logic states of a number of components or circuits

logic symbol /'lɒdʒɪk ˌsɪmbəl/ *noun* a graphical symbol used to represent a type of logic function in a diagram

log in script /'lɒg ɪn ˌskrɪpt/ *noun* a series of instructions that are automatically run when you log into a network. For example, if you log into your office network in the morning by typing your name and password, the login script might remind you of important information or just display 'good morning'.

logo /'ləʊgəʊ/ *noun* a special printed set of characters or symbols used to identify a company or product

LOGO /'ləʊgəʊ/ *noun* a high-level programming language used mainly for educational purposes, with graphical commands that are easy to use

logoff /lɒg'ɒf/ *verb* same as **logging off**

logon /lɒg'ɒn/ *verb* same as **logging in**

log on server /l'ɒg ɒn ˌsɜːvə/ *noun* a computer that checks user identification and password data against a user database to authorise connection to a network or server

long filename /lɒŋ 'faɪlˌneɪm/ *noun* a feature of Windows 95 that lets a user give files names up to 254 characters in length

long haul network /ˌlɒŋ hɔːl 'netwɜːk/ *noun* a communications network between distant computers that usually uses the public telephone system

long integer /lɒŋ 'ɪntɪdʒə/ *noun* (*in programming languages*) an integer represented by several bytes of data

longitudinal redundancy check /ˌlɒŋgɪtjuːdɪn(ə)l rɪ'dʌndənsi ˌtʃek/ *noun* a check on received blocks of data to detect any errors

longitudinal time code /ˌlɒŋgɪtjuːdɪn(ə)l 'taɪm kəʊd/ *noun* full form of **LTC**

long persistence phosphor /lɒŋ pə ˌsɪstəns 'fɒsfə/ *noun* a television screen coating that retains the displayed image for a period of time longer than the refresh rate, so reducing flicker effects

look-ahead /'lʊk əˌhed/ *noun* an action performed by some CPUs that fetch instructions and examine them before they

are executed in order to speed up operations

look-up /'lʊk ʌp/ *noun* a computer procedure in which a term or value is matched against a table of stored information

look-up table /'lʊk ʌp ˌteɪb(ə)l/ *noun* full form of **LUT** ○ *Lookup tables are pre-programmed then used in processing so saving calculations for each result required.*

'...a lookup table changes a pixel's value based on the values in a table' [*Byte*]

loop /luːp/ *noun* a procedure or series of instructions in a computer program that are performed again and again until a test shows that a specific condition has been met or until the program is completed

loopback /'luːpbæk/ *noun* a diagnostic test that returns the transmitted signal to the sending device after it has passed through another device or across a link

loopback test /'luːpbæk test/ *noun* a test mode for a modem in which any information sent to the modem from a local computer is immediately sent back to prove that the connection between the computer and modem is working

loop body /luːp 'bɒdi/ *noun* the main section of instructions within a loop. The loop body carries out the loop's primary function rather than being used to enter, leave or set up the loop.

loop check /'luːp ˌtʃek/ *noun* a check that data has been correctly transmitted down a line by returning the data to the transmitter

loop counter /luːp 'kaʊntə/ *noun* a register that contains the number of times a loop has been repeated

looping program /luːpɪŋ 'prəʊgræm/ *noun* a computer program that runs continuously

loop program /luːp 'prəʊgræm/ *noun* a sequence of instructions that are repeated until a condition is met

lo-res /ləʊ riːs/ *noun* same as **low resolution**

lossless compression /ˌlɒsləs kəm 'preʃ(ə)nn/ *noun* image compression techniques that can reduce the number of bits used for each pixel in an image, without losing any information or quality. ◊ **Huffman code**

lossy compression /'ˌlɒsi kəm ˌpreʃ(ə)n/ *noun* image compression techniques that can reduce the number of bits used for each pixel in an image, but in doing so lose information. ◊ **JPEG**

lost cluster /lɒst ˈklʌstə/ *noun* a number of sectors on a disk whose identification bits have been corrupted. The operating system has marked this area of disk as being used by a file, but the data it contains can no longer be identified with a particular file.

Lotus /ˈləʊtəs/ a software company best known for its spreadsheet program, 1–2–3

loudspeaker /ˌlaʊdˈspiːkə/ *noun* an electromagnetic device that converts electrical signals into audible noise

low-end /ˌləʊ ˈend/ *adjective* referring to hardware or software that is not very powerful or sophisticated and is designed for beginners

lower case /ˌləʊə ˈkeɪs/ *noun* small characters, e.g. a, b and c, as opposed to upper case, A, B, C

low frequency effects channel /ləʊ ˌfriːkwənsi ɪˈfekts ˌtʃæn(ə)l/ *noun* a separate audio channel in a multichannel system that provides very low frequency bass sounds. ◊ **Dolby Digital**. Also called **LFE channel**

low-level format /ˌləʊ ˈlev(ə)l ˌfɔːmæt/ *noun* a process that defines the physical pattern and arrangement of tracks and sectors on a disk

low-level language /ˌləʊ ˌlev(ə)l ˈlæŋgwɪdʒ/ *noun* a programming language, particular to one system or computer, in which each instruction has a single equivalent machine code instruction, so that programming in it is a long and complex task. Abbr **LLL**

low memory /ˌləʊ ˈmem(ə)ri/ *noun* (*in a PC*) available memory locations up to 640Kb. Compare **high memory**

low-order digit /ˌləʊ ˌɔːdə ˈdɪdʒɪt/ *noun* a digit in the position within a number that represents the lowest weighting of the number base ○ *The number 234156 has a low-order digit of 6.*

low-power standby /ˌləʊ ˈpaʊə ˌstændbaɪ/ *noun* an energy-saving feature of laptop computers and many monitors connected to a desktop

low-priority work /ˌləʊ praɪˌɒrɪti ˈwɜːk/ *noun* work that is not particularly important

low resolution /ˌləʊ ˌrezəˈluːʃ(ə)n/ *noun* the ability of a display system to control a number of pixels at a time rather than individual pixels

low-resolution graphics, low-res graphics *plural noun* the ability to display character-sized graphic blocks or preset shapes on a screen rather than to create graphics using individual pixels. Compare **high-resolution**

low-speed communications /ˌləʊ spiːd kəˌmjuːnɪˈkeɪʃ(ə)nz/ *plural noun* data transmission at less than 2400 bits per second

LPM *abbr* lines per minute

LPT1 /ˌel piː tiː ˈwʌn/ *noun* (*in a PC*) the name given to the first, main parallel printer port in the system

LRU *abbr* least recently used algorithm

LSB /ˌel es ˈbiː/ *noun* a binary digit occupying the right hand position of a word and carrying the least power of two in the word, usually equal to two raised to zero = 1. Full form **least significant bit**

LSD /ˌel es ˈdiː/ *noun* the digit which occupies the right hand position in a number and so carries least power, being equal to the number radix raised to zero = 1. Full form **least significant digit**

LSI /ˌel es ˈaɪ/ *noun* a configuration with between 500 and 10,000 circuits on a single IC. Full form **large scale integration**

LTC /ˌel tiː ˈsiː/ *noun* a method of recording a time code signal on a linear audio track along a video tape. The disadvantage of this method is that the code is not readable at slow speeds or when the tape has stopped. Full form **longitudinal time code**

LU /ˌel ˈjuː/ *noun* a set of protocols developed by IBM to allow communication over an SNA network. LU1, LU2 and LU3 provide control of the session, LU4 supports communication between the devices and LU6.2 is a peer-to-peer protocol. Full form **logical unit**

luggable /ˈlʌgəb(ə)l/ *noun* a personal computer that is just about portable and usually will not run off batteries. A luggable is much heavier and less compact than a laptop or true transportable machine.

luma /ˈluːmə/ *noun* the black and white parts of an image or video signal, represented by the symbol Y. ◊ **S-Video, Y/C**

luminance /ˈluːmɪn(ə)ns/ *noun* the part of a video signal or image that defines the brightness at each point. ◊ **YUV encoding**

lurk /lɜːk/ *verb* to join an online conference, discussion group or chat room and listen to the messages without contributing anything yourself. Most discussion forums do not mind people lurking, since it helps to build confidence in new users and lets them check the content before joining in, however some chat rooms do not approve of lurking and immediately identify anyone joining to discourage people who do not contribute to the forum.

LUT /ˌel ju: 'ti:/ *noun* a collection of stored results that can be accessed very rapidly by a program without the need to calculate each result whenever needed. Full form **look-up table**

'...an image processing system can have three LUTs that map the image memory to the display device' [*Byte*]

LV-ROM /ˌel vi: 'rɒm/ *noun* a 12-inch diameter optical disc, developed by Philips, that can store both analog video and digital data

M

M *abbr* mega-

mA /ˌem 'eɪ/ *noun* an electrical current measure equal to one thousandth of an ampere. Full form **milliampere**

Mac /mæk/ *noun* same as **Macintosh**

MAC /ˌem eɪ 'si:/ *noun* a special code transmitted at the same time as a message as proof of its authenticity. Full form **message authentication code** ■ *abbr* media access control

MacBinary /mæk'baɪnəri/ a trade name for a file storage and transfer system that allows Macintosh files, together with their icons and long file names, to be stored on other computer systems

machine /məˈʃiːn/ *noun* **1.** a number of separate moving parts or components, acting together to carry out a process **2.** a computer, system or processor made up of various components connected together to provide a function or perform a task

machine address /məˈʃiːn əˌdres/ *noun* same as **absolute address**

machine check /məˈʃiːn tʃek/ *noun* a fault caused by equipment failure

machine code /məˈʃiːn kəʊd/ *noun* a programming language that consists of commands in binary code that can be directly understood by the central processing unit without the need for translation. Also called **computer code**

machine code format /məˈʃiːn kəʊd ˌfɔːmæt/ *noun* a format for machine code instructions, usually made up of 1,2 or 3 bytes for operand, data and address

machine code instruction /məˈʃiːn kəʊd ɪnˌstrʌkʃən/ *noun* an instruction that directly controls the CPU and is recognised without the need for translation

machine cycle /məˈʃiːn ˌsaɪk(ə)l/ *noun* the minimum period of time taken by the CPU for the execution of an instruction

machine-dependent /məˌʃiːn dɪ'pendənt/ *adjective* not standardised, or unable to be used on hardware or software from a different manufacturer without modifications

machine equation /məˈʃiːn ɪˌkweɪʒ(ə)n/ *noun* a formula which an analog computer has been programmed to solve

machine error /məˈʃiːn ˌerə/ *noun* an error caused by a hardware malfunction

machine-independent /məˌʃiːn ˌɪndɪ'pendənt/ *adjective* referring to computer software that can be run on any computer system

machine-independent language /məˌʃiːn ˌɪndɪpendənt 'læŋgwɪdʒ/ *noun* a programming language that can be translated and executed on any computer that has a suitable compiler

machine instruction /məˈʃiːn ɪnˌstrʌkʃən/ *noun* an instruction which can be recognised by a machine and is part of its limited set of commands

machine intelligence /məˈʃiːn ɪnˌtelɪdʒ(ə)ns/ *noun* the design of computer programs and devices that attempt to imitate human intelligence and decision-making functions, providing basic reasoning and other human characteristics

machine-intimate /məˌʃiːn ˈɪntɪmət/ *adjective* referring to software that operates and interacts closely with the hardware in a system

machine language /məˈʃiːn ˌlæŋgwɪdʒ/ *noun* **1.** same as **machine code 2.** the way in which machine code is written

machine language compile /mə ˌʃiːn ˌlæŋgwɪdʒ kəmˈpaɪl/ *noun* the process of generating a machine code program from a HLL program by translating and assembling each HLL instruction

machine language programming /məˌʃiːn ˌlæŋgwɪdʒ ˈprəʊgræmɪŋ/ *noun* the slowest and most complex method of programming a CPU, but the fastest in execution, achieved by entering directly into RAM or ROM the binary representation for the machine code instructions to be carried out (NOTE: The alternative methods are to use an assembler with assembly language programs or a compiler with HLL programs.)

machine readable /məˌʃiːn ˈriːdəb(ə)l/ *adjective* referring to commands or data stored on a medium that can be directly input into the computer

machine-readable code /məˌʃiːn ˌriːdəb(ə)l ˈkəʊd/ *noun* a set of signs or letters, e.g. a bar code or post code, that can be read by computers

machine run /məˈʃiːn rʌn/ *noun* the action of processing instructions in a program by a computer

machine translation /məˌʃiːn træns ˈleɪʃ(ə)n/ *noun* a computer system that is used to translate text and commands from one language and syntax to another

machine word /məˈʃiːn wɜːd/ *noun* a number of bits of data operated on simultaneously by a CPU in one machine cycle, often 8, 16 or 32 bits

Macintosh /ˈmækɪntɒʃ/ a trade name for a range of personal computers designed by Apple Corporation. The Macintosh uses the Motorola family of proces-sors, the 68000, and offers similar computing power to a PC. The Macintosh is best known for its graphical user interface which allows a user to control the computer using icons and a mouse. ○ *Macintosh computers are not compatible with an IBM PC unless you use special emulation software.* Also called **Mac**

macro /ˈmækrəʊ/ *noun* a program routine or block of instructions identified by a single word or label

macro- /ˈmækrəʊ/ *prefix* very large or applying to the whole system

macro block /ˈmækrəʊ blɒk/ *noun* a grid of 16x16 pixels used to analyse and compress video data in the MPEG compression system

macro call /ˈmækrəʊ kɔːl/ *noun* the use of a label in an assembly language program to indicate to an assembler that the macro routine is to be inserted at that point

macro code /ˈmækrəʊ kəʊd/ *noun* one word that is used to represent a number of instructions, simplifying program writing

macro command /ˈmækrəʊ kə ˌmɑːnd/ *noun* same as **macro code**

macro definition /ˈmækrəʊ ˌdefənɪʃ(ə)n/ *noun* a description, in a program or to the operating system, of the structure, function and instructions that make up a macro operation

macroelement /ˈmækrəʊˌelɪmənt/ *noun* a number of data items treated as one element

macro expansion /ˈmækrəʊ ɪk ˌspænʃ(ə)n/ *noun* a process in which a macro call is replaced with the instructions in the macro

macro flowchart /ˈmækrəʊ ˌfləʊtʃɑːt/ *noun* a graphical representation of the logical steps, stages and actions within a routine

macroinstruction /ˈmækrəʊ ˌɪnstrʌkʃən/ *noun* one programming instruction that refers to a number of instructions within a routine or macro

macro language /ˈmækrəʊ ˌlæŋgwɪdʒ/ *noun* a programming language that allows the programmer to define and use macro instructions

'Microsoft has released a developer's kit for its Word 6.0 for Windows wordprocessing package. The 900-page kit explains how to use the WordBasic macro language supplied with the software.' [*Computing*]

macro library /ˈmækrəʊ ˌlaɪbrəri/ *noun* a number of useful, independent routines that can be incorporated into any program to ease program writing

Macromedia Director /ˌmækrəʊmiːdiə daɪˈrektə/ a trade name for authoring software for the PC and Macintosh that uses the Lingo scripting language

macro programming /ˌmækrəʊ ˌprəʊɡræmɪŋ/ *noun* the process of writing a program using macro instructions or defining macro instructions

macro virus /ˈmækrəʊ ˌvaɪrəs/ *noun* a type of virus that is stored as a macro attached to a document or e-mail message. Most advanced software applications provide a macro language that lets users extend the application and automate features. However, as macro languages become more advanced and powerful, they also provide an opportunity for someone to create a macro that can delete files or corrupt data when run.

COMMENT: A macro virus will run when the document is opened. Some viruses are benign, others carry out malicious damage on your files and data. The virus will also try and spread to other compatible documents and applications on your computer, so that any new documents you create are also infected. Current macro virus attacks have used the macro features of advanced e-mail software to re-send the virus to all the e-mail addresses stored in your e-mail address book. The last major macro virus created so much extra network e-mail traffic on the Internet that many servers were overloaded. The best way to avoid a macro virus is to regularly run virus detection software that can check and remove viruses attached to documents and new e-mail messages.

magazine /ˌmæɡəˈziːn/ *noun* a number of pages in a videotext system

magnet /ˈmæɡnɪt/ *noun* something that produces a magnetic field

magnetic /mæɡˈnetɪk/ *adjective* that has a magnetic field associated with it

magnetic bubble memory /mæɡ ˌnetɪk ˈbʌb(ə)l ˌmem(ə)ri/ *noun* ♦ **bubble memory**

magnetic card /mæɡˈnetɪk kɑːd/ *noun* a plastic card with a strip of magnetic recording material on its surface, allowing data to be stored

magnetic card reader /mæɡˌnetɪk ˈkɑːd ˌriːdə/ *noun* a machine that can read data stored on a magnetic card

magnetic cartridge /mæɡˌnetɪk ˈkɑːtrɪdʒ/ *noun* a small box containing a reel of magnetic tape and a pick up reel

magnetic cassette /mæɡˌnetɪk kəˈset/ *noun* same as **magnetic cartridge**

magnetic cell /mæɡˈnetɪk sel/ *noun* a small piece of material whose magnetic field can be altered to represent the two states of binary data

magnetic core /mæɡˈnetɪk kɔː/ *noun* an early main memory system for storing data in the first types of computer, where each bit of data was stored in a magnetic cell

magnetic disk /mæɡˈnetɪk dɪsk/ *noun* a flat circular piece of material coated with a substance, allowing signals and data to be stored magnetically

magnetic disk unit /mæɡˌnetɪk ˈdɪsk ˌjuːnɪt/ *noun* a computer peripheral made up of a disk drive and the necessary control electronics

magnetic drum /mæɡˈnetɪk drʌm/ *noun* a cylindrical magnetic storage device

magnetic encoding /mæɡˌnetɪk ɪn ˈkəʊdɪŋ/ *noun* the storage of binary data signals on a magnetic medium

magnetic field /mæɡˌnetɪk ˈfiːld/ *noun* a description of the polarity and strength of magnetic effects at a point

magnetic flux /mæɡˈnetɪk flʌks/ *noun* a measure of magnetic field strength per unit area

magnetic head /mæɡˈnetɪk hed/ *noun* an electromagnetic component that converts electrical signals into a magnetic field, allowing them to be stored on a magnetic medium

magnetic ink /mæɡˌnetɪk ˈɪŋk/ *noun* printing ink that contains a magnetic material, used in some character recognition systems

magnetic ink character recognition /mæɡˌnetɪk ɪŋk ˌkærɪktə ˌrekəɡ ˈnɪʃ(ə)n/ *noun* full form of **MICR**

magnetic master /mæɡˌnetɪk ˈmɑːstə/ *noun* the original version of a recorded tape or disk

magnetic material /mæɡˌnetɪk mə ˈtɪəriəl/ *noun* a substance that will retain a magnetic flux pattern after a magnetic field is removed

magnetic media /mæɡˌnetɪk ˈmiːdiə/ *plural noun* magnetic materials used to store signals, e.g. disk and tape

magnetic medium /mæɡˌnetɪk ˈmiːdiəm/ *noun* same as **magnetic material**

magnetic memory /mæg,netɪk 'mem(ə)ri/ *noun* storage that uses a medium that can store data bits as magnetic field changes

magnetic polarity /mæg,netɪk pəʊ 'lærɪti/ *noun* a method of indicating if a point is a source or collector of magnetic flux patterns

magnetic recording /mæg,netɪk rɪ 'kɔːdɪŋ/ *noun* the process of transferring an electrical signal onto a moving magnetic tape or disk by means of an magnetic field generated by a magnetic head

magnetic screen /mæg'netɪk skriːn/ *noun* a metal screen to prevent stray magnetic fields affecting electronic components

magnetic storage /mæg,netɪk 'stɔːrɪdʒ/ *noun* a method of storing information as magnetic changes on a sensitive disk, such as a floppy disk or hard disk

magnetic strip /mæg,netɪk 'strɪp/ *noun* a layer of magnetic material on the surface of a plastic card, used for recording data

magnetic stripe /mæg,netɪk 'straɪp/ *noun* a strip of magnetic material, containing information in coded form, on a plastic card such as a credit card

magnetic strip reader /mæg,netɪk 'strɪp ˌriːdə/ *noun* same as **magnetic card reader**

magnetic tape /mæg'netɪk teɪp/ *noun* a narrow length of thin plastic coated with a magnetic material used to store signals magnetically

COMMENT: Magnetic tape is available on spools of between 200 and 800 metres. The tape is magnetised by the read/write head. Tape is a storage medium that only allows serial access, that is, all the tape has to be read until the required location is found, as opposed to disk storage, which can be accessed randomly.

magnetic tape cartridge /mæg ,netɪk teɪp 'kɑːtrɪdʒ/ *noun* a small box containing a reel of magnetic tape and a pick up reel, used in a cassette player or tape drive

magnetic tape cassette /mæg,netɪk teɪp kə'set/ *noun* same as **magnetic tape cartridge**

magnetic tape encoder /mæg,netɪk teɪp en'kəʊdə/ *noun* a device that directly writes data entered at a keyboard onto magnetic tape

magnetic tape reader /mæg,netɪk teɪp 'riːdə/ *noun* a machine that can read

signals stored on magnetic tape and convert them to an electrical form that can be understood by a computer

magnetic tape recorder /mæg,netɪk 'teɪp rɪ,kɔːdə/ *noun* a device with a magnetic head, motor and circuitry to allow electrical signals to be recorded onto or played back from a magnetic tape

magnetic tape transport /mæg ,netɪk teɪp 'trænspɔːt/ *noun* a computer-controlled magnetic tape drive mechanism

magnetic transfer /mæg,netɪk 'trænsfɜː/ *noun* the copying of signals stored on one type of magnetic medium to another

magnetise /'mægnəˌtaɪz/, **magnetize** *verb* to convert a material or object into a magnet

magneto-optical disc /mæg,niːtəʊ ˌɒptɪk(ə)l 'dɪsk/ *noun* an optical disc that is used in a magneto-optical recording device

magneto-optical recording /mæg ,niːtəʊ ˌɒptɪk(ə)l rɪ'kɔːdɪŋ/ *noun* a method of recording that uses an optical disc covered with a thin layer of magnetic film that is heated by a laser. The particles are then polarised by a weak magnetic field. (NOTE: Magneto-optical discs have very high capacity, over 600Mb, and are re-writable.)

magnitude /'mægnɪtjuːd/ *noun* a level or strength of a signal or variable

mag tape /'mæg teɪp/ *noun* same as **magnetic tape** (*informal*)

mail /meɪl/ *noun* electronic messages to and from users of a bulletin board or network

mail application programming interface /ˌmeɪl ˌæplɪkeɪʃ(ə)n 'prəʊgræmɪŋ ˌɪntəfeɪs/ *noun* full form of **MAPI**

mailbox /'meɪlbɒks/, **mail box** /'meɪl bɒks/ *noun* an electronic storage space with an address in which a user's incoming messages are stored

mail-enabled /meɪl ɪn'eɪb(ə)ld/ *adjective* referring to an application that has access to an electronic mail system without leaving the application ○ *This word-processor is mail-enabled – you can send messages to other users from within it.*

mail exchange record /ˌmeɪl ɪks 'tʃeɪndʒ ˌrekɔːd/ *noun* (*in an electronic mail system*) information stored in the DNS, a database that helps locate a domain name on the Internet or a Unix network, that tells a mail system how to deliver a mail message to a particular domain ○ *Mail sent to 'smith&pcp.co.uk' will be sent to the 'pcp.co.uk' server by the MX record, the local server then has to send the message to the user 'smith'.* Also called **MX record**

mail gateway /'meɪl ˌɡeɪtweɪ/ *noun* a software program, or a combination of server and software, that links two different electronic mail systems together so that mail messages can be transferred from one system to another. For example, if you are using Lotus cc:Mail as the electronic mail product within your company, you would need to fit a gateway function to allow messages to be sent to and received by users on the Internet. (NOTE: LAN e-mail systems normally use one of three main standards, MAPI, MHS or VIM, to send mail messages. If you are sending mail from a LAN e-mail system to the Internet the mail gateway needs to convert this standard to one of the Internet mail standards such as POP3 or SMTP before it can be delivered.)

mailing /'meɪlɪŋ/ *noun* the process of sending something using the post or e-mail

mailing list /'meɪlɪŋ lɪst/ *noun* (*in electronic mail*) list of the e-mail addresses of users who receive information on a regular basis from a company, a person or from other people on the list. An Internet mailing list allows any person whose name and address are on the list to send a message to the list, which will then automatically distribute a copy of this message to all the other people on the list.

mailmerge /'meɪlmɜːdʒ/ *noun* a word-processing program which allows a standard form letter to be printed out to a series of different names and addresses

'Spreadsheet views for data and graphical forms for data entry have been added to the Q&A database, with the traditional reporting, mailmerge, and labels improved through Windows facilities.' [*Computing*]

mail server /meɪl 'sɜːvə/ *noun* a computer that stores incoming mail and sends it to the correct user and stores outgoing mail and transfers it to the correct destination server on the Internet

mail transfer agent /ˌmeɪl 'trænsfɜː ˌeɪdʒənt/ *noun* a software program that manages the way electronic mail messages are transferred over a network. On computers running the Unix operating system and the Internet the 'sendmail' software is the most popular mail transfer agent. Abbr **MTA**

mail user agent /ˌmeɪl 'juːzə ˌeɪdʒənt/ *noun* full form of **MUA**

main /meɪn/ *adjective* most important

main body /ˌmeɪn 'bɒdi/ *noun* a set of instructions that form the main part of a program and from which other subroutines are called

main clock /'meɪn klɒk/ *noun* a clock signal that synchronises all the components in a system

main entry /meɪn 'entri/ *noun* an entry in a catalogue that contains the most important information about a particular document

mainframe /'meɪnfreɪm kəmˌpjuːtə/, **mainframe computer** /ˌmeɪnfreɪm kəm 'pjuːtə/ *noun* a large-scale high-power computer system that can handle high-capacity memory and backing storage devices as well as a number of operators simultaneously

mainframe access /'meɪnfreɪm ˌækses/ *noun* the process of using microcomputers to access a mainframe computer

main index /meɪn 'ɪndeks/ *noun* a general index that directs the user gradually to more specific index areas

main loop /ˌmeɪn 'luːp/ *noun* a series of instructions performed repeatedly that carry out the main action of a program. This loop is often used to wait for user input before processing the event.

main memory /meɪn 'mem(ə)ri/ *noun* a fast-access RAM whose locations can be directly and immediately addressed by the CPU ○ *The 16-bit system includes up to 3Mb of main memory.*

main menu /meɪn 'menjuː/ *noun* a list of the primary options available

main routine /meɪn ruː'tiːn/ *noun* a section of instructions that make up the main part of a program (NOTE: A program often consists of a main routine and several subroutines, which are called from the main routine.)

mains electricity /meɪnz ɪˌlek'trɪsəti/ *noun* the normal domestic electricity supply to consumers (NOTE: In the UK this is 240 volts at 50Hz. In the US, it is 110 volts at 60Hz.)

main storage /meɪn 'stɔːrɪdʒ/ *noun* same as **main memory**

maintain /meɪn'teɪn/ *verb* to ensure a system is in good condition and functioning correctly □ **well maintained** well looked after

maintainability /ˌmeɪnteɪnəˈbɪlɪti/ *noun* the ability to have repairs carried out quickly and efficiently if a failure occurs

maintenance /ˈmeɪntənəns/ *noun* **1.** the task of keeping a machine in good working condition **2.** tasks carried out in order to keep a system running, e.g. repairing faults and replacing components

maintenance contract /ˈmeɪntənəns ˌkɒntrækt/ *noun* an arrangement with a repair company that provides for regular checks and special repair prices in the event of a fault

maintenance release /ˈmeɪntənəns rɪˌliːs/ *noun* a program revision that corrects a minor problem or bug but does not offer any major new features ○ *The maintenance release of the database program, version 2.01, corrects the problem with the margins.*

maintenance routine /ˈmeɪntənəns ruːˌtiːn/ *noun* a software diagnostic tool used by an engineer during preventative maintenance operations

major cycle /ˌmeɪdʒə ˈsaɪk(ə)l/ *noun* the minimum access time of a mechanical storage device

majordomo /ˌmeɪdʒəˈdəʊməʊ/ *noun* same as **listserv**

make directory /ˌmeɪk daɪˈrekt(ə)ri/ *noun* full form of **MD**

male connector /meɪl kəˈnektə/ *noun* a plug with conducting pins that can be inserted into a female connector to provide an electrical connection

malfunction /mælˈfʌŋkʃən/ *noun* (*of hardware or software*) the fact of not working correctly ○ *The data was lost due to a software malfunction.* ■ *verb* not to work properly ○ *Some of the keys on the keyboard have started to malfunction.*

malfunctioning /mælˈfʌŋkʃənɪŋ/ *adjective* not working properly

malfunction routine /mælˈfʌŋkʃən ruːˌtiːn/ *noun* a software routine used to find and help diagnose the cause of an error or fault

MAN /mæn/ *noun* a network extending over a limited geographical area, normally a city. Full form **metropolitan area network**. Compare **LAN, WAN**

manageable /ˈmænɪdʒəb(ə)l/ *adjective* that can be dealt with easily ○ *processing problems which are still manageable.*

management information service /ˌmænɪdʒmənt ˌɪnfəˈmeɪʃ(ə)n ˌsɜːvɪs/ *noun* a department within a company that is responsible for information and data processing. Abbr **MIS** (NOTE: In practice, this department is often responsible for the computer system in a company.)

management information system /ˌmænɪdʒmənt ˌɪnfəˈmeɪʃ(ə)n ˌsɪstəm/ *noun* software that allows managers in a company to access and analyse data. Abbr **MIS**

manager /ˈmænɪdʒə/ *noun* a user-friendly front end software that allows easy access to operating system commands

Manchester coding /ˈmæntʃestə ˌkəʊdɪŋ/ *noun* a method of encoding data and timing signals that is used in communications. The first half of the bit period indicates the value of the bit (1 or 0), and the second half is used as a timing signal.

Mandlebrot set /ˈmænd(ə)lbrɒt set/ *noun* a mathematical equation that is called recursively to generate a set of values. When plotted these form a fractal image. ◊ **fractal**

manipulate /məˈnɪpjʊˌleɪt/ *verb* to move, edit and change text or data ○ *An image processor that captures, displays and manipulates video images.*

manipulation /məˌnɪpjʊˈleɪʃ(ə)n/ *noun* the process of moving or editing or changing text or data ○ *The high-speed database management program allows the manipulation of very large amounts of data.*

man machine interface /ˌmæn mə ˌʃiːn ˈɪntəfeɪs/ *noun* full form of **MMI**

mantissa /mænˈtɪsə/ *noun* the fractional part of a number ○ *The mantissa of the number 45.897 is 0.897.*

manual /ˈmænjuəl/ *noun* a document containing instructions about the operation of a system or piece of software ○ *The manual is included with the system.*

manual data processing /ˌmænjuəl ˈdeɪtə ˌprəʊsesɪŋ/ *noun* the process of sorting and processing information without the help of a computer

manual entry /ˌmænjʊəl ˈentri/ *noun* the act of entering data into a computer by an operator via a keyboard

manual input /ˌmænjʊəl ˈɪnpʊt/ *noun* same as **manual entry**

manually /'mænjuəli/ *adverb* done by hand, not automatically ○ *The paper has to be fed into the printer manually.*

map /mæp/ *noun* a diagram representing the internal layout of a computer's memory or communications regions ■ *verb* **1.** to retrieve data and display it as a map **2.** to represent a network directory path on a remote computer with a local drive letter, enabling a user to view the contents of the remote directory by simply typing in the drive letter rather than the often long and complex directory path **3.** to represent a network printer connected to another computer on a network with a local printer identifier, so a user can treat the remote network printer as if it is directly connected to their computer **4.** to connect to a disk drive or a printer that is connected to another computer on a network. ◊ **texture mapping 5.** to transform a two-dimensional image into a three-dimensional form that can then be rotated or manipulated **6.** (*in an image*) to transform a graphical object from one coordinate system to another so that it can be displayed; e.g., to transform a three-dimensional wire frame model to a solid shaded object. ◊ **texture mapping**

MAPI /ˌem eɪ piː 'aɪ/ *noun* a set of standards, developed by Microsoft, that defines how electronic mail is sent and delivered. Full form **mail application programming interface**

MAR /ˌem eɪ 'ɑː/ *noun* a register within the CPU that contains the next location to be accessed. Full form **memory address register**

marching display /mɑːtʃɪŋ dɪ'spleɪ/ *noun* a display device that contains a buffer to show the last few characters entered

margin /'mɑːdʒɪn/ *noun* **1.** the blank space around a section of printed text ○ *When typing the contract leave wide margins.* □ **to set the margin** to define the size of a margin **2.** an extra time or space

margin of error /ˌmɑːdʒɪn əv 'erə/ *noun* the number of mistakes that is acceptable in a document or in a calculation

mark /mɑːk/ *noun* **1.** a sign put on a page to show something **2.** a transmitted signal that represents a logical one or true condition ■ *verb* to put a mark on something

mark block /ˌmɑːk 'blɒk/ *verb* to put a block marker at the beginning and end of a block of text

marker /'mɑːkə/ *noun* a code inserted in a file or text to indicate a special section

mark sense /ˌmɑːk 'sens/ *verb* to write characters with conductive or magnetic ink so that they are then machine readable

mark sense device /ˌmɑːk 'sens dɪˌvaɪs/ *noun* a device that reads data from special cards containing conductive or magnetic marks

mark sense reader /ˌmɑːk 'sens ˌriːdə/ *noun* same as **mark sense device**

mark sensing card /'mɑːk ˌsensɪŋ kɑːd/ *noun* a preprinted card with spaces for mark sense characters

mark space /ˌmɑːk 'speɪs/ *noun* a two-state transmission code using a mark and a space (without a mark) as signals

markup /'mɑːkʌp/ *noun* the addition of instructions for layout and style to a text that is to be printed out

markup language /'mɑːkʌp ˌlæŋgwɪdʒ/ *noun* a computer coding system that gives instructions relating to the layout and style to be used for a document

marquee /mɑː'kiː/ *noun* **1.** (*in graphics*) the area selected by a selection tool **2.** (*in a website*) a piece of text that moves slowly across the screen, used as a special feature of a webpage

mask /mɑːsk/ *noun* **1.** an integrated circuit layout that is used to define the pattern to be etched or doped onto a slice of semiconductor ○ *A mask or stencil is used to transfer the transistor design onto silicon.* **2.** a pattern of binary digits used to select various bits from a binary word. A one in the mask retains that bit in the word. ■ *verb* to cover an area of something with something

maskable /'mɑːskəb(ə)l/ *adjective* that can be masked

maskable interrupt /ˌmɑːskəb(ə)l 'ɪntərʌpt/ *noun* an interrupt which can be activated by using an interrupt mask

mask bit /'mɑːsk bɪt/ *noun* one bit in a mask, used to select the required bit from a word or string

masked ROM /'mɑːskt rɒm/ *noun* a read-only memory device that is programmed during manufacture, by depositing metal onto selected regions dictated by the shape of a mask

masking /'mɑːskɪŋ/ *noun* an operation used to select various bits in a word

mask register /mɑːsk 'redʒɪstə/ *noun* a storage location in a computer that contains the pattern of bits used as a mask

mass production /mæs prəˈdʌkʃən/ noun the process of manufacturing large quantities of goods ○ *mass production of monitors*

mass storage /mæs ˈstɔːrɪdʒ/ noun the storage and retrieval of large amounts of data

mass storage device /ˌmæs ˈstɔːrɪdʒ dɪˌvaɪs/ noun a computer backing store device that is able to store large amounts of data ○ *The hard disk is a mass storage device.*

mass storage system /ˌmæs ˈstɔːrɪdʒ ˌsɪstəm/ noun a data storage system that can hold more than one million million bits of a data

master /ˈmɑːstə/ adjective referring to the main or most important device or person in a system ○ *The master computer controls everything else.* ■ verb to learn and understand a language or process ○ *We mastered the new word-processor quite quickly.*

master card /ˈmɑːstə kɑːd/ noun the first punched card in a pack that provides information about the rest of the pack

master clock /ˈmɑːstə klɒk/ noun a timing signal to which all components in a system are synchronised

master computer /ˈmɑːstə kəmˌpjuːtə/ noun a computer in a multiprocessor system that controls the other processors and allocates jobs

master control program /ˌmɑːstə kənˈtrəʊl ˌprəʊɡræm/ noun software that controls the operations in a system. Abbr **MCP**

master data /ˌmɑːstə ˈdeɪtə/ noun reference data which is stored in a master file

master disc /ˈmɑːstə dɪsk/ noun a glass disc onto which a laser etches pits to represent data, and which is then used to create plastic compact discs ready for distribution

master disk /ˈmɑːstə dɪsk/ noun **1.** a disk containing all the files for a task **2.** a disk containing the code for a computer's operating system that must be loaded before the system will operate

master file /ˈmɑːstə faɪl/ noun a set of all the reference data required for an application, which is updated periodically

mastering /ˈmɑːstərɪŋ/ noun a process used to convert finished data to a master disc

master/master computer system /ˌmɑːstə ˈmɑːstə kəmˌpjuːtə ˌsɪstəm/ noun a system in which each processor is a master, dedicated to one task

master program file /ˌmɑːstə ˈprəʊɡræm ˌfaɪl/ noun a magnetic medium which contains all the programs required for an application

master/slave computer system /ˌmɑːstə ˈsleɪv kəmˌpjuːtə ˌsɪstəm/ noun a system with a master controlling computer and a slave that takes commands from the master

master tape /ˈmɑːstə teɪp/ noun a magnetic tape which contains all the vital operating system routines, loaded by the initial program loader once when the computer is switched on or hard reset

master terminal /ˌmɑːstə ˈtɜːmɪn(ə)l/ noun one terminal in a network which has priority over any other, used by the system manager to set up the system or carry out privileged commands ○ *The system manager uses the master terminal to restart the system.*

mat /mæt/ noun a plain coloured border that is displayed around an image that is smaller than the window in which it is displayed

match /mætʃ/ verb **1.** to search through a database for a similar piece of information **2.** to set a register equal to another

material /məˈtɪəriəl/ noun a substance which can be used to make a finished product ○ *Gold is the ideal material for electrical connections.*

math /mæθ/ noun US same as **mathematics** (*informal*)

mathematical /ˌmæθəˈmætɪk(ə)l/ adjective referring to mathematics

mathematical model /ˌmæθəmætɪk(ə)l ˈmɒd(ə)l/ noun a representation of a system using mathematical ideas and formulae

mathematical subroutines /ˌmæθəmætɪk(ə)l ˈsʌbruːtiːnz/ plural noun library routines that carry out standard mathematical functions such as square root, logarithm, cosine and sine

mathematics /ˌmæθəˈmætɪks/ noun the science of the relationship between numbers, their manipulation and organisation to (logically) prove facts and theories. ◊ **algebra**

maths chip /ˈmæθs ˌtʃɪp/ noun a dedicated IC that can be added to a system to carry out mathematical functions far more rapidly than a standard CPU, speeding up the execution of a program

maths coprocessor /ˈmæθs kəʊˌprəʊsesə/ *noun* same as **maths chip**

matrix /ˈmeɪtrɪks/ *noun* **1.** an array of numbers or data items arranged in rows and columns **2.** an array of connections between logic gates providing a number of possible logical functions **3.** a pattern of the dots that make up a character on a computer screen, dot-matrix or laser printer

matrix printer /ˈmeɪtrɪks ˌprɪntə/ *noun* ♦ **dot-matrix printer**

matrix rotation /ˈmeɪtrɪks rəʊˌteɪʃ(ə)n/ *noun* the process of swapping the rows with the columns in an array, equal to rotating by 90 degrees

matrix transform /ˌmeɪtrɪks trænsˈfɔːm/ *noun* a mathematical process used to rotate a line in any direction. The process involves multiplying a 4x4 transform matrix with the matrix of the line's coordinates.

matte /mæt/ *noun* (*in video or film*) a specified region within an image, which can be coded to appear transparent or opaque. A matte is reveals or masks off part of an image in another plane, and is normally used for special effects in which an object is photographed against a specially coloured background that is then replaced with another image to give the impression that the object appears against that image. ◊ **chroma key**

matter /ˈmætə/ *noun* the main section of text on a page as opposed to titles or headlines

MAU *abbr* multistation access unit

maximise /ˈmæksɪmaɪz/, **maximize** *verb* (*in MS-Windows*) to expand an application icon back to its original display window. Compare **minimise**

maximum /ˈmæksɪməm/ *noun* the highest value used or that is allowed

maximum capacity /ˌmæksɪməm kəˈpæsɪti/ *noun* the greatest amount of data that can be stored

maximum transmission rate /ˌmæksɪməm trænzˈmɪʃ(ə)n ˌreɪt/ *noun* the greatest amount of data that can be transmitted every second

maximum users /ˌmæksɪməm ˈjuːzəz/ *plural noun* the greatest number of users that a system can support at any one time

Mb *abbr* megabit

MB *abbr* megabyte

Mbps *abbr* megabits per second

MBR /ˌem biː ˈɑː/ *noun* a register in a CPU that temporarily buffers all inputs and outputs. Full form **memory buffer register**

Mbyte /ˈem baɪt/ *abbr* megabyte ○ *The latest model has a 30Mbyte hard disk.*

MCA /ˌem siː ˈeɪ/ a trade name for the expansion bus within IBM's PS/2 range of personal computers that has taken over from the older ISA/AT bus. MCA is a 32-bit bus that supports bus master devices. Full form **Micro Channel Architecture** ■ *abbr* media control architecture

MCA chipset /ˌem siː eɪ ˈtʃɪpset/ *noun* the number of electronic components required to manage the timing and data signals over an MCA expansion bus

MCGA /ˌem siː ˈdʒiː eɪ/ *noun* a colour graphics adapter standard fitted in low-end IBM PS/2 computers. Full form **multi-color graphics adapter**

MCI /ˌem siː ˈaɪ/ *noun* an interface that allow any program to control a multimedia device such as a sound card or video clip. Full form **media control interface**

MCI device /ˌem siː ˈaɪ dɪˌvaɪs/ *noun* a recognised multimedia device that is installed in a computer with the correct drivers

MCP /ˌem siː ˈpiː ˌdʒɔɪnt/ *abbr* master control program

MD /ˌem ˈdiː/ *noun* a DOS command used to create a new directory on a disk. Full form **make directory**

MDA /ˌem diː ˈeɪ/ *noun* a video adapter standard used in early PC systems that could display text in 25 lines of 80 columns. Full form **monochrome display adapter**

MDK /ˌem diː ˈkeɪ/ *noun* a product developed by Microsoft that allows developers to produce multimedia applications more easily using the supplied libraries of routines to control video playback, process images and display text. Full form **multimedia developer's kit**

MDR /ˌem diː ˈɑː/ *noun* a register in a CPU that holds data before it is processed or moved to a memory location. Full form **memory data register**

MDRAM /ˌem diː ˈræm/ *noun* a type of high-performance memory normally used in video adapter cards to provide fast graphic display. Full form **multibank dynamic random access memory**

mean /miːn/ *noun, adjective* the average value of a set of numbers or values ■ *verb* to signify something ○ *The message DISK FULL means that there is no more room on the disk for further data.*

mean time between failures /ˌmiːn taɪm bɪˌtwiːn 'feɪljəz/ *noun* full form of **MTBF**

mean time to failure /ˌmiːn taɪm tə 'feɪljə/ *noun* full form of **MTF**

measure /'meʒə/ *noun* **1.** a way of calculating size or quantity **2.** the total width of a printed line of text **3.** a type of action □ **to take measures to prevent something happening** to act to stop something happening ■ *verb* **1.** to find out the size or quantity of something **2.** to be of a certain size or quantity

measurement /'meʒəmənt/ *noun* a way of judging something ○ *Performance measurement or measurement of performance is carried out by running a benchmark program.*

measurements /'meʒəmənts/ *plural noun* size ○ *to write down the measurements of a package*

mechanical /mɪ'kænɪk(ə)l/ *adjective* referring to machines

mechanical mouse /mɪ'kænɪk(ə)l maʊs/ *noun* pointing device that is operated by moving it across a flat surface. As the mouse is moved, a ball inside spins and turns two sensors that feed the horizontal and vertical movement back to the computer. Compare **optical mouse**

mechanism /'mekəˌnɪz(ə)m/ *noun* a piece of machinery ○ *The printer mechanism is very simple.*

medallion /mə'dæliən/ *noun* the microchip inside a smart card

media /'miːdiə/ *plural noun* physical materials that can be used to store data ○ *Computers can store data on a variety of media, such as disk or CD-ROM.*

media access control /ˌmiːdiə 'ækses kənˌtrəʊl/ *noun* a sublayer within the data-link layer of the OSI network model that provides access to the transmission media. Abbr **MAC**

media control architecture /ˌmiːdiə kənˌtrəʊl 'ɑːkɪˌtektʃə/ *noun* full form of **MCA**

media control interface /ˌmiːdiə kən ˌtrəʊl 'ɪntəfeɪs/ *noun* full form of **MCI**

media conversion /ˌmiːdjə kən 'vɜːʃ(ə)n/ *noun* the process of copying data from one type of storage medium to another

media error /ˌmiːdjə 'erə/ *noun* a fault in the storage media that corrupts data

Media Player /'miːdiə ˌpleɪə/ a trade name for a Windows utility program that allows a user to control installed multimedia hardware including video disc or audio CDs, or play back multimedia files including sound, animation and video files

MediaServer /'miːdiəˌsɜːvə/ a trade name for a system developed by Netscape to provide audio and video delivery over the Internet

medical telematics /ˌmedɪk(ə)l ˌtelɪ 'mætɪks/ *noun* the development and use of computer networks to enable medical data to be accessed from different countries and exchanged between one country and another

medium /'miːdiəm/ *adjective* middle or average ○ *a medium-sized computer system* ■ *noun* any physical material that can be used to store date

medium model /ˌmiːdiəm 'mɒd(ə)l/ *noun* memory model of the Intel 80x86 processor family that allows 64Kb of data and up to 1MB of code

medium scale integration /ˌmiːdiəm skeɪl ˌɪntɪ'greɪʃ(ə)n/ *noun* an integrated circuit with 10 – 500 components. Abbr **MSI**

medium speed /'miːdiəm spiːd/ *noun* a data communication speed between 2400 and 9600 bits per second (NOTE: Medium speed transmission describes the maximum rate of transfer for a normal voice grade channel.)

meet /miːt/ *noun* a logical function whose output is true if both inputs are true

meg /meg/ *noun* same as **megabyte** (*informal*) ○ *This computer has a ninety-meg hard disk.*

mega- /megə/ *prefix* **1.** one million **2.** 1,048,576 (equal to 2^{20}) and used only in computing and electronic related applications

megabit /'megəbɪt/ *noun* equal to 1,048,576 bits. Abbr **Mb**

megabits per second /ˌmegəbɪts pɜː 'sekənd/ *noun* a number of million bits transmitted every second. Abbr **Mbps**

megabyte /'megəbaɪt/ *noun* a measure of the data capacity of a storage device that is equal to 1,048,576 bytes or 2^{20} bytes. Megabytes are used to measure the storage capacity of hard disk drives or main memory (RAM). Abbr **MB**

'Doing this reduced a bitmap of my desktop from 2.25 megabytes to a 58K GIF' [*The Guardian*]

mega floating point instructions per second /ˌmegə ˌfləʊtɪŋ pɔɪnt ɪnˌstrʌkʃənz pɜː sɪ'kɒnd/ *noun* full form of **MFLOPS**

megaflop /'megəflɒp/ *noun* a measure of computing power and speed equal to one million floating point instructions per second. Abbr **MFLOPS**

megahertz /'megəˌhɜːts/ *noun* a measure of frequency equal to one million cycles per second. Abbr **MHz**

megapixel display /megəˌpɪks(ə)l dɪ'spleɪ/ *noun* a display adapter and monitor that are capable of displaying over one million pixels. This means a resolution of at least 1,024x1,024 pixels.

Megastream /'megəstriːm/ a trade name for a data link provided by British Telecom that offers data transfer at rates up to 8Mbits/second

Mega VGA /ˌmegə viː dʒiː 'eɪ/ *noun* a 256 colour Super VGA mode with a resolution of 1024x768 that requires one megabyte of video RAM

member /'membə/ *noun* **1.** one object on a page of a multimedia book **2.** an individual record or item in a field

membrane keyboard /ˌmembreɪn 'kiːbɔːd/ *noun* a keyboard that uses a thin plastic or rubber sheet with key shapes moulded into it. When the user presses on a key, it activates a pressure sensor. (NOTE: The keys in a membrane keyboard have less travel than normal mechanical keys, but since they have no moving parts, they are more robust and reliable.)

memo field /'meməʊ fiːld/ *noun* a field in a database or text window in an application that allows a user to add comments or a memo about the entry

memorise /'meməˌraɪz/, **memorize** *verb* to remember or to retain in the memory

memory /'mem(ə)ri/ *noun* storage space in a computer system or medium that is capable of retaining data or instructions

'The lower-power design, together with an additional 8Kb of on-board cache memory, will increase the chip's performance to 75 million instructions per second.' [*Computing*]

'…when a program is loaded into memory, some is used for the code, some for the permanent data, and some is reserved for the stack which grows and shrinks for function calls and local data' [*Personal Computer World*]

memory access time /ˌmem(ə)ri 'ækses ˌtaɪm/ *noun* a time delay between requesting access to a location and actually gaining access to it

memory address register /ˌmem(ə)ri ə'dres ˌredʒɪstə/ *noun* full form of **MAR**

memory allocation /'mem(ə)ri ˌæləkeɪʃ(ə)n/ *noun* a process in which an operating system provides an application with the memory it requires in order to run

memory backup capacitor /ˌmem(ə)ri 'bækʌp kəˌpæsɪtə/ *noun* a very high-capacitance, small device that can be used instead of a battery to provide power for volatile RAM chips for up to two weeks

memory bank /'mem(ə)ri bæŋk/ *noun* a number of smaller storage devices connected together to form one large area of memory

memory board /'mem(ə)ri bɔːd/ *noun* a printed circuit board containing memory chips

memory buffer register /'mem(ə)ri ˌbʌfə ˌredʒɪstə/ *noun* full form of **MBR**

memory bus /'mem(ə)ri bʌs/ *noun* a bus carrying address data between a CPU and memory devices

memory capacity /'mem(ə)ri kə ˌpæsɪti/ *noun* the number of bits or bytes that can be stored within a memory device

memory cell /'mem(ɔ)ri sel/ *noun* the smallest location in a memory that can be individually accessed

memory chip /'mem(ə)ri tʃɪp/ *noun* an electronic component that is able to store binary data

memory cycle /'mem(ə)ri ˌsaɪk(ə)l/ *noun* the period of time from when the CPU reads or writes to a location and to when the action is actually performed

memory data register /ˌmem(ə)ri 'deɪtə ˌredʒɪstə/ *noun* full form of **MDR**

memory diagnostic /'mem(ə)ri ˌdaɪəgnɒstɪk/ *noun* a software routine that checks each memory location in main memory for faults

memory dump /'mem(ə)ri dʌmp/ *noun* a printout of all the contents of an area of memory

memory edit /'mem(ə)ri ˌedɪt/ *verb* to change the contents of various memory locations

memory effect /'mem(ə)ri ɪˌfekt/ *noun* a feature of nickel-cadmium, or

NiCad, rechargeable batteries where the battery's capacity to hold charge is reduced if the battery is recharged before it has been fully discharged. For example, if a battery still has half its original charge when it is recharged, it appears only to have the capacity to carry the new half-charge rather than a full charge. It seems, in effect, to have a memory of the last level of its charge. (NOTE: This problem was particularly noticeable on older NiCad batteries. Modern NiCad batteries suffer very little from this effect, and other types of battery such as the lithium ion battery do not suffer from it at all.)

memory expansion /'mem(ə)ri ɪk ˌspænʃ(ə)n/ *noun* the action of adding more electronic memory chips to a computer

memory hierarchy /ˌmem(ə)ri ˌhaɪərɑːki/ *noun* the different types of memory available in a system, arranged according to their capacity and access time

memory-intensive software /ˌmem(ə)ri ɪnˌtensɪv 'sɒftweə/ *noun* software that uses large amounts of RAM or disk storage during run-time, such as programs whose entire code has to be in main memory during execution

memory management /'mem(ə)ri ˌmænɪdʒmənt/ *noun* software that controls and regulates the flow and position in memory of files and data

memory management unit /'mem(ə)ri ˌmænɪdʒmənt ˌjuːnɪt/ *noun* full form of **MMU**

memory map /'mem(ə)ri mæp/ *noun* a diagram indicating the allocation of address ranges to various memory devices, such as RAM, ROM and memory-mapped input/output devices

memory-mapped /'mem(ə)ri ˌmæpt/ *adjective* referring to a computer's input or output devices that have addresses allocated to them so that they can be accessed as if they were a memory location ○ *A memory-mapped screen has an address allocated to each pixel, allowing direct access to the screen by the CPU.*

memory-mapped input/output /ˌmem(ə)ri ˌmæpt ˌɪnpʊt 'aʊtpʊt/ *noun* same as **memory-mapped I/O**

memory-mapped I/O /ˌmem(ə)ri ˌmæpt aɪ 'əʊ/ *noun* an I/O port which can be accessed as if it were a memory location within the CPU's normal address range

memory model /'mem(ə)ri ˌmɒd(ə)l/ *noun* a method used in a program to address the code and data that is used within that program. The memory model defines how much memory is available for code and data. (NOTE: Processors with a segmented address space, like the Intel 80x86 range, can support multiple memory models.)

memory page /'mem(ə)ri peɪdʒ/ *noun* one section of a main store containing data or programs that is divided into pages

memory protect /'mem(ə)ri prəˌtekt/ *noun* a feature on most storage systems to prevent the accidental overwriting of data

memory-resident software /ˌmem(ə)ri ˌrezɪd(ə)nt 'sɒftweə/ *noun* same as **resident software**

memory stick /'mem(ə)ri stɪk/ *noun* a tiny memory expansion device, developed by Sony, that can store up to 128Mb of data, often used in MP3 music players and digital cameras

memory switching system /'mem(ə)ri ˌswɪtʃɪŋ ˌsɪstəm/ *noun* a system which communicates information, stores it in memory and then transmits it according to instructions

memory workspace /'mem(ə)ri ˌwɜːkspeɪs/ *noun* the amount of extra memory required by a program to store data used during execution

menu /'menjuː/ *noun* a list of options or programs available to the user

menu-bar /'menjuː bɑː/ *noun* (*in a GUI*) a list of options available to a user which are displayed on a horizontal line along the top of the screen or window. Each menu option activates a pull-down menu.

menu-driven software /ˌmenjuː ˌdrɪv(ə)n 'sɒftweə/ *noun* a program in which commands or options are selected from a menu by the operator rather than typed in by the user at a prompt

menu item /'menjuː ˌaɪtəm/ *noun* one of the choices in a menu

menu selection /'menjuː sɪˌlekʃən/ *noun* the act of choosing commands from a list of options presented to the operator

menu shortcut /ˌmenjuː 'ʃɔːtkʌt/ *noun* a key combination of two or more keys that is the same are selecting a menu option

merchant account /'mɜːtʃənt ə ˌkaʊnt/ *noun* a bank account that enables its user to deposit payments made by credit card, used especially for trading on the Internet

mercury delay line /ˌmɜːkjʊri dɪˈleɪ ˌlaɪn/ *noun* an obsolete method of storing serial data as pulses in a length of mercury (NOTE: The data was constantly read, regenerated and fed back into the input.)

merge /mɜːdʒ/ *verb* to combine two data files retaining an overall order ○ *The system automatically merges text and illustrations into the document.* (NOTE: merges – merging – merged)

merge sort /ˌmɜːdʒ ˈsɔːt/ *noun* a software application in which the sorted files are merged into a new file

mesh /meʃ/ *noun* any system with two or more possible paths at each interconnection

mesh model /meʃ ˈmɒd(ə)l/ *noun* a graphical object that is displayed as a mesh, with crossing lines. ◊ **wire frame model** (NOTE: The mesh is actually created from polygons and can be used to shade the object.)

mesh network /meʃ ˈnetwɜːk/ *noun* a method of connecting several machines together, where each device is directly connected to every other device in the network

message /ˈmesɪdʒ/ *noun* **1.** a piece of information sent from one person to another **2.** a defined amount of information

message authentication code /ˌmesɪdʒ ɔːˌθentɪˈkeɪʃ(ə)n kəʊd/ *noun* full form of **MAC**

message board /ˈmesɪdʒ bɔːd/ *noun* same as **bulletin board**

message box /ˈmesɪdʒ bɒks/ *noun* a small window that is displayed on screen to warn of an event, condition or error

message code authentication /ˌmesɪdʒ kəʊd ɔːˌθentɪˈkeɪʃ(ə)n/ *noun* a coding system that enables the author of an email message to be identified and ensures that the message is genuine

message format /ˈmesɪdʒ ˌfɔːmæt/ *noun* a set of predetermined rules defining the coding, size and speed of transmitted messages

message handling service /ˌmesɪdʒ ˈhændlɪŋ ˌsɜːvɪs/ *noun* full form of **MHS**

message header /ˈmesɪdʒ ˌhedə/ *noun* a sequence of data at the beginning of a message that contains routing and destination information

message routing /ˈmesɪdʒ raʊtɪŋ/ *noun* selection of a suitable path between the source and destination of a message in a network

message slot /ˈmesɪdʒ slɒt/ *noun* the number of bits that can hold a message that circulates around a ring network

message text /ˈmesɪdʒ tekst/ *noun* information that concerns the user at the destination without routing or network control data

message transfer agent /ˌmesɪdʒ ˈtrænsfɜː ˌeɪdʒənt/ *noun* full form of **MTA**

messaging /ˈmesɪdʒɪŋ/ *noun* the process of sending a message to other people, e.g. by computer, telephone or pager

metabit /ˈmetəbɪt/ *noun* an extra identifying bit for each data word

metacompilation /ˌmetəkɒmpɪˈleɪʃ(ə)n/ *noun* the process of compiling a program that will compile other programs when executed

metacompiler /ˈmetəkɒmˌpaɪlə/ *noun* a compiler that is used to create another compiler

metafile /ˈmetəfaɪl/ *noun* **1.** a file that contains other files ○ *The operating system uses a metafile to hold data that defines where each file is stored on disk.* **2.** a file that defines or contains data about other files

metalanguage /ˈmetəˌlæŋgwɪdʒ/ *noun* a language that describes a programming language

metal oxide semiconductor /ˌmet(ə)l ˌɒksaɪd ˈsemikənˌdʌktə/ *noun* full form of **MOS**

metal oxide semiconductor field effect transistor /ˌmet(ə)l ˌɒksaɪd ˌsemikəndʌktə fiːld ɪˌfekt trænˈzɪstə/ *noun* full form of **MOSFET**

meter – power supply /ˌmiːtə ˈpaʊə səˌplaɪ/ *noun* a utility within Windows that indicates how much power is left in a laptop's battery and whether a laptop is running from a battery or mains electricity power

metropolitan area network /ˌmetrəpɒlɪt(ə)n ˌeəriə ˈnetwɜːk/ *noun* full form of **MAN**

MFLOPS /ˈem flɒps/ *noun* a measure of computing speed calculated as the number of floating point instructions that can be processed each second. Full form **mega floating point instructions per second**

MFM /ˌem ef ˈem/ *noun* a method of storing data on magnetic media, e.g. a magnetic disk that encodes the data bit according to the state of the previous bit. Full form **modified frequency modulation** (NOTE: MFM is more efficient than FM, but less efficient than RLL encoding.)

MFS *abbr* Macintosh filing system

MHS /ˌem eɪtʃ 'es/ *noun* a store-and-forward message transfer mechanism used mainly by Novell. Full form **message handling service**

MHz *abbr* megahertz

MICR /ˌem aɪ siː 'ɑː/ *noun* a system that identifies characters by sensing magnetic ink patterns, as used on bank cheques. Full form **magnetic ink character recognition**

micro /'maɪkrəʊ/ *noun* same as **microcomputer**

micro- /maɪkrəʊ/ *prefix* **1.** very small **2.** one millionth of a unit

microcassette /'maɪkrəʊkəˌset/ *noun* a small format audio cassette used mainly in pocket dictating equipment

Micro Channel Architecture /ˌmaɪkrəʊ ˌtʃæn(ə)l 'ɑːkɪtektʃə/ full form of **MCA**

Micro Channel Architecture chipset /ˌmaɪkrəʊ ˌtʃæn(ə)l ˌɑːkɪtektʃə 'tʃɪpset/ same as **MCA chipset**

Micro Channel Bus /ˌmaɪkrəʊ ˌtʃæn(ə)l 'bʌs/ a proprietary 32-bit expansion bus defined by IBM in its Micro Channel Architecture

microchip /'maɪkrəʊˌtʃɪp/ *noun* a circuit in which all the active and passive components are formed on one small piece of semiconductor, by means of etching and chemical processes

microcircuit /'maɪkrəʊˌkɜːkɪt/ *noun* a complex integrated circuit

microcode /'maɪkrəʊkəʊd/ *noun* a set of ALU control instructions implemented as hardwired software

Microcom Networking Protocol /ˌmaɪkrəkɒm 'netwɜːkɪŋ ˌprəʊtəkɒl/ full form of **MNP**

microcomputer[1] /'maɪkrəʊkəm ˌpjuːtə/ *noun* a complete small-scale, cheap, low-power computer system based around a microprocessor chip and having limited memory capacity

COMMENT: Microcomputers are particularly used as home computers or as small office computers.

microcomputer[2] /'maɪkrəʊkəm ˌpjuːtə/ *noun* a complete small-scale, cheap, low-power computer system based around a microprocessor chip and having limited memory capacity. Also called **micro**

microcomputer architecture /ˌmaɪkrəʊkəmpjuːtə 'ɑːkɪtektʃə/ *noun* the layout and interconnection of a microcomputer's internal hardware

microcomputer backplane /ˌmaɪkrəʊkəmpjuːtə 'bækpleɪn/ *noun* the main printed circuit board of a system, containing most of the components and connections for expansion boards

microcomputer bus /'maɪkrəʊkəm ˌpjuːtə ˌbʌs/ *noun* the set of the main data, address and control buses in a microcomputer

microcomputer development kit /ˌmaɪkrəʊkəmpjuːtə dɪ'veləpmənt ˌkɪt/ *noun* a basic computer based around a new CPU chip that allows hardware and software designers to experiment with the new device

microcomputing /'maɪkrəʊkəm ˌpjuːtɪŋ/ *adjective* referring to microcomputers and their use ○ *the microcomputing industry*

microcontroller /'maɪkrəʊkən ˌtrəʊlə/ *noun* a small selfcontained microcomputer for use in dedicated control applications

microcycle /'maɪkrəʊˌsaɪk(ə)l/ *noun* a unit of time, (usually a multiple of the system clock period) used to give the execution time of instructions

microdevice /'maɪkrəʊdɪˌvaɪs/ *noun* a very small device, e.g. a microprocessor

microelectronics /ˌmaɪkrəʊɪlek 'trɒnɪks/ *noun* the design and manufacture of electronic circuits with integrated circuits and chips

microfloppy /'maɪkrəʊˌflɒpi/ *noun* a small size magnetic floppy disk, usually a 3.5 inch disk

microinstruction /'maɪkrəʊɪn ˌstrʌkʃən/ *noun* a hardwired instruction, part of a microcode, that controls the actions of the ALU in a processor

micrometre /'maɪkrəʊˌmiːtə/ *noun* one millionth of a metre

micron /'maɪkrɒn/ *noun* one millionth of a metre

microphone /'maɪkrəfəʊn/ *noun* a device that converts sound waves into electrical signals

microprocessor /'maɪkrəʊˌprəʊsesə/ *noun* a set of central processing unit elements, often contained on a single integrated circuit chip, which when combined with other memory and I/O chips will make up a microcomputer

microprocessor addressing capabilities /ˌmaɪkrəʊprəʊsesə əˈdresɪŋ ˌkeɪpəbɪlɪtiz/ *noun* the highest address that a CPU can directly address, without special features (NOTE: This depends on the address word size: the bigger the word the greater the addressing capacity.)

microprocessor architecture /ˈmaɪkrəʊprəʊsesə ˌɑːkɪtektʃə/ *noun* the layout of the basic parts within a CPU

microprocessor chip /ˈmaɪkrəʊprəʊsesə tʃɪp/ *noun* an integrated circuit that contains all the elements of a central processing unit, connected with other memory and I/O chips to make a microcomputer

microprocessor timing /ˈmaɪkrəʊprəʊsesə ˌtaɪmɪŋ/ *noun* the correct selection of system clock frequency to allow for factors such as slower peripherals

microprocessor unit /ˈmaɪkrəʊprəʊsesə ˌjuːnɪt/ *noun* a unit containing the main elements of a microprocessor. Abbr **MPU**

microprogram /ˈmaɪkrəʊˌprəʊɡræm/ *noun* a series of microinstructions

microprogram assembly language /ˌmaɪkrəʊprəʊɡræm əˈsembli ˌlæŋɡwɪdʒ/ *noun* a computer language consisting of microprograms each of which carries out an assembly language instruction

microprogram counter /ˈmaɪkrəʊˌprəʊɡræm ˌkaʊntə/ *noun* a register that stores the address of the next microinstruction to be carried out (NOTE: The microprogram counter is the same as the memory address register.)

microprogram instruction set /ˌmaɪkrəʊprəʊɡræm ɪnˈstrʌkʃən ˌset/ *noun* a complete set of basic microinstructions available in a CPU

microprogramming /ˈmaɪkrəʊˌprəʊɡræmɪŋ/ *noun* the writing of microcode using microinstructions

microprogram store /ˈmaɪkrəʊˌprəʊɡræm ˌstɔː/ *noun* a storage device used to hold a microprogram

microsecond /ˈmaɪkrəʊˌsekənd/ *noun* one millionth of a second

microsequence /ˈmaɪkrəʊˌsiːkwəns/ *noun* a series of microinstructions

Microsoft /ˈmaɪkrəsɒft/ the biggest developer and publisher of software for the PC and Apple Mac. Microsoft developed the MS-DOS operating system for the IBM PC and later Windows together with a range of application software.

Microsoft Compact Disc Extensions /ˌmaɪkrəsɒft ˌkɒmpækt ˈdɪsk ɪkˌstenʃ(ə)nz/ full form of **MSCDEX**

Microsoft DOS /ˌmaɪkrəsɒft ˈdɒs/ full form of **MS-DOS**

Microsoft Exchange /ˌmaɪkrəsɒft ɪksˈtʃeɪndʒ/ a program included with Windows 95 that coordinates the email, fax and network messages sent and received on a PC

Microsoft Exchange Server /ˌmaɪkrəsɒft ɪksˈtʃeɪndʒ ˌsɜːvə/ a program that runs on a server under Microsoft Windows NT and provides sophisticated groupware functions using the Exchange client software supplied with Windows 95

Microsoft Fax /ˌmaɪkrəsɒft ˈfæks/ a series of programs supplied with Windows 3.1 and 95 that let a user send and receive fax transmissions from a PC

Microsoft Internet Explorer /ˌmaɪkrəsɒft ˌɪntənet ɪksˈplɔːrə/ ⧫ **Internet Explorer**

Microsoft Network /ˌmaɪkrəsɒft ˈnetwɜːk/ full form of **MSN**

Microsoft Outlook /ˌmaɪkrəsɒft ˈaʊtlʊk/ a trade name for an application that provides a range of features to manage email, fax messages, contacts, diary appointments, notes and projects

Microsoft Outlook Express /ˌmaɪkrəsɒft ˌaʊtlʊk ɪkˈspres/ a trade name for a free version of Outlook that is normally used for email (NOTE: It has fewer extra features for managing contacts and appointments than Microsoft Outlook.)

Microsoft Windows /ˌmaɪkrəsɒft ˈwɪndəʊz/ same as **Windows**

microwriter /ˈmaɪkrəʊˌraɪtə/ *noun* a portable keyboard and display, used for keyboarding when travelling

middleware /ˈmɪd(ə)lweə/ *noun* system software that has been customised by a dealer for a particular user

MID-F1 /ˌmɪd ef ˈwʌn/ *noun* (in CD-i) mid-quality sound at Level B. ⧫ **Level B**

MIDI /ˈmɪdi/ *noun* a serial interface that connects electronic instruments. Full form **musical instrument digital interface** (NOTE: The MIDI interface carries signals from a controller or computer that instructs the different instruments to play notes.)

MIDI channel /'mɪdi ˌtʃæn(ə)l/ *noun* any one of 15 independent connections that is supported by the MIDI system, allowing 16 different electronic devices to be connected to one main sequencer

MIDI connector /'mɪdi kəˌnektə/ *noun* a standard 5-pin, round DIN connector used to connect MIDI devices

MIDI control-change message /ˌmɪdi kən'trəʊl tʃeɪndʒ ˌmesɪdʒ/ *noun* a message sent to a synthesiser to control the volume or pitch of a sound or to change the instrument patch used to generate a sound

MIDI device /'mɪdi ðɪˌvaɪs/ *noun* a device that can receive or send MIDI data

MIDI file /'mɪdi faɪl/ *noun* a file format used to store a MIDI song, made up of notes and control-change messages (NOTE: It usually has a MID file extension.)

MIDI interface card /ˌmɪdi 'ɪntəfeɪs kɑːd/ *noun* an adapter card that plugs into an expansion connector in a PC and allows it to send and receive MIDI data

MIDI Mapper /'mɪdi ˌmæpə/ *noun* a program supplied with Windows 3.1x that allows experienced MIDI users to change the way in which musical notes are sent to each instrument that is connected to the PC ○ *You could use the MIDI Mapper to re-direct all the notes meant for the drum machine to the electronic piano.*

MIDI mapping /'mɪdi ˌmæpɪŋ/ *noun* the process of translating and redirecting MIDI messages between channels according to settings in a MIDI map

MIDI program-change message /ˌmɪdi 'prəʊgræm tʃeɪndʒ ˌmesɪdʒ/ *noun* a message sent to a synthesiser to request a patch change for a particular MIDI channel

MIDI sequence /'mɪdi ˌsiːkwəns/ *noun* data that has time-sequence data embedded and that can be played by a MIDI sequencer

MIDI sequencer /ˌmɪdi 'siːkwənsə/ *noun* **1.** a piece of software that allows a user to record, edit, add special effects and play back MIDI data through a synthesiser **2.** a hardware device that records or plays back stored MIDI data

MIDI setup map /ˌmɪdi 'setʌp mæp/ *noun* a file that contains all the data required to define the settings for MIDI Mapper

MIDI time code /ˌmɪdi 'taɪm kəʊd/ *noun* full form of **MTC**

mid-user /mɪd 'juːzə/ *noun* an operator who retrieves relevant information from a database for a customer or end user

migrate /maɪ'greɪt/ *verb* to transfer a file from one computer system or database to another (NOTE: migrates – migrating – migrated)

migration /maɪ'greɪʃ(ə)n/ *noun* the process of moving users from one hardware platform to another

milk disk /'mɪlk dɪsk/ *noun* a disk used to transfer data from a small machine onto a larger computer, which provides greater processing power

milking machine /'mɪlkɪŋ məˌʃiːn/ *noun* a portable machine which can accept data from different machines, then transfer it to another larger computer

millennium bug /mɪ'leniəm bʌg/ *noun* the inability to handle dates later than 1999. This problem, which came to light in the 1990s, affected old hardware and software that stored dates as two digits, with the '19' being assumed. Such dates would not move to '2000' at the turn of the millennium but would revert to '1900', with unpredictable and possibly serious results for the affected systems. In the event, the affected systems were nearly all modified in time. There were very few problems when the year 2000 arrived, and the more apocalyptic predictions did not come to pass.

milli- /mɪlɪ/ *prefix* one thousandth. Abbr **m**

milliampere /ˌmɪli'æmpeə/ *noun* an electrical current measure equal to one thousandth of an ampere. Abbr **mA**

million instructions per second /ˌmɪljən ɪnˌstrʌkʃənz pɜː sɪ'kɒnd/ *noun* full form of **MIPS**

millisecond /'mɪliˌsekənd/ *noun* one thousandth of a second. Abbr **ms**

MIMD /ˌem aɪ em 'diː/ *noun* architecture of a parallel processor that uses a number of ALUs and memory devices in parallel to provide high speed processing. Full form **multiple instruction stream – multiple data stream**

MIME /ˌem aɪ em 'iː/ *noun* a standard that defines a way of sending files using email software. Full form **multipurpose Internet mail extensions**

COMMENT: MIME allows a user to send files over the Internet to another user without having to carry out any other encoding or conversion actions. MIME was developed to get around a problem of many email systems that could only transmit text which is stored in a 7-bit data format; programs, multimedia, graphics and other files are stored using an 8-bit data format.

mini /'mɪni/ *noun* same as **minicomputer**

mini- /mɪni/ *prefix* small

miniaturisation, **miniaturization** *noun* the process of making something very small

minicomputer /'mɪnikəmˌpjuːtə/ *noun* a small computer with a greater range of instructions and processing power than a microcomputer but not able to compete with the speed or data-handling capacity of a mainframe computer. Also called **mini**

minidisk /'mɪnidɪsk/ *noun* a magnetic disk smaller than the 5.25 inch standard, usually 3.5 inch

minifloppy /'mɪniˌflɒpi/ *noun* a magnetic disk, usually of the 5.25 inch standard (NOTE: The plural is **minifloppies**.)

minimal latency coding /ˌmɪnɪməl 'leɪtənsi ˌkəʊdɪŋ/ *noun* ♦ **optimum code**

minimal tree /'mɪnɪm(ə)l triː/ *noun* a tree whose nodes are organised in the optimum way, providing maximum efficiency

minimise /'mɪnɪmaɪz/, **minimize** *verb* **1.** to make something as small as possible ○ *We minimised costs by cutting down the number of components.* **2.** (*in MS-Windows*) to shrink an application window to an icon. Compare **maximise** (NOTE: minimises – minimising – minimised)

COMMENT: The application can continue to run in the background. You minimise a window by clicking once on the down arrow in the top right hand corner.

miniwinny /'mɪniˌwɪni/ *noun* a small Winchester hard disk (*slang*) (NOTE: The plural is **miniwinnies**.)

minmax /'mɪnimæks/ *noun* a method used in artificial intelligence to solve problems

minuend /'mɪnjuːend/ *noun* a number from which another is subtracted

minus /'maɪnəs/, **minus sign** /'maɪnəs saɪn/ *noun* a printed or written sign, like a small dash, to indicate subtraction or to show a negative value

MIP mapping /ˌem aɪ piː 'mæpɪŋ/ *noun* a method of calculating pixels within texture mapping to take into account the perceived distance of the scene from the viewer

MIPS /mɪps/ *noun* a measure of processor speed that defines the number of instructions it can carry out per second. Full form **million instructions per second**. Compare **megaflop**

'ICL has staked its claim to the massively parallel market with the launch of the Goldrush MegaServer, providing up to 16,000 Unix MIPS of processing power.' [*Computing*]

mirror /'mɪrə/ *verb* **1.** to create an identical copy of something **2.** to duplicate all disk operations onto a second disk drive that can be used if the first breaks down

'Network-attached storage systems which aim to make it easy to mirror data between units' [*The Guardian*]

mirror site /'mɪrə saɪt/ *noun* an exact copy of a website kept on a different file server so that the main site does not become overloaded and its data is protected against loss if there is a hardware or software failure

MIS *abbr* **1.** management information service **2.** management information system

MISD /ˌem aɪ es 'diː/ *noun* architecture of a parallel computer that has a single ALU and data bus with a number of control units. Full form **multiple instruction stream-single data stream**

mission-critical /ˌmɪʃ(ə)n 'krɪtɪk(ə)l/ *adjective* referring to an application or hardware on which a company depends

MJPEG /ˌem 'dʒeɪ peg/ *noun* a version of the JPEG image compression system that supports video. Full form **motion JPEG**

MKDIR *abbr* make directory. ♦ **MD**

MMC /ˌem em 'siː/ *noun* a compact memory expansion device that includes digital copyright control features and is often used in MP3 music players and digital cameras. Full form **multimedia card**. Also called **SD card**

MMI /ˌem em 'aɪ/ *noun* hardware and software designed to make it easier for users to communicate effectively with a machine. Full form **man-machine interface**

MMU /ˌem em 'juː/ *noun* a set of electronic logic circuits that generate the memory refresh signals and manage the mapping of virtual memory addresses to physical memory locations. Full form **memory management unit** (NOTE: The MMU is normally integrated into the processor chip.)

MMX a trade name for an enhanced Intel processor chip that includes special features and components that are used to improve the performance when dealing with multimedia and communications. Full form **multimedia extensions**

mnemonic /nɪˈmɒnɪk/ *noun* a shortened form of a word or function that is helpful as a reminder, e.g. INCA for increment register A

mnemonic operation code /nɪ ˌmɒnɪk ˌɒpəˈreɪʃ(ə)n kəʊd/ *noun* same as **assembler mnemonic**

MNP /ˌem en ˈpiː/ *noun* an error detection and correction system developed by Microcom Inc. used in modems and some communications software. Full form **Microcom Networking Protocol**

MNP 2–4 *noun* an error-correcting communications protocol developed by Microcom Inc. and adopted into the CCITT V.42 standard.

MNP 5 *noun* a communications standard that provides data compression, providing up to 2-to-1 compression, though averaging less

MNP 10 *noun* an error correcting communications protocol that can transfer data accurately even over poor-quality telephone connections

mobile phone /ˌməʊbaɪl ˈfəʊn/ *noun* a small, portable device that lets someone make and receive telephone calls. Also called **cellular phone**

COMMENT: Older mobile phone standards transmitted the user's voice as an analog radio signal; current phones convert the voice to digital data and transmit this via a radio signal. New mobile phones provide data and messaging services as well as basic telephone functions: some include built-in modems to provide dial-up access to the Internet, many allow text messages to be transmitted to other phone users and some incorporate an electronic diary, organiser and address book. Current mobile telephones transmit information using the GSM, PCS or GPRS standard and can provide basic Internet access using WAP and GPRS.

mock-up /ˈmɒk ʌp/ *noun* a model of a new product for testing or to show to possible customers

MOD /mɒd/ *noun* the remainder after the division of one number by another. Full form **modulus**

modal /ˈməʊd(ə)l/ *adjective* **1.** referring to modes ○ *Dialog boxes are normally modal windows.* **2.** (*in Windows*) referring to a window that is displayed and does not allow a user to do anything outside it

mode /məʊd/ *noun* a way of doing something

'The approach being established by the Jedec committee provides for burst mode data transfer clocked at up to 100MHz.' [*Computing*]

Mode 1 /ˈməʊd wʌn/ *noun* an encoding format used on compact discs that has error-detection and -correction codes

Mode 2 /ˈməʊd tuː/ *noun* an encoding format with two forms, form 1, which is the same as Mode 1, and form 2, which requires no processing and allows data to be sent straight to the output channel

model /ˈmɒd(ə)l/ *noun* **1.** a small copy of something to show what it will look like when finished ○ *He showed us a model of the new computer centre building.* **2.** a style, type or version of a product ○ *The new model B has taken the place of model A.* ■ *adjective* which is a perfect example to be copied ○ *a model agreement* ■ *verb* to make a computerised model of a new product or of a system, e.g. the economic system (NOTE: **modelling – modelled.** The US spellings are **modeling – modeled.**)

modelling /ˈmɒd(ə)lɪŋ/ *noun* the process of creating computer models

modem /ˈməʊˌdem/, **MODEM** *noun* a device that allows data to be sent over telephone lines by converting binary signals from a computer into analog sound signals which can be transmitted over a telephone line. Full form **modulator/demodulator**

'AST Research has bundled together a notebook PC with a third-party PCMCIA fax modem technology for a limited-period special offer.' [*Computing*]

COMMENT: The process of converting binary signals to analog is called 'modulation'. When the signal is received, another converter reverses the process (called 'demodulation'). Both parts must be working according to the same standards.

modem eliminator /ˌməʊdem ɪˈlɪmɪneɪtə/ *noun* a cable or device that allows two computers to communicate via their serial ports without using modems

modem standards /ˈməʊdem ˌstændədz/ *plural noun* rules defining transmitting frequencies and other factors which allow different modems to communicate

moderated list /ˌmɒd(ə)rətɪd ˈlɪst/, **moderated mailing list** *noun* a mailing list in which a moderator reads all the material that has been submitted before it is distributed to the users on the list

moderated newsgroup /ˌmɒd(ə)rətɪd ˈnjuːzgruːp/ *noun* a newsgroup in which a moderator reads all the material that has been submitted before it is published in the newsgroup (NOTE: Most newsgroups are not moderated and anyone can write anything. Moderated newsgroups usually have a -d after their name.)

moderator /'mɒdə,reɪtə/ *noun* a person responsible for reading messages sent to a mailing list or newsgroup and editing any messages that do not conform to the rules of the list, e.g. by deleting commercial messages

modification /,mɒdɪfɪ'keɪʃ(ə)n/ *noun* a change made to something ○ *The modifications to the system allow it to be run as part of a LAN.*

modification loop /,mɒdɪfɪ'keɪʃ(ə)n luːp/ *noun* a set of instructions within a loop that change other instructions or data within a program

modified frequency modulation /,mɒdɪfaɪd 'friːkwənsi ,mɒdjʊleɪʃ(ə)n/ *noun* full form of **MFM**

modifier /'mɒdɪ,faɪə/ *noun* a programming instruction that alters the normal action of a command

modify /'mɒdɪ,faɪ/ *verb* to change something or make something fit a different use ○ *The keyboard was modified for European users.* (NOTE: modifies – modifying – modified)

Modula-2 /,mɒdjulə 'tuː/ *noun* a high-level programming language derived from Pascal that supports modular programming techniques and data abstraction

modular /'mɒdjʊlə/ *adjective* referring to a method of constructing hardware or software products by connecting several smaller blocks together to produce a customised product

modularisation, **modularization** *noun* the process of designing programs from a set of standard modules

modularity /,mɒdjʊ'lærɪti/ *noun* the state or fact of being made up from modules ○ *The modularity of the software or hardware allows the system to be changed.*

modular programming /,mɒdjʊlə 'prəʊɡræmɪŋ/ *noun* programming with small individually written sections of computer code that can be made to fit into a structured program and can be called up from a main program

modulate /'mɒdjʊ,leɪt/ *verb* to change a carrier wave so that it can carry data

(NOTE: modulates – modulating – modulated)

modulated signal /,mɒdjʊleɪtɪd 'sɪɡn(ə)l/ *noun* a constant frequency and amplitude carrier signal that is used in a modulated form to transmit data

modulating signal /'mɒdjuleɪtɪŋ ,sɪɡn(ə)l/ *noun* a signal to be transmitted that is used to modulate a carrier

modulator /'mɒdjʊleɪtə/ *noun* an electronic circuit that varies a carrier signal according to an applied signal

modulator/demodulator /,mɒdjʊleɪtə diː'mɒdjʊleɪtə/ *noun* full form of **modem**

module /'mɒdjuːl/ *noun* **1.** a small section of a large program that can, if required, function independently as a program in its own right **2.** a self-contained piece of hardware that can be connected with other modules to form a new system ○ *A multifunction analog interface module includes analog-to-digital and digital-to-analog converters.*

modulo arithmetic /'mɒdjuləʊ ə ,rɪθmətɪk/ *noun* a branch of arithmetic that uses the remainder of one number when divided by another

modulo-N /,mɒdjuləʊ 'en/ *noun* modulo arithmetic using base N

modulo-N check /,mɒdjuləʊ 'en tʃek/ *noun* an error detection test using the remainder from a modulo arithmetic operation on data

modulus /'mɒdjʊləs/ *noun* full form of **MOD**

moiré effect /'mwɑːreɪ ɪ,fekt/ *noun* an interference pattern caused by printing with the wrong screen angle

momentary switch /'məʊmənt(ə)ri swɪtʃ/ *noun* a switch that only conducts while it is being pressed

monadic Boolean operation /mɒ ,nædɪk ,buːliən ,ɒpə'reɪʃ(ə)n/ *noun* a logical operation on only one word, such as NOT. Also called **monadic operator**

monadic operation /mɒ,nædɪk ,ɒpə 'reɪʃ(ə)n/ *noun* an operation that uses one operand to produce one result

monitor /'mɒnɪtə/ *noun* **1.** a VDU used to display high quality text or graphics, generated by a computer **2.** a system that watches for faults or failures in a circuit ■ *verb* **1.** to check or to examine how something is working ○ *He is monitoring the progress of the trainee programmers.* **2.** to look after and supervise a process or experiment to make sure it is operating correctly ○ *The machine monitors each signal as it is sent out.*

monitor program /'mɒnɪtə ˌprəʊɡræm/ *noun* a computer program that allows basic commands. e.g. load a program or examine the state of devices, to be entered to operate a system.

monitor unit /'mɒnɪtə ˌjuːnɪt/ *noun* same as **VDU**

mono- /mɒnəʊ/ *prefix* single or one

monoaural /ˌmɒnəʊ'ɔːrəl/ *adjective* having one source of sound or one sound signal. Compare **stereo**

monochrome /'mɒnəkrəʊm/ *adjective*, *noun* referring to an image in one colour, usually shades of grey and black and white

monochrome display adapter /ˌmɒnəkrəʊm dɪ'spleɪ əˌdæptə/ *noun* a video adapter standard used in early PC systems that could display text in 25 lines of 80 columns. Abbr **MDA**

monochrome monitor /ˌmɒnəkrəʊm 'mɒnɪtə/ *noun* a computer monitor that displays text and graphics in black, white and shades of grey instead of colours

monolithic driver /mɒnəˌlɪθɪk 'draɪvə/ *noun* a piece of driver software that has a range of different functions or applications within one program

monomode fibre /'mɒnəʊməʊd ˌfaɪbə/ *noun* same as **single mode fibre**

monoprogramming system /'mɒnəʊˌprəʊɡræmɪŋ ˌsɪstəm/ *noun* a computer batch processing system that executes one program at a time. Compare **multi-programming system**

monospaced /'mɒnəʊspeɪst/ *adjective* referring to a font in which each character has the same width. Compare **proportionally spaced**

monospaced font /ˌmɒnəʊspeɪst 'fɒnt/ *noun* a font in which each character has the same width, making it easy to align tables and columns ○ *In Windows, the monospaced font is called Courier.*

Monte Carlo method /ˌmɒnti 'kɑːləʊ ˌmeθəd/ *noun* a statistical analysis technique

morphing /'mɔːfɪŋ/ *noun* a special effect used in multimedia and games in which one image gradually turns into another

MOS /ˌem əʊ 'es/ *noun* a production and design method for a certain family of inte-

grated circuits using patterns of metal conductors and oxide deposited onto a semiconductor. Full form **metal oxide semiconductor.** ◊ **MOSFET**

mosaic /məʊ'zeɪɪk/ *noun* a display character used in videotext systems that is made up of small dots

Mosaic /məʊ'zeɪɪk/ a trade name for a popular browser software used to view webpages on the Internet

MOSFET /'mɒsfet/ *noun* a high power and high speed field effect transistor manufactured using MOS techniques. Full form **metal oxide semiconductor field effect transistor**

MOS memory /ˌem əʊ es 'mem(ə)ri/ *noun* a solid-state memory using MOSFETs to store binary data

most significant bit /ˌməʊst sɪɡ ˌnɪfɪkənt 'bɪt/ *noun* full form of **msb** ○ *The most significant bit in an eight bit binary word represents 128 in decimal notation.*

most significant digit, most significant character *noun* full form of **MSD**

motherboard /'mʌðəbɔːd/ *noun* the main printed circuit board of a system, containing most of the components and connections for expansion boards and other features

motion JPEG /ˌməʊʃ(ə)n 'dʒeɪ ˌpeɡ/ *noun* full form of **MJPEG**

motion picture experts group /ˌməʊʃ(ə)n ˌpɪktʃə 'ekspɜːts ɡruːp/ *noun* full form of **MPEG**

Motorola /ˌməʊtə'rəʊlə/ a company that designs and makes the 68000 range of processors that were used in the original Apple Mac computers. Its latest processor is the PowerPC chip that is used in workstations and newer Apple Mac computers. Compare **Intel**

mount /maʊnt/ *verb* **1.** to fix a device or circuit onto a base ○ *The chips are mounted in sockets on the PCB.* **2.** to insert a disk in a disk drive or inform an operating system that a disk drive is ready to be used

mouse /maʊs/ *noun* a small hand-held input device moved on a flat surface to control the position of a cursor on the screen (NOTE: The plural is **mouses** or **mice**.)

'This project has now borne fruit, with the announcement last week of Windots, a project which allows users to 'see' Windows screens in a Braille form of Ascii. Other areas of research include a sound system which allows a sound to 'move', mirroring the movement of a mouse.' [*Computing*]

mouse acceleration /maʊs ək͵selə
'reɪʃ(ə)n/ *noun* a feature of some mouse
driver software that will move the mouse
pointer at different speeds according to the
speed at which you move the mouse rather
than the distance

mouse-driven /maʊs 'drɪv(ə)n/ *adjective* referring to software which uses a
mouse rather than a keyboard for input

mouse driver /maʊs 'draɪvə/ *noun* a
program which converts positional data
sent from a mouse to a standard form of
coordinates that can be used by any software

mouse pointer /maʊs 'pɔɪntə/ *noun* a
small arrow displayed on screen that
moves around as the mouse is moved

mouse sensitivity /maʊs ͵sensə
'tɪvəti/ *noun* the ratio of how far the
pointer moves on screen in relation to the
distance you move the mouse (NOTE: High
mouse sensitivity means that a small
movement of the mouse results in a
small movement of the pointer.)

mouse tracking /maʊs 'trækɪŋ/ *noun*
inverse of mouse sensitivity (NOTE: High
mouse tracking means that a small
movement of the mouse results in a large
movement of the pointer.)

M out of N code /͵em aʊt əv 'en
͵kəʊd/ *noun* a coding system providing
error detection on the basis that each valid
character which is N bits long must contain M binary 'one' bits

movable /'muːvəb(ə)l/ *adjective* which
can be moved

movable head disk /͵muːvəb(ə)l hed
'dɪsk/ *noun* a magnetic disk head assembly that moves across the disk until the required track is reached

move /muːv/ *verb* to change the position
of something

move block /'muːv ͵blɒk/ *noun* a command which changes the place of a block
of text identified by block markers

movement /'muːvmənt/ *noun* the act
of changing position or of changing the
position of something

movement file /'muːvmənt faɪl/ *noun*
a file which continues recent changes or
transactions to records, which is then used
to update a master file

movie file /'muːvi faɪl/ *noun* a file
stored on disk that contains a series of images that make up an animation or video
clip

Moving Pictures Expert Group
/͵muːvɪŋ ͵pɪktʃəs 'ekspɜːt ͵gruːp/ *noun*
full form of **MPEG**

MP3 /͵em piː 'θriː/ *noun* a way of encoding digital audio data into a compressed
data format that is approximately one
twelfth the size of the original without per-
ceptible loss of quality. MP3 files (that
normally have the file name extension
'MP3') are now one of the most popular
ways of storing and distributing music
over the Internet. Because MP3 files are
compact and easy to copy, they are relatively quick to download and very easy to
distribute – which is causing problems for
the original artists who are trying to protect their copyright material. Once you
have an MP3 file you can listen to it by
opening it and playing it with special software on your computer or by transferring
it to a dedicated pocket-sized device that
stores the file in its memory, has no moving parts and but can play back CD-quality
music. Full form **MPEG audio level 3**

COMMENT: MP3 files, which usually have the
file name extension MP3, are now one of the
most popular ways of storing and distributing
music over the Internet. Because MP3 files
are compact and easy to copy, they are relatively quick to download and very easy to distribute, which is causing problems for the original artists who are trying to protect their copyright material. Once you have an MP3 file
you can listen to it by opening it and playing it
with special software on your computer or by
transferring it to a dedicated pocket-sized device that stores the file in its memory, and has
no moving parts but that can play back CD-
quality music.

MPC /͵em piː 'siː/ *noun* an outdated set
of minimum requirements for a PC that
will allow it to run most multimedia software. Full form **multimedia PC**

MPEG /'em peg/ *noun* a group of developers that have defined a series of standards to improve audio and video quality
but at the same time increase data compression so that the audio or video information takes less space but retains its quality. Full form **moving pictures expert
group**. ◊ **JPEG** (NOTE: MPEG is often
used to compress video clips and its de-
rivative standard MP3 provides one of
the most popular ways of compressing
and storing audio information, while
JPEG provides a popular way to store
compressed still images.)

MPEG audio level 3 /͵em peg ͵ɔːdiəʊ
͵lev(ə)l 'θriː/ *noun* full form of **MP3**

MPPP /ˌem piː piː 'piː/ *noun* communications protocol used with ISDN to link the two B-channels in a standard ISDN adapter to create a transmission channel that can transfer data at a higher speed. Full form **multi-link point to point protocol**

MPS *abbr* microprocessor system

MPU *abbr* microprocessor unit

ms *abbr* millisecond

msb /ˌem es 'biː/, **MSB** *noun* a bit in a word that represents the greatest value or weight, usually the bit furthest to the left. Full form **most significant bit**

MSCDEX /ˌem es siː diː 'eks/ *noun* driver software installed on a PC to allow DOS and Windows to control a CD-ROM drive. Full form **Microsoft Compact Disc Extensions**

MSD /ˌem es 'diː/ *noun* the digit at the far left of a number, which represents the greatest power of the base. Full form **most significant digit**

MS-DOS /ˌem es 'dɒs/ a trade name for an operating system for the IBM PC range of personal computers that managed data storage onto disks, display output and user input. Windows supports MS-DOS programs through the Command Prompt, which emulates MS-DOS. Full form **Microsoft DOS** (NOTE: MS-DOS is a single-user, single-tasking operating system that is controlled by a command-line interface.)

MSF time format /ˌem es ef 'taɪ ˌfɔːmæt/ *noun* a time format that counts frames per second used by MCI, usually used by CD-audio devices, in which there are 75 frames per second

MSI *abbr* medium scale integration

MSN a trade name for an Internet portal. Full form **Microsoft Network**

MS-Windows /ˌem es 'wɪndəʊz/ same as **Windows**

MSX /ˌem es 'eks/ *noun* a hardware and software standard for home computers that can use interchangeable software

MTA /ˌem tiː 'eɪ/ *noun* software that temporarily stores a new email message and then sends it to its correct destination. Full form **message transfer agent** (NOTE: In some email software applications, there are several message transfer agents, one for each type of delivery method such as Internet, fax or LAN.)

MTBF /ˌem tiː biː 'ef/ *noun* the average period of time that a piece of equipment will operate between failures. Full form **mean time between failures**

MTC /ˌem tiː 'siː/ *noun* a system of messages used to synchronise MIDI sequences with an external device, e.g. an SMPTE time code. Full form **MIDI time code**

MTF /ˌem tiː 'ef/ *noun* the average period of time for which a device will operate, usually continuously, before failing. Full form **mean time to failure**

MUA /ˌem juː 'eɪ/ *noun* software used to create and read email messages that creates a message in the correct format and standard and passes this to the mail transfer agent that is responsible for transferring the message over the network. Full form **mail user agent**

MUD /ˌem tiː 'eɪ/ *noun* **1.** a virtual online space in which several people can participate in collaborative projects at the same time. Full form **multiuser domain 2.** an adventure game played by multiple users over the Internet. Full form **multiuser dungeon**

multi- /mʌlti/ *prefix* many or more than one

multi-access system /ˌmʌltɪ ˌækses 'sɪstəm/ *noun* a computer system that allows several users to access one file or program at the same time. Also called **multiple access system**

multi-address /ˌmʌltɪ ə'dres/, **multi-address instruction** /ˌmʌltɪ əˌdres ɪn 'strʌkʃən/ *noun* an instruction that contains more than one address of data , locations or input/output

multibank dynamic random access memory /ˌmʌltɪbæŋk daɪ ˌnæmɪk ˌrændəm ˌækses 'mem(ə)ri/ *noun* full form of **MDRAM**

multi-board computer /ˌmʌlti bɔːd kəm'pjuːtə/ *noun* a computer which has several integrated circuit boards connected with a motherboard

multibus system /ˌmʌltɪbʌs 'sɪstəm/, **multibus architecture** /ˌmʌltɪbʌs 'ɑːkɪtektʃə/ *noun* computer architecture that uses a high speed bus between CPU and main memory and a slower bus between CPU and other peripherals. Also called **multiple bus system, multiple bus architecture**

multicast /'mʌltɪkɑːst/ *verb* to transmit one message to a group of recipients

COMMENT: This could be as simple as sending an email message to a list of email addresses or posting a message to a mailing list. It can also refer to more complex transfers such as a teleconference or videoconference in which several users link together by telephone or video link. A broadcast, in comparison, refers to the process of sending a message to anyone who could receive the message rather than a select group of recipients. Narrowcasting is very similar in concept to a multicasting, but is normally used to refer to the concept, whereas multicasting refers to the technology used.

multicast packet /ˌʌltɪkɑːst 'pækɪt/ noun a data packet that is sent to a selected set of network addresses, as opposed to a broadcast packet, which is sent to all stations in a network

multichannel /ˌmʌlti'tʃæn(ə)l/ adjective with more than one channel

multicolour /ˌmʌlti'kʌlə/ adjective with several colours

multicolour graphics adapter /ˌmʌltikʌlə 'græfɪks əˌdæptə/ noun full form of **MCGA**

multidimensional /ˌmʌltidaɪ'menʃən(ə)l/ adjective with features in more than one dimension

multidimensional array /ˌmʌltɪdaɪmenʃ(ə)n(ə)l ə'reɪ/ noun a number of arrays arranged in parallel, providing depth

multidimensional language /ˌmʌltɪdaɪmenʃ(ə)n(ə)l 'læŋgwɪdʒ/ noun a programming language that can be represented in a number of ways

multi-disk /ˌmʌltɪ 'dɪsk/ adjective referring to several types of disk

multi-disk option /'mʌltɪ dɪsk ˌɒpʃ(ə)n/ noun a system that can have disk drives installed in a number of sizes

multi-disk reader /ˌmʌltɪ dɪsk 'riːdə/ noun a device which can read from various sizes and formats of disk

multidrop circuit /'mʌltɪdrɒp ˌsɜːkɪt/ noun a network allowing communications between a number of terminals and a central computer, but not directly between terminals

MultiFinder /'mʌltifaɪndə/ noun a version of Apple Macintosh Finder that supports multitasking

multifrequency monitor /ˌmʌltifriːkwənsi 'mɒnɪtə/ noun same as **multisync monitor**

multifunction, multifunctional adjective which has several functions ○ A multifunction analog interface module includes analog to digital and digital to analog converters.

multifunction card /ˌmʌltɪfʌnkʃ(ə)n 'kɑːd/ noun an add-on circuit board that

provides many features to upgrade a computer

multifunction workstation /ˌmʌltɪfʌnkʃ(ə)n 'wɜːkˌsteɪʃ(ə)n/ noun a workstation where several tasks can be carried out

multilayer /ˌmʌlti'leɪə/ adjective referring to a printed circuit board that has several layers or interconnecting conduction tracks

multilevel /ˌmʌlti'lev(ə)l/ adjective referring to a signal with a number of possible values

multiline adjective in a text box, referring to a display of text broken into several lines rather than as a single continuous line. Also called **multiple line**

multi-link point to point protocol /ˌmʌlti lɪŋk ˌpɔɪnt tə ˌpɔɪnt 'pəʊtəkɒl/ noun full form of **MPPP**

multilink system /'mʌltɪlɪŋk ˌsɪstəm/ noun a system in which there is more than one connection between two points

multimedia /ˌmʌlti'miːdiə/ adjective combining sound, graphics, animation, video and text within an application

'The Oracle Media Server is a multimedia database designed to run on massively parallel computers, running hundreds of transactions per second and managing multiple data types, such as video, audio and text.' [*Computing*]

multimedia card /ˌmʌltimiːdiə 'kɑːd/ noun full form of **MMC**

multimedia developer's kit /ˌmʌltimiːdiə dɪ'veləpəz kɪt/ noun full form of **MDK**

multimedia extensions /ˌmʌlti miːdiə ɪk'stenʃ(ə)nz/ plural noun full form of **MMX**

multimedia Internet mail extensions /ˌmʌltimiːdiə ˌɪntənet 'meɪl ɪkˌstenʃ(ə)nz/ noun full form of **MIME**

multimedia PC /ˌmʌltimiːdiə ˌpiː 'siː/ noun full form of **MPC**

multimedia-ready /ˌmʌltimiːdiə 'redi/ adjective referring to a PC that has all the extra equipment requirement to run most multimedia software

multimode fibre /ˌmʌltɪməʊd 'faɪbə/ noun a commonly used type of optic fibre that uses a glass fibre with a diameter of between 50 and 125 microns and can carry several different frequencies of light with a maximum bandwidth of 2.5 Gbps (NOTE: The disadvantage is that because the fibre is wide, the light disperses quickly and so repeaters need to be installed to boost the signal.)

multipass overlap /ˌmʌltɪpɑːs ˈəʊvəlæp/ *noun* a system of producing higher quality print from a dot matrix printer by repeating the line of characters but shifted slightly, so making the dots less noticeable

multiphase program /ˌmʌltɪfeɪz ˈprəʊgræm/ *noun* a program that requires more than one fetch operation before execution is complete

multi platform /ˌmʌltɪ ˈplætˌfɔːm/ *adjective* referring to software that can run on several different hardware platforms

multiple /ˈmʌltɪp(ə)l/ *adjective* having many parts

multiple access system /ˌmʌltɪp(ə)l ˈækses ˌsɪstəm/ *noun* same as **multi-access system**

multiple address code /ˌmʌltɪp(ə)l ə ˈdres ˌkəʊd/ *noun* an instruction with more than one address for the operands, result and the location of the next instruction to be executed

multiple base page /ˌmʌltɪp(ə)l beɪs ˈpeɪdʒ/ *noun* a multi-user system in which each user and the operating system have one page of main memory, which can then call up other pages within main memory

multiple instruction stream-multiple data stream /ˌmʌltɪp(ə)l ɪn ˌstrʌkʃən ˌstriːm ˌmʌltɪp(ə)l ˈdeɪtə ˌstriːm/ *noun* full form of **MIMD**

multiple instruction stream-single data stream /ˌmʌltɪp(ə)l ɪnˌstrʌkʃən ˌstriːm ˌsɪŋg(ə)l ˈdeɪtə ˌstriːm/ *noun* full form of **MISD**

multiple line *adjective* same as **multi-line**

multiple precision /ˌmʌltɪp(ə)l prɪ ˈsɪʒ(ə)n/ *noun* the use of more than one byte of data for number storage to increase possible precision

multiplex /ˈmʌltɪpleks/ *verb* to combine several messages in the same transmission medium

multiplexed bus /ˌmʌltɪpleksd ˈbʌs/ *noun* one bus used to carry address, data and control signals at different times

multiplexor /ˈmʌltɪpleksə/ *noun* full form of **MUX** ○ *A 4 to 1 multiplexor combines four inputs into a single output.*

multiplicand /ˌmʌltɪplɪˈkænd/ *noun* a number which is multiplied by another number, the multiplier

multiplication /ˌmʌltɪplɪˈkeɪʃ(ə)n/ *noun* a mathematical operation that adds one number to itself a number of times ○ *The multiplication of 5 and 3 = 15.*

multiplication sign /ˌmʌltɪplɪ ˈkeɪʃ(ə)n saɪn/ *noun* a printed or written sign (x) used to show that numbers are multiplied

multiplier /ˈmʌltɪplaɪə/ *noun* a number which multiplies a multiplicand

multiply /ˈmʌltɪˌplaɪ/ *verb* to perform the mathematical operation of multiplication (NOTE: multiplies – multiplying – multiplied)

multipoint /ˈmʌltɪpɔɪnt/ *adjective* referring to a connection with several lines, attaching several terminals to a single line to a single computer

multiprecision /ˌmʌltɪprɪˈsɪʒ(ə)n/ *noun* the use of more than one data word to represent numbers, increasing the range or precision possible

multiprocessing system /ˌmʌltɪ ˈprəʊsesɪŋ ˌsɪstəm/ *noun* a system where several processing units work together sharing the same memory

multiprocessor /ˈmʌltɪˌprəʊsesə/ *noun* a number of processing units acting together or separately but sharing the same area of memory

multiprocessor interleaving /ˌmʌltɪprəʊsesə ˌɪntəˈliːvɪŋ/ *noun* an operation in which each processor in a multiprocessor system deals with a section of one or more processes

multi-programming system /ˌmʌltɪ ˈprəʊgræmɪŋ ˌsɪstəm/ *noun* an operating system used to execute more than one program apparently simultaneously, each program being executed a little at a time. Compare **monoprogramming system**

multipurpose Internet mail extensions /ˌmʌltɪpɜːpəs ˌɪntənet ˈmeɪl ɪk ˌstenʃ(ə)nz/ *noun* full form of **MIME**

multi-scan monitor /ˌmʌltɪ skæn ˈmɒnɪtə/ *noun* same as **multisync monitor**

multisession-compatible /ˌmʌltɪseʃ(ə)n kəmˈpætɪb(ə)l/ *adjective* referring to a CD-ROM drive that can read PhotoCD discs or other discs that have been created in several goes

multi statement line /ˌmʌltɪ ˌsteɪtmənt ˈlaɪn/ *noun* a line from a computer program that contains more than one instruction or statement

multistation access unit /ˌmʌltɪsteɪʃ(ə)n ˈækses ˌjuːnɪt/ *noun* a central hub used to connect together cables in a Token Ring network. Abbr **MAU**

multisync monitor /mʌltɪˌsɪŋk ˈmɒnɪtə/ *noun* a monitor which contains circuitry to lock onto the required scanning frequency of any type of graphics card ○ *If you want to plug a monitor into PCs with VGA, EGA and MDA adapters, you'll need a multisync monitor.* Also called **multifrequency monitor, multiscan monitor**

multitasking /ˈmʌltiˌtɑːskɪŋ/ *noun* the ability of a computer system to run two or more programs at the same time ○ *The system is multi-user and multi-tasking.*

'X is the underlying technology which allows Unix applications to run under a multi-user, multitasking GUI. It has been adopted as the standard for the Common Open Software Environment, proposed recently by top Unix vendors including Digital, IBM and Sun.' [*Computing*]

COMMENT: Few small systems are capable of simultaneous multitasking, since each program would require its own processor. This is overcome by allocating to each program an amount of processing time, executing each a little at a time so that they will appear to run simultaneously due to the speed of the processor and the relatively short gaps between programs.

multi terminal system /ˌmʌltɪ ˌtɜːmɪn(ə)l ˈsɪstəm/ *noun* a system where several terminals are linked to a single CPU

multithread /ˈmʌltiθred/ *noun* a program design using more than one logical path through it, each path being concurrently executed

multiuser domain /ˌmʌltijuːzə də ˈmeɪn/ *noun* full form of **MUD**

multiuser dungeon /ˌmʌltijuːzə ˈdʌndʒən/ *noun* full form of **MUD**

multiuser program /ˌmʌltijuːzə ˈprəɡræm/ *noun* a software diary utility that allows many users to enter appointments and schedule meetings with other users. Also called **network calendar program**

multiuser system /ˌmʌltijuːzə ˈsɪstəm/ *noun* a computer system that can support more than one user at a time ○ *The program runs on a standalone machine or a multi-user system.*

multi-window editor /ˌmʌlti ˌwɪndəʊ ˈedɪtə/ *noun* a program used for creating and editing a number of applications programs independently, each in a separate window on screen at the same time

Murray code /ˈmʌri kəʊd/ *noun* a code used for teleprinters that uses only 5 bits

musical instrument digital interface /ˌmjuːzɪk(ə)l ˌɪnstrʊmənt ˌdɪdʒɪt(ə)l ˈɪntəfeɪs/ *noun* full form of **MIDI**

music chip /ˈmjuːzɪk tʃɪp/ *noun* an integrated circuit capable of generating musical sounds and tunes

MUX /ˌem juː ˈeks/ *noun* a circuit that combines a number of inputs into a smaller number of outputs. Full form **multiplexor**. Compare **demultiplexor**

MX record /ˌem eks ˈrekɔːd/ *noun* same as **mail exchange record** ○ *Mail sent to 'smith&pcp.co.uk' will be sent to the 'pcp.co.uk' server by the MX record, the local server then has to send the message to the user 'smith'.*

My Computer /ˌmaɪ kəmˈpjuːtə/ *noun* an icon that is normally in the upper left-hand corner of the screen on a computer running Windows, containing an overview of the PC

N

n *abbr* nano-

NAK *abbr* negative acknowledgement

name /neɪm/ *noun* an ordinary word used to identify an address in machine language

name registration /neɪm ˌredʒɪ ˈstreɪʃ(ə)n/ *noun* same as **domain name registration**

name resolution /neɪm ˌrezə ˈluːʃ(ə)n/ *noun* the process of converting a domain name into its numerical IP address

name server /neɪm ˈsɜːvə/ *noun* a computer on the Internet that provides a domain name service to any other computer

namespace /ˈneɪmspeɪs/ *noun* a group of unique names (NOTE: In a small office network the namespace might include 20 users; in the Internet the namespace runs into hundreds of millions.)

name table /neɪm ˈteɪb(ə)l/ *noun* a list of reserved words or commands in a language and the addresses in the computer that refer to them

naming services /ˈneɪmɪŋ ˌsɜːvɪsɪz/ *noun* a method of assigning each user or node or computer on a network a unique name that allows other users to access shared resources even over a wide area network

NAND function /ˈnænd ˌfʌŋkʃ(ə)n/ *noun* a logical function whose output is false if all inputs are true, and true if any input is false

COMMENT: The NAND function is equivalent to an AND function with a NOT function at the output. The output is 0 only if both inputs are 1; if one input is 1 and the other 0, or if both inputs are 0, then the output is 1.

NAND gate /ˈnænd geɪt/ *noun* an electronic circuit that provides a NAND function

nano- /nænəʊ/ *prefix* one thousand millionth. Abbr **n**

nanocircuit /ˈnænəʊˌsɜːkɪt/ *noun* a set of electronic and logic circuits that can re-

spond to impulses within nanoseconds. Also called **nanosecond circuit**

nanosecond /ˈnænəʊˌsekənd/ *noun* one thousand millionth of a second

nanosecond circuit /ˈnænəʊˌsekənd ˌsɜːkɪt/ *noun* same as **nanocircuit**

Napster /ˈnæpstə/ a trade name for software that allows users to share files, normally MP3-format music files, over the Internet

COMMENT: Napster was originally used to distribute and share MP3 files with a personal recording of a commercial artist in an efficient way. The software, developed by Shawn Fanning, allowed anyone to download music from any another Napster user's computer. Once installed, the free software searches your hard disk for any MP3 music files, then allows other Napster users online to access these files from your hard disk, via the Internet. Because it allows music to be copied and shared very easily, Napster has become unpopular with the recording and music industry and was the subject of a legal case enforcing copyright over the Internet.

narrative /ˈnærətɪv/ *noun* a set of explanatory notes or comments to help a user operate a program

narrative statement /ˈnærətɪv ˌsteɪtmənt/ *noun* a statement which sets variables and allocates storage at the start of a program

narrow band ISDN /ˌnærəʊ bænd ˌaɪ es diː ˈen/ *noun* the ISDN communications system

narrowcast /ˈnærəʊkɑːst/ *verb* same as **multicast**

NAT /ˌen eɪ ˈtiː/ *noun* a system that allows a local area network to work with two sets of IP addresses for each computer or node in the network. Full form **network address translation**

COMMENT: The first set of addresses is used for internal traffic and the second set (often just one or two addresses) is used for external traffic, for example when accessing resources on the public Internet via a router. This system provides basic security against external attacks, for example using IP spoofing. Its main purpose is that it allows the local area network to use as many IP addresses as are required, but only using a minimal number of public IP addresses, which must be registered and allocated by an organisation such as InterNIC.

National Center for Supercomputing Applications /ˌnæʃ(ə)nəl ˌsentə fə ˈsuːpəkəmˌpjuːtɪŋ ˌæplɪkeɪʃ(ə)nz/ *noun* full form of **NCSA**

National Television System Committee /ˌnæʃ(ə)nəl ˌtelɪˈvɪʒ(ə)n ˌsɪstəm kəˌmɪti/ *noun* full form of **NTSC**

native compiler /ˌneɪtɪv kəmˈpaɪlə/ *noun* a compiler that produces code that will run on the same system on which it is running (NOTE: A cross-compiler produces code that will run on another hardware platform.)

native file format /ˌneɪtɪv ˈfaɪl ˌfɔːmæt/ *noun* a default file format, usually proprietary, that is used by an application to store its data on disk

native format /ˌneɪtɪv ˈfɔːmæt/ *noun* the first or basic format

native language /ˌneɪtɪv ˈlæŋgwɪdʒ/ *noun* a computer language that can be executed by a processor without the need for any special software, usually the processor's machine code

natural binary coded decimal /ˌnætʃ(ə)rəl ˌbaɪnəri ˌkəʊdɪd ˈdesɪm(ə)l/ *noun* a representation of single decimal digits as a pattern of 4 bits. Abbr **NBCD**

natural language /ˌnætʃ(ə)rəl ˈlæŋgwɪdʒ/ *noun* a language that is used or understood by humans ○ *The expert system can be programmed in a natural language.*

natural language processing /ˌnætʃ(ə)rəl ˈlæŋgwɪdʒ ˌprəʊsesɪŋ/ *noun* the use of artificial intelligence to process ordinary human languages, e.g. in machine translation

navigable /ˈnævɪgəb(ə)l/ *adjective* referring to a website that has been designed in such a way that the user can move from one section of the site to another by clicking on highlighted computer links

navigation /ˌnævɪˈgeɪʃ(ə)n/ *noun* the process of moving around a multimedia title using hotspots, buttons and a user interface

NBCD *abbr* natural binary coded decimal

NC *abbr* **1.** network computer **2.** numerical control

NCR paper /ˌen siː ˈɑː ˌpeɪpə/ *noun* a special type of paper impregnated with chemicals and used in multipart forms. Full form **no carbon required paper** (NOTE: When NCR paper is printed on by an impact printer, the writing also appears on the sheets below.)

NCSA /ˌen siː es ˈeɪ/ *noun* an organisation that helped define and create the World Wide Web with its Mosaic web browser. Full form **National Center for Supercomputing Applications**

NDIS /ˌen diː eɪ ˈes/ *noun* a standard command interface, defined by Microsoft, between network driver software and NICs, Full form **network driver interface specification**

NDR /ˌen diː ˈɑː/ *noun* a display system that continues to display previous characters when new ones are displayed. Full form **non destructive readout**

NEAR /nɪə/ *noun* a binary operator used in searches of computer text that returns true if it finds two words within a specified distance of each other within the text, and false otherwise

needle /ˈniːd(ə)l/ *noun* a tiny metal pin on a dot matrix printer which prints one of the dots

negate /nɪˈgeɪt/ *verb* to reverse the sign of a number ○ *If you negate 23.4 the result is –23.4.* (NOTE: negates – negating – negated)

negation /nɪˈgeɪʃ(ə)n/ *noun* the reversing of the sign of a number, e.g. from 5 to –5

negation gate /nɪˈgeɪʃ(ə)n geɪt/ *noun* a single input gate whose output is equal to the logical inverse of the input. Also called **NOT gate**

negative /ˈnegətɪv/ *adjective* meaning 'no'

negative acknowledgement /ˌnegətɪv əkˈnɒlɪdʒmənt/ *noun* a signal sent by a receiver to indicate that data has been incorrectly or incompletely received. Abbr **NAK**

negative number /ˌnegətɪv ˈnʌmbə/ *noun* a number which represents the number subtracted from zero, indicated by a minus sign in front of the number

negative-true logic /ˌnegətɪv ˈtruː ˌlɒdʒɪk/ *noun* the use of a lower voltage level to represent binary 1 than for binary 0

neither-nor function /ˌnaɪðə ˈnɔːr ˌfʌŋkʃ(ə)n/ *noun* a logical function whose output is false if any input is true

NEQ *abbr* nonequivalence function

NEQ function /'nek ˌfʌŋkʃ(ə)n/ *noun*
a logical function in which the output is
true if the inputs are not the same, otherwise the output is false

NEQ gate /'nek geɪt/ *noun* an electronic
implementation of a nonequivalence function

nerd /nɜːd/ *noun* a person who is ob-
sessed with computers and rarely talks or
thinks about anything that is not technologically exciting (*slang*)

nest /nest/ *verb* **1.** to insert a subroutine
within a program or another routine **2.** to
use a routine that calls itself recursively

nested loop /ˌnestd 'luːp/ *noun* a loop
inside another loop in the same program

nested macro call /ˌnestɪd 'mækrəʊ
ˌkɔːl/ *noun* a macro called from within another macro

nested structure /nestd 'strʌktʃə/
noun a section of a program in which one
control loop or subroutine is used within
another

nesting level /nestɪŋ 'lev(ə)l/ *noun* a
number of subroutines within a subroutine

nesting store /ˌnestɪŋ 'stɔː/ *noun* a
hardware stack (NOTE: Usually stacks are
implemented with software.)

NetBEUI /'net bjuːi/ *noun* an extended
version of the NetBIOS network protocol
developed by Microsoft, which cannot be
routed in a network. Full form **NetBIOS
Extended User Interface**

NetBIOS /'net ˌbaɪɒs/ *noun* a commonly used standard set of commands, originally developed by IBM, that allow application programs to carry out basic operations such as file sharing and transferring
data between nodes over a network ○ *This
software uses NetBIOS calls to manage
file sharing.* Full form **Network Basic Input Output System**

netiquette /'netɪket/ *noun* a set of unofficial rules that define good manners on
the Internet

netphone /'netfəʊn/ *noun* a phone that
uses the Internet to make connections and
carry voice messages

NetScape /'netskeɪp/ a software company that develops Internet applications

Netscape Navigator /ˌnetskeɪp
'nævɪgeɪtə/ a trade name for one of the
most popular web browsers that provides
many features including a news reader and
that supports Java applets

NetShow /'netʃəʊ/ a system developed by Microsoft to provide audio and
video delivery over the Internet without interruption or glitches in the video sequence

NetView /'netvjuː/ a trade name for a
network management architecture developed by IBM

NetWare /'netweə/ a trade name for a
network operating system, developed by
Novell, that runs on a range of hardware
platforms and supports file and print sharing and client-server applications

NetWare Loadable Module
/ˌnetweə ˌləʊdəb(ə)l 'mɒdjuːl/ a trade
name for an application that can run under
the NetWare operating system

network /'netwɜːk/ *noun* a system
made of a number of points or circuits that
are interconnected ■ *verb* to link points together in a network ○ *They run a system of
networked micros.*

'Asante Technologies has expanded its range of
Ethernet-to-LocalTalk converters with the release of
AsantePrint 8, which connects up to eight LocalTalk
printers, or other LocalTalk devices, to a high-speed
Ethernet network.' [*Computing*]

network adapter /'netwɜːk əˌdæptə/
noun same as **NIC**

network address /'netwɜːk əˌdres/
noun a part of an IP address that defines
the main network on which the domain is
located (NOTE: For class A networks this
is the first byte of the address, for class B
networks it is the first two bytes and for
class C networks it is the first three bytes.
The rest of the IP address forms the host
address.)

network address translation
/ˌnetwɜːk əˌdres trænsˈleɪʃ(ə)n/ *noun*
full form of **NAT** (*see*)

network administrator /ˌnetwɜːk əd
'mɪnɪstreɪtə/ *noun* a person who is responsible for looking after a network, with
responsibilities including installing, configuring and maintaining the network

network alert /ˌnetwɜːk əˈlɜːt/ *noun* a
message sent from the network operating
system to the user warning that the network hardware is not working properly

network analysis /'netwɜːk ə
ˌnæləsɪs/ *noun* the study of messages,
destinations and routes in a network to
provide a better operation

network architecture /ˌnetwɜːk
'ɑːkɪtektʃə/ *noun* the way in which a network is constructed, e.g. layers in an OSI
system

Network Basic Input Output System /ˌnetwɜːk ˌbeɪsɪk ˌɪnpʊt ˈaʊtpʊt ˌsɪstəm/ *noun* full form of **NetBIOS**

network computer /ˌnetwɜːk kəmˈpjuːtə/ *noun* a computer that is designed to run Java programs and access information using a web browser. Abbr **NC**

COMMENT: The network computer has a small desktop box that does not have a floppy disk drive. Instead it downloads any software it requires from a central server. Network computers are simpler and cheaper than current PCs and Apple Mac computers, and are designed to be easier to manage in a large company.

network controller /ˌnetwɜːk kənˈtrəʊlə/ *noun* a network user responsible for allocating disk space, answering queries and solving problems from other users of the same network

network control program /ˌnetwɜːk kənˈtrəʊl ˌprəʊgræm/ *noun* a piece of software that regulates the flow of and channels for data transmitted in a network

network database /ˌnetwɜːk ˈdeɪtəbeɪs/ *noun* a database structure in which data items can be linked together

network device driver /ˌnetˌwɜːk dɪ ˈvaɪs ˌdraɪvə/ *noun* a piece of software which controls and manages a n NIC to ensure that it functions correctly with other hardware and software in the computer

network diagram /ˌnetwɜːk ˈdaɪəgræm/ *noun* a graphical representation of the interconnections between points in a network

network directory /ˌnetwɜːk daɪ ˈrekt(ə)ri/ *noun* a directory that is stored on a disk drive on another computer in the network but can be accessed by anyone on the network

network drive /ˈnetwɜːk draɪv/ *noun* a disk drive that is part of another computer on a network but can be used by anyone on the network

network driver interface specification /ˌnetwɜːk ˌdraɪvə ˈɪntəfeɪs ˌspesɪfɪkeɪʃ(ə)n/ *noun* full form of **NDIS**

network file system /ˌnetwɜːk ˈfaɪl ˌsɪstəm/ *noun* a network protocol developed by Sun Microsystems that allows a computer to share its local disk drives with other users on a network and is now used as a standard across most of the Internet. Abbr **NFS**

network hardware /ˌnetwɜːk ˈhɑːdweə/ *noun* same as **networking hardware**

networking /ˈnetwɜːkɪŋ/ *noun* **1.** the working or organisation of a network **2.** the process of interconnecting two or more computers either in the same room or different buildings, in the same town or different towns, allowing them to exchange information

COMMENT: Networking allows a machine with a floppy disk drive to use another PC's hard disk when both machines are linked by a cable and are using networking software.

networking hardware /ˌnetwɜːkɪŋ ˈhɑːdweə/ *noun* the physical links, computers and control equipment that make up a network. Also called **network hardware**

networking software /ˌnetwɜːkɪŋ ˈsɒftweə/ *noun* software that is used to establish the link between a user's program and the network. Also called **network software**

networking specialist /ˈnetwɜːkɪŋ ˌspeʃəlɪst/ *noun* a company or person who specialises in designing and setting up networks ○ *This computer firm is a UK networking specialist.*

network interface card /ˌnetwɜːk ˈɪntəfeɪs ˌkɑːd/ *noun* full form of **NIC**

network-intrinsic application /ˌnetwɜːk ɪnˈtrɪnsɪk ˌæplɪkeɪʃ(ə)n/ *noun* an application that makes use of a network and its shared resources

network layer /ˈnetwɜːk ˌleɪə/ *noun* the third ISO/OSI layer that decides on the route to be used to send a packet of data

network management /ˌnetwɜːk ˈmænɪdʒmənt/ *noun* the organisation, planning, running and upkeep of a network

Network Neighborhood /ˌnetwɜːk ˈneɪbəhʊd/ *noun* a Windows 95 utility that allows you to view and manage connections to your computer

network news transfer protocol /ˌnetwɜːk njuːz ˈtrænsfɜː ˌprəʊtəkɒl/ *noun* full form of **NNTP**

network operating system /ˌnetwɜːk ˈɒpəreɪtɪŋ ˌsɪstəm/ *noun* an operating system running on a server computer, usually a dedicated one, that controls access to the network resources, managing network links, printing and users. Abbr **NOS**

network printer /ˌnetwɜːk ˈprɪntə/ *noun* a printer attached to a server or workstation that can be used by any user connected to the network

network processor /ˌnetwɜːk ˈprəʊsesə/ *noun* a signal multiplexor controlled by a microprocessor in a network

network protocol /ˌnetwɜːk ˈprəʊtəkɒl/ *noun* a set of handshaking signals that defines how a workstation sends data over a network without clashing with other data transmissions

network redundancy /ˌnetwɜːk rɪˈdʌndənsi/ *noun* the existence of extra links between points allowing continued operation in the event of one point failing

network server /ˌnetwɜːk ˈsɜːvə/ *noun* a computer which runs a network operating system and controls the basic network operations (NOTE: All the workstations in a LAN are connected to the central network server and users log onto a network server,)

network software /ˌnetwɜːk ˈsɒftweə/ *noun* same as **networking software**

network structure /ˌnetwɜːk ˈstrʌktʃə/ *noun* a data structure which allows each node to be connected to any of the others

network time protocol /ˌnetwɜːk ˈtaɪm ˌprəʊtəkɒl/ *noun* a protocol which provides an accurate time signal to computers on the Internet based on an atomic clock, allowing local computers to synchronise their clocks. Abbr **NTP**

network timing /ˌnetwɜːk ˈtaɪmɪŋ/ *noun* signals which correctly synchronise the transmission of data

network topology /ˌnetwɜːk təˈpɒlədʒi/ *noun* the layout of machines in a network, e.g. a star network, ring network or bus network, which will determine what cabling and interfaces are needed and what possibilities the network can offer

neural network /ˌnjʊərəl ˈnetwɜːk/ *noun* a system running an artificial intelligence program that attempts to simulate the way the brain works, how it learns and remembers

neutral /ˈnjuːtrəl/ *adjective* with no state, bias or voltage

neutral transmission /ˌnjuːtrəl trænzˈmɪʃ(ə)n/ *noun* a transmission system in which a voltage pulse and zero volts represent the binary digits 1 and 0

new /njuː/ *adjective* recent or not old ○ *They have installed a new computer system.*

newbie /ˈnjuːbi/ *noun* a new user of the Internet (*slang*)

new line character /ˌnjuː ˈlaɪn ˌkærɪktə/ *noun* a character that moves a cursor or printhead to the beginning of the next line

newsgroup /ˈnjuːzˌgruːp/ *noun* a feature of the Internet that provides free-for-all discussion forums

news reader /ˈnjuːz ˌriːdə/ *noun* a piece of software that allows a user to view the list of newsgroups and read the articles posted in each group or submit a new article

newswire /ˈnjuːzwaɪə/ *noun* an Internet service providing the latest information on current events

new technology /njuː tekˈnɒlədʒi/ *noun* electronic instruments which have recently been developed

Newton /ˈnjuːtən/ a trade name for a range of PDAs developed by the Apple Computer Corporation

next instruction register /ˌnekst ɪnˈstrʌkʃən ˌredʒɪstə/ *noun* a register in a CPU that contains the location where the next instruction to be executed is stored

nexus /ˈneksəs/ *noun* a connection point between units in a network

NFS *abbr* network file system

nibble /ˈnɪb(ə)l/ *noun* another spelling of **nybble**

NIC /ˌen aɪ ˈsiː/ *noun* an add-in board that connects a computer to a network. Full form **network interface card**. Also called **network adapter** (NOTE: The board converts the computer's data into electrical signals that are then transmitted along the network cable.)

NiCad /ˈnaɪkæd/ *noun* a type of rechargeable battery used in laptops but now superseded by the NiMH battery. Full form **nickel-cadmium**

COMMENT: NiCad batteries unfortunately have one problem called 'memory' which gradually reduces their ability to retain charge. To remove the memory you should condition a battery by running it right down so that it has no charge, before re-charging it.

nil pointer /nɪl ˈpɔɪntə/ *noun* a pointer used to indicate the end of a chained list of items

NiMH /ˌen aɪ em ˈeɪtʃ/ *noun* a type of rechargeable battery now used in laptops that has better charge-carrying ability than a NiCad battery, is quicker to charge and does not suffer from 'memory.' Full form **nickel metal hydride**

nine's complement /ˈnaɪnz ˌkɒmplɪmənt/ *noun* a decimal complement, equivalent to the binary one's complement, formed by subtracting each digit in the number from nine. ◊ **ten's complement**

n-key rollover /ˌen kiː ˈrəʊləʊvə/ *noun* a facility on a keyboard where each keystroke, (up to a maximum of n, is registered in sequence even if they are struck very fast (NOTE: Up to n keys can be stored.)

NLB *abbr* nonlinear behaviour

n-level logic /ˌen ˌlev(ə)l ˈlɒdʒɪk/ *noun* logic gate design in which no more than n gates occur in a series

NLP *abbr* neurolinguistic programming

NLQ *abbr* near-letter-quality

NMI *abbr* non maskable interrupt

NNTP /ˌen en tiː ˈpiː/ *noun* a standard method of distributing news messages on the Internet, one of the protocols within the TCP/IP protocol suite, that provides a way of creating, reading and distributing messages within newsgroups over the Internet. Full form **network news transfer protocol**

no-address operation /ˌnəʊ əˈdres ˌɒpəreɪʃ(ə)n/ *noun* an instruction which does not require an address within it

node /nəʊd/ *noun* an interconnection point in a structure or network ○ *A tree is made of branches that connect together at nodes.*

no-drop image /ˌnəʊ ˈdrɒp ˌɪmɪdʒ/ *noun* (*in a GUI*) an icon image displayed during a drag and drop operation when the pointer is over an object that cannot be the destination object and onto which it cannot be dropped

noise /nɔɪz/ *noun* a random signal present in addition to any wanted signal, caused by static, temperature, power supply, magnetic or electric fields and also from stars and the Sun

noise immunity /nɔɪz ɪˈmjuːnəti/ *noun* the ability of a circuit to ignore or filter out noise or to be protected from noise

noisy digit /ˌnɔɪzi ˈdɪdʒɪt/ *noun* a digit, usually not zero, added during the normalisation of a floating point number when in noisy mode

noisy mode /ˈnɔɪzi məʊd/ *noun* a floating point arithmetic system in which a digit other than a zero is deliberately added in the least significant position during the normalisation of a floating point number

nomenclature /nəʊˈmeŋklətʃə/ *noun* a predefined system for assigning words and symbols to represent numbers or terms

nomogram /ˈnɒməɡræm/, **nomograph** /ˈnɒməɡrɑːf/ *noun* a graphical system for solving one value given two others

non- /nɒn/ *prefix* not

nonaligned /ˌnɒnəˈlaɪnd/ *adjective* referring to two devices which are not correctly positioned in relation to each other, for optimum performance

nonaligned read head /nɒnəˌlaɪnd ˈriːd hed/ *noun* a read head that is not in the same position on a magnetic medium as the write head was, producing a loss of signal quality

non arithmetic shift /ˌnɒn ˌærɪθmetɪk ˈʃɪft/ *noun* same as **logical shift**

non breaking space /ˌnɒn ˌbreɪkɪŋ ˈspeɪs/ *noun* (*in word-processing or DTP software*) a space character that prevents two words being separated by a line break

noncompatibility /ˌnɒnkəmˌpætɪ ˈbɪlɪti/ *noun* inability of two or more pieces of hardware or software to exchange data or use the same peripherals

non dedicated server /ˌnɒn ˌdedɪkeɪtɪd ˈsɜːvə/ *noun* a computer that runs a network operating system in the background and can also be used to run normal applications at the same time

non destructive cursor /ˌnɒn dɪ ˌstrʌktɪv ˈkɜːsə/ *noun* a cursor on a display that does not erase characters already displayed as it passes over them ○ *The screen quickly became unreadable when using a non-destructive cursor.*

non destructive readout /ˌnɒn dɪ ˌstrʌktɪv ˈriːdaʊt/ *noun* full form of **NDR**

non destructive test /ˌnɒn dɪ ˌstrʌktɪv ˈtest/ *noun* a series of tests carried out on a piece of equipment without destroying it ○ *I will carry out a number of non-destructive tests on your computer, if it passes, you can start using it again.*

nonequivalence function /ˌnɒnɪ ˈkwɪvələns ˌfʌŋkʃən/ *noun* a logical function in which the output is true if the inputs are not the same, otherwise the output is false. Abbr **NEQ**

nonequivalence gate /ˌnɒnɪ ˈkwɪvələns ɡeɪt/ *noun* an electronic implementation of an NEQ function

nonerasable storage /ˈnɒnɪˌreɪzəb(ə)l ˈstɔːrɪdʒ/ *noun* a storage medium that cannot be erased and reused

non impact printer /ˌnɒn ɪmˌpækt ˈprɪntə/ *noun* a printer such as an ink-jet printer in which the character form does not hit a ribbon onto the paper

non interlaced /ˌnɒn ˈɪntəleɪsd/ *adjective* (*in a monitor*) referring to a system in which the picture electron beam scans each line of the display once during each refresh cycle (NOTE: The beam in an interlaced display scans every alternate line.)

nonlinear /nɒnˈlɪniə/ *adjective* referring to an electronic circuit whose output does not change linearly in proportion to its input

nonlinear video editing /nɒnˌlɪniə ˈvɪdiəʊ ˌedɪtɪŋ/ *noun* a method of editing a video sequence in which the video is digitised and stored in a computer and the editor can then cut and move frames in any order before outputting the finished sequence (NOTE: The finished sequence can either be produced directly from the computer output – though this is normally at a lower quality than the original because of compression losses – or the computer can output timecode instructions that can be used to edit the original videotape.)

non maskable interrupt /ˌnɒn ˌmɑːskəb(ə)l ˈɪntərʌpt/ *noun* a high priority interrupt signal that cannot be blocked and overrides all other commands. Abbr **NMI**

nonmodal /nɒnˈməʊd(ə)l/ *adjective* (*in a GUI*) displaying a window but still allowing a user to access other windows that are on-screen before closing the nonmodal window

non operable instruction /ˌnɒn ˌɒp(ə)rəb(ə)l ɪnˈstrʌkʃən/ *noun* an instruction that does not carry out any function, but increments the program counter

nonprinting code /ˌnɒnprɪntɪŋ ˈkəʊd/ *plural noun* a code that represents an action of the printer rather than a printed character ○ *The line width can be set using one of the non-printing codes, .LW, then a number.*

non-procedural language /nɒn prəˌsiːdʒ(ə)rəl ˈlæŋgwɪdʒ/ *noun* a programming language which does not execute statements one after another or calls subroutines, but instead defines a set of facts that can be queried

nonrepudiation /ˌnɒnrɪˌpjuːdiˈeɪʃ(ə)n/ *noun* the ability of the person who receives a message to identify its sender, especially by means of the digital signature on the message

non-return to zero /ˌnɒn rɪˌtɜːn tə ˈzɪərəʊ/ *noun* a representation of binary data in which the signal changes when the data changes state, and does not return to zero volts after each bit of data. Abbr **NRZ**

non scrollable /ˌnɒn ˈskrəʊləb(ə)l/ *adjective* referring to part of the screen display which is always displayed (NOTE: In a WP the text can scroll while instructions are nonscrollable.)

non volatile memory /ˌnɒn ˌvɒlətaɪl ˈmem(ə)ri/ *noun* a storage medium or memory that retains data even when the power has been switched off ○ *Bubble memory is a non-volatile storage.* Also called **nonvolatile storage, nonvolatile store**

non-volatile random access memory /ˌnɒn ˌvɒlətaɪl ˌrændəm ˌækses ˈmem(ə)ri/ *noun* full form of **NVRAM**

non volatile storage /ˌnɒn ˌvɒlətaɪl ˈstɔːrɪdʒ/, **nonvolatile store** *noun* same as **non volatile memory**

no-op instruction /nəʊ ɒp/, **no op** *noun* an instruction that does not carry out any functions but increments the program counter

no parity /nəʊ ˈpærəti/ *noun* data transmission which does not use a parity bit

NOR function /nɔːr ˈfʌŋkʃən/ *noun* a logical function whose output is false if either input is true

> COMMENT: The output is 1 only if both inputs are 0; if the two inputs are different or if both are 1, the output is 0.

NOR gate /ˈnɔːr geɪt/ *noun* an electric circuit or chip which performs a NOR function

normal /ˈnɔːm(ə)l/ *adjective* usual or which happens regularly ○ *The normal procedure is for backup copies to be made at the end of each day's work.*

normal form /ˈnɔːm(ə)l fɔːm/ *noun* a method of structuring information in a database to avoid redundancy and improve storage efficiency

normal format /ˈnɔːm(ə)l ˌfɔːmæt/ *noun* a standardised format for data storage

normalisation /ˌnɔːməlaɪˈzeɪʃ(ə)n/, **normalization** *noun* the process of normalising data

normalisation routine /ˌnɔːmələɪ 'zeɪʃ(ə)n ruːˌtiːn/ *noun* a routine that normalises a floating point number and adds extra, noisy digits in the least significant position

normalise /'nɔːməˌlaɪz/, **normalize** *verb* **1.** to convert data into a form which can be read by a particular computer system **2.** to convert characters into just capitals or into just a lowercase form **3.** to store and represent numbers in a pre-agreed form, usually to provide maximum precision ○ *All the new data has been normalised to 10 decimal places.* (NOTE: normalises – normalising – normalised)

normalised form /'nɔːməlaɪzd fɔːm/ *noun* a floating point number that has been normalised so that its mantissa is within a certain range

normal range /'nɔːm(ə)l reɪndʒ/ *noun* the expected range for a result or number (NOTE: Any outside this range are errors.)

normals /'nɔːm(ə)lz/ *plural noun* (*in a three-dimensional scene*) lines that are perpendicular to a tangent

normal-vector interpolation shading /ˌnɔːm(ə)l ˌvektə ɪnˌtɜːpə'leɪʃ(ə)n ˌʃeɪdɪŋ/ *noun* same as **Phong shading**

NOS *abbr* network operating system

NOT-AND /nɒt ən/ *noun* an equivalent to the NAND function

notation /nəʊ'teɪʃ(ə)n/ *noun* a method of writing or representing numbers

notched /nɒtʃd/ *adjective* ♦ **edge notched card**

notebook computer /ˌnəʊtbʊk kəm 'pjuːtə/ *noun* a very small portable computer, usually smaller than a laptop computer, that has a small keyboard and display and can be carried easily

NOT function /nɒt 'fʌŋkʃən/ *noun* a logical inverse function in which the output is true if the input is false

COMMENT: If the input is 1, the output is 0; if the input is 0, the output is 1.

NOT gate /'nɒt geɪt/ *noun* same as **negation gate**

notice board /'nəʊtɪs bɔːd/ *noun* **1.** a board fixed to a wall where notices can be pinned up **2.** a type of bulletin board on which messages to all users can be left

notification message /ˌnəʊtɪfɪ 'keɪʃ(ə)n ˌmesɪdʒ/ *noun* a message within authoring software to notify other objects that a particular task has been completed ○ *If an object is moved, the application will generate a notification message* to tell other processes when it has finished moving the object.

notify handler /'nəʊtɪfaɪ ˌhændlə/ *noun* a series of commands that are executed when a particular notification message is received

Novell /nəʊ'vel/ a large company that produces network software and is best known for its NetWare range of network operating system software that runs on a PC server

n-plus-one address instruction /en plʌs wʌn ə'dres/ *noun* an instruction made up of a number (n) of addresses and one other address that is the location of the next instruction

n-plus-one instruction /'en plʌs wʌn/ *noun* an instruction made up of a number (n) of addresses and one other address that is the location of the next instruction to be executed

npn transistor /ˌen piː 'en trænˌzɪstə/ *noun* a bipolar transistor design using p-type semiconductor for the base and n-type for the collector and emitter

NRZ *abbr* non return to zero

ns *abbr* nanosecond

NSFnet /ˌen es 'ef net/ *noun* a wide area network developed by the National Science Foundation to replace ArpaNet as the main US government-funded network linking together universities and research laboratories (NOTE: NSFnet was a crucial stepping-stone in the development history of the Internet. It was closed down in 1995 and replaced by a commercial high-speed network backbone that formed one of the foundations for the current commercial Internet.)

NT /ˌen 'tiː/ *noun* ♦ **Windows NT**

NTFS *abbr* Windows NT file system

NTP *abbr* network time protocol

NTSC /ˌen tiː es 'siː/ *noun* a US committee that defines standards for television and video. Full form **National Television System Committee**

n-type material /en taɪp/, **n-type semiconductor** *noun* a semiconductor doped with a substance which provides extra electrons in the material, giving it an overall negative charge compared to the intrinsic semiconductor

NuBus /'njuːbʌs/ *noun* a high-speed 96-pin expansion bus used within Apple Mac II computers

NUL character /'nʌl ˌkærɪktə/ *noun* same as **null character**

null /nʌl/ *noun* nothing

null character /'nʌl ˌkærɪktə/ *noun* a character which means nothing, usually code 0

null instruction /nʌl ɪn'strʌkʃən/ *noun* same as **blank instruction**

null modem /nʌl 'məʊˌdem/ *noun* a circuit or cable which allows two computers to communicate via their serial ports ○ *This cable is configured as a null modem, which will allow me to connect these two computers together easily.*

null string /ˌnʌl 'strɪŋ/ *noun* a string which contains nothing

null terminated string /ˌnʌl ˌtɜːmɪneɪtɪd 'strɪŋ/ *noun* a string of characters which has a null character to indicate the end of the string

number /'nʌmbə/ *noun* **1.** a representation of a quantity **2.** a written figure ○ *Each piece of hardware has a production number.* ■ *verb* **1.** to put a figure on a document ○ *The pages of the manual are numbered 1 to 196.* **2.** to assign digits to a list of items in an ordered manner

number cruncher /'nʌmbə ˌkrʌntʃə/ *noun* a dedicated processor used for high-speed calculations

number crunching /'nʌmbə krʌntʃɪŋ/ *noun* the process of performing high-speed calculations ○ *A very powerful processor is needed for graphics applications which require extensive number crunching capabilities.*

number range /'nʌmbə reɪndʒ/ *noun* a set of allowable values

numeral /'njuːm(ə)rəl/ *noun* a character or symbol which represents a number

numeric /njuː'merɪk/ *adjective* **1.** referring to numbers **2.** which contains only numbers ○ *a numeric field*

numerical /njuː'merɪk(ə)l/ *adjective* referring to numbers

numerical analysis /njuːˌmerɪk(ə)l ə'næləsɪs/ *noun* the study of ways of solving mathematical problems

numerical control /njuːˌmerɪk(ə)l kən'trəʊl/ *noun* a machine operated automatically by computer or a set of circuits controlled by stored data. Abbr **NC**

numeric array /njuːˌmerɪk ə'reɪ/ *noun* an array containing numbers

numeric character /njuːˌmerɪk 'kærɪktə/ *noun* a letter used in some notations to represent a number. For example, in hex the letters A-F are numeric characters.

numeric keypad /njuːˌmerɪk 'kiːpæd/ *noun* a set of ten keys with figures 0–9, included in most computer keyboards as a separate group, used for entering large amounts of data in numeric form. Also called **numeric pad**

numeric operand /njuːˌmerɪk 'ɒpərænd/ *noun* an operand that only contains numerals

numeric pad /njuːˌmerɪk 'pæd/ *noun* same as **numeric keypad**

numeric punch /njuːˌmerɪk 'pʌntʃ/ *noun* a punched hole in rows 0–9 of a punched card

numeric string /njuːˌmerɪk 'strɪŋ/ *noun* a string which contains only numbers

Num Lock key /'nʌm lɒk kiː/ *noun* (*on a keyboard*) a key that switches the function of a numeric keypad from cursor control to numeric entry

NVRAM /ˌen viː 'ræm/ *noun* memory that can permanently retain information. Full form **non-volatile random access memory**

nybble /'nɪb(ə)l/, **nibble** *noun* half the length of a standard byte (*informal*)

COMMENT: A nybble is normally 4 bits, but can vary according to different micros.

O

OA *abbr* office automation

object /ˈɒbdʒekt/ *noun* **1.** the data that makes up a particular image or sound **2.** a variable used in an IKBS within a reasoning operation **3.** the data in a statement which is to be operated on by the operator

object animation /ˌɒbdʒekt ˌænɪˈmeɪʃ(ə)n/ *noun* same as **cast-based animation**

object architecture /ˌɒbdʒekt ˈɑːkɪtektʃə/ *noun* a structure where all features such as files or outputs in a system are represented as objects. Also called **object-orientated architecture**

object code /əbˈdʒekt kəʊd/ *noun* program code after it has been translated, compiled or assembled into machine code

object computer /ˌɒbdʒekt kəmˈpjuːtə/ *noun* a computer system for which a program has been written and compiled

object deck /əbˈdʒekt dek/ *noun* a set of punched cards that contain a program

object file /əbˈdʒekt faɪl/ *noun* a file that contains object code for a routine or program

object hierarchy /ˌɒbdʒekt ˈhaɪərɑːki/ *noun* the order in which messages are passed from one object to another

objective /əbˈdʒektɪv/ *noun* something which someone tries to do

object language /ˌɒbdʒekt ˈlæŋgwɪdʒ/ *noun* the language of a program after it has been translated. Opposite **source language**

object linking and embedding /ˌɒbdʒekt ˌlɪŋkɪŋ ənd ɪmˈbedɪŋ/ *noun* full form of **OLE**

object linking and embedding 2 /ˌɒbdʒekt ˌlɪŋkɪŋ ənd ɪmˌbedɪŋ ˈtuː/ *noun* full form of **OLE-2**

object-orientated architecture /ˌɒbdʒekt ˌɔːriənteɪtɪd ˈɑːkɪtektʃə/ *noun* same as **object architecture**

object-oriented /ˌɒbdʒekt ˈɔːrientɪd/ *adjective* referring to a system or language that uses objects

object-oriented graphics /ˌɒbdʒekt ˌɔːrientɪd ˈgræfɪks/ *plural noun* graphics which use lines and curves, vector definitions, to describe the shapes of the image rather than pixels in a bitmap image ○ *This object-oriented graphics program lets you move shapes around very easily.*

object-oriented language /ˌɒbdʒekt ˌɔːrientɪd ˈlæŋgwɪdʒ/ *noun* a programming language that is used for object-oriented programming, e.g. C++

object-oriented programming /ˌɒbdʒekt ˌɔːrientɪd ˈprəʊgræmɪŋ/ *noun* a method of programming, as in C++, in which each element of the program is treated as an object that can interact with other objects within the program. Abbr **OOP**

Object Packager /ˈɒbdʒekt ˌpækɪdʒə/ *noun* a utility included with Windows 3.x that lets you convert data from an application that does not support OLE so that it can be used as an OLE object in another application.

object program /ˈɒbdʒekt ˌprəʊgræm/ *noun* a computer program in object code form, produced by a compiler or assembler

Object Request Broker /əbˌdʒekt rɪˈkwest ˌbrəʊkə/ *noun* software that links objects together using the CORBA standard. Abbr **ORB**

obtain /əbˈteɪn/ *verb* to get or receive something ○ *to obtain data from a storage device*

OCCAM /ˈɒkəm/ *noun* a computer programming language used in large multi-processor or multi-user systems

COMMENT: This is the development language for transputer systems.

occur /əˈkɜː/ *verb* to happen or take place ○ *Data loss can occur because of* *power supply variations.* (NOTE: occurring – occurred)

OCE /ˌəʊ siː 'iː/ *noun* a set of standards that allow networked Apple Mac users to share objects and files. Full form **open collaboration environment**

OCP /ˌəʊ siː 'piː/ *noun* (*in a multiprocessor system*) a processor which decides and performs the arithmetic and logical operations according to the program code. Full form **order code processor**

OCR /ˌəʊ siː 'ɑː/ *noun* **1.** a device which scans printed or written characters, recognises them and converts them into machine-readable form for processing in a computer. Full form **optical character reader 2.** software or a process that allows printed or written characters to be recognised optically and converted into machine-readable code that can be input into a computer, using an optical character reader. Full form **optical character recognition**

'In 1986, Calera Recognition Systems introduced the first neural-network-based OCR system that could read complex pages containing any mixture of nondecorative fonts without manual training.' [*Computing*]

COMMENT: There are two OCR fonts in common use: OCR-A, which is easy for scanners to read, and OCR-B, which is easier for people to read than the OCR-A font.

OCR font /ˌəʊ siː 'ɑː fɒnt/ *noun* same as **optical font**

octal /'ɒkt(ə)l/, **octal notation** /ˌɒkt(ə)l nəʊ'teɪʃ(ə)n/ *noun* a number notation using base 8, with digits 0 to 7

COMMENT: In octal, the digits used are 0 to 7; so decimal 9 is octal 11.

octal digit /ˌɒkt(ə)l 'dɪdʒɪt/ *noun* a digit, 0 to 7 used in octal notation

octal scale /'ɒkt(ə)l skeɪl/ *noun* the power of eight associated with each digit position in a number

octet /ɒk'tet/ *noun* a group of eight bits treated as one unit or word. ◊ **byte**

OCX /ˌəʊ siː 'eks/ *noun* the file extension of an ActiveX component or add-in that is used by an application such as a web browser or custom application running under Windows 95 or 98

ODBC *noun* a software interface that allows an application to access any compatible data source. Full form **open database connectivity** (NOTE: The standard was developed by Microsoft but is used by many different developers as a standard method of providing access to a wide range of databases.)

odd-even check /ˌɒd 'iːv(ə)n ˌtʃek/ *noun* a method of checking that transmitted binary data has not been corrupted

odd parity /ˌɒd 'pærɪti/, **odd parity check** /ˌɒd 'pærɪti tʃek/ *noun* an error checking system in which any series of bits transmitted must have an odd number of binary ones

ODI a trade name for a standard interface, defined by Novell, for an NIC that allows users to have just one network driver that will work with all NICs. Full form **open datalink interface**. Compare **NDIS** (NOTE: The standard also supports more than one protocol, e.g. IPX and NetBEUI.)

OEM /ˌəʊ iː 'em/ *noun* a company which produces equipment using basic parts made by other manufacturers, and customises the product for a particular application ○ *One OEM supplies the disk drive, another the monitor.* Full form **original equipment manufacturer**

off-hook /ˌɒf hʊk/ *adverb* in or into the condition of a modem when it is connected to answer a call. Compare **on-hook**

office automation /ˌɒfɪs ˌɔːtə 'meɪʃ(ə)n/ *noun* the use of machines and computers to carry out ordinary office tasks. Abbr **OA**

office computer /ˌɒfɪs kəm'pjuːtə/ *noun* a small computer, sometimes with a hard disk and several terminals, suitable for office use

off-line /ˌɒf laɪn/ *adverb, adjective* **1.** referring to a processor, printer or terminal that is not connected to a network or central computer, usually temporarily ○ *Before changing the paper in the printer, switch it off-line.* **2.** referring to a peripheral connected to a network but not available for use. Compare **online**

off-line editing /ˌɒf laɪn 'edɪtɪŋ/ *noun* an editing process in which copies of the original sound tape or videotape are used, cut and edited to create an EDL that is then used in an on-line editing suite to automatically assemble all the sectors of the tape according to the instructions in the EDL (NOTE: Off-line editing software allows two or more video clips to be edited and merged with effects.)

off-line newsreader /ˌɒf laɪn 'njuːzriːdə/ *noun* a piece of software that allows a user to read newsgroup articles when the computer is not connected to the Internet

off-line printing /ˌɒf laɪn ˈprɪntɪŋ/ *noun* a printout operation that is not supervised by a computer

off-line processing /ˌɒf laɪn ˈprəʊsesɪŋ/ *noun* processing performed by devices not under the control of a central computer

off-line storage /ˌɒf laɪn ˈstɔːrɪdʒ/ *noun* storage that is not currently available for access

offload /ɒfˈləʊd/ *verb* to transfer data from one computer to another to create more usable space on the first computer

off-screen buffer /ˌɒf skriːn ˈbʌfə/ *noun* the area of RAM used to hold an off-screen image before it is displayed on screen

off-screen image /ˌɒf skriːn ˈɪmɪdʒ/ *noun* an image that is first drawn in memory and then is transferred to the display memory to give the impression of fast display action

offset /ˈɒfset/ *noun* a quantity added to a number or address to give a final number

offset value /ˌɒfˌset ˈvæljuː/, **offset word** /ˌɒfˈset wɜːd/ *noun* a value to be added to a base address to provide a final indexed address

ohm /əʊm/ *noun* a unit of measurement of electrical resistance ○ *this resistance has a value of 100 ohms*

OK /ˌəʊ ˈkeɪ/ *noun* used as a prompt in place of 'ready' in some systems

OK button /ˌəʊˈkeɪ ˌbʌt(ə)n/ *noun* (*in a GUI*) a button with an 'OK' label that is used to start or confirm an action

OLE /ˌəʊ el ˈiː/ *noun* (*in Microsoft Windows*) a facility for including data formatted in one application within another application; e.g. insertion of an object such as an image or sound into a document or spreadsheet. Full form **object linking and embedding**. ◊ DDE

OLE-2 /ˌəʊ el iː ˈtuː/ *noun* (*in Microsoft Windows*) a facility that extends the functions of OLE to include visual editing to allow the embedded object to be edited without leaving the document in which it is embedded. Full form **object linking and embedding 2** (NOTE: If you insert an image into a document, you can now edit the image without leaving the word-processor. OLE2 also allows applications to exchange information.)

OLE object /ˌəʊ el ˌiː ˈɒbdʒekt/, **OLE container object** /ˌəʊ el ˌiː kənˈteɪnə ˌɒbdʒekt/ *noun* an object that contains a

reference to a linked object or a copy of an embedded object

omission factor /əʊˈmɪʃ(ə)n ˌfæktə/ *noun* the number of relevant documents that were missed in a search

OMR /ˌəʊ em ˈɑː/ *noun* **1.** a device that can recognise marks or lines on a special forms such as an order form or a reply to a questionnaire and convert them into a form a computer can process. Full form **optical mark reader 2.** process that allows certain marks or lines on special forms such as an order form or a reply to a questionnaire to be recognised by an OMR and input into a computer. Full form **optical mark recognition**

on-board /ɒn bɔːd/ *adjective* referring to a feature or circuit which is contained on a motherboard or main PCB

'…the electronic page is converted to a printer-readable video image by the on-board raster image processor the key intelligence features of these laser printers are emulation modes and on-board memory' [*Byte*]

on chip /ˌɒn ˈtʃɪp/ *noun* a circuit constructed on a chip

on-chip /ɒn tʃɪp/ *adjective* referring to a circuit constructed on a chip ○ *The processor uses on-chip bootstrap software to allow programs to be loaded rapidly.*

on-chip cache /ˌɒn tʃɪp ˈkæʃ/ *noun* cache memory and controller circuitry built into a processor chip

one-address computer /ˌwʌn əˌdres kəmˈpjuːtə/ *noun* a computer structure whose machine code only uses one address at a time

one-address instruction /ˌwʌn əˌdres ɪnˈstrʌkʃən/ *noun* an instruction made up of an operator and one address

one element /wʌn ˈelɪmənt/ *noun* a logical function that produces a true output if any input is true

one for one /ˌwʌn fə ˈwʌn/ *noun* a programming language, usually assembler, that produces one machine code instruction for each instruction or command word in the language

COMMENT: Compilers and interpreters are usually used for translating high-level languages that use more than one machine code instruction for each high-level instruction.

one-level address /ˌwʌn ˌlev(ə)l əˈdres/ *noun* a storage address that directly, without any modification, accesses a location or device

one-level code /ˌwʌn ˌlev(ə)l ˈkəʊd/ *noun* same as **direct code**

one-level store /ˌwʌn ˌlev(ə)l ˈstɔː/
noun the organisation of storage in which each different type of storage device is treated as if it were the same

one-level subroutine /ˌwʌn ˌlev(ə)l ˈsʌbruːtiːn/ *noun* a subroutine which does not call another subroutine during its execution

one-pass assembler /ˌwʌn pɑːs ə ˈsemblə/ *noun* an assembler program that translates the source code in one action ○ *This new one-pass assembler is very quick in operation.*

one-plus-one address /ˈwʌn plʌs wʌn/ *noun* an address format that provides the location of one register and the location of the next instruction

one's complement /ˈwʌnz ˌkɒmplɪment/ *noun* the inverse of a binary number ○ *The one's complement of 10011 is 01100.*

one-time pad /ˌwʌn ˈtaɪm pæd/ *noun* a coding system that uses a unique cipher key each time it is used
COMMENT: Two identical pieces of paper with an encrypted alphabet printed on each one are used, one by the sender, one by the receiver. This is one of the most secure cipher systems.

one to zero ratio /wʌn tə, tʊ ˈzɪərəʊ/ *noun* the ratio between the amplitude of a binary one and zero output

on-hook /ɒn hʊk/ *adverb* in or into the condition of a modem when it is not connected to make a call

onion skin architecture /ˈʌnjən skɪn ˌɑːkɪtektʃə/ *noun* a design of a computer system in layers, according to function or priority ○ *The onion skin architecture of this computer is made up of a kernel at the centre, an operating system, a low-level language and then the user's program.*

onion skin language /ˈʌnjən skɪn ˌlæŋɡwɪdʒ/ *noun* a database manipulation language that can process hierarchical data structures

online /ɒnˈlaɪn/ *adverb*, *adjective* referring to a terminal or device connected to and under the control of a central processor ○ *The terminal is on-line to the mainframe.*

online database /ˌɒnlaɪn ˈdeɪtəbeɪs/ *noun* an interactive search, retrieve and update of database records using an online terminal

online editing /ɒnˌlaɪn ˈedɪtɪŋ/ *noun* the process of creating a finished audio or film sequence from original tape using editing instructions in an EDL list

online help /ˌɒnlaɪn ˈhelp/ *noun* a text screen displayed from within an application that explains how to use the application

online information retrieval /ˌɒnlaɪn ˌɪnfəˈmeɪʃ(ə)n rɪˌtriːvəl/ *noun* a system that allows an operator of an online terminal to access, search and display data held in a main computer

online processing /ˌɒnlaɪn ˈprəʊsesɪŋ/ *noun* processing by devices connected to and under the control of the central computer, during which the user remains in contact with the central computer

online storage /ˌɒnlaɪn ˈstɔːrɪdʒ/ *noun* data storage equipment that is directly controlled by a computer

online system /ˌɒnlaɪn ˈsɪtsəm/ *noun* a computer system that allows users who are online to transmit and receive information

online transaction processing /ˌɒnlaɪn trænˈzækʃən ˌprəʊsesɪŋ/ *noun* an interactive processing in which a user enters commands and data on a terminal which is linked to a central computer, with results being displayed on the screen

OnNow /ˌɒnˈnaʊ/ *noun* a standard that provides a way of integrating power management and control within all types of computer (NOTE: The main benefit of OnNow is that it allows the development of a computer that is dormant but will be ready to use almost immediately after it has been switched on, unlike current computers that can take a minute to configure and load the operating system.)

on-screen /ɒn skriːn/ *adjective* referring to information that is displayed on a computer screen rather than printed out

on-site /ɒn saɪt/ *adjective* located at the place where a particular thing is ○ *The new model has an on-site upgrade facility.*

on the fly /ˌɒn ðə ˈflaɪ/ *adverb* (*to examine and modify data*) during a program run without stopping the run

OOP *abbr* object-oriented programming

o/p, O/P *abbr* output

op code /ˈɒp kəʊd/ *noun* a part of the machine code instruction that defines the action to be performed. Also called **operation code, order code**

open /ˈəʊpən/ *adjective* **1.** called up and prepared before reading or writing actions can occur ○ *You cannot access the data unless the file is open.* **2.** not closed ■ *verb* to call up and prepare a file before accessing, editing or carrying out other transactions on stored records ○ *You cannot access the data unless the file has been opened.*

open access /ˌəʊpən ˈækses/ *noun* a system in which many workstations are available for anyone to use

open architecture /ˌəʊpən ˈɑːkɪtektʃə/ *noun* computer architecture with a published expansion interface that has been designed to allow add-on hardware to be plugged in

open code /ˈəʊpən kəʊd/ *noun* a set of extra instructions required in a program that mainly uses macroinstructions

open collaboration environment /ˌəʊpən kəˌlæbəˈreɪʃ(ə)n ɪn ˌvaɪrənmənt/ *noun* full form of **OCE**

open database connectivity /ˌəʊpən ˌdeɪtəbeɪs ˌkɒnekˈtɪvɪti/ *noun* full form of **ODBC**

open datalink interface /ˌəʊpən ˈdeɪtəlɪŋk ˌɪntəfeɪs/ *noun* full form of **ODI**

open-ended program /ˌəʊpən ˌendɪd ˈprəʊɡræm/ *noun* a program designed to allow future expansion and easy modification

open file /ˈəʊpən faɪl/ *noun* a file that can be read from or written to (NOTE: An application opens the file which locates the file on disk and prepares it for an operation.)

open reel /ˈəʊpən riːl/ *noun* a magnetic tape on a reel that is not enclosed in a cartridge or cassette

open routine /ˌəʊpən ruːˈtiːn/ *noun* a routine which can be inserted into a larger routine or program without using a call instruction

OpenScript /ˈəʊpənskrɪpt/ *noun* an object-oriented programming language used in the Asymetrix Toolbook authoring software

open shortest path first /ˌəʊpən ˌʃɔːtəst pɑːθ ˈfɜːʃθ/ *noun* full form of **OSPF**

open source *adjective* describes a program for which the source code is freely available and which anyone is legally able to modify and improve

'In yet another initiative, aimed at cutting the upfront costs of big IT projects, the OGC is tipping towards a preference for open source software.' [*The Guardian*]

open subroutine /ˌəʊpən ˈsʌbruːtiːn/ *noun* a code for a subroutine which is copied into memory whenever a call instruction is found, rather than executing a jump to the subroutine's address

open system /ˈəʊpən ˌsɪstəm/ *noun* **1.** a nonproprietary system that is not under the control of one company **2.** a system that is constructed in such a way that different operating systems can work together

open system interconnection /ˌəʊpən ˌsɪstəm ˌɪntəkəˈnekʃ(ə)n/ *noun* e. Full form of **OSI**

open trading protocol /ˌəʊpən ˈtreɪdɪŋ ˌprəʊtəkɒl/ *noun* a standardised computer protocol for transactions involving payments and for methods of payment. Abbr **OTP**

operand /ˈɒpərænd/ *noun* the data in a computer instruction which is to be operated on by the operator ○ *In the instruction ADD 74, the operator ADD will add the operand 74 to the accumulator.*

operand field /ˈɒpərænd fiːld/ *noun* a part of a computer instruction containing the location of the operand

operate /ˈɒpəreɪt/ *verb* to work or to make a machine work ○ *Do you know how to operate the telephone switchboard?* (NOTE: operates – operating – operated)

operating code /ˈɒpəreɪtɪŋ kəʊd/ *noun* a part of the machine code instruction that defines the action to be performed. Also called **op code**

operating console /ˈɒpəreɪtɪŋ ˌkɒnsəʊl/ *noun* a terminal in an interactive system that sends and receives information

operating instructions /ˈɒpəreɪtɪŋ ɪnˌstrʌkʃ(ə)nz/ *plural noun* commands and instructions used to operate a computer

operating system /ˈɒpəreɪtɪŋ ˌsɪstəm/ *noun* full form of **OS**

operating time /ˈɒpəreɪtɪŋ taɪm/ *noun* the total time required to carry out a task

operation /ˌɒpəˈreɪʃ(ə)n/ *noun* the working of a machine

operational /ˌɒpəˈreɪʃ(ə)nəl/ *adjective* which is working

operational information /ˌɒpə ˌreɪʃ(ə)nəl ˌɪnfəˈmeɪʃ(ə)n/ *noun* information about the normal operations of a system

operation code /ˌɒpəˈreɪʃ(ə)n kəʊd/ *noun* same as **op code**

operation cycle /ˌɒpəˈreɪʃ(ə)n ˌsaɪk(ə)l/ *noun* a section of the machine cycle during which the instruction is executed

operation decoder /ˌɒpəˈreɪʃ(ə)n diːˌkəʊdə/ *noun* a piece of hardware that converts a machine-code instruction in binary form into actions

operation field /ˌɒpəˈreɪʃ(ə)n ˌfiːld/ *noun* a part of an assembly language statement that contains the mnemonic or symbol for the op code

operation priority /ˌɒpəreɪʃ(ə)n praɪˈɒrɪti/ *noun* the sequence order in which the operations within a statement are carried out

operation register /ˌɒpəˈreɪʃ(ə)n ˌredʒɪstə/ *noun* a register that contains the op code during its execution

operations manual /ˌɒpəˌreɪʃ(ə)nz ˈmænjʊəl/ *noun* same as **instruction manual**

operation time /ˌɒpəˈreɪʃ(ə)n taɪm/ *noun* a period of time that an operation requires for its operation cycle

operation trial /ˌɒpəˈreɪʃ(ə)n ˌtraɪəl/ *noun* a series of tests to check programs and data preparation

operator /ˈɒpəˌreɪtə/ *noun* **1.** a person who makes a machine or process work ○ *The operator was sitting at his console.* **2.** a character, symbol or word that defines a function or operation ○ *x is the multiplication operator.*

operator overloading /ˌɒpəreɪtə ˈəʊvələʊdɪŋ/ *noun* the process of assigning more than one function to a particular operator (NOTE: the function often depends on the type of data being operated on and is used in the C++ and Ada programming languages.)

operator precedence /ˌɒpəreɪtə ˈpresɪdəns/ *noun* the order in which a number of mathematical operations will be carried out

operator procedure /ˈɒpəreɪtə prəˌsiːdʒə/ *noun* a set of actions that an operator has to carry out to work a machine or process

operator's console /ˈɒpəreɪtəz ˌkɒnsəʊl/ *noun* a unit with the input and output devices used by an operator to control a computer, usually consisting of a keyboard and VDU

op register /ɒp ˈredʒɪstə/ *noun* a register that contains the op code for the instruction that is being executed

optical /ˈɒptɪk(ə)l/ *adjective* referring to or making use of light ○ *An optical reader uses a light beam to scan characters.*

optical bar reader /ˌɒptɪk(ə)l ˈbɑː ˌriːdə/ *noun* an optical device that reads data from a bar code

optical character reader /ˌɒptɪk(ə)l ˈkærɪktə ˌriːdə/ *noun* full form of **OCR 1**

optical character recognition /ˌɒptɪk(ə)l ˌkærɪktə ˌrekəgˈnɪʃ(ə)n/ *noun* full form of **OCR 2**

optical communication system /ˌɒptɪk(ə)l kəˌmjuːnɪˈkeɪʃ(ə)n ˌsɪstəm/ *noun* a communication system using fibre optics

optical computer /ˌɒptɪk(ə)l kəm ˈpjuːtə/ *noun* a proposed computer that would use optical fibres and switches and laser light, instead of wires, transistors and printed circuits, and that would process information much faster than conventional computers

optical data link /ˌɒptɪk(ə)l ˈdeɪtə ˌlɪŋk/ *noun* a connection between two devices to allow the transmission of data using light signals, either line-of-sight or optic fibre

optical disk /ˈɒptɪk(ə)l dɪsk/ *noun* a disk that contains binary data in the form of small holes in a metal layer under the surface which are read with a laser beam (NOTE: One example is a WORM disk (write once, read many times) which can be programmed once or a compact disc (CD) which is programmed at manufacture)

optical fibre /ˌɒptɪk(ə)l ˈfaɪbə/ *noun* a fine strand of glass or plastic protected by a surrounding material, that is used for the convenient transmission of light signals. ◊ **fibre optics**. Also called **optic fibre**

optical font /ˈɒptɪk(ə)l fɒnt/ *noun* a character design that can be easily read using an OCR. Also called **OCR font**

optical mark reader /ˌɒptɪk(ə)l ˈmɑːk ˌriːdə/ *noun* full form of **OMR 1**

optical mark recognition /ˌɒptɪk(ə)l mɑːk ˌrekəgˈnɪʃ(ə)n/ *noun* full form of **OMR 2**

optical memory /ˌɒptɪk(ə)l ˈmem(ə)ri/ *noun* the capacity of optical disks

optical mouse /ˈɒptɪk(ə)l maʊs/ *noun* a pointing device that is operated by moving it across a special flat mat; (NOTE: On the mat is printed a grid of lines. As the mouse is moved, two light sensors count the number of lines that have been passed to produce a measure of the distance and direction of travel. An optical mouse has fewer moving parts than a mechanical mouse and so is more reliable, but requires an accurately printed mat.)

optical scanner /ˌɒptɪk(ə)l 'skænə/ noun a piece of equipment that converts an image into electrical signals which can be stored in and displayed on a computer

optical storage /ˌɒptɪk(ə)l 'stɔːrɪdʒ/ noun data storage using mediums such as optical disk

optical transmission /ˌɒptɪk(ə)l trænz'mɪʃ(ə)n/ noun the use of fibre optic cables, laser beams and other light sources to carry data, in the form of pulses of light

optic fibre /ˌɒptɪk 'faɪbə/ noun same as **optical fibre**

optimisation, optimization noun the process of making something work as efficiently as possible

optimise /'ɒptɪˌmaɪz/, **optimize** verb to make something work as efficiently as possible (NOTE: optimises – optimising – optimised)

optimised code /'ɒptɪˌmaɪzd kəʊd/, **optimized code** noun a program that has been passed through an optimiser to remove any inefficient code or statements

optimiser /'ɒptɪmaɪzə/, **optimizer** noun a program that adapts another program to run more efficiently

optimising compiler /ˌɒptɪmaɪzɪŋ kəm'paɪlə/ noun a compiler that analyses the machine code it produces in order to improve the speed or efficiency of the code

optimum /'ɒptɪməm/ adjective best possible

optimum code /'ɒptɪməm kəʊd/ noun a coding system that provides the fastest access and retrieval time for stored data items

opt-in mailing list /ˌɒpt ɪn 'meɪlɪŋ lɪst/ noun a list of email addresses in which each recipient has specifically asked to receive advertising email messages, usually so that he or she can keep up to date with a topic or industry

option /'ɒpʃən/ noun an action which can be chosen ○ *There are usually four options along the top of the screen.*

optional /'ɒpʃ(ə)n(ə)l/ adjective which can be chosen ○ *The system comes with optional 3.5 or 5.25 disk drives.*

Option key /'ɒpʃ(ə)n kiː/ noun a key on an Apple Mac keyboard that gives access to other functions of keys, similar to Ctrl or Alt keys on an IBM PC keyboard

optomechanical mouse /ˌɒptəʊmɪˌkænɪk(ə)l 'maʊs/ noun same as **mechanical mouse**

OR /ˌəʊ 'ɑː/ noun a Boolean function that is often used in searches to ask the search engine to find text that contains any of the search words. Compare **AND** (NOTE: For example, the phrase 'dog OR cat' will include all documents that contain the words dog or cat.)

Orange Book /'ɒrɪndʒ bʊk/ noun a set of standards published by Philips that define the format for a recordable CD-ROM

ORB abbr Object Request Broker (see)

order /'ɔːdə/ noun 1. an instruction 2. an arrangement sorted according to a key ○ *in alphabetical order* ■ verb 1. to direct or instruct a person to do something 2. to sort data according to a key

order code /'ɔːdə kəʊd/ noun same as **op code**

order code processor /'ɔːdə kəʊd ˌprəʊsesə/ noun full form of **OCP**

ordered list /'ɔːdəd lɪst/ noun a list of data items which have been sorted into an order

OR function /ɔː 'fʌŋkʃən/ noun a logical function that produces a true output if any input is true

COMMENT: The result of the OR function will be 1 if either or both inputs are 1; if both inputs are 0, then the result is 0.

organisation /ˌɔːɡənaɪ'zeɪʃ(ə)n/, **organization** noun a way of arranging something so that it works efficiently or has a logical structure

organisational /ˌɔːɡənaɪ'zeɪʃ(ə)n(ə)l/, **organizational** adjective referring to the way in which something is organised

organise /'ɔːɡəˌnaɪz/, **organize** verb to arrange something so that it works efficiently or has a logical structure (NOTE: organises – organising – organised)

OR gate /'ɔː ɡeɪt/ noun an electronic circuit that provides the OR function

orientated /'ɔːriənteɪtɪd/ adjective aimed towards something

orientation /ˌɔːriən'teɪʃ(ə)n/ noun 1. the direction or position of an object 2. (in *word-processing or DTP software*) the direction of a page, either landscape, with long edge horizontal, or portrait, with long edge vertical

origin /'prɪdʒɪn/ *noun* **1.** the position on a display screen to which all coordinates are referenced, usually the top left hand corner of the screen **2.** a location in memory at which the first instruction of a program is stored

original /ə'rɪdʒən(ə)l/ *adjective* used or made first ■ *noun* the master data disk, from which a copy can be made

original equipment manufacturer /ə,rɪdʒən(ə)l ɪ,kwɪpmənt ,mænjʊ 'fæktʃərə/ *noun* full form of **OEM**

originate /ə'rɪdʒɪneɪt/ *verb* to start or come from a place or source ○ *The data originated from the new computer.* (NOTE: originates – originating – originated)

originate modem /ə'rɪdʒəneɪt ,məʊdem/ *noun* a modem that makes a call to another modem that is waiting to answer calls (NOTE: The originate modem emits a carrier in response to an answer-tone from the remote modem.)

origination /ə,rɪdʒɪ'neɪʃ(ə)n/ *noun* the work involved in creating something

OROM /'əʊ rɒm/ *abbr* optical read-only memory

orphan /'ɔːf(ə)n/ *noun* the first line of a paragraph of text printed alone at the bottom of a column, with the rest of the paragraph at the top of the next column or page. Compare **widow** (NOTE: An orphan makes a page look ugly.)

orthogonal /,ɔː'θɒgənəl/ *adjective* referring to an instruction made up of independent parameters or parts

OS /,əʊ 'es/ *noun* software that controls the basic, low-level hardware operations, and file management of a computer, without the user having to operate it. Full form **operating system** (NOTE: The OS is usually supplied with the computer as part of the bundled software in ROM.)

OS/2 a trade name for a multitasking operating system for PC computers developed by IBM and Microsoft (NOTE: Development is now continued by IBM to make it an alternative to Microsoft Windows.)

OSF *abbr* Open Software Foundation

OSI /,əʊ es 'aɪ/ *noun* a standard theoretical model of a network that is created from seven different layers each with a different function. This model provides the basis of

almost all networks in use. Full form **open system interconnection**

OSPF /,əʊ es pi: 'ef/ *noun* a protocol used with a TCP/IP network that will send packets of data on a route that has the least amount of traffic. Full form **open shortest path first**

OTP *abbr* open trading protocol

outage /'aʊtɪdʒ/ *noun* the time during which a system is not operational

outlet /'aʊtlet/ *noun* a connection or point in a circuit or network where a signal or data can be accessed

outline /'aʊtlaɪn/ *noun* the main features of something

outline flowchart /'aʊt(ə)laɪn ,fləʊtʃɑːt/ *noun* a flowchart of the main features, steps and decisions in a program or system

outline font /'aʊt(ə)laɪn fɒnt/ *noun* a printer or display font stored as a set of outlines that mathematically describe the shape of each character, and which are then used to draw each character rather than actual patterns of dots (NOTE: Outline fonts can be easily scaled, unlike bitmap fonts.)

outliner /'aʊtlaɪnə/ *noun* a utility program used to help a user order sections and subsections of a list of things to do or parts of a project

out of alignment /,aʊt əv ə'laɪnmənt/ *adjective* not aligned correctly

out of control /,aʊt əv kən'trəʊl/ *adjective* not kept in check

out of date /,aʊt əv 'deɪt/ *adjective* old-fashioned or no longer current ○ *Their computer system is years out of date.*

out of range /,aʊt əv 'reɪndʒ/ *adjective* referring to a number or quantity that is outside the limits of a system

output /'aʊtpʊt/ *noun* **1.** information or data that is transferred from a CPU or the main memory to another device such as a monitor, printer or secondary storage device **2.** the action of transferring information or data from store to a user ▶ *abbr* **o/p, O/P** ■ *verb* to transfer data from a computer to a monitor or printer ○ *Finished documents can be output to the laser printer.*

output area /'aʊtpʊt ,eəriə/, **output block** *noun* a section of memory that contains data to be transferred to an output device

output-bound /'aʊtpʊt ,baʊnd/ *adjective* referring to a processor that cannot function at normal speed because of a slower peripheral

output buffer register /ˌaʊtpʊt ˌbʌfə 'redʒɪstə/ *noun* a temporary store for data that is waiting to be output

output bureau /'aʊtpʊt ˌbjʊərəʊ/ *noun* an office that converts data from a DTP program or a drawing stored on disk into typeset artwork

output device /'aʊtpʊt dɪˌvaɪs/ *noun* a device such as a monitor or printer which allows information to be displayed

output file /'aʊtpʊt faɪl/ *noun* a set of records that have been completely processed according to various parameters

output formatter /'aʊtpʊt ˌfɔːmætə/ *noun* **1.** a piece of software used to format data or programs, and output them, so that they are compatible with another sort of storage medium **2.** a part of a word-processor program that formats text according to embedded commands

output-limited /ˌaʊtpʊt 'lɪmɪtɪd/ *adjective* same as **output-bound**

output mode /'aʊtpʊt məʊd/ *noun* a computer mode in which data is moved from internal storage or the CPU to external devices

output port /'aʊtpʊt pɔːt/ *noun* a circuit and connector that allow a computer to output or transmit data to other devices or machines ○ *Connect the printer to the printer output port.*

output register /'aʊtpʊt ˌredʒɪstə/ *noun* a register that stores data to be output until the receiver is ready or the channel is free

output stream /'aʊtpʊt striːm/ *noun* a communications channel carrying data output to a peripheral

outsource /'aʊtˌsɔːs/ *verb* to employ another company to manage and support a network for your company

OV *abbr* overflow

OverDrive /'əʊvədraɪv/ a trade name for a processor chip that is used as a more powerful replacement for a conventional Intel 80486 processor

overflow /'əʊvəfləʊ/ *noun* **1.** a mathematical result that is greater than the limits of the computer's number storage system **2.** a situation in a network when the number of transmissions is greater than the line capacity and they are transferred by another route ▶ *abbr* **OV**

overflow check /ˌəʊvə'fləʊ tʃek/ *noun* a process of examining an overflow flag to see if an overflow has occurred

overhead /'əʊvəhed/ *noun* an extra code that has to be stored to organise the program ○ *The line numbers in a BASIC program are overhead.*

overhead bit /ˌəʊvər'hed bɪt/ *noun* a single bit used for error detection in a transmission

overheat /ˌəʊvə'hiːt/ *verb* to become too hot ○ *The system may overheat if the room is not air-conditioned.*

overlap /ˌəʊvə'læp/ *noun* a situation in which one thing covers part of another or two sections of data are placed on top of each other ■ *verb* to cover part of an item with another (NOTE: overlapping – overlapped)

overlay /'əʊvəleɪ/ *noun* a small section of a program that is bigger than the main memory capacity of a computer, loaded into memory when required, so that main memory only contains the sections it requires

'Many packages also boast useful drawing and overlay facilities which enable the user to annotate specific maps.' [*Computing*]

overlay card /'əʊvəleɪ kɑːd/ *noun* same as **video graphics card**

overlay function /'əʊvəleɪ ˌfʌŋkʃ(ə)n/ *noun* ♦ matte, chroma key

overlay manager /'əʊvəleɪ ˌmænɪdʒə/ *noun* a piece of system software that manages the loading and execution of sections of a program when they are required during run-time

overlay region /'əʊvəleɪ ˌriːdʒ(ə)n/ *noun* an area of main memory that can be used by the overlay manager to store the current section of the program being run

overlay segments /'əʊvəleɪ ˌsegmənts/ *plural noun* short sections of a long program that can be loaded into memory when required, and executed

overload /ˌəʊvə'ləʊd/ *verb* to demand more than the device is capable of ○ *The computer is overloaded with that amount of processing.*

overpunching /ˌəʊvə'pʌntʃɪŋ/ *noun* the process of altering data on a paper tape by punching additional holes

overrun /ˌəʊvə'rʌn/ *noun* data that was missed by a receiver because it was not synchronised with the transmitter or because it operates at a slower speed than the transmitter and has no buffer

overscan /'əʊvəskæn/ *noun* **1.** a faulty or badly adjusted monitor in which the displayed image runs off the edge of the screen **2.** display equipment in which the picture beam scans past the screen boundaries to ensure that the image fills the screen

over-voltage protection /,əʊvə'vəʊltɪdʒ prə,tekʃ(ə)n/ *noun* a safety device that prevents a power supply voltage exceeding certain specified limits

overwrite /,əʊvə'raɪt/ *verb* to write data to a location, e.g. memory or disk, and, in doing so, to destroy any data already contained in that location ○ *The latest data input has overwritten the old information.* (NOTE: overwriting – overwrote – overwritten)

P

p *abbr* pico-
P *abbr* peta
pack /pæk/ *noun* a number of disks sold or kept together ■ *verb* to store a quantity of data in a reduced form, often by representing several characters of data with one stored character
package deal /'pækɪdʒ diːl/ *noun* an agreement in which several different items are agreed at the same time ○ *They agreed a package deal, which involves the development of software, customising hardware and training of staff.*
packaged software /,pækɪdʒd 'sɒftweə/ *noun* same as **software package**
packed decimal /pækt 'desɪm(ə)l/ *noun* a sequence of decimal digits stored in a small space, by using only four bits for each digit
packed format /pækt 'fɔːmæt/ *noun* two binary coded decimal digits stored within one computer word or byte, usually achieved by removing the check or parity bit
packet /'pækɪt/ *noun* a group of data bits which can be transmitted as a group from one node to another over a network
packet assembler/disassembler /,pækɪt ə,semblə ,dɪsə'semblə/ *noun* a dedicated computer which converts serial data from asynchronous terminals to a form that can be transmitted along a pack-

et-switched, synchronous network. Abbr **PAD**
packet Internet groper /,pækɪt ,ɪntənet 'grəʊpə/ *noun* full form of **PING** (*see*)
packet scheduler /'pækɪt ,ʃedjuːlə/ *noun* a part of a network router that determines when to transmit the packet of data to the final destination based on the route that has been selected
packet switching /'pækɪt swɪtʃɪŋ/ *noun* a method of sending data across a WAN in small packets, which are then reassembled in the correct order at the receiving end
'The network is based on Northern Telecom DPN data switches over which it will offer X.25 packet switching, IBM SNA, and frame-relay transmission.' [*Computing*]
packet switching service /'pækɪt ,swɪtʃɪŋ ,sɜːvɪs/ *noun* a commercial data transmission service that sends data over its WAN using packet switching. Abbr **PSS**
packing /'pækɪŋ/ *noun* the process of putting large amounts of data into a small area of storage
packing density /'pækɪŋ ,densɪti/ *noun* the number of bits that can be stored in a unit area
packing routine /'pækɪŋ ruː,tiːn/ *noun* a program which packs data into a small storage area

pad /pæd/ *noun* a number of keys arranged together

PAD *abbr* packet assembler/disassembler

pad character /pæd ˈkærɪktə/ *noun* an extra character added to a string or packet or file until it is a required size

padding /ˈpædɪŋ/ *noun* a character or set of digits added to fill out a string or packet until it is the right length

paddle /ˈpæd(ə)l/ *noun* a computer peripheral consisting of a knob or device which is turned to move a cursor or pointer on the screen

page /peɪdʒ/ *noun* 1. a sheet of paper 2. an amount of text displayed on a computer monitor or screen which would fill a page of paper if printed out or which fills the screen 3. a section of main store, which contains data or programs 4. one section of a main program which can be loaded into main memory when required ■ *verb* 1. to make up a text into pages 2. to divide computer backing store into sections to allow long programs to be executed in a small main memory (NOTE: pages – paging – paged)

page addressing /peɪdʒ əˈdresɪŋ/ *noun* main memory which has been split into blocks, with a unique address allocated to each block of memory which can then be called up and accessed individually, when required

page boundary /peɪdʒ ˈbaʊnd(ə)ri/ *noun* a point where one page ends and the next starts

page break /ˌpeɪdʒ ˈbreɪk/ *noun* 1. the point in continuous text at which a page ends and a new page starts 2. a marker used when word-processing to show where a new page should start

paged address /ˌpeɪdʒd əˈdres/ *noun* (*in a paged-memory scheme*) the actual physical memory address that is calculated from a logical address and its page address

page description language /ˌpeɪdʒ dɪˈskrɪpʃən ˌlæŋgwɪdʒ/ *noun* software that controls a printer's actions to print a page of text to a particular format according to a user's instructions. Abbr **PDL**

page description programming language /peɪdʒ dɪˌskrɪpʃ(ə)n ˈprəʊgræmɪŋ ˌlæŋgwɪdʒ/ *noun* a programming language that accepts commands to define the size, position and type style for text or graphics on a page

page display /peɪdʒ dɪˈspleɪ/ *noun* the process of showing a page of text on the screen as it will appear when printed out

paged-memory management unit /ˌpeɪdʒd ˌmem(ə)ri ˈmænɪdʒmənt ˌjuːnɪt/ *noun* an electronic logic circuit that manages the translation between logical addresses that refer to a particular page and the real physical address that is being referenced

paged-memory scheme /ˌpeɪdʒd ˈmem(ə)ri ˌskiːm/ *noun* a way of dividing memory into areas or pages which are then allocated a page number (NOTE: Memory addresses are relative to a page that is then mapped to the real, physical memory. This system is normally used to implement virtual memory.)

page down key /ˌpeɪdʒ ˈdaʊn ˌkiː/ *noun* a keyboard key that moves the cursor position down by the number of lines on one screen. Abbr **PgDn**

page frame /ˌpeɪdʒ ˈfreɪm/ *noun* a physical address to which a page of virtual or logical memory can be mapped

page image buffer /ˌpeɪdʒ ˈɪmɪdʒ ˌbʌfə/ *noun* memory in a page printer that holds the image as it is built up before it is printed

page impression /ˌpeɪdʒ ɪmˈpreʃ(ə)n/ *noun* a measure used to count how many times a webpage has been displayed to a visitor to a website

page layout /peɪdʒ ˈleɪaʊt/ *noun* the arrangement of text and pictures within a page of a document ○ *We do all our page layout using desktop publishing software.*

page length /ˌpeɪdʒ ˈleŋθ/ *noun* the length of a page in word-processing

page makeup /ˌpeɪdʒ ˈmeɪkʌp/ *noun* the action of pasting images and text into a page ready for printing

page-mode RAM /ˌpeɪdʒ məʊd ˈræm/ *noun* dynamic RAM designed to access sequential memory locations very quickly ○ *The video adapter uses page-mode RAM to speed up the display.*

page number /peɪdʒ ˈnʌmbə/ *noun* a unique number assigned to each page within a multimedia application, to be used within hyperlinks and when moving between pages

page orientation /peɪdʒ ˌɔːriənˈteɪʃ(ə)n/ *noun* the direction of the long edge of a piece of paper

page preview /peɪdʒ ˈpriːˌvjuː/ *noun* (*in WP or DTP software*) a graphical representation of how a page will look when printed, with different type styles, margins and graphics correctly displayed

page printer /peɪdʒ 'prɪntə/ *noun* a printer, usually a laser printer, which composes one page of text within memory and then prints it in one pass

page protection /peɪdʒ prə'tekʃən/ *noun* the set of software controls used to ensure that pages are not overwritten by accident or copied into a reserved section of memory

page reader /peɪdʒ 'riːdə/ *noun* a device which converts written or typed information to a form that a computer can understand and process

page requests /peɪdʒ rɪ'kwestz/ *plural noun* a measure of the number of pages viewed in a day, providing an indication of the popularity of your website

page setup /'peɪdʒ ˌsetʌp/ *noun* the set of software options that allow a user to set up how the page will look when printed, – usually setting the margins, size of paper, and scaling of a page

pages per minute /ˌpeɪdʒɪz pɜː 'mɪnət/ *noun* full form of **ppm** ○ *This laser printer can output eight pages per minute.*

page table /peɪdʒ 'teɪb(ə)l/ *noun* a list of all the pages and their locations within main memory, used by the operating system when accessing a page

page up key /ˌpeɪdʒ 'ʌp ˌkiː/ *noun* a keyboard key that moves the cursor position up by the number of lines in one screen. Abbr **PgUp**

page width /ˌpeɪdʒ ', wɪdθ/ *noun* the number of characters across a page or line

pagination /ˌpædʒɪ'neɪʃ(ə)n/ *noun* the process of dividing text into pages

paging /'peɪdʒɪŋ/ *noun* a virtual memory technique of splitting main memory into small blocks or pages which are allocated an address and which can be called up when required

COMMENT: A virtual memory management system stores data as pages in memory to provide an apparently larger capacity main memory by storing unused pages in backing store, copying them into main memory only when required.

paging algorithm /'peɪdʒɪŋ ˌælgərɪð(ə)m/ *noun* a formula by which the memory management allocates memory to pages, also covering the transfer from backing storage to main memory in the most efficient way

paint /peɪnt/ *noun* (*in a graphics program*) colour and pattern used to fill an area ■ *verb* (*in a graphics program*) to fill an enclosed graphics shape with a colour

Paintbrush/Paint /ˌpeɪntbrʌʃ 'peɪnt/ *noun* an application supplied with Microsoft Windows 3.1x and Windows 95 for creating or editing bitmap images

paint object /'peɪnt ˌɒbdʒekt/ *noun* a bitmap image

paint program /'peɪnt ˌprəʊgræm/ *noun* software that allows a user to draw pictures on screen in different colours, with different styles of brush and special effects ○ *I drew a rough of our new logo with this paint program.*

COMMENT: Paint programs normally operate on bitmap images. Drafting or design software normally works with vector-based images.

paired register /ˌpeəd 'redʒɪstə/ *noun* a set of two basic word size registers used together as one large word size register, often for storing address words ○ *The 8-bit CPU uses a paired register to provide a 16-bit address register.*

PAL /ˌpiː eɪ 'el/ *noun* a standard for television transmission and reception using a 625-line picture transmitted at 25 frames per second. Full form **phase alternation line** (NOTE: PAL provides a clearer image than NTSC and is used in most of Europe, except for France, which uses SECAM. The USA and Japan use NTSC.)

palette /'pælət/ *noun* the range of colours which can be used on a printer or computer display

palette shift /'pælət ʃɪft/ *noun* an image displayed using the wrong palette with the unwanted effect that the colours appear distorted

palmtop /'pɑːmtɒp/ *noun* a personal computer that is small enough to be held in one hand and operated with the other ○ *This palmtop has a tiny keyboard and twenty-line LCD screen.*

pan /pæn/ *verb* **1.** (*in computer graphics*) to smoothly move a viewing window horizontally across an image that is too wide to display all at once **2.** (*in MIDI or sound*) to adjust the balance of a sound between the two stereo channels (NOTE: panning – panned)

panel /'pæn(ə)l/ *noun* a flat section of a casing with control knobs or sockets ○ *The socket is on the back panel.*

Pantone Matching System /ˌpæntəʊn 'mætʃɪŋ ˌsɪstəm/ a trade name for a standard method of matching ink colours on screen and on printed output using a book of pre-defined colours. Abbr **PMS**

paper-fed /'peɪpə fed/ *adjective* referring to a device which is activated when paper is introduced into it ○ *a paper-fed scanner*

paper feed /'peɪpə fiːd/ *noun* a mechanism which pulls paper through a printer

paperless /'peɪpələs/ *adjective* without using paper

paperless office /ˌpeɪpələs 'ɒfɪs/ *noun* an office which uses computers and other electronic devices for office tasks and avoids the use of paper

'Indeed, the concept of the paperless office may have been a direct attack on Xerox and its close ties to the paper document. Yet, as we all know, the paperless office has so far been an empty promise.' [*Computing*]

paper tape /'peɪpə teɪp/ *noun* a long strip of paper on which data can be recorded, usually in the form of punched holes

paper tape feed /ˌpeɪpə 'teɪp ˌfiːd/ *noun* a method by which paper tape is passed into a machine

paper tape punch /ˌpeɪpə 'teɪp ˌpʌntʃ/ *noun* a device which punches holes in paper tape to carry data

paper tape reader /ˌpeɪpə 'teɪp ˌriːdə/ *noun* a device which accepts punched paper tape and converts the punched information stored on it into signals which a computer can process

paper throw /'peɪpə θrəʊ/ *noun* rapid vertical movement of paper in a printer

paper tray /'peɪpə treɪ/ *noun* a container used to hold paper to be fed into a printer

paper-white monitor /ˌpeɪpə 'waɪt ˌmɒnɪtə/ *noun* a monitor that normally displays black text on a white background, rather than the normal illuminated text on a black background

paragraph /'pærəgrɑːf/ *noun* **1.** (*in a document*) the section of text between two carriage return characters, with a unified subject **2.** (*in a memory map*) a 16-byte section of memory which starts at a hexadecimal address that can be evenly divided by 16

paragraph marker /'pærəgrɑːf ˌmɑːkə/ *noun* (*in a document*) a nonprinting character that shows where a carriage return is within a document

parallel /'pærəlel/ *adjective* **1.** referring to a computer system in which two or

more processors operate simultaneously on one or more items of data **2.** referring to two or more bits of a word transmitted over separate lines at the same time

parallel access /ˌpærəlel 'ækses/ *noun* data transfer between two devices with a number of bits, usually one byte wide, being sent simultaneously

parallel adder /ˌpærəlel 'ædə/ *noun* a number of adders joined together, allowing several digits to be added at once

parallel broadcast /ˌpærəlel 'brɔːdkɑːst/ *noun* a broadcast that is transmitted simultaneously by radio or television and over the Internet

parallel computer /ˌpærəlel kəm 'pjuːtə/ *noun* a computer with one or more logic or arithmetic units, allowing parallel processing

parallel connection /ˌpærəlel kə 'nekʃ(ə)n/ *noun* a connector on a computer allowing parallel data to be transferred ○ *Their transmission rate is 60,000 bps through parallel connection.*

parallel data transmission /ˌpærəlel 'deɪtə trænzˌmɪʃ(ə)n/ *noun* the transmission of bits of data simultaneously along a number of data lines

parallel input/output /ˌpærəlel ˌɪnpʊt 'aʊtpʊt/ *noun* full form of **PIO**

parallel input/output chip /ˌpærəlel ˌɪnpʊt 'aʊtpʊt ˌtʃɪp/ *noun* a dedicated integrated circuit that performs all handshaking, buffering and other operations needed when transferring parallel data to and from a CPU

parallel input/parallel output /ˌpærəlel ˌɪnpʊt ˌpærəlel 'aʊtpʊt/ *noun* full form of **PIPO**

parallel input/serial output /ˌpærəlel ˌɪnpʊt ˌsɪəriəl 'aʊtpʊt/ *noun* full form of **PISO**

parallel interface /ˌpærəlel 'ɪntəfeɪs/ *noun* a circuit and connector that allows parallel data to be received or transmitted. Also called **parallel port**

parallel operation /ˌpærəlel ˌɒpə 'reɪʃ(ə)n/ *noun* a number of processes carried out simultaneously on a number of inputs

parallel printer /ˌpærəlel 'prɪntə/ *noun* a printer that is connected to a computer via a parallel interface and accepts character data in parallel form

'The Wheelwriter 7000 offers 172Kb of document storage and mail-merge capabilities: it can be connected to a PC using the parallel printer port.' [*Computing*]

parallel priority system /ˌpærəlel praɪˈprɪti ˌsɪstəm/ *noun* a number of peripherals connected in parallel to one bus, which, if they require attention, send their address and an interrupt signal, which is then processed by the computer according to device priority

parallel processing /ˌpærəlel ˈprəʊsesɪŋ/ *noun* computer operation on several tasks simultaneously

parallel running /ˌpærəlel ˈrʌnɪŋ/ *noun* the running of an old and a new computer system together to allow the new system to be checked before it becomes the only system used

parallel search storage /ˌpærəlel ˈsɜːtʃ ˌstɔːrɪdʒ/ *noun* data retrieval from storage that uses part of the data other than an address to locate the data

parallel transfer /ˌpærəlel ˈtrænsfɜː/ *noun* data transfer between two devices with a number of bits, usually one byte wide, being sent simultaneously

parallel transmission /ˌpærəlel trænzˈmɪʃ(ə)n/ *noun* data transmitted over a number of data lines carrying all the bits of a data word simultaneously. Compare **serial transmission**

parameter /pəˈræmɪtə/ *noun* an item of information which defines the limits or actions of something, e.g. a variable, routine or program ○ *The X parameter defines the number of characters displayed across a screen.*

parameter-driven software /pəˌræmɪtə ˌdrɪv(ə)n ˈsɒftweə/ *noun* software whose main functions can be modified and tailored to a user's needs by a number of variables

parameterisation /pəˌræmɪtəraɪˈzeɪʃ(ə)n/, **parameterization** *noun* the action of setting parameters for software

parameter passing /pəˈræmɪtə ˌpɑːsɪŋ/ *noun* (*in a program*) a value passed to a routine or program when it is called

parameter testing /pəˈræmɪtə ˌtestɪŋ/ *noun* the process of using a program to examine the parameters and set up the system or program accordingly

parameter word /pəˈræmɪtə wɜːd/ *noun* a data word that contains information defining the limits or actions of a routine or program

parametric equaliser /ˌpærəmetrɪk ˈiːkwəlaɪzə/ *noun* a device that can enhance or reduce the levels of particular frequencies within an audio signal

parametric subroutine /ˌpærəmetrɪk ˈsʌbruːtiːn/ *noun* a subroutine that uses parameters to define its limits or actions

parent directory /ˈpeərənt daɪˌrekt(ə)ri/ *noun* (*in a DOS filing system*) the directory above a subdirectory

parent folder /ˈpeərənt ˌfəʊldə/ *noun* (*in an Apple Mac filing system*) one folder that contains other folders

parent object /ˈpeərənt ˌɒbdʒekt/ *noun* a page that contains the object that is being referenced

parent program /ˈpeərənt ˌprəʊgræm/ *noun* a program that starts another program, a child program, while it is still running (NOTE: Control passes back to the parent program when the child program has finished.)

parity /ˈpærɪti/ *noun* the fact of being equal

'The difference between them is that RAID level one offers mirroring, whereas level five stripes records in parity across the disks in the system.' [*Computing*]

parity bit /ˈpærɪti bɪt/ *noun* an extra bit added to a data word as a parity checking device

parity check /ˈpærɪti tʃek/ *noun* a method of checking for errors and that transmitted binary data has not been corrupted by adding an extra bit

parity flag /ˈpærɪti flæg/ *noun* an indicator that shows if data has passed a parity check or if data has odd or even parity

parity interrupt /ˈpærɪti ˌɪntərʌpt/ *noun* an interrupt signal from an error checking routine which indicates that received data has failed a parity check and is corrupt

parity track /ˈpærɪti træk/ *noun* a track on magnetic or paper tape that carries the parity bit

park /pɑːk/ *verb* to move the read/write head of a hard disk drive over a point on the disk where no data is stored ○ *When parked, the disk head will not damage any data if it touches the disk surface.*

parse /pɑːz/ *verb* to break down high-level language code into its element parts when translating into machine code (NOTE: parses – parsing – parsed)

parser /ˈpɑːzə/ *noun* a program that parses computer input (NOTE: Using the grammar of the language involved, it works out how a sentence can be constructed from the input and produces a parse tree to show this.)

part /pɑːt/ *noun* a section of something

part exchange /ˌpɑːt ɪksˈtʃeɪndʒ/ *noun* the act of giving an old product as part of the payment for a new one

partial carry /ˌpɑːʃ(ə)l ˈkæri/ *noun* temporary storage of all carries generated by parallel adders rather than a direct transfer

partial RAM /ˈpɑːʃ(ə)l ræm/ *noun* a RAM chip in which only a certain area of the chip functions correctly, usually in newly released chips (NOTE: Partial RAMs can be used by employing more than one to make up the capacity of one fully functional chip.)

partition /pɑːˈtɪʃ(ə)n/ *noun* **1.** an area of a hard disk that is treated as a logical drive and can be accessed as a separate drive ○ *I defined two partitions on this hard disk – called drive C: and D:.* **2.** a section of computer memory set aside as foreground or background memory ■ *verb* **1.** to divide a hard disk into two or more logical drives that can be accessed as separate drives **2.** to divide a large file or block into several smaller units which can be accessed and handled more easily

partitioned file /pɑːˈtɪʃ(ə)nd faɪl/ *noun* one file made up of several smaller sequential files, each part of which can be accessed individually by the control program

part page display /ˌpɑːt peɪdʒ dɪˈspleɪ/ *noun* a display of only a section of a page, and not the whole page

parts per quarter note /ˌpɑːts pɜː ˈkɔːtə ˌnəʊt/ *noun* full form of **PPQN**

PASCAL /ˈpæskæl/ *noun* a high-level structured programming language used both on micros and for teaching programming

pass /pɑːs/ *noun* **1.** the execution of a loop, once **2.** a single operation **3.** the action of moving the whole length of a magnetic tape over the read/write heads

password /ˈpɑːsˌwɜːd/ *noun* a word or series of characters which identifies a user so that he or she can access a system

'…the system's security features let you divide the disk into up to 256 password-protected sections' [*Byte*]

password protection /ˌpɑːswɜːd prəˈtekʃ(ə)n/ *noun* a computer software that requires the user to enter a password before he or she can gain access

paste /peɪst/ *verb* to insert text or graphics that has been copied or cut into a file ○ *Now that I have cut this paragraph from the end of the document, I can paste it in here.* (NOTE: pastes – pasting – pasted)

Paste Special /ˌpeɪst ˈspeʃ(ə)l/ *noun* a facility for inserting a special object such as sound, images or data from other applications into a document

patch /pætʃ/ *noun* a temporary correction made to a program by a user, often on the instructions of the software publisher

patch cord /ˈpætʃ kɔːd/ *noun* a short cable with a connector at each end, used to make an electrical connection on a patch panel

patch panel /pætʃ ˈpæn(ə)l/ *noun* a set of electrical terminals that can be interconnected using short patch cords, allowing quick and simple reconfiguration of a network

path /pɑːθ/ *noun* **1.** a possible route or sequence of events or instructions within the execution of a program **2.** a route from one point in a communications network to another **3.** (*in the DOS operating system*) a list of subdirectories in which the operating system should look for a named file ○ *You cannot run the program from the root directory until its directory is added to the path*

pathname /ˌpɑːθˈneɪm/ *noun* the location of a file with a listing of the subdirectories leading to it ○ *The pathname for the letter file is .DOC.*

pattern /ˈpæt(ə)n/ *noun* a series of regular lines or shapes which are repeated again and again

patterned /ˈpæt(ə)nd/ *adjective* with patterns

pattern palette /ˈpæt(ə)n ˌpælət/ *noun* a range of predefined patterns that can be used to fill an area of an image

pattern recognition /ˌpæt(ə)n ˌrekəgˈnɪʃ(ə)n/ *noun* algorithms or program functions that can identify a shape, e.g. from a video camera

pause key /ˈpɔːz kiː/ *noun* a keyboard key that temporarily stops a process, often a scrolling screen display, until the key is pressed a second time

payment gateway /ˈpeɪmənt ˌɡeɪtweɪ/ *noun* a server or organisation that acts as an interface between the payment systems of the seller and the buyer when payments are made over the Internet

payment gateway certificate authority /ˌpeɪmənt ˌɡeɪtweɪ səˈtɪfɪkət ɔːˌθɒrɪti/ *noun* an organisation that issues, renews or cancels the certificates that identify an Internet payment gateway. Abbr **PGCA**

PB *abbr* petabyte

PBX *abbr* private branch exchange

PC /ˌpiː ˈsiː/ *noun* a computer that uses an Intel 80x86 processor and is based on the IBM PC-style architecture. Full form **personal computer** (NOTE: PC originally referred to a microcomputer specification with an 8086-based low-power computer.)

PC-97 *noun* the set of basic requirements for the hardware of a PC system that can run the Windows 95 operating system

PC-98 *noun* the set of basic requirements for the hardware of a PC system that can run the Windows 98 operating system

PC/AT /ˌpiː siː eɪ ˈtiː/ *noun* a PC-compatible computer that used an Intel 80286 processor and was fitted with 16-bit ISA expansion connectors

PC/AT keyboard /ˌpiː siː eɪ tiː ˈkiːbɔːd/ *noun* a keyboard that features 12 function keys arranged in one row along the top of the keyboard

PCB *abbr* printed circuit board

PC Card /ˌpiː siː ˈkɑːd/ *noun* an electronic device, about the same size as a thick credit card, that can be plugged into a PCMCIA adapter to provide a particular function. ◊ **PCMCIA** (NOTE: For example, PC Cards are available that provide a modem, NIC, extra memory and hard disk drive functions.)

PC-compatible /ˌpiː ˌsiː kəmˈpætəb(ə)l/ *adjective* referring to a computer that is compatible with the IBM PC

PC-DOS /ˌpiː siː ˈdɒs/ *noun* a version of MS-DOS that is sold by IBM

p-channel metal oxide semiconductor /piː ˌtʃæn(ə)l ˌmet(ə)l ˌɒksaɪd ˌsemikənˈdʌktə/ *noun* full form of **PMOS**

PCI /ˌpiː siː ˈeɪ/ *noun* a specification produced by Intel defining a type of fast local bus that allows high-speed data transfer between the processor and expansion cards. Full form **peripheral component interconnect**

PCL /ˌpiː siː ˈel/ *noun* standard set of commands, defined by Hewlett Packard,

that allow a computer to control a printer. Full form **printer control language**

PCM /ˌpiː siː ˈem/ *noun* **1.** a company that produces add-on boards which are compatible with another manufacturer's computer. Full form **plug-compatible manufacturer 2.** a way of storing sounds in an accurate, compact format that is used by high-end sound cards. Full form **pulse-code modulation**

PCMCIA /ˌpiː siː em siː aɪ ˈeɪ/ *noun* a specification for add-in expansion cards that are the size of a credit card with a connector at one end ○ *The extra memory is stored on this PCMCIA card and I use it on my laptop.* Full form **Personal Computer Memory Card International Association**

PCMCIA card /ˌpiː siː ˌem ˌsiː aɪ ˈeɪ kɑːd/ *noun* add-in memory or a peripheral which complies with the PCMCIA standard

PCMCIA connector /ˌpiː siː ˌem ˌsiː aɪ ˌeɪ kəˈnektə/ *noun* a 68-pin connector that is inside a PCMCIA slot and on the end of a PCMCIA card

PCMCIA slot /ˌpiː siː ˌem ˌsiː aɪ ˈeɪ slɒt/ *noun* an expansion slot, normally on a laptop, that can accept a PCMCIA expansion card

P-code /piː kəʊd/ *noun* an intermediate code produced by a compiler that is ready for an interpreter to process, usually for PASCAL programs

PCS *abbr* personal communications services

PC/TV /ˌpiː siː tiː ˈviː/ *noun* a personal computer that can receive, decode and display standard television images

PCU /ˌpiː siː ˈjuː/ *noun* a device used to convert input and output signals and instructions to a form that a peripheral device will understand. Full form **peripheral control unit**

PCX file /ˌpiː siː siː eks ˈfaɪl/ *noun* a method of storing a bitmap graphic image file on disk

PC/XT /ˌpiː siː siː eks ˈtiː/ *noun* a PC-compatible computer that was fitted with a hard disk drive and used a 8086 Intel processor

PC/XT keyboard /ˌpiː siː siː eks tiː ˈkiːbɔːd/ *noun* a keyboard that features 10 function keys arranged in two columns along the left hand side of the keyboard

PD *abbr* public domain

PDA /ˌpiː diː 'eɪ/ *noun* a lightweight palmtop computer that provides the basic functions of a diary, notepad, address-book and to-do list together with fax or modem communications. Full form **personal digital assistant** (NOTE: Current PDA designs do not have a keyboard, but use a touch-sensitive screen with a pen and handwriting-recognition to control the software.)

PDF /ˌpiː diː 'ef/ *noun* a file format used by Adobe Acrobat. Full form **portable document format**

PDL *abbr* **1.** page description language **2.** program design language

PDN *abbr* public data network

peak /piːk/ *noun* the highest point ■ *verb* to reach the highest point

peak output /piːk 'aʊtpʊt/ *noun* the highest output

peak period /'piːk ˌpɪəriəd/ *noun* the time of the day when most power is being used

peek /piːk/ *noun* a BASIC computer instruction that allows the user to read the contents of a memory location ○ *You need the instruction PEEK 1452 here to examine the contents of memory location 1452.* Compare **poke**

peer /pɪə/ *noun* each of two similar devices operating on the same network protocol level

peer-to-peer network /ˌpɪə tə 'pɪə/ *noun* a local area network, usually using NICs in each computer, that does not use a central dedicated server, but instead each computer in the network shares the jobs ○ *We have linked the four PCs in our small office using a peer-to-peer network.*

pel /pel/ *noun* same as **pixel**

pen /pen/ *noun* same as **light pen**

pen computer /pen kəm'pjuːtə/ *noun* a type of computer that uses a light pen instead of a keyboard for input (NOTE: The computer has a touch-sensitive screen and uses handwriting-recognition software to interpret the commands written on the screen using the light pen.)

pen plotter /'pen ˌplɒtə/ *noun* a plotter that uses removable pens to draw an image on paper

pen recorder /pen rɪ'kɔːdə/ *noun* a peripheral which moves a pen over paper according to an input

Pentium /'pentiəm/ a trade name for a range of electronic processor components developed by Intel (NOTE: They are back-wards-compatible with the 80x86 family used in IBM PCs. The processor uses a 32-bit address bus and a 64-bit data bus.)

per □ **as per** according to ■ *noun* **1.** at a rate of **2.** out of or for each ○ *The rate of imperfect items is about 25 per 1.000.*

per cent /pə 'sent/ *adjective, adverb* out of each hundred or for each hundred □ **10 per cent** ten in every hundred ○ *what is the increase per cent? fifty per cent of nothing is still nothing*

percentage point /pə'sentɪdʒ pɔɪnt/ *noun* one per cent

percentile /pə'sen̩taɪl/ *noun* one of a series of 99 figures below which a certain percentage of the total falls

per day /pə 'deɪ/ *phrase* for each day

perforated tape /'pɜːfəˌreɪtɪd teɪp/ *noun* a paper tape or long strip of tape on which data can be recorded in the form of punched holes

perforation /ˌpɜːfə'reɪʃ(ə)n/ *noun* any one of a line of very small holes in a sheet of paper or continuous stationery, to help when tearing

perforator /'pɜːfəreɪtə/ *noun* a machine that punches holes in a paper tape

perform /pə'fɔːm/ *verb* to do well or badly

performance /pə'fɔːməns/ *noun* the way in which someone or something works

per hour /ˌpə 'aʊə/ *adverb* for each hour

period /'pɪəriəd/ *noun* **1.** a length of time ○ *for a period of time* or *for a period of months* or *for a six-year period* **2.** a printing sign used at the end of a piece of text, the full stop

periodic /ˌpɪəri'ɒdɪk/, **periodical** /ˌpɪəri'ɒdɪk(ə)l/ *adjective* **1.** happening from time to time ○ *a periodic review of the company's performance* **2.** referring to a signal or event that occurs regularly ○ *The clock signal is periodic.*

periodically /ˌpɪəri'ɒdɪkli/ *adverb* from time to time

peripheral /pə'rɪf(ə)rəl/ *adjective* which is not essential ■ *noun* **1.** an item of hardware such as a terminals, printers or monitors which is attached to a main computer system ○ *Peripherals such as disk drives* or *printers allow data transfer and are controlled by a system, but contain independent circuits for their operation.* Also called **peripheral unit 2.** any device that allows communication between a system and itself but is not directly operated by the system

peripheral component interconnect /pə,rɪf(ə)rəl kəm,pəʊnənt 'ɪntəkənekt/ *noun* full form of **PCI**

peripheral control unit /pə,rɪf(ə)rəl kən'trəʊl ,juːnɪt/ *noun* full form of **PCU**

peripheral driver /pə,rɪf(ə)rəl 'draɪvə/ *noun* a program or routine used to interface, manage and control an input/output device or peripheral

peripheral equipment /pə,rɪf(ə)rəl ɪ'kwɪpmənt/ *noun* **1.** external devices that are used with a computer, e.g. a printer or scanner **2.** communications equipment external to a central processor that provides extra features

peripheral interface adapter /pə,rɪf(ə)rəl 'ɪntəfeɪs ə,dæptə/ *noun* full form of **PIA**

peripheral limited /pə,rɪf(ə)rəl 'lɪmɪtɪd/ *noun* a CPU that cannot execute instructions at normal speed because of a slow peripheral

peripheral memory /pə,rɪf(ə)rəl 'mem(ə)ri/ *noun* storage capacity available in a peripheral

peripheral processing unit /pə,rɪf(ə)rəl 'prəʊsesɪŋ ,juːnɪt/ *noun* a device used for input, output or storage which is controlled by the CPU. Abbr **PPU**

peripheral software driver /pə,rɪf(ə)rəl 'sɒftweə ,draɪvə/ *noun* a short section of computer program that allows a user to access and control a peripheral easily

peripheral transfer /pə,rɪf(ə)rəl 'trænsfɜː/ *noun* the movement of data between a CPU and peripheral

peripheral unit /pə,rɪf(ə)rəl 'juːnɪt/ *noun* **1.** an item of hardware such as a terminal, printer or monitor which is attached to a main computer system. Also called **peripheral 2.** any device that allows communication between a system and itself, but is not operated only by the system

Perl /pɜːl/ *noun* an interpreted programming language, usually used under Unix, used to create CGI scripts that can process forms or carry out functions on a web server to enhance a website. Full form **practical extraction and report language**

permanent dynamic memory /,pɜːmənənt daɪ,næmɪk 'mem(ə)ri/

noun a storage medium which retains data even when power is removed

permanent error /,pɜːmənənt 'erə/ *noun* an error in a system which cannot be repaired

permanent file /'pɜːmənənt faɪl/ *noun* a data file that is stored in a backing storage device such as a disk drive

permanent memory /,pɜːmənənt 'mem(ə)ri/ *noun* a computer memory that retains data even when power is removed

permanent swap file /,pɜːmənənt 'swɒp ,faɪl/ *noun* a file on a hard disk, made up of contiguous disk sectors, which stores a swap file for software that implements virtual memory, e.g. Microsoft Windows

permission /pə'mɪʃ(ə)n/ *noun* authorisation given to a particular user to access a certain shared resource or area of disk ○ *This user cannot access the file on the server because he does not have permission.*

permutation /,pɜːmjʊ'teɪʃ(ə)n/ *noun* each of a number of different ways in which something can be arranged ○ *The cipher system is very secure since there are so many possible permutations for the key.*

persistence /pə'sɪstəns/ *noun* the length of time that a CRT will continue to display an image after the picture beam has stopped tracing it on the screen ○ *Slow scan rate monitors need long persistence phosphor to prevent the image flickering.*

personal communications services /,pɜːs(ə)n(ə)l kə,mjuːnɪ'keɪʃ(ə)nz ,sɜːvɪsɪz/ *plural noun* a range of wireless communication systems that allow computers to exchange data with other devices such as a printer or PDA. Abbr **PCS**

personal computer /,pɜːs(ə)n(ə)l kəm'pjuːtə/ *noun* full form of **PC**

Personal Computer Memory Card International Association /,pɜːs(ə)nəl kəm,pjuːtə ,mem(ə)ri kɑːd ,ɪntənæʃ(ə)nəl ə,səʊsi'eɪʃ(ə)n/ *noun* full form of **PCMCIA** (*see*)

personal digital assistant /,pɜːs(ə)n(ə)l ,dɪdʒɪt(ə)l ə'sɪstənt/ *noun* full form of **PDA**

personal identification device /,pɜːs(ə)n(ə)l aɪ,dentɪfɪ'keɪʃ(ə)n dɪ ,vaɪs/ *noun* full form of **PID**

personal identification number /,pɜːs(ə)n(ə)l aɪ,dentɪfɪ'keɪʃ(ə)n ,nʌmbə/ *noun* full form of **PIN**

personal information manager /ˌpɜːs(ə)n(ə)l ˌɪnfə'meɪʃ(ə)n ˌmænɪdʒə/ *noun* full form of **PIM**

personalise /'pɜːs(ə)nəlaɪz/, **personalize** *verb* to customise or adapt a product specially for a certain user (NOTE: personalises – personalising – personalised)

personalising, personalizing *noun* the process of changing the settings of Windows from their default

COMMENT: For example, you can change the background wallpaper to display a different image behind your windows or you could change the colours of the title bars, the font used by Windows and so on. To make these changes, use the Start/Settings menu item in Windows or the Control Panel icon in the Main program group of Windows 3.1x.

perspective /pə'spektɪv/ *noun* the appearance of depth in an image in which objects that are further away from the viewer appear smaller

perspective correction /pə'spektɪv kəˌrekʃ(ə)n/ *noun* (*in a three-dimensional scene*) a method that is used to change the size and shape of an object to give the impression of depth and distance

PERT /pɜːt/ *noun* a definition of tasks or jobs and the time each requires, arranged in order to achieve a goal. Full form **program evaluation and review technique**

per week /pə 'wiːk/ *adverb* for each week

per year /pə 'jɪə/ *adverb* for each year

peta /petə/ *prefix* one quadrillion (2^{50}). Abbr **P**

petabyte /'petəbaɪt/ *noun* one quadrillion bytes. Abbr **PB**

PGCA *abbr* Payment Gateway Certificate Authority

PgDn /ˌpeɪdʒ 'daʊn/ *abbr* page down key

PGP /ˌpiː dʒiː 'piː/ *noun* an encryption system developed to allow anyone to protect the contents of his or her email messages from unauthorised readers. Full form **pretty good privacy** (NOTE: This system is often used when sending credit card or payment details over the Internet.)

PgUp /ˌpeɪdʒ 'ʌp/ *abbr* page up key

phantom ROM /'fæntəm rɒm/ *noun* a duplicate area of read-only memory that is accessed by a special code

phase /feɪz/ *noun* one part of a larger process ■ *verb* □ **to phase in, to phase out** to introduce something gradually or to reduce something gradually

phase alternation line /ˌfeɪz ˌɔːltə'neɪʃ(ə)n ˌlaɪn/ *noun* full form of **PAL**

phased change-over /ˌfeɪzd 'tʃeɪndʒ/ *noun* gradually introduction of a new device as the old one is used less and less

PHIGS /fɪgz/ *noun* a standard application interface between software and a graphics adapter that uses a set of standard commands to draw and manipulate 2D and 3D images. Full form **programmer's hierarchical interactive graphics standard**

phone /fəʊn/ *noun* a telephone or machine used for speaking to someone over a long distance ○ *We had a new phone system installed last week.*

Phone Dialer /'fəʊn ˌdaɪələ/ *noun* same as **Dialer**

phoneme /'fəʊniːm/ *noun* one small meaningful sound, several of which may make up a spoken word (NOTE: Phonemes are relevant to the analysis of voice input to recognise words and in the reproduction of speech.)

phone number /'fəʊn ˌnʌmbə/ *noun* a set of figures for a particular telephone ○ *He keeps a list of phone numbers in a little black book.*

Phong shading /'fɒŋ ˌʃeɪdɪŋ/ *noun* the most complex method of applying shading to a three-dimensional scene that creates the smoothest shading effects and is better than a Gouraud shading (NOTE: The disadvantage is that this method is very processor-intensive and so takes a long time to process each scene.)

phosphor /'fɒsfə/ *noun* a substance that produces light when excited by some form of energy, usually an electron beam, used for coating the inside of a cathode ray tube

COMMENT: A thin layer of phosphor is arranged in a pattern of small dots on the inside of a television screen which produces an image when scanned by the picture beam.

phosphor coating /'fɒsfə ˌkəʊtɪŋ/ *noun* a thin layer of phosphor on the inside of a CRT screen

phosphor dots /'fɒsfə dɒtz/ *plural noun* individual dots of red, green and blue phosphor on a colour CRT screen

phosphor efficiency /'fɒsfə ɪˌfɪʃ(ə)nsi/ *noun* a measure of the amount of light produced in ratio to the energy received from an electron beam

phosphor triad /'fɒsfə ˌtraɪæd/ *noun* a group of three individual phosphor dots,

photo- 254

representing red, green and blue, that together form a single pixel on a colour screen

photo- /ˈfəʊtəʊ/ *prefix* light

PhotoCD /ˈfəʊtəʊ siː ˌdiː/ *noun* a standard developed to store 35 mm photographic slides or negatives in digital format on a CD-ROM

photodigital memory /ˈfəʊtəʊ ˌdɪdʒɪt(ə)l ˈmem(ə)ri/ *noun* a computer memory system that uses a laser to write data onto a piece of film which can then be read many times but not written to again. Also called **WORM**

photorealistic /ˌfəʊtəʊrɪəˈlɪstɪk/ *adjective* referring to a computer image that has almost the same quality and clarity as a photograph

photoresist /ˌfəʊtəʊrɪˈzɪst/ *noun* a chemical or material that hardens into an etch resistant material when light is shone on it ○ *To make the PCB, coat the board with photoresist, place the opaque pattern above, expose, then develop and etch, leaving the conducting tracks.*

phototypesetter /ˌfəʊtəʊˈtaɪpsetə/ *noun* a device that can produce very high-resolution text on photosensitive paper or film

physical address /ˌfɪzɪk(ə)l əˈdres/ *noun* a memory address that corresponds to a hardware memory location in a memory device

physical database /ˌfɪzɪk(ə)l ˈdeɪtəbeɪs/ *noun* the organisation and structure of a stored database

physical layer /ˌfɪzɪk(ə)l ˈleɪə/ *noun* the lowest ISO/OSI standard network layer that defines rules for bit rate, power and medium for signal transmission

physical memory /ˌfɪzɪk(ə)l ˈmem(ə)ri/ *noun* memory fitted in a computer

physical parameter /ˌfɪzɪk(ə)l pə ˈræmɪtə/ *noun* a description of the size, weight, voltage or power of a system

physical record /ˌfɪzɪk(ə)l ˈrekɔːd/ *noun* **1.** the maximum unit of data that can be transmitted in a single operation **2.** all the information, including control data, for one record stored in a computer system

physical topology /ˌfɪzɪk(ə)l tə ˈpɒlədʒi/ *noun* the actual arrangement of the cables in a network

PIA /ˌpiː aɪ ˈeɪ/ *noun* a circuit which allows a computer to communicate with a peripheral by providing serial and parallel

ports and other handshaking signals required to interface the peripheral. Full form **peripheral interface adapter**

PIC /ˌpiː aɪ ˈsiː/ *noun* an image compression algorithm used in Intel's DVI video system. Full form **picture image compression**

pica /ˈpaɪkə/ *noun* a typeface used on a printer to giving 10 characters to the inch

PICK /pɪk/ *noun* a multi-user, multitasking operating system that runs on mainframe, mini or PC computers

pickup reel /ˈpɪkʌp riːl/ *noun* an empty reel used to take the tape as it is played from a full reel

pico- /ˈpiːkəʊ/ *prefix* one million millionth of a unit. Abbr **p**

picosecond /ˈpiːkəʊˌsekənd/ *noun* one million millionth of a second. Abbr **pS**

PICS /pɪks/ *noun* a file format used to import a sequence of PICT files on an Apple Mac

PICT /pɪkt/ *noun* a method of storing vector graphic images, developed by Lotus for its 1–2–3 spreadsheet charts and graphs. Full form **PICture**

picture /ˈpɪktʃə/ *noun* a printed or drawn image of an object or scene ○ *This picture shows the new design.* ■ *verb* to visualise an object or scene ○ *Try to picture the layout before starting to draw it in.* (NOTE: pictures – picturing – pictured)

PICture /ˈpɪktʃə/ *noun* full form of **PICT**

picture beam /ˈpɪktʃə biːm/ *noun* a moving electron beam in a TV that produces an image on the screen by illuminating the phosphor coating and by varying its intensity according to the received signal

picture element /ˈpɪktʃə ˌelɪmənt/ *noun* same as **pixel**

picture image compression /ˌpɪktʃə ˈɪmɪdʒ kəmˌpreʃ(ə)n/ *noun* full form of **PIC**

picture level benchmark /ˌpɪktʃə ˌlev(ə)l ˈbentʃmɑːk/ *noun* full form of **PLB**

picture object /ˈpɪktʃə ˌɒbdʒekt/ *noun* an image created with a vector drawing package and stored as vectors rather than as a bitmap

picture processing /ˌpɪktʃə ˌprə ˈsesɪŋ/ *noun* the analysis of information contained in an image, usually by computer or electronic methods, providing analysis or recognition of objects in the image

picture transmission /'pɪktʃə trænz ˌmɪʃ(ə)n/ *noun* the transmission of images over a telephone line

PID /ˌpiː aɪ 'diː/ *noun* a device such as a bank card connected with or inserted into a system to identify or provide authorisation for a user. Full form **personal identification device**

pie chart /'paɪ tʃɑːt/ *noun* a diagram in which ratios are shown as slices of a circle ○ *The memory allocation is shown on this pie chart.*

PIF /ˌpiː aɪ 'et/ *noun* a Microsoft Windows file that contains the environment settings for a particular program. Full form **program information file**

piggyback /'pɪgibæk/ *verb* to connect two integrated circuits in parallel, one on top of the other to save space ○ *Piggyback those two memory chips to boost the memory capacity.*

piggyback entry /'pɪgibæk ˌentri/ *noun* unauthorised access to a computer system gained by using an authorised user's password or terminal

piggybacking /'pɪgibækɪŋ/ *noun* the process of using transmitted messages to carry acknowledgements from a message which has been received earlier

pilot /'paɪlət/ *adjective* used as a test, which if successful will then be expanded into a full operation ○ *The company set up a pilot project to see if the proposed manufacturing system was efficient.* ■ *verb* to test something ○ *They are piloting the new system.*

PILOT /'paɪlət/ *noun* a computer programming language that uses a text-based format and is mainly used in computer-aided learning

pilot system /'paɪlət ˌsɪstəm/ *noun* a system constructed to see if it can be manufactured, if it works and if the end user likes it

PIM /ˌpiː aɪ 'em/ *noun* a software utility that stores and manages a user's everyday data such as diary, telephone numbers, address book and notes. Full form **personal information manager**

pin /pɪn/ *noun* **1.** one of several short pieces of wire attached to an integrated circuit package that allows the IC to be connected to a circuit board **2.** a short piece of metal, part of a plug which fits into a hole

in a socket ○ *Use a three-pin plug to connect the printer to the mains.*

PIN /pɪn/ *noun* a unique sequence of digits that identifies a user to provide authorisation to access a system, often used on automatic cash dispensers or with a PID or password to enter a system. Full form **personal identification number**

pinchwheel /'pɪntʃwiːl/ *noun* a small rubber wheel in a tape machine that holds the tape in place and prevents flutter

pin-compatible /ˌpɪn kəm'pætɪb(ə)l/ *adjective* referring to an electronic chip that can directly replace another because the arrangement of the pins is the same and they carry the same signals ○ *It's easy to upgrade the processor because the new one is pin-compatible.*

pincushion distortion /ˌpɪnkʊʃ(ə)n dɪ'stɔːʃ(ə)n/ *noun* a fault with a monitor that causes the distortion of an image displayed in which the edges curve in towards the centre

pinfeed /'pɪnfiːd/ *noun* same as **tractor feed**

PING /pɪŋ/ *noun* a software utility that will test all the nodes on a network or Internet to ensure that they are working correctly. Full form **packet Internet groper**

pinout /'pɪnaʊt/ *noun* a description of the position of all the pins on an integrated circuit together with their function and signal

PIO /ˌpiː aɪ 'əʊ/ *noun* data input or output from a computer in a parallel form. Full form **parallel input/output**. ◊ **PIPO, PISO**

pipe /paɪp/ *noun* (*in DOS and UNIX*) a symbol, usually (), that tells the operating system to send the output of one command to another command, instead of displaying it

pipeline /'paɪplaɪn/ *verb* **1.** to schedule inputs to arrive at the microprocessor when nothing else is happening, so increasing apparent speed **2.** to carry out more than one task at a time: e.g., to compress and store an image on disk as it is being scanned (NOTE: pipelines – pipelining – pipelined)

pipeline burst cache /ˌpaɪplaɪn bɜːst 'kæʃ/ *noun* a secondary synchronous cache that uses very high speed memory chips, with access speeds of around 9 ns

PIPO /ˌpiː aɪ piː 'əʊ/ *noun* a device that can accept and transmit parallel data. Full form **parallel input/parallel output**

piracy /'paɪrəsi/ *noun* the process of copying patented inventions or copyright works

pirate /'paɪrət/ *noun* a person who copies a patented invention or a copyright work and sells it ○ *The company is trying to take the software pirates to court.* ■ *verb* to manufacture copies of an original copyrighted work illegally ○ *a pirated DVD* or *a pirated design* (NOTE: pirates – pirating – pirated)

COMMENT: The items most frequently pirated are programs on magnetic disks and tapes, which are relatively simple to copy.

pirate copy /ˌpaɪrət 'kɒpi/ *noun* a copy of software or other copyright material which has been made illegally

pirate software /ˌpaɪrət 'sɒftweə/ *noun* an illegal copy of a software package

PISO /ˌpi: aɪ es 'əʊ/ *noun* a device that can accept parallel data and transmit serial data. Full form **parallel input/serial output**

pit /pɪt/ *noun* a bump or impression on the surface of an optical disk that represents a bit of data, created by a master disk during manufacture

pitch /pɪtʃ/ *noun* the number of characters which will fit into one inch of line, when the characters are typed in single spacing (NOTE: Pitch is used on line printers, the normal pitches available being 10, 12 and 17 characters per inch.)

pitch scale factor /ˌpɪtʃ 'skeɪl ˌfæktə/ *noun* an instruction to a waveform audio device to change the pitch of the sound by a factor

pix /pɪks/ *plural noun* pictures

pixel /'pɪksəl/ *noun* the smallest single unit or point of a display whose colour or brightness can be controlled. Also called **picture element**

'…adding 40 to each pixel brightens the image and can improve the display's appearance' [*Byte*]

COMMENT: In high resolution display systems the colour or brightness of a single pixel can be controlled; in low resolution systems a group of pixels are controlled at the same time.

pixelated /'pɪksəleɪtɪd/ *adjective* referring to an image on a computer or television screen that is made up of pixels, especially one that is unclear or distorted

PLA /ˌpi: el 'eɪ/ *noun* an integrated circuit that can be permanently programmed to perform logic operations on data using a matrix of links between input and output pins. Full form **programmable logic array**

COMMENT: A PLA consists of a large matrix of paths between input and output pins, with logic gates and a fusible link at each connection point that can be broken or left to conduct when programming to define a function from input to output.

place /pleɪs/ *noun* the position of a digit within a number

plain old telephone service /ˌpleɪn əʊld 'telɪfəʊn ˌsɜːvɪs/ *noun* full form of **POTS**

plaintext /ˌpleɪn'tekst/ *noun* text or information that has not been encrypted or coded ○ *The messages were sent as plaintext by telephone.* Opposite **ciphertext**

plan /plæn/ *noun* **1.** an organised way of doing something **2.** a drawing which shows how something is arranged or how something will be built ■ *verb* to organise carefully how something should be done (NOTE: planning – planned)

PLAN /plæn/ *noun* a low-level programming language

planar /'pleɪnə/ *adjective* referring to a method of producing integrated circuits by diffusing chemicals into a slice of silicon to create the different components ■ *noun* referring to graphical objects or images arranged on the same plane

plane /pleɪn/ *noun* one layer of an image that can be manipulated independently within a graphics program

planner /'plænə/ *noun* a software program that allows appointments and important meetings to be recorded and arranged in the most efficient way

planning /'plænɪŋ/ *noun* the activity of organising how something should be done ○ *long-term planning* or *short-term planning*

plant /plɑːnt/ *verb* to store a result in memory for later use

plasma display /'plæzmə dɪˌspleɪ/ *noun* same as **gas discharge display**

COMMENT: This is a thin display usually used in small portable computers.

plastic bubble keyboard /ˌplæstɪk ˌbʌb(ə)l 'kiːbɔːd/ *noun* a keyboard whose keys are small bubbles in a plastic sheet over a contact which when pressed completes a circuit

COMMENT: These are very solid and cheap keyboards but are not ideal for rapid typing.

platform /'plætˌfɔːm/ *noun* a standard type of hardware that makes up a particular range of computers ○ *This software will only work on the IBM PC platform.*

platform independence /ˌplætfɔːm ˌɪndɪ'pendəns/ *noun* the fact that software or a network can work with or connect to different types of incompatible hardware

platter /'plætə/ *noun* one disk within a hard disk drive

COMMENT: The disks are made of metal or glass and coated with a magnetic compound; each platter has a read/write head that moves across its surface to access stored data.

play back /ˌpleɪ 'bæk/ *verb* to read data or a signal from a recording ○ *After you have recorded the music, press this button to play it back and hear what it sounds like.*

playback head /'pleɪˌbæk hed/ *noun* a piece of equipment that reads signals recorded on a storage medium and usually converts them to an electrical signal ○ *disk playback head*

playback rate scale factor /'pleɪbæk reɪt skeɪl ˌfæktə/ *noun* **1.** (in *waveform audio*) sound played back at a different rate, directed by another application, to create a special effect **2.** (in *video displayed on a computer*) the point at which video playback is no longer smooth and appears jerky because of missed frames

playback speed /'pleɪˌbæk spiːd/ *noun* the rate at which tape travels past a playback head

PLB /ˌpiː el 'biː/ *noun* benchmark used to measure the performance (not the quality) of a graphics adapter or workstation. Full form **picture level benchmark**

PLD *abbr* programmable logic device

plex database /'pleks ˌdeɪtəbeɪs/ *noun* a database structure in which data items can be linked together

plex structure /'pleks ˌstrʌktʃə/ *noun* a network structure or data structure in which each node is connected to all the others

PL/M /ˌpiː el 'em/ *noun* a high level programming language derived for use on microprocessors. Full form **programming language for microprocessors**

plot /plɒt/ *noun* a graph or map ■ *verb* to draw an image (especially a graph) based on information supplied as a series of coordinates

plotter /'plɒtə/ *noun* a computer peripheral that draws straight lines between two coordinates

COMMENT: Plotters are used for graph and diagram plotting and can plot curved lines as a number of short straight lines.

plotter driver /'plɒtə ˌdraɪvə/ *noun* dedicated software that converts simple instructions issued by a user into complex control instructions to direct the plotter

plotter pen /'plɒtə pen/ *noun* an instrument used in a plotter to mark the paper with ink as it moves over the paper

plotting mode /'plɒtɪŋ məʊd/ *noun* the ability of some word-processors to produce graphs by printing a number of closely spaced characters rather than individual pixels, which results in a broad low-resolution line

plug /plʌg/ *noun* a connector with protruding pins that is inserted into a socket to provide an electrical connection ○ *The printer is supplied with a plug.* ■ *verb* □ **plug in** to make an electrical connection by pushing a plug into a socket ○ *No wonder the computer does nothing, you have not plugged it in at the mains.*

plug and play /ˌplʌg ən 'pleɪ/ *noun* a facility in PCs that allows a user to plug a new adapter card into their PC without having to configure it or set any switches. Abbr **PNP**

plug-compatible /plʌg kəm'pætəb(ə)l/ *adjective* referring to equipment that can work with several different types of computer, so long as they have the correct type of connector

plug-compatible manufacturer /ˌplʌg kəmˌpætɪb(ə)l ˌmænjʊ'fæktʃərə/ *noun* full form of **PCM**

plug-in /'plʌg ɪn/ *noun* a program that works with a web browser to increase the functionality of the browser. ♦ **browser, helper application**

plug-in unit /'plʌg ɪn ˌjuːnɪt/ *noun* a small electronic circuit that can be simply plugged into a system to increase its power

plus /plʌs/, **plus sign** /'plʌs saɪn/ *noun* a printed or written sign (+) showing that figures are added or showing a positive value

PLV /ˌpiː el 'viː/ *noun* the highest-quality video compression algorithm used with DVI full-motion video sequences. Full form **production level video**

PMOS /'piː mɒs/ *noun* a metal oxide semiconductor transistor that conducts via a small region of p-type semiconductor. Full form **p-channel metal oxide semiconductor**

PMS /ˌpiː em 'es/ *abbr* Pantone Matching System

PNP /ˌpiː en 'piː/ *abbr* plug and play

pnp transistor /ˌpiː en 'piː trænˌzɪstə/ *noun* the layout of a bipolar transistor whose collector and emitter are of p-type semiconductor and whose base is n-type semiconductor

pointer /'pɔɪntə/ *noun* **1.** a variable in a computer program that contains the address to a data item or instruction ○ *Increment the contents of the pointer to the address of the next instruction.* **2.** a graphical symbol used to indicate the position of a cursor on a computer display ○ *Desktop publishing on a PC is greatly helped by the use of a pointer and mouse.*

pointer file /'pɔɪntə faɪl/ *noun* a file of pointers referring to large amounts of stored data

pointing device /'pɔɪntɪŋ dɪˌvaɪs/ *noun* an input device that controls the position of a cursor on screen as it is moved by the user. ♢ **mouse**

point of presence /ˌpɔɪnt əv 'prezəns/ *noun* full form of **POP**

point-of-sale /ˌpɔɪnt əv 'seɪl/ *noun* a place in a shop where goods are paid for. Abbr **POS**

point sampling /pɔɪnt 'sɑːmplɪŋ/ *noun* a method of adding texture and shading to a three-dimensional scene or object, in which the algorithm calculates the perceived depth, position and shade of each point on the image and applies a texture map pixel, or texel, to that point

point size /ˌpɔɪnt 'saɪz/ *noun* (*in typography*) a unit of measure equal to 1/72-inch, used to measure type or text

point to point /'pɔɪnt tə, tʊ/ *noun* **1.** a direct link between two devices **2.** communications network in which every node is directly connected to every other node

point to point protocol /ˌpɔɪnt tə ˌpɔɪnt 'prəʊtəkɒl/ *noun* full form of **PPP**

point-to-point tunneling protocol /pɔɪnt tə, tʊ pɔɪnt ˌ'tʌn(ə)lɪŋ/ *noun* full form of **PPTP**

poke /pəʊk/ *noun* a computer instruction that modifies an entry in a memory by writing a number to an address in memory ○ *Poke 1423,74 will write the data 74 into location 1423.* Compare **peek**

POL *abbr* problem-orientated language

polar /'pəʊlə/ *adjective* referring to poles

polar coordinates /ˌpəʊlə kəʊ 'ɔːdɪnəts/ *noun* a system of defining positions as an angle and distance from the origin

polarised edge connector /ˌpəʊləraɪzd 'edʒ kəˌnektə/ *noun* an edge connector that has a hole or key to prevent it being plugged in the wrong way round

polarised plug /ˌpəʊləraɪzd 'plʌg/ *noun* a plug which has a feature (usually a peg or a special shape) which allows it to be inserted into a socket only in one way

polarity /pəʊ'lærəti/ *noun* the definition of direction of flow of flux or current in an object

polarity test /pəʊ'lærəti test/ *noun* a check to see which electrical terminal is positive and which negative

policy /'pɒlisi/ *noun* ♦ **acceptable use policy**

Polish notation /ˌpəʊliʃ nəʊ'teɪʃ(ə)n/ ♦ **reverse Polish notation**

poll /pəʊl/ *verb* (*of a computer*) to determine the state of a peripheral in a network

polled interrupt /ˌpəʊld 'ɪntərʌpt/ *noun* an interrupt signal determined by polling devices

polling /'pəʊlɪŋ/ *noun* a system of communication between a controlling computer and a number of networked terminals (the computer checks each terminal in turn to see if it is ready to receive or transmit data, and takes the required action)

COMMENT: The polling system differs from other communications systems in that the computer asks the terminals to transmit *or* receive, not the other way round.

polling characters /ˌpəʊlɪŋ 'kærɪktəz/ *plural noun* a special sequence of characters for each terminal to be polled, which ensures that when a terminal recognises its sequence, it responds

polling interval /'pəʊlɪŋ ˌɪntəv(ə)l/ *noun* a period of time between two polling operations

polling list /'pəʊlɪŋ lɪst/ *noun* the order in which terminals are to be polled by a computer

polling overhead /'pəʊlɪŋ ˌəʊvəhed/ *noun* the amount of time spent by a computer calling and checking each terminal in a network

polygon /'pɒlɪgən/ *noun* a graphics shape with three or more sides

polygon mesh model /ˌpɒlɪgən ˈmeʃ ˌmɒd(ə)l/ *noun* same as **wire frame model**

polynomial code /ˌpɒliˈnəʊmiəl kəʊd/ *noun* an error detection system that uses a set of mathematical rules applied to the message before it is transmitted and again when it is received to reproduce the original message

polyphony /pəˈlɪfəni/ *noun* a device that can play more than one musical note at a time

pop /pɒp/ *verb* to read and remove the last piece of data from a stack

POP /pɒp/ *noun* telephone access number for a service provider that can be used to connect to the Internet via a modem. Full form **point of presence**

POP 2 /ˈpɒp tuː/ *noun* a high level programming language used for list processing applications

POP 3 /ˌpɒp ˈθriː/ *noun* a system used to transfer electronic mail messages between a user's computer and a server at an ISP

pop-down menu /ˌpɒp daʊn ˈmenjuː/ *noun* a menu that can be displayed on the screen at any time by pressing the appropriate key, usually displayed over material already on the screen. Also called **pop-up menu**

populate /ˈpɒpjʊleɪt/ *verb* to fill the sockets on a printed circuit board with components

pop-up menu /ˌpɒp ʌp ˈmenjuː/ *noun* same as **pop-down menu**

pop-up window /ˌpɒp ʌp ˈwɪndəʊ/ *noun* a window that can be displayed on the screen at any time on top of anything that is already on the screen

'…you can use a mouse to access pop-up menus and a keyboard for word processing' [*Byte*]

port /pɔːt/ *noun* a socket or physical connection allowing data transfer between a computer's internal communications channel and another external device

portability /ˌpɔːtəˈbɪlɪti/ *noun* an extent to which software or hardware can be used on several systems

'…although portability between machines is there in theory, in practice it just isn't that simple' [*Personal Computer World*]

portable /ˈpɔːtəb(ə)l/ *noun* a compact self-contained computer that can be carried around and used either with a battery pack or mains power supply ■ *adjective* referring to any hardware or software or

data files that can used on a range of different computers

portable document format /ˌpɔːtəb(ə)l ˈdɒkjʊmənt ˌfɔːmæt/ *noun* full form of **PDF**

portable operating system interface /ˌpɔːtəb(ə)l ˈɒpəreɪtɪŋ ˌsɪstəm ˌɪntəfeɪs/ *noun* full form of **POSIX**

portable programs /ˌpɔːtəb(ə)l ˈprəʊgræmz/ *noun* same as **portable software**

portable software /ˌpɔːtəb(ə)l ˈsɒftweə/ *noun* programs that can be run on several different computer systems

portal /ˈpɔːt(ə)l/ *noun* a website that provides links to information and other websites

portrait /ˈpɔːtrɪt/ *adjective* the orientation of a page or piece of paper in which the longest edge is vertical

port replicator /ˈpɔːt ˌreplɪkeɪtə/ *noun* a version of a docking station that allows a laptop computer to be connected to duplicate the connection ports on the back of the laptop, allowing a user to keep a mouse, power cable, and printer connected to the port replicator and easily insert the laptop to use these ports without having to plug in cables each time the machine is used

port selector /pɔːt sɪˈlektə/ *noun* a switch that allows the user to choose which peripheral a computer is connected to, via its o/p port

port sharing /pɔːt ˈʃeərɪŋ/ *noun* a device that is placed between one I/O port and a number of peripherals, allowing the computer access to all of them

POS /pɒz/ *abbr* point-of-sale

positional /pəˈzɪʃ(ə)nəl/ *adjective* referring to position

positioning time /pəˈzɪʃ(ə)nɪŋ taɪm/ *noun* the amount of time required to access data stored in a disk drive or tape machine, including all mechanical movements of the read head and arm

positive /ˈpɒzɪtɪv/ *adjective* **1.** meaning 'yes' **2.** referring to an image that shows objects as they are seen **3.** an electrical voltage greater than zero

positive display /ˌpɒzɪtɪv dɪˈspleɪ/ *noun* a display in which the text and graphics are shown as black on a white background to imitate a printed page

positive logic /ˌpɒzɪtɪv ˈlɒdʒɪk/ *noun* a logic system in which a logical one is represented by a positive voltage level, and a logical zero represented by a zero or negative voltage level

positive photoresist /ˌpɒzɪtɪv ˌfəʊtəʊriˈzɪst/ *noun* a method of forming photographic images where exposed areas of photoresist are removed, used in making PCBs

positive presentation /ˌpɒzɪtɪv ˌprez(ə)nˈteɪʃ(ə)n/ *noun* a screen image which is coloured on a white background

positive response /ˌpɒzɪtɪv rɪ ˈspɒns/ *noun* a communication signal that indicates correct reception of a message

positive terminal /ˌpɒzɪtɪv ˈtɜːmɪn(ə)l/ *noun* a connection to a power supply source that is at a higher electrical potential than ground and supplies current to a component

POSIX /ˈpɒsɪks/ *noun* the IEEE standard that defines software that can be easily ported between hardware platforms. Full form **portable operating system interface**

post /pəʊst/ *verb* to enter data into a record in a file

postbyte /ˈpəʊstbaɪt/ *noun* in a program instruction, the data byte following the op code that defines the register to be used

post-editing /pəʊst ˈedɪtɪŋ/ *noun* the process of editing and modifying text after it has been compiled or translated by a machine

post-filtering /ˌpəʊst ˈfɪltərɪŋ/ *noun* image processing carried out after the image has been compressed

postfix /ˈpəʊstfɪks/ *noun* a word or letter written after another

postfix notation /ˌpəʊstfɪks nəʊ ˈteɪʃ(ə)n/ *noun* mathematical operations written in a logical way, so that the operator appears after the operands, which removes the need for brackets

post-formatted /ˌpəʊst ˈfɔːmætɪd/ *adjective* referring to text arranged at printing time rather than on screen

posting /ˈpəʊstɪŋ/ *noun* an online message, especially a message sent to an Internet newsgroup or bulletin board

postmaster /ˈpəʊstmɑːstə/ *noun* the email address of the person nominally in charge of email within a company

post mortem /pəʊst ˈmɔːtəm/ *noun* an examination of a computer program or piece of hardware after it has failed, designed to find out why the failure took place

post office /ˈpəʊst ˌɒfɪs/ *noun* the central store for the messages for users on a local area network

post office protocol /pəʊst ˈɒfɪs/ *noun* ♦ POP 3

postprocessor /ˌpəʊstˈprəʊsesə/ *noun* **1.** a microprocessor that handles semi-processed data from another device **2.** a program that processes data from another program, which has already been processed

post production /ˌpəʊst prəˈdʌkʃən/ *noun* the final editing process of a video or animation in which titles are added and sequences finalised

PostScript /ˈpəʊstskrɪpt/ a trade name for a standard page description language developed by Adobe Systems that offers flexible font sizing and positioning and is most often found in laser printers

potential difference /pəˌtenʃəl ˈdɪf(ə)rəns/ *noun* the voltage difference between two points in a circuit

POTS /pɒts/ *noun* the simplest, standard telephone line without any special features such as call waiting or forwarding, and without high-speed digital access such as ADSL. Full form **plain old telephone service**

power /ˈpaʊə/ *noun* **1.** the unit of energy in electronics equal to the product of voltage and current, measured in watts **2.** a mathematical term describing the number of times a number is to be multiplied by itself ○ *5 to the power 2 is equal to 25.* (NOTE: written as small figures in superscript: 10^5: say: 'ten to the power five') ■ *verb* to provide electrical or mechanical energy to a device ○ *The monitor is powered from a supply in the main PC.*

PowerBook /ˈpaʊəbʊk/ a trade name for a laptop version of a Macintosh computer, designed by Apple Corp

PowerCD /ˈpaʊə siː ˌdiː/ a trade name for a CD-ROM player produced by Apple that can connect to a television to display Photo CD images, or to a Macintosh as a standard CD-ROM drive, or to play back music CDs

power down /ˈpaʊə daʊn/ *verb* to turn off the electricity supply to a computer or other electronic device

power dump /ˈpaʊə dʌmp/ *verb* to remove all power from a computer

power failure /ˈpaʊə ˌfeɪljə/ *noun* the loss of the electric power supply

power loss /'paʊə lɒs/ *noun* the amount of power lost in transmission or through connection equipment

power management /'paʊə ˌmænɪdʒmənt/ *noun* software built into laptop computers and some newer desktop PCs and monitors that, to save energy, will automatically turn off components that are not being used

power monitor /'paʊə ˌmɒnɪtə/ *noun* a circuit that shuts off the electricity supply if it is faulty or likely to damage equipment

power-on reset /ˌpaʊə 'ɒn ˌriːset/ *noun* the automatic reset of a CPU to a known initial state immediately after power is applied

power on self test /ˌpaʊə ɒn ˌself 'test/ *noun* a series of hardware tests that a computer carries out when it is first switched on. Abbr **POST**

power pack /'paʊə pæk/ *noun* a self-contained box that will provide a voltage and current supply for a circuit

PowerPC /'paʊə piː ˌsiː/ a trade name for a high-performance RISC-based processor developed by Motorola

power supply /ˌpaʊə sə'plaɪ/ *noun* a PSU

power transient /ˌpaʊə 'trænziənt/ *noun* a very short duration voltage pulse or spike

power up /'paʊə ʌp/ *verb* to switch on or apply a voltage to a electrical device

power user /'paʊə ˌjuːzə/ *noun* a user who needs the latest, fastest model of computer because he or she runs complex or demanding applications

ppm /ˌpiː piː 'em/ *noun* the number of pages that a printer can print in one minute, used for describing the speed of a printer. Full form **pages per minute**

PPP /ˌpiː piː 'piː/ *noun* a protocol that supports a network link over an asynchronous (modem) connection and is normally used to provide data transfer between a user's computer and a remote server on the Internet using the TCP/IP network protocol. Full form **point to point protocol**

PPQN /ˌpiː piː kjuː 'en/ *noun* the most common time format used with standard MIDI sequences. Full form **parts per quarter note**

PPTP /ˌpiː piː tiː 'piː/ *noun* a protocol that allows a standard local-area network protocol (such as Novell's IPX or Microsoft's NetBEUI) to be sent over the Inter-net in a transparent manner without the user or operating system noticing, used by companies that want to use the Internet to connect servers in different offices. Full form **point-to-point tunneling protocol**

practical extraction and report language /ˌpræktɪk(ə)l ɪkˌstrækʃ(ə)n ən rɪ'pɔːt ˌlæŋgwɪdʒ/ *noun* full form of **Perl**

pre- /priː/ *prefix* before

pre-agreed /pri ə'griːd/ *adjective* which has been agreed in advance

pre-allocation /pri ˌælə'keɪʃ(ə)n/ *noun* the execution of a process which does not begin until all memory and peripheral requirements are free for use

pre-amplifier /pri 'æmplɪˌfaɪə/ *noun* an electronic circuit which amplifies a signal to a particular level, before it is fed to an amplifier for output

precede /prɪ'siːd/ *verb* to come before something ○ *This instruction cancels the instruction which precedes it.*

precedence /'presɪd(ə)ns/ *noun* a set of computational rules defining the order in which mathematical operations are calculated

precise /prɪ'saɪs/ *adjective* very exact ○ *The atomic clock will give the precise time of starting the process.*

precision /prɪ'sɪʒ(ə)n/ *noun* the fact that something is very accurate

precision of a number /prɪˌsɪʒ(ə)n əv ə 'nʌmbə/ *noun* the number of digits in a number

precompiled code /prɪkəmˌpaɪld 'kəʊd/ *noun* a code that is output from a compiler, ready to be executed

precondition /ˌpriːkən'dɪʃ(ə)n/ *verb* to condition data before it is processed

predefined /ˌpriːdɪ'faɪnd/ *adjective* which has been defined in advance

predicate /'predɪkət/ *noun* a function or statement used in rule-based programs such as expert systems

predictive /prɪ'dɪktɪv/ *adjective* using technology that works out which word a computer or mobile phone user is keying from its first few letters and automatically completes the word

pre-edit /pri 'edɪt/ *verb* to change text before it is run through a machine to make sure it is compatible

preemptive multitasking /pri ˌemptɪv 'mʌltitɑːskɪŋ/ *noun* a form of multitasking in which the operating system executes a program for a period of time, then passes control to the next program so preventing any one program using all the processor time

pre-fetch /priː'fetʃ/ *noun* CPU instructions stored in a short temporary queue before being processed, increasing the speed of execution

prefetch unit /priː'fetʃ ˌjuːnɪt/ *noun* part of a microprocessor that sorts out which instruction and data is next to be processed by looking in the main memory and the instruction cache and passing the next instruction on to the decode unit

pre-filtering /priː'fɪltərɪŋ/ *noun* image processing before the image is compressed (e.g., scaling the image)

prefix /'priːˌfɪks/ *noun* a code, instruction or character at the beginning of a message or instruction

prefix notation /'priːfɪks nəʊ ˌteɪʃ(ə)n/ *noun* mathematical operations written in a logical way, so that the operator appears before the operands, removing the need for brackets

preformatted /priː'fɔːmætɪd/ *adjective* which has been formatted already ○ *a preformatted disk*

pre-imaging /pri 'ɪmɪdʒɪŋ/ *noun* the process of generating one frame of an animation or video in a memory buffer before it is transferred on screen for display

preprinted stationery /priˌprɪntɪd 'steɪʃ(ə)n(ə)ri/ *noun* computer stationery which is preprinted with the company heading and form layout onto which the details will be printed by the computer

preprocess /priː'prəʊses/ *verb* to carry out initial organisation and simple processing of data

preprocessor /priː'prəʊsesə/ *noun* **1.** software that partly processes or prepares data before it is compiled or translated **2.** a small computer that carries out some initial processing of raw data before passing it to the main computer

'...the C preprocessor is in the first stage of converting a written program into machine instructions the preprocessor can be directed to read in another file before completion, perhaps because the same information is needed in each module of the program' [*Personal Computer World*]

preprogram /priː'prəʊɡræm/ *verb* to program a computer in advance

preprogrammed /priː'prəʊɡræmd/ *adjective* referring to a chip that has been programmed in the factory to perform one function

prescan /'priːskæn/ *noun* a feature of many flat-bed scanners that carry out a quick, low-resolution scan to allow you to re-position the original or mark the area that is to be scanned at a higher resolution

presentation graphics /ˌprez(ə)nteɪʃ(ə)n 'ɡræfɪks/ *plural noun* graphics used to represent business information or data

presentation layer /ˌprez(ə)n 'teɪʃ(ə)n ˌleɪə/ *noun* the sixth ISO/OSI standard network layer that agrees on formats, codes and requests for the start and end of a connection

Presentation Manager /ˌprez(ə)n 'teɪʃ(ə)n ˌmænɪdʒə/ *noun* a graphical user interface supplied with the OS/2 operating system

presentation software /ˌprez(ə)nteɪʃ(ə)n 'sɒftweə/ *noun* a software application that allows a user to create a business presentation with graphs, data, text and images

preset /ˌpriː'set/ *verb* to set something in advance ○ *The printer was preset with new page parameters.*

prestore /priː'stɔː/ *verb* to store data in memory before it is processed

presumptive address /prɪˌzʌmptɪv ə'dres/ *noun* the initial address in a program, used as a reference for others

presumptive instruction /prɪ ˌzʌmptɪv ɪn'strʌkʃən/ *noun* an unmodified program instruction that is processed to obtain the instruction to be executed

pretty good privacy /ˌprɪti ɡʊd 'prɪvəsi/ *noun* full form of **PGP**

preventative /prɪ'ventətɪv/, **preventive** /prɪ'ventɪv/ *adjective* which tries to stop something happening

preventive maintenance /prɪ ˌventɪv 'meɪntənəns/ *noun* a regular inspection and cleaning of a system to prevent faults occurring

preview /'priːˌvjuː/ *verb* to display text or graphics on a screen as it will appear when it is printed out

previewer /'priːvjuːə/ *noun* a feature that allows a user to see on screen what a page will look like when printed ○ *The built-in previewer allows the user to check for mistakes.*

PRI /ˌpiː ɑː 'aɪ/ *noun* a high-performance ISDN communications link that supports 23 separate B channels that can transfer 64Kbits/second plus one D channel for signalling and control. Full form **primary rate interface**

primary /ˈpraɪməri/ *adjective* first or basic or most important

primary channel /ˌpraɪməri ˈtʃæn(ə)l/ *noun* a channel that carries the data transmission between two devices

primary key /ˈpraɪməri kiː/ *noun* a unique identifying word that selects one entry from a database

primary memory /ˌpraɪməri ˈmem(ə)ri/ *noun* same as **core memory**

primary rate interface /ˌpraɪməri reɪt ˈɪntəfeɪs/ *noun* full form of **PRI**

primary station /ˌpraɪməri ˈsteɪʃ(ə)n/ *noun* the single station in a data network that can select a path and transmit

primary storage /ˌpraɪməri ˈstɔːrɪdʒ/ *noun* **1.** a small fast-access internal memory of a system which contains the program currently being executed **2.** the main internal memory of a system

prime /praɪm/ *adjective* very important

prime attribute /ˌpraɪm əˈtrɪbjuːt/ *noun* the most important feature or design of a system

primer /ˈpraɪmə/ *noun* a manual or simple instruction book with instructions and examples to show how a new program or system operates

primitive /ˈprɪmɪtɪv/ *noun* **1.** (*in programming*) a basic routine that can be used to create more complex routines **2.** (*in graphics*) a simple shape such as circle, square, line or curve used to create more complex shapes in a graphics program

print /prɪnt/ *noun* characters made in ink on paper ○ *The print from the new printer is much clearer than that from old one.* ■ *verb* to put letters or figures in ink on paper ○ *printed agreement* □ **print out** to print information stored in a computer with a printer

print control character /prɪnt kən ˈtrəʊl/, **print control code** *noun* a special character sent to a printer that directs it to perform an action or function, e.g. to change font, rather than print a character

printed circuit /ˌprɪntɪd ˈsɜːkɪt/, **printed circuit board** *noun* a flat insulating material that has conducting tracks of metal printed or etched onto its surface which complete a circuit when components are mounted on it. Abbr **PCB**

printer /ˈprɪntə/ *noun* a device that converts input data in an electrical form into a printed readable form. Abbr **PRN**

printer buffer /ˈprɪntə ˌbʌfə/ *noun* a temporary store for character data waiting to be printed, used to free the computer before the printing is completed making the operation faster

printer control characters /ˌprɪntə kənˈtrəʊl ˌkærɪktəz/ *noun* a command characters in a text which transmit printing commands to a printer

printer control language /ˌprɪntə kənˈtrəʊl ˌlæŋgwɪdʒ/ *noun* full form of **PCL**

printer driver /ˈprɪntə ˌdraɪvə/ *noun* dedicated software that converts and formats users' commands ready for a printer

printer emulation /ˈprɪntə emjuˌleɪʃ(ə)n/ *noun* a printer that is able to interpret the standard set of commands used to control another brand of printer ○ *This printer emulation allows my NEC printer to emulate an Epsom.*

printer-plotter /ˈprɪntə ˌplɒtə/ *noun* a high-resolution printer that is able to mimic a plotter and produce low-resolution plots

printer port /ˈprɪntə pɔːt/ *noun* the output port of a computer with a standard connector to which a printer is connected to receive character data

printer quality /ˈprɪntə ˌkwɒlɪti/ *noun* the standard of printed text from a particular printer

printer ribbon /ˈprɪntə ˌrɪbən/ *noun* a roll of inked material that passes between a printhead and the paper

printer's controller /ˌprɪntəz kən ˈtrəʊlə/ *noun* the main device in a printer that translates output from the computer into printing instructions

print format /prɪnt ˈfɔːmæt/ *noun* a way in which text is arranged when printed out, according to embedded codes, used to set features such as margins and headers

print formatter /ˈprɪnt ˌfɔːmætə/ *noun* a piece of software that converts embedded codes and print commands to printer control signals

print hammer /prɪnt ˈhæmə/ *noun* a moving arm in a daisy-wheel printer that presses the metal character form onto the printer ribbon leaving a mark on the paper

printhead /ˈprɪnthed/ *noun* **1.** a row of needles in a dot-matrix printer that produce characters as a series of dots **2.** the metal form of a character that is pressed onto an inked ribbon to print the character on paper

printing /'prɪntɪŋ/ *noun* the action of putting text and graphics onto paper

print job /'prɪnt dʒɒb/ *noun* a file in a print queue that contains all the characters and printer control codes needed to print one document or page

print life /ˌprɪnt 'laɪf/ *noun* the number of characters a component can print before needing to be replaced ○ *The printhead has a print life of over 400 million characters.*

Print Manager /'prɪnt ˌmænɪdʒə/ a software utility that is part of Microsoft Windows and is used to manage print queues

print modifiers /prɪnt 'mɒdɪˌfaɪəs/ *plural noun* codes in a document that cause a printer to change mode, e.g., from bold to italic

printout /'prɪntˌaʊt/ *noun* the final printed page

print pause /ˌprɪnt 'pɔːz/ *noun* the process of temporarily stopping a printer while printing, e.g. in order to change paper

print preview /prɪnt 'priːˌvjuː/ *noun* a function of a software product that lets the user see how a page will appear when printed

print quality /prɪnt 'kwɒlɪti/ *noun* the quality of the text or graphics printed, normally measured in dots per inch ○ *A desktop printer with a resolution of 600dpi provides good print quality.*

print queue /ˌprɪnt 'kjuː/ *noun* an area of memory that stores print jobs ready to send to the printer when it has finished its current work

Print Screen key /ˌprɪnt 'skriːn ˌkiː/ *noun* a key in the top right-hand side of the keyboard that sends the characters that are displayed on the screen to the printer

print server /prɪnt 'sɜːvə/ *noun* a computer in a network which is dedicated to managing print queues and printers

print spooling /ˌprɪnt 'spuːlɪŋ/ *noun* the automatic printing of a number of different documents in a queue at the normal speed of the printer, while the computer is doing some other task

print style /ˌprɪnt 'staɪl/ *noun* a typeface used on a certain printer or for a certain document

printwheel /'prɪntwiːl/ *noun* a daisy-wheel or the wheel made up of a number of arms, with a character shape at the end of each arm, used in a daisy-wheel printer

priority /praɪ'ɒrɪti/ *noun* the importance of a device or software routine in a computer system ○ *The operating system has priority over the application when disk space is allocated.*

priority interrupt /praɪˌɒrɪti 'ɪntərʌpt/ *noun* a signal to a computer that takes precedence over any other task

priority interrupt table /praɪˌɒrɪti 'ɪntərʌpt ˌteɪb(ə)l/ *noun* a list of peripherals and their priorities when they send an interrupt signal, used instead of a hardware priority scheduler

priority scheduler /praɪ'ɒrɪti ˌʃedjuːlə/ *noun* a system that organises tasks into correct processing priority to improve performance

priority sequence /praɪ'ɒrɪti ˌsiːkwəns/ *noun* the order in which various devices that have sent an interrupt signal are processed, according to their importance or urgency

privacy /'prɪvəsi/ *noun* the right of an individual to limit the extent of and control the access to the data that is stored about him

privacy of data /ˌprɪvəsi əv 'deɪtə/ *noun* the fact that particular data is secret and must not be accessed by users who have not been authorized

privacy of information /ˌprɪvəsi əv ˌɪnfə'meɪʃ(ə)n/ *noun* the fact that unauthorized users must not obtain data about private individuals from databases, or that each individual has the right to know what information is being held about him or her on a database

privacy statement /'prɪvəsi ˌsteɪtmənt/ *noun* the policy of a company, published on their website, that explains to visitors and customers what the company will or will not do with a customer's personal details

private /'praɪvət/ *adjective* belonging to an individual or to a company, not to the public

private address space /ˌpraɪvət ə 'dres ˌspeɪs/ *noun* a memory address range that is reserved for a single user, not for public access

private branch exchange /ˌpraɪvət 'brɑːntʃ ɪksˌtʃeɪndʒ/ *noun* a small telephone exchange located within a company that allows the people in the company to dial each other or to dial out to an external telephone number. Abbr **PBX**

private key cryptography /ˌpraɪvət kiː krɪpˈtɒɡrəgi/ *noun* a method of encrypting Internet messages that uses a single key both to encode and decode them

privilege /ˈprɪvɪlɪdʒ/ *noun* the status of a user as regards to the type of program he or she can run and the resources he or she can use

privileged account /ˌprɪvəlɪdʒd əˈkaʊnt/ *noun* a computer account that allows special programs or access to sensitive system data

privileged instructions /ˌprɪvəlɪdʒd ɪnˈstrʌkʃənz/ *plural noun* computer commands that can only be executed via a privileged account

privileged mode /ˈprɪvəlɪdʒd məʊd/ *noun* a mode of an Intel 80286 processor that is in protected mode and allows a program to modify vital parts of the operating environment

PRN /ˌpiː ɑː ˈen/ *noun* an acronym used in MS-DOS to represent the standard printer port. Full form **printer**

problem /ˈprɒbləm/ *noun* a malfunction or fault with hardware or software

problem definition /ˈprɒbləm ˌdefənɪʃ(ə)n/ *noun* the clear explanation, in logical steps, of a problem that is to be solved

problem diagnosis /ˈprɒbləm ˌdaɪəgnəʊsɪs/ *noun* the process of finding the cause of a fault or error and finding the method of repairing it

problem-orientated language /ˌprɒbləm ˌɔːriənteɪtɪd ˈlæŋgwɪdʒ/ *noun* a high-level programming language that allows certain problems to be expressed easily. Abbr **POL**

procedural /prəˈsiːdʒərəl/ *adjective* using a procedure to solve a problem

procedural language /prəˌsiːdʒ(ə)rəl ˈlæŋgwɪdʒ/ *noun* a high-level programming language in which the programmer enters the actions required to achieve the result wanted

procedure /prəˈsiːdʒə/ *noun* **1.** a small section of computer instruction code that provides a frequently used function and can be called upon from a main program ○ *This procedure sorts all the files into alphabetical order.* ◊ **subroutine 2.** a method or route used when solving a problem ○ *You should use this procedure to retrieve lost files.*

procedure declaration /prəˈsiːdʒə ˌdekləreɪʃ(ə)n/ *noun* the process of writing and declaring the variable types of procedure used and the routine name and location

procedure-orientated language /prəˌsiːdʒə ˌɔːriənteɪtɪd ˈlæŋgwɪdʒ/ *noun* a high-level programming language that allows procedures to be programmed easily

process /ˈprəʊses/ *noun* a number of tasks that must be carried out to achieve a goal ○ *The process of setting up the computer takes a long time.* ■ *verb* to carry out a number of tasks to produce a result ○ *We processed the new data.*

process bound /ˈprəʊses baʊnd/ *noun* a program that spends more time executing instructions and using the CPU than in I/O operations

process chart /ˈprəʊses tʃɑːt/ *noun* a diagram that shows each step of the computer procedures needed in a system

process control /ˈprəʊses kənˌtrəʊl/ *noun* the automatic control of a process by a computer

process control computer /ˌprəʊses kənˌtrəʊl kəmˈpjuːtə/ *noun* a dedicated computer that controls and manages a process

process control system /ˌprəʊses kənˈtrəʊl ˌsɪstəm/ *noun* a system that completely monitors, manages and regulates a process, comprising input and output modules, a CPU with memory, a program and control and feedback devices such as A/D and D/A converters

processing /ˈprəʊsesɪŋ/ *noun* the use of a computer to solve a problem or organise data ○ *Page processing time depends on the complexity of a given page.* ◊ **CPU**

processor /ˈprəʊˌsesə/ *noun* a hardware or software device that is able to manipulate or modify data according to instructions

processor controlled keying /ˌprəʊsesə kənˌtrəʊld ˈkiːɪŋ/ *noun* data entry by an operator which is prompted and controlled by a computer

processor interrupt /ˌprəʊsesə ˈɪntərʌpt/ *noun* the process of sending an interrupt signal to a processor requesting attention, usually causing it to stop what it is doing and attend to the calling device

processor-limited /ˌprəʊsesə ˈlɪmɪtɪd/ *adjective* referring to operation or execution time that is set by the speed of the processor rather than a peripheral

processor status word /ˌprəʊsesə
ˈsteɪtəs ˌwɜːd/ *noun* a word that contains
a number of status bits, e.g. as carry flag,
zero flag and overflow flag. Abbr **PSW**

produce /prəˈdjuːs/ *verb* to make or
manufacture something

producer /prəˈdjuːsə/ *noun* a person,
company or country that manufactures ○
*Country which is a producer of high qual-
ity computer equipment.*

producing capacity /prəˈdjuːsɪŋ kə
ˌpæsəti/ *noun* the capacity to produce

product /ˈprɒdʌkt/ *noun* **1.** an item that
is made or manufactured **2.** a manufactured item for sale **3.** the result after multiplication

product design /ˈprɒdʌkt dɪˌzaɪn/
noun the activity of designing products

product engineer /ˌprɒdʌkt ˌendʒɪ
ˈnɪə/ *noun* an engineer in charge of the
equipment for making a product

production /prəˈdʌkʃən/ *noun* the
process of making or manufacturing of
goods for sale ○ *Production will probably
be held up by industrial action.*

production control /prəˈdʌkʃən kən
ˌtrəʊl/ *noun* the control of the manufacturing of a product (using computers)

production level video /prəˌdʌkʃən
ˌlev(ə)l ˈvɪdiəʊ/ *noun* full form of **PLV**

production rate /prəˈdʌkʃ(ə)n reɪt/
noun same as **rate of production**

production standards /prəˈdʌkʃən
ˌstændədz/ *plural noun* the quality of production

productive /prəˈdʌktɪv/ *adjective* during or in which something useful is produced

productive time /prəˌdʌktɪv ˈtaɪm/
noun a period of time during which a computer can run error-free tasks

product line /ˈprɒdʌkt laɪn/, **product
range** /ˈprɒdʌkt reɪndʒ/ *noun* a series of
different products made by the same company, which form a group

product range /ˈprɒdʌkt reɪndʒ/
noun same as **product line**

profile /ˈprəʊfaɪl/ *noun* a feature of Windows 95 that stores the settings for different users on one PC

PROFS /prɒfs/ a trade name for an electronic mail system developed by IBM that
runs on mainframe computers

program /ˈprəʊɡræm/ *noun* a complete
set of instructions which direct a computer
to carry out a particular task □ **assembly**

program a number of assembly code instructions that perform a task ■ *verb* to
write or prepare a set of instructions that
direct a computer to perform a certain task

program address counter
/ˌprəʊɡræm əˈdres ˌkaʊntə/ *noun* a register in a CPU that contains the location of
the next instruction to be processed

program branch /ˈprəʊɡræm
brɑːntʃ/ *noun* one or more paths that can
be followed after a conditional statement

program cards /ˈprəʊɡræm kɑːdz/
plural noun punched cards that contain the
instructions that make up a program

program coding sheet /ˌprəʊɡræm
ˈkəʊdɪŋ ˌʃiːt/ *noun* a specially preprinted
form on which computer instructions can
be written, simplifying program writing

program compatibility /ˌprəʊɡræm
kəmˌpætəˈbɪlɪti/ *noun* the ability of two
pieces of software to function correctly together

program compilation /ˌprəʊɡræm
ˌkɒmpəˈleɪʃ(ə)n/ *noun* the translation of
an encoded source program into machine
code

program counter /ˈprəʊɡræm
ˌkaʊntə/ *noun* a register in a CPU that
contains the location of the next instruction to be processed. Abbr **PC**

program crash /ˈprəʊɡræm kræʃ/
noun an unexpected failure of a program
owing to a programming error or a hardware fault

program design language
/ˌprəʊɡræm dɪˈzaɪn ˌlæŋɡwɪdʒ/ *noun* a
programming language used to design the
structure of a program. Abbr **PDL**

program development /ˈprəʊɡræm
dɪˌveləpmənt/ *noun* all the operations involved in creating a computer program
from first ideas to initial writing, debugging and the final product

program development system
/ˌprəʊɡræm dɪˈveləpmənt ˌsɪstəm/
noun all the hardware and software needed for program development on a system

program documentation
/ˌprəʊɡræm ˌdɒkjʊmenˈteɪʃ(ə)n/ *noun*
a set of instruction notes, examples and
tips on how to use a program

program editor /ˈprəʊɡræm ˌedɪtə/
noun a piece of software that allows the
user to alter, delete and add instructions to
a program file

**program evaluation and review
technique** /ˌprəʊɡræm ɪˌvæljueɪʃ(ə)n

ən rɪ'vjuː tek,niːk/ *noun* full form of **PERT**

program execution /,prəʊɡræm ,eksɪ'kjuːʃ(ə)n/ *noun* the process of instructing a processor to execute in sequence the instructions in a program

program file /'prəʊɡræm faɪl/ *noun* a file containing a program rather than data

program flowchart /,prəʊɡræm 'fləʊtʃɑːt/ *noun* a diagram that graphically describes the various steps in a program

program generation /,prəʊɡræm ,dʒenə'reɪʃ(ə)n/ *noun* ⏺ **generator**

program generator /'prəʊɡræm ,dʒenəreɪtə/ *noun* a piece of software that allows users to write complex programs using a few simple instructions

program group /'prəʊɡræm ɡruːp/ *noun* (*in Windows 3.1x*) a window that contains icons relating to a particular subject or program

program icon /'prəʊɡræm ,aɪkɒn/ *noun* (*in a GUI*) an icon that represents an executable program file ○ *To run the program, double-click on the program icon.*

program information file /,prəʊɡræm ,ɪnfə'meɪʃ(ə)n ,faɪl/ *noun* full form of **PIF**

program instruction /'prəʊɡræm ɪn,strʌkʃən/ *noun* a single word or expression that represents one operation

program item /'prəʊɡræm ,aɪtəm/ *noun* (*in a GUI*) an icon that represents a program

program library /'prəʊɡræm ,laɪbrəri/ *noun* a collection of useful procedures and programs which can be used for various purposes and included into new software

program line /'prəʊɡræm laɪn/ *noun* one row of commands or arguments in a computer program

program line number /,prəʊɡræm 'laɪn ,nʌmbə/ *noun* a number that refers to a line of program code in a computer program

program listing /'prəʊɡræm ,lɪstɪŋ/ *noun* a list of the instructions that make up a program, displayed in an ordered manner

programmable /'prəʊɡræməb(ə)l/ *adjective* referring to a device that can accept and store instructions then execute them

programmable calculator /,prəʊɡræməb(ə)l 'kælkjʊleɪtə/ *noun* a small calculator that can hold certain basic mathematical calculating programs

programmable clock /,prəʊɡræməb(ə)l 'klɒk/ *noun* a circuit whose frequency can be set by the user

programmable interrupt controller /,prəʊɡræməb(ə)l 'ɪntərʌpt kən,trəʊlə/ *noun* a circuit or chip that can be programmed to ignore certain interrupts, accept only high priority interrupts and select the priority of interrupts

programmable key /,prəʊɡræməb(ə)l 'kiː/ *noun* a special key on a computer terminal keyboard that can be programmed with various functions or characters

programmable logic array *noun* full form of **PLA**

programmable logic device /,prəʊɡræməb(ə)l 'lɒdʒɪk dɪ,vaɪs/ *noun* full form of **PLD**

programmable memory /,prəʊɡræməb(ə)l 'mem(ə)ri/ *noun* full form of **PROM**

programmable read only memory /,prəʊɡræməb(ə)l riːd ,əʊnli 'mem(ə)ri/ *noun* full form of **PROM**

program maintenance /'prəʊɡræm ,meɪntənəns/ *noun* the process of keeping a program free of errors and up to date

Program Manager /,prəʊɡræm 'mænɪdʒə/ *noun* (*in Windows 3.x*) the main part of Windows that the user sees

programmatic /,prəʊɡrə'mætɪk/ *adjective* relating to computer programs

programmed halt /'prəʊɡræmd hɔːlt/ *noun* an instruction within a program which, when executed, halts the processor

programmed learning /,prəʊɡræmd 'lɜːnɪŋ/ *noun* the process of using educational software which allows a learner to follow a course of instruction

programmer /'prəʊ,ɡræmə/ *noun* **1.** a person who is capable of designing and writing a working program ○ *The programmer is still working on the new software.* **2.** a device that allows data to be written into a programmable read only memory

programmer's hierarchical interactive graphics standard /,prəʊɡræməz haɪə,rɑːkɪk(ə)l ɪntər,æktɪv 'ɡræfɪks ,stændəd/ *noun* full form of **PHIGS**

programming /'prəʊɡræmɪŋ/ *noun* **1.** the activity of writing programs for computers **2.** the activity of writing data into a PROM device

COMMENT: Programming languages are grouped into different levels: the high-level languages such as BASIC and PASCAL are easy to understand and use, but offer slow execution time since each instruction is made up of a number of machine code instructions; low-level languages such as assembler are more complex to read and program in but offer faster execution time.

programming in logic /ˌprəʊgræmɪŋ ɪn ˈlɒdʒɪk/ *noun* full form of **PROLOG**

programming language /ˈprəʊgræmɪŋ ˌlæŋgwɪdʒ/ *noun* a piece of software that allows a user to write a series of instructions to define a particular task, which will then be translated to a form that is understood by the computer

programming language for microprocessors /ˌprəʊgræmɪŋ ˌlæŋgwɪdʒ fə ˈmaɪkrəɪˌprəʊsesəz/ *noun* full form of **PL/M**

programming standards /ˈprəʊgræmɪŋ ˌstændədz/ *plural noun* rules to which programs must conform to produce compatible code

program name /ˈprəʊgræm neɪm/ *noun* an identification name for a stored program file

program origin /ˌprəʊgræm ˈɒrɪdʒɪn/ *noun* the address at which the first instruction of a program is stored

program overlay /ˌprəʊgræm ˈəʊvəleɪ/ *noun* a portion of a big program that is loaded from disk into memory when it is needed

program register /ˈprəʊgræm ˌredʒɪstə/ *noun* a register in a CPU that contains an instruction during decoding and execution operations

program relocation /ˌprəʊgræm ˌriːləʊˈkeɪʃ(ə)n/ *noun* the process of moving a stored program from one area of memory to another

program report generator /ˌprəʊgræm rɪˈpɔːt ˌdʒenəreɪtə/ *noun* a piece of software that allows users to create reports from files, databases and other stored data

program run /ˈprəʊgræm rʌn/ *noun* the process of executing, in correct order, the instructions in a program

program segment /ˈprəʊgræm ˌsegmənt/ *noun* a section of a main program that can be executed in its own right, without the rest of the main program being required

Programs menu /ˈprəʊgræmz ˌmenjuː/ *noun* a sub-menu, accessed from the Start button in Windows, that lists all the programs that are installed on the computer

program specification /ˌprəʊgræm ˌspesɪfɪˈkeɪʃ(ə)n/ *noun* detailed information about a program's abilities, features and methods

program stack /ˈprəʊgræm stæk/ *noun* a section of memory reserved for storing temporary system or program data

program statement /ˈprəʊgræm ˌsteɪtmənt/ *noun* a high level program instruction that is made up of a number of machine code instructions

program status word /ˌprəʊgræm ˈsteɪtəs ˌwɜːd/ *noun* a word which contains a number of status bits, such as carry flag, zero flag, overflow bit, etc. Abbr **PSW**

program status word register /ˌprəʊgræm ˈsteɪtəs wɜːd ˌredʒɪstə/ *noun* a register which contains a number of status bits, such as carry flag, zero flag, overflow flag. Also called **PSW register**

program step /ˈprəʊgræm step/ *noun* one operation within a program, usually a single instruction

program storage /ˌprəʊgræm ˈstɔːrɪdʒ/ *noun* a section of main memory in which programs, rather than operating system or data, can be stored

program structure /ˌprəʊgræm ˈstrʌktʃə/ *noun* the way in which sections of program code are interlinked and operate

program testing /ˈprəʊgræm ˌtestɪŋ/ *noun* the process of testing a new program with test data to ensure that it functions correctly

program trading /ˈprəʊgræm ˌtreɪdɪŋ/ *noun* the automatic buying and selling of large quantities of shares using computer programs that monitor price changes

program verification /ˌprəʊgræm ˌverɪfɪˈkeɪʃ(ə)n/ *noun* a number of tests and checks performed to ensure that a program functions correctly

progressive scanning /prəʊˌgresɪv ˈskænɪŋ/ *noun* a method of displaying and transmitting video images in which each line of the image is displayed consecutively, unlike non-interlaced image, which shows alternate lines. ◊ **scan conversion**

project *noun* /ˈprɒdʒekt/ a planned task ○ *His latest project is computerising the sales team.* ■ *verb* /prəˈdʒekt/ to forecast future figures from a set of data ○ *The projected sales of the new PC.*

projection /prəˈdʒekʃən/ *noun* the forecasting of a situation from a set of data ○ *The projection indicates that sales will increase.*

PROLOG /ˈprəʊlɒg/ *noun* a high-level programming language using logical operations for artificial intelligence and data retrieval applications. Full form **programming in logic**

PROM /prɒm/ *noun* **1.** read-only memory that can be programmed by the user, as distinct from ROM, which is programmed by the manufacturer. Full form **programmable read-only memory 2.** an electronic device in which data can be stored. Full form **programmable memory**

PROM blaster /ˈbɜːnə/, **PROM burner**, **PROM programmer** /ˈprəʊˌgræmə/ *noun* an electronic device used to program a PROM

prompt /prɒmpt/ *noun* a message or character displayed to remind the user that an input is expected ○ *The prompt READY indicates that the system is available to receive instructions.*

propagate /ˈprɒpəˌgeɪt/ *verb* to travel or spread

propagated error /ˌprɒpəgeɪtɪd ˈerə/ *noun* one error in a process that has affected later operations

propagating error /ˈprɒpəgeɪtɪŋ ˌerə/ *noun* an error that occurs in one place or operation and affects another operation or process

propagation delay /ˌprɒpəˈgeɪʃ(ə)n dɪˌleɪ/ *noun* **1.** the time taken for an output to appear in a logic gate after the input is applied **2.** the time taken for a data bit to travel over a network from the source to the destination

propagation time /ˌprɒpəˈgeɪʃ(ə)n ˌtaɪm/ *noun* same as **gate delay**

properties /ˈprɒpətiz/ *noun* (*in Windows*) the attributes of a file or object

proportionally   spaced /prə ˌpɔːʃ(ə)nəli ˈspeɪst/ *adjective* referring to a font in which each letter takes a space proportional to the character width. Compare **monospaced**

proprietary   file   format /prə ˌpraɪət(ə)ri ˈfaɪl ˌfɔːmæt/ *noun* a method of storing data devised by a company for

its products and incompatible with other products ○ *You cannot read this spreadsheet file because my software saves it in a proprietary file format.*

protected field /prəˈtektɪd fiːld/ *noun* a storage or display area that cannot be altered by the user

protected location /prəˌtektɪd ləʊ ˈkeɪʃ(ə)n/ *noun* a memory location that cannot be altered or cannot be accessed without authorisation

protected mode /prəˈtektɪd məʊd/ *noun* the operating mode of an 80286 Intel processor or higher that supports multitasking, virtual memory and data security

protected   storage /prəˌtektɪd ˈstɔːrɪdʒ/ *noun* a section of memory that cannot be altered

protection key /prəˈtekʃən kiː/ *noun* a signal checked to see if a program can access a section of memory

protection   master /prəˈtekʃən ˌmɑːstə/ *noun* a spare copy of a master film or tape

protocol /ˈprəʊtəkɒl/ *noun* the pre-agreed signals, codes and rules to be used for data exchange between systems

protocol stack /ˈprəʊtəʊkɒl stæk/ *noun* the separate parts of a protocol, each with a different function, that work together to provide a complete set of network functions

protocol   standards /ˈprəʊtəʊkɒl ˌstændədz/ *plural noun* standards laid down to allow data exchange between any computer system conforming to the standard

prototype /ˈprəʊtəˌtaɪp/ *noun* the first working model of a device or program, which is then tested and adapted to improve it

prototyping /ˈprəʊtətaɪpɪŋ/ *noun* the process of making a prototype

proximity   operator /prɒkˈsɪmɪti ˌɒpəreɪtə/ *noun* a Boolean operator that directs a search engine making a text search to locate pages in which the words it is looking for are near one another in any direction

proxy agent /ˈprɒksi ˌeɪdʒənt/ *noun* a piece of software that can translate network management commands to allow management software to control a device that uses a different protocol

proxy server /ˌprɒksi ˈsɜːvə/ *noun* a computer that stores copies of files and data normally held on a slow server and so allows users to access files and data quickly. Proxy servers are often used as a firewall between an intranet in a company and the public Internet.

PrtSc /ˌprɪnt 'skriːn/ *noun* (*on an IBM PC keyboard*) a key that sends the contents of the current screen to the printer. Full form **print screen**

pS /ˌpi: 'es/ *abbr* picosecond

PS/2 a trade name for a range of IBM PC computers that are software compatible with the original IBM PC, but use a different MCA expansion bus. ◊ **MCA**

pseudo- /sjuːdəʊ/ *prefix* similar to something, but not genuine

pseudo-code /'sjuːdəʊ kəʊd/ *noun* English sentence structures, used to describe program instructions that are translated at a later date into machine code

pseudo-digital /ˌsjuːdəʊ 'dɪdʒɪt(ə)l/ *adjective* referring to modulated analog signals that are produced by a modem and transmitted over telephone lines

pseudo-instruction /ˌsjuːdəʊ ɪn 'strʌkʃən/ *noun* a label in an assembly language program that represents a number of instructions

pseudo-operation /ˌsjuːdəʊ ˌɒpə 'reɪʃ(ə)n/ *noun* a command in an assembler program that controls the assembler rather than producing machine code

pseudo-random /ˌsjuːdəʊ 'rændəm/ *noun* a generated sequence that appears random but is repeated over a long period

pseudo-random number generator /ˌsjuːdəʊ ˌrændəm 'nʌmbə ˌdʒenəreɪtə/ *noun* a piece of hardware or software that produces pseudo-random numbers

pseudo-static /ˌsjuːdəʊ 'stætɪk/ *adjective* referring to dynamic RAM memory chips that contain circuitry to refresh the contents and so have the same appearance as a static RAM component

PSN *abbr* packet switched network

PSS *abbr* packet switching system

PSU /ˌpi: es 'juː/ *noun* an electrical circuit that provides certain direct current voltage and current levels from an alternating current source to other electrical circuits. Full form **power supply unit**

COMMENT: A PSU will regulate, smooth and step down a higher voltage supply for use in small electronic equipment.

PSW *abbr* processor status word

PTR *abbr* paper tape reader

public access terminal /ˌpʌblɪk ˌækses 'tɜːmɪn(ə)l/ *noun* a terminal that can be used by anyone to access a computer

public data network /ˌpʌblɪk ˌdeɪtə 'netwɜːk/ *noun* a data transmission service for the public, e.g. the main telephone system in a country. Abbr **PDN**

public domain /ˌpʌblɪk dəʊ'meɪn/ *noun* the status of documents, text or programs that are not protected by copyright and can be copied by anyone. Abbr **PD** Compare **shareware** □ **program which is in the public domain** a program which is not protected by copyright

public key cipher system /ˌpʌblɪk kiː 'saɪfə ˌsɪstəm/ *noun* a cipher that uses a public key to encrypt messages and a secret key to decrypt them. Conventional cipher systems use one secret key to encrypt and decrypt messages.

public key encryption /ˌpʌblɪk kiː ɪn 'krɪpʃ(ə)n/ *noun* a method of encrypting data that uses one key to encrypt the data and another different key to decrypt the data

publish /'pʌblɪʃ/ *verb* to produce and sell software

pull /pʊl/ *verb* to remove data from a stack

pull-down menu /'pʊl daʊn ˌmenjuː/ *noun* a set of options that are displayed below the relevant entry on a menu-bar. Compare **pop-down menu**

pull up /ˌpʊl 'ʌp/ *verb* □ **to pull up a line** to connect or set a line to a voltage level ○ *Pull up the input line to a logic one by connecting it to 5 volts.*

pulse /pʌls/ *noun* a short period of a voltage level ■ *verb* to apply a short-duration voltage level to a circuit ○ *We pulsed the input but it still would not work.*

COMMENT: Electric pulse can be used to transmit information, as the binary digits 0 and 1 correspond to 'no pulse' and 'pulse' (the voltage level used to distinguish the binary digits 0 and 1, is often zero and 5 or 12 volts, with the pulse width depending on transmission rate).

pulse-code modulation /ˌpʌls kəʊd ˌmɒdjʊ'leɪʃ(ə)n/ *noun* full form of **PCM**

pulse-dialling /'pʌls ˌdaɪəlɪŋ/ *noun* telephone dialling that dials a telephone number by sending a series of pulses along the line

pulse stream /ˌpʌls 'striːm/ *noun* a continuous series of similar pulses

pulse train /'pʌls treɪn/ *noun* same as **pulse stream**

punch /pʌntʃ/ *noun* a device for making holes in punched cards ■ *verb* to make a hole in something

punch card /'pʌntʃ kɑːd/ *noun* a small piece of card which contains holes representing various instructions or data

punch-down block /,pʌntʃ daʊn 'blɒk/ *noun* a device used in a local area network to connect UTP cable

punched card /,pʌntʃt 'kɑːd/ *noun* same as **punch card**

punched card reader /,pʌntʃd 'kɑːd ,riːdə/ *noun* a device that transforms data on a punched card to a form that can be recognized by a computer

punched code /,pʌntʃd 'kəʊd/ *noun* a combination of holes that represent characters in a punched card

punched tag /,pʌntʃd 'tæg/ *noun* a card attached to a product in a shop, with punched holes containing data about the product

punched tape[1] /,pʌntʃd 'teɪp/, **punched paper tape** *noun* a strip of paper tape that contains holes to represent data

punched tape[2] /,pʌntʃd 'teɪp/ *noun* same as **paper tape**

punctuation mark /,pʌŋktʃu'eɪʃ(ə)n mɑːk/ *noun* a printing symbol such as a comma or full stop, used for making the meaning of text clear

pure code /,pjʊə 'kəʊd/ *noun* a code that does not modify itself during execution

purge /pɜːdʒ/ *verb* to remove unnecessary or out-of-date data from a file or disk ○ *Each month, I purge the disk of all the old email messages.*

pushbutton /'pʊʃbʌt(ə)n/ *adjective* which works by pressing on a button

push-down list /,pʊʃdaʊn 'lɪst/, **push-down stack** /pʊʃ daʊn/ *noun* a method of storing data in which the last item stored is always at the same location, the rest of the list being pushed down by one address

push instruction /pʊʃ ɪn'strʌkʃən/, **push operation** *noun* **non-synchronous sound, non-sync sound** a computer instruction that stores data on a LIFO list or stack

push technology /'pʊʃ tek,nɒlədʒi/ *noun* Internet technology that allows subscribers to receive customised information directly

push-up list /stæk/, **push-up stack** *noun* a method of storing data in which the last item stored is added at the bottom of the list. ◊ **FIFO**

put /pʊt/ *verb* to push or place data onto a stack

Q

QAM *abbr* quadrature amplitude modulation

QBE /,kjuː biː 'iː/ *noun* a simple language used to retrieve information from a database management system by, normally, entering a query with known values, which is then matched with the database and used to retrieve the correct data ○ *In most QBE databases, the query form looks like the record format in the database – re-* *trieving data is as easy as filling in a form.* Full form **query by example**

Q Channel /kjuː 'tʃæn(ə)l/ *noun* (*in a CD audio disc*) one of the eight information channels that holds data identifying the track and the absolute playing time

QISAM *noun* an indexed sequential file that is read item by item into a buffer. Full form **queued indexed sequential access method**

QL *abbr* query language

QOS *abbr* quality of service

QSAM /ˌkjuː es eɪ 'em/ *noun* queue of blocks waiting to be processed, which are retrieved using a sequential access method. Full form **queued sequential access method**

quad /kwɒd/ *adjective* operating at four times the standard speed, or processing four times the standard amount of data

quadbit /'kwɒdbɪt/ *noun* four bits that are used by modems to increase transmission rates when using QAM

quad density /kwɒd 'densəti/ *noun* four bits of data stored in the usual place of one

quadding /'kwɒdɪŋ/ *noun* the insertion of spaces into text to fill out a line

quadr- /kwɒdr/ *prefix* four

quadrature amplitude modulation /ˌkwɒdrətʃə 'æmplɪtjuːd mɒdjuˌleɪʃ(ə)n/ *noun* a data encoding method used by high-speed modems (transmitting at rates above 2,400bps). It combines amplitude modulation and phase modulation to increase the data transmission rate. Abbr **QAM**

quadrature encoding /'kwɒdrətʃə ɪnˌkəʊdɪŋ/ *noun* a system used to determine the direction in which a mouse is being moved. In a mechanical mouse, two sensors send signals that describe its horizontal and vertical movements, these signals being transmitted using quadrature encoding.

quadruplex /'kwɒdrʊpleks/ *noun* a set of four signals combined into a single one

quad-speed drive /ˌkwɒd spiːd 'draɪv/ *noun* a CD-ROM drive that spins the disc at four times the speed of a single-speed drive, providing higher data throughput of 600Kbps and shorter seek times

quality control /'kwɒlɪti kənˌtrəʊl/ *noun* the process of checking that the quality of a product is good

quality of service /ˌkwɒlɪti əv 'sɜːvɪs/ *noun* the degree to which a network can transfer information without error or fault

Quantel /'kwɒntel/ the hardware graphics company that developed Paintbox and Harry production graphics systems

quantifiable /'kwɒntɪfaɪəb(ə)l/ *adjective* which can be quantified ○ *The effect of the change in the pricing structure is not quantifiable.*

quantifier /'kwɒntɪˌfaɪə/ *noun* a sign or symbol that indicates the quantity or range of a predicate

quantify /'kwɒntɪˌfaɪ/ *verb* □ **to quantify the effect of something** to show the effect of something in figures ○ *It is impossible to quantify the effect of the new computer system on our production.*

quantisation, quantization *noun* the conversion of an analog signal to a numerical representation

quantisation error /ˌkwɒn'teɪʃ(ə)n ˌerə/ *noun* an error in converting an analog signal into a numerical form, owing to limited accuracy or a rapidly changing signal

quantise, quantize *verb* to convert an analog signal into a numerical representation ○ *The input signal is quantized by an analog to digital converter.*

quantiser, quantizer *noun* a device used to convert an analog input signal to a numerical form, that can be processed by a computer

quantising noise /ˌkwɒntaɪzɪŋ 'nɔɪz/ *noun* noise on a signal caused by inaccuracies in the quantising process

quantity /'kwɒntɪti/ *noun* the amount or number of items ○ *A small quantity of illegal copies of the program have been imported.* ■ *adjective* in large amounts ○ *The company offers a discount for quantity purchases.*

quantum /'kwɒntəm/ *noun* (*in communications*) a packet of data that is the result of a signal being quantised

quartz clock /ˌkwɔːts 'klɒk/, **quartz crystal clock** /ˌkwɔːts ˌkrɪstəl 'klɒk/ *noun* a small slice of quartz crystal that vibrates at a certain frequency when an electrical voltage is supplied, used as a very accurate clock signal for computers and other high precision timing applications

quasi- /kweɪzaɪ/ *prefix* almost, or similar to

quasi-instruction /ˌkweɪzaɪ ɪn 'strʌkʃən/ *noun* a label in an assembly program that represents a number of instructions

quaternary /'kwɔːtɜːnəri/ *adjective* existing as four bits, levels or objects

quaternary level quantization /kwə ˌtɜːnəri ˌlev(ə)l ˌkwɒntaɪ'zeɪʃ(ə)n/ *noun* the use of four bits of data in an A/D conversion process

query by example /ˌkwɪəri baɪ ɪg 'zɑːmpəl/ *noun* full form of **QBE**

query facility /'kwɪəri fə,sɪlɪti/ *noun* a program, usually a database or retrieval system, that allows the user to ask questions and receive answers or access certain information according to the query

query language /'kwɪəri ,læŋgwɪdʒ/ *noun* a language in a database management system that allows a database to be searched and queried easily. Abbr **QL**

query message /'kwɪəri ,mesɪdʒ/ *noun* a message sent to an object to find out the value of one of the object's properties, e.g. its name, active state or position

query processing /'kwɪəri ,prəʊsesɪŋ/ *noun* the processing of queries, either by extracting information from a database or by translating query commands from a query language

query window /'kwɪəri ,wɪndəʊ/ *noun* **1.** a window that appears when an error has occurred, asking the user what action they would like to take **2.** a window that is displayed with fields a user can fill in to search a database

question mark /'kweʃtʃən mɑːk/ *noun* the character (?) that is often used as a wildcard to indicate that any single character in the position will produce a match ○ *To find all the letters, use the command DIR LETTER?DOC which will list LETTER1.DOC, LETTER2.DOC and LETTER3.DOC.* ◊ **asterisk**

queue /kjuː/ *noun* a list of data or tasks that are waiting to be processed, or a series of documents that are dealt with in order ■ *verb* to add more data or tasks to the end of a queue

queued access method /,kjuːd 'ækses ,meθəd/ *noun* a programming method that minimises input/output delays by ensuring that data transferred between software and an I/O device is synchronised with the I/O device

queued indexed sequential access method /,kjuːd ,ɪndeksd sɪ ,kwenʃəl 'ækses ,meθəd/ *noun* full form of **QISAM**

queue discipline /kjuː 'dɪsə,plɪn/ *noun* a method used as the queue structure, either LIFO or FIFO

queued sequential access method /,kjuːd sɪ,kwenʃəl 'ækses ,meθəd/ *noun* full form of **QSAM**

queue management /kjuː 'mænɪdʒmənt/, **queue manager** /kjuː 'mænɪdʒə/ *noun* software which orders tasks to be processed ○ *This is a new soft-*

ware spooler with a built-in queue management.

queuing time /'kjuːɪŋ taɪm/ *noun* the period of time messages have to wait before they can be processed or transmitted

QuickDraw /'kwɪkdrɔː/ (*in an Apple Macintosh*) a trade name for the graphics routines built into the Macintosh's operating system that control displayed text and images

quick format /kwɪk 'fɔːmæt/ *noun* a command that does not delete all the existing data on a floppy disk during a format process. It is faster than a full format and allows data to be recovered.

quicksort /'kwɪksɔːt/ *noun* a very rapid file sorting and ordering method

QuickTime /'kwɪktaɪm/ (*in an Apple Macintosh*) a trade name for the graphics routines built into the Macintosh's operating system that allow windows, boxes and graphic objects, including animation and video files, to be displayed

quiescent /kwi'es(ə)nt/ *adjective* referring to a process, circuit or device in a state in which no input signal is applied

quintet /kwɪn'tet/ *noun* a byte made up of five bits

quit /kwɪt/ *verb* to leave a system or a program ○ *Do not forget to save your text before you quit the system.*

quotation /kwəʊ'teɪʃ(ə)n/ *noun* part of a text borrowed from another text

quotation marks /kwəʊ'teɪʃ(ə)n mɑːks/ *noun* punctuation marks used for enclosing text to show that it has been quoted from another source

quote /kwəʊt/ *verb* to repeat words used by someone else

quotes /kwəʊts/ *plural noun* quotation marks (*informal*)

quotient /'kwəʊʃ(ə)nt/ *noun* the result of one number divided by another

COMMENT: When two numbers are divided, the answer is made up of a quotient and a remainder (the fractional part). 16 divided by 4 is equal to a quotient of 4 and zero remainder; 16 divided by 5 is equal to a quotient of 3 and a remainder of 1.

quoting /'kwəʊtɪŋ/ *noun* a feature of many electronic mail applications that allows you to reply to a message and include the text of the original message

QWERTY keyboard /,kwɜːti 'kiːbɔːd/ *noun* a standard English language key layout. The first six letters on the top left row of keys are QWERTY.

R

race /reɪs/ *noun* an error condition in a digital circuit, in which the state or output of the circuit is very dependent on the exact timing between the input signals. Faulty output is due to unequal propagation delays on the separate input signals at a gate.

rack /ræk/ *noun* a metal supporting frame for electronic circuit boards and peripheral devices such as disk drives

rack mounted /ræk 'maʊntɪd/ *plural noun* referring to a system consisting of removable circuit boards in a supporting frame

radial transfer /ˌreɪdiəl 'trænsfɜː/ *noun* data transfer between two peripherals or programs that are on different layers of a structured system (such as an ISO/OSI system)

radio button /'reɪdiəʊ ˌbʌt(ə)n/ *noun* (*in a GUI*) a circle displayed beside an option that, when selected, has a dark centre. Only one radio button can be selected at one time.

radio frequency /'reɪdiəʊ ˌfriːkwənsi/ *noun* full form of **RF**

radix /'reɪdɪks/ *noun* the value of the base of the number system being used ○ *The hexadecimal number has a radix of 16.*

radix complement /'reɪdɪks ˌkɒmplɪmənt/ *noun* ♦ **ten's complement, two's complement**

radix notation /'reɪdɪks nəʊˌteɪʃ(ə)n/ *noun* numbers represented to a certain radix

radix point /'reɪdɪks pɔɪnt/ *noun* a dot which indicates the division between a whole unit and its fractional parts

ragged left /'rægɪd left/ *noun* printed text with a flush right-hand margin and uneven left-hand margin

ragged right /'rægɪd raɪt/ *noun* printed text with a flush left-hand margin and uneven right-hand margin

ragged text /'rægɪd tekst/ *noun* text with a ragged right margin

RAID /reɪd/ *noun* a fast, fault tolerant disk drive system that uses multiple drives which would, typically, each store one byte of a word of data, so allowing the data to be saved faster. Full form **redundant array of inexpensive disks**

'A Japanese investor group led by system distributor Technography has pumped $4.2 million (#2.8 million) into US disk manufacturer Storage Computer to help with the development costs of RAID 7 hard disk technology.' [*Computing*]

RAM /ræm/ *noun* memory that allows access to any location in any order, without having to access the rest first. Full form **random access memory**. Compare **sequential access**

'The HP Enterprise Desktops have hard-disk capacities of between 260Mb and 1Gb, with RAM ranging from 16Mb up to 128Mb.' [*Computing*]

'…fast memory is RAM that does not have to share bus access with the chip that manages the video display' [*Byte*]

COMMENT: Dynamic RAM, which uses a capacitor to store a bit of data, needs to have each location refreshed from time to time to retain the data, but is very fast and can contain more data per unit area than static RAM, which uses a latch to store the state of a bit. Static RAM, however, has the advantage of not requiring to be refreshed to retain its data, and will keep data for as long as power is supplied.

RAM cache /'ræm kæʃ/ *noun* a section of high-speed RAM that is used to buffer data transfers between the faster processor and a slower disk drive

RAM card /'ræm kɑːd/ *noun* an expansion card that contains RAM chips. It is plugged into a computer or device to increase the main memory capacity.

RAM cartridge /ræm 'kɑːtrɪdʒ/ *noun* a plug-in device that contains RAM chips and increases the memory of a computer or device

RAM chip /'ræm tʃɪp/ *noun* a chip that stores data, allowing random access

RAMDAC /'ræmdæk/ *noun* an electronic component on a video graphics adapter that converts the digital colour signals into electrical signals that are sent to the monitor

RAM disk /'ræm dɪsk/ *noun* same as **silicon disk**

RAM loader /'ræm ˌləʊdə/ *noun* a routine that will transfer a program from external backing store into RAM

RAM refresh /ræm rɪ'freʃ/ *noun* signals used to update the contents of dynamic RAM chips every few thousandths of a second, involving reading and rewriting the contents

RAM refresh rate /ˌræm rɪ'freʃ ˌreɪt/ *noun* the number of times every second that the data in a dynamic RAM chip has to be read and rewritten

RAM resident program /ˌræm ˌrezɪd(ə)nt 'prəʊɡræm/ *noun* a program that loads itself into main memory and carries out a function when activated ○ *When you hit Ctrl-F5, you will activate the RAM resident program and it will display your day's diary.*

R & D /ˌɑːr ən 'diː/ *noun* investigation of new products, discoveries and techniques. Full form **research and development**

R & D department /ˌɑːr ən 'diː dɪˌpɑːtmənt/ *noun* a department in a company that investigates new products, discoveries and techniques

random access /ˌrændəm 'ækses/ *noun* the ability to access immediately memory locations in any order ○ *Disk drives are random access, whereas magnetic tape is sequential access memory.*

random access device /ˌrændəm 'ækses dɪˌvaɪs/ *noun* a device whose access time to retrieve data is not dependent on the location or type of data

random access digital to analog converter /ˌrændəm ˌækses ˌdɪdʒɪt(ə)l tə ˌænəlɒɡ kən'vɜːtə/ *noun* an electronic component on a video graphics adapter that converts the digital colour signals into electrical signals that are sent to the monitor. Abbr **RAMDAC**

random access files /ˌrændəm 'ækses ˌfaɪlz/ *noun* a file in which each item or record can be immediately accessed by its address, without searching through the rest of the file, and is not dependent on the previous location

random access memory /ˌrændəm 'ækses ˌmem(ə)ri/ *noun* full form of **RAM**

random access storage /ˌrændəm 'ækses ˌstɔːrɪdʒ/ *noun* a storage medium that allows access to any location in any order

random number /ˌrændəm 'nʌmbə/ *noun* a number which cannot be predicted

random number generation /ˌrændəm 'nʌmbə ˌdʒenəreɪʃ(ə)n/ *noun* a method of creating a sequence of numbers that appears to be random so that no number appears more often than another

random number generator /ˌrændəm 'nʌmbə ˌdʒenəreɪtə/ *noun* a program that generates random numbers, used in lotteries, games, etc.

random process /ˌrændəm 'prəʊses/ *noun* a system whose output cannot be related to its input or internal structure

random processing /ˌrændəm 'prəʊsesɪŋ/ *noun* the processing of data in the order required rather than the order in which it is stored

range /reɪndʒ/ *noun* **1.** a set of allowed values between a maximum and minimum **2.** (*in a spreadsheet*) a cell or group of cells □ **range left** to move text to align it to the left margin ■ *verb* **1.** to vary or to be different ○ *The company's products range from a cheap lapheld micro to a multistation mainframe.* **2.** to put text in order to one side

range left /'reɪndʒ left/ *noun* to move text to align it to the left margin

rank /ræŋk/ *verb* to sort data into an order, usually according to size or importance

rapid access /ˌræpɪd 'ækses/ *noun* a device or memory whose access time is very short

rapid access memory /ˌræpɪd ˌækses 'mem(ə)ri/ *noun* storage locations that can be read from or written to very quickly

raster /'ræstə/ *noun* a system of scanning the whole of a CRT screen with a picture beam by sweeping across it horizontally, moving down one pixel or line at a time

raster font /'ræstə fɒnt/ *noun* a computer font formed from pixels and based on a bit map

raster graphics /'ræstə ˌɡræfɪks/ *plural noun* graphics in which the picture is built up in lines across the screen or page

raster image processor /ˌræstə ˈɪmɪdʒ ˌprəʊsesə/ *noun* raster which translates software instructions into an image or complete page which is then printed by the printer ○ *An electronic page can be converted to a printer-readable video image by an on-board raster image processor.* Abbr **RIP**

raster scan /ˈræstə skæn/ *noun* one sweep of the picture beam horizontally across the front of a CRT screen

rate /reɪt/ *noun* the quantity of data or tasks that can be processed in a set time ○ *The processor's instruction execution rate is better than the older version.*

rated throughput /ˌreɪtɪd ˈθruːpʊt/ *noun* the maximum throughput of a device which will still meet original specifications

rate of production /ˌreɪt əv prə ˈdʌkʃən/ *noun* the speed at which items are made

ratio /ˈreɪʃiəʊ/ *noun* the proportion of one number to another ○ *The ratio of 10 to 5 is 2:1.*

rational number /ˌræʃ(ə)nəl ˈnʌmbə/ *noun* a number that can be written as the ratio of two whole numbers ○ *24 over 7 is a rational number.*

raw data /rɔː ˈdeɪtə/ *noun* **1.** pieces of information which have not been input into a computer system **2.** data in a database which has to be processed to provide information to the user **3.** unprocessed data

raw mode /ˌrɔː ˈməʊd/ *noun* a method of accessing a file which, when data is read from the file, does not carry out any data translation or filtering

ray tracing /reɪ ˈtreɪsɪŋ/ *noun* (*in graphics*) a method of creating life-like computer-generated graphics which correctly show shadows and highlights on an object to suggest the existence of a light source

RD /ˌɑː ˈdiː/ *noun* (*in DOS*) a command to remove an empty subdirectory. Full form **remove directory**

RDBMS *abbr* relational database management system

react /riˈækt/ *verb* □ **to react to something** to act in response to something □ **to react with something** to change because a substance is present

reaction time /riˈækʃən taɪm/ *noun* same as **access time**

reactive mode /riˈæktɪv məʊd/ *noun* a computer operating mode in which each entry by the user causes something to happen but does not provide an immediate response

read /riːd/ *verb* **1.** (*of an electronic device*) to scan printed text ○ *Can the OCR read typeset characters?* **2.** to retrieve data from a storage medium ○ *This instruction reads the first record of a file.*

read in /ˌriːd ˈɪn/ *verb* to transfer data from an external source to main memory ○ *The computer automatically read-in thirty values from the A/D converter.*

readable /ˈriːdəb(ə)l/ *adjective* that can be read or understood by someone or by an electronic device ○ *The electronic page is converted to a printer-readable video image.*

read back check /ˈriːd bæk ˌtʃek/ *noun* a system that ensures that data was correctly received, in which the transmitted data is sent back and checked against the original for any errors

read cycle /riːd ˈsaɪk(ə)l/ *noun* the period of time between address data being sent to a storage device and the data being returned

reader /ˈriːdə/ *noun* a device that reads data stored on one medium and converts it into another form

reader level /ˈriːdə ˌlev(ə)l/ *noun* (*in authoring software*) one of two modes that allows a user to run and interact with a multimedia application, but not modify it in any way

read error /riːd ˈerə/ *noun* an error that occurs during a read operation, often because the stored data has been corrupted

read head /ˌriːd ˈhed/ *noun* a transducer that reads signals stored on a magnetic medium and converts them back to their original electrical form

reading /ˈriːdɪŋ/ *noun* a note taken of figures or degrees, especially of degrees on a scale

readme file /ˈriːdmi faɪl/ *noun* a file that contains last-minute information about an application

read only /ˈriːd ˌəʊnli/ *noun* a device or circuit whose stored data cannot be changed

read only attribute /ˌriːd ˈəʊnli ˌætrɪbjuːt/ *noun* a special attribute attached to a file which, when switched on, only allows the contents of the file to be viewed, the contents cannot be changed

read only memory /ˌriːd ˌəʊnli ˈmem(ə)ri/ *noun* a memory device that has had data written into it at the time of manufacture, and now its contents can only be read ○ *The manufacturer provided the monitor program in two ROM chips.* Abbr **ROM**

readout /ˈriːdaʊt/ *noun* a display of data ○ *The readout displayed the time.*

readout device /ˈriːdaʊt dɪˌvaɪs/ *noun* a device that allows information (numbers or characters) to be displayed

read rate /ˌriːd ˈreɪt/ *noun* the number of bytes or bits that a reader can read in a certain time

read/write channel /ˌriːd ˈraɪt ˌtʃæn(ə)l/ *noun* a channel that can carry signals travelling in two directions

read/write cycle /ˌriːd ˈraɪt ˌsaɪk(ə)l/ *noun* a sequence of events used to retrieve and store data

read/write head /ˌriːd ˈraɪt hed/ *noun* same as **combined head**

read/write memory /ˌriːd ˌraɪt ˈmem(ə)ri/ *noun* a storage medium that can be written to and read from

ready /ˈredi/ *adjective* waiting and able to be used ○ *The green light indicates the system is ready for another program.*

ready state /ˈredi steɪt/ *noun* the state of a communications line or device that is waiting to accept data

Real /rɪəl/ a trade name for a system used to transmit sound and video over the Internet, normally used to transmit live sound, e.g. from a radio station, over the Internet.
◊ **plug-in, streaming data**

real address /rɪəl əˈdres/ *noun* an absolute address that directly accesses a memory location. Compare **paged address**

RealAudio /ˌrɪəlˈɔːdiəʊ/ a trade name for a system used to transmit sound, usually live, over the Internet

realise /ˈrɪəlaɪz/, **realise the palette** *verb* to select a particular set of colours for a 256-colour palette and use this palette when displaying an image, normally by mapping the colours in a logical palette into the system palette

real memory /rɪəl ˈmem(ə)ri/ *noun* the actual physical memory that can be addressed by a CPU. Compare **virtual memory**

RealNames /ˌrɪəlˈneɪmz/ a system of assigning a trade name or descriptive name to a website address

real number /rɪəl ˈnʌmbə/ *noun* (*in computing*) a number that is represented with a fractional part, or a number represented in floating point notation

real time /ˈrɪəl taɪm/ *noun* the instant nature of the responses of some computer system to events, changes and other stimuli ○ *A navigation system needs to be able to process the position of a ship in real time and take suitable action before it hits a rock.*

'Quotron provides real-time quotes, news and analysis on equity securities through a network of 40,000 terminals to US brokers and investors.' [*Computing*]

'…define a real-time system as any system which is expected to interact with its environment within certain timing constraints' [*British Telecom Technology Journal*]

real-time animation /ˌrɪəl taɪm ˌænɪˈmeɪʃ(ə)n/ *noun* an animation in which objects appear to move at the same speed as they would in real life. Real-time animation requires display hardware capable of displaying a sequence with tens of different images every second.

real-time authorisation /ˌrɪəl taɪm ˌɔːθəraɪˈzeɪʃ(ə)n/, **real-time authentication** /ˌrɪəl taɪm ˌɔːθentɪˈkeɪʃ(ə)n/ *noun* an online system that can check the authenticity and validity of a customer's credit card within a few seconds, allowing the Internet shop to deliver goods or confirm an order immediately

real-time clock /ˌrɪəl taɪm ˈklɒk/ *noun* a clock in a computer that provides the correct time of day

real-time input /ˌrɪəl taɪm ˈɪnpʊt/ *noun* data input to a system as it happens or is required

real-time multi-tasking /ˌrɪəl taɪm ˈmʌltiˌtɑːskɪŋ/ *noun* the process of executing several real-time tasks simultaneously without slowing the execution of any of the processes

real-time operating system /ˌrɪəl taɪm ˈɒpəreɪtɪŋ ˌsɪstəm/ *noun* an operating system designed to control a real-time system or process-control system

real-time processing /ˌrɪəl taɪm ˈprəʊsesɪŋ/ *noun* processing operations that take place instantly

real-time simulation /ˌrɪəl taɪm ˌsɪmjʊˈleɪʃ(ə)n/ *noun* a computer model of a process where each process is executed in a similar time to the real process

real-time system /'rɪəl taɪm ˌsɪstəm/ *noun* a computer system that responds instantly to events, changes and other stimuli

real time transport protocol /ˌrɪəl taɪm 'trænspɔːt ˌprəʊtəkɒl/ *noun* a data transport protocol developed by the IETF that provides guaranteed data delivery over a network that does not normally provide this quality of service. Abbr **RTP**

real-time video /ˌrɪəl taɪm 'vɪdiəʊ/ *noun* full form of **RTV**

reboot /riː'buːt/ *verb* to reload an operating system during a computing session ○ *We rebooted and the files reappeared.* ◊ **boot**

recall /rɪ'kɔːl/ *noun* the process of bringing back text or files from store ■ *verb* to bring back text or files from store for editing

receipt notification /rɪ'siːt ˌnəʊtɪfɪkeɪʃ(ə)n/ *noun* a feature of many electronic mail applications that will send an automatic message to confirm that the recipient has received the message

receive /rɪ'siːv/ *verb* to accept data from a communications link ○ *The computer received data via the telephone line.*

receive only /rɪˌsiːv 'əʊnli/ *noun* full form of **RO**

receiver /rɪ'siːvə/ *noun* an electronic device that can detect transmitted signals and present them in a suitable form

receiver register /rɪ'siːvə ˌredʒɪstə/ *noun* a temporary storage register for data inputs, before processing

re-chargeable battery /riːˌtʃɑːdʒəb(ə)l 'bæt(ə)ri/ *noun* a battery that can be used to supply power, and then have its charge replenished ○ *A re-chargeable battery is used for RAM back-up when the system is switched off.*

reciprocal link /rɪˌsɪprək(ə)l 'lɪŋk/ *noun* a link connecting two websites and working in both directions so that each site is effectively providing advertising space for the other

recode /riː'kəʊd/ *verb* to code a program which has been coded for one system, so that it will work on another

recognisable /'rekəɡnaɪzəb(ə)l/, **recognizable** *adjective* which can be recognised

recognise /'rekəɡˌnaɪz/, **recognize** *verb* to see something and remember that it has been seen before ○ *The scanner will recognize most character fonts.*

recognition /ˌrekəɡ'nɪʃ(ə)n/ *noun* a process that allows something such as letters on a printed text or bars on bar codes to be recognised,

recognition logic /ˌrekəɡ'nɪʃ(ə)n ˌlɒdʒɪk/ *noun* logical software used in OCR, AI, etc.

recompile /ˌriːkəm'paɪl/ *verb* to compile a source program again, usually after changes or debugging

reconfiguration /ˌriːkənfɪɡə'reɪʃ(ə)n/ *noun* the process of altering the structure of data in a system

reconfigure /ˌriːkən'fɪɡə/ *verb* to alter the structure of data in a system ○ *I reconfigured the field structure in the file.* ◊ **configure, set up**

reconstitute /riː'kɒnstɪtjuːt/ *verb* to return a file to a previous state, usually to restore a file after a crash or corruption

record *noun* /'rekɔːd/ a set of items of related data ○ *Your record contains several fields that have been grouped together under the one heading.* ■ *verb* /rɪ'kɔːd/ to store data or signals ○ *Record the results in this column.*

recordable CD /rɪˌkɔːdəb(ə)l siː 'diː/ *noun* full form of **CD-R**

record button /rɪ'kɔːd ˌbʌt(ə)n/ *noun* a key pressed on a recorder when ready to record signals onto a medium

record count /'rekɔːd kaʊnt/ *noun* the number of records within a stored file

recorder /rɪ'kɔːdə/ *noun* equipment able to transfer input signals onto a storage medium

COMMENT: The signal recorded is not always in the same form as the input signal. Many recorders record a modulated carrier signal for better quality. A recorder is usually combined with a suitable playback circuit since the read and write heads are often the same physical device.

record format /'rekɔːd ˌfɔːmæt/ *noun* the organisation and length of separate fields in a record

record gap /'rekɔːd ɡæp/ *noun* a blank section of magnetic tape between two consecutive records

record head /re'kɔːd ˌhed/ *noun* a transducer that converts an electrical signal into a magnetic field to write the data onto a magnetic medium. Also called **write head**

recording /rɪ'kɔːdɪŋ/ *noun* the action of storing signals or data

recording density /rɪ'kɔːdɪŋ ˌdensɪti/ *noun* same as **packing density**

recording indicator /rɪˈkɔːdɪŋ ˌɪndɪkeɪtə/ *noun* a light or symbol that shows when a device is recording

recording level /rɪˈkɔːdɪŋ ˌlev(ə)l/ *noun* the amplification of an input signal before it is recorded

record layout /ˌrekɔːd ˈleɪaʊt/ *noun* same as **record format**

record length /ˈrekɔːd leŋθ/ *noun* the total number of characters contained in the various fields within a stored record

record locking /ˈrekɔːd lɒkɪŋ/ *noun* (*in a multiuser system*) a software method of preventing more than one user writing data to a record at the same time. The first user's software sets a locked flag for the record during write operations, preventing other users from corrupting data by also writing data.

recordset /ˈrekɔːdset/ *noun* a group of records selected from a main database by a filter, search or query

records manager /ˈrekɔːdz ˌmænɪdʒə/ *noun* a program which maintains records and can access and process them to provide information

record structure /ˈrekɔːd ˌstrʌktʃə/ *noun* a list of the fields that make up a record, together with their length and data type

recover /rɪˈkʌvə/ *verb* to get back something which has been lost ○ *It is possible to recover the data but it can take a long time.*

recoverable error /rɪˌkʌv(ə)rəb(ə)l ˈerə/ *noun* an error type that allows program execution to be continued after it has occurred

recovery /rɪˈkʌv(ə)ri/ *noun* **1.** the process of returning to normal operating after a fault **2.** the process of getting back something that has been lost ○ *The recovery of lost files can be carried out using the recovery procedure.*

recovery procedure /rɪˈkʌv(ə)ri prəˌsiːdʒə/ *noun* the processes required to return a system to normal operation after an error

recursion /rɪˈkɜːʒ(ə)n/ *noun* a subroutine in a program that calls itself during execution. Also called **recursive routine**

recursive call /rɪˌkɜːsɪv ˈkɔːl/ *noun* a subroutine that calls itself when it is run

recursive routine /rɪˌkɜːsɪv ˈruːtiːn/ *noun* same as **recursion**

Recycle Bin /riːˈsaɪk(ə)l bɪn/ *noun* a folder in Windows 95 where deleted files

are automatically stored, with an icon on the Desktop that looks like a wastepaper bin

red, green, blue /ˌred griːn ˈbluː/ *noun* the three colour picture beams used in a colour TV

COMMENT: There are three colour guns producing red, green and blue beams acting on groups of three phosphor dots at each pixel location.

red, green, blue display /ˌred griːn ˈbluː dɪˌspleɪ/ *noun* full form of **RGB display**

red book audio /ˌred bʊk ˈɔːdiəʊ/ *noun* ♦ **compact disc-digital audio**

redefinable /ˌriːdɪˈfaɪnəb(ə)l/ *adjective* which can be redefined

redefine /ˌriːdɪˈfaɪn/ *verb* to change the function or value assigned to a variable or object ○ *We redefined the initial parameters.* □ **to redefine a key** to change the function of a programmable key ○ *I have redefined this key to display the figure five when pressed.*

'…one especially useful command lets you redefine the printer's character-translation table' [*Byte*]

redirect /ˌriːdaɪˈrekt/ *verb* **1.** to send a message to its destination by another route **2.** (*in DOS and UNIX operating systems*) to treat the output of one program as input for another program

redirection /ˌriːdaɪˈrekʃən/ *noun* the process of sending a message to its destination by another route ○ *Call forwarding is automatic redirection of calls.*

redirect operator, redirection operator *noun* a character used by an operating system to indicate that the output of one program is to be sent as input to another

redliner /ˈredlaɪnə/ *noun* a feature of workgroup or word-processor software that allows a user to highlight text in a different colour

redo from start /ˌriːduː frəm ˈstɑːt/ *verb* to start something again from the beginning

reduce /rɪˈdjuːs/ *verb* to convert raw data into a more compact form which can then be easily processed

reduced instruction set computer /rɪˌdjuːst ɪnˌstrʌkʃən set kəmˈpjuːtə/ *noun* full form of **RISC**

redundancy /rɪˈdʌndənsi/ *noun* the process of providing extra components in a system in case there is a breakdown

redundancy checking /rɪˈdʌndənsi tʃekɪŋ/ *noun* the checking of received data for correct redundant codes to detect any errors

redundant /rɪˈdʌndənt/ *adjective* 1. referring to data that can be removed without losing any information ○ *The parity bits on the received data are redundant and can be removed.* 2. referring to an extra piece of equipment kept ready for a task in case of faults

redundant array of inexpensive disks /rɪˌdʌndənt əˌreɪ əv ˌɪnɪkspensɪv ˈdɪsks/ *noun* full form of **RAID**

redundant character /rɪˌdʌndənt ˈkærɪktə/ *noun* a character added to a block of characters for error detection or protocol purposes. It carries no information.

redundant code /rɪˈdʌndənt kəʊd/ *noun* a check bit or item of data added to a block of data for error detection purposes. It carries no information.

reel to reel /ˌriːl tə ˈriːl/ *noun* the process of copying one tape of data onto another magnetic tape

reel to reel recorder /ˌriːl tə riːl rɪˈkɔːdə/ *noun* a magnetic tape recording machine that uses tape held on one reel and feeds it to a pick-up reel

re-entrant program /kəʊd/, **re-entrant code, re-entrant routine** /ruːˈtiːn/ *noun* one program or code shared by many users in a multi-user system. It can be interrupted or called again by another user before it has finished its previous run, and will return to the point at which it was interrupted when it has finished that run.

re-entry /reɪ ˈentri/ *noun* the process of calling a routine from within that routine, or of running a program from within that program

re-entry point /ˌriː ˈentri ˌpɔɪnt/ *noun* a point in a program or routine where it is re-entered

reference /ˈref(ə)rəns/ *noun* 1. a value used as a starting point for other values, often zero 2. the act of mentioning or dealing with something ■ *verb* to access a location in memory ○ *The access time taken to reference an item in memory is short.*

reference address /ˈref(ə)rəns əˌdres/ *noun* the initial address in a program used as an origin or base for others

reference file /ˈref(ə)rəns faɪl/ *noun* a file of data which is kept so that it can be referred to

reference instruction /ˈref(ə)rəns ɪnˌstrʌkʃən/ *noun* a command that provides access to sorted or stored data

reference list /ˈref(ə)rəns lɪst/ *noun* a list of routines or instructions and their location within a program

reference mark /ˈref(ə)rəns mɑːk/ *noun* a printed symbol that indicates the presence of a note or reference not in the text

reference program table /ˌref(ə)rəns ˈprəʊgræm ˌteɪb(ə)l/ *noun* a list produced by a compiler or system of the location, size and type of the variables, routines and macros within a program

reference retrieval system /ˌref(ə)rəns rɪˈtriːv(ə)l ˌsɪstəm/ *noun* an index that provides a reference to a document

reference table /ˈref(ə)rəns ˌteɪb(ə)l/ *noun* a list of ordered items

reference time /ˈref(ə)rəns taɪm/ *noun* a point in time that is used as an origin for further timings or measurements

reflectance /rɪˈflektəns/ *noun* the difference between the amount of light or signal incident and the amount that is reflected back from a surface. Opposite **absorptance** (NOTE: the opposite is **absorptance**)

reflected code /rɪˈflektd kəʊd/ *noun* a coding system in which the binary representation of decimal numbers changes by only one bit at a time from one number to the next

reformat /ˌriːˈfɔːmæt/ *verb* to format a disk that already contains data, and erasing the data by doing so ○ *Do not reformat your hard disk unless you can't do anything else.*

reformatting /riːˈfɔːmætɪŋ/ *noun* the act of formatting a disk which already contains data ○ *Reformatting destroys all the data on a disk.* ◊ **format**

refraction /rɪˈfrækʃən/ *noun* the apparent bending of light or sound that occurs when it travels through a material

refresh /rɪˈfreʃ/ *verb* to update regularly the contents of dynamic RAM by reading and rewriting stored data to ensure data is retained ○ *memory refresh signal*

refresh cycle /rɪˈfreʃ ˌsaɪk(ə)l/ *noun* the period of time during which a controller updates the contents of dynamic RAM chips

refresh rate /rɪˈfreʃ reɪt/ *noun* the number of times every second that the image on a CRT is redrawn

'Philips autoscan colour monitor, the 4CM6099, has SVGA refresh rates of 72Hz (800 x 600) and EVGA refresh rates of 70Hz (1,024 x 768).' [*Computing*]

regenerate /rɪˈdʒenəˌreɪt/ *verb* **1.** to redraw an image on a screen many times a second so that it remains visible **2.** to receive distorted signals, process and error check them, then retransmit the same data

regenerative memory /rɪˌdʒenərətɪv ˈmem(ə)ri/ *noun* a storage medium whose contents need to be regularly refreshed to retain its contents ○ *Dynamic RAM is regenerative memory – it needs to be refreshed every 250ns.*

regenerative reading /rɪˌdʒenərətɪv ˈriːdɪŋ/ *noun* a reading operation that automatically regenerates and rewrites the data back into memory

regenerator /riːˈdʒenəreɪtə/ *noun* a device used in communications that amplifies or regenerates a received signal and transmits it on. Regenerators are often used to extend the range of a network.

region /ˈriːdʒən/ *noun* a special or reserved area of memory or program or screen

regional breakpoint /ˌriːdʒ(ə)nəl ˈbreɪkpɔɪnt/ *noun* a breakpoint that can be inserted anywhere within a program that is being debugged. ◊ **breakpoint, debug**

region fill /ˈriːdʒ(ə)n fɪl/ *noun* the process of filling an area of the screen or a graphics shape with a particular colour

register /ˈredʒɪstə/ *noun* **1.** a special location within a CPU that is used to hold data and addresses to be processed in a machine code operation **2.** a reserved memory location used for special storage purposes ■ *verb* to react to a stimulus

register addressing /ˌredʒɪstə əˈdresɪŋ/ *noun* an instruction whose address field contains the register in which the operand is stored

register file /ˈredʒɪstə faɪl/ *noun* a number of registers used for temporary storage

register length /ˈredʒɪstə leŋθ/ *noun* the number of bits that make up a register

register map /ˈredʒɪstə mæp/ *noun* a display of the contents of all the registers

Registry /ˈredʒɪstri/ *noun* a database of information about configuration and program settings that forms the basis of Windows

regulate /ˈregjʊleɪt/ *verb* to control a process, usually using sensors and a feedback mechanism

regulated power supply /ˌregjʊleɪtɪd ˈpaʊə səˌplaɪ/ *noun* a constant, controlled voltage or current source whose output will not vary with input supply variation

COMMENT: A regulated power supply is required for all computers where components cannot withstand voltage variations.

rehyphenation /riːˌhaɪfəˈneɪʃ(ə)n/ *noun* the process of changing the hyphenation of words in a text after it has been put into a new page format or line width

rejection error /rɪˈdʒekʃən ˌerə/ *noun* an error by a scanner which cannot read a character and so leaves a blank

rekey /riːˈkiː/ *verb* to use a keyboard to re-enter lost text or data into a computer or to input text or data in a different form

relational database /rɪˌleɪʃ(ə)n(ə)l ˈdeɪtəbeɪs/, **relational database management system** *noun* a database in which all the items of data can be interconnected. Data is retrieved by using one item of data to search for a related field. ○ *If you search the relational database for the surname, you can pull out his salary from the related accounts database.* Abbr **RDBMS**

relational operator /rɪˌleɪʃ(ə)n(ə)l ˈɒpəreɪtə/ *noun* a symbol that compares two items

relational query /rɪˌleɪʃ(ə)n(ə)l ˈkwɪəri/ *noun* a database query that contains relational operators ○ *The relational query 'find all men under 35 years old' will not work on this system.*

relative address /ˌrelətɪv əˈdres/ *noun* a location specified in relation to a reference or base address

relative coding /ˈrelətɪv kɒdɪŋ/ *noun* the writing of a program using relative address instructions

relative coordinates /ˌrelətɪv kəʊˈɔːdɪnəts/ *plural noun* positional information given in relation to a reference point

relative data /ˌrelətɪv ˈdeɪtə/ *noun* data that gives new coordinate information relative to previous coordinates

relative error /ˌrelətɪv ˈerə/ *noun* the difference between a number and its correct value, caused by rounding off

relative pointing device /ˌrelətɪv ˈpɔɪntɪŋ dɪˌvaɪs/ *noun* an input device, e.g. a mouse, in which the movement of a pointer on screen is relative to the movement of the input device

relative-time clock /ˌrelətɪv taɪm 'klɒk/ *noun* regular pulses that allow software in a computer to calculate the real time

relay /'riːleɪ/ *noun* an electromagnetically controlled switch ○ *There is a relay in the circuit.* ■ *verb* to receive data from one source and then retransmit it to another point ○ *All messages are relayed through this small micro.*

release /rɪ'liːs/ *noun* **1.** a version of a product ○ *The latest software is release 5.* **2.** the shape of a sound signal that shows the speed at which a sound signal decreases in strength after a note has stopped playing. ◊ **decay** ■ *verb* **1.** to put a new product on the market **2.** (*of software*) to relinquish control of a block of memory or file

release number /rɪ'liːs ˌnʌmbə/ *noun* the number of the version of a product

release rate /rɪ'liːs reɪt/ *noun* the speed at which a sound signal decreases in strength after a note has stopped playing. ◊ **decay**

reliability /rɪˌlaɪə'bɪlɪti/ *noun* the ability of a device to function as intended, efficiently and without failure ○ *It has an excellent reliability record.*

reliable /rɪ'laɪəb(ə)l/ *adjective* which can be trusted to work properly ○ *The early versions of the software were not completely reliable.*

reliable connection /rɪˌlaɪəb(ə)l kə 'nekʃən/ *noun* a connection between two modems that are both using an error correction protocol to ensure that data is transmitted without errors

reload /riː'ləʊd/ *verb* to load something again ○ *We reloaded the program after the crash.* ◊ **load**

relocatable /ˌriːləʊ'keɪtəb(ə)l/ *adjective* which can be moved to another area of memory without affecting its operation

relocatable program /ˌriːləʊkeɪtəb(ə)l 'prəʊɡræm/ *noun* a computer program that can be loaded into and executed from any area of memory ○ *The operating system can load and run a relocatable program from any area of memory.*

relocate /ˌriːləʊ'keɪt/ *verb* to move data from one area of storage to another ○ *The data is relocated during execution.*

relocation /ˌriːləʊ'keɪʃ(ə)n/ *noun* the process of moving to another area in memory

relocation constant /ˌriːləʊ'keɪʃ(ə)n ˌkɒnstənt/ *noun* a quantity added to all addresses to move them to another section of memory, equal to the new base address

REM /rem/ *noun* a statement in a BASIC program that is ignored by the interpreter, allowing the programmer to write explanatory notes. Full form **remark**

remainder /rɪ'meɪndə/ *noun* a number equal to the dividend minus the product of the quotient and divider ○ *7 divided by 3 is equal to 2 remainder 1.* Compare **quotient**

remark /rɪ'mɑːk/ *noun* full form of **REM**

remedial maintenance /rɪˌmiːdiəl 'meɪntənəns/ *noun* maintenance to repair faults which have developed in a system

remote /rɪ'məʊt/ *adjective* referring to communications with a computer at a distance from the systems centre ○ *Users can print reports on remote printers.*

remote access /rɪˌməʊt 'ækses/ *noun* a link that allows a user to access a computer from a distance, normally using a modem

remote client /rɪˌməʊt 'klaɪənt/ *noun* a user who is accessing mail without being connected to the mail server's local network

remote console /rɪˌməʊt 'kɒnsəʊl/ *noun* an input/output device located away from the computer. Data is sent between the two by line or modem.

remote control /rɪˌməʊt kən'trəʊl/ *noun* a system that allows a remote user to control a computer from a distance

remote control software /rɪˌməʊt kən'trəʊl ˌsɒftweə/ *noun* software that runs on a local computer and a remote computer allowing a user to control the remote computer

remote device /rɪˌməʊt dɪ'vaɪs/ *noun* same as **remote console**

remote job entry /rɪˌməʊt dʒɒb 'entri/ *noun* full form of **RJE**

remote procedure call /rɪˌməʊt prə 'siːdʒə ˌkɔːl/ *noun* full form of **RPC**

remote station /rɪˌməʊt 'steɪʃ(ə)n/ *noun* a communications station that can be controlled by a central computer

remote terminal /rɪˌməʊt 'tɜːmɪn(ə)l/ *noun* a computer terminal connected to a distant computer system

removable /rɪˈmuːvəb(ə)l/ *adjective* which can be removed ○ *a removable hard disk*

removable Winchester /rɪ ˌmuːvəb(ə)l ˈwɪntʃestə/ *noun* a small hard disk in a sealed unit, which can be detached from a computer when full or when not required

remove directory /rɪˌmuːv daɪ ˈrekt(ə)ri/ *noun* full form of **RD**

REN /ren/ *noun* a number that defines the load a device places on a telephone network. Full form **ringer equivalence number**

rename /riːˈneɪm/ *verb* to give a new name to a file

render /ˈrendə/ *verb* to colour and shade a graphic object so that it looks solid and real ○ *We rendered the wire-frame model.*

renumber /ˈriːnʌmbə/ *noun* a feature of some computer languages which allows the programmer to allocate new values to all or some of a program's line numbers. ♢ **line number**

reorganise /riːˈɔːgənaɪz/, **reorganize** *verb* to organise something again or in a different way ○ *Wait while the spelling checker database is being reorganized.*

repaginate /riːˈpædʒɪneɪt/ *verb* to change the lengths of pages of text before they are printed ○ *The text was repaginated with a new line width.*

repagination /riːˌpædʒɪˈneɪʃ(ə)n/ *noun* the action of changing pages lengths ○ *The dtp package allows simple repagination.*

repeat counter /rɪˌpiːt ˈkaʊntə/ *noun* a register that holds the number of times a routine or task has been repeated

repeater /rɪˈpiːtə/ *noun* a device used in communications that amplifies or regenerates a received signal and transmits it on. Regenerators are often used to extend the range of a network, while the repeater works at the physical layer of the OSI network model. ♢ **bridge, OSI, router**

repeating group /rɪˈpiːtɪŋ gruːp/ *noun* a pattern of data that is duplicated in a bit stream

repeat key /rɪˈpiːt kiː/ *noun* a key on a keyboard which repeats the character pressed

repeat rate /rɪˈpiːt reɪt/ *noun* the number of times that a character will be entered on screen if you press and hold down one key on the keyboard

reperforator /riːˈpɜːfəreɪtə/ *noun* a machine that punches paper tape according to received signals

reperforator transmitter /riː ˈpɜːfəreɪtə trænzˌmɪtə/ *noun* a reperforator and a punched tape transmitter connected together

repertoire /ˈrepəˌtwɑː/ *noun* the range of functions of a device or software ○ *The manual describes the full repertoire.*

repetitive letter /rɪˌpetətɪv ˈletə/ *noun* a form letter or standard letter into which the details of each addressee are inserted

repetitive strain injury /rɪˌpetɪtɪv ˈstreɪn ˌɪndʒəri/, **repetitive stress injury** *noun* pain in the arm, wrist or hands felt by someone who performs the same movement many times over a certain period, as when operating a computer. Abbr **RSI**

replace /rɪˈpleɪs/ *verb* to find a certain item of data and put another in its place. ♢ **search and replace**

replace mode /rɪˈpleɪs məʊd/ *noun* an interactive computer mode in which new text entered replaces any previous text

replay *noun* /ˈriːpleɪ/ the playing back or reading back of data or a signal from a recording ■ *verb* /riːˈpleɪ/ to play back something that has been recorded

replenish /rɪˈplenɪʃ/ *verb* to charge a battery with electricity again

replication /ˌreplɪˈkeɪʃ(ə)n/ *noun* **1.** extra components in a system provided in case there is a breakdown or fault in one **2.** the process of copying a record or data to another location

reply /rɪˈplaɪ/ *verb* to answer an electronic mail message

report generator /rɪˌpɔːt ˈdʒenəreɪtə/ *noun* software that allows data from database files to be merged with a document, in the form of graphs or tables, in order to provide a complete report

report program generator /rɪˈpɔːt ˌprəʊgræm ˌdʒenəreɪtə/ *noun* a programming language used mainly on personal computers for the preparation of business reports, allowing data in files, databases, etc., to be included. Abbr **RPG**

reproduce /ˌriːprəˈdjuːs/ *verb* to copy data or text from one material or medium to another similar one

reprogram /riːˈprəʊgræm/ *verb* to alter a program so that it can be run on another type of computer

request for comment /rɪ,kwest fə 'kɒment/ *noun* full form of **RFC**

request to send /rɪ,kwest tə 'send/ *noun* a signal used in an RS-232C serial port to control the flow of data from another device, e.g. a modem. When the computer is ready to receive more data, it sends a RTS signal to the modem that replies with a signal on the CTS pin of the RS-232C connector and then sends the next batch of data to the computer. Abbr **RTS**

request to send signal /rɪ,kwest tə 'send ,sɪgn(ə)l/ *noun* a signal sent by a transmitter to a receiver asking if the receiver is ready to accept data, used in the RS232C serial connection. Abbr **RTS**

requirements /rɪ'kwaɪəmənts/ *noun* things which are needed ○ *Memory requirements depend on the application software in use.*

re-route /riː ruːt/ *verb* to send something by a different route

rerun /,riː'rʌn/ *verb* to run a program or a printing job again

rerun point /'riː,rʌn pɔɪnt/ *noun* a place in the program from where to start a running again after a crash or halt

res /rez/ *noun* same as **resolution**

resample /riː'saːmp(ə)l/ *verb* to change the number of pixels used to make up an image

resave /riː'seɪv/ *verb* to save a document or file again ○ *It automatically resaves the text.*

rescue dump /'reskjuː dʌmp/ *noun* data automatically saved on disk when a computer fault occurs. The rescue dump describes the state of the system at that time, and is used to help in debugging.

research /rɪ'sɜːtʃ/ *noun* scientific investigation carried out in order to learn new facts about a field of study

research and development /rɪ,sɜːtʃ ən dɪ'veləpmənt/ *noun* full form of **R & D**

reserved character /rɪ,zɜːvd 'kærɪktə/ *noun* a special character which is used by the operating system or which has a particular function to control an operating system and cannot be used for other uses

reserved sector /rɪ,zɜːvd 'sektə/ *noun* the area of disk space that is used only for control data storage

reserved word /rɪ'zɜːvd wɜːd/ *noun* a word or phrase used as an identifier in a programming language. It performs a par-

ticular operation or instruction and so cannot be used for other purposes by the programmer or user.

reset /,riː'set/ *verb* **1.** to return a system to its initial state, in order to allow a program or process to be started again **2.** to set a register or counter to its initial state ○ *When it reaches 999 this counter resets to zero.*

> COMMENT: Hard reset is similar to soft reset but with a few important differences. Hard reset is a switch that directly signals the CPU, while soft reset signals the operating system; hard reset clears all memory contents, while a soft reset does not affect memory contents; hard reset should always reset the system, while a soft reset does not always work if the operating system has been upset in a significant way.

reset button /,riː,set 'bʌt(ə)n/, **reset key** *noun* a switch that allows a program to be terminated and reset manually

reshape handle /'riːʃeɪp ,hænd(ə)l/ *noun* (*in a GUI*) a small square displayed on a frame around an object or image that a user can select and drag to change the shape of the frame or graphical object

resident /'rezɪd(ə)nt/ *adjective* referring to data or a program that is always in a computer

resident engineer /,rezɪd(ə)nt ,endʒɪ'nɪə/ *noun* an engineer who works permanently for one company

resident fonts /,rezɪd(ə)nt 'fɒntz/ *plural noun* font data which is always present in a printer or device and which does not have to be downloaded

resident software /,rezɪd(ə)nt 'sɒftweə/ *noun* a program that is held permanently in memory (whilst the machine is on)

residual /rɪ'zɪdjuəl/ *adjective* remaining after the rest or the others have disappeared or have been dealt with

residual error rate /rɪ,zɪdjuəl 'erə ,reɪt/ *noun* the ratio between incorrect and undetected received data and total data transmitted

residue check /'rezɪ,djuː tʃek/ *noun* an error detection check in which the received data is divided by a set number and the remainder is checked against the required remainder

resist /rɪ'zɪst/ *noun* a substance used to protect a pattern of tracks on a PCB, which is not affected by etching chemicals. ◊ **photoresist**

resolution /,rezə'luːʃ(ə)n/ *noun* the number of pixels that a screen or printer can display per unit area ○ *The resolution of most personal computer screens is not much more than 70 dpi (dots per inch).* Also called **res**

'Group IV fax devices can send a grey or colour A4 page in about four seconds, at a maximum resolution of 15.7 lines per millimetre over an Integrated Services Digital Network circuit.' [*Computing*]

resolving power /rɪ'zɒlvɪŋ ,paʊə/ *noun* a measurement of the ability of an optical system to detect fine black lines on a white background, given as the number of lines per millimetre

resonance /'rez(ə)nəns/ *noun* a situation in which a body oscillates with a very large amplitude because the frequency applied to it is the same as its natural frequency

resource /rɪ'zɔːs/ *noun* a useful device, product, program or graphic object

resource allocation /rɪ'zɔːs ,æləkeɪʃ(ə)n/ *noun* the process of dividing available resources in a system between jobs

resource fork /rɪ'zɔːs fɔːk/ *noun* (*in an Apple Macintosh*) one of two forks of a file. The resource fork contains resources such as fonts, codes or icons that the file needs.

resource interchange file format /rɪ,zɔːs ,ɪntətʃeɪndʒ 'faɪl ,fɔːmæt/ *noun* full form of **RIFF**

resource sharing /rɪ'zɔːs ,ʃeərɪŋ/ *noun* the use of one resource in a network or system by several users

response frame /rɪ'spɒns freɪm/ *noun* a page in a videotext system that allows a user to enter data

response position /rɪ'spɒns pə ,zɪʃ(ə)n/ *noun* the area of a form that is to be used for optical mark reading data

response time /rɪ'spɒns taɪm/ *noun* **1.** the time which passes between the user starting an action, by pressing a key, and the result appearing on the screen **2.** the speed with which a system responds to a stimulus

restart /rɪ'stɑːt/ *verb* to start something again ○ *First try to restart your system.*

restore /rɪ'stɔː/ *verb* to put something back into an earlier state

'...first you have to restore the directory that contains the list of deleted files' [*Personal Computer World*]

restrict /rɪ'strɪkt/ *verb* to keep something within a certain limit

restriction /rɪ'strɪkʃ(ə)n/ *noun* something that restricts data flow or access

result /rɪ'zʌlt/ *noun* the answer or outcome of an arithmetic or logical operation

result code /rɪ'zʌlt kəʊd/ *noun* a message sent from a modem to the local computer indicating the state of the modem

resume /rɪ'zjuːm/ *verb* to restart the program from the point where it was left, without changing any data

retrain /,riː'treɪn/ *verb* to re-establish a better quality connection when the quality of a line is very bad

retrieval /rɪ'triːv(ə)l/ *noun* the process of searching, locating and recovering information from a file or storage device

retrieve /rɪ'triːv/ *verb* to extract information from a file or storage device ○ *These are the records retrieved in that search.*

retro- /retrəʊ/ *prefix* relating to an earlier time, state, or stage of development

retrofit /'retrəʊ,fɪt/ *noun* a new device or accessory added to an existing system to upgrade it

retrospective parallel running /,retrəʊspektɪv 'pærəlel ,rʌnɪŋ/ *noun* running a new computer system with old data to check if it is accurate

retrospective search /,retrəʊspektɪv 'sɜːtʃ/ *noun* a search of documents on a certain subject since a certain date

return /rɪ'tɜːn/ *noun* **1.** an instruction that causes program execution to return to the main program from a subroutine ○ *The program is not working because you missed out the return instruction at the end of the subroutine.* **2.** a key on a keyboard used to indicate that all the required data has been entered ○ *You type in your name and code number then press return.* **3.** the indication of an end of line (in printing)

return address /rɪ'tɜːn ə,dres/ *noun* the address to be returned to after a called routine finishes

COMMENT: The return address is put on the stack by the call instruction and provides the address of the instruction after the call, which is to be returned to after the called routine has finished.

return to zero signal /rɪ,tɜːn tə 'zɪərəʊ ,sɪgn(ə)l/ *noun* a recording reference mark taken as the level of unmagnetised tape

reveal /rɪ'viːl/ *verb* to display previously hidden information once a condition has been met

reverb, reverberation *noun* a musical effect that gives the impression of depth in the sound

reverse /rɪ'vɜːs/ *verb* to go or travel in the opposite direction

'…the options are listed on the left side of the screen, with active options shown at the top left in reverse video' [*PC User*]

reverse channel /rɪˌvɜːs 'tʃæn(ə)l/ *noun* a low speed control data channel between a receiver and transmitter

reverse characters /rɪˌvɜːs 'kærɪktəz/ *plural noun* characters which are displayed in the opposite way to other characters for emphasis

reverse engineering /rɪˌvɜːs ˌendʒɪ'nɪərɪŋ/ *noun* a method of product design in which the finished item is analysed to determine how it should be constructed

reverse index /rɪˌvɜːs 'ɪndeks/ *noun* the movement of a printer head up half a line to print superscripts

reverse interrupt /rɪˌvɜːs 'ɪntərʌpt/ *noun* a signal sent by a receiver to request the termination of transmissions

reverse polarity /rɪˌvɜːs pəʊ'lærɪti/ *noun* a situation in an electric or electronic circuit in which the positive and negative terminals have been confused, resulting in the equipment not functioning

reverse Polish notation /rɪˌvɜːs ˌpəʊlɪʃ nəʊ'teɪʃ(ə)n/ *noun* mathematical operations written in a logical way, so that the operator appears after the numbers to be acted upon, removing the need for brackets. Abbr **RPN**

reverse video /rɪˌvɜːs 'vɪdiəʊ/ *noun* a screen display mode in which white and black are reversed and colours are complemented

revert command /rɪ'vɜːt kəˌmɑːnd/ *noun* a command in text that returns a formatted page to its original state

revise /rɪ'vaɪz/ *verb* to update or correct a version of a document or file

rewind /ˌriː'waɪnd/ *verb* to return a tape or film or counter to its starting point ○ *The tape rewinds onto the spool automatically.*

RF, R/F *noun* the electromagnetic spectrum that lies between the frequency range 10KHz and 3000GHz. Full form **radio frequency**

RFC /ˌɑː ef 'siː/ *noun* a document that contains information about a proposed new standard and asks users to look at the document and make any comments. Full form **request for comment**

RF shielding /ˌɑː ef 'ʃiːldɪŋ/ *noun* thin metal foil wrapped around a cable that prevents the transmission of radio frequency interference signals ○ *Without RF shielding, the transmitted signal would be distorted by the interference.*

RGB /ˌɑː dʒiː 'biː/ *noun* a high-definition monitor system that uses three separate input signals controlling red, green and blue colour picture beams. Full form **red, green, blue**

COMMENT: There are three colour guns producing red, green and blue beams acting on groups of three phosphor dots at each pixel location.

RGB display /'mɒnɪtə/, **RGB monitor** *noun* a monitor that uses RGB

ribbon cable /'rɪbən ˌkeɪb(ə)l/ *noun* same as **tape cable**

rich e-mail /ˌrɪtʃ 'iː meɪl/ *noun* an e-mail that has a voice message attached to it

rich text /ˌrɪtʃ 'tekst/ *noun* text that includes formatting such as bold, italics, etc

rich text format /ˌrɪtʃ 'tekst ˌfɔːmæt/ *noun* a way of storing a document that includes all the commands that describe the page, type, font and formatting. Abbr **RTF**

RIFF /rɪf/ *noun* a multimedia data format jointly introduced by IBM and Microsoft that uses tags to identify parts of a multimedia file structure and allows the file to be exchanged between platforms. Full form **resource interchange file format**

RIFF chunk /'rɪf tʃʌŋk/ *noun* a chunk with the ID RIFF

RIFF file /'rɪf faɪl/ *noun* a file that contains tagged information that complies with the RIFF file format

right-click /ˌraɪt 'klɪk/ *verb* to press and release the right-hand button of a computer mouse

right-click menu /ˌraɪt 'klɪk ˌmenjuː/ *noun* a small pop-up menu that appears when you click on the right-hand button of a two-button mouse

right-hand button /ˌraɪt hænd 'bʌt(ə)n/ *noun* a button on the right-hand side of a two or three-button mouse

right justification /raɪt ˌdʒʌstɪfɪ'keɪʃ(ə)n/ *noun* the process of aligning the text and spacing characters so that the right margin is straight

right justify /raɪt 'dʒʌstɪˌfaɪ/ *verb* to align the right margin so that the text is straight

right shift /ˌraɪt 'ʃɪft/ *verb* to move a section of data one bit to the right

rightsizing /'raɪtsaɪzɪŋ/ *noun* the process of moving a company's information technology structure to the most cost-effective hardware platform, which in practice often means moving from a mainframe-based network to a PC-based network

rigid disk /'rɪdʒɪd dɪsk/ *noun* a rigid magnetic disk that is able to store many times more data than a floppy disk, and usually cannot be removed from the disk drive

ring /rɪŋ/ *noun* **1.** a data list whose last entry points back to the first entry. ◊ **chained list 2.** the topology of a network in which the wiring sequentially connects one workstation to another

ring back system /'rɪŋ bæk ˌsɪstəm/ *noun* a remote computer system in which a user attempting to access it phones once, allows it to ring a number of times, disconnects, waits a moment, then redials

ringer equivalence number /ˌrɪŋər ɪ 'kwɪvələns ˌnʌmbə/ *noun* full form of **REN**

ring shift /ˌrɪŋ 'ʃɪft/ *noun* data movement to the left or right in a word. The bits falling outside the word boundary are discarded, and the free positions are filled with zeros.

ring topology /'rɪŋ təˌpɒlədʒi/ *noun* network architecture in which each computer or printer is connected together in a loop

ring topology network /rɪŋ tə ˌpɒlədʒi 'netwɜːk/ *noun* a type of network in which each terminal is connected one after the other in a circle

RIP *abbr* **1.** raster image processor **2.** routing information protocol

ripper /'rɪpə/ *noun* a program that can be used to copy digital music from a compact disc onto a computer before converting it into a format in which it can be stored as a computer file

ripple-through carry /'rɪp(ə)l θruː ˌkæri/ *noun* the fact that one operation produces a carry out from a sum and a carry in to

ripple-through effect /'rɪp(ə)l θruː ɪ ˌfekt/ *noun* (*in a spreadsheet*) the results, changes or errors appearing in a spreadsheet as a result of the value in one cell being changed

RISC /ˌɑː aɪ es 'siː/ *noun* a CPU design whose instruction set contains a small number of simple fast-executing instructions, which makes program writing more complex but increases speed. Full form **reduced instruction set computer**. ◊ **WISC**

Rivest, Shamir, Adleman /ˌrɪvest ʃə ˌmɪə 'æd(ə)lmən/ *noun* full form of **RSA** (*see*)

RJ-11 /ˌɑː dʒeɪ ɪ'lev(ə)n/ *noun* a connector with four connections, normally used in telephone sockets in the USA

RJ-45 /ˌɑː dʒeɪ ˌfɔːti 'faɪv/ *noun* a connector used in telephone systems with eight connections. A similar looking connector, often referred to as an RJ-45 connector, is used to connect 10BaseT UTP cable in an Ethernet local area network.

RJE /ˌɑː dʒeɪ 'iː/ *noun* a batch processing system in which instructions are transmitted to the computer from a remote terminal. Full form **remote job entry**

RLE /ˌɑː el 'iː/ *noun* a data compression technique that stores any sequence of bits of data with the same value to a single value. Full form **run-length encoding**

RLL encoding /ˌɑː el el ɪn'kəʊdɪŋ/ *noun* a fast and efficient method of storing data onto a disk in which the changes in a run of data bits is stored. Full form **run-length limited encoding**

rm /ˌɑː 'em/ *noun* (*in UNIX*) a command to remove an empty subdirectory

RMDIR *abbr* remove directory. Same as **RD**

RO /ˌɑː 'əʊ/ *noun* a computer terminal that can only accept and display data, not transmit. Full form **receive only**

roam /rəʊm/ *verb* (*in wireless communications*) to move around freely and still be in contact with a wireless communications transmitter

robot /'rəʊˌbɒt/ *noun* **1.** a device that can be programmed to carry out certain manufacturing tasks which are similar to tasks carried out by people **2.** same as **bot[2]**

robotics /rəʊ'bɒtɪks/ *noun* the study of artificial intelligence, programming and building involved with robot construction

robust /rəʊ'bʌst/ *adjective* referring to a system which can resume working after a fault

robustness /rəʊ'bʌstnəs/ *noun* a system's ability to continue functioning even with errors or faults during a program execution

rogue indicator /rəʊg 'ɪndɪˌkeɪtə/ *noun* a special code used only for control applications, e.g. an end of file marker

rogue value /ˌrəʊg 'væljuː/ *noun* an item in a list of data which shows that the list is terminated. Also called **terminator**

role indicator /rəʊl 'ɪndɪˌkeɪtə/ *noun* a symbol used to show the role of a index entry in its particular context

roll back /'rəʊl bæk/ *noun* a function of a database application that stops a transaction and returns the database to its previous state

roll forward /rəʊl 'fɔːwəd/ *noun* a function of a database application that allows the user to recover from an event such as a power cut by reading the transaction log and re-executing all the instructions to return the database to the state just before the event

roll in /ˌrəʊl 'ɪn/ *verb* to transfer data from backing store into main memory

roll out /ˌrəʊl 'aʊt/ *verb* to save the contents of main memory onto backing store

rollover /'rəʊləʊvə/ *noun* a keyboard with a small temporary buffer so that it can still transmit correct data when several keys are pressed at once

roll scroll /'rəʊl skrəʊl/ *noun* displayed text that moves up or down the computer screen one line at a time

ROM /rɒm/ *abbr* read only memory

Roman numerals /ˌrəʊmən 'njuːmərəlz/ *plural noun* numbers represented using the symbols I, V, X, L, C, D and M

ROM BIOS /rɒm 'baɪɒs/ *noun* a code which makes up the BIOS routines stored in a ROM chip, normally executed automatically when the computer is switched on

ROM cartridge /rɒm 'kɑːtrɪdʒ/ *noun* software stored in a ROM mounted in a cartridge which can easily be plugged into a computer

romware /'rɒmweə/ *noun* software which is stored in ROM

root /ruːt/ *noun* **1.** the starting node from which all paths branch in a data tree structure **2.** a fractional power of a number

root directory /ruːt də'rekt(ə)ri/ *noun* the topmost directory from which all other directories branch ○ *In DOS, the root directory on drive C: is called C:.*

rot13 /ˌrɒt θɜː'tiːn/ *noun* simple encoding that is used to scramble offensive messages posted in newsgroups

rotate /rəʊ'teɪt/ *verb* to move data within a storage location in a circular manner

rotate operation /rəʊ'teɪt ˌɒpəreɪʃ(ə)n/ *noun* same as **bit rotation**

rotating helical aperture scanner /rəʊˌteɪtɪŋ ˌhelɪk(ə)l 'æpətʃə ˌskænə/ *noun* a type of scanner in which the original image is lit and the reflection sent, through a lens and mirror, through a rotating spiral slit and finally onto a photodetector cell; as the spiral slit turns, it has the effect of moving up the image

rotation /rəʊ'teɪʃ(ə)n/ *noun* the degree to which an object has been rotated

rough copy /ˌrʌf 'kɒpi/ *noun* a draft of a program which, it is expected, will have changes made to it before it is complete

round /raʊnd/ *verb* □ **to round down** to approximate a number to a slightly lower one of lower precision ○ *We can round down 2.651 to 2.65.* □ **to round off** to approximate a number to a slightly larger or smaller one of lower precision ○ *Round off 23.456 to 23.46.* □ **to round up** to approximate a number to a slightly larger one of lower precision ○ *We can round up 2.647 to 2.65.*

round brackets /ˌraʊnd 'brækɪts/ *plural noun* brackets in the form ( )

rounding /'raʊndɪŋ/ *noun* **1.** an approximation of a number to a slightly larger or smaller one of lower precision **2.** the process of giving graphics a smoother look

rounding error /'raʊndɪŋ ˌerə/, **round-off error** /'raʊnd ɒf ˌerə/ *noun* an error in a result caused by rounding off the number

round robin /raʊnd 'rɒbɪn/ *noun* a way of organising the use of a computer by several users, who each use it for a time and then pass it on the next in turn

route /ruːt/ *noun* the path taken by a message between a transmitter and receiver in a network ○ *The route taken was not the most direct since a lot of nodes were busy.*

routed /ˌruːt 'diː/ *noun* software that manages the routes taken by traffic across a network. Full form **route-daemon**. ◊ **gated**

router /'ruːtɪd/ *noun* **1.** a communications device that receives data packets in a particular protocol and forwards them to their correct location via the most efficient route **2.** (*in a LAN*) a device that connect two or more LANs that use the same protocol and allows data to be transmitted between each network. The router works at the network-layer level of the OSI model. ◊ **bridge, OSI**

routine /ruːˈtiːn/ *noun* a number of instructions that perform a particular task, but are not a complete program. They are included as part of a program. ○ *The routine copies the screen display onto a printer.*

'Hewlett-Packard has announced software which aims to reduce PC-network downtime and cut support costs by automating housekeeping routines such as issuing alerts about potential problems.' [*Computing*]

COMMENT: Routines are usually called from a main program to perform a task. Control is then returned to the part of the main program from which the routine was called once that task is complete.

routing /ˈruːtɪŋ/ *noun* the process of determining a suitable route for a message through a network

routing information protocol /ˈruːtɪŋ ˌɪnfəmeɪʃ(ə)n ˌprəʊtəkɒl/ *noun* a protocol used on the Internet to calculate the best route by which to transfer information over the Internet. RIP bases its selection on the distance that each route takes. Abbr **RIP**

routing overheads /ˌraʊtɪŋ ˈəʊvəhedz/ *plural noun* actions that have to be taken when routing messages ○ *The information transfer rate is very much less once all routing overheads have been accommodated.*

routing page /ˌraʊtɪŋ ˈpeɪdʒ/ *noun* a videotext page describing the routes to other pages

routing table /ˌraʊtɪŋ ˈteɪb(ə)l/ *noun* a list of preferred choices for a route for a message stored within a router

row /raʊ/ *noun* **1.** a line of printed or displayed characters ○ *The figures are presented in rows, not in columns.* **2.** a horizontal line on a punched card ○ *Each entry is separated by a row of dots.* **3.** a horizontal set of data elements in an array or matrix

RPC /ˌɑː piː ˈsiː/ *noun* a method of communication between two programs running on two separate, but connected, computers. A software routine asks another computer on the network to process a problem and then displays the results. Full form **remote procedure call**

RPG *abbr* report program generator

RS-232C *noun* an EIA approved standard used in serial data transmission, covering voltage and control signals

RS-422 *noun* an EIA approved standard that extends the RS-232's 50ft limit

RS-423 *noun* an EIA approved standard that extends the RS-232's 50ft limit, introduced at the same time as the RS-422 standard, but less widely used

COMMENT: The RS232C has now been superseded by the RS423 and RS422 interface standards, which are similar to the RS232 but allow higher transmission rates.

RS-485 *noun* a standard that defines how serial devices are connected together for multipoint communications. This standard, approved by the EIA, supports higher rates of data transfer than the older RS-232C standard and allows more connections to one line than the RS-422 standard.

RSA *noun* a public-key cryptography system used to provide high-level of security (*see*) Full form **Rivest, Shamir, Adleman.** ◊ **public key cipher system**

RSI *abbr* repetitive strain injury

RTDS *abbr* real-time data system

RTE *abbr* real time execution

RTF *abbr* rich text format

RTFM *abbreviation* a euphemistic abbreviation used in messages as an instruction to someone to 'read the manual'

RTP *abbr* real time transport protocol (*see*)

RTS *abbr* request to send signal

RTV /ˌɑː tiː ˈviː/ *noun* real-time video compression used within DVI software to provide usable, but lower-quality, images that are compressed in real-time at 10 frames per second. Full form **real-time video**

rubber banding /ˌrʌbə ˈbændɪŋ/ *noun* ♦ **elastic banding**

rub out /ˌrʌb ˈaʊt/ *verb* ♦ **erase**

rule /ruːl/ *noun* **1.** a set of conditions that describe a function ○ *The rule states that you wait for the clear signal before transmitting.* **2.** in printing, a thin line

rule-based system /ˌruːl beɪst ˈsɪstəm/ *noun* software that applies the rules and knowledge defined by experts in a particular field to a user's data to solve a problem

ruler /ˈruːlə/ *noun* a bar displayed on screen that indicates a unit of measurement, often used in DTP or word-processor software to help with layout

ruler line /'ruːlə laɪn/ *noun* same as **tab rack**

rules /ruːlz/ *noun* a method of testing incoming messages for certain conditions, e.g. the name of the sender or the contents, and acting upon them

run /rʌn/ *noun* the execution by a computer of a set of instructions, programs or procedures ○ *The next invoice run will be on Friday.* ■ *verb* to operate, or to make a device operate ○ *The computer has been running ten hours a day.*

> **run around** /rʌn ə'raʊnd/ *verb* to fit text around an image on a printed page
> **run in** /'rʌn ɪn/ *verb* to operate a system at a lower capacity for a time in case of any faults
> **run on** /ˌrʌn 'ɒn/ *verb* to make text continue without a break ○ *The line can run on to the next without any space.*

runaway /'rʌnəˌweɪ/ *noun* an uncontrolled operation of a device or computer that occurs as a result of a malfunction or error

Run command /'rʌn kəˌmɑːnd/ *noun* (*in Windows*) a command that lets the user type in the name of a program that they want to run or a DOS command they want to execute

run-duration /'rʌn djʊˌreɪʃ(ə)n/ *noun, adjective* same as **run-time**

run indicator /rʌn 'ɪndɪˌkeɪtə/ *noun* an indicator bit or LED which shows that a computer is currently executing a program

run length encoding /ˌrʌn leŋθ en 'kəʊdɪŋ/ *noun* full form of **RLE**

run-length limited encoding /ˌrʌn leŋθ ˌlɪmɪtɪd en'kəʊdɪŋ/ *noun* full form of **RLL encoding**

running head /'rʌnɪŋ hed/ *noun* the title line of each page in a document

run phase /'rʌn feɪz/ *noun* same as **target phase**

run-time, run duration *noun* **1.** the period of a time that a program takes to run **2.** the time during which a computer is executing a program ▶ also called **run-duration** ■ *adjective* referring to an operation carried out only when a program is running

run-time error /'rʌn taɪm ˌerə/ *noun* a fault only detected when a program is run

run-time library /'rʌn taɪm ˌlaɪbrəri/ *noun* a library of routines that are only accessed by an application when it is running

run-time licence /'rʌn taɪm ˌlaɪs(ə)ns/ *noun* a licence granted to a user to run an application

run-time system /'rʌn taɪm ˌsɪstəm/ *noun* software that is required in main storage while a program is running, to execute instructions to peripherals, etc.

run-time version /'rʌn taɪm ˌvɜːʒ(ə)n/ *noun* **1.** a program code that has been compiled and is in a form that can be directly executed by the computer **2.** a commercial interpreter program that is sold with an application developed in a high-level language that allows it to run

R/W *abbr* read/write

R/W cycle /ˌɑː 'dʌb(ə)l juː ˌsaɪ(ə)l/ *noun* a sequence of events used to retrieve or store data. Full form **read/write cycle**

R/W head /ˌɑː 'dʌb(ə)l juː ˌhed/ *noun* an electromagnetic device that allows data to be read from or written to a storage medium. Full form **read/write head**

RX *abbr* receive ○ *The RXed signal needs to be amplified.*

S

S100 bus, S-100 bus *noun* an IEEE-696 standard bus, a popular 8– and 16-bit microcomputer bus using 100 lines and a 100-pin connector. ◊ **bus** (NOTE: say 'S one hundred bus')

SAA a trade name for a standard developed by IBM which defines the look and feel of an application regardless of the hardware platform. SAA defines which keystrokes carry out standard functions, the application's display and how the application interacts with the operating system. Full form **Systems Application Architecture**

safe format /seɪf 'fɔːmæt/ *noun* a format operation that does not destroy the existing data and allows the data to be recovered in case the wrong disk was formatted

safe mode /ˌseɪf 'məʊd/ *noun* a special operating mode of Windows 95 that is automatically selected if Windows 95 detects that there is a problem when starting

safety margin /'seɪfti ˌmɑːdʒɪn/ *noun* an extra amount of time or space provided so that errors can be absorbed

safety measures /'seɪfti ˌmeʒəz/ *plural noun* actions taken to make sure that something is safe

safety net /'seɪfti net/ *noun* a software or hardware device that protects the system or files from excessive damage in the event of a system crash ○ *If there is a power failure, we have a safety net in the form of a UPS.*

sag /sæg/ *noun* a short drop in the voltage level from a power supply

salami technique /səˈlɑːmi tekˌniːk/ *noun* computer fraud involving many separate small transactions that are difficult to detect and trace

SAM /ˌes eɪ 'em/ *noun* a type of storage in which a particular data item can only be accessed by reading through all the previous items in the list. Full form **serial access memory**

COMMENT: Magnetic tape is a form of SAM. You have to go through the whole tape to access one item, while disks provide random access to stored data.

sample /'sɑːmpəl/ *noun* a measurement of a signal at a point in time ○ *The sample at three seconds showed an increase.* ■ *verb* to obtain a number of measurements of a signal which can be used to provide information about the signal

sample and hold circuit /ˌsɑːmpəl ən 'həʊld ˌsɜːkɪt/ *noun* a circuit that freezes an analog input signal for long enough for an A/D converter to produce a stable output

sample interval /'sɑːmpəl ˌɪntəv(ə)l/ *noun* a time period between two consecutive samples

sampler /'sɑːmplə/ *noun* an electronic circuit that takes many samples of a signal and stores them for future analysis

sample rate /'sɑːmpəl reɪt/ *noun* a number of measurements of a signal that are recorded every second. A PC sound card normally supports one of the following three standard rates: 11,025, 22,050 and 44,100 samples per second, normally written as 11.025KHz, 22.05KHz and 44.1KHz.

sample size /'sɑːmpəl saɪz/ *noun* the size of the word used to measure the level of the signal when it is sampled

sampling interval /'sɑːmplɪŋ ˌɪntəv(ə)l/ *noun* a time period between two consecutive samples

sampling rate /'sɑːmplɪŋ reɪt/ *noun* a number of measurements of a signal recorded every second

SAR /ˌes eɪ 'ɑː/ *noun* a register within the CPU that contains the address of the next location to be accessed. Full form **store address register**

SAS *abbr* single attachment station

satellite /'sætəˌlaɪt/ *noun* a small system that is part of a larger system

COMMENT: In a network the floppy disk units are called 'satellites' and the hard disk unit the 'server'. In a star network each satellite is linked individually to a central server.

satellite computer /ˌsætəlaɪt kəm'pjuːtə/ *noun* a computer doing various tasks under the control of another computer

satellite terminal /'sætəlaɪt ˌtɜːmɪn(ə)l/ *noun* a computer terminal that is outside the main network

saturated colour /ˌsætʃ əreɪtɪd 'kʌlə/ *noun* bright colours such as red and orange that do not reproduce well on video and can cause distortion or can spread over the screen

saturation /ˌsætʃə'reɪʃ(ə)n/ *noun* a point where a material cannot be further magnetized

saturation noise /ˌsætʃə'reɪʃ(ə)n nɔɪz/ *noun* errors that occur as a result of saturation of a magnetic storage medium

saturation testing /ˌsætʃə'reɪʃ(ə)n ˌtestɪŋ/ *noun* the process of testing a communications network by transmitting large quantities of data and messages over it

save /seɪv/ *verb* to store data or a program on an auxiliary storage device ○ *This WP saves the text every 15 minutes in case of a fault.*

save area /seɪv 'eəriə/ *noun* a temporary storage area of main memory, used for registers and control data

save as /'seɪv əz/ *noun* an option in an application that allows the user to save the current work in a file with a different name

SBC /ˌes biː 'siː/ *noun* a computer whose main components such as processor, input/output and memory are all contained on one PCB. Full form **single board computer**

SBM /ˌes biː 'em/ *noun* an extension to the Red Book CD-Audio specification in which studio-quality 20-bit sound samples are stored in the 16-bit data format used by CD-Audio. Full form **super bit mapping**

scalable /'skeɪləb(ə)l/ *adjective* **1.** used to describe a computer, component or network that can be expanded to meet future needs **2.** referring to fonts used for computer graphics that can be made to appear in a wide range of sizes

scalable software /ˌskeɪləb(ə)l 'sɒftweə/ *noun* a groupware application that can easily accommodate more users on a network without the need for investment in new software

scalar /'skeɪlə/ *noun* a variable that has a single value assigned to it

scalar data /'skeɪlə ˌdeɪtə/ *noun* a data type containing single values that are predictable and follow a sequence

scalar processor /ˌskeɪlə 'prəʊsesə/ *noun* a processor designed to operate at high-speed on scalar values

Scalar Processor Architecture /ˌskeɪlə 'prəʊsesə ˌɑːkɪtektʃə/ full form of **SPARC**

scalar value /'skeɪlə ˌvæljuː/ *noun* a single value rather than a matrix or record

scalar variable /ˌskeɪlə 'veəriəb(ə)l/ *noun* a variable that can contain a single value rather than a complex data type such as an array or record

scale /skeɪl/ *noun* the ratio of two values ■ *verb* □ **to scale down, scale up** to lower or increase in proportion

scan /skæn/ *noun* an examination of an image or object or list of items to obtain data describing it ○ *The heat scan of the computer quickly showed which component was overheating.* ■ *verb* to examine and produce data from the shape or state of an object or drawing or file or list of items ○ *The facsimile machine scans the picture and converts this to digital form before transmission.*

scan area /skæn 'eəriə/ *noun* a section of an image read by a scanner

scan code /ˌskæn 'kəʊd/ *noun* a number transmitted from the keyboard to an IBM PC compatible computer to indicate that a key has been pressed and to identify the key

scan conversion /skæn kən'vɜːʃ(ə)n/ *noun* the process of converting an interlaced video signal to a non-interlaced signal or a composite to a separated RGB signal

ScanDisk /'skændɪsk/ *noun* a utility that will check the hard disk for any problems and will try and correct problems that it finds

scan head /'skæn hed/ *noun* a device used in scanners, photocopiers and fax machines, which uses photo-electric cells to turn an image into a pattern of pixels ○ *This model uses a scan head that can distinguish 256 different colours.*

scan length /ˌskæn 'leŋθ/ *noun* the number of items in a file or list that are examined in a scan

scan line /ˌskæn 'laɪn/ *noun* one of the horizontal lines of phosphor, or phosphor dots, on the inside of a CRT or monitor. The monitor's picture beam sweeps along each scan line to create the image on the screen.

scanner /'skænə/ *noun* a device that converts an image or document into graphical data which can be manipulated by a computer

'Ricoh's Fax 300L Computer Link is connected to a PC via a RS232C serial interface, and enables users to send faxes from within Dos and Windows applications without printing a hard copy: It can also act as a scanner for graphics, and a printer for documents.' [*Computing*]

scanner memory /'skænə ˌmem(ə)ri/ *noun* the memory area allocated to store images which can be scanned

scanning /'skænɪŋ/ *noun* the action of examining and producing data from the shape of an object or drawing

COMMENT: A modem with auto-baud scanning can automatically sense which baud rate to operate on and switches automatically to that baud rate.

scanning error /'skænɪŋ ˌerə/ *noun* an error introduced while scanning an image

scanning line /'skænɪŋ laɪn/ *noun* a path traced on a CRT screen by the picture beam

scanning rate /'skænɪŋ reɪt/ *noun* the time taken to scan one line of a CRT image

scanning resolution /'skænɪŋ rezə ˌluːʃ(ə)n/ *noun* the ability of a scanner to distinguish between small points. The usual resolution is 300 dpi.

scanning software /'skænɪŋ ˌsɒf(t)weə/ *noun* a dedicated program that controls a scanner and allows certain operations, e.g. rotate, edit or store, to be performed on a scanned image

scanning speed /'skænɪŋ spiːd/ *noun* the speed at which a line or image is scanned

scan rate /ˌskæn 'reɪt/ *noun* the number of times every second that the image on a CRT is redrawn

SCART connector /'skɑːt kəˌnektə/ *noun* a special connector normally used to carry video or audio signals between video equipment

scatter-load /'skætə ləʊd/ *verb* to load sequential data into various non-continuous locations in memory

scatter-read /'skætə riːd/ *verb* to access and read sequential data stored in various non-continuous locations

scavenging /'skævɪndʒɪŋ/ *noun* the act of searching through and accessing database material without permission

schedule /'ʃedjuːl/ *noun* the order in which tasks are to be done, or the order in which CPU time will be allocated to processes in a multi-user system

Schedule+ /ˌʃedjuːl'plʌs/ *noun* a Microsoft Windows 95 software program that provides personal information management features, including a diary

scheduled circuits /ˌʃedʒuːld 'sɜːkɪts/ *noun* telephone lines for data communications only

scheduler /'ʃedjuːlə/ *noun* **1.** a program that organises the use of a CPU or of peripherals which are shared by several users **2.** utility software that helps users organise their meetings, appointments or the use of a resource

scheduling /'ʃedjuːlɪŋ/ *noun* a method of working that allows several users to share the use of a CPU

schema /'skiːmə/ *noun* a graphical description of a process or database structure

schematic /skiː'mætɪk/ *noun* a diagram showing system components and how they are connected

scissor /'sɪzə/ *verb* **1.** to define an area of an image and then cut out this part of the image so it can then be pasted into another image **2.** to define an area of an image and delete any information that is outside this area

scope /skəʊp/ *noun* the range of values that a variable can contain

SCR *abbr* sequence control register

scramble /'skræmb(ə)l/ *verb* to code speech or data which is transmitted in such a way that it cannot be understood unless it is decoded

scrambler /'skræmblə/ *noun* a device that codes a data stream into a pseudo-random form before transmission to eliminate any series of ones or zeros or alternate ones and zeros that would cause synchronisation problems at the receiver

scrapbook /'skræpˌbʊk/ *noun* a utility on an Apple Macintosh that stores frequently used graphic images ○ *We store our logo in the scrapbook.*

scratch /skrætʃ/ *noun* an area of memory or of a file used for the temporary storage of data ■ *verb* to delete or move an area of memory to provide room for other data

scratch file /'skrætʃ faɪl/ *noun* same as **work file**

scratchpad /'skrætʃpæd/ *noun* a workspace or area of high speed memory used for temporary storage of data currently in use

'Mathcad is described as an easy-to-use 'handy scratch pad for quick number crunching', which is positioned as an alternative to popular spreadsheets.' [*Computing*]

scratchpad memory /'skrætʃpæd ˌmem(ə)ri/ *noun* cache memory used to buffer data being transferred between a fast processor and a slow I/O device such as a disk drive

scratch tape /'skrætʃ teɪp/ *noun* magnetic tape used for a scratch file

screen /skriːn/ *noun* a display device capable of showing a quantity of information, such as a CRT or VDU. ◊ **readout**

screen angle /skriːn 'æŋg(ə)l/ *noun* the angle at which a screen is set before the photograph is taken

screen attribute /skriːn 'ætrɪˌbjuːt/ *noun* a set of attribute bits which define how each character will be displayed on screen. They set background and foreground colour and bold, italic or underline.

screen border /skriːn 'bɔːdə/ *noun* a margin around text displayed on a screen

screen buffer /skriːn 'bʌfə/ *noun* a temporary storage area for characters or graphics before they are displayed

screen burn /'skriːn bɜːn/ *noun* a problem caused if a stationary image is displayed for too long on a monitor, burning the phosphor. This problem was the original reason why screen savers were developed. Now, screens are better made and the phosphor is more resilient. As a result, it is very difficult to cause screen burn, but the screen savers look good and are still used.

screen capture /skriːn 'kæptʃə/ *verb* to store the image currently displayed on screen in a file

screen cleaning kit /'skriːn ˌkliːnɪŋ ˌkɪt/ *noun* the liquids and cloth which remove any static and dirt from a VDU screen

screen dump /'skriːn ˌdʌmp/ *noun* the process of outputting the text or graphics displayed on a screen to a printer

screen editor /skriːn 'edɪtə/ *noun* software which allows the user to edit text on-screen, with one complete screen of information being displayed at a time

screen flicker /skriːn 'flɪkə/ *noun* (*on a display*) an image that moves slightly or whose brightness alternates due to a low image refresh rate or signal corruption

screen font /ˌskriːn 'fɒnt/ *noun* (*in a GUI*) typeface and size designed to be used to display text on screen rather than be printed out ○ *The screen font is displayed at 72dpi on a monitor, rather than printed at 300dpi on this laser printer.*

screen format /skriːn 'fɔːmæt/ *noun* a way in which a screen is laid out

screenful /'skriːnfʊl/ *noun* a complete frame of information displayed on a screen

screen grab /ˌskriːn 'græb/ *noun* **1.** the process of digitising a single frame from a display or television **2.** the process of capturing what is displayed on a monitor and storing it as a graphics file

screen memory /skriːn 'mem(ə)ri/ *noun* in a memory-mapped screen, the area of memory representing the whole screen, usually with one byte representing one or a number of pixels

screen notepad /skriːn 'nəʊtˌpæd/ *noun* the part of the screen used to store information even when the terminal is switched off

screen refresh /skriːn rɪ'freʃ/ *verb* to update regularly the images on a CRT screen by scanning each pixel with a picture beam to make sure the image is still visible

screen saver /skriːn 'seɪvə/ *noun* software which, after a pre-determined period of user inactivity, replaces the existing image on screen and displays moving objects to protect against screen burn

screen shot /ˌskriːn 'ʃɒt/ *noun* ♦ **screen capture**

screen size /ˌskriːn 'saɪz/ *noun* **1.** the number of characters a computer display can show horizontally and vertically **2.** the size of a monitor screen based on international paper sizes

script /skrɪpt/ *noun* a set of instructions which carry out a function, normally used with a macro language or batch language ○ *I log in automatically using this script with my communications software.*

script channel /skrɪpt 'tʃæn(ə)l/ *noun* (*in Movie Player*) one channel in a score that contains instructions

script editor /skrɪpt 'edɪtə/ *noun* an editor that lets a user edit a script or program in an authoring package

scripting language /skrɪptɪŋ
'læŋgwɪdʒ/ *noun* a simple programming
language (normally proprietary to an application) that allows a user to automate
the application's functions ○ *This communications software has a scripting language that lets me dial and log in automatically.*

script recorder /skrɪpt rɪ'kɔːdə/ *noun*
a function of an authoring package that
records the functions and actions a user
carries out and converts these into commands in a script

ScriptX /ˌskrɪpt'eks/ *noun* an authoring
tool and utilities that allow a developer to
write multimedia applications that can be
played (unchanged) on a range of different
platforms

scroll /skrəʊl/ *verb* to move displayed
text vertically up or down the screen, one
line or pixel at a time

scroll arrows /skrəʊl 'ærəʊz/ *plural
noun* (*in a GUI*) arrows that when clicked,
move the contents of the window up or
down or sideways

scroll bar /'skrəʊl bɑː/ *noun* (*in a GUI*)
a bar displayed along the side of a window
with a marker which indicates how far you
have scrolled ○ *The marker is in the middle of the scroll bar so I know I am in the
middle of the document.*

Scroll Lock key /'skrəʊl lɒk ˌkiː/ *noun*
a key on an IBM PC keyboard that changes
how the cursor control keys operate, their
function being dependent on the application

scroll mode /ˌskrəʊl 'məʊd/ *noun* a
terminal mode which transmits every key
press and displays what is received

scrub /skrʌb/ *verb* to wipe information
off a disk or remove data from store ○
Scrub all files with the .BAK extension.

SCSI /ˌes siː es 'aɪ/ *noun* a standard
high-speed parallel interface used to connect computers to peripheral devices (such
as disk drives and scanners). Full form
small computer system interface

'…the system uses SCSI for connecting to the host
and ESDI for interconnecting among drives within a
multidrive system' [*Byte*]

COMMENT: SCSI is the current standard used
to interface high-capacity, high-performance
disk drives to computers. Smaller disk drives
are connected with an IDE interface, which is
slower, but cheaper. SCSI replaced the older
ESDI interface and allows several (normally
eight) peripherals to be connected, in a daisy-
chain, to one controller.

SCSI-2 /ˌskʌzi tuː/ *noun* a standard that
provides a wider data bus and transfers
data faster than the original SCSI specification that supports 16-bit data transfers
and can control 15 devices

'The Tricord ES4000 is an entry-level superserver
machine, with 525Mb of SCSI-2 fixed disk, 64Mb of
ECC memory, and support for Raid levels 0, 1 and
10.' [*Computing*]

SD *abbr* single density

SDLC /ˌes diː el 'siː/ *noun* data transmission protocol most often used in IBM's
Systems Network Architecture (SNA). It
defines how synchronous data is transmitted. Full form **synchronous data link
control**

SDR /ˌes diː 'ɑː/ *noun* the register in a
CPU which holds data before it is processed or moved to memory location. Full
form **store data register**

SDRAM /ˌes 'diː ˌræm/ *noun* the enhanced memory component that is replacing traditional DRAM; the memory access
cycle is synchronised with the main processor clock, eliminating wait time between
memory operations. Full form **synchronised dynamic ram**

seamless integration /ˌsiːmləs ˌɪntɪ
'greɪʃ(ə)n/ *noun* the process of including
a new device or software into a system
without any problems ○ *It took a lot of
careful planning, but we succeeded in a
seamless integration of the new application.*

search /sɜːtʃ/ *noun* the process of looking for and identifying a character or word
or section of data in a document or file ■
verb to look for an item of data

'…a linear search of 1,000 items takes 500 compar-
isons to find the target, and 1,000 to report that it
isn't present. A binary search of the same set of items
takes roughly ten divisions either to find or not to
find the target' [*Personal Computer World*]

searchable *adjective* able to be accessed by a search facility

search and replace /ˌsɜːtʃ ənd rɪ
'pleɪs/ *noun* a feature on word-processors
which allows the user to find certain words
or phrases, then replace them with another
word or phrase

search directory /'sɜːtʃ daɪˌrekt(ə)ri/
noun a website in which links to information are listed in categories or in alphabetical order

search engine /'sɜːtʃ ˌendʒɪn/ *noun*
(*on the Internet*) software that searches a
database (*see also*) ◊ **agent, Gopher**

searching storage /'sɜːtʃɪŋ ˌstɔːrɪdʒ/ *noun* a method of data retrieval that uses part of the data rather than an address to locate the data

search key /'sɜːtʃ kiː/ *noun* **1.** a word or phrase that is to be found in a text **2.** a field and other data used to select various records in a database

search memory /sɜːtʃ 'mem(ə)ri/ *noun* a method of data retrieval that uses part of the data rather than an address to locate the data

SECAM /ˌes iː siː eɪ 'em/ *noun* a standard for television transmission and reception similar to PAL except that SECAM uses frequency modulation to transmit the chroma signal. SECAM is used in France and Eastern Europe. Full form **Système Electronique Couleur Avec Mémoire**

secondary /'sekənd(ə)ri/ *adjective* second in importance or less important than the first

secondary channel /ˌsekənd(ə)ri 'tʃæn(ə)l/ *noun* a second channel containing control information transmitted at the same time as data

secondary memory /ˌsekənd(ə)ri 'mem(ə)ri/ *noun* a permanent storage device in a computer that is used for storing files and data. Compare **main memory, RAM**

secondary service provider /ˌsekənd(ə)ri 'sɜːvɪs prəˌvaɪdə/ *noun* an organisation that provides Internet access for a particular region of a country

secondary station /ˌsekənd(ə)ri 'steɪʃ(ə)n/ *noun* the temporary status of a station receiving data

secondary storage /ˌsekənd(ə)ri 'stɔːrɪdʒ/ *noun* any data storage medium that is not the main, high-speed computer storage (RAM)

COMMENT: This type of storage is usually of a higher capacity, lower cost and slower access time than main memory.

second generation computers /ˌsekənd ˌdʒenəreɪʃ(ə)n kəm'pjuːtə/ *noun* computers which used transistors instead of valves

second hand /ˌsekənd 'hænd/ *adjective* same as **second user**

second-level addressing /ˌsekənd ˌlev(ə)l ə'dresɪŋ/ *noun* an instruction that contains an address at which the operand is stored

second sourcing /ˌsekənd 'sɔːsɪŋ/ *noun* the process of granting a licence to another manufacturer to produce an electronic item or component when production capacity is not great enough to meet demand

second user /ˌsekənd 'juːzə/ *adjective* referring to old equipment which has already been used and is being sold again

section /'sekʃən/ *noun* part of a main program which can be executed in its own right, without the rest of the main program being required

sector /'sektə/ *noun* the smallest area on a magnetic disk which can be addressed by a computer; the disk is divided into concentric tracks, and each track is divided into sectors which, typically, can store 512 bytes of data ■ *verb* to divide a disk into a series of sectors

COMMENT: A disk is divided into many tracks, each of which is then divided into a number of sectors which can hold a certain number of bits.

sectoring hole /'sektərɪŋ həʊl/ *noun* a hole in the edge of a disk to indicate where the first sector is located

sector interleave /ˌsektə 'ɪntəliːv/ *noun* the ratio of sectors skipped between access operations on a hard disk; in a hard disk with an interleave of 3, the first sector is read, then three sectors are skipped and the next sector is read; this is used to allow hard disks with slow access time to store more data on the disk

sector map /'sektə mæp/ *noun* a table which contains the addresses of unusable sectors on a hard disk

secured /sɪ'kjʊəd/ *adjective* (*of a file*) protected against accidental writing or deletion or against unauthorised access

Secure Digital Card /sɪˌkjʊə ˌdɪdʒɪt(ə)l 'kɑːd/ *noun* same as **MMC**

secure electronic transactions /sɪˌkjʊə ˌelektrɒnɪk trænz'ækʃənz/ *plural noun* full form of **SET**

secure encryption payment protocol /sɪˌkjʊə ɪnˌkrɪpʃən 'peɪmənt ˌprəʊtəkɒl/ *noun* full form of **SEPP**

secure hypertext transfer protocol /sɪˌkjʊə ˌhaɪpətekst 'trænsfɜː ˌprəʊtəkɒl/ *noun* full form of **S-HTTP**

secure/multipurpose Internet mail extension /sɪˌkjʊə ˌmʌltipɜːpəs ˌɪntənet 'meɪl ɪkˌstenʃ(ə)n/ *noun* a method of providing secure electronic mail messages; the system encrypts the main message using a standard cipher such as DES then sends the key in encrypted form using a second, public-key encryption system. Abbr **S/MIME**

secure server /sɪˌkjʊə ˈsɜːvə/ *noun* an Internet server that allows data to be encrypted and thus is suitable for use in e-commerce

secure site /sɪˌkjʊə ˈsaɪt/ *noun* a website that includes features to ensure that any information transferred between the user and the website is encrypted and cannot be read by a hacker. Also called **secure website**

COMMENT: A secure website is normally used in a shopping site to allow a customer to type in their personal details (such as their credit card number) without risk. Secure websites almost always use a system called SSL (secure sockets layer) that creates a secure channel when you visit the site; when you visit a secure site, the small padlock icon in the status bar at the bottom of your web browser is locked. If the padlock icon is open, this is not a secure site and you should not type in sensitive information, such as a credit-card number.

secure sockets layer /sɪˌkjʊə ˈsɒkɪts ˌleɪə/ *noun* full form of **SSL**

secure system /sɪˌkjʊə ˈsɪstəm/ *noun* a system that cannot be accessed without authorisation

secure transaction technology /sɪ ˌkjʊə trænˈzækʃən tekˌnɒlədʒi/ *noun* full form of **STT**

secure website /sɪˌkjʊə ˈwebsaɪt/ *noun* same as **secure site**

security backup /sɪˈkjʊərɪti ˌbækʌp/ *noun* a copy of a disk, tape or file kept in a safe place in case the working copy is lost or damaged

security check /sɪˈkjʊərɪti tʃek/ *noun* identification of authorised users (by a password) before granting access

seed /siːd/ *noun* the starting value used when generating random or pseudorandom numbers

seek area /siːk ˈeəriə/ *noun* a section of memory to be searched for a particular item of data or a word

seek time /ˌsiːk ˈtaɪm/ *noun* the time taken by a read/write head to find the right track on a disk ○ *The new hard disk drive has a seek time of just 35mS.*

segment /ˈsegmənt/ *noun* a section of a main program which can be executed in its own right, without the rest of the main program being required ■ *verb* to divide a long program into shorter sections which can then be called up when required. ◊ **overlay**

'…you can also write in smaller program segments. This simplifies debugging and testing' [*Personal Computer World*]

segmented address space /seg ˌmentɪd əˈdres ˌspeɪs/ *noun* memory address space divided into areas called segments; to address a particular location, the segment and offset values must be specified

select /sɪˈlekt/ *verb* to find and retrieve specific information from a database

selectable /sɪˈlektəb(ə)l/ *adjective* which can be selected □ **this modem has user-selectable baud rates** the receive and transmit baud rates of the modem can be chosen by the user, and are not preset

selectable attributes /sɪˌlektəb(ə)l ˈætrɪbjuːtz/ *plural noun* the attributes of a device which can be chosen by the user

selection handle /sɪˈlekʃən ˌhænd(ə)l/ *noun* a small square displayed on a frame around a selected area that allows the user to change the shape of the area

selection tool /sɪˈlekʃən tuːl/ *noun* (*in a paint or drawing program*) an icon in a toolbar that allows a user to select an area of an image which can then be cut, copied or processed in some way

selective dump /sɪˈlektɪv dʌmp/ *noun* a display or printout of a selected area of memory

selective sort /sɪˈlektɪv sɔːt/ *noun* the process of sorting a section of data items into order

selector /sɪˈlektə/ *noun* a mechanical device which allows a user to choose an option or function

self- /self/ *prefix* oneself or itself

self-adapting system /ˌself ə ˌdæptɪŋ ˈsɪstəm/ *noun* a system which is able to adapt itself to various tasks

self-checking code /ˌself ˌtʃekɪŋ ˈkəʊd/ *noun* a character coding system which is able to detect an error or bad character but not correct it

self-checking system /ˌself ˌtʃekɪŋ ˈsɪstəm/ *noun* a system which carries out diagnostic tests on itself usually at switch on

self-correcting /ˌselfkəˈrektɪŋ/ *adjective* referring to a word processor that automatically corrects any typing errors made by the user as soon as he or she makes them

self-correcting codes % /self kə ˌrektɪŋ ˈkəʊdz/ *plural noun* a character coding system which is able to detect and correct an error or bad character

self-diagnostic /self ˌdaɪəgˈnɒstɪk/ *noun* a computer that runs a series of diagnostic programs (usually when the computer is switched on) to ensure that all circuits, memory and peripherals are working correctly

self-documenting program /ˌself ˌdɒkjʊmentɪŋ ˈprəʊgræm/ *noun* a computer program providing the user with operating instructions as it runs

self extracting archive /ˌself ɪk ˌstræktɪŋ ˈɑːkaɪv/ *noun* a compressed file that includes the program to de-compress the contents

self-learning /self ˈlɜːnɪŋ/ *adjective* referring to an expert system that adds each new piece of information or rule to its database, improving its knowledge, expertise and performance as it is used

self-refreshing RAM /ˌself rɪˌfreʃɪŋ ˈræm/ *noun* a dynamic RAM chip with built-in circuitry to generate refresh signals, allowing data to be retained when the power is off, using battery back-up

self-relocating program /self riːləʊ ˌkeɪtɪŋ ˈprəʊgræm/ *noun* a program that can be loaded into any part of memory (that will modify its addresses depending on the program origin address)

self-resetting loop /ˌself riːˌsetɪŋ ˈluːp/ *noun* a loop that returns any locations or registers accessed during its execution to the state they were in

self-restoring loop /ˌself rɪˌstɔːrɪŋ ˈluːp/ *noun* same as **self-resetting loop**

semantic error /səˌmæntɪk ˈerə/ *noun* an error due to use of an incorrect symbol within a program instruction

semantics /sɪˈmæntɪks/ *noun* (*in computing*) meanings of words or symbols used in programs

semaphore /ˈseməˌfɔː/ *noun* coordination of two jobs and appropriate handshaking to prevent lock-outs or other problems when both require a peripheral or function

semi- /semi/ *prefix* half or partly

semicolon /ˌsemiˈkəʊlɒn/ *noun* a printed sign (;) which marks the end of a program line or statement in some languages (such as C and Pascal)

semicompiled /ˌsemikəʊˈpaɪld/ *adjective* (object code) program converted from a source code program, but not containing the code for functions from libraries, etc., that were used in the source code

semiconductor /ˌsemikənˈdʌktə/ *noun* a material with conductive properties between those of a conductor (such as a metal) and an insulator

COMMENT: Semiconductor material (such as silicon) is used as a base for manufacturing integrated circuits and other solid-state components, usually by depositing various types of doping substances on or into its surface.

semiconductor device /ˌsemikəndʌktə dɪˈvaɪs/ *noun* an electronic component constructed on a small piece of semiconductor (the components on the device are constructed using patterns of insulator or conductor or semiconductor material whose properties can be changed by doping)

semiconductor memory /ˌsemikəndʌktə ˈmem(ə)ri/ *noun* storage using capacitors (dynamic memory) or latches and bistables (static memory) constructed as a semiconductor device to store bits of data

semi-processed data /ˌsemi ˌprəʊsesd ˈdeɪtə/ *noun* raw data which has had some processing carried out, such as sorting, recording, error detection, etc.

sender /ˈsendə/ *noun* a person who sends a message

send-only device /ˌsend ˈəʊnli dɪ ˌvaɪs/ *noun* a device such as a terminal which cannot receive data, but can only transmit it

Send To command /ˈsend tʊ kə ˌmɑːnd/ *noun* a menu command, available from the File menu of Windows applications, that allows a user to send the file or data currently open in the application to another application

sense /sens/ *verb* to examine the state of a device or electronic component ○ *The condition of the switch was sensed by the program.*

sense recovery time /ˌsens rɪ ˈkʌv(ə)ri ˌtaɪm/ *noun* the time that a RAM device takes to switch from read to write mode

sense switch /ˈsens swɪtʃ/ *noun* a switch on a computer front panel whose state can by examined by the computer

sensitive /ˈsensɪtɪv/ *adjective* which can sense even small changes ○ *The computer is sensitive even to very slight changes in current.*

sensitivity /ˌsensɪˈtɪvɪti/ *noun* **1.** being sensitive to something ○ *The scanner's sensitivity to small objects.* **2.** the minimum power of a received signal that is necessary for a receiver to distinguish the signal

sensor /'sensə/ *noun* an electronic device which produces an output dependent upon the condition or physical state of a process ○ *The sensor's output varies with temperature.* ◊ **transducer**

sensor glove /'sensə glʌv/ *noun* a glove, used with virtual reality applications, that fits over a user's hand and has sensors that detect when the user moves his fingers or arm and so control an image on screen

sentinel /'sentɪn(ə)l/ *noun* **1.** a marker or pointer to a special section of data **2.** a flag which reports the status of a register after a mathematical or logical operation

separate channel signalling /ˌsep(ə)rət ˌtʃæn(ə)l 'sɪgn(ə)lɪŋ/ *noun* the process of using independent communications channels or bands in a multichannel system to send the control data and messages

separated graphics /ˌsepəreɪtɪd 'ɡræfɪks/ *plural noun* displayed characters that do not take up the whole of a character matrix, resulting in spaces between them

separator /'sepəˌreɪtə/ *noun* a symbol used to distinguish parts of an instruction line in a program, such as command and argument. ◊ **delimiter**

SEPP /ˌes iː piː 'piː/ *noun* a system developed to provide a secure link between a user's browser and a vendor's Website to allow the user to pay for goods over the Internet. Full form **secure encryption payment protocol**. ◊ PGP, S-HTTP, SSL, STT

septet /sep'tet/ *noun* a word made up of seven bits

sequence /'siːkwəns/ *noun* a number of items or data arranged as a logical, ordered list ○ *The sequence of names is arranged alphabetically.* □ **the logon sequence** the order in which user number, password and other authorisation codes are to be entered when attempting to access a system

sequence check /'siːkwəns tʃek/ *noun* a check to ensure that sorted data is in the correct order

sequence control register, sequence counter *noun* a CPU register which contains the address of the next instruction to be processed. Abbr **SCR**. Also

called **sequence register, instruction address register, instruction counter**

sequenced packet exchange /ˌsiːkwənsd 'pækɪt ɪksˌtʃeɪndʒ/ *noun* full form of **SPX**

sequencer /'siːkwənsə/ *noun* a section within a bit-slice microprocessor which contains the next microprogram address

sequence register /'siːkwəns ˌredʒɪstə/ *noun* same as **sequence control register**

sequential /sɪ'kwenʃ(ə)l/ *adjective* arranged in an ordered manner

sequential access /sɪˌkwenʃ(ə)l 'ækses/ *noun* a method of retrieving data from a storage device by starting at the beginning of the medium and reading each record until the required data is found

COMMENT: A tape storage system uses sequential access, since the tape has to be played through until the section required is found. The access time of sequential access storage is dependent on the position in the file of the data, compared with random access which has the same access time for any piece of data in a list.

sequential access storage /sɪˌkwenʃ(ə)l 'ækses ˌstɔːrɪdʒ/ *noun* a storage medium in which the data is accessed sequentially

sequential batch processing /sɪˌkwenʃ(ə)l 'bætʃ ˌprəʊsesɪŋ/ *noun* the process of completing one job in a batch before the next can be started

sequential computer /sɪˌkwenʃ(ə)l kəm'pjuːtə/ *noun* a type of computer, for which each instruction must be completed before the next is started, and so cannot handle parallel processing

sequential file /sɪ'kwenʃ(ə)l faɪl/ *noun* a stored file whose records are accessed sequentially

sequential logic /sɪˌkwenʃ(ə)l 'lɒdʒɪk/ *noun* a logic circuit whose output depends on the logic state of the previous inputs

sequentially /sɪ'kwenʃəli/ *adverb* (done) one after the other, in sequence

sequential mode /sɪ'kwenʃ(ə)l məʊd/ *noun* a mode in which each instruction in a program is stored in consecutive locations

sequential operation /sɪˌkwenʃ(ə)l ˌɒpə'reɪʃ(ə)n/ *noun* operations executed one after the other

sequential packet exchange /sɪˌkwenʃ(ə)l 'pækɪt ɪksˌtʃeɪndʒ/ *noun* a network transport protocol developed by

Novell and used to carry IPX network traffic. Abbr **SPX**

sequential processing /sɪˌkwenʃ(ə)l ˈprəʊsesɪŋ/ *noun* data or instructions processed sequentially, in the same order as they are accessed

sequential search /sɪˌkwenʃ(ə)l ˈsɜːtʃ/ *noun* a search where each item in a list (starting at the beginning) is checked until the required one is found

serial /ˈsɪəriəl/ *adjective* referring to data or instructions which are ordered sequentially (one after the other) and not in parallel

serial access /ˌsɪəriəl ˈækses/ *noun* one item of the data accessed by reading through all the data in a list until the correct one is found (as on a tape)

serial-access memory /ˌsɪəriəl ˌækses ˈmem(ə)ri/ *noun* full form of **SAM**

serial adder /ˌsɪəriəl ˈædə/ *noun* an addition circuit which acts on one digit at a time from a larger number

serial computer /ˌsɪəriəl kəmˈpjuːtə/ *noun* a computer system which has a single ALU and carries out instructions one at a time

serial data communications /ˌsɪəriəl ˌdeɪtə kəˌmjuːnɪˈkeɪʃ(ə)nz/ *noun* same as **serial data transmission**

serial data transmission /ˌsɪəriəl ˈdeɪtə trænzˌmɪʃ(ə)n/ *noun* the transmission of the separate bits that make up data words, one at a time down a single line

serial file /ˌsɪəriəl ˈfaɪl/ *noun* same as **sequential file**

serial input/output /ˌsɪəriəl ˌɪnpʊt ˈaʊtpʊt/ *noun* full form of **SIO**

serial input/parallel output /ˌsɪəriəl ˌɪnpʊt ˌpærəlel ˈaʊtpʊt/ *noun* a device which can accept serial data and transmit parallel data. Abbr **SIPO**. Also called **serial to parallel converter**

serial input/serial output /ˌsɪəriəl ˌɪnpʊt ˌsɪəriəl ˈaʊtpʊt/ *noun* full form of **SISO**

serial line Internet protocol /ˌsɪəriəl laɪn ˈɪntənet ˌprəʊtəkɒl/ *noun* full form of **SLIP**

serially /ˈsɪəriəli/ *adverb* one after the other or in a series ○ *Their transmission rate is 64,000 bits per second through a parallel connection* or *19,200 serially.*

serial memory /ˌsɪəriəl ˈmem(ə)ri/ *noun* storage whose locations can only be accessed in a serial way: locating one item requires a search through every location

serial mouse /ˌsɪəriəl ˈmaʊs/ *noun* a mouse that connects to the serial port of a PC and transfers positional data via the serial port (NOTE: the plural is **serial mice**)

serial operation /ˌsɪəriəl ˌɒpəˈreɪʃ(ə)n/ *noun* the working of a device on data in a sequential manner

serial port /ˈsɪəriəl pɔːt/ *noun* a connector and circuit used to convert the data in a computer to and from a form in which each bit is transmitted one at a time over a single wire. Normally, data in a computer is transferred around the computer in parallel form that is eight or 16 bits wide. If you want to use a modem, you need to send the modem serial data that it can convert into sound signals that can be sent one at a time over a telephone line.

serial printer /ˌsɪəriəl ˈprɪntə/ *noun* a printer which prints characters one at a time

serial processing /ˌsɪəriəl ˈprəʊsesɪŋ/ *noun* data or instructions processed sequentially, in the same order as they are retrieved

serial storage /ˌsɪəriəl ˈstɔːrɪdʒ/ *noun* storage which only allows sequential access

serial to parallel converter /ˌsɪəriəl tə ˌpærəlel kənˈvɜːtə/ *noun* same as **serial input/parallel output**

serial transmission /ˌsɪəriəl trænz ˈmɪʃ(ə)n/ *noun* data transmitted one bit at a time (this is the normal method of transmission over long distances, since although slower it uses fewer lines and so is cheaper than parallel transmission)

series /ˈsɪəriːz/ *noun* a group of related items ordered sequentially

series circuit /ˈsɪəriːz ˌsɜːkɪt/ *noun* a circuit in which the components are connected serially

COMMENT: In a series circuit the same current flows through each component; in a parallel circuit the current flow is dependent upon the component impedance.

server /ˈsɜːvə/ *noun* a dedicated computer which provides a function to a network

'Sequent Computer Systems' Platform division will focus on hardware and software manufacture, procurement and marketing, with the Enterprise division concentrating on services and server implementation.' [*Computing*]

COMMENT: In a network the hard disk machine is called the 'server' and the floppy disk units the 'satellites'. In a star network each satellite is linked individually to a central server.

server access log /ˌsɜːvə ˈækses lɒg/ *noun* same as **access log** (*see*)

server-based application /ˌsɜːvə beɪst ˌæplɪˈkeɪʃ(ə)n/ *noun* an application program, stored on a server's hard disk, which can be accessed (and executed) by several users at one time

server farm /ˈsɜːvə fɑːm/ *noun* a business consisting of a group of Internet servers, all of which are linked to one another and are engaged in web hosting

server message block /ˌsɜːvə ˈmesɪdʒ blɒk/ *noun* full form of **SMB**

service /ˈsɜːvɪs/ *verb* to check or repair or maintain a system ○ *The disk drives were serviced yesterday and are working well.*

service bit /ˈsɜːvɪs bɪt/ *noun* a transmitted bit used for control rather than data

service bureau /ˈsɜːvɪs ˌbjʊərəʊ/ *noun* a company which provides a specialist service, such as outputting DTP files to a typesetter, converting files or creating slides from graphics files

service contract /ˈsɜːvɪs ˌkɒntrækt/ *noun* an agreement that an engineer will service equipment if it goes wrong

service program /ˈsɜːvɪs ˌprəʊgræm/ *noun* a program used for routine activities such as file searching, copying, sorting, debugging, etc.

service provider /ˈsɜːvɪs prəˌvaɪdə/ *noun* a company that offers users a connection to the Internet; the service provider has a computer that acts as a domain name server and has a high-speed link to the Internet. It provides modem access to the Internet via point-of-presence telephone numbers. You connect to the Internet by setting up an account with the service provider then dialling into its point-of-presence telephone number with a modem.

services /ˈsɜːvɪsɪz/ *plural noun* **1.** a set of functions provided by a device **2.** (*in an OSI network model*) a set of functions provided by one OSI layer for use by a higher layer

service side includes /ˌsɜːvɪs saɪd ɪnˈkluːdz/ *plural noun* special extensions to a web server that allow the webpage, scripts and programs to access special features, such as a count of visitors to a site. Abbr **SSI**

session /ˈseʃ(ə)n/ *noun* the time during which a program or process is running or active

session layer /ˈseʃ(ə)n ˌleɪə/ *noun* the fifth layer in the ISO/OSI standard model which makes the connection/disconnection between transmitter and receiver

set /set/ *noun* a number of related data items ■ *verb* **1.** to make one variable equal to a value ○ *We set the right-hand margin at 80 characters.* **2.** to define a parameter value **3.** to give a binary data bit the value of one

SET /set/ *plural noun* the standards created by a group of banks and Internet companies that allow users to buy goods over the Internet without risk of hackers. Full form **secure electronic transactions**. Same as **SSL**

set breakpoints /set ˈbreɪkpɔɪnts/ *verb* to define the position of breakpoints within a program being debugged

set theory /set ˈθɪəri/ *noun* mathematics related to numerical sets

set up /ˈset ʌp/ *verb* to configure, initialize, define or start an application or system ○ *The new computer worked well as soon as the engineer had set it up.*

setup option /ˈsetʌp ˌɒpʃ(ə)n/ *noun* the choices available when setting up a system

setup program /ˈsetʌp ˌprəʊgræm/ *noun* a utility program that helps a user configure their computer or new software application

setup time /ˈsetʌp taɪm/ *noun* a period of time between a signal to start an operation and the start

sexadecimal /ˌseksəˈdesɪməl/ *noun* ♦ **hex**

sex changer /ˈseks ˌtʃeɪndʒə/ *noun* a device for changing a female connection to a male or vice versa

sextet /ˌseksˈtet/ *noun* a byte made up of six bits

sf signalling /ˌes ef ˈsɪgn(ə)lɪŋ/ *noun* same as **single frequency signalling**

SGML /ˌes dʒiː em ˈel/ *noun* a hardware-independent standard which defines how documents should be marked up to indicate bolds, italics, margins and so on. Full form **Standard Generalized Markup Language**

shading /ˈʃeɪdɪŋ/ *noun* a simple method of applying shading to a three-dimensional scene using a single point of light and calculating the shade and highlights on each object; this type of shading is calculated for each polygon that makes up an object and can sometimes causes unwanted effects as shading may differ on each polygon

shadowmask /'ʃædəʊmɑːsk/ *noun* a sheet with holes placed just behind the front of a colour monitor screen to separate the three-colour picture beams

shadow memory, shadow page *noun* duplicate memory locations accessed by a special code

shadow page table /'ʃædəʊ peɪdʒ ˌteɪb(ə)l/ *noun* a conversion table which lists real memory locations with their equivalent shadow memory locations

shadow RAM /'ʃædəʊ ræm/ *noun* a method of improving the performance of a PC by copying the contents of a (slow) ROM chip to a faster RAM chip when the computer is first switched on

shadow ROM /'ʃædəʊ rɒm/ *noun* read-only shadow memory

shannon /'ʃænən/ *noun* a measure of the information content of a transmission

Shannon's Law /'ʃænənz lɔː/ *noun* a law defining the maximum information-carrying capacity of a transmission line

COMMENT: Shannon's Law is defined as B lg(1 + S/N) where B = Bandwidth, lg is logarithm to the base two and S/N is Signal to Noise ratio.

shared access /ʃeəd 'ækses/ *noun* the use of a computer or peripheral by more than one person or system

shared bus /ˌʃeəd 'bʌs/ *noun* one bus used (usually) for address and data transfer between the CPU and a peripheral

shared directory /ʃeəd də'rekt(ə)ri/ *noun* a directory (on a file server or workstation) which can be accessed by several users connected to a network

shared file /ˌʃeəd 'faɪl/ *noun* a stored file which can be accessed by more than one user or system

shared folder /ʃeəd 'fəʊldə/ *noun* a folder of files stored on a computer's local hard disk drive that can be used (or shared) by other users on the network

shared logic system /ˌʃeəd 'lɒdʒɪk ˌsɪstəm/ *noun* one computer and backing storage device used by a number of people in a network for an application

shared logic text processor /ˌʃeəd ˌlɒdʒɪk 'tekst ˌprəʊsesə/ *noun* word-processing available to a number of users of a shared logic system

shared memory /ʃeəd 'mem(ə)ri/ *noun* memory accessed by more than one CPU

shared network directory /ˌʃeəd 'netwɜːk daɪˌrekt(ə)ri/ *noun* a directory (on a file server or workstation) which can be accessed by several users connected to a network

shared resources system /ˌʃeəd rɪ'zɔːsɪz ˌsɪstəm/ *noun* a system where one peripheral or backing storage device or other resource is used by a number of users

share-level access /ˌʃeə ˌlev(ə)l 'ækses/ *noun* a method used to set up network security to protect local resources

share level security /ˌʃeə ˌlev(ə)l sɪ'kjʊərɪti/ *noun* a network operating system which assigns passwords to resources rather than setting up user accounts to limit access

shareware /'ʃeəˌweə/ *noun* software which is available free to try, but if kept the user is expected to pay a fee to the writer (often confused with public domain software which is completely free)

'Bulletin board users know the dangers of 'flaming' (receiving hostile comments following a naive or ridiculous assertion) and of being seen 'troughing' (grabbing every bit of shareware on the network).' [*Computing*]

sheet /ʃiːt/ *noun* a large piece of paper

sheet feed /'ʃiːt fiːd/ *noun* a device which puts one sheet at a time into a printer

shell /ʃel/ *noun* software which operates between the user and the operating system, often to try and make the operating system more friendly or easier to use

shell out /ˌʃel 'aʊt/ *verb* (when running an application) to exit to the operating system, whilst the original application is still in memory; the user then returns to the application ○ *I shelled out from the word-processor to check which files were on the floppy, then went back to the program.*

shell script /ˌʃel 'skrɪpt/ *noun* a scripting language (such as Perl) that is used to create programs that can enhance a website, e.g. to search a site for a key word

shell sort /ˌʃel 'sɔːt/ *noun* an algorithm for sorting data items, in which items can be moved more than one position per sort action

shield /ʃiːld/ *noun* a metal screen connected to earth, used to prevent harmful voltages or interference reaching sensitive electronic equipment ■ *verb* to protect a signal or device from external interference or harmful voltages

shielded cable /ˌʃiːldɪd 'keɪb(ə)l/ *noun* a cable made up of a conductive core surrounded by an insulator, then a conductive layer to protect the transmitted signal against interference

shielded twisted pair cable /ˌʃiːldɪd ˌtwɪstɪd ˈpeə ˌkeɪb(ə)l/ *noun* a cable consisting of two insulated copper wires twisted around each other (to reduce induction and so interference), then wrapped in an insulated shielding layer to further reduce interference. Also called **STP cable**

shift /ʃɪft/ *verb* **1.** to move a bit or word of data left or right by a certain amount (usually one bit) **2.** to change from one character set to another, allowing other characters (such as capitals) to be used

shift character /ʃɪft ˈkærɪktə/ *noun* a transmitted character code which indicates that the following code is to be shifted

shift code /ˌʃɪft ˈkəʊd/ *noun* a method of increasing total possible bit combinations by using a number of bits to indicate if the following code is to be shifted

shift instruction /ʃɪft ɪnˈstrʌkʃən/ *noun* a computer command to shift the contents of a register to the left or right

Shift key /ˈʃɪft kiː/ *noun* the key on a keyboard which switches on secondary functions for keys, such as another character set, by changing the output to upper case

shift left /ˈʃɪft ˌleft/ *noun* a left arithmetic shift of data in a word (the number is doubled for each left shift)

shift register /ʃɪft ˈredʒɪstə/ *noun* temporary storage into which data can be shifted

shift right /ˈʃɪft ˌraɪt/ *noun* a right arithmetic shift of data in a word (the number is halved for each right shift)

Shockwave /ˈʃɒkweɪv/ a trade name for a system developed by Macromedia that allows web browsers to display complex multimedia effects

shoot /ʃuːt/ *verb* to take a picture or record a video sequence with a camera

shopping agent /ˈʃɒpɪŋ ˌeɪdʒənt/ *noun* a computer program used to browse websites searching for a product or service

shopping basket /ˈʃɒpɪŋ ˌbɑːskɪt/, **shopping cart** /ˈʃɒpɪŋ kɑːt/ *noun* software that runs on a web server and provides an electronic version of a real shopping basket; the software allows a visitor to the website to view items in the catalogue, add items to their shopping basket and then pay for the goods at an electronic checkout. ◊ **real-time authorisation**

short card /ˌʃɔːt ˈkɑːd/ *noun* an add-on expansion board which is shorter than a standard size

shortcut /ˈʃɔːtˌkʌt/ *noun* a feature of Windows that allows a user to define an icon that links to another file or application, e.g., you could place shortcut icons on the Windows Desktop to allow you to start an application without using the menu commands. The shortcut has the same icon as the original file but has a tiny arrow in the bottom left-hand corner. It is not a duplicate of the original, rather it is a pointer to the original file.

short haul modem /ˌʃɔːt hɔːl ˈməʊdem/ *noun* a modem used to transmit data over short distances (often within a building), usually without using a carrier

short message service /ˌʃɔːt ˈmesɪdʒ ˌsɜːvɪs/ *noun* a system that allows short text messages to be sent between and to mobile telephones; the service depends upon the telephone company. Abbr **SMS**

shout /ʃaʊt/ *verb* to type a message or electronic mail in capital letters

S-HTTP /es ˌeɪtʃ tiː tiː ˈpiː/ *noun* a system developed to provide a secure link between a user's browser and a vendor's Website to allow the user to pay for goods over the Internet. Full form **secure hypertext transfer protocol**. ◊ **PGP, SEPP, SET, SSL, STT**

shut down /ˌʃʌt ˈdaʊn/ *verb* to switch off and stop the functions of a machine or system

ShutDown /ˈʃʌtdaʊn/ *noun* (*in Windows*) a command that will close down Windows and, if the user has a compatible PC, will switch off the computer

shut-off mechanism /ˈʃʌt ɒf ˌmekənɪz(ə)m/ *noun* a device which stops a process in case of fault

COMMENT: Most hard disks have an automatic shut-off mechanism to pull the head back from the read position when the power is turned off.

sideways ROM /ˈsaɪdweɪz rɒm/ *noun* software which allows selection of a particular memory bank or ROM device

SIG /sɪg/ *noun* a group within a larger club which is interested in a particular aspect of software or hardware ○ *Our local computer club has a SIG for comms and networking.* Full form **special interest group**

sign /saɪn/ *noun* polarity of a number or signal (whether it is positive or negative) ■

verb to identify oneself to a computer using a personalised signature □ **to sign off** to log off a system □ **to sign on** to log on to a system

signal /'sɪgn(ə)l/ *noun* **1.** a generated analog or digital waveform used to carry information ○ *The signal received from the computer contained the answer.* **2.** a short message used to carry control codes ■ *verb* to send a message to a computer ○ *Signal to the network that we are busy.*

signal conditioning /'sɪgn(ə)l kən‚dɪʃ(ə)nɪŋ/ *noun* the process of converting or translating a signal into a form that is accepted by a device

signal conversion /'sɪgn(ə)l kən‚vɜːʃ(ə)n/ *noun* the process of processing, changing or modulating a signal

signal distance /'sɪgn(ə)l ‚dɪstəns/ *noun* a number of bit positions with different contents in two data words

signal element /'sɪgn(ə)l ‚elɪmənt/ *noun* the smallest basic unit used when transmitting digital data

signalling /'sɪgn(ə)lɪŋ/ *noun* **1.** a method used by a transmitter to warn a receiver that a message is to be sent **2.** a communication to the transmitter about the state of the receiver □ **in band signalling** use of a normal voice grade channel for data transmission

signal processing /'sɪgn(ə)l ‚prəʊsesɪŋ/ *noun* processing of signals to extract the information contained ○ *The system is used by students doing research on signal processing techniques.*

signal to noise ratio /‚sɪgn(ə)l tə 'nɔɪz ‚reɪʃiəʊ/ *noun* the difference between the power of the transmitted signal and the noise on the line. Abbr **S/N**

sign and magnitude /‚saɪn ən 'mægnɪtjuːd/ *noun* a number representation in which the most significant bit indicates the sign of the number, the rest of the bits its value

sign and modulus /‚saɪn ən 'mɒdjʊləs/ *noun* a way of representing numbers, where one bit shows if the number is positive or negative (usually 0 = positive, 1 = negative)

signature /'sɪgnɪtʃə/ *noun* a special authentication code, such as a password, which a user gives prior to access to a system or prior to the execution of a task (to prove identity)

signature file /'sɪgnɪtʃə faɪl/ *noun* a short text file, containing information such as the user's name and address, that is used as a signature at the end of e-mails and Usenet messages

sign bit /‚saɪn 'bɪt/ *noun* a single bit which indicates if a binary number is positive or negative (usually 0 = positive, 1 = negative)

sign digit /saɪn 'dɪdʒɪt/ *noun* one digit which indicates if a number is positive or negative

signed field /‚saɪnd 'fiːld/ *noun* a storage field which can contain a number and a sign bit

signed magnitude /‚saɪnd 'mægnɪtjuːd/ *noun* same as **sign and magnitude**

significance /sɪg'nɪfɪkəns/ *noun* a special meaning

significant /sɪg'nɪfɪkənt/ *adjective* which has a special meaning

significant digit codes /sɪg‚nɪfɪkənt 'dɪdʒɪt ‚kəʊdz/ *plural noun* codes which indicate various details of an item, by assigning each one a value

signify /'sɪgnɪ‚faɪ/ *verb* to mean ○ *A carriage return code signifies the end of an input line.*

sign indicator /saɪn 'ɪndɪ‚keɪtə/ *noun* same as **sign bit**

sign position /saɪn pə'zɪʃ(ə)n/ *noun* a digit or bit position which contains the sign bit or digit

silicon /'sɪlɪkən/ *noun* an element with semiconductor properties, used in crystal form as a base for IC manufacture

COMMENT: Silicon is used in the electronics industry as a base material for integrated circuits. It is grown as a long crystal which is then sliced into wafers before being etched or treated, producing several hundred chips per wafer. Other materials, such as germanium or gallium arsenide, are also used as a base for ICs.

silicon chip /'sɪlɪkən tʃɪp/ *noun* a small piece of silicon in and on the surface of which a complete circuit or logic function has been produced by depositing other substances or by doping

silicon disk /'sɪlɪkən dɪsk/ *noun* a section of RAM made to look and behave like a high speed disk drive. Also called **RAM disk**

silicon foundry /'sɪlɪkən ‚faʊndri/ *noun* a machine used to create crystals of silicon, then slice them into silicon wafers

Silicon Valley /‚sɪlɪkən 'væli/ *noun* an area in California where many US semiconductor device manufacturers are based

silicon wafer /ˌsɪlɪkən ˈweɪfə/ *noun* a thin slice of a pure silicon crystal, usually around 4 inches in diameter on which integrated circuits are produced (these are then cut out of the wafer to produce individual chips)

SIMD /ˌes aɪ em ˈdiː/ *noun* the architecture of a parallel computer which has a number of ALUs and data buses with one control unit. Full form **single instruction stream multiple data stream**

SIMM /ˌes aɪ em ˈem/ *noun* a small, compact circuit board with an edge connector along one edge that carries densely-packed memory chips ○ *You can expand the main memory of your PC by plugging in two more SIMMs.* Full form **single in-line memory module**

simple device /ˌsɪmp(ə)l dɪˈvaɪs/ *noun* a multimedia device that does not require a data file for playback, such as a CD drive used to play audio CDs

simple mail transfer protocol /ˌsɪmpəl meɪl ˈtrænsfɜː ˌprəʊtəkɒl/ *noun* full form of **SMTP**

simple network management protocol /ˌsɪmpəl ˌnetwɜːk ˈmænɪdʒmənt ˌprəʊtəkɒl/ *noun* a network management system which defines how status data is sent from monitored nodes back to a control station; SNMP is able to work with virtually any type of network hardware and software. Abbr **SNMP**

simple to use /ˈsɪmp(ə)l tə ˌtuː/ *adjective* (*of a machine or software*) easy to use and operate

simplex /ˈsɪmpleks/ *noun* full form of **SPX**. opposite **duplex**

simulate /ˈsɪmjuˌleɪt/ *verb* to copy the behaviour of a system or device with another ○ *This software simulates the action of an aircraft.*

simulation /ˌsɪmjuˈleɪʃ(ə)n/ *noun* an operation where a computer is made to imitate a real life situation or a machine, and shows how something works or will work in the future ○ *Simulation techniques have reached a high degree of sophistication.*

simulator /ˈsɪmjuˌleɪtə/ *noun* a device which simulates another system

simultaneity /ˌsɪm(ə)ltəˈniːəti/ *noun* in which the CPU and the I/O sections of a computer can handle different data or tasks at the same time

simultaneous /ˌsɪm(ə)lˈteɪniəs/ *adjective* which takes place at the same time as something else

simultaneous processing /ˌsɪm(ə)lteɪniəs ˈprəʊsesɪŋ/ *noun* two or more processes executed at the same time

COMMENT: True simultaneous processing requires two processors, but can be imitated by switching rapidly between two tasks with a single processor.

simultaneous transmission /ˌsɪm(ə)lteɪniəs trænzˈmɪʃ(ə)n/ *noun* the transmission of data or control codes in two directions at the same time (NOTE: same as **duplex**)

single address code /ˌsɪŋg(ə)l ə ˈdres ˌkəʊd/ *noun* a machine code instruction which contains one operator and one address

single address instruction /ˌsɪŋg(ə)l əˌdres ɪnˈstrʌkʃən/ *noun* same as **single address code**

single address message /ˌsɪŋg(ə)l ə ˈdres ˌmesɪdʒ/ *noun* a message with a single destination

single attachment station /ˌsɪŋg(ə)l əˌtætʃmənt ˈsteɪʃ(ə)n/ *noun* (*in an FDDI network*) a station with only one port through which to attach to the network; SAS stations are connected to the FDDI ring through a concentrator. Abbr **SAS**

single board computer /ˌsɪŋg(ə)l bɔːd kəmˈpjuːtə/ *noun* full form of **SBC**

single-board microcomputer /ˌsɪŋg(ə)l bɔːd ˈmaɪkrəʊkɒmˌpjuːtə/ *noun* a microcomputer whose components are all contained on a single printed circuit board

single chip computer /ˌsɪŋg(ə)l tʃɪp kəmˈpjuːtə/ *noun* a complete simple computer including CPU, memory and input/output ports on one chip

single-chip microcontroller /ˌsɪŋg(ə)l tʃɪp ˈmaɪkrəkənˌtrəʊlə/ *noun* one integrated circuit that contains a CPU, I/O ports, RAM and often a basic programming language

single density disk /ˌsɪŋg(ə)l ˌdensɪti ˈdɪsk/ *noun* a standard magnetic disk able to store data. Abbr **SD**

single frequency signalling /ˌsɪŋg(ə)l ˈfriːkwənsi ˌsɪgn(ə)lɪŋ/ *noun* the use of various frequency signals to represent different control codes. Also called **sf signalling**

single function software /ˌsɪŋg(ə)l ˈfʌŋkʃən ˌsɒftweə/ *noun* an applications program used for one kind of task only

single in-line memory module
/ˌsɪŋg(ə)l ɪn laɪn 'mem(ə)ri ˌmɒdjuːl/
noun full form of **SIMM**

single in-line package /ˌsɪŋg(ə)l ɪn
laɪn 'pækɪdʒ/ *noun* an electronic component which has all its leads on one side of
its package. Abbr **SIP**

**single instruction stream multiple
data stream** /ˌsɪŋg(ə)l ɪnˌstrʌkʃən
striːm ˌmʌltɪp(ə)l 'deɪtə ˌstriːm/ *noun*
full form of **SIMD**

**single instruction stream single
data stream** /ˌsɪŋg(ə)l ɪnˌstrʌkʃən
striːm ˌsɪŋg(ə)l 'deɪtə striːm/ *noun* full
form of **SISD**

single key response /ˌsɪŋg(ə)l 'kiː rɪ
ˌspɒns/ *noun* software which requires
only one key to be pressed to select an option

single length precision /ˌsɪŋg(ə)l
leŋθ prɪ'sɪʒ(ə)n/ *noun* a number stored in
one word

single length working /ˌsɪŋg(ə)l leŋθ
'wɜːkɪŋ/ *noun* the process of using numbers that can be stored within a single
word

single line display /ˌsɪŋg(ə)l laɪn dɪs
'pleɪ/ *noun* a small screen which displays
a single line of characters at a time

single mode fibre /ˌsɪŋg(ə)l məʊd
'faɪbə/ *noun* an optic fibre that has a very
narrow diameter (of 10 microns or less)
and is designed to transmit a single light
signal over a long distance; this type of fibre has a bandwidth of 5Gbits/second and
is normally used for long distance telephone networks

single operand instruction
/ˌsɪŋg(ə)l ˌɒpərænd ɪn'strʌkʃən/ *noun*
same as **single address code**

single operation /ˌsɪŋg(ə)l ˌɒpə
'reɪʃ(ə)n/ *noun* a communications system
which allows data to travel in only one direction at a time (controlled by codes S/O
= send only, R/O = receive only, S/R =
send or receive)

single-pass assembler /ˌsɪŋg(ə)l
pɑːs ə'semblə/ *noun* an object code produced in one run through the assembler of
the source program

single pass operation /ˌsɪŋg(ə)l
pɑːs ˌɒpə'reɪʃ(ə)n/ *noun* software which
produces the required result or carries out
a task after one run

single precision /ˌsɪŋg(ə)l prɪ
'sɪʒ(ə)n/ *noun* a number stored in one
word

single quotes /'sɪŋg(ə)l kwəʊtz/ *plural noun* single inverted commas

single sheet feed /ˌsɪŋg(ə)l ʃiːt 'fiːd/
noun a paper feed system which puts single sheets of paper into a printer, one at a
time

single-sided disk /ˌsɪŋg(ə)l ˌsaɪdɪd
'dɪsk/ *noun* a floppy disk that can only
store data on one side, because of the way
it is manufactured or formatted. Abbr **SSD**

single speed /'sɪŋg(ə)l spiːd/ *noun* the
speed at which a CD-ROM is spun by a
drive, usually 230rpm

single step /'sɪŋg(ə)l step/ *noun* the
process of executing a computer program
one instruction at a time, used for debugging

single-strike ribbon /ˌsɪŋg(ə)l straɪk
'rɪbən/ *noun* a printer ribbon which can
only be used once

single-system image /ˌsɪŋg(ə)l
ˌsɪstəm 'ɪmɪdʒ/ *noun* an operational view
of multiple networks, distributed databases or multiple computer systems as if they
were one system

single-user system /ˌsɪŋg(ə)l ˌjuːzə
'sɪstəm/ *noun* a computer system which
can only be used by a single user at a time
(as opposed to a multi-user system)

sink /sɪŋk/ *noun* the receiving end of a
communications line. Opposite **source**

sink tree /ˌsɪŋk 'triː/ *noun* a description
in a routing table of all the paths in a network to a destination

SIO *abbr* serial input/output

SIP *abbr* single in-line package

SIPO *abbr* serial input/parallel output

SISD /ˌes aɪ es 'diː/ *noun* the architecture
of a serial computer, which has one ALU
and data bus, with one control unit. Full
form **single instruction stream single
data stream**

SISO *abbr* serial input/serial output

site /saɪt/ *noun* a place where something
is based

site licence /saɪt 'laɪs(ə)ns/ *noun* a licence between a software publisher and a
user which allows any number of users in
that site to use the software ○ *We have ne-
gotiated a good deal for the site licence for
the 1200 employees in our HQ.*

site poll /ˌsaɪt 'pəʊl/ *verb* to poll all the
terminals or devices in a particular location or area. ◊ **polling**

6 degrees of freedom /ˌsɪks dɪˌgriːz
əv 'friːdəm/ *noun* (*in virtual reality*) a de-

scription of the movements and vision that a user can interpret: normally three visual dimensions together with movement

16-bit /'sɪksti:n bɪt/ data that is transferred sixteen bits at a time along sixteen parallel conductors; in a processor this refers to its ability to manipulate data that is sixteen bits wide representing numbers up to 65,536

sixteen-bit /ˌsɪks'ti:n bɪt/ *adjective* (*of a microcomputer system or CPU*) which handles data in sixteen bit words, providing much faster operation than older eight-bit systems

16-bit sample /ˌsɪksti:n bɪt 'sɑːmp(ə)l/ *noun* single sample of an analog signal which is stored as a 16-bit number, meaning that there are 65,536 possible levels. A '16-bit sound card' can sometimes mean that the card generates 16-bit samples, but it can also mean that it generates 8-bit samples, but fits into a 16-bit expansion slot. ◊ **8-bit sample, 24-bit sample**

size /saɪz/ *noun* the physical dimensions of an image, object or page ■ *verb* to calculate the resources available, and those required, to carry out a particular job

skeletal code /'skelɪt(ə)l kəʊd/ *noun* a program which is not complete, with the basic structure coded

skew /skjuː/ *noun* the amount by which something is not correctly aligned ■ *verb* to align something incorrectly ○ *This page is badly skewed.*

skin /skɪn/ *noun* **1.** a piece of software that changes the appearance of images produced by existing software without changing their function **2.** the changed image that is produced by a piece of skin software ■ *verb* to change the appearance of images produced by existing software, without changing their function

skip /skɪp/ *verb* to ignore an instruction in a sequence of instructions ○ *The printer skipped the next three lines of text.*

skip capability /skɪp ˌkeɪpə'bɪləti/ *noun* a feature of certain word-processors to allow the user to jump backwards or forwards by a quantity of text in a document

skip instruction /skɪp ɪn'strʌkʃən/ *noun* a null computer command which directs the CPU to the next instruction

slash /slæʃ/ *noun* a punctuation mark (/) that is used to separate optional items in a list and to express fractions or ratios, and that has various uses in computer pro-

gramming, e.g. to separate off certain sections of an Internet address

slashed zero /slæʃd 'zɪərəʊ/ *noun* a printed or written sign (Ø)

slave /sleɪv/ *noun* a remote secondary computer or terminal controlled by a central computer

slave cache /ˌsleɪv 'kæʃ/ *noun* a section of high-speed memory which stores data that the CPU can access quickly

slave processor /sleɪv 'prəʊˌsesə/ *noun* a dedicated processor controlled by a master processor

slave store /'sleɪv stɔː/ *noun* same as **slave cache**

slave terminal /sleɪv 'tɜːmɪn(ə)l/ *noun* a terminal controlled by a main computer or terminal

slave tube /ˌsleɪv 'tjuːb/ *noun* a second CRT display connected to another so that it shows exactly the same information

sleep /sliːp/ *noun* the state of a system that is waiting for a signal (log-on) before doing anything

sleeve /sliːv/ *noun* a paper or plastic cover for a magnetic disk

slew /sluː/ *noun* a rapid movement of paper in a printer, ignoring the normal line advance

slide /slaɪd/ *noun* one image in a presentation or a single frame of positive photographic film

slide show /'slaɪd ʃəʊ/ *noun* a feature of a presentation graphics software in which slides (static images) are displayed in a sequence under the control of the presenter

SLIP /slɪp/ *noun* a method of sending TCP/IP network traffic over a serial line, such as a telephone modem connection (normally used to connect a user's computer to the Internet via a modem link). Full form **serial line internet protocol**

slot /slɒt/ *verb* to insert an object into a hole ○ *The disk slots into one of the floppy drive apertures.*

slow peripheral /sləʊ pə'rɪf(ə)rəl/ *noun* a peripheral in which mechanical movement determines speed

slow scan TV /ˌsləʊ skæn ti: 'vi:/ *noun* a system used to transmit still video frames over a telephone line

SLSI *abbr* super large scale integration

small computer systems interface /ˌsmɔːl kəmˌpjuːtə 'sɪstəmz ˌɪntəfeɪs/ *noun* full form of **SCSI**

small-scale /'smɔːl skeɪl/ *adjective* working with small amounts of data. Compare **large-scale**

small scale integration /ˌsmɔːl skeɪl ˌɪntɪ'greɪʃ(ə)n/ *noun* an integrated circuit with 1 to 10 components. Abbr **SSI**

Smalltalk /'smɔːltɔːk/ an object-oriented programming language developed by Xerox

smart card /'smɑːt kɑːd/ *noun* a plastic card with a memory and microprocessor device embedded in it, so that it can be used for electronic funds transfer or for identification of the user

smart terminal /smɑːt 'tɜːmɪn(ə)l/ *noun* a computer terminal which can process information. Compare **dumb terminal**

smart wiring hub /ˌsmɑːt 'waɪərɪŋ ˌhʌb/ *noun* a network hub or concentrator which can transmit status information back to a managing station and allows management software to configure each port remotely ○ *Using this management software, I can shut down Tom's port on the remote smart wiring hub.*

SMB /ˌes em 'biː/ *noun* a system developed by Microsoft which allows a user to access another computer's files and peripherals over a network as if they were local resources. Full form **server message block**

smiley /'smaɪli/ *noun* a face created with text characters, used to provide the real meaning to an email message; e.g., :-) means laughter or a joke, and :-(means sad

S/MIME *abbr* secure/multipurpose Internet mail extension

smooth scroll /ˌsmuːð 'skrəʊl/ *noun* text which is moved up a screen pixel by pixel rather than line by line, which gives a smoother movement

SMPTE /ˌes em pi: ti: 'iː/ *noun* an organisation that defines standards for television production systems; e.g., the SMPTE time code standard is widely used to synchronise audio and video equipment using hours, minutes, seconds, frame data that is stored in an 80-bit word. Full form **Society for Motion Picture and TV Engineers**

SMPTE division type /ˌes em pi: ti: ˌiː dɪ'vɪʒ(ə)n ˌtaɪp/ *noun* a timing format which specifies the number of frames per second used, and in which time is shown as hours, minutes, seconds, frames; standard SMPTE division types are 24, 25 and 30 frames per second

SMPTE offset /ˌes em pi: ti: iː 'ɒfset/ *noun* a MIDI event that defines when a MIDI file is to be played back

SMPTE time code /ˌes em pi: ti: iː 'taɪm ˌkəʊd/ *noun* a method of assigning a unique identifying number to each frame in a video sequence

SMS *abbr* short message service

SMT /ˌes em 'tiː/ *noun* a method of manufacturing circuit boards in which the electronic components are bonded directly onto the surface of the board rather than being inserted into holes and soldered into place ○ *Surface-mount technology is faster and more space-efficient than soldering.* Full form **surface-mount technology**

SMTP /ˌes em ti: 'piː/ *noun* a standard protocol which allows electronic mail messages to be transferred from one system to another, normally used as the method of transferring mail from one Internet server to another or to send mail from a computer to a server. Full form **simple mail transfer protocol**. Compare **POP 3**

S/N *abbr* signal to noise ratio

SNA /ˌes en 'eɪ/ *noun* design methods developed by IBM which define how communications in a network should occur and allow different hardware to communicate. Full form **systems network architecture**

snail mail /'sneɪl meɪl/ *noun* a slang term used to refer to the normal (slow) postal delivery rather than (near instant) electronic mail delivery

snapshot /'snæp‚ʃɒt/ *noun* **1.** a recording of all the states of a computer at a particular instant **2.** the process of storing in main memory the contents of a screen full of information at an instant

snapshot dump /'snæp‚ʃɒt dʌmp/ *noun* a printout of all the registers and a section of memory at a particular instant, used when debugging a program

snd /saʊnd/ *noun* a filename extension used to indicate a file that contains digitised sound data. Full form **SouND**

sniffer /'snɪfə/ *noun* a device or program that monitors and analyses network traffic, in order to detect bottlenecks and problems

SNMP *abbr* simple network management protocol

SNOBOL /'snəʊbɒl/ *noun* a high-level programming language which uses string processing methods. Full form **string orientated symbolic language**

snow /snəʊ/ *noun* interference displayed as flickering white flecks on a monitor

soak /səʊk/ *verb* to run a program or device continuously for a period of time to make sure it functions correctly

Society for Motion Picture and TV Engineers /sə,saɪəti fə ,məʊʃ(ə)n ,pɪktʃə ən ,tiː 'viː/ *noun* full form of **SMPTE**

socket /'sɒkɪt/ *noun* a device with a set of holes, into which a plug fits

socket driver /'sɒkɪt ,draɪvə/ *noun* same as **Winsock**

SOCKS /sɒks/ *noun* a network protocol developed to support the transfer of TCP/IP (Internet) traffic through a proxy server. It is commonly used to provide a way for users on a local area network to access the Internet via a single shared connection.

soft /sɒft/ *adjective* **1.** referring to material which loses its magnetic effects when removed from a magnetic field **2.** referring to data which is not permanently stored in hardware. Soft usually refers to data stored on magnetic medium.

soft copy /sɒft 'kɒpi/ *noun* text listed on screen (as opposed to hard copy on paper)

soft error /sɒft 'erə/ *noun* a random error caused by software or data errors which is very difficult to trace and identify since it only appears under certain conditions

soft-fail /sɒft feɪl/ *adjective* referring to a system which is still partly operational even after a part of the system has failed

soft font /,sɒft 'fɒnt/ *noun* fonts or typefaces stored on a disk, which can be downloaded or sent to a printer and stored in temporary memory or RAM

soft goods /sɒft gʊdz/ *plural noun* software that can be purchased and paid for in an online shop, and which is then downloaded directly onto a computer instead of receiving a CD-ROM sent by post

soft keyboard /sɒft 'kiː,bɔːd/ *noun* a keyboard where the functions of the keys can be changed by programs

soft keys /,sɒft 'kiːz/ *plural noun* keys which can be changed by means of a program

soft reset /sɒft ,riː'set/ *noun* an instruction that terminates any program execution and returns the user to the monitor or BIOS

soft-sectored disk /,sɒft ,sektəd 'dɪsk/ *noun* a disk where the sectors are described by an address and start code data written onto it when the disk is formatted

software /'sɒftweə/ *noun* any program or group of programs which instructs the hardware on how it should perform, including operating systems, word processors and applications programs

software compatible /,sɒftweə kəm'pætɪb(ə)l/ *adjective* referring to a computer which will load and run programs written for another computer

software developer /'sɒftweə dɪ,veləpə/ *noun* a person or company which writes software

software development /'sɒftweə dɪ,veləpmənt/ *noun* the processes required to produce working programs from an initial idea

software documentation /,sɒftweə ,dɒkjʊmen'teɪʃ(ə)n/ *noun* information, notes and diagrams describing the function, use and operation of a piece of software

software engineer /'sɒftweə ,endʒɪnɪə/ *noun* a person who can write working software to fit an application

software engineering /'sɒftweə ,endʒɪnɪərɪŋ/ *noun* a field of study covering all software-related subjects

software house /'sɒftweə haʊs/ *noun* a company which develops and sells computer programs

software interrupt /,sɒftweə 'ɪntərʌpt/ *noun* a high priority program-generated signal, requesting the use of the central processor

software library /'sɒftweə ,laɪbrəri/ *noun* a number of specially written routines, stored in a library file which can be inserted into a program, saving time and effort. Abbr **H**

software licence /'sɒftweə ,laɪs(ə)ns/ *noun* an agreement between a user and a software house, giving details of the rights of the user to use or copy the software

software life cycle /,sɒftweə 'laɪf ,saɪk(ə)l/ *noun* the period of time when a piece of software exists, from its initial design to the moment when it becomes out of date

software maintenance /ˈsɒftweə ˌmeɪntənəns/ *noun* the process of carrying out updates and modifications to a software package to make sure the program is up to date

software modem /ˈsɒftweə ˌməʊdem/ *noun* a modem that uses the main computer's processor to carry out all the signal processing required to modulate and demodulate data signals that can be sent to a dedicated serial port. New PCs are often fitted with a software modem (often called a WinModem) that takes advantage of the powerful processors to provide a very cheap way of adding a modem function and providing dial-up Internet access to a computer.

software-only video playback /ˌsɒftweə ˌəʊnli ˌvɪdiəʊ ˈpleɪbæk/ *noun* the ability to display full-motion video standard on any multimedia computer, without requiring special hardware

software package /ˈsɒftweə ˌpækɪdʒ/ *noun* computer programs and manuals designed for a special purpose

software piracy /ˈsɒftweə ˌpaɪrəsi/ *noun* the illegal copying of software for sale

software quality assurance /ˌsɒftweə ˌkwɒlɪti əˈʃʊərəns/ *noun* the process of making sure that software will perform as intended. Abbr **SQA**

software reliability /ˌsɒftweə rɪˌlaɪəbɪlɪti/ *noun* the ability of a piece of software to perform the task required correctly

software specification /ˌsɒftweə ˌspesɪfɪˈkeɪʃ(ə)n/ *noun* detailed information about a piece of software's abilities, functions and methods

software system /ˈsɒftweə ˌsɪstəm/ *noun* all the programs required for one or more tasks

software tool /ˈsɒftweə tuːl/ *noun* a program used in the development of other programs

soft zone /ˌsɒft ˈzəʊn/ *noun* a text area to the left of the right margin in a word-processed document, where if a word does not fit completely, a hyphen is automatically inserted

solid colour /ˌsɒlɪd ˈkʌlə/ *noun* a colour that can be displayed on a screen or printed on a colour printer without dithering

solid error /ˌsɒlɪd ˈerə/ *noun* an error that is always present when certain equipment is used

solid font printer /ˌsɒlɪd fɒnt ˈprɪntə/ *noun* a printer which uses a whole character shape to print in one movement, such as a daisy wheel printer

solid modelling /ˌsɒlɪd ˈmɒd(ə)lɪŋ/ *noun* a function in a graphics program that creates three-dimensional solid-looking objects by shading

solid-state /ˈsɒlɪd steɪt/ *adjective* referring to semiconductor devices

solid-state device /ˌsɒlɪd steɪt dɪ ˈvaɪs/ *noun* an electronic device which operates by using the effects of electrical or magnetic signals in a solid semiconductor material

solid state disk /ˌsɒlɪd steɪt ˈdɪsk/ *noun* a mass storage device that uses electronic memory components with a backup battery to store data rather than a magnetic medium (such as a magnetic disk used in a hard disk drive)

solid-state memory device /ˌsɒlɪd steɪt ˈmem(ə)ri dɪˌvaɪs/ *noun* a solid-state memory storage device (usually in the form of RAM or ROM chips)

son file /ˈsʌn faɪl/ *noun* the latest working version of a file. Compare **father file, grandfather file**

song key /ˈsɒŋ kiː/ *noun* a musical key used to play a MIDI song

Sony /ˈsəʊni/ an electronics company that has developed a wide range of consumer and computer electronic products

sophisticated /səˈfɪstɪkeɪtɪd/ *adjective* technically advanced ○ *A sophisticated desktop publishing program.*

sophistication /səˌfɪstɪˈkeɪʃ(ə)n/ *noun* the state of being technically advanced ○ *The sophistication of the new package is remarkable.*

sort /sɔːt/ *verb* to put data in order, according to a system, on the instructions of the user ○ *To sort addresses into alphabetical order.*

sorting pass /ˌsɔːtɪŋ ˈpɑːs/ *noun* a single run through a list of items to put them into order

sortkey /ˈsɔːtkiː/, **sort field** /ˈsɔːt fiːld/ *noun* a field in a stored file which is used to sort the file ○ *The orders were sorted according to dates by assigning the date field as the sortkey.*

sort/merge /ˌsɔːt ˈmɜːdʒ/ *noun* a program which allows new files to be sorted and then merged in correct order into existing files

sound /saʊnd/ *noun* **1.** in a PC, a filename extension used to indicate a file that contains digitised sound data **2.** in a Macintosh, the resource that contains sound information ▶ abbr **snd**

sound bandwidth /saʊnd 'bænd ˌwɪdθ/ *noun* the range of frequencies that a human ear can register, normally from 20Hz to 20KHz

Sound Blaster /'saʊnd ˌblɑːstə/ a trade name for a type of sound card for PC compatibles developed by Creative Labs that allows sounds to be recorded to disk (using a microphone) and played back

sound capture /saʊnd 'kæptʃə/ *noun* the conversion of an analog sound into a digital form that can be used by a computer

sound card /ˌsaʊnd 'kɑːd/ *noun* an expansion card which produces analog sound signals under the control of a computer ○ *This software lets you create almost any sound – but you can only hear them if you have a sound card fitted.*

sound chip /ˌsaʊnd 'tʃɪp/ *noun* a device that will generate a sound or tune

sound file /ˌsaʊnd 'faɪl/ *noun* a file stored on disk that contains sound data

sound hood /ˌsaʊnd 'hʊd/ *noun* a cover which cuts down the noise from a noisy printer

sound pressure level /ˌsaʊnd 'preʃə ˌlev(ə)l/ *noun* full form of **SPL**

Sound Recorder /'saʊnd rɪˌkɔːdə/ a utility included with Microsoft Windows that allows a user to play back digitised sound files or record sound onto disk and carry out very basic editing

sound waves /ˌsaʊnd 'weɪvz/ *plural noun* pressure waves produced by vibrations, which are transmitted through air (or a solid) and detected by the human ear or a microphone (in which they are converted to electrical signals)

source /sɔːs/ *noun* a point where a transmitted signal enters a network. Opposite **sink**

source address filtering /'sɔːs ə ˌfɪltərɪŋ/ *noun* a feature of some bridges which detects a particular address in the received packet and either rejects or forwards the data

source book /ˌsɔːs 'bʊk/ *noun* a library file from which elements or objects are copied and used

source code /ˌsɔːs 'kəʊd/ *noun* a set of codes (as a program) written by the programmer which cannot be directly executed by the computer, but have to be translated into an object code program by a compiler, assembler or interpreter

source deck /ˌsɔːs 'dek/ *noun* a set of punched cards which contain the source code for a program

source document /sɔːs 'dɒkjuˌment/ *noun* a form or document from which data is extracted prior to entering it into a database

source editor /sɔːs 'edɪtə/ *noun* software which allows the user to alter, delete or add instructions in a program source file

source file /ˌsɔːs 'faɪl/ *noun* a program written in source language, which is then converted to machine code by a compiler

source language /sɔːs 'læŋgwɪdʒ/ *noun* **1.** a language in which a program is originally written **2.** a language of a program prior to translation. Opposite **object language, target language**

source listing /sɔːs 'lɪstɪŋ/ *noun* **1.** listing of a text in its original form **2.** listing of a source program

source machine /sɔːs mə'ʃiːn/ *noun* a computer which can compile source code

source object /sɔːs 'ɒbdʒekt/ *noun* (*in Windows*) the object within a drag and drop operation that is first clicked on and then dragged

source pack /'sɔːs pæk/ *noun* same as **source deck**

source program /sɔːs 'prəʊgræm/ *noun* a program, prior to translation, written in a programming language by a programmer

source routing /ˌsɔːs 'raʊtɪŋ/ *noun* a method, originally developed by IBM for its Token Ring networks, of moving data between two networks, which examines the data within the token and passes the data to the correct station

source transparent routing /ˌsɔːs trænsˌpærənt 'ruːtɪŋ/ *noun* a standard developed by IBM and the IEEE, allowing IBM networks and non-IBM Token Ring networks to be bridged and so exchange data. Abbr **SRT**

SP *abbr* stack pointer

space /speɪs/ *noun* a gap between characters or lines ■ *verb* to spread out text ○ *The line of characters was evenly spaced out across the page.*

space bar /'speɪs bɑː/ *noun* a long bar at the bottom of a keyboard, which inserts a space into the text when pressed

space character /speɪs 'kærɪktə/ *noun* a character code which prints a space

spacing /'speɪsɪŋ/ *noun* the process of putting spaces between characters or lines of printed text ○ *The spacing on some lines is very uneven.*

spam /spæm/ *noun* an article that has been posted to more than one newsgroup, so is likely to contain commercial messages (*slang*)

spam killer /'spæm ˌkɪlə/ *noun* a piece of software that automatically identifies and deals with spam in incoming e-mail

span /spæn/ *noun* a set of allowed values between a maximum and minimum

spanning tree /'spænɪŋ triː/ *noun* a method of creating a network topology that does not contain any loops and provides redundancy in case of a network fault or problem

SPARC /spɑːk/ *noun* a RISC processor designed by Sun Microsystems which is used in its range of workstations. Full form **Scalar Processor Architecture**

spare part /ˌspeə 'pɑːt/ *noun* a small piece of a machine which is needed to replace a piece which is broken or missing

spark printer /spɑːk 'prɪntə/ *noun* a thermal printer which produces characters on thermal paper by electric sparks

sparse array /spɑːs ə'reɪ/ *noun* a data matrix structure containing mainly zero or null entries

spatial measurement /ˌspeɪʃ(ə)l 'meʒəmənt/ *noun* a method of allowing a computer to determine the position of a pointer within three dimensions (often using a sensitive glove)

spec /spek/ *noun* same as **specification** (*informal*)

special character /ˌspeʃ(ə)l 'kærɪktə/ *noun* a character which is not a standard one in a certain font (such as a certain accent or a symbol)

special interest group /ˌspeʃ(ə)l 'ɪntrəst ˌgruːp/ *noun* full form of **SIG**

specialise /'speʃəlaɪz/ *verb* to study and be an expert in a subject ○ *He specialises in the design of CAD systems.*

specialist /'speʃəlɪst/ *noun* an expert in a certain field of study ○ *You need a specialist programmer to help devise a new word-processing program.*

special purpose /ˌspeʃ(ə)l 'pɜːpəs/ *noun* a system designed for a specific or limited range of applications

special sort /'speʃ(ə)l sɔːt/ *noun* an extra printing character not in the standard font range

specific address /spəˌsɪfɪk ə'dres/ *noun* a storage address which directly, without any modification, accesses a location or device

specification /ˌspesɪfɪ'keɪʃ(ə)n/ *noun* detailed information about what is to be supplied or about a job to be done. Also called **spec** □ **to work to standard specifications** to work to specifications which are accepted anywhere in the same industry □ **the work is not up to specification** *or* **does not meet the customer's specifications** the product was not manufactured in the way which was detailed in the specifications

specific code /spəˈsɪfɪk kəʊd/ *noun* a binary code which directly operates the central processing unit, using only absolute addresses and values

specific coding /spəˈsɪfɪk kɒdɪŋ/ *noun* a program code which has been written so that it only uses absolute addresses and values

specificity /ˌspesɪ'fɪsəti/ *noun* the ratio of non-relevant entries not retrieved to the total number of non-relevant entries contained in a file, database or library

speech chip /ˌspiːtʃ 'tʃɪp/ *noun* an integrated circuit which generates sounds (usually phonemes) which when played together sound like human speech

speech quality /spiːtʃ 'kwɒlɪti/ *noun* a sound recorded at a low bandwidth with a small sample size; e.g., in CD-i it is Level C with 4-bit samples and a rate of 18.9KHz

speech recognition /spiːtʃ ˌrekəg'nɪʃ(ə)n/ *noun* the process of analysing spoken words in such a way that a computer can recognize spoken words and commands

speech synthesis /spiːtʃ 'sɪnθəsɪs/ *noun* the production of spoken words by a speech synthesiser

speech synthesiser /'spiːtʃ ˌsɪnθəsaɪzə/ *noun* a device which takes data from a computer and outputs it as spoken words

speed /spiːd/ *noun* the time taken for a movement divided by the distance travelled

speed of loop /ˌspiːd əv 'luːp/ *noun* a method of benchmarking a computer by measuring the number of loops executed in a certain time

spellcheck /'speltʃek/ *verb* to check the spelling in a text by comparing it with a dictionary held in the computer

spellchecker /'speltʃekə/, **spelling checker** *noun* a dictionary of correctly spelled words, held in a computer, and used to check the spelling of a text ○ *The program will be upgraded with a word-processor and a spelling checker.*

spherisation /ˌsfɪəraɪ'zeɪʃ(ə)n/ *noun* a special effect provided by a computer graphics program that converts an image into a sphere, or 'wraps' the image over a spherical shape

spider /'spaɪdə/ *noun* a program that searches through the millions of pages that make up the world wide web for new information, changes or pages that have been deleted. These changes are then added to a search engine index to ensure that it is always up to date.

spike /spaɪk/ *noun* a very short duration voltage pulse

spillage /'spɪlɪdʒ/ *noun* a situation when too much data is being processed and cannot be contained in a buffer

spindle /'spɪnd(ə)l/ *noun* an object which grips and spins a disk in the centre hole

spindling /'spɪndlɪŋ/ *noun* the process of turning a disk by hand

SPL /ˌes piː 'el/ *noun* a measure of loudness, in decibels (dB). Full form **sound pressure level**

splash screen /'splæʃ skriːn/ *noun* the initial screen that is displayed for a few seconds when a program is started ○ *The splash screen normally displays the product logo and gives basic copyright information.*

splice /splaɪs/ *verb* to join two lengths of magnetic tape, forming a continuous length

splicing tape /'splaɪsɪŋ teɪp/ *noun* a non-magnetic tape which is applied to the back of the two ends of tape to be spliced

split baud rate /ˌsplɪt 'bɔːd ˌreɪt/ *noun* a feature of a modem which receives data at one baud rate but transmits data at another ○ *The viewdata modem uses a 1200/75 split baud rate.*

split screen /'splɪt skriːn/ *noun* software which can divide the display into two

or more independent areas, to display two text files or a graph and a text file ○ *We use split screen mode to show the text being worked on and another text from memory for comparison.*

spoof /spuːf/ *verb* to send e-mail using a false name or e-mail address

spool /spuːl/ *noun* a reel on which a tape or printer ribbon is wound ■ *verb* to transfer data from a disk to a tape

spooler *noun* a device which holds a tape and which receives information from a disk for storage

spooling /'spuːlɪŋ/ *noun* the process of transferring data to a disk from which it can be printed at the normal speed of the printer, leaving the computer available to do something else

sporadic fault /spə'rædɪk fɔːlt/ *noun* an error which occurs occasionally

spreadsheet /'spredˌʃiːt/ *noun* **1.** a program which allows calculations to be carried out on several columns of numbers **2.** a printout of calculations on wide computer stationery

sprite /spraɪt/ *noun* an object which moves round the screen in computer graphics

sprocket *noun* a wheel with teeth round it which fit into holes in continuous stationery or punched tape

sprocket feed /'sprɒkɪt fiːd/ *noun* a paper feed where the printer pulls the paper by turning sprocket wheels which fit into a series of holes along each edge of the sheet. ◊ **tractor feed**

sprocket holes /'sprɒkɪt həʊlz/ *plural noun* a series of small holes on each edge of continuous stationery, which allow the sheet to be pulled through the printer

spurious data /ˌspjʊəriəs 'deɪtə/ *noun* unexpected or unwanted data or an error in a signal, often due to noise

SPX /ˌes piː 'eks/ a trade name for a network transport protocol developed by Novell and used to carry IPX network traffic. Full form **sequenced packet exchange** ■ *noun* data transmission in only one direction. Full form **simplex**. Opposite **duplex**

spyware /'spaɪweə/ *noun* a type of software that can be installed on someone's hard disk without that person's knowledge. It is designed to send back encoded information about the computer owner's identity and the way he or she uses the Internet to the person who installed it.

SQA *abbr* software quality assurance

SQL /ˌes kjuː 'el/ *noun* a simple, commonly used standard, database programming language that is only used to create queries to retrieve data from the database. Full form **structured query language**

square brackets /skweə 'brækɪts/ *plural noun* brackets with straight sides ([ ])

square measure /skweə 'meʒə/ *noun* an area in square feet or square metres, calculated by multiplying width and length

square root /skweə 'ruːt/ *noun* a number raised to the power one half ○ *The square root of 25 is 5.*

square wave /ˌskweə 'weɪv/ *noun* a pulse that rises vertically, levels off, then drops vertically; the ideal shape for a digital signal

SRAM /'es ræm/ *noun* RAM which retains data for as long as the power supply is on, and where the data does not have to be refreshed. Full form **static RAM**

S-registers /'es ˌredʒɪstəz/ *plural noun* memory storage locations in a modem that contain the current configuration details for the way the modem operates. ◊ **AT command set**

SRT *abbr* source transparent routing

SSD *abbr* single-sided disk

SSI *abbr* small scale integration

SSL /ˌes es 'el/ *noun* a protocol designed by Netscape that provides secure communications over the Internet. Full form **secure sockets layer**. ◊ **PGP, SEPP, SET, STT**

ST506 standard /ˌes tiː ˌfaɪv əʊ 'sɪks ˌstændəd/ *noun* (*old*) a disk interface standard used in early IBM PCs, developed by Seagate, now replaced by IDE and SCSI

stable state /'steɪb(ə)l steɪt/ *noun* the state of a system when no external signals are applied

stack /stæk/ *noun* temporary storage for data, registers or tasks where items are added and retrieved from the same end of the list. ◊ **LIFO**

stackable hub /ˌstækəb(ə)l 'hʌb/ *noun* a hub device that has an external connector to allow several devices to be connected together so that network information can pass from one network ring to another

stack address /stæk ə'dres/ *noun* a location pointed to by the stack pointer

stack base /'stæk beɪs/ *noun* the address of the origin or base of a stack

stacked job control /ˌstækt 'dʒɒb kən,trəʊl/ *noun* a queue of job control instructions that are processed in the order in which they were received

stack job processing /ˌstæk dʒɒb 'prəʊsesɪŋ/ *noun* the process of storing a number of jobs to be processed in a stack and automatically executing one after the other

stack overflow /stæk ˌəʊvə'fləʊ/ *noun* an error message that is sometimes displayed when there is not enough free memory on a computer for a program's needs

stack pointer /'stæk ˌpɔɪntə/ *noun* the address register containing the location of the most recently stored item of data or the location of the next item of data to be retrieved. Abbr **SP**

stackware /'stækweə/ *noun* an application developed using the Apple Macintosh HyperCard system

stage /steɪdʒ/ *noun* one of several points in a process ○ *The text is ready for the printing stage.*

staged /steɪdʒd/ *adjective* carried out in stages, one after the other

staged change-over /ˌstæɡd 'tʃeɪndʒ/ *noun* a change between an old and a new system in a series of stages

stage window /ˌsteɪdʒ 'wɪndəʊ/ *noun* a window in which a video or animation sequence is viewed (normally refers to a window in which a Movie Player sequence is played)

stand-alone, standalone *adjective* referring to a device or system that can operate without the need of any other devices ○ *The workstations have been networked together rather than used as stand-alone systems.*

stand-alone system /'stænd əˌləʊn ˌsɪstəm/ *noun* a system which can operate independently

stand-alone terminal /'stænd əˌləʊn ˌtɜːmɪn(ə)l/ *noun* a computer terminal with a processor and memory which can be directly connected to a modem, without being a member of a network or cluster

standard /'stændəd/ *noun* the normal quality or normal conditions which are used to judge other things

COMMENT: Modem standards are set by the CCITT in the UK, the Commonwealth and most of Europe, while the USA and part of

South America use modem standards set by Bell.

standard colours /ˌstændəd ˈkʌləz/ *plural noun* the range of colours that are available on a particular system and can be shared by all applications

standard document /ˌstændəd ˈdɒkjʊmənt/, **standard form** *noun* a printed document or form which is used many times (with different names and addresses often inserted – as in a form letter)

standard function /ˌstændəd ˈfʌŋkʃən/ *noun* a special feature included as normal in a computer system

Standard Generalized Markup Language /ˌstændəd ˌdʒen(ə)rəlaɪzd ˈmɑːkʌp ˌlæŋgwɪdʒ/ *noun* full form of **SGML**

standard interface /ˌstændəd ˈɪntəfeɪs/ *noun* an interface between two or more systems which conforms to pre-defined standards

standardise /ˈstændədaɪz/ *verb* to make a series of things conform to a standard ○ *to standardize control of transmission links*

standard letter /ˌstændəd ˈletə/ *noun* a letter which is sent without any change to the main text, but which is personalised by inserting the names and addresses of different people

standard memory /ˌstændəd ˈmem(ə)ri/ *noun* the first 1Mb of memory in a PC

standard paragraph /ˌstændəd ˈpærəgrɑːf/ *noun* a printed paragraph which is used many times (with different names and addresses often inserted – as in a form letter)

standards converter /ˈstændədz kən ˌvɜːtə/ *noun* a device to convert received signals conforming to one standard into a different standard

standard subroutine /ˌstændəd ˈsʌbruːtiːn/ *noun* a routine which carries out an often used function, such as keyboard input or screen display

standard text /ˌstændəd ˈtekst/ *noun* a printed text which is used many times (with different names and addresses often inserted – as in a form letter)

standby /ˈstændbaɪ/ *adjective* referring to a device or program that is ready for use in case of failure

standby equipment /ˈstændbaɪ ɪ ˌkwɪpmənt/ *noun* a secondary system

identical to the main system, to be used if the main system breaks down

star network /ˈstɑː ˌnetwɜːk/ *noun* a network of several machines where each node is linked individually to a central hub. Compare **bus network**

star program /stɑː ˈprəʊgræm/ *noun* a perfect program which runs (first time) without any errors or bugs

start /stɑːt/ *noun* the beginning or first part

start bit /ˈstɑːt ˌbɪt/ *noun* a transmitted bit used (in asynchronous communications) to indicate the start of a character. Opposite **stop bit**

Start button /ˈstɑːt ˌbʌt(ə)n/ *noun* a button that is normally in the bottom left-hand corner of a Windows 95 Desktop screen and provides a convenient route to the programs and files on the computer

start element /ˈstɑːt ˌelɪmənt/ *noun* same as **start bit**

starting point /ˈstɑːtɪŋ pɔɪnt/ *noun* a place where something starts

start of header /ˌstɑːt əv ˈhedə/ *noun* a transmitted code indicating the start of header (address or destination) information for a following message

start of text /ˌstɑːt əv ˈtekst/ *noun* a transmitted code indicating the end of control or address information and the start of the message. Abbr **SOT, STX**

star topology /ˈstɑː təˌpɒlədʒi/ *noun* a network topology in which all devices are connected by individual cable to a single central hub ○ *If one workstation cable snaps in a star topology, the rest continue, unlike a bus topology.*

start page /ˈstɑːt peɪdʒ/ *noun* **1.** the page to which a user is automatically taken first whenever he or she goes online **2.** the webpage to which a visitor to a website is automatically taken first

startup disk /ˈstɑːtʌp dɪsk/ *noun* a floppy disk which holds the operating system and system configuration files which can, in case of hard disk failure, be used to boot the computer

Startup folder /ˈstɑːtʌp ˌfəʊldə/ *noun* a special folder on a hard disk that contains programs that will be run automatically when the user next starts Windows

startup screen /ˈstɑːtʌp skriːn/ *noun* text or graphics displayed when an application or multimedia book is run

statement /ˈsteɪtmənt/ *noun* **1.** an expression used to convey an instruction or define a process **2.** an instruction in a source language which is translated into several machine code instructions

statement number /ˈsteɪtmənt ˌnʌmbə/ *noun* a number assigned (in a sequential way) to a series of instruction statements

state-of-the-art /ˌsteɪt əv ði ˈɑːt/ *adjective* very modern or technically as advanced as possible

'…the main PCB is decidedly non-state-of-the-art' [*Personal Computer World*]

static /ˈstætɪk/ *adjective* **1.** referring to data that does not change with time **2.** referring to a system that is not dynamic

COMMENT: Static RAM uses bistable devices such as flip-flops to store data; these take up more space on a chip than the capacitative storage method of dynamic RAM but do not require refreshing.

static colours /ˌstætɪk ˈkʌləz/ *plural noun* ♦ default palette

static dump /ˈstætɪk dʌmp/ *noun* a printout of the state of a system when it has finished a process

static electricity /ˌstætɪk ɪlekˈtrɪsɪti/ *noun* an electrical charge that can build up in a person or electronic component

static memory /ˌstætɪk ˈmem(ə)ri/ *noun* nonvolatile memory that does not require refreshing

static object /ˌstætɪk ˈɒbdʒekt/ *noun* an object in an animation or video that does not move within the frame

static RAM /ˌstætɪk ˈræm/ *noun* full form of **SRAM**

static relocation /ˌstætɪk ˌriːləʊˈkeɪʃ(ə)n/ *noun* the process of moving data or coding or assigning absolute locations before a program is run

static storage /ˌstætɪk ˈstɔːrɪdʒ/ *noun* nonvolatile memory which does not require refreshing

static subroutine /ˌstætɪk ˈsʌbruːtiːn/ *noun* a subroutine which uses no variables apart from the operand addresses

station /ˈsteɪʃ(ə)n/ *noun* a point in a network or communications system which contains devices to control the input and output of messages, allowing it to be used as a sink or source

station management /ˌsteɪʃ(ə)n ˈmænɪdʒmənt/ *noun* software and hardware within the FDDI specification which provides control information. Abbr **SMT**

statistical /stəˈtɪstɪk(ə)l/ *adjective* based on statistics

statistics /stəˈtɪstɪks/ *noun* the study of facts in the form of figures

status bar /ˈsteɪtəs bɑː/ *noun* a line at the top or bottom of a screen which gives information about the task currently being worked on, e.g. position of cursor, number of lines, filename, time

status bit /ˈsteɪtəs bɪt/ *noun* a single bit in a word used to provide information about the state or result of an operation

status line /ˈsteɪtəs laɪn/ *noun* same as **status bar**

status poll /ˈsteɪtəs pəʊl/ *noun* a signal from a computer requesting information on the current status of a terminal

status register /ˈsteɪtəs ˌredʒɪstə/ *noun* a register containing information on the status of a peripheral device

ST connector /ˌes tiː kəˈnektə/ *noun* a connector used to terminate optical fibres

steady state /ˈstedi steɪt/ *noun* a circuit, device or program state in which no action is occurring but an input can be accepted

steep learning curve /ˌstiːp ˈlɜːnɪŋ ˌkɜːv/ *adjective* referring to a product that is very difficult to use

steg analysis /ˈsteg əˌnæləsɪs/ *noun* the process of searching through computerised graphics or music files to find slight changes in the normal patterns that may show the presence of hidden messages

steganography /ˌstegəˈnɒgrəfi/ *noun* the practice of placing secret messages in computerised graphics and music files. These messages are so small that they can only be detected by special software.

step /step/ *noun* a single unit ■ *verb* to move forward or backwards by one unit ○ *We stepped forward through the file one record at a time.*

step frame /step freɪm/ *verb* to capture a video sequence one frame at a time, used when the computer is not powerful or fast enough to capture real-time full-motion video

stepper motor, stepping motor *noun* a motor which turns in small steps as instructed by a computer (used in printers, disk drives and robots)

step through /step θruː/ *noun* a function of a debugger that allows a developer to execute a program one instruction at a time to see where the fault lies

stereo /ˈsteriəʊ/, **stereophonic** /ˌsteriəˈfɒnɪk/ *adjective* referring to sound recorded onto two separate channels from two separate microphone elements and played back through a pair of headphones or two speakers

stickiness /'stɪkinəs/ *noun* the ability of a website to attract visitors and to keep them interested for a long time

stick model /stɪk 'mɒd(ə)l/ *noun* same as **wire frame model** (*see*)

sticky /'stɪki/ *adjective* used to describe an Internet site that attracts visitors, especially one that keeps them interested for a long time

still /stɪl/ *noun* a single image or frame within a video or film sequence

stochastic model /stə'kæstɪk ˌmɒd(ə)l/ *noun* a mathematical representation of a system which includes the effects of random actions

stock control program /ˌstɒk kən 'trəʊl ˌprəʊɡræm/ *noun* software designed to help manage stock in a business

stop and wait protocol /ˌstɒp ən 'weɪt ˌprəʊtəkɒl/ *noun* communications protocol in which the transmitter waits for a signal from the receiver that the message was correctly received before transmitting further data

stop bit /stɒp bɪt/ *noun* a transmitted bit used in asynchronous communications to indicate the end of a character. Opposite **start bit**

stop code /stɒp kəʊd/ *noun* an instruction which temporarily stops a process to allow the user to enter data

stop element /stɒp 'elɪmənt/ *noun* same as **stop bit**

stop instruction /stɒp ɪn'strʌkʃən/ *noun* a computer programming instruction which stops program execution

stop list /stɒp lɪst/ *noun* a list of words which are not to be used or are not significant for a file or library search

stop time /stɒp taɪm/ *noun* the time taken for a spinning disk to come to a stop after it is no longer powered

storage /'stɔːrɪdʒ/ *noun* memory or the part of a computer system in which data or programs are kept for further use

storage allocation /'stɔːrɪdʒ ˌæləkeɪʃ(ə)n/ *noun* a method by which memory is allocated for different uses, e.g. programs, variables, data

storage capacity /'stɔːrɪdʒ kə ˌpæsɪti/ *noun* the amount of space available for storage of data

storage density /'stɔːrɪdʒ ˌdensɪti/ *noun* the number of bits which can be recorded per unit area of storage medium

storage device /'stɔːrɪdʒ dɪˌvaɪs/ *noun* any device which can store data and then allow it to retrieved when required

storage disk /'stɔːrɪdʒ dɪsk/ *noun* a disk used to store data

storage dump /'stɔːrɪdʒ dʌmp/ *noun* a printout of all the contents of an area of storage space

storage medium /'stɔːrɪdʒ ˌmiːdiəm/ *noun* any physical material that can be used to store data for a computer application

storage tube /'stɔːrɪdʒ tjuːb/ *noun* a special CRT used for computer graphics, which retains an image on screen without the need for refresh actions

store /stɔː/ *noun* memory or the part of a computer system in which data or programs are kept for further use ■ *verb* to save data, which can then be used again as necessary ○ *Storing a page of high resolution graphics can require 3Mb.*

COMMENT: Storage devices include hard and floppy disk, RAM, punched paper tape and magnetic tape.

store address register /ˌstɔː ə'dres ˌredʒɪstə/ *noun* full form of **SAR**

store and forward /ˌstɔː ən 'fɔːwəd/ *noun* an electronic mail communications system which stores a number of messages before retransmitting them

store cell /'stɔː sel/ *noun* same as **store location**

store data register /ˌstɔː 'deɪtə ˌredʒɪstə/ *noun* full form of **SDR**

stored program /stɔːd 'prəʊɡræm/ *noun* a computer program which is stored in memory. If it is stored in dynamic RAM it will be lost when the machine is switched off, if stored on disk or tape (backing store) it will be permanently retained.

stored program signalling /ˌstɔːd ˌprəʊɡræm 'sɪɡn(ə)lɪŋ/ *noun* a system of storing communications control signals on computer in the form of a program

store location /stɔː ləʊ'keɪʃ(ə)n/ *noun* a unit in a computer system which can store information

story board /'stɔːri bɔːd/ *noun* a series of pictures or drawings that show how a video or animation progresses

STP *abbr* shielded twisted pair

straight-line coding /ˌstreɪt laɪn ɪn 'kəʊdɪŋ/ *noun* a program written to avoid the use of loops and branches, providing a faster execution time

stream /striːm/ *noun* a long flow of serial data

streaming audio /ˌstriːmɪŋ 'ɔːdiəʊ/ *noun* digital audio data that is continuously transmitted (normally over the Internet) using a streaming protocol to provide stereo sound

streaming data, streaming protocol *noun* a method of sending a continuous stream of data over the Internet to provide live video or sound transmission

COMMENT: Older methods of sending continuous live data used a standard web server (an HTTP server) to transmit the data. However, an HTTP server is designed to send data when it is ready rather than sending a regular stream of data that is required by multimedia. If you have ever tried to view a video clip over the Internet, you will have encountered this burst-transmission problem: when traffic or server load lightens, you can watch 20 frames per second, when the server is busy, you can watch one frame per minute. To provide a good multimedia server, the data delivery must be regulated and ideally synchronised. There are many different standards used to deliver sound and video over the Internet including Progressive Network's RealAudio, Microsoft's NetShow server (that supports both audio and video) and Netscape's MediaServer. Each of these streaming data technologies allows the user or publisher to limit the delivery of data to a maximum data rate. There are several standard formats used including Microsoft's multimedia delivery format, ASF (active streaming format) and other standards developed by Macromedia, VDOnet, Vivo, and VXtreme.

streaming tape drive /ˌstriːmɪŋ 'teɪp ˌdraɪv/ *noun* same as **tape streamer**

streaming video /ˌstriːmɪŋ 'vɪdiəʊ/ *noun* video image data that is continuously transmitted (normally over the Internet) using a streaming protocol to provide smooth moving images

STRESS /stres/ *abbr* structural engineering system solver

strikethrough *noun* a horizontal line used for indicating deleted text

string /strɪŋ/ *noun* any series of consecutive alphanumeric characters or words that are manipulated and treated as a single unit by the computer □ **alphanumeric** *or* **character string** storage allocated for a series of alphanumeric characters

string area /strɪŋ 'eəriə/ *noun* a section of memory in which strings of alphanumeric characters are stored

string array /strɪŋ ə'reɪ/ *noun* an array whose elements can be strings (of alphanumeric characters)

string concatenation /strɪŋ kənˌkætə'neɪʃ(ə)n/ *noun* the process of linking a series of strings together

string function /strɪŋ 'fʌŋkʃən/ *noun* a program operation which can act on strings

string length /strɪŋ leŋθ/ *noun* the number of characters in a string

string name /strɪŋ neɪm/ *noun* identification label assigned to a string

string orientated symbolic language /ˌstrɪŋ ˌɔːriənteɪtɪd sɪmˌbɒlɪk 'læŋgwɪdʒ/ *noun* full form of **SNOBOL**

string type /strɪŋ taɪp/ *noun* a variable that can contain alphanumeric characters only

string variable /strɪŋ 'veəriəb(ə)l/ *noun* a variable used in a computer language that can contain alphanumeric characters as well as numbers

stringy floppy /ˌstrɪŋi 'flɒpi/ *noun* same as **tape streamer**

strip /strɪp/ *verb* to remove the control data from a received message, leaving only the relevant information

strip window /strɪp 'wɪndəʊ/ *noun* a display which shows a single line of text

strobe /strəʊb/ *verb* to send a pulse, usually on the selection line, of an electronic circuit ■ *noun* the pulse of an electric circuit

stroke /strəʊk/ *noun* **1.** the width (in pixels) of a pen or brush used to draw onscreen **2.** the thickness of a printed character

structure /'strʌktʃə/ *noun* a way in which something is organized or formed ■ *verb* to organise or to arrange in a certain way ○ *You first structure a document to meet your requirements and then fill in the blanks.* □ **structured programming** well-ordered and logical technique of assembling programs

structured cabling /ˌstrʌktʃəd 'keɪb(ə)lɪŋ/ *noun* a method of cabling using UTP cable feeding into hubs designed in such a way that it is easy to trace and repair cable faults and also to add new stations or more cable

structured design /ˌstrʌktʃəd dɪ 'zaɪn/ *noun* a number of interconnected modules which are intended to solve problems

structured programming
/ˌstrʌktʃəd 'prəʊgræmɪŋ/ *noun* a style
of computer programming in which a program consists of a hierarchy of simple subroutines

structured query language
/ˌstrʌktʃəd 'kwɪəri ˌlæŋgwɪdʒ/ *noun*
full form of **SQL**

structured wiring /ˌstrʌktʃəd
'waɪərɪŋ/ *noun* the planned installation of
all the cables that will be required in an office or building for computer networks and
telephone

STT /ˌes tiː 'tiː/ *noun* a system developed
to provide a secure link between a user's
browser and a vendor's Website to allow
the user to pay for goods over the Internet.
Full form **secure transaction technology.** ◊ **PGP, SEPP, SET, S-HTTP, SSL**

stub /stʌb/ *noun* a short program routine
which contains comments to describe the
executable code that will, eventually, be
inserted into the routine

stuck beacon /stʌk 'biːkən/ *noun* an
error condition in which a station continuously transmits beacon frames

STX *abbr* start of text

style /staɪl/ *noun* the typeface, font,
point size, colour, spacing and margins of
text in a formatted document

style sheet /staɪl ʃiːt/ *noun* a template
which can be preformatted to generate automatically the style or layout of a document such as a manual, book or newsletter

stylus /'staɪləs/ *noun* a pen-like device
which is used in computer graphics systems to dictate cursor position on the
screen

stylus printer /'staɪləs ˌprɪntə/ *noun* ◗
dot-matrix printer

sub- /sʌb/ *prefix* less than, less important
than or lower than

subaddress /'sʌbəˌdres/ *noun* a peripheral identification code, used to access
one peripheral. This is then followed by
address data to access a location within the
peripheral's memory.

subclass /'sʌbklɑːs/ *noun* a number of
data items related to one item in a master
class

subdirectory /'sʌbdɪˌrekt(ə)ri/ *noun* a
directory of disk or tape contents contained within the main directory

'…if you delete a file and then delete the subdirectory where it was located, you cannot restore the file
because the directory does not exist'
[*Personal Computer World*]

sub-domain /sʌb dəʊ'meɪn/ *noun* a
second level of addressing on the Internet
that normally refers to a department name
within a larger organisation

subdomain name /ˌsʌbdə'meɪn
ˌneɪm/ *noun* an organisational name consisting of two or three letters, e.g. ac or
.com, that precedes the two-letter country
domain name in an Internet address, as in
'.com.au', the address for Australian commercial sites.

subject line /'sʌbdʒɪkt laɪn/ *noun* a
line in an e-mail that indicates the subject
of the message

submenu /'sʌbmenjuː/ *noun* a secondary menu displayed as a choice from a
menu

submit button /səb,mɪt 'bʌt(ə)n/
noun a button displayed on a webpage that
sends information entered by a user on a
web form to a program running on a web
server for processing, e.g., the submit button could be used to start a search query

subnet /'sʌbnet/ *noun* a self-contained
part of a large network, normally referring
to one, independently-managed part of the
Internet

subnet address /'sʌbnet əˌdres/,
subnet number /'sʌbnet ˌnʌmbə/ *noun*
the part of an IP address that identifies a
subnet that is connected to a larger network. The first part of the IP address identifies the network, the next part of the IP
address identifies the subnet and the last
part of the IP address identifies a single
host server. ◊ **IP address**

subnet mask /'sʌbnet mɑːsk/ *noun* a
filter that is used to select the portion of an
IP address that contains the subnet address

subnotebook /sʌb'nəʊtbʊk/ *noun* a
very small portable computer, smaller and
lighter than a standard full-size notebook
or laptop computer. A subnotebook often
has a smaller keyboard and display and often only includes a hard disk drive with
any floppy disk drive or CD-ROM drive in
a separate, external unit that can be
plugged in when needed.

subprogram /'sʌbprəʊgræm/ *noun* **1.**
a subroutine in a program **2.** a program
called up by a main program

subroutine /'sʌbruːˌtiːn/ *noun* a section of a program which performs a required function and can be called upon at
any time from inside the main program □
closed *or* **linked subroutine** a number of
computer instructions in a program which

can be called at any time, with control being returned on completion to the next instruction after the call

COMMENT: A subroutine is executed by a call instruction which directs the processor to its address; when finished it returns to the instruction after the call instruction in the main program.

subroutine call /'sʌbruːˌtiːn kɔːl/ *noun* a computer programming instruction which directs control to a subroutine

subscribe /səb'skraɪb/ *verb* to add your name to a mailing list or listserv list so that you will receive any messages for the group

subscriber /səb'skraɪbə/ *noun* **1.** a person who has a telephone **2.** a person who pays for access to a service such as a BBS

subscript /'sʌbskrɪpt/ *noun* a small character which is printed below the line of other characters. ◊ **superscript** (NOTE: used in chemical formulae: CO_2)

subscripted variable /ˌsʌbskrɪptɪd 'veəriəb(ə)l/ *noun* an element in an array, which is identified by a subscript

subsegment /'sʌbsegmənt/ *noun* a small section of a segment

subset /'sʌbˌset/ *noun* a small set of data items which forms part of a another larger set

substitute /'sʌbstɪtjuːt/ *verb* to put something in the place of something else (NOTE: you substitute one thing **for** another)

substitute character /ˌsʌbstɪtjuːt 'kærɪktə/ *noun* a character which is displayed if a received character is not recognized

substitution error /ˌsʌbstɪ'tjuːʃ(ə)n ˌerə/ *noun* an error made by a scanner which mistakes one character or letter for another

substitution table /ˌsʌbstɪ'tjuːʃ(ə)n ˌteɪb(ə)l/ *noun* a list of characters or codes which are to be inserted instead of received codes

substrate /'sʌbstreɪt/ *noun* a base material on which an integrated circuit is constructed. ◊ **integrated circuit**

subsystem /'sʌbsɪstəm/ *noun* one smaller part of a large system

subtraction /səb'trækʃən/ *noun* the process of taking one number away from another

subtrahend /'sʌbtrəhend/ *noun* in a subtraction operation, the number to be subtracted from the minuend

sub-woofer /sʌb 'wʊfə/ *noun* a large loudspeaker that can reproduce very low frequency sounds, normally with frequencies between 20 to 100Hz, used with normal loudspeakers to enhance the overall sound quality

suffix notation /ˌsʌfɪks nəʊ'teɪʃ(ə)n/ *noun* mathematical operations written in a logical way, so that the symbol appears after the numbers to be acted upon. ◊ **postfix notation**

suitcase /'suːtkeɪs/ *noun* (*in the Apple Macintosh environment*) an icon which contains a screen font and allows fonts to be easily installed onto the system

suite of programs /ˌswiːt əv 'prəʊgræmz/ *noun* **1.** a group of programs which run one after the other ○ *The word-processing system uses a suite of three programs, editor, spelling checker and printing controller.* **2.** a number of programs used for a particular task

sum /sʌm/ *noun* total of a number of items added together

summation check /sʌ'meɪʃ(ə)n tʃek/ *noun* an error detection check performed by adding together the characters received and comparing with the required total

Sun Microsystems /ˌsʌn 'maɪkrəʊsɪstəmz/ a company that developed the Java programming system used to extend webpages

super- /suːpə/ *prefix* very good or very powerful

super bit mapping /ˌsuːpə 'bɪt ˌmæpɪŋ/ *noun* full form of **SBM**

supercomputer /ˌsuːpəkəm'pjuːtə/ *noun* a very powerful mainframe computer used for high speed mathematical tasks

superimpose /ˌsuːpərɪm'pəʊz/ *verb* to place something on top of something else

superior number /suˌpɪəriə 'nʌmbə/ *noun* a superscript figure

super large scale integration /ˌsuːpə ˌlaːdʒ skeɪl ˌɪntɪ'greɪʃ(ə)n/ *noun* an integrated circuit with more than 100,000 components. Abbr **SLSI**

superscript /'suːpəˌskrɪpt/ *noun* a small character printed higher than the normal line of characters. Compare **subscript** (NOTE: used often in mathematics: 10^5 say: ten to the power five)

supersede /ˌsuːpəˈsiːd/ *verb* to take the place of something which is older or less useful ○ *The new program supersedes the earlier one, and is much faster.*

super VGA /ˌsuːpə viː dʒiː ˈeɪ/ *noun* full form of **SVGA**

supervisor /ˈsuːpəˌvaɪzə/ *noun* **1.** a person who makes sure that equipment is always working correctly **2.** a section of a computer operating system that regulates the use of peripherals and the operations undertaken by the CPU

supervisor program /ˈsuːpəvaɪzə ˌprəʊɡræm/ *noun* same as **supervisory program**

supervisory /ˈsuːpəvaɪzəri/ *adjective* as a supervisor

supervisory instruction /ˌsuːpəvaɪzəri ɪnˈstrʌkʃən/ *noun* an instruction used to control and execute programs under the control of an operating system

supervisory program /ˌsuːpəvaɪzəri ˈprəʊɡræm/ *noun* a master program in a computer system that controls the execution of other programs

supervisory sequence /ˈsuːpəvaɪzəri ˌsiːkwəns/ *noun* a combination of control codes that perform a controlling function in a data communications network

supervisory signal /ˌsuːpəvaɪzəri ˈsɪɡn(ə)l/ *noun* **1.** a signal that indicates if a circuit is busy **2.** a signal which provides an indication of the state of a device

supplier /səˈplaɪə/ *noun* a company which supplies something ○ *a supplier of computer parts*

supply /səˈplaɪ/ *noun* the process of providing goods, products or services ○ *The electricity supply has failed.* ■ *verb* to provide something which is needed and for which someone will pay ○ *The computer was supplied by a recognised dealer.*

support /səˈpɔːt/ *verb* to give help to or to help to run ○ *The main computer supports six workstations.*

support chip /səˈpɔːt tʃɪp/ *noun* a dedicated IC which works with a CPU and carries out an additional function or a standard function very rapidly, so speeding up the processing time ○ *The maths support chip can be plugged in here.*

suppressor /səˈpresə/ *noun* a device which suppresses interference

surf /sɜːf/ *verb* to explore a website looking at the webpages in no particular order, but simply moving between pages using the links

surface-mount technology /ˌsɜːfɪs maʊnt tekˈnɒlədʒi/ *noun* full form of **SMT**

surge /sɜːdʒ/ *noun* a sudden increase in electrical power in a system, due to a fault, noise or component failure

COMMENT: Power surges can burn out circuits before you have time to pull the plug. A surge protector between your computer and the wall outlet will help prevent damage.

surge protector /sɜːdʒ prəˈtektə/ *noun* an electronic device which cuts off the power supply to sensitive equipment if it detects a power surge that could cause damage

suspend /səˈspend/ *noun* a command that is used when running Windows on a battery-powered laptop computer to shut down almost all of the electronic components of the laptop

SVGA /ˌes viː dʒiː ˈeɪ/ *noun* an enhancement to the standard VGA graphics display system which allows resolutions of up to 800x600pixels with 16million colours. Full form **super VGA**

S-Video /ˌes ˈvɪdiəʊ/ *noun* a method of transmitting a video signal in which the luminance and colour components (the luma, Y, and chroma, C) are transmitted over separate wires to improve the quality of the video, used in Hi8, S-VHS and other video formats to provide better quality than composite video. Also called **Y/C video**

swap /swɒp/ *noun* same as **swapping** ■ *verb* to stop using one program, put it into store temporarily, run another program, and when that is finished, return to the first one

swap file /swɒp faɪl/ *noun* a file stored on the hard disk used as a temporary storage area for data held in RAM, to provide virtual memory

swapping /ˈswɒpɪŋ/ *noun* (*in a virtual memory system*) an activity in which program data is moved from main memory to disk, while another program is loaded or run. ◊ **virtual memory**. Also called **swap**

swim /swɪm/ *noun* computer graphics which move slightly due to a faulty display unit

switch /swɪtʃ/ *noun* **1.** (*in some command-line operating systems*) an additional character entered on the same line as the program command, which affects how the program runs **2.** a point in a computer program where control can be passed to one of a number of choices **3.** a mechanical or solid state device that can electrically connect or isolate two or more lines ■ *verb* **1.** to connect or disconnect two lines by activating a switch □ **to switch on** to start to provide power to a system by using a switch to connect the power supply lines to the circuit **2.** □ **to switch over** to start using an alternative device when the primary one becomes faulty

switched network backup /ˌswɪtʃ ˈnetwɜːk ˌbækʌp/ *noun* a user's choice of a secondary route through a network if the first is busy

switching /ˈswɪtʃɪŋ/ *noun* a constant update of connections between changing sinks and sources in a network

switching centre /ˈswɪtʃɪŋ ˌsentə/ *noun* a point in a communications network where messages can be switched to and from the various lines and circuits that end there

switching circuit /ˈswɪtʃɪŋ ˌsɜːkɪt/ *noun* an electronic circuit that can direct messages from one line or circuit to another in a switching centre

SX /ˌes ˈeks/ *noun* a type of processor chip derived from the basic 80386 or 80486 processor that is slightly cheaper to manufacture and buy

symbol /ˈsɪmbəl/ *noun* a sign or picture which represents something ○ *This language uses the symbol ? to represent the print command.*

Symbol font /ˈsɪmb(ə)l fɒnt/ *noun* a TrueType font that is included with Windows and includes all sorts of symbols and Greek characters. ◊ **TrueType**

symbolic /sɪmˈbɒlɪk/ *adjective* which acts as a symbol or which uses a symbol name or label

symbolic address /sɪmˌbɒlɪk əˈdres/ *noun* the address represented by a symbol or name

symbolic code /sɪmˌbɒlɪk ˈkəʊd/ *noun* an instruction that is in mnemonic form rather than a binary number

symbolic-coding format /sɪmˌbɒlɪk ˈkəʊdɪŋ ˌfɔːmæt/ *noun* assembly language instruction syntax, using a label, operation and operand fields

symbolic debugger /sɪmˌbɒlɪk diː ˈbʌɡə/ *noun* a debugger that allows symbolic representation of variables or locations

symbolic instruction /sɪmˌbɒlɪk ɪn ˈstrʌkʃən/ *noun* same as **symbolic code**

symbolic language /sɪmˌbɒlɪk ˈlæŋɡwɪdʒ/ *noun* **1.** any computer language where locations are represented by names **2.** any language used to write source code

symbolic logic /sɪmˌbɒlɪk ˈlɒdʒɪk/ *noun* the study of reasoning and thought (formal logic)

symbolic name /sɪmˌbɒlɪk ˈneɪm/ *noun* a name used as a label for a variable or location

symbolic programming /sɪmˌbɒlɪk ˈprəʊɡræmɪŋ/ *noun* the process of writing a program in a source language

symbolic table /sɪmˌbɒlɪk ˈteɪb(ə)l/ *noun* a list of labels or names in a compiler or assembler, which relate to their addresses in the machine code program

symmetrical compression /sɪ ˌmetrɪk(ə)l kəmˈpreʃ(ə)n/ *noun* a compression system that requires the same processing power and time scale to compress and decompress an image

symmetric difference /sɪˌmetrɪk ˈdɪfrəns/ *noun* a logical function whose output is true if either of 2 inputs is true, and false if both inputs are the same

sync /sɪŋk/ *noun* same as **synchronisation** (*informal*) □ **in sync** synchronised □ **the two devices are out of sync** the two devices are not properly synchronised

sync bit /sɪŋk bɪt/ *noun* a transmitted bit used to synchronise devices

sync character /sɪŋk ˈkærɪktə/ *noun* a transmitted character used to synchronise devices

synchronisation /ˌsɪŋkrənaɪ ˈzeɪʃ(ə)n/ *noun* the action of synchronising two or more devices

synchronisation pulses /ˌsɪŋkrənaɪ ˈzeɪʃ(ə)n ˌpʌlsɪz/ *plural noun* transmitted pulses used to make sure that the receiver is synchronised with the transmitter

synchronise /ˈsɪŋkrəˌnaɪz/ *verb* to make sure that two or more devices or processes are coordinated in time or action

synchronised dynamic RAM /ˌsɪŋkrənaɪzd daɪˌnæmɪk ˈræm/ *noun* full form of **SDRAM**

synchroniser /ˈsɪŋkrənaɪzə/ *noun* a device that will perform a function when it receives a signal from another device

synchronous /'sɪŋkrənəs/ *adjective* which runs in sync with something else (such as a main clock)

synchronous cache /'sɪŋkrənəs kæʃ/ *noun* a high-speed secondary cache system used in many computers that use the Pentium processor chip

synchronous computer /ˌsɪŋkrənəs kəm'pjuːtə/ *noun* a computer in which each action can only take place when a timing pulse arrives

synchronous data link control /ˌsɪŋkrənəs 'deɪtə lɪŋk kənˌtrəʊl/ *noun* full form of **SDLC**

synchronous data network /ˌsɪŋkrənəs 'deɪtə ˌnetwɜːk/ *noun* a communications network in which all the actions throughout the network are controlled by a single timing signal

synchronous DRAM /'sɪŋkrənəs dræm/ *noun* new high-speed memory technology in which the memory components work from the same clock signal as the main processor, so are synchronised

synchronous idle character /ˌsɪŋkrənəs ˌaɪd(ə)l 'kærɪktə/ *noun* a character transmitted by a DTE to ensure correct synchronisation when no other character is being transmitted

synchronous mode /'sɪŋkrənəs məʊd/ *noun* a system mode in which operations and events are synchronised with a clock signal

synchronous network /ˌsɪŋkrənəs 'netwɜːk/ *noun* a network in which all the links are synchronised with a single timing signal

synchronous system /ˌsɪŋkrənəs 'sɪstəm/ *noun* a system in which all devices are synchronised to a main clock signal

synchronous transmission /ˌsɪŋkrənəs trænz'mɪʃ(ə)n/ *noun* the transmission of data from one device to another, where both devices are controlled by the same clock, and the transmitted data is synchronised with the clock signal

sync pulses /sɪŋk 'pʌlsɪz/ *plural noun* transmitted pulses used to make sure that the receiver is synchronised with the transmitter

syntactic error /sɪnˌtæktɪk 'erə/ *noun* a programming error in which the program statement does not follow the syntax of the language

syntax /'sɪntæks/ *noun* grammatical rules which apply to a programming language

syntax analysis /'sɪntæks əˌnæləsɪs/ *noun* a stage in compilation where statements are checked to see if they obey the rules of syntax

syntax error /'sɪntæks ˌerə/ *noun* an error resulting from incorrect use of programming language syntax

synthesis /'sɪnθəsɪs/ *noun* the process of producing something artificially from a number of smaller elements

synthesise /'sɪnθəsaɪz/ *verb* to produce something artificially from a number of smaller elements

'…despite the fact that speech can now be synthesized with very acceptable quality, all it conveys is linguistic information' [*Personal Computer World*]

synthesised voice /ˌsɪnθəsaɪzd 'vɔɪs/ *noun* speech created by an electronic device that uses phonemes

synthesiser /'sɪnθəsaɪzə/ *noun* a device which generates signals, sound or speech

synthetic address /sɪnˌθetɪk ə'dres/ *noun* a location used by a program produced by instructions within the program

synthetic language /sɪnˌθetɪk 'læŋgwɪdʒ/ *noun* programming language in which the source program is written

SyQuest /'saɪkwest/ a manufacturer of storage devices, including a range of removable hard disk drives and backup units. ◊ **Zip disk**

sysgen /'sɪsdʒen/ *noun* same as **system generation**

sysop /'sɪsˌɒp/ *noun* a person who maintains a bulletin board system or network

system /'sɪstəm/ *noun* any group of hardware or software or peripherals, etc., which work together

system administrator /ˌsɪstəm əd 'mɪnɪstreɪtə/ *noun* ♦ **network administrator**

system attribute /ˌsɪstəm 'ætrɪbjuːt/ *noun* a special attribute attached to a file used by the operating system, the file being hidden from normal users

system backup /ˌsɪstəm 'bækʌp/ *noun* a copy of all the data stored on a computer, server or network

system board /'sɪstəm bɔːd/ *noun* ♦ **motherboard**

system check /'sɪstəm tʃek/ *noun* the process of running diagnostic routines to ensure that there are no problems

system clock /'sɪstəm klɒk/ *noun* an electronic component that generates a regular signal that is used to synchronise all the components in the computer

system colours /ˌsɪstəm ˈkʌləz/ *plural noun* same as **default palette**

system console /ˌsɪstəm ˈkɒnsəʊl/ *noun* the main terminal or control centre for a computer which includes status lights and control switches

system control panel /ˌsɪstəm kən ˈtrəʊl ˌpæn(ə)l/ *noun* main computer system control switches and status indicators

system crash /ˈsɪstəm kræʃ/ *noun* a situation where the operating system stops working and has to be restarted

system design /ˌsɪstəm dɪˈzaɪn/ *noun* the process of identifying and investigating possible solutions to a problem, and deciding upon the most appropriate system to solve the problem

system diagnostics /ˌsɪstəm ˌdaɪəg ˈnɒstɪks/ *noun* tests, features and messages that help find hardware or software faults

system disk /ˈsɪstəm dɪsk/ *noun* a disk which holds the system software

Système Electronique Couleur Avec Mémoire *noun* full form of **SECAM**

system exclusive data /ˌsɪstəm ɪk ˌskluːsɪv ˈdeɪtə/ *noun* MIDI messages that can only be understood by a MIDI device from a particular manufacturer

system firmware /ˌsɪstəm ˈfɜːmweə/ *noun* basic operating system functions and routines in a ROM device

system flowchart /ˈsɪstəm ˌfləʊtʃɑːt/ *noun* a diagram which shows each step of the computer procedures needed in a system

system folder /ˈsɪstəm ˌfəʊldə/ *noun* (*in the Apple Macintosh environment*) a folder that contains the program files for the operating system and Finder

system generation /ˌsɪstəm ˌdʒenə ˈreɪʃ(ə)n/ *noun* the process of producing an optimum operating system for a particular task. Also called **sysgen**

system library /ˌsɪstəm ˈlaɪbrəri/ *noun* stored files that hold the various parts of a computer's operating system

system life cycle /ˌsɪstəm ˈlaɪf ˌsaɪk(ə)l/ *noun* the time when a system exists, between its initial design and its becoming out of date

system log /ˈsɪstəm lɒg/ *noun* a record of computer processor operations

system manager /ˌsɪstəm ˈmænɪdʒə/ *noun* a person responsible for the computers or network in a company

System Monitor /ˈsɪstəm ˌmɒnɪtə/ *noun* a Windows utility that allows a user to view how the resources on their PC are performing and, if they have shared the device, who else on the network is using the resources

system operator /ˌsɪstəm ˈɒpəreɪtə/ *noun* a person who manages an online bulletin board or maintains a computer network

system palette /ˌsɪstəm ˈpælət/ *noun* the range of colours that are available on a particular operating system and can be shared by all applications

system prompt /ˈsɪstəm prɒmpt/ *noun* a prompt which indicates the operating system is ready and waiting for the user to enter a system command

systems analysis /ˈsɪstəmz əˌnæləsɪs/ *noun* **1.** the process of analysing a process or system to see if it could be more efficiently carried out by a computer **2.** the process of examining an existing system with the aim of improving or replacing it

systems analyst /ˈsɪstəmz ˌænəlɪst/ *noun* a person who specialises in systems analysis

Systems Application Architecture /ˌsɪstəmz ˌæplɪkeɪʃ(ə)n ˈɑːkɪtektʃə/ *noun* full form of **SAA**

system security /ˌsɪstəm sɪˈkjʊərɪti/ *noun* measures, such as password, priority protection, authorisation codes, designed to stop browsers and hackers

systems integration /ˌsɪstəmz ˌɪntɪ ˈgreɪʃ(ə)n/ *noun* the process of combining different products from different manufacturers to create a system

Systems Network Architecture /ˌsɪstəmz ˈnetwɜːk ˌɑːkɪtektʃə/ *noun* full form of **SNA**

system software /ˌsɪstəm ˈsɒftweə/ *noun* programs which direct the basic functions, input-output control, etc., of a computer

system specifications /ˌsɪstəm ˌspesɪfɪˈkeɪʃ(ə)nz/ *plural noun* details of hardware and software required to perform certain tasks

systems program /ˈsɪstəmz ˌprəʊgræm/ *noun* a program which controls the way in which a computer system works

systems programmer /ˌsɪstəmz ˈprəʊɡræmə/ *noun* a programmer who specialises in writing systems software

system support /ˌsɪstəm səˈpɔːt/ *noun* a group of people who maintain and operate a system

system tray /ˈsɪstəm treɪ/ *noun* (*in Windows*) an area of the taskbar normally in the bottom right-hand corner next to the clock. The system tray displays tiny icons that show which system software pro-

grams were run automatically when Windows started and are now running in the background.

system unit /ˈsɪstəm ˌjuːnɪt/ *noun* the main terminal or control centre for a computer which includes status lights and control switches

system variable /ˌsɪstəm ˈveəriəb(ə)l/ *noun* a variable that contains data generated by the system software that can be used by applications

T

T *abbr* tera-

T1 /ˌtiː ˈwʌn/ *noun* a term that refers to a leased line connection that transfers data at 1.544Mbits per second in the US (in the UK and Europe, the transfer rate is 2.048Mbits per second) and can carry either data or 24 voice channels. If the link uses only part of this capacity, it is called a fractional T1 link. These links are normally used to connect ISPs together or to connect offices of a large organisation. ◊ **ADSL, leased line**

T1 committee /ˌtiː ˈwʌn kəˌmɪti/ *noun* an ANSI committee which sets digital communications standards for the US, particularly ISDN services

T1 link /ˌtiː ˈwʌn ˌlɪŋk/ *noun* (*in the US*) a high speed, long distance data transmission link not related to the T1 committee, that can carry data at 1.544Mbits per second

T2 link /ˌtiː ˈtuː ˌlɪŋk/ *noun* (*in the US*) a high speed, long distance data transmission link equivalent to four T1 lines that can carry data at 6.3Mbits per second

T3 link /ˌtiː ˈθriː ˌlɪŋk/ *noun* (*in the US*) a high speed, long distance data transmission link equivalent to 28 T1 lines that can carry data at 44.736Mbits per second

tab /tæb/ *verb* to tabulate or to arrange text in columns with the cursor automati-

cally running from one column to the next in keyboarding ○ *The list was neatly lined up by tabbing to column 10 at the start of each new line.*

TAB *abbr* tabulate

tabbing /ˈtæbɪŋ/ *noun* the movement of the cursor in a word-processing program from one tab stop to the next ○ *Tabbing can be done from inside the program.*

tabbing order /ˈtæbɪŋ ˌɔːdə/ *noun* the order in which the focus moves from one button or field to the next as the user presses the tab key

tab character /tæb ˈkærɪktə/ *noun* the ASCII character 09hex which is used to align text at a preset tab stop

tab key /ˈtæb kiː/ *noun* a key on a keyboard, normally positioned on the far left, beside the 'Q' key, with two arrows pointing in opposite horizontal directions, used to insert a tab character into text and so align the text at a preset tab stop

table /ˈteɪb(ə)l/ *noun* **1.** a list of data in columns and rows on a printed page or on the screen **2.** (*in a relational database*) a structure which shows how records and data items are linked by relations between the rows and columns of the table

table lookup /ˈteɪb(ə)l ˌlʊkʌp/ *noun* the process of using one known value to select one entry in a table, providing a secondary value

table of contents /ˌteɪb(ə)l əv 'kɒntents/ *noun* **1.** a list of the contents of a book, usually printed at the beginning **2.** data at the start of a disc that describes how many tracks are on the CD, their position and length

tablet /'tæblət/ *noun* a graphics pad or flat device which allows a user to input graphical information into a computer by drawing on its surface

tab memory /tæb 'mem(ə)ri/ *noun* the ability of an editing program, usually a word-processor, to store details about various tab settings

tab rack /tæb ræk/ *noun* a graduated scale, displayed on the screen, showing the position of tabulation columns ○ *The tab rack shows you the left and right margins.*

tab settings /tæb 'setɪŋz/, **tab stops** /tæb stɒpz/ *plural noun* preset points along a line, where the printing head or cursor will stop for each tabulation command

tabular /'tæbjʊlə/ *adjective* □ **in tabular form** arranged in a table

tabulate /'tæbjʊˌleɪt/ *verb* to arrange text in columns, with the cursor moving to each new column automatically as the text is keyboarded

tabulating /'tæbjʊleɪtɪŋ/ *noun* the action of processing punched cards, such as a sorting operation

tabulation /ˌtæbjʊ'leɪʃ(ə)n/ *noun* **1.** arrangement of a table of figures **2.** the process of moving a printing head or cursor a preset distance along a line

tabulation markers /ˌtæbju'leɪʃ(ə)n ˌmɑːkəz/ *plural noun* symbols displayed to indicate the position of tabulation stops

tabulation stops /ˌtæbju'leɪʃ(ə)n stɒpz/ *plural noun* preset points along a line at which a printing head or cursor will stop for each tabulation command

tabulator /'tæbjʊleɪtə/ *noun* part of a word-processor which automatically sets words or figures into columns

tactile keyboard /ˌtæktaɪl 'kiːbɔːd/ *noun* a keyboard that provides some indication that a key has been pressed, such as a beep

tag /tæg/ *noun* **1.** one section of a computer instruction **2.** a set of identifying characters attached to a file or item (of data) ○ *Each file has a three letter tag for rapid identification.*

tag image file format /ˌtæg ˌɪmɪdʒ 'faɪl ˌfɔːmæt/ *noun* full form of **TIFF**

tail /teɪl/ *noun* **1.** data recognised as the end of a list of data **2.** a control code used to signal the end of a message

takedown /'teɪkdaʊn/ *verb* to remove something such as paper or disks from a peripheral after one job and prepare it for the next

takedown time /'teɪkdaʊn taɪm/ *noun* the amount of time required to takedown a peripheral ready for another job

take-up reel /'teɪk ʌp ˌriːl/ *noun* a reel onto which magnetic tape is collected

Taligent /'tælɪdʒənt/ *noun* an operating system developed by IBM and Apple that can be used on both PC and Macintosh platforms

tandem processors /ˌtændəm 'prəʊsesəz/ *plural noun* two processors connected so that if one fails, the second takes over

tape archive /teɪp 'ɑːkaɪv/ *noun* ♦ **tar**

tape backup /teɪp 'bækʌp/ *noun* the process of using (usually magnetic) tape as a medium for storing back-ups from faster main or secondary storage, such as RAM or hard disk

tape cable /teɪp 'keɪb(ə)l/ *noun* a number of insulated conductors arranged next to each other forming a flat cable

tape cartridge /teɪp 'kɑːtrɪdʒ/ *noun* a cassette box containing magnetic tape (on a reel)

tape cassette /teɪp kə'set/ *noun* a small box containing a reel of magnetic tape and a pickup reel

tape code /teɪp kəʊd/ *noun* a coding system used for punched data representation on paper tape

tape deck /'teɪp dek/ *noun* a device which plays back and records data onto magnetic tape

tape drive /teɪp draɪv/ *noun* a mechanism which controls magnetic tape movement over the tape heads ○ *Our new product has a 96Mb streaming tape drive.*

tape format /teɪp 'fɔːmæt/ *noun* a way in which blocks of data, control codes and location data is stored on tape

tape guide /teɪp gaɪd/ *noun* a method by which the tape is correctly positioned over the tape head ○ *The tape is out of alignment because one of the tape guides has broken.*

tape head /teɪp hed/ *noun* a head which reads or writes signals on a magnetic tape

tape header /teɪp 'hedə/ *noun* identification information at the beginning of a tape

tape label /teɪp 'leɪb(ə)l/ *noun* a tape header and trailer containing information about the contents of a tape

tape library /teɪp 'laɪbrəri/ *noun* **1.** a secure area for the storage of computer data tapes **2.** a series of computer tapes kept in store for reference

tape loadpoint /'teɪp ˌləʊdpɔɪnt/ *noun* the position on a magnetic tape at which reading should commence to load a file

tape punch /teɪp pʌntʃ/ *noun* a machine that punches holes into paper tape

tape reader /teɪp 'riːdə/ *noun* a machine which reads punched holes in paper tape or signals on magnetic tape

tape streamer /teɪp 'striːmə/ *noun* a device containing a continuous loop of tape, used as backing storage. Also called **stringy floppy**

tape to card converter /teɪp tə, tʊ kɑːd/ *noun* a device which reads data from magnetic tape and stores it on punched cards

tape trailer /teɪp 'treɪlə/ *noun* identification information at the beginning of a tape

tape transmitter /teɪp trænz'mɪtə/ *noun* a device which reads data from paper tape and transmits it to another point

tape transport /teɪp 'trænspɔːt/ *noun* a method by which the tape in a magnetic tape recorder is moved smoothly from reel to reel over the magnetic heads

TAPI *abbr* telephony application programming interface

tar /tɑː/ *noun* a file compression system used on a computer running the Unix operating system. Full form **tape archive**

Targa /'tɑːgə/ *noun* **1.** a graphics file format which uses the .TGA extension on a PC, developed by Truevision to store raster graphic images in 16–, 24– and 32-bit colour. **2.** a high-resolution colour graphics adapter made by Truevision

targetcast /'tɑːgɪtkɑːst/ *verb* to broadcast a website only to a group of people who are known to be potentially interested in it, and not to everyone on the Internet

target computer /ˌtɑːgɪt kəm'pjuːtə/ *noun* a computer on which software is to be run

target disk /'tɑːgɪt dɪsk/ *noun* a disk onto which a file is to be copied

target language /'tɑːgɪt ˌlæŋgwɪdʒ/ *noun* a language into which a language will be translated from its source language ○ *The target language for this PASCAL program is machine code.* Opposite **source language**

target level /'tɑːgɪt ˌlev(ə)l/ *noun* an interpretative processing mode for program execution

target phase /'tɑːgɪt feɪz/ *noun* the period of time during which the target program is run

target program /ˌtɑːgɪt 'prəʊgræm/ *noun* an object program or computer program in object code form, produced by a compiler

target window /'tɑːgɪt ˌwɪndəʊ/ *noun* a window in which text or graphics will be displayed

tariff /'tærɪf/ *noun* a charge incurred by a user of a communications or computer system ○ *There is a set tariff for logging on, then a rate for every minute of computer time used.*

task /tɑːsk/ *noun* a job which is to be carried out by a computer

taskbar /'tɑːskˌbɑː/ *noun* a bar that normally runs along the bottom of the screen in Windows and displays the Start button and a list of other programs or windows that are currently active

task management /tɑːsk 'mænɪdʒmənt/ *noun* system software which controls the use and allocation of resources to programs

task queue /tɑːsk kjuː/ *noun* temporary storage of jobs waiting to be processed

task swapping /'tɑːsk ˌswɒpɪŋ/ *noun* the process of exchanging one program in memory for another which is temporarily stored on disk. Task switching is not the same as multitasking which can execute several programs at once.

task switching /'tɑːsk ˌswɪtʃɪŋ/ *noun* same as **task swapping**

TAT *abbr* turnaround time

T carrier /'tiː ˌkæriə/ *noun* a US standard for digital data transmission lines, such as T1, T1C, and corresponding signal standards DS1, DS1C

T-commerce /ˌtiː 'kɒmɜːs/ *noun* a business conducted by means of interactive television

T connector /tiː kəˈnektə/ *noun* a coaxial connector, shaped like the letter 'T', which connects two thin coaxial cables using BNC plugs and provides a third connection for another cable or network interface card

TCP /ˌtiː siː 'piː/ *noun* standard data transmission protocol that provides full duplex transmission, bundles data into packets and checks for errors. Full form **transmission control protocol**

TCP/IP /ˌtiː siː piː aɪ 'piː/ *noun* a data transfer protocol used in networks and communications systems, often used in Unix-based networks. This protocol is used for all communications over the internet. Full form **transmission control protocol/interface program**

TDM /ˌtiː diː 'em/ *noun* a method of combining several signals into one high-speed transmission carrier, each input signal being sampled in turn and the result transmitted to a the receiver which re-constructs the signals. Full form **time division multiplexing**

TDR /ˌtiː diː 'ɑː/ *noun* a test that identifies where cable faults lie by sending a signal down the cable and measuring how long it takes for the reflection to come back. Full form **time domain reflectometry**

TDS /ˌtiː diː 'es/ *noun* a computer system that will normally run batch processing tasks until interrupted by a new transaction, at which point it allocates resources to the new transaction. Full form **transaction-driven system**

technical /ˈteknɪk(ə)l/ *adjective* referring to a particular machine or process ○ *The document gives all the technical details on the new computer.*

technical support /ˌteknɪk(ə)l sə 'pɔːt/ *noun* technical advice to a user to explain how to use software or hardware or explain why it might not work

technician /tekˈnɪʃ(ə)n/ *noun* a person who is specialised in industrial work

technique /tekˈniːk/ *noun* a skilled way of doing a job ○ *The company has developed a new technique for processing customers' disks.*

technological /ˌteknəˈlɒdʒɪk(ə)l/ *adjective* referring to technology □ **the technological revolution** the changing of industrial methods by introducing new technology

technology /tekˈnɒlədʒi/ *noun* the process of applying scientific knowledge to industrial processes □ **the introduction of new technology** the process of putting new electronic equipment into a business or industry

tele- /teli/ *prefix* long distance

telecommunications /ˌtelikəmjuːnɪ 'keɪʃ(ə)nz/ *noun* the technology of passing and receiving messages over a distance, as in radio, telephone, telegram, satellite broadcast, etc.

telecommuting /ˈtelikəmjuːtɪŋ/ *noun* the practice of working on a computer in one place (normally from home) that is linked by modem to the company's central office allowing messages and data to be transferred

teleconferencing /ˈteli ˌkɒnf(ə)rənsɪŋ/ *noun* the process of linking video, audio and computer signals from different locations so that distant people can talk and see each other, as if in a conference room

teleinformatic services /teliɪn ˌfɔːmətɪk 'sɜːvɪsɪz/ *plural noun* any of various data only services, such as telex, facsimile, which use telecommunications

telematics /ˌteliˈmætɪks/ *noun* the interaction of all data processing and communications devices

telephone /ˈtelɪfəʊn/ *noun* a machine used for speaking to someone or communicating with another computer (using modems) over a long distance

telephone line /ˈtelɪfəʊn laɪn/ *noun* a cable used to connect a telephone handset with a central exchange

telephony /təˈlefəni/ *noun* a series of standards that define the way in which computers can work with a telephone system to provide voice-mail, telephone answering, and fax services

telephony application programming interface /təˌlefəni ˌæplɪkeɪʃ(ə)n 'prəʊɡræmɪŋ ˌɪntəfeɪs/ *noun* a system developed by Microsoft and Intel that allows a PC to control a single telephone. Abbr **TAPI**

telephony services application programming interface /təˌlefəni ˌsɜːvɪsɪz ˌæplɪkeɪʃ(ə)n 'prəʊɡræmɪŋ ˌɪntəfeɪs/ *noun* a system developed by Novell and AT&T that allows a PC to control a PBX telephone exchange. Abbr **TSAPI**

teleprinter /'teli,printə/ *noun* a device that is capable of sending and receiving data from a distant point by means of a telegraphic circuit, and printing out the message on a printer ○ *You can drive a teleprinter from this modified serial port.*

teleprinter interface /'teliprintə ,intəfeis/ *noun* a terminal interface or hardware and software combination required to control the functions of a terminal

teleprinter roll /'teliprintə ,rəʊl/ *noun* a roll of paper onto which messages are printed

teleprocessing /'teli,prəʊsesiŋ/ *noun* the processing of data at a distance (as on a central computer from outside terminals). Abbr **TP**

telesoftware /'teli,sɒftweə/ *noun* software which is received from a viewdata or teletext service. Abbr **TSW**

teletext /'teli,tekst/ *noun* a method of transmitting text and information with a normal television signal, usually as a serial bit stream which can be displayed using a special decoder

teletype /'telitaip/ *noun* a term used for teleprinter equipment. Abbr **TTY**

teletypewriter /,teli'taipraitə/ *noun* a keyboard and printer attached to a computer system which can input data either direct or by making punched paper tape

television /,teli'viʒ(ə)n/ *noun* a device which can receive (modulated) video signals from a computer or broadcast signals with an aerial and display images on a CRT screen with sound. Abbr **TV**

television monitor /,teli'viʒ(ə)n ,mɒnitə/ *noun* a device able to display signals from a computer without sound, but is not able to broadcast signals, usually because there is no demodulator

television receiver/monitor /,teliviʒ(ə)n ri,si:və 'mɒnitə/ *noun* a device able to act as a TV receiver or monitor

television scan /'teli,viʒ(ə)n skæn/ *noun* a horizontal movement of the picture beam over the screen, producing one line of an image

television tube /'teli,viʒ(ə)n tju:b/ *noun* a CRT with electronic devices which provide the line by line horizontal and vertical scanning movement of the picture beam

telnet /'telnet/ *noun* a TCP/IP protocol that allows a user to connect to and control via the Internet a remote computer as if they were there and type in commands as if they were sitting in front of the computer

template /'tem,pleit/ *noun* **1.** a plastic or metal sheet with cut-out symbols to help in the drawing of flowcharts and circuit diagrams **2.** (*in text processing*) standard text, such as a standard letter or invoice, into which specific details can be added

template command /'templeit kə ,ma:nd/ *noun* a command which allows functions or other commands to be easily set ○ *A template paragraph command enables the user to specify the number of spaces each paragraph should be indented.*

tempo /'tempəʊ/ *noun* **1.** (*in MIDI or music*) the speed at which the notes are played, measured in beats per minute ○ *A typical MIDI tempo is 120bpm.* **2.** (*in a multimedia title*) the speed at which frames are displayed

temporary *adjective* not permanent

temporary register /,temp(ə)rəri 'redʒistə/ *noun* a register used for temporary storage for the results of an ALU operation

temporary storage /,temp(ə)rəri 'stɔːridʒ/ *noun* storage which is not permanent

temporary swap file /,temp(ə)rəri 'swɒp ,fail/ *noun* a file on a hard disk which is used by software to store data temporarily or for software that implements virtual memory, such as Microsoft's Windows

10Base2 /,ten beis 'tuː/ IEEE standard specification for running Ethernet over thin coaxial cable

10Base5 /,ten beis 'faiv/ IEEE standard specification for running Ethernet over thick coaxial cable

10BaseT /,ten beis 'tiː/ IEEE standard specification for running Ethernet over unshielded twisted pair cable

ten's complement /'tenz ,kɒmplimənt/ *noun* formed by adding one to the nine's complement of a decimal number

tera- /terə/ *prefix* 10^{12}; one million million. Abbr **T**

terabyte /'terə,bait/ *noun* one thousand gigabytes or one million megabytes of data

teraflop /'terəflɒp/ *noun* one million million floating-point operations per second, a measure of computer speed

terminal /'tɜːmɪn(ə)l/ *noun* **1.** a device usually made up of a display unit and a keyboard which allows entry and display of information when on-line to a central computer system □ **intelligent terminal**, **smart terminal** a computer terminal which contains a CPU and memory, allowing basic data processing to be carried out, usually with the facility to allow the user to program it independently of the host computer ○ *The new intelligent terminal has a built-in text editor.* **2.** an electrical connection point **3.** a point in a network where a message can be transmitted or received. ◊ **source, sink** ■ *adjective* fatal or which cannot be repaired ○ *The computer has a terminal fault.*

terminal adapter /'tɜːmɪn(ə)l ə ˌdæptə/ *noun* a device that connects a computer to a digital communications line; e.g., to link a PC to an ISDN line. A terminal adapter transfers digital signals from the computer to the line, whereas a modem is used to connect a computer to an analogue communications line, such as a telephone line, and needs to convert digital signals to and from an analogue form.

terminal area /'tɜːmɪn(ə)l ˌeəriə/ *noun* part of a printed circuit board at which edge connectors can be connected

terminal character set /ˌtɜːmɪn(ə)l 'kærɪktə ˌset/ *noun* the range of characters available for a particular type of terminal, which might include graphics or customized characters

terminal controller /'tɜːmɪn(ə)l kən ˌtrəʊlə/ *noun* a hardware device or IC which controls a terminal including data communications and display

terminal emulation /'tɜːmɪn(ə)l emjuˌleɪʃ(ə)n/ *noun* the ability of a terminal to emulate the functions of another type of terminal so that display codes can be correctly decoded and displayed and keystrokes correctly coded and transmitted

terminal emulation software /ˌtɜːmɪn(ə)l ˌemjuˈleɪʃ(ə)n ˌsɒftweə/ *noun* a software program that is used to allow a computer to interpret the special display codes used to control a specialist workstation, normally used with a modem to allow you to connect to a remote mainframe computer system

terminal identity /ˌtɜːmɪn(ə)l aɪ ˈdentɪti/ *noun* a unique code transmitted by a viewdata terminal to provide identification and authorisation of a user

terminal interface /'tɜːmɪn(ə)l ˌɪntəfeɪs/ *noun* a hardware and software combination required to control the functions of a terminal from a computer ○ *The network controller has 16 terminal interfaces.*

terminal keyboard /ˌtɜːmɪn(ə)l 'kiːbɔːd/ *noun* a standard QWERTY or special keyboard allowing input at a terminal

terminal session /'tɜːmɪn(ə)l ˌseʃ(ə)n/ *noun* a period of time when a terminal is on-line or in use

terminal strip /'tɜːmɪn(ə)l strɪp/ *noun* a row of electrical connectors that allow pairs of wires to be electrically connected using a screw-down metal plate

terminate /'tɜːmɪˌneɪt/ *verb* to end

terminate and stay resident program /ˌtɜːmɪneɪt ən steɪ 'rezɪd(ə)nt ˌprəʊgræm/ *noun* a program which loads itself into main memory and carries out a function when activated ○ *When you hit Ctrl-F5, you will activate the TSR program and it will display your day's diary.* Also called **TSR program**

terminate and stay resident software /ˌtɜːmɪneɪt ən steɪ 'rezɪd(ə)nt ˌsɒftweə/ *noun* a program that is started from the command line, then loads itself into memory, ready to be activated by an action, and passes control back to the command line. Abbr **TSR**

termination /ˌtɜːmɪ'neɪʃ(ə)n/ *noun* the process of ending or stopping

terminator /'tɜːmɪneɪtə/ *noun* **1.** (*in a LAN*) a resistor that fits onto each end of a coaxial cable in a bus network to create an electrical circuit **2.** (*in a SCSI installation*) a resistor that fits onto the last SCSI device in the daisy-chain, creating an electrical circuit **3.** same as **rogue value**

ternary /'tɜːnəri/ *adjective* referring to a number system with three possible states

tessellate /'tesəleɪt/ *verb* to reduce a complex shape into a collection of simple shapes, often triangles

test /test/ *noun* the action carried out on a device or program to establish whether it is working correctly, and if not, which component or instruction is not working ■ *verb* to carry out an examination of a device or program to see if it is working correctly

test bed /test bed/ *noun* an environment used to test programs

test data /test 'deɪtə/ *noun* data with known results prepared to allow a new program to be tested

test equipment /test ɪ'kwɪpmənt/ *noun* special equipment which tests hardware or software

test numeric /'test njuː,merɪk/ *noun* a check to ensure that numerical information is numerical

test run /'test rʌn/ *noun* a program run with test data to ensure that the software is working correctly ○ *A test run will soon show up any errors.*

texel /'teksəl/ *noun* a collection of pixels that are treated as a single unit when applying a texture map over an object

text /tekst/ *noun* a set of alphanumeric characters that convey information □ **text processing** word-processing or the practice of using a computer to keyboard, edit and output text, in the forms of letters, labels, etc.

text compression /tekst kəm'preʃ(ə)n/ *noun* the process of reducing the space required by a section of text, using one code to represent more than one character, and removing spaces and punctuation marks, etc.

text-editing facilities /'tekst ,edɪtɪŋ fə,sɪlɪtiz/ *plural noun* a word-processing system which allows the user to add, delete, move, insert and correct sections of text

text-editing function /'tekst ,edɪtɪŋ ,fʌŋkʃ(ə)n/ *noun* an option in a program which provides text-editing facilities ○ *The program includes a built-in text-editing function.*

text editor /tekst 'edɪtə/ *noun* same as **screen editor**

text file /tekst faɪl/ *noun* a file that contains text rather than digits or data

text formatter /'tekst ,fɔːmætə/ *noun* a program that converts text to a new form or layout according to parameters or embedded codes such as line width, page size, justification, etc.

text management /tekst 'mænɪdʒmənt/ *noun* facilities which allow text to be written, stored, retrieved, edited and printed

text manager /'tekst ,mænɪdʒə/ *noun* facilities that allow text to be written, stored, retrieved, edited and printed

text manipulation /tekst mə,nɪpjʊ 'leɪʃ(ə)n/ *noun* facilities which allow text editing, changing, inserting and deleting

text message /'tekst ,mesɪdʒ/ *noun* a message sent in the form of text, especially one that appears on the viewing screen of a mobile phone or pager

text mode /tekst məʊd/ *noun* an operating mode of a computer or display screen that will only display pre-defined characters and will not allow graphic images to be displayed

text processing /'tekst ,prəʊsesɪŋ/ *noun* the use of a computer to create, store, edit and print or display text

text register /tekst 'redʒɪstə/ *noun* a temporary computer storage register for text characters only

text retrieval /tekst rɪ'triːv(ə)l/ *noun* an information retrieval system that allows the user to examine complete documents rather than just a reference to a document

text screen /tekst skriːn/ *noun* the area of a computer screen set up to display text

text-to-speech converter /tekst tə, tʊ spiːtʃ/ *noun* an electronic device which uses a speech synthesiser to produce the spoken equivalent of a piece of text that has been entered

texture /'tekstʃə/ *noun* a surface detail that is added to basic shapes

texture mapping /'tekstʃə ,mæpɪŋ/ *noun* **1.** a special computer graphics effect using algorithms to produce an image that looks like the surface of something such as marble, brick, stone or water **2.** the process of covering one image with another to give the first a texture

text window /tekst 'wɪndəʊ/ *noun* a window in a graphics system, where the text is held in a small space on the screen before being allocated to a final area

TFTP /,tiː ef tiː 'piː/ *noun* a simple form of the standard FTP (file transfer protocol) system, commonly used to load the operating system software onto a diskless workstation from a server when the workstation boots up when it is switched on. Full form **trivial file transfer protocol**. ◊ **FTP**

TFT screen /,tiː ef 'tiː ,skriːn/ *noun* a method of creating a high-quality LCD display often used in laptop computers. Full form **thin film transistor screen**

thermal dye diffusion /ˌθɜːm(ə)l daɪ dɪˈfjuːʒ(ə)n/ *noun* a method of printing similar to thermal wax transfer, except that a dye is used instead of coloured wax. Thermal dye diffusion can print continuous colour to produce a near-photographic output.

thermal inkjet printer /ˌθɜːm(ə)l ˌɪnkdʒet ˈprɪntə/ *noun* a computer printer which produces characters by sending a stream of tiny drops of electrically charged ink onto the paper, the movement of the ink drops being controlled by an electric field. This is a non-impact printer with few moving parts.

COMMENT: This type of printer is very quiet in operation since the printing head does not strike the paper.

thermal paper /ˌθɜːm(ə)l ˈpeɪpə/ *noun* a special paper whose coating turns black when heated, allowing characters to be printed by using a matrix of small heating elements

thermal printer /ˌθɜːm(ə)l ˈprɪntə/ *noun* a printer where the character is formed on thermal paper with a printhead containing a matrix of small heating elements

thermal transfer, thermal wax, thermal wax transfer printer *noun* a method of printing where the colours are produced by melting coloured wax onto the paper ○ *Thermal wax transfer technology still provides the best colour representation on paper for PC output.*

thesaurus /θɪˈsɔːrəs/ *noun* a file which contains synonyms that are displayed as alternatives to a misspelt word during a spell-check

thick-Ethernet /θɪk ˈiːθəˌnet/ *noun* a network implemented using thick coaxial cable and transceivers to connect branch cables. ◊ **Ethernet, thin-Ethernet**

thick film /θɪk fɪlm/ *noun* a miniature electronic circuit design in which miniature components are mounted on an insulating base, then connected as required

thimble printer /ˈθɪmb(ə)l ˌprɪntə/ *noun* a computer printer using a printing head similar to a daisy wheel but shaped like a thimble

thin-Ethernet /θɪn ˈiːθəˌnet/ *noun* the most popular type of Ethernet network implemented using thin coaxial cable and BNC connectors. ◊ **Ethernet, thick-Ethernet** (NOTE: It is limited to distances of around 1000 m)

thin film /θɪn fɪlm/ *noun* a method of constructing integrated circuits by depositing in a vacuum very thin patterns of various materials onto a substrate to form the required interconnected components

thin-film memory /ˌθɪn fɪlm ˈmem(ə)ri/ *noun* a high-speed access RAM device using a matrix of magnetic cells and a matrix of read/write heads to access them

thin-film transistor screen /ˌθɪn fɪlm trænˈzɪstə ˌskriːn/ *noun* full form of **TFT screen**

thin window /θɪn ˈwɪndəʊ/ *noun* a single line display window

third generation /ˌθɜːd ˌdʒenəˈreɪʃ(ə)n/ *noun* the latest specification for mobile communication systems, including mobile telephones. Abbr **3G**

COMMENT: The third generation includes very fast data transfer rates of between 128 Kbps and 2 Mbps, depending on whether the person is walking, in a car or at his or her base station. This will allow high-speed Internet access and even live video links, to a portable telephone. The first generation of mobile telephones were analog cellular telephones, the second generation were digital PCS.

third generation computer /ˌθɜːd ˌdʒenəreɪʃ(ə)n kəmˈpjuːtə/ *noun* a computer in which integrated circuits were used instead of transistors

third party /ˌθɜːd ˈpɑːti/ *noun* a company which supplies items or services for a system sold by one party, the seller, to another, the buyer

COMMENT: A third party might supply computer maintenance or write programs, for example.

32-bit /ˈθɜːti tuː ˌbɪt/ *data* that is transferred thirty-two bits at a time along thirty-two parallel conductors; in a processor this refers to its ability to manipulate numbers that are thirty-two bits long

thirty-two bit system /ˌθɜːti tuː ˌbɪt ˈsɪstəm/, **32-bit system** *noun* a microcomputer system or CPU that handles data in 32 bit words

thrashing /ˈθræʃɪŋ/ *noun* **1.** excessive disk activity **2.** a configuration or program fault in a virtual memory system that results in a CPU wasting time moving pages of data between main memory and disk or backing store

thread /θred/ *noun* a program which consists of many independent smaller sections or beads

'WigWam makes it easier for a user to follow a thread in a bulletin-board conference topic by ordering responses using a hierarchical indent similar to that found in outline processor.' [*Computing*]

threaded file /ˌθredɪd 'faɪl/ *noun* a file in which an entry contains data and an address to the next entry that contains the same data, allowing rapid retrieval of all identical entries

threaded language /ˌθredɪd 'læŋgwɪdʒ/ *noun* a programming language which allows many small sections of code to be written then used by a main program

threaded tree /ˌθredɪd 'triː/ *noun* a structure in which each node contains a pointer to other nodes

three-address instruction /ˌθriː ə'dres ɪnˌstrʌkʃən/ *noun* an instruction which contains the addresses of two operands and the location where the result is to be stored

3D /ˌθriː 'diː/ *adjective* referring to an image which has three dimensions (width, breadth and depth), and therefore gives the impression of being solid. Full form **three-dimensional**

three-dimensional /ˌθriː daɪ 'menʃ(ə)nəl/ *adjective* full form of **3D**

three-dimensional array /θriː daɪ ˌmenʃ(ə)nəl ə'reɪ/ *noun* an array made up of a number of two-dimensional arrays, arranged in parallel, giving rows, columns and depth

3G /ˌθriː 'dʒiː/ *noun* ♦ **third generation**

three input adder /ˌθriː ˌɪnpʊt 'ædə/ *noun* ♦ **full adder**

three state logic /ˌθriː steɪt 'lɒdʒɪk/ *noun* a logic gate or IC which has three possible output states, logic high, logic low and high impedance (NOTE: Most logic gates and ICs have only two possible output states.)

threshold /'θreʃhəʊld/ *noun* a preset level which causes an action if a signal exceeds or drops below it

throughput /'θruːˌpʊt/ *noun* the rate of production by a machine or system, measured as total useful information processed in a set period of time ○ *For this machine throughput is 1.3 inches per second scanning speed.*

thumbnail /'θʌmˌneɪl/ *noun* a miniature graphical representation of an image, used as a quick and convenient method of viewing the contents of graphics or DTP files before they are retrieved

TIFF /tɪf/ *noun* standard file format used to store graphic images. Full form **tag image file format**

tile /taɪl/ *verb* (*in a GUI*) to arrange a group of windows so that they are displayed side by side without overlapping (NOTE: **tiles – tiling – tiled**)

tilt and swivel /ˌtɪlt ən 'swɪv(ə)l/ *adjective* referring to a monitor which is mounted on a pivot so that it can be moved to point in the most convenient direction for the operator

timbre /'tæmbə/ *noun* the shape of a particular sound that can be identified by the human ear (NOTE: The same musical note played on two different musical instruments will not sound the same.)

time /taɪm/ *verb* to measure the time taken by an operation

time base /taɪm beɪs/ *noun* **1.** a signal used as a basis for timing purposes **2.** a regular sawtooth signal used in an oscilloscope to sweep the beam across the screen

time bomb /'taɪm bɒm/ *noun* a computer virus that is designed to take effect on a particular date or when a computer application is used for a particular length of time

time code /taɪm kəʊd/ *noun* a sequence of timing information recorded on an audio track in a videotape

timed backup /taɪmd 'bækʌp/ *noun* a backup which occurs automatically after a period of time or at a particular time each day

time division multiplexing /ˌtaɪm dɪ ˌvɪʒ(ə)n 'mʌltɪpleksɪŋ/ *noun* full form of **TDM**

time domain reflectometry /ˌtaɪm dəʊˌmeɪn ˌriːflek'tɒmətri/ *noun* full form of **TDR**

time of peak demand /ˌtaɪm əv piːk dɪ'mɑːnd/ *noun* the time when something is being used most

timeout /'taɪmaʊt/ *noun* **1.** a logoff procedure carried out if no data is entered on an online terminal **2.** a period of time reserved for an operation

timer /'taɪmə/ *noun* a device which records the time taken for an operation to be completed

time-sharing /'taɪm ˌʃeərɪŋ/ *noun* an arrangement which allows several independent users to use a computer system or be online at the same time

COMMENT: In time-sharing, each user appears to be using the computer all the time, when in fact each is using the CPU for a short time slice only. The CPU processes one user for a short time then moves on to the next.

time slice /taɪm slaɪs/ *noun* a period of time allocated for a user or program or job within a multitasking system

time stamp /taɪm stæmp/ *noun* a MIDI message that is tagged with a time so that a sequencer can play it at the correct moment

timing loop /'taɪmɪŋ luːp/ *noun* a computer program loop which is repeated a number of times to produce a certain time delay

timing master /'taɪmɪŋ ˌmɑːstə/ *noun* a clock signal which synchronises all the components in a system

tint /tɪnt/ *noun* ◗ **hue**

tiny model /ˌtaɪni 'mɒd(ə)l/ *noun* a memory model of the Intel 80x86 processor family that allows a combined total of 64 Kb for data and code

title /'taɪt(ə)l/ *noun* an identification name given to a file or program or disk

title bar /'taɪt(ə)l bɑː/ *noun* a horizontal bar at the top of a window which displays the title of the window or application

T junction /tiː 'dʒʌŋkʃ(ə)n/ *noun* a connection at right angles to a cable carrying the main signal or power

TMSF time format /ˌtiː em es ef 'taɪm ˌfɔːmæt/ *noun* a time format used mainly by audio CD devices to measure time in frames and tracks. Full form **tracks, minutes, seconds, frames time format**

toggle /'tɒg(ə)l/ *verb* to switch something between two states (NOTE: **toggles – toggling – toggled**)

toggle switch /'tɒg(ə)l swɪtʃ/ *noun* an electrical switch which has only two positions

token /'təʊkən/ *noun* **1.** an internal code which replaces a reserved word or program statement in a high-level language **2.** (*in a local area network*) a control packet which is passed between workstations to control access to the network

token bus network /ˌtəʊkən 'bʌs ˌnetwɜːk/ *noun* an IEEE 802.4 standard for a local area network formed with a bus-topology cable, in which workstations transfer data by passing a token

token-passing /'təʊkən ˌpɑːsɪŋ/ *noun* a method of controlling access to a local area network by using a token (NOTE: A workstation cannot transmit data until it receives the token.)

Token Ring network /'təʊkən rɪŋ ˌnetwɜːk/ *noun* an IEEE 802.5 standard that uses a token passed from one worksta-tion to the next in a ring network ○ *Token Ring networks are very democratic and retain performance against increasing load.* (NOTE: A workstation can only transmit data if it captures the token. Token Ring networks, although logically rings, are often physically wired in a star topology.)

tone dialling /'təʊn ˌdaɪəlɪŋ/ *noun* a method of dialling a telephone number using sounds to represent the digits of the number (NOTE: This method of dialling is the current standard method of dialling numbers and has generally replaced the older pulse dialling system. A Hayes-compatible modem can dial the number '123' using tone dialling with the AT command 'ATDT123' or using pulse dialling with the AT command 'ATDP123')

toner /'təʊnə/ *noun* a finely powdered ink, usually black, that is used in laser printers ○ *If you get toner on your hands, you can only wash it off with cold water.* (NOTE: The toner is transferred onto the paper by electrical charge, then fixed permanently to the paper by heating.)

toner cartridge /'təʊnə ˌkɑːtrɪdʒ/ *noun* a plastic container which holds powdered toner for use in a laser printer

tool /tuːl/ *noun* (*in a graphical front end*) a function accessed from an icon in a toolbar, e.g. a circle-draw option

toolbar /'tuːlˌbɑː/ *noun* a window that contains a range of icons that access tools

Toolbook /'tuːlbʊk/ *noun* a multimedia authoring tool developed by Asymetrix which uses the OpenScript script language to control objects and actions

toolbox /'tuːlbɒks/ *noun* **1.** a box containing instruments needed to repair or maintain or install equipment **2.** a set of predefined routines or functions that are used when writing a program

Toolbox /'tuːlbɒks/ *noun* (*in an Apple Mac*) a set of utility programs stored in ROM to provide graphic functions

toolkit /'tuːlkɪt/ *noun* a series of functions which help a programmer to write or debug programs

tools /tuːlz/ *noun* a set of utility programs such as backup and format in a computer system

ToolTips /'tuːltɪps/ *noun* a feature of applications that work under Windows that display a line of descriptive text under an icon when the user moves the pointer over the icon

top down programming /ˌtɒp daʊn
'prəʊgræmɪŋ/ *noun* same as **structured
programming**

top-level domain /ˌtɒp ˌlev(ə)l dəʊ
'meɪn/ *noun* the part of an Internet address
that identifies an Internet domain, e.g. a
two-letter country code or a three-letter
code such as .edu for education or .com for
commercial when used without a country
code.

topology /tɒ'pɒlədʒi/ *noun* a way in
which the various elements in a network
are interconnected (NOTE: The plural is
topologies.)

TOPS /tɒps/ *noun* software that allows
IBM PCs and Apple Macs to share files on
a network

touch pad /tʌtʃ pæd/ *noun* a flat device
which can sense where on its surface and
when it is touched, used to control a cursor
position or switch a device on or off

touch screen /tʌtʃ skriːn/ *noun* a
computer display which has a grid of infrared transmitters and receivers, positioned on either side of the screen used to
control a cursor position (NOTE: When a
user wants to make a selection or move
the cursor, he or she points to the screen,
breaking two of the beams, which gives
the position of the pointing finger.)

touch-sensitive keyboard /ˌtʌtʃ
ˌsensətɪv 'kiːbɔːd/ *noun* a thin, flat membrane type keyboard whose keys are activated by touching and operate without
movement (NOTE: It is often used in heavy
duty or dirty environments where normal
keys would not function correctly.)

TP *abbr* teleprocessing

TPI *abbr* tracks per inch

trace /treɪs/ *noun* a method of verifying
that a program is functioning correctly, in
which the current status and contents of
the registers and variables used are displayed after each instruction step

trace program /treɪs 'prəʊgræm/
noun a diagnostic program which executes
a program that is being debugged, one instruction at a time, displaying the states
and registers

traceroute /'treɪsruːt/ *noun* a software
utility that finds and displays the route tak-
en for data travelling between a computer
and a distant server on the Internet

COMMENT: The display shows the different
servers that the data travels through, together
with the time taken to travel between each
server (called a hop). Traceroute works by
sending out a time-to-live (TTL) query data

packet to the distant server. It starts by sending out packets with a very low time-to-live,
then gradually increases the length of time
that the packet can survive until one is returned by the host – this then provides the
shortest time it will take to reach the host. If
you are trying to view a website you can use
traceroute to check which section of the link to
the website's server is the slowest. Windows
includes a traceroute utility 'tracert'. Click the
Start button and select the Run option then
type in 'tracert' followed by the domain name
of the distant web server, e.g. tracert
'www.bloomsbury.com"

trace trap /treɪs træp/ *noun* a selective
breakpoint where a tracing program stops,
allowing registers to be examined

tracing /'treɪsɪŋ/ *noun* a function of a
graphics program that takes a bitmap image and processes it to find the edges of the
shapes and so convert these into a vector
line image that can be more easily manipulated

track /træk/ *noun* any one of a series of
thin concentric rings on a magnetic disk
which the read/write head accesses and
along which the data is stored in separate
sectors ■ *verb* to follow a path or track
correctly ○ *The read head is not tracking
the recorded track correctly.*

COMMENT: The first track on a tape is along the
edge and the tape may have up to nine different tracks on it, while a disk has many concentric tracks around the central hub. The
track and sector addresses are set up during
formatting.

track address /træk ə'dres/ *noun* the
location of a particular track on a magnetic
disk

trackball /'trækˌbɔːl/ *noun* a device
used to move a cursor on-screen which is
controlled by turning a ball contained in a
case

tracking /'trækɪŋ/ *noun* **1.** the correct
alignment of a read head and the tape in a
tape player **2.** degradation of a video clip
because the action moves too fast to be accurately captured by the camera

**tracks, minutes, seconds, frames
time format** /ˌtræks ˌmɪnəts ˌsekəndz
ˌfreɪmz 'taɪm ˌfɔːmæt/ *noun* full form of
TMSF time format

tracks per inch /ˌtræks pɜːr 'ɪntʃ/
noun a measure of the number of concentric data tracks on a disk surface per inch.
Abbr **TPI**

tractor feed /'træktə fiːd/ *noun* a
method of feeding paper into a printer, in
which sprocket wheels on the printer connect with the sprocket holes on either edge
of the paper to pull the paper through

traffic /'træfɪk/ *noun* the totality of messages and other signals processed by a system or carried by a communications link ○ *Our Ethernet network begins to slow down if the traffic reaches 60 per cent of the bandwidth.*

traffic analysis /'træfɪk ə,næləsɪs/ *noun* the study of the times, types and quantities of messages and signals being processed by a system

traffic density /'træfɪk ,densɪti/ *noun* the number of messages and data transmitted over a network or system in a period of time

traffic intensity /'træfɪk ɪn,tensɪti/ *noun* the ratio of messages entering a queue to those leaving the queue within a certain time

trailer /'treɪlə/ *noun* the final byte of a file containing control or file characteristics

trailer record /'treɪlə ,rekɔːd/ *noun* the last record in a file containing control or file characteristics

transaction /træn'zækʃən/ *noun* a single action which affects a database, e.g. a sale, a change of address or a new customer

transaction-driven system /træn 'zækʃən ,drɪv(ə)n ,sɪstəm/ *noun* full form of **TDS**

transaction file /træn'zækʃən faɪl/ *noun* same as **update file**

transaction processing /træn 'zækʃən ,prəʊsesɪŋ/ *noun* interactive processing in which a user enters commands and data on a terminal which is linked to a central computer, with results being displayed on-screen. Abbr **TP**

'At present, users implementing client-server strategies are focusing on decision support systems before implementing online transaction processing and other mission-critical applications.' [*Computing*]

transaction record /træn'zækʃən ,rekɔːd/ *noun* same as **change record**

transceiver /træn'siːvə/ *noun* a transmitter and receiver, or a device which can both transmit and receive signals, e.g. a terminal or modem

transcribe /træn'skraɪb/ *verb* to copy data from one backing storage unit or medium to another (NOTE: **transcribes – transcribing – transcribed**)

transducer /trænz'djuːsə/ *noun* an electronic device which converts signals in one form into signals in another ○ *the pressure transducer converts physical pressure signals into electrical signals*

transfer /'trænsfɜː/ *verb* **1.** to change command or control of something ○ *All processing activities have been transferred to the mainframe.* **2.** to copy a section of memory to another location (NOTE: **transferring – transferred**) ■ *noun* the process of changing command or control

transfer check /træns'fɜː tʃek/ *noun* a check that a data transfer is correct according to a set of rules

transfer command /'trænsfɜː kə ,maːnd/ *noun* an instruction that directs processor control from one part of a program to another

transfer control /'trænsfɜː kən,trəʊl/ *noun* a change in the command or control of something, e.g. to another point in the program when a branch or jump instruction within a program is executed

transfer rate /'trænsfɜː reɪt/ *noun* the speed at which data is transferred from backing store to main memory or from one device to another ○ *With a good telephone line, this pair of modems can achieve a transfer rate of 14.4Kbps.*

transfer time /træns'fɜː taɪm/ *noun* the time taken to transfer data between devices or locations

transform /træns'fɔːm/ *verb* to change something from one state to another

transformational rules /trænzfə 'meɪʃ(ə)n(ə)l ruːlz/ *noun* a set of rules applied to data which is to be transformed into coded form

transient /'trænziənt/ *adjective* referring to a state or signal which is present for a short period of time ■ *noun* something which is present for a short period

transient area /,trænziənt 'eəriə/ *noun* a section of memory for user programs and data

transient error /,trænziənt 'erə/ *noun* a temporary error which occurs for a short period of time

transient read error /,trænziənt 'riːd ,erə/ *noun* an error, caused by bad data recording, from which a program can recover

transient suppressor /,trænziənt sə 'presə/ *noun* a device which suppresses voltage transients

transistor /træn'zɪstə/ *noun* an electronic semiconductor device which can control the current flow in a circuit (NOTE:

There are two main types of transistor, bipolar and unipolar.)

transistor-transistor logic /træn ˌzɪstə træn ˌzɪstə ˈlɒdʒɪk/ *noun* full form of **TTL**

transition point /trænˈzɪʃ(ə)n pɔɪnt/ *noun* a point in a program or system where a transition occurs

translate /trænsˈleɪt/ *verb* to convert data from one form into another (NOTE: **translates – translating – translated**)

translation tables /trænsˈleɪʃ(ə)n ˌteɪb(ə)lz/ *plural noun* same as **conversion tables**

translator program /trænsˈleɪtə ˌprəʊɡræm/ *noun* a program which translates a high level language program into another language, usually machine code. ◊ **interpreter, compiler**

transmission /trænzˈmɪʃ(ə)n/ *noun* the process of sending signals from one device to another

transmission channel /trænz ˈmɪʃ(ə)n ˌtʃæn(ə)l/ *noun* a physical connection between two points which allows data to be transmitted, e.g. a link between a CPU and a peripheral

transmission control protocol /trænz ˌmɪʃ(ə)n kənˈtrəʊl ˌprəʊtəkɒl/ *noun* full form of **TCP**

transmission control protocol/interface program /trænz ˌmɪʃ(ə)n kən ˈtrəʊl ˌprəʊtəʊkɒl ˈɪntəfeɪs ˌprəʊɡræm/ *noun* full form of **TCP/IP**

transmission error /trænz ˌmɪʃ(ə)n ˈerə/ *plural noun* an error due to noise on the line

transmission medium /trænz ˈmɪʃ(ə)n ˌmiːdiəm/ *noun* a means by which data can be transmitted, e.g. radio or light

transmission rate /trænzˈmɪʃ(ə)n reɪt/ *noun* a measure of the amount of data transmitted in a certain time ○ *Their average transmission is 64,000 bits per second (bps) through a parallel connection* or *19,200 bps through a serial connection.*

transmissive disk /trænzˈmɪsɪv dɪsk/ *noun* an optical data storage disk in which the reading laser beam shines through the disk to a detector below

transmit /trænzˈmɪt/ *verb* to send information from one device to another, using any medium such as radio, cable or wire link (NOTE: **transmitting – transmitted**)

transmitter /trænzˈmɪtə/ *noun* a device which will take an input signal, process it, e.g. to modulate or convert it to sound, then transmit it by a medium such as radio or light. Abbr **TX**

transparency /trænsˈpærənsi/ *noun* (*in graphics*) the degree to which one image shows another image beneath it

transparent /trænsˈpærənt/ *adjective* referring to a computer program which is not obvious to the user or which cannot be seen by the user when it is running

transparent GIF /træns ˌpærənt ˌdʒiː aɪ ˈef/ *noun* a graphic image stored in the GIF file format with one colour from the palette assigned as a transparent colour (NOTE: When the image is displayed, any part of the image in this colour will be transparent to allow any image beneath to show through. This feature is used a lot in webpages to place images on a patterned background.)

transparent interrupt /træns ˌpærənt ˈɪntərʌpt/ *noun* a mode in which if an interrupt occurs, all machine and program states are saved, the interrupt is serviced, then the system restores all previous states and continues normally

transparent paging /træns ˌpærənt ˈpeɪdʒɪŋ/ *noun* software which allows the user to access any memory location in a paged memory system as if it were not paged

transphasor /trænzˈfeɪzə/ *noun* an optical transistor constructed from a crystal which is able to switch a main beam of light according to a smaller input signal

COMMENT: This is used in the latest research for an optical computer that could run at the speed of light.

transportable /trænsˈpɔːtəb(ə)l/ *adjective* which can be carried, though perhaps requiring a vehicle ○ *A transportable computer is not as small as a portable* or *a laptop.*

transport layer /trænsˈpɔːt ˌleɪə/ *noun* the fourth layer in the ISO/OSI network model that provides a reliable connection and checks and controls the quality of the connection

trap /træp/ *noun* a device or piece of software or hardware that will catch something such as a variable, fault or value

trapdoor /ˈtræpˌdɔː/ *noun* a way of getting into a system to change data, browse or hack

trapezoidal distortion /ˌtræpɪzɔɪdəl dɪsˈtɔːʃ(ə)n/ *noun* same as **keystone distortion**

trap handler /træp ˈhændlə/ *noun* a piece of software that accepts interrupt signals and acts on them, e.g. running a special routine or sending data to a peripheral

trashcan /ˈtræʃkæn/ *noun* (*in a GUI*) an icon which looks like a dustbin that deletes any file that is dragged onto it

tree and branch network system /ˌtriː ən brɑːntʃ ˈnetwɜːk ˌsɪstəm/ *noun* a system of networking in which data is transmitted along a single output line, from which other lines branch out, forming a tree structure that feeds individual stations

tree of folders /ˌtriː əv ˈfəʊldəz/ *noun* a view of all the folders stored on a disk arranged to show folders and subfolders

tree selection sort /ˌtriː sɪˈlekʃən ˌpɔːt/ *noun* a rapid form of selection in which the information from the first sort pass is used in the second pass to speed up selection

trellis coding /ˈtrelɪs kɒdɪŋ/ *noun* a method of modulating a signal that uses both amplitude and phase modulation to give a greater throughput and lower error rates for data transmission speeds of over 9,600 bits per second

triad /ˈtraɪæd/ *noun* **1.** a group of three elements, characters or bits **2.** a triangular shaped grouping of the red, green and blue colour phosphor spots at each pixel location on the screen of a colour RGB monitor

trichromatic /ˌtraɪkrəʊˈmætɪk/ *adjective* ♦ RGB

trivial file transfer protocol /ˌtrɪviəl ˈfaɪl ˌtrænsfɜː ˌprəʊtəkɒl/ *noun* full form of **TFTP**

Trojan Horse /ˈtrəʊdʒ(ə)n hɔːs/ *noun* a program inserted into a system by a hacker that will perform a harmless function while copying information held in a classified file into a file with a low priority, which the hacker can then access without the authorised user's knowledge

troubleshoot /ˈtrʌb(ə)lʃuːt/ *verb* **1.** to debug computer software **2.** to locate and repair faults in hardware

troubleshooter /ˈtrʌb(ə)lʃuːtə/ *noun* a person who troubleshoots hardware or software (NOTE: **troubleshot**)

true /truː/ *adjective* referring to a logical condition representing a non-zero value. Compare **false**

TrueType /ˈtruːtaɪp/ a trade name for an outline font technology introduced by Apple and Microsoft as a means of printing exactly what is displayed on screen

truncate /trʌŋˈkeɪt/ *verb* **1.** to cut something short **2.** to give an approximate value to a number by reducing it to a certain number of digits ○ *3.5678 truncated to 3.56* (NOTE: **truncates – truncating – truncated**)

truncation /trʌŋˈkeɪʃ(ə)n/ *noun* removal of digits from a number so that it is a particular length

truncation error /trʌŋˈkeɪʃ(ə)n ˌerə/ *noun* an error caused when a number is truncated

trunk /trʌŋk/ *noun* a bus or communication link consisting of wires or leads which connect different parts of a hardware system

truth table /truːθ ˈteɪb(ə)l/ *noun* a method of defining a logic function as the output state for all possible inputs

truth value /truːθ ˈvæljuː/ *noun* each of two values, true or false, T or F, 1 or 0, used in Boolean algebra

TSAPI *abbr* telephony services application programming interface

Tseng Labs /ˈseŋ læbz/ a manufacturer of chipsets used in graphics adapters

TSR *abbr* terminate and stay resident

TSW *abbr* telesoftware

TTL /ˌtiː tiː ˈel/ *noun* the most common family of logic gates and high-speed transistor circuit designs in which the bipolar transistors are directly connected, usually collector to base. Full form **transistor-transistor logic**

TTL-compatible /ˌtiː tiː el kəm ˈpɒtɪb(ə)l/ *adjective* referring to MOS or other electronic circuits or components that can directly connect to and drive TTL circuits

TTL logic /ˌtiː tiː el ˈlɒdʒɪk/ *noun* the use of TTL design and components to implement logic circuits and gates

TTL monitor /ˌtiː tiː el ˈmɒnɪtə/ *noun* a monitor which can only accept digital signals, so can only display monochrome images or a limited range of colours

TTY *abbr* teletype

tune /tjuːn/ *verb* to set a system at its optimum point by careful adjustment (NOTE: **tunes** – **tuning** – **tuned**)

tunnelling /'tʌn(ə)lɪŋ/ *noun* a method of enclosing a packet of data from one type of network within another packet so that it can be sent over a different, incompatible network

Turing machine /'tjʊərɪŋ məˌʃiːn/ *noun* a mathematical model of a device which could read and write data to a controllable tape storage while altering its internal states

Turing test /'tjʊərɪŋ test/ *noun* a test to decide if a computer is 'intelligent'

turnaround document /'tɜːnəˌraʊnd ˌdɒkjʊmənt/ *noun* a document which is printed out from a computer, sent to a user and returned by the user with new notes or information written on it, which can be read by a document reader

turnaround time /'tɜːnəraʊnd ˌtaɪm/ *noun* **1.** the length of time it takes to switch data flow direction in a half duplex system **2.** the time taken to activate a program and produce the result which the user has asked for (*US*) ▶ abbr **TAT**

turnkey system /'tɜːnkiː ˌsɪstəm/ *noun* a complete system which is designed to a customer's needs and is ready to use (NOTE: To operate it, the user only has to switch it on or turn a key.)

turtle /'tɜːt(ə)l/ *noun* a device whose movements and position are controllable, used to draw graphics with instructions in the computer language LOGO (NOTE: It is either a device which works on a flat surface (floor turtle) or one which draws on a VDU screen (screen turtle), and is often used as a teaching aid.)

turtle graphics /'tɜːt(ə)l ˌɡræfɪks/ *plural noun* graphic images created using a turtle and a series of commands ○ *The charts were prepared using turtle graphics.*

TV /ˌtiː 'viː/ *abbr* television

TV-out /ˌtiː 'viː aʊt/ *noun* a connector on a computer or graphics adapter that provides a modulated signal that can be displayed on a standard television or recorded on a video recorder

TWAIN /tweɪn/ *noun* an application programming interface standard developed by Hewlett-Packard, Logitech, Eastman Kodak, Aldus, and Caere that allows software to control image hardware

tweak /twiːk/ *verb* to make small adjustments to a program or hardware to improve performance

tweening /'twiːnɪŋ/ *noun* (*in computer graphics*) the process of calculating the intermediate images that lead from a starting image to a different finished image ○ *Using tweening, we can show how a frog turns into a princess in five steps.*

24/96 /ˌtwenti fɔː ˌnaɪnti 'sɪks/ popular standard for high-performance digital audio equipment that provides 24-bit samples and a sample rate of 96KHz

24-bit sample /ˌtwenti fɔː bɪt 'saːmp(ə)l/ *noun* single sample of an analogue signal which is stored as three bytes (a 24-bit digital number), meaning that there are 16,777,216 possible levels. ◊ **8-bit sample, 16-bit sample**

twisted-pair cable /ˌtwɪstɪd peə 'keɪb(ə)l/ *noun* a cable which consists of two insulated copper wires twisted around each other, to reduce induction and so interference

COMMENT: The EIA specifies five levels of cable for different purposes. The Category 1 standard defines an older-style unshielded twisted-pair cable that is formed by loosely twisting two insulated wires together to reduce noise and interference; this type of cable is not suitable for data transmission. The Category 2 (part of the EIA/TIA 568 specification) standard defines a type of unshielded twisted-pair cable that can be used to transmit data at rates up to 4MHz. The Category 3 (part of the EIA/TIA 568 specification) standard defines a type of unshielded twisted-pair cable that can be used to transmit data at rates up to 10MHz; this type of cable is the minimum standard of cable required for a 10BaseT network. The standard suggests that the cable should have three twists per foot of cable. The Category 4 (part of the EIA/TIA 568 specification) standard defines a type of unshielded twisted-pair cable that is the minimum standard of cable required for data transmission rates up to 16Mbit/second on a Token Ring network. The Category 5 (part of the EIA/TIA 568 specification) standard defines a type of cable that can carry data transmitted at up to 100MHz and is suitable for FDDI over copper wire, 100BaseT or other high-speed networks.

twisted-pair Ethernet /ˌtwɪstɪd peə 'iːθənet/ *noun* a star-topology network that uses twisted-pair cable and transmits data at 10 Mbps;. Also called **10BaseT**

two-address instruction /ˌtuː əˈdres ɪnˌstrʌkʃən/ *noun* an instruction format containing the location of two operands, the result being stored in one of the operand locations

2D /ˌtuː 'diː/ object in a graphic image that has only the appearance of width and height, not depth, so does not look like a solid object

two-dimensional /ˌtuː daɪ'menʃən(ə)l/ *adjective* which has two dimensions, i.e. flat, with no depth

two-dimensional array /ˌtuː daɪ ˌmenʃ(ə)nəl ə'reɪ/ *noun* an ordered structure whose elements are arranged as a table of rows and columns

two-input adder /ˌtuː ˌɪnpʊt 'ædə/ *adjective* ♦ **half adder**

two-level subroutine /ˌtuː ˌlev(ə)l 'sʌbruːtiːn/ *noun* a subroutine containing another subroutine

two-part /tuː pɑːt/ *noun* referring to paper with a top sheet for the original and a second sheet for a copy ○ *two-part invoices*

two-pass assembler /ˌtuː pɑːs ə 'semblə/ *noun* an assembler which converts an assembly language program into machine code in two passes (NOTE: The first pass stores symbolic addresses, the second converts them to absolute addresses.)

two-phase commit /ˌtuː feɪz kə'mɪt/ *noun* (*in a database*) a function that ensures that each step of a transaction is correct and valid before committing the changes to the database

two-plus-one-address instruction /tuː plʌs wʌn ə'dres/, **two-plus-one instruction** /tuː plʌs wʌn/ *noun* an instruction containing locations of two operands and an address for the storage of the result

two's complement /'tuːz ˌkɒmplɪmənt/ *noun* a complement formed by adding one to the one's complement of a binary number, often used to represent negative binary numbers

TX *abbr* transmitter

type /taɪp/ *noun* **1.** printed characters on a page ○ *they switched to italic type for the heading* **2.** the definition of the processes or sorts of data which a variable in a computer can contain ■ *verb* to enter information via a keyboard ○ *I typed in the command again, but it still didn't work.* (NOTE: **types – typing – typed**)

Type 1 /taɪp wʌn/ *noun* a set of four wires arranged as two pairs of solid wires surrounded by a braided shield to reduce interference

Type 2 /taɪp tuː/ *noun* a set of twelve wires arranged as six pairs of wire, used for voice transmission

Type 3 /taɪp 'θriː/ *noun* a twisted pair of wires, used for telephone wire

Type 5 /taɪp 'faɪv/ *noun* 100–140 micron diameter fibre optic cable

Type 6 /ˌtaɪp 'sɪks/ *noun* a set of four separate wires arranged as two pairs, with each wire made up of strands of fine wire

Type 8 /taɪp eɪt/ *noun* a set of four separate wires arranged as two pairs, forming shielded cable with no twists

Type cable /taɪp 'keɪb(ə)l/ *noun* a specification for cables defined by IBM

typeface /'taɪpˌfeɪs/ *noun* a set of characters in a particular design and particular weight ○ *Most of this book is set in the Times typeface.*

typesetter /'taɪpˌsetə/ *noun* a machine which produces very high-quality text output using a laser to create an image on photosensitive paper, usually at a resolution of 1275 or 2450 dpi

type size /taɪp saɪz/ *noun* the size of a font, measured in points

type style /taɪp staɪl/ *noun* the weight and angle of a font, e.g. bold or italic

U

UA /ˌjuː ˈeɪ/ *noun* (*in an X.400 email system*) software that ensures a mail message has the correct header information and then delivers it to the message transfer agent which sends the message to its destination. Full form **user agent**

UART /ˈjuːɑːt/ *noun* a chip which converts asynchronous serial bit streams to a parallel form or parallel data to a serial bit stream. Full form **universal asynchronous receiver/transmitter**

UART controller /ˈjuːɑːt kənˌtrəʊlə/ *noun* a circuit that uses a UART to convert serial data from a terminal into a parallel form, then transmits it over a network

UBC *abbr* universal block channel

UDP /ˌjuː diː ˈpiː/ *noun* a protocol that is part of TCP/IP that is often used in network management and SNMP applications. Full form **user datagram protocol**

UHF /ˌjuː eɪtʃ ˈef/ *noun* a range of frequencies normally used to transmit television signals. Full form **ultra high frequency**

ULA /ˌjuː el ˈeɪ/ *noun* a chip containing a number of unconnected logic circuits and gates which can then be connected by a customer to provide a required function. Full form **uncommitted logic array**

ulaw /ˈjuːlɔː/ *noun* a method of encoding digital sound samples so that an 8-bit word can store a 14-bit sound sample

Ultimedia /ˌʌltiˈmɪdiə/ a trade name for a multimedia concept developed by IBM that combines sound, video, images and text, and defines the hardware required to run it

ultra- /ˈʌltrə/ *prefix* very large

Ultra-2 SCSI /ˌʌltrə ˈtuː es siː es ˌaɪ/ *noun* an extension to the SCSI hard disk interface that supports either 8-bit data transfers at a rate of 40 Mbits/second or 16-bit data transfers at a rate of 80 Mbits/second (NOTE: This standard can support 15 devices.)

Ultra ATA /ˌʌltrə eɪ tiː ˈeɪ/ *noun* a version of the AT Attachment hard disk drive interface standard that can support a data transfer rate of up to 33 MBps (NOTE: To manage this high-speed data transfer from the hard disk interface to the rest of your PC, it needs to have a high-speed version of DMA.)

ultra high frequency /ˌʌltrə haɪ ˈfriːkwənsi/ *noun* full form of **UHF**

Ultra SCSI /ˌʌltrə es siː es ˈaɪ/ *noun* an extension to the SCSI hard disk interface that supports either 8-bit data transfers at a rate of 20 Mbits/second or 16-bit data transfers at a rate of 40 Mbits/second (NOTE: This standard can support 15 devices.)

ultraviolet erasable PROM /ˌʌltrə ˌvaɪələt ɪˌreɪzəb(ə)l ˈpiː rɒm/ *noun* an EPROM whose contents are erased by exposing to UV light

ultraviolet light /ˌʌltrəvaɪələt ˈlaɪt/ *noun* full form of **UV light**

UMTS /ˌjuː em tiː ˈes/ *noun* a third generation mobile communication system that supports voice data, and video signals to the handset. Full form **universal mobile telecommunications system**

unallowable digit /ˌʌnəˌlaʊəb(ə)l ˈdɪdʒɪt/ *noun* an illegal combination of bits in a word, according to predefined rules

unarchive /ʌnˈɑːkaɪv/ *verb* to retrieve a computer file from an archive where it has been stored (NOTE: **unarchives – unarchiving – unarchived**)

unary operation /ˌjuːnəri ˌɒpə ˈreɪʃ(ə)n/ *noun* a computing operation on only one operand, e.g. the logical NOT operation

unattended operation /ˌʌnətendɪd ˌɒpəˈreɪʃ(ə)n/ *noun* an operation that can proceed without the need for a person to supervise

unauthorised /ʌnˈɔːθəraɪzd/, **unauthorized** *adjective* which has not been authorised ○ *The use of a password is to prevent unauthorised access to the data.*

unbundled software /ʌnˌbʌnd(ə)ld ˈsɒftweə/ *noun* software which is not included in the price of the equipment

unclocked /ʌnˈklɒkd/ *adjective* referring to an electronic circuit or flip-flop which changes state as soon as an input changes, not with a clock signal

uncommitted logic array /ˌʌnkəmɪtɪd ˈlɒdʒɪk əˌreɪ/ *noun* full form of **ULA**

uncommitted storage list /ˌʌnkəmɪtɪd ˈstɔːrɪdʒ ˌlɪst/ *noun* a table of the areas of memory in a system that are free or have not been allocated

unconditional /ˌʌnkənˈdɪʃ(ə)nəl/ *adjective* which does not depend on any condition being met

unconditional branch /ˌʌnkən ˈdɪʃ(ə)nəl brɑːntʃ/, **unconditional jump** /ˌʌnkənˈdɪʃ(ə)nəl dʒʌmp/, **unconditional transfer** *noun* an instruction which transfers control from one point in the program to another, without depending on any condition being met

uncorrupted /ˌʌnkəˈrʌptɪd/ *adjective* referring to a computer file or database that is free of errors or viruses

undelete /ˈʌndɪliːt/ *verb* to restore deleted information or a deleted file ○ *Don't worry, this function will undelete your cuts to the letter.* (NOTE: **undeletes – undeleting – undeleted**)

underflow /ˈʌndəfləʊ/ *noun* the result of a numerical operation that is too small to be represented with the given accuracy of a computer

underline *noun* a line drawn or printed under a piece of text. Also called **underscore** ■ *verb* to print or write a line under a piece of text (NOTE: **underlines – underlining – underlined**)

underlining /ˌʌndəˈlaɪnɪŋ/ *noun* a word-processing command which underlines text

underscore /ˈʌndəskɔː/ *noun, verb* same as **underline** (NOTE: **underscores – underscoring – underscored**)

undetected error /ˌʌndɪtektɪd ˈerə/ *noun* an error which is not detected by a coding system

undo /ʌnˈduː/ *verb* to reverse the previous action, normally an editing command ○ *You've just deleted the paragraph, but you can undo it from the option in the Edit menu.* (NOTE: **undoes – undoing – undid**)

unedited /ʌnˈedɪtɪd/ *adjective* which has not been edited

unformatted /ʌnˈfɔːmætɪd/ *adjective* **1.** referring to a text file which contains no formatting commands, margins or typographical commands ○ *It is impossible to copy to an unformatted disk.* **2.** referring to a disk which has not been formatted ○ *The cartridge drive provides 12.7Mbyte of unformatted storage.*

unformatted capacity /ʌnˌfɔːmætɪd kəˈpæsɪti/ *noun* the capacity of a magnetic disk before it has been formatted

unformatted disk /ʌnˌfɔːmætɪd ˈdɪsk/ *noun* a magnetic disk which has not been formatted (NOTE: Disks must be formatted before use.)

ungroup /ʌnˈgruːp/ *verb* to convert a single complex object back into a series of separate objects

uni- /juːni/ *prefix* one or single

unicast /ˈjuːnikɑːst/ *noun* a transmission from a single computing terminal to one other terminal

uniform resource locator /ˌjuːnifɔːm rɪˈzɔːs ləʊˌkeɪtə/ *noun* full form of **URL**

uninstall /ˌʌnɪnˈstɑːl/ *verb* to remove a piece of software from a computer

uninterruptible power supply /ˌʌnɪntərʌptɪb(ə)l ˈpaʊə səˌplaɪ/ *noun* full form of **UPS**

union /ˈjuːnjən/ *noun* a logical function which produces a true output if any input is true

unipolar /ˌjuːniˈpəʊlə/ *adjective* **1.** (*referring to a transistor*) which can act as a variable current flow control (NOTE: An external signal varies the resistance of the device.) **2.** referring to a transmission system in which a positive voltage pulse and zero volts represents the binary bits 1 and 0

unipolar signal /juːniˌpəʊlə ˈsɪgn(ə)l/ *noun* a signal that uses only positive voltage levels

unique identifier /juːˌniːk aɪ ˈdentɪfaɪə/ *noun* a set of characters used to distinguish between different resources in a multimedia book

unit /ˈjuːnɪt/ *noun* **1.** the smallest element **2.** a single machine, possibly with many different parts

unit buffer /'juːnɪt ˌbʌfə/ *noun* a buffer which is one character long (NOTE: Usually used to mean that there are no buffering facilities)

unit record /'juːnɪt ˌrekɔːd/ *noun* a single record of information

universal /ˌjuːnɪ'vɜːs(ə)l/ *adjective* which applies everywhere or which can be used everywhere or used for a number of tasks

universal asynchronous receiver/transmitter /ˌjuːnɪvɜːsəl ˌeɪsɪŋkrənəs rɪˌsiːvə trænz'mɪtə/ *noun* full form of **UART**

universal block channel /ˌjuːnɪvɜːs(ə)l 'blɒk ˌtʃæn(ə)l/ *noun* a communications channel allowing high speed transfer of blocks of data to and from high speed peripherals. Abbr **UBC**

universal device /ˌjuːnɪvɜːs(ə)l dɪ'vaɪs/ *noun* **1.** same as **UART 2.** same as **USRT 3.** same as **USART**

universal mobile telecommunications system /ˌjuːnɪvɜːs(ə)l ˌməʊbaɪl ˌtelikəmjuːnɪ'keɪʃ(ə)nz ˌsɪstəm/ *noun* full form of **UMTS**

universal product code /ˌjuːnɪvɜːs(ə)l 'prɒdʌkt ˌkəʊd/ *noun* a standard printed bar coding system used to identify products in a shop using a bar code reader or at a EPOS. Abbr **UPC**

universal programming /ˌjuːnɪvɜːs(ə)l 'prəʊgræmɪŋ/ *noun* the writing of a program which is not specific to one machine, so that it can run on several machines

universal resource locator /ˌjuːnɪvɜːs(ə)l rɪ'zɔːs ləʊˌkeɪtə/ *noun* full form of **URL**

universal serial bus /ˌjuːnɪvɜːs(ə)l 'sɪəriəl ˌbʌs/ *noun* full form of **USB**

universal set /ˌjuːnɪ'vɜːs(ə)l set/ *noun* a complete set of elements which conform to a set of rules ○ *The universal set of prime numbers less than 10 and greater than 2 is 3,5,7.*

universal synchronous asynchronous receiver/transmitter /ˌjuːnɪvɜːsəl ˌsɪŋkrənəs ˌeɪsɪŋkrənəs rɪˌsiːvə trænz'mɪtə/ *noun* full form of **USART**

universal synchronous receiver/transmitter /ˌjuːnɪvɜːs(ə)l ˌsɪŋkrənəs rɪˌsiːvə træns'mɪtə/ *noun* full form of **USRT**

UNIX /'juːnɪks/ *noun* a popular multiuser, multitasking operating system devel-oped by AT&T Bell Laboratories to run on almost any computer, from PCs to minicomputers and large mainframes

'Hampshire fire brigade is investing £2 million in a command and control system based on the new SeriesFT fault-tolerant Unix machine from Motorola.' [*Computing*]

UNIX-to-UNIX copy /ˌjuːnɪks tə ˌjuːnɪks 'kɒpi/ *noun* a software utility that helps make it easier for a user to copy data from one computer running UNIX via a serial link to another computer running UNIX. Abbr **UUCP**

unjustified /ʌn'dʒʌstɪfaɪd/ *adjective* referring to text which has not been justified

unjustified tape /ʌn'dʒʌstɪˌfaɪd teɪp/ *noun* a tape containing unformatted text, which cannot be printed until formatting data such as justification, line width and page size has been added by a computer

unlock /ʌn'lɒk/ *verb* to make it possible for other users to write to a file or access a system

unmoderated list /ʌnˌmɒdəreɪtɪd 'lɪst/ *noun* a mailing list that sends any material submitted to the listserv on to all the subscribers without a person reading or checking the content

unmodified instruction /ʌn ˌmɒdɪfaɪd ɪn'strʌkʃən/ *noun* a program instruction which is directly processed without modification to obtain the operation to be performed

unmodulated /ʌn'mɒdjʊleɪtɪd/ *adjective* referring to a signal which has not been modulated

unmount /ʌn'maʊnt/ *verb* **1.** to remove a disk from a disk drive **2.** to inform the operating system that a disk drive is no longer in active use

unpack /ʌn'pæk/ *verb* to remove packed data from storage and expand it to its former state ○ *This routine unpacks the archived file.*

unplug /ʌn'plʌg/ *verb* to take a plug out of a socket ○ *Do not move the system without unplugging it.* (NOTE: **unplugging – unplugged**)

unpopulated /ʌn'pɒpjʊleɪtɪd/ *adjective* referring to a printed circuit board which does not yet contain any components or whose sockets are empty

unprotected /ˌʌnprə'tektɪd/ *adjective* referring to data which can be modified and is not protected by a security measure

unprotected field /ˌʌnprəˈtektɪd fiːlⁿd/ *noun* a section of a computer display that a user can modify

unrecoverable error /ʌnrɪˌkʌvərəb(ə)l ˈerə/ *noun* a computer hardware or software error which causes a program to crash

unshielded twisted-pair cable /ˌʌnʃiːldɪd ˌtwɪstɪd ˈpeə ˌkeɪb(ə)l/ *noun* full form of **UTP cable**

unsigned /ʌnˈsaɪnd/ *adjective* referring to a number system which does not represent negative numbers

unsolicited mail /ˌʌnsəˈlɪsɪtɪd meɪl/ *noun* an advertising email message that has not been requested. ◊ **spam** (NOTE: Do not send out unsolicited mail to unknown email addresses unless you want to annoy the recipients and damage your company's reputation)

unsorted /ʌnˈsɔːtɪd/ *adjective* referring to data which has not been sorted ○ *It took four times as long to search the unsorted file.*

unsubscribe /ˌʌnsəbˈskraɪb/ *verb* to cancel a subscription to or registration with something, especially an email mailing list (NOTE: **unsubscribes – unsubscribing – unsubscribed**)

'All commercial messages will have to include full details of the sender's name and physical address, as well as an unsubscribe option allowing recipients to stop any further messages.' [*The Guardian*]

unsupported /ˌʌnsəˈpɔːtɪd/ *adjective* having no technical support system

unzip /ʌnˈzɪp/ *verb* to restore a compressed computer file to its original size (NOTE: **unzipping – unzipped**)

up /ʌp/ *adverb* referring to a computer or program that is working or running ○ *They must have found the fault – the computer is finally up and running.*

UPC *abbr* universal product code

up conversion /ʌp kənˈvɜːʃ(ə)n/ *noun* same as **scan conversion**

update *noun* /ˈʌpdeɪt/ **1.** a master file which has been made up -to date by adding new material **2.** a piece of printed information which is an up-to-date revision of earlier information **3.** a new version of a system which is sent to users of the existing system ■ *verb* /ʌpˈdeɪt/ to change or add to specific data in a master file so as to make the information up -to date ○ *He has the original and updated documents on disks.* (NOTE: **updates – updating – updated**)

update file /ʌpˈdeɪt faɪl/ *noun* a file containing recent changes or transactions to records which is used to update the master file. Also called **detail file, transaction file**

up/down counter /ʌp ˈdaʊn ˌkaʊntə/ *noun* an electronic counter which can increment or decrement a counter with each input pulse

upgrade /ʌpˈgreɪd/ *verb* to make a system more powerful or more up -to-date by adding new equipment or facilities ○ *They can upgrade the printer.* (NOTE: **upgrades – upgrading – upgraded**)

upkeep /ˈʌpkiːp/ *noun* the process of keeping data up-to-date ○ *The upkeep of the files means reviewing them every six months.*

uplink /ˈʌplɪŋk/ *noun* a transmission link from an earth station to a satellite

upload /ˈʌpˌləʊd/ *verb* **1.** to transfer data files or programs from a small computer to a main CPU ○ *The user can upload PC data to update mainframe applications.* **2.** to transfer a file from one computer to a BBS or host computer ○ *The image can be manipulated before it is uploaded to the host computer.* ▶ opposite **download**

uppercase /ˌʌpəˈkeɪs/ *noun* the style of capital letters and other symbols on a keyboard which are accessed by pressing the shift key

upper memory /ˌʌpə ˈmem(ə)ri/ *noun* (*in an IBM PC*) 384 Kb of memory located between the 640 Kb and 1 Mb limits, after the 640 Kb conventional memory but before the high memory areas above the 1 Mb range

UPS /ˌju: pi: ˈes/ *noun* a power supply which can continue to provide a regulated supply to equipment even after a mains power failure, using a battery. Full form **uninterruptible power supply**

'Magnum Power Systems has launched a new UPS for PCs. The BI-UPS prevents loss of data due to power dips or 'brown-outs' – voltage drops because of circuit overload.' [*Computing*]

uptime, up time *noun* the time during which a device is operational and error-free. Opposite **downtime**

upward compatible, upwards compatible *adjective* referring to hardware or software designed to be compatible either with earlier models or with future models which have not yet been developed

URL /ˌju: ɑː ˈel/ *noun* an Internet system used to standardise the way in which World Wide Web addresses are written;

made up of three parts: the first is the protocol (such as HTTP or FTP), then the domain name of the service and finally the directory or file name ○ *The URL of the Bloomsbury Publishing home page is 'http://www.bloomsbury.com'*. Full form **uniform resource locator**

COMMENT: It is made up of three parts: the first is the protocol, e.g. HTTP or FTP, then the domain name of the service and finally the directory or file name – 'http://www.bloomsbury.com/index.html'

usability /ˌjuːzəˈbɪlɪti/ *noun* the ease with which hardware or software can be used ○ *We have studied usability tests and found that a GUI is easier for new users than a command line.*

USART /ˈjuːzɑːt/ *noun* a chip which can be instructed by a CPU to communicate with asynchronous or synchronous bit streams or parallel data lines. Full form **universal synchronous asynchronous receiver-transmitter**

USASCII /ˌjuː es ˈæskiː/ *abbr* USA standard code for information interchange. ♦ **ASCII**

USB /ˌjuː es ˈbiː/ *noun* a standard defining a high-speed serial interface that transfers data at up to 12Mbps and allows up to 127 compatible peripherals to be connected to a computer. Full form **universal serial bus**. ♦ **Firewire**

Usenet /ˈjuːzˌnet/ *noun* a section of the Internet that provides forums, called newsgroups, in which any user can add a message or comment on any other message

user /ˈjuːzə/ *noun* **1.** a person who uses a computer, machine or software **2.** a keyboard operator

'...the user's guides are designed for people who have never seen a computer, but some sections have been spoiled by careless checking' [*PC User*]

user account /ˈjuːzə əˌkaʊnt/ *noun* (*in a network or multiuser system*) a record which identifies a user, contains his or her password and holds his or her rights to use resources ○ *I have a new user account on this LAN but I cannot remember my password.*

user agent /ˈjuːzə ˌeɪdʒənt/ *noun* full form of **UA**

user area /ˈjuːzə ˌeəriə/ *noun* a part of memory which is available for the user, and does not contain the operating system

user datagram protocol /ˌjuːzə ˈdeɪtəɡræm ˌprəʊtəkɒl/ *noun* full form of **UDP**

user-definable /ˈjuːzə dɪˌfaɪnəb(ə)l/ *adjective* referring to a feature or section of a program that a user can customise as required ○ *The style sheet contains 125 user-definable symbols.*

user-defined character /ˌjuːzə dɪˌfaɪnd ˈkærɪktə/ *plural noun* a character which is created by the user and added to the standard character set

user documentation /ˌjuːzə ˌdɒkjʊmenˈteɪʃ(ə)n/ *noun* documentation provided with a program which helps the user run it ○ *Using the package was easy with the excellent user documentation.*

user-friendly /ˌjuːzə ˈfrendli/ *adjective* referring to a language, system or program which is easy to use and interact with

'ModelMaker saves researchers a great deal of time and effort, and provides a highly user-friendly environment using menus and 'buttons', instant output, and instant access to a wide variety of mathematical techniques built into the system.' [*Computing*]

user-friendly software /ˌjuːzə ˌfrendli ˈsɒftweə/ *noun* a program which is easy for a nonexpert to use and interact with

user group /ˈjuːzə ɡruːp/ *noun* an association or club of users of a particular system or computer ○ *I found how to solve the problem by asking people at the user group meeting.*

user guide /ˈjuːzə ɡaɪd/ *noun* a manual describing how to use a software package or system

user ID /ˌjuːzə aɪ ˈdiː/ *noun* a unique identification code which allows a computer to recognise a user ○ *If you forget your user ID, you will not be able to log on.*

user interface /ˈjuːzə ˌɪntəfeɪs/ *noun* hardware or software designed to make it easier for a user to communicate with a machine

user level /ˈjuːzə ˌlev(ə)l/ *noun* (*in authoring software*) one of two modes that allows a user to run and interact with a multimedia application but not to modify it in any way

user name /ˈjuːzə neɪm/ *noun* (*in a network or multi-user system*) a name by which a user is known to the system and which opens the correct user account

user-operated language /ˌjuːzə ˌɒpəreɪtɪd ˈlæŋɡwɪdʒ/ *noun* a high-level programming language which allows certain problems or procedures to be easily expressed

user port /'juːzə pɔːt/ *noun* a socket which allows peripherals to be connected to a computer

user program /'juːzə ˌprəʊɡræm/ *noun* a program written by a user, often in a high-level language

user-selectable /ˌjuːzə sɪˈlektəb(ə)l/ *adjective* which can be chosen or selected by the user

user's manual /'juːzəz ˌmænjʊəl/ *noun* a booklet showing how a device or system should be used

user's program /'juːzəz ˌprəʊɡræm/ *noun* a computer software written by a user rather than a manufacturer

USRT /ˌjuː es ɑː 'tiː/ *noun* a single integrated circuit which can carry out all the serial to parallel and interfacing operations required between a computer and transmission line. Full form **universal synchronous receiver/transmitter**

utility program /juːˈtɪlɪti ˌprəʊɡræm/ *noun* a program which is concerned with such routine activities as file searching, copying files, file directories, sorting and debugging and various mathematical functions

UTP cable /ˌjuː tiː 'piː ˌkeɪb(ə)l/ *noun* a cable consisting of two insulated copper wires twisted around each other, to reduce induction and so interference. Full form **unshielded twisted-pair cable**

COMMENT: UTP is normally used for telephone cabling, but is also the cabling used in the IEEE 802.3 (10BaseT) standard that defines Ethernet running over UTP at rates of up to 10 Mbits per second. Unlike STP cable, the pair of wires are not wrapped in any other layer.

UUCP *abbr* Unix-to-Unix copy

Uuencoding /ˌjuː juː ɪnˈkəʊdɪŋ/ *noun* a method of converting documents and files to a pseudo-text format that allows them to be transmitted as an email message

COMMENT: This gets around the Internet's inability to transfer messages that are not text. It has now been largely replaced by MIME.

V

V *abbr* voltage

V20 *noun* a range of processor chips made by NEC, which are compatible with the Intel 8088 and 8086. Also called **V30**

V.21 *noun* an outdated full duplex communications standard at 300 baud (NOTE: In the USA, the Bell 103 standard was used instead.)

V.22 *noun* a half-duplex communication standard at 1,200 bps (NOTE: In the USA, the Bell 212A standard was more commonly used.)

V.22bis *noun* a full-duplex modem communication standard transferring data at up to 2,400 bps

V.29 *noun* a half-duplex modem communication standard transferring data at up to 9,600 bps (NOTE: This standard is generally used by fax modems.)

V30 *noun* ♦ V20

V.32 *noun* a full-duplex modem communication standard that can transfer data at up to 9,600 bps but can also automatically adjust its speed based on the quality of the telephone line, in order to avoid errors

V.32bis *noun* a protocol similar to the V.32 protocol but able to transfer data at rates up to 14,400 bps.

V.42 *noun* an error-detection system that can be used to reduce errors due to poor telephone line quality. ♦ **MNP**

V.42bis *noun* a data compression system that increases the data transfer rate up to 34,000 bps

V.90 *noun* a full-duplex modem data communication standard at up to 56,600 bps

vaccine /'væksiːn/ *noun* a software utility used to check a system to see if any viruses are present, and remove any that are found

valid /'vælɪd/ *adjective* correct, according to a set of rules

validate /'vælɪˌdeɪt/ *verb* to check that an input or data is correct according to a set of rules (NOTE: **validates – validating – validated**)

validation /ˌvælɪ'deɪʃ(ə)n/ *noun* a check performed to validate data. ◊ **verification**

validity /və'lɪdɪti/ *noun* the correctness of an instruction or password

validity check /və'lɪdəti tʃek/ *noun* a check that data or results are realistic

valid memory address /ˌvælɪd 'mem(ə)ri əˌdres/ *noun* a signal on a control bus indicating that an address is available on the address bus

value /'væljuː/ *noun* what something is worth, either in money or as a quantity

value-added /ˌvæljuː 'ædɪd/ *adjective* (with extra benefit for a user)

value-added network /ˌvæljuː ˌædɪd 'netwɜːk/ *noun* a commercial network which offers information services, e.g. stock prices, weather, email or advice, as well as basic file transfer. Abbr **VAN**

value-added reseller /ˌvæljuː ædɪd 'riːselə/ *noun* a company that buys hardware or software and adds another feature, customises or offers an extra service to attract customers. Abbr **VAR**

VAN /væn/ *abbr* value-added network

V & V /ˌviː ənd 'viː/ *noun* the process of testing a system to check that it is functioning correctly and that it is suitable for the tasks intended. Full form **verification and validation**

vanishing point perspective /'vænɪʃɪŋ pɔɪnt pəˌspektɪv/ *noun* graphics displayed in two dimensions that have the appearance of depth as all lines converge at a vanishing point and objects appear smaller as they are further from the user

vapourware /'veɪpəweə/ *noun* products which exist in name only (*informal*)

'Rivals dismissed the initiative as IBM vapourware, designed to protect its installed base of machines running under widely differing operating systems.' [*Computing*]

VAR *abbr* value-added reseller

variable /'veəriəb(ə)l/ *adjective* which is able to change ■ *noun* a register or storage location which can contain any number or characters and which may vary during the program run. Opposite **constant**

variable data /ˌveəriəb(ə)l 'deɪtə/ *noun* data which can be modified, and is not write protected

variable data rate video /ˌveəriəb(ə)l ˌdeɪtə reɪt 'vɪdiəʊ/ *noun* full form of **VDRV**

variable data type /ˌveəriəb(ə)l 'deɪtə ˌtaɪp/ *noun* a variable that can contain any sort of data, e.g. numerical or text

variable format /ˌveəriəb(ə)l 'fɔːmæt/ *noun* a changing method of arranging data or text within an area

variable length record /ˌveəriəb(ə)l leŋθ 'rekɔːd/ *noun* a record which can be of any length

variable name /'veəriəb(ə)l neɪm/ *noun* a word used to identify a variable in a program

variable word length computer /ˌveəriəb(ə)l wɜːd leŋθ kəm'pjuːtə/ *noun* a computer in which the number of bits which make up a word is variable, and varies according to the type of data

VB *abbr* Visual Basic

VBA *abbr* Visual Basic for Applications

Vbox /'viːbɒks/ *noun* a device that allows several VCRs, videodiscs and camcorders to be attached and controlled by one unit, developed by Sony. Full form **video box**

VBScript /viː 'biː ˌskrɪpt/ *abbr* Visual Basic Script. Compare **JavaScript**

VBX *abbr* Visual Basic Extension (NOTE: Originally developed as a way of adding extra programming features to the Microsoft VB programming language, it is now a standard that can be used by many Windows programming tools; a VBX can be used in 16-bit or 32-bit Windows (versions 3.x or 95) whereas an OCX control will only work with 32-bit Windows (version 95 and later).)

VCR /ˌviː siː 'ɑː/ *noun* a machine that can record analog video signals onto a magnetic cassette tape and play back the tape to display video on a monitor. Full form **video cassette recorder**

COMMENT: The most popular formats are: 1-inch tape, used for studio-quality mastering; 3/4-inch tape, which was widely used but has now been mostly replaced by 1/2-inch tape; 1/2-inch VHS format tape, which was first used only in the home but has now mostly replaced 3/4-inch tape; 1/2-inch Beta format tape, which was the first home VCR format but is no longer used. Some VCRs can be used to store digital data for data backup.

VDRV /ˌviː diː ɑː 'viː/ *noun* a digital video system that can adjust the amount of data used to represent each different frame and so adjust image quality or stay within bandwidth limits. Full form **variable data rate video**

VDU /ˌviː diː 'juː/ *noun* a terminal with a screen and a keyboard, on which text or graphics can be viewed and information entered. Full form **visual display unit**

vector /'vektə/ *noun* **1.** the address which directs a computer to a new memory location **2.** a coordinate that consists of a magnitude and direction

vectored interrupt /ˌvektəd 'ɪntərʌpt/ *noun* an interrupt signal which directs the processor to a routine at a particular address

vector font /'vektə fɒnt/ *noun* the shape of characters within a font that are drawn vector graphics, allowing the characters to be scaled to almost any size without changing the quality

vector graphics /'vektə ˌɡræfɪks/, **vector image** *noun* a system of drawing objects using curves and lines. Also called **vector scan**

COMMENT: The images are described by line length and direction from an origin to plot lines and so build up an image rather than a description of each pixel, as in a bitmap. A vector image can be easily and accurately resized with no loss of detail.

vector processor /'vektə ˌprəʊsesə/ *noun* a coprocessor that operates on one row or column of an array at a time

Veitch diagram /'vaɪtʃ ˌdaɪəɡræm/ *noun* a graphical representation of a truth table

vendor /'vendə/ *noun* a person who manufactures, sells or supplies hardware or software products

vendor-independent /ˌvendə ˌɪndɪ 'pendənt/ *adjective* referring to hardware or software that will work with hardware and software manufactured by other vendors

vendor-independent messaging /ˌvendə ˌɪndɪpendənt 'mesɪdʒɪŋ/ *noun* full form of **VIM**

Venn diagram /'ven ˌdaɪəɡræm/ *noun* a graphical representation of the relationships between the states in a system or circuit

verification /ˌverɪfɪ'keɪʃ(ə)n/ *noun* the process of checking that data has been keyboarded correctly or that data transferred from one medium to another has been transferred correctly

verification and validation /ˌverɪfɪkeɪʃ(ə)n ən ˌvælɪ'deɪʃ(ə)n/ *noun* full form of **V & V**

verifier /'verɪfaɪə/ *noun* a special device for verifying input data

verify /'verɪˌfaɪ/ *verb* to check that data recorded or entered is correct (NOTE: **verifies – verifying – verifies**)

Veronica /və'rɒnɪkə/ a tool that works with Gopher to help a user find information or files on the World Wide Web

version /'vɜːʃ(ə)n/ *noun* a copy or program or statement which is slightly different from others ○ *The latest version of the software includes an improved graphics routine.*

version control /'vɜːʃ(ə)n kənˌtrəʊl/ *noun* a utility software that allows several programmers to work on a source file and monitors the changes that have been made by each programmer

version number /'vɜːʃ(ə)n ˌnʌmbə/ *noun* the number of the version of a product

vertex /'vɜːteks/ *noun* a point in space defined by the three coordinates x, y and z

vertical /'vɜːtɪk(ə)l/ *adjective* at right angles to the horizontal

vertical application /ˌvɜːtɪk(ə)l ˌæplɪ 'keɪʃ(ə)n/ *noun* application software that has been designed for a specific use, rather than for general use ○ *Your new software to manage a florist's is a good vertical application.*

vertical axis /ˌvɜːtɪk(ə)l 'æksɪs/ *noun* a reference line used for vertical coordinates on a graph

vertical blanking interval /ˌvɜːtɪk(ə)l 'blæŋkɪŋ ˌɪntəvəl/ *noun* ♦ **raster**

vertical format unit /ˌvɜːtɪk(ə)l 'fɔːmæt ˌjuːnɪt/ *noun* a part of the control system of a printer which governs the vertical format of the document to be printed, e.g. vertical spacing or page length. Abbr **VFU**

vertical interval time code /ˌvɜːtɪk(ə)l ˌɪntəv(ə)l 'taɪm ˌkəʊd/ *noun* full form of **VITC**

vertical justification /ˌvɜːtɪk(ə)l ˌdʒʌstɪfɪ'keɪʃ(ə)n/ *noun* the adjustment of the spacing between lines of text to fit a section of text into a page

vertically /'vɜːtɪkli/ *adverb* from top to bottom or going up and down at right angles to the horizontal ○ *The page has been justified vertically.*

vertical parity check /ˌvɜːtɪk(ə)l 'pærɪti ˌtʃek/ *noun* an error detection test in which the bits of a word are added and compared with a correct total

vertical portal /ˌvɜːtɪk(ə)l 'pɔːt(ə)l/ *noun* full form of **VORTAL**

vertical redundancy check /ˌvɜːtɪk(ə)l rɪ'dʌndənsi ˌtʃek/ *noun* full form of **VRC**

vertical scan frequency /ˌvɜːtɪk(ə)l 'skæn ˌfriːkwənsi/ *noun* the number of times a picture beam in a monitor moves from the last line back up to the first

vertical scrolling /ˌvɜːtɪk(ə)l 'skrəʊlɪŋ/ *noun* displayed text which moves up or down the computer screen one line at a time

vertical sync signal /ˌvɜːtɪk(ə)l 'sɪŋk ˌsɪgn(ə)l/ *noun* (*in a video signal*) a signal which indicates the end of the last trace at the bottom of the display

vertical tab /ˌvɜːtɪk(ə)l 'tæb/ *noun* the number of lines that should be skipped before printing starts again

very large scale integration /ˌveri lɑːdʒ skeɪl ˌɪntɪ'ɡreɪʃ(ə)n/ *noun* full form of **VLSI**

VESA *abbr* Video Electronics Standards Association

VESA local bus /ˌviː iː es eɪ 'ləʊk(ə)l bʌs/ *noun* full form of **VL-bus**

vestigial side band /vesˌtɪdʒiəl 'saɪd ˌbænd/ *noun* full form of **VSB**

V format /viː 'fɔːmæt/ *noun* data organisation, in which variable length records are stored with a header which contains their length

VFU *abbr* vertical format unit

VFW *abbr* Video for Windows

VGA /ˌviː dʒiː 'eɪ/ *noun* (*in an IBM PC*) a standard of video adapter developed by IBM that can support a display with a resolution up to 640 x 480 pixels in up to 256 colours, superseded by SVGA

VGA feature connector /ˌviː dʒiː eɪ 'fiːtʃə kəˌnektə/ *noun* a 26-pin edge connector or port of a VGA display adapter, usually at the top edge, that allows another device to access its palette information and clock signals

via /'vaɪə/ *preposition* going through something or using something to get to a destination ○ *The signals have reached us via satellite.*

VidCap /'vɪdkæp/ *noun* a utility program used in the Microsoft VFW system to capture a video sequence

video /'vɪdiəʊ/ *noun* text or images or graphics viewed on television or a monitor

video adapter /'vɪdiəʊ əˌdæptə/ *noun* an add-in board which converts data into electrical signals to drive a monitor and display text and graphics. Also called **video board**, **video controller**

video bandwidth /ˌvɪdiəʊ 'bændwɪdθ/ *noun* the maximum display resolution, measured in MHz, and calculated by horizontal x vertical resolution x refreshes/sec (NOTE: TV studio recording is limited to 5 MHz; TV broadcasting is limited to 3.58 MHz)

video board /'vɪdiəʊ bɔːd/ *noun* same as **video adapter**

video buffer /'vɪdiəʊ ˌbʌfə/ *noun* memory in a video adapter that is used to store the bitmap of the image being displayed

video capture board /ˌvɪdiəʊ 'kæptʃə ˌbɔːd/ *noun* a board that plugs into an expansion socket inside a PC and lets a user capture a TV picture and store it in memory so that it can then be processed by a computer

video cassette recorder /ˌvɪdiəʊ kə'set rɪˌkɔːdə/ *noun* full form of **VCR**

video-CD /ˌvɪdiəʊ ˌsiː 'diː/ *noun* a CD-ROM that stores digital video data conforming to the Philips White Book standard and uses MPEG compression for the full-motion video data

video clip *noun* a short video sequence

video codec /ˌvɪdiəʊ 'kəʊdek/ *noun* an electronic device to convert a video signal to or from a digital form

video compression /ˌvɪdiəʊ kəm'preʃ(ə)n/ *noun* algorithms used to compress analog television signals so that they can be efficiently broadcast over a digital channel

video conferencing /'vɪdiəʊ ˌkɒnf(ə)rənsɪŋ/ *noun* the linking of video, audio and computer signals from different locations so that distant people can talk and see each other, as if in a conference room

video controller /ˌvɪdiəʊ kən'trəʊlə/ *noun* same as **video adapter**

video digitiser /ˌvɪdiəʊ ˈdɪdʒɪtaɪzə/ *noun* a high-speed digital sampling circuit which stores a TV picture in memory so that it can then be processed by a computer

videodisc /ˈvɪdiəʊdɪsk/ *noun* a read-only optical disc that can store up to two hours of video data, usually used either to store a complete film, as a rival to video cassette, or to use in an interactive system with text, video and still images (NOTE: For interactive use, a videodisc can store 54,000 frames of information. If the videodisc contains a complete film, the data is recorded using a constant linear velocity format; if it is used to store interactive data, it is stored in a constant angular velocity format.)

video display /ˈvɪdiəʊ dɪˌspleɪ/ *noun* a device which can display text or graphical information, e.g. a CRT

video editing /ˌvɪdiəʊ ˈedɪtɪŋ/ *noun* a method of editing a video sequence in which the video is digitised and stored in a computer

video editor /ˈvɪdiəʊ ˌedɪtə/ *noun* a computer that controls two videotape recorders to allow an operator to play back sequences from one and record these on the second machine

Video Electronics Standards Association /ˌvɪdiəʊ elekˌtrɒnɪks ˈstændədz əˌsəʊsieɪʃ(ə)n/ *noun* full form of **VESA**

Video for Windows /ˌvɪdiəʊ fə ˈwɪndəʊz/ a trade name for a set of software drivers and utilities for Microsoft Windows 3.1, developed by Microsoft, that allows AVI-format video files to be played back in a window. Abbr **VFW**

video game /ˈvɪdiəʊ ɡeɪm/ *noun* a game played on a computer, with action shown on a video display

video graphics array /ˌvɪdiəʊ ˈɡræfɪks əˌreɪ/ *noun* (*in an IBM PC*) a standard of video adapter developed by IBM that can support a display with a resolution up to 640 x 480 pixels in up to 256 colours, superseded by SVGA. Abbr **VGA**

video graphics card /ˌvɪdiəʊ ˈɡræfɪks ˌkɑːd/ *noun* an expansion card that fits into an expansion slot inside a PC and that allows a computer to display both generated text and graphics and moving video images from an external camera or VCR. Also called **overlay card**

video interface chip /ˌvɪdiəʊ ˈɪntəfeɪs ˌtʃɪp/ *noun* a chip which controls a video display allowing information such as text or graphics stored in a computer to be displayed

video lookup table /ˌvɪdiəʊ ˈlʊkʌp ˌteɪb(ə)l/ *noun* a collection of precalculated values of the different colours that are stored in memory and can be examined very quickly to produce an answer without the need to recalculate

video memory /ˌvɪdiəʊ ˈmem(ə)ri/ *noun* a high speed random access memory used to store computer-generated or digitised images

video monitor /ˈvɪdiəʊ ˌmɒnɪtə/ *noun* a device able to display, without sound, signals from a computer

video random access memory /ˌvɪdiəʊ ˌrændəm ˌækses ˈmem(ə)ri/, **video RAM** /ˌvɪdiəʊ ˈræm/ *noun* full form of **VRAM**. same as **video memory**

video scanner /ˈvɪdiəʊ ˌskænə/ *noun* a device which allows images of objects or pictures to be entered into a computer ○ *New video scanners are designed to scan three-dimensional objects.*

video server /ˈvɪdiəʊ ˌsɜːvə/ *noun* a dedicated computer on a network used to store video sequences

video signal /ˈvɪdiəʊ ˌsɪɡn(ə)l/ *noun* a signal which provides line picture information and synchronisation pulses (*informal*)

video system control architecture /ˌvɪdiəʊ ˌsɪstəm kənˈtrəʊl ˌɑːkɪtektʃə/ *noun* full form of **ViSCA**

video tape recorder /ˌvɪdiəʊ ˈteɪp rɪ ˌkɔːdə/ *noun* full form of **VTR**

video teleconferencing /ˌvɪdiəʊ ˈteliˌkɒnf(ə)rənsɪŋ/ *noun* the linking of computers that can capture and display video so that distant people can talk to and see each other, as if in a conference room

video terminal /ˈvɪdiəʊ ˌtɜːmɪn(ə)l/ *noun* a keyboard with a monitor

videotext /ˈvɪdiəʊtekst/, **videotex** /ˈvɪdiəʊteks/ *noun* a system for transmitting text and displaying it on a screen

COMMENT: This covers information transmitted either by TV signals (teletext) *or* by signals sent down telephone lines (viewdata).

video window /ˈvɪdiəʊ ˌwɪndəʊ/ *noun* a window that displays a moving video image, independent of other displayed material

view /vjuː/ *verb* to look at something, especially something displayed on a screen

○ *The user has to pay a charge for viewing pages on a bulletin board.*

viewdata /'vjuːdeɪtə/ *noun* an interactive system for transmitting text or graphics from a database to a user's terminal by telephone lines, providing facilities for information retrieval, transactions, education, games and recreation

COMMENT: The user calls up the page of information required, using the telephone and a modem, as opposed to teletext, where the pages of information are repeated one after the other automatically.

viewer /'vjuːə/ *noun* a utility that allows a user to see what is contained in an image or formatted document file without having to start the program that created it

VIM /vɪm/ *noun* a set of standards developed by IBM, Borland, Novell and Apple that provides a way of sending email messages between applications. Full form **vendor-independent messaging**. Compare **MAPI**

viral /'vaɪrəl/ *adjective* referring to unsolicited emails that automatically forward themselves from one user to another, or to activities that use such emails

viral marketing /'vaɪrəl ˌmɑːkɪtɪŋ/ *noun* a form of marketing in which an organisation's customers act as advertisers for its products by spreading knowledge of them to other people, especially over the Internet

virgin /'vɜːdʒɪn/ *adjective* referring to a medium that has not been recorded on before

virtual /'vɜːtʃuəl/ *adjective* referring to a feature or device which does not actually exist but which is simulated by a computer and can be used by a user as if it did exist

virtual address /ˌvɜːtʃuəl ə'dres/ *noun* an address referring to virtual memory

virtual assistant /ˌvɜːtʃuəl ə'sɪst(ə)nt/ *noun* an employee who works as a personal assistant to somebody but does the job from another place solely by using computer and phone links

virtual circuit /ˌvɜːtʃuəl 'sɜːkɪt/ *noun* a link established between a source and sink in a packet-switching network for the duration of the call

virtual community /ˌvɜːtʃuəl kə'mjuːnɪti/ *noun* a group of people who communicate with each other via the Internet

virtual desktop /ˌvɜːtʃuəl 'desktɒp/ *noun* an area that is bigger than the physical limits of the monitor, and which can contain text, images, windows and other facilities. Also called **virtual screen**

virtual disk /ˌvɜːtʃuəl 'dɪsk/ *noun* a section of RAM used with a short controlling program as if it were a fast disk storage system

virtual image /ˌvɜːtʃuəl 'ɪmɪdʒ/ *noun* a complete image stored in memory rather than the part of it that is displayed

virtual machine /ˌvɜːtʃuəl mə'ʃiːn/ *noun* a piece of software that allows a Java application to run on a computer. Abbr **VM**

COMMENT: When a developer writes a program in Java, it is compiled to a file format called bytecode (or pseudocode). This file can then be run using another application (the virtual machine) that is specific to the particular computer platform – there are virtual machine applications for PCs, Apple Macs and Sun computers, and each can run the same Java bytecode file, making Java a platform-independent language.

virtual memory /ˌvɜːtʃuəl 'mem(ə)ri/ *noun* a system of providing extra main memory by using a disk drive as if it were RAM. Also called **virtual storage**

virtual memory stack /ˌvɜːtʃuəl 'mem(ə)ri ˌstæk/ *noun* a temporary store for pages in a virtual memory system

virtual reality /ˌvɜːtʃuəl ri'ælɪti/ *noun* full form of **VR** ○ *This new virtual reality software can create a three-dimensional room that you can navigate around.*

'Autodesk suggests that anyone wishing to build Virtual Reality applications with the Cyberspace Developer's Kit should have solid knowledge of programming in C++ along with general knowledge of computer graphics.' [*Computing*]

virtual reality modelling language /ˌvɜːtʃuəl ri ˌælɪti 'mɒd(ə)lɪŋ ˌlæŋgwɪdʒ/ *noun* full form of **VRML**

virtual screen /ˌvɜːtʃuəl 'skriːn/ *noun* same as **virtual desktop**

virtual storage /ˌvɜːtʃuəl 'stɔːrɪdʒ/ *noun* abbr **VS**. same as **virtual memory**

virtual terminal /ˌvɜːtʃuəl 'tɜːmɪn(ə)l/ *noun* a set of ideal terminal specifications used as a model by a real terminal

virus /'vaɪrəs/ *noun* a program which adds itself to an executable file and copies itself to other executable files each time an infected file is run ○ *If your PC is infected with a virus, your data is at risk.*

COMMENT: Viruses can corrupt data, display a message or do nothing. They are spread by downloading unchecked files from a bulletin board system or via unregulated networks or by inserting an unchecked floppy disk into your PC – always use a virus detector.

virus checker /'vaɪrəs ˌtʃekə/ *noun* a piece of software that is used to try and detect and remove unwanted virus programs from the hard disk of a computer

virus detector /'vaɪrəs dɪˌtektə/ *noun* a utility software which checks executable files to see if they contain a known virus

ViSCA /'vɪskə/ *noun* a protocol used to synchronise multiple video devices, developed by Sony. Full form **video system control architecture**

visual /'vɪʒuəl/ *adjective* which can be seen or which is used by sight

Visual Basic /ˌvɪʒuəl 'beɪsɪk/ a trade name for a programming tool, developed by Microsoft, that allows users to create Windows applications very easily. Abbr **VB**

Visual Basic Extension /ˌvɪʒuəl ˌbeɪsɪk ɪk'stenʃ(ə)n/ a trade name for a Windows custom software module that adds functionality to another application, similar to the OCX control. Abbr **VBX**

Visual Basic for Applications /ˌvɪʒuəl ˌbeɪsɪk fər ˌæplɪ'keɪʃ(ə)nz/ a trade name for a complex macro language developed by Microsoft from its VB programming tool. Abbr **VBA**

Visual Basic Script /ˌvɪʒuəl ˌbeɪsɪk 'skrɪpt/ a trade name for a set of programming commands that can be included within a normal webpage, written using HTML commands. Abbr **VBScript**

Visual C /ˌvɪʒuəl 'siː/ a trade name for a development product by Microsoft that allows Windows applications to be created by drawing the user interface and attaching C code

visualisation /ˌvɪʒuəlaɪ'zeɪʃ(ə)n/, **visualization** *noun* the conversion of numbers or data into a graphical format that can be more easily understood

visual programming /ˌvɪʒuəl ˌprəʊ'græmɪŋ/ *noun* a method of programming a computer by dragging icons into a flowchart that describes the program's actions rather than by writing a series of instructions

VITC /ˌviː aɪ tiː 'siː/ *noun* a time code recorded onto tape between video frames. Full form **vertical interval time code**

COMMENT: This is preferred to LTC because it does not use the audio track and can be read at slow playback speeds.

Vivo /'viːvəʊ/ data format used to deliver video over the Internet

VL-bus, VL local bus *noun* a standard defined by the Video Electronics Standards Association which allows up to three special expansion slots that provide direct, bus-master control of the central processor and allow very high speed data transfers between main memory and the expansion card without using the processor ○ *For a high-performance PC, choose one with a VL-bus.* Full form **VESA local bus**

VLSI /ˌviː el es 'aɪ/ *noun* a system with between 10,000 and 100,000 components on a single IC. Full form **very large scale integration**

VM *abbr* virtual machine

v-mail /'viː ˌmeɪl/ *noun* an email message with a video clip as an attachment

VME bus /ˌviː em 'iː bʌs/ *noun* an expansion bus standard that supports 32-bit data transfer, mostly used in industrial and test equipment. Full form **versamodule eurocard bus**

voice answer back /ˌvɔɪs 'ɑːnsə ˌbæk/ *noun* a computerised response service using a synthesised voice to answer enquiries

voice coil /vɔɪs kɔɪl/ *noun* **1.** an element in a dynamic microphone which vibrates when sound waves strike it and cause variations in an electrical signal **2.** an element in a loudspeaker that vibrates according to a signal and so produces sound waves

voice data entry /ˌvɔɪs ˌdeɪtə 'entri/, **voice data input** /ˌvɔɪs ˌdeɪtə 'ɪnpʊt/ *noun* the input of information into a computer using a speech recognition system and the user's voice

voicemail /'vɔɪsmeɪl/ *noun* a computer linked to a telephone exchange that answers a person's telephone when no one is there and allows messages to be recorded, in digital form ○ *I checked my voice mail to see if anyone had left me a message.*

voice output /vɔɪs 'aʊtˌpʊt/ *noun* the production of sounds which sound like human speech, made as a result of voice synthesis

'…the technology of voice output is reasonably difficult, but the technology of voice recognition is much more complex' [*Personal Computer World*]

voice over Internet protocol /ˌvɔɪs əʊvə 'ɪntənet ˌprəʊtəkɒl/ *noun* full form of **VoIP**

voice-over-the-Net /ˌvɔɪs əʊvə ðə 'net/ *adjective* used to describe voice communication using VoIP technology

voice recognition /vɔɪs ˌrekəg'nɪʃ(ə)n/ *noun* the ability of a computer to recognise certain words in a human voice and provide a suitable response

voice synthesis /vɔɪs 'sɪnθəsɪs/ *noun* the reproduction of sounds similar to those of the human voice

voice synthesiser /'vɔɪs ˌsɪnθəsaɪzə/ *noun* a device which generates sounds which are similar to the human voice

VoIP /vɔɪp/ *noun* a technology that enables voice messages to be sent over the Internet, often at the same time as data in text or other forms. Full form **voice over Internet protocol**

volatile memory /ˌvɒlə ˌtaɪl 'mem(ə)ri/, **volatile store, volatile dynamic storage** *noun* memory or storage medium which loses data stored in it when the power supply is switched off

volatility /ˌvɒlə'tɪlɪti/ *noun* the number of records that are added or deleted from a computer system compared to the total number in store

volt /vəʊlt/ *noun* an SI unit of electrical potential, defined as voltage across a one ohm resistance when one amp is flowing

voltage /'vəʊltɪdʒ/ *noun* an electromotive force expressed in volts. Abbr **V**

COMMENT: Electricity supply can have peaks and troughs of current, depending on the users in the area. Fluctuations in voltage can affect computers; a voltage regulator will provide a steady supply of electricity.

voltage regulator /'vəʊltɪdʒ ˌregjʊleɪtə/ *noun* a device which provides a steady output voltage even if the input supply varies

voltage transient /ˌvəʊltɪdʒ 'trænziənt/ *noun* a spike of voltage which is caused by a time delay in two devices switching or by noise on the line

volume /'vɒljuːm/ *noun* **1.** a disk or storage device **2.** the total space occupied by data in a storage system

volume label /'vɒljuːm ˌleɪb(ə)l/, **volume name** /'vɒljuːm neɪm/ *noun* a name assigned to identify a particular disk

VORTAL /'vɔːtəl/ *noun* a portal website that contains information for just one particular industry or interest group. Full form **vertical portal**

COMMENT: General-interest portals such as AOL, Yahoo! and Excite provide a whole range of general-interest information for users, including news, weather, sports and financial information. An example of a vertical portal is Buzzsaw (www.buzzsaw.com), which provides news and resources for the construction industry.

voxel /'vɒksəl/ *noun* the smallest unit of three-dimensional space in a computer image, equivalent to a three-dimensional pixel

VR /ˌviː 'ɑː/ *noun* a simulation of a real-life scene or environment by computer. Full form **virtual reality**

VRAM /'viː ræm/ *noun* high speed random access memory used to store computer-generated or digitised images. Full form **video random access memory**. Also called **video RAM**

VRC /ˌviː ɑː 'siː/ *noun* an odd parity check on each character of a block received, to detect any errors. Full form **vertical redundancy check**

VRML /ˌviː ɑːr em 'el/ *noun* a system that allows developers to create three-dimensional worlds within a webpage. Full form **virtual reality modelling language**

VS *abbr* virtual storage

VSB /ˌviː es 'biː/ *noun* a method of transferring data over coaxial cable, used to modulate and transmit digital television signals. Full form **vestigial side band**

V series /'viː ˌsɪəriːz/ *noun* a series of CCITT standards for data transmission using a modem, used in the UK and Europe

COMMENT: V.21 = 300 bits/second transmit and receive; full duplex V.22 = 1200 bits/second transmit and receive; half duplex V.22 BIS = 1200 bits/second transmit and receive; full duplex V.23 = 75 bits/second transmit, 1,200 bits/second receive; half duplex V.24 = interchange circuits between a DTE and a DCE; V.25 BIS = automatic calling and answering equipment on a PSTN; V.26 = 2,400 bits/second transmission over leased lines; V.26 BIS = 2,400 bits/second transmit, 1,200 bits/second receive, half duplex for use on a PSTN; V.26 TER = 2,400 bits/second transmit, 1,200 bits/second receive, full duplex for use on a PSTN ; V.27 = 4,800 bits/second modem for use on a leased line; V.27 BIS = 4,800 bits/second transmit, 2,400 bits/second receive for use on a leased line ; V.27 TER = 4,800 bits/second transmit, 2,400 bits/second receive for use on a PSTN; V.29 = 9,600 bits/second modem for use on a PSTN or leased line; V.32 = data transmission rate 9,600 bits/second; V.32BIS = data transmission rate 14,400 bits/second; V.34 = full-duplex modem communication standard that can transfer data at up to 28,800 bps (like V.32, the V.34 standard allows the modem to automatically adjust its speed based on the quality of the telephone line to avoid errors); V.42 = error control and correction protocol; V.42 BIS = data compression used with V.42 error control.

VT-52 /ˌviː tiː ˌfɪfti ˈtuː/ *noun* a popular standard of a terminal that defines the codes used to display text and graphics

VTR /ˌviː tiː ˈɑː/ *noun* a machine used to record and play back video signals that are stored on open reels of magnetic tape rather than on the sealed, enclosed cassette used by a VCR. Full form **video tape recorder**

VT-terminal emulation /ˌviː tiː ˈtɜːmɪn(ə)l emjuˌleɪʃ(ə)n/ *noun* a standard set of codes developed by Digital Equipment Corporation to control how text and graphics are displayed on its range of terminals

VxD /ˌviː eks ˈdiː/ *noun* a device driver used to control one part of the Windows operating system or to link a peripheral to the Windows operating system. Full form **virtual device driver**

Vxtreme /ˌviː eksˈtriːm/ *noun* a format used to deliver streaming video sequences over the Internet

W

W3 *abbr* World Wide Web

W3C /ˌdʌb(ə)l juː θriː ˈsiː/ *noun* a group of international industry members that work together to develop common standards for the World Wide Web. Full form **world wide web consortium**

> COMMENT: Visit the www.w3.org website for new standards and developments.

wafer /ˈweɪfə/ *noun* a thin round slice of a large single crystal of silicon onto which hundreds of individual integrated circuits are constructed, before being cut into individual chips

wafer scale integration /ˌweɪfə skeɪl ˌɪntɪˈgreɪʃ(ə)n/ *noun* one large chip, the size of a wafer, made up of smaller integrated circuits connected together (NOTE: These are still in the research stage.)

WAIS /ˌdʌb(ə)l eɪ aɪ ˈes/ *noun* a system that allows a user to search for information stored on the Internet. Full form **wide area information server**

wait condition /ˈweɪt kənˌdɪʃ(ə)n/ *noun* **1.** a state in which a processor is not active, but waiting for input from peripherals **2.** a null instruction which is used to slow down a processor so that slower memory or a peripheral can keep up ▶ also called **wait state**

waiting list /ˈweɪtɪŋ lɪst/ *noun* ♦ queue

waiting state /ˈweɪtɪŋ steɪt/ *noun* a computer state in which a program requires an input or signal before continuing execution

wait loop /weɪt luːp/ *noun* a processor that repeats one loop of program until some action occurs

wait state /ˈweɪt steɪt/ *noun* same as **wait condition**

wait time /weɪt taɪm/ *noun* a time delay between the moment when an instruction is given and the execution of the instruction or return of a result, e.g. the delay between a request for data and the transfer of the data from memory

wake-on-LAN /weɪk ɒn/ *noun* technology that allows a personal computer or workstation to be switched on automatically by sending it a signal over a local area network connection (NOTE: The system is built into the network interface card fitted to the computer and allows a network manager or network server software to manage the computers linked to the network.)

wake-up code /ˈweɪk ʌp kəʊd/ *noun* a code entered at a remote terminal to indicate to the central computer that someone is trying to log on at that location

wallpaper /'wɔːl,peɪpə/ noun (in a GUI) an image or pattern used as a background in a window

WAN /wæn/ noun a network in which the various terminals are far apart and linked by radio or satellite. Full form **wide area network**. Opposite **LAN**

wand /wɒnd/ noun a bar-code reader or optical device which is held in the hand to read bar codes on products in a store

WAP /wæp/ noun **1.** a system that allows a user to access information on an Internet server using a wireless handheld device such as a mobile telephone. Full form **Wireless Application Protocol 2.** a device that connects to a LAN and allows a computer to access the network using a wireless data transmission ○ The WAP has an aerial and a built-in hub. Full form **wireless access point**

> COMMENT: WAP can be used over almost all of the current wireless networks, including the popular GSM mobile telephone standard, and can run on almost any operating system or hardware device. A device that supports WAP provides a very simple browser that can display basic graphics and text-based pages of information on a small, monochrome, 6–10 line display, similar to a tiny, simple web page. The user can navigate between pages using two or three buttons on the handheld device or mobile telephone. The arrival of WAP allows users to access email and news-based websites from a mobile telephone, but users have been put off by the very slow speed (no more than 9,600bps) at which data can be transferred over current wireless telephone systems.

WAP browser /wæp 'braʊzə/ noun a simple web browser that works on a handheld WAP device

> COMMENT: A WAP browser supports the HTML and XML webpage markup standards, but also supports its own markup system, WML (WAP markup language) that allows designers to create simple pages that can be transferred efficiently over the often slow wireless link (normally at a maximum of 9,600 bps) and navigated using two or three buttons on the handheld device or mobile telephone.

WAP markup language /,wæp 'mɑːkʌp ,læŋgwɪdʒ/ noun full form of **WML**

WAP markup language script /,wæp ,mɑːkʌp ,læŋgwɪdʒ 'skrɪpt/ noun same as **WMLScript**

warm boot /,wɔːm 'buːt/ noun the act of restarting a computer without switching it off. Compare **cold boot**

warm standby /wɔːm 'stændbaɪ/ noun a secondary backup device which can be switched into action a short time af-

ter the main system fails. Compare **cold standby, hot standby**

warm start /wɔːm stɑːt/ noun the process of restarting a program which has stopped, without losing any data. Compare **cold start**

warn /wɔːn/ verb to say that something dangerous is about to happen or that there is a possible danger ○ He warned the keyboarders that the system might become overloaded. (NOTE: You warn someone **of** something, or **that** something may happen)

warning light /'wɔːnɪŋ laɪt/ noun a small light which lights up to show that something dangerous may happen ○ When the warning light on the front panel comes on, switch off the system.

waste instruction /weɪst ɪn'strʌkʃən/ noun an instruction that does not carry out any action other than increasing the program counter to the location of next instruction

watermark /'wɔːtəmɑːk/ noun a pattern of bits that is digitally embedded in a data file in order to make it possible to detect unauthorised copies

watt /wɒt/ noun an SI unit of measurement of electrical power, defined as power produced when one amp of current flows through a load that has one volt of voltage across it

wave /weɪv/ noun a signal motion which rises and falls periodically as it travels through a medium

WAVE /weɪv/ noun a standard method of storing an analog signal in digital form under Microsoft Windows. Also called **WAV file** (NOTE: Files have the .WAV extension.)

waveform /'weɪvfɔːm/ noun the shape of a wave

waveform audio /'weɪvfɔːm ,ɔːdiəʊ/ noun a method of storing analog audio signals as digital data

waveform digitisation /,weɪvfɔːm ,dɪdʒɪtaɪ'zeɪʃ(ə)n/ noun the conversion and storing of a waveform in numerical form using an A/D converter

waveform editor /'weɪvfɔːm ,edɪtə/ noun a software program that displays a graphical representation of a sound wave and allows a user to edit, adjust levels and frequencies or add special effects

waveform synthesiser /'weɪvfɔːm ,sɪnθəsaɪzə/ noun a musical device that creates sounds of an instrument by using recorded samples of the original waveform produced by the instrument

waveform table /'weɪvfɔːm ˌteɪb(ə)l/ *noun* a set of data that describes a sound clip

wavelength /'weɪvˌleŋθ/ *noun* the distance between two adjacent peaks of a wave, equal to the speed divided by the frequency

wavelength division multiplexing /ˌweɪvleŋθ dɪˌvɪʒ(ə)n 'mʌltɪpleksɪŋ/ *noun* a method of increasing the data capacity of an optic fibre by transmitting several light signals at different wavelengths along the same fibre. Abbr **WDM**

wavetable /'weɪvteɪb(ə)l/ *noun* memory in a sound card that contains a recording of a real musical instrument that is played back

WAV file /'weɪv faɪl/ *noun* same as **WAVE**

WDM *abbr* wavelength division multiplexing

wearable computer /ˌweərəb(ə)l kəm'pjuːtə/ *noun* a battery-powered computer small enough to be worn on the body

web /web/ *noun* same as **World Wide Web**

web application /web ˌæplɪ'keɪʃ(ə)n/ *noun* a software program that works behind the scenes at a website, runs on a web server and uses the HTTP protocol to deliver information to a user (NOTE: An example is a database of information that can be searched from a webpage or a method of ordering and paying for a product using a webpage.)

WebBot /'webbɒt/ a trade name for a utility used in Microsoft Internet software that helps a user create a particular function in a webpage

web browser /'web ˌbrauzə/ *noun* same as **browser**

web cam /web kæm/ *noun* a video camera linked to a website that allows visitors to see live video images of a scene

COMMENT: These devices have become very popular and have been used to display the inside of an office, the view over a city, an office coffee machine, the inside of a bedroom and many other scenes.

webcast /'webkɑːst/ *noun* a broadcast made on the World Wide Web

'It is spending $450m on a community support programme for developers: webcasts, free on-site training, seminars, roadshows and 125 new books.' [*The Guardian*]

web crawler /'web ˌkrɔːlə/ *noun* software that moves over every webpage on the Internet and produces an index based on the content of the webpages

web designer /'web ðɪˌzaɪnə/ *noun* a person who designs websites

webmaster /'webmɑːstə/ *noun* a person in charge of a website

webpage /'webpeɪdʒ/ *noun* a single file stored on a web server that contains formatted text, graphics and hypertext links to other pages on the Internet or within a website

webpage design software /ˌwebpeɪdʒ dɪˌzaɪn 'sɒftweə/ *noun* software that provides features that make it easier for a user to create webpages

COMMENT: The design software is similar to desktop publishing software and allows you to drag text and images onto a page, create tables and change the style of text from menu options, without having to edit complex HTML commands.

web portal /web 'pɔːt(ə)l/ *noun* a website that provides a wide range of information and resources that include everything a particular user might want from the Internet, on one site

COMMENT: The biggest web portals include AOL, MSN, Yahoo! and Excite, which offer a wide range of general services including news, sports, email, weather, shopping and a search engine.

web ring /'web rɪŋ/ *noun* a series of linked websites that are designed to be visited one after the other until the visitor reaches the first website again

web server /web 'sɜːvə/ *noun* a computer that stores the collection of webpages that make up a website

website /'websaɪt/ *noun* a collection of webpages that are linked and related and can be accessed by a user with a web browser ○ *The Bloomsbury website, http://www.bloomsbury.com, contains information about all the books Bloomsbury publish.*

WebTV /ˌweb tiː 'viː/ a trade name for a television that also lets a user view webpages

COMMENT: Some TVs include a computer and modem, other systems use an external box that links to the TV and a telephone socket. Some interactive television and cable television installations do not use a telephone socket but instead download and display webpages via the television cable.

webzine /'webziːn/ *noun* same as **e-zine**

weighted   average   /ˌweɪtɪd
'æv(ə)rɪdʒ/ *noun* an average which is calculated taking several factors into account,
giving some more value than others

weighted bit /'weɪtɪd bɪt/ *noun* each
bit having a different value depending on
its position in a word

weighting /'weɪtɪŋ/ *noun* the sorting of
users, programs or data by their importance or priority

well-behaved /ˌwel bɪ'heɪvd/ *adjective* referring to a program which does not
make any nonstandard system calls, using
only the standard BIOS input/output calls
rather than directly addressing peripherals
or memory

> COMMENT: If well-behaved, the software
> should work on all machines using the same
> operating system.

wetware /'wet,weə/ *noun* the human
brain, intelligence which writes software
to be used with hardware (*informal; US*)

What-You-See-Is-All-You-Get /ˌwɒt
juː siː ɪz ˌɔːl juː 'get/ *noun* full form of
WYSIAYG

What-You-See-Is-What-You-Get
/ˌwɒt juː siː ɪz ˌwɒt juː 'get/ *noun* full
form of **WYSIWYG**

while-loop /waɪl luːp/ *noun* a conditional program instructions that carries out
a loop while a condition is true

White Book /waɪt bʊk/ *noun* a formal
video-CD standard published by Philips
and JVC that defines how digital video can
be stored on a CD-ROM

white pages /waɪt peɪdʒz/ *plural noun*
a database of users and their email address
stored on the Internet to help other users
find an email address

white writer /waɪt 'raɪtə/ *noun* a laser
printer which directs its laser beam on the
points that are not printed. Opposite **black
writer**

> COMMENT: With a white writer, the black areas
> are printed evenly but edges and borders are
> not so sharp.

whois /'huː ɪz/ *noun* an Internet utility
that displays information about the owner
of a particular domain name

wide   area   information   server
/ˌwaɪd ˌeəriə ˌɪnfə'meɪʃ(ə)n ˌsɜːvə/
noun full form of **WAIS**

wide   area   network /ˌwaɪd ˌeəriə
'netwɜːk/ *noun* full form of **WAN**

wideband /'waɪdbænd/ *noun* same as
broadband

widescreen display /ˌwaɪdskriːn dɪ
'spleɪ/ *noun* a film, video or TV display
with an aspect ratio greater than 1.37, or
the same as the full size of a 35 mm film
image

Wide-SCSI /waɪd 'skʌzi/ *noun* a development that provides a wider data bus than
the original SCSI specification, so can
transfer more data at a time

widow /'wɪdəʊ/ *noun* the first line of a
paragraph which is printed by itself at the
bottom of a column. Compare **orphan**

wild   card /'waɪldkɑːd/,   **wild   card
character** /'waɪldkɑːd ˌkærɪktə/ *noun* a
symbol used when searching for files or
data which represents all files ◇ *A wild
card can be used to find all files names beginning DIC.*

> COMMENT: In DOS, UNIX and PC operating
> systems, the wild card character '?' will match
> any single character in this position; the wild
> card character ' or ' means match any number
> of any characters.

WIMP /wimp/ *noun* a program display
which uses graphics or icons to control the
software and make it easier to use. Full
form **window, icon, mouse, pointers.** ◇
environment, GUI. Compare **command
line interface**

> COMMENT: WIMPs normally use a combination
> of windows, icons and a mouse to control the
> operating system. In many GUIs, such as Mi-
> crosoft Windows, Apple Mac System 7 and
> DR-GEM, you can control all the functions of
> the operating system just using the mouse.
> Icons represent programs and files; instead of
> entering the file name, you select it by moving
> a pointer with a mouse.

Winchester disk /draɪv/, **Winchester
drive** *noun* a compact high-capacity hard
disk which is usually built into a computer
system and cannot be removed

window /'wɪndəʊ/ *noun* **1.** a reserved
section of screen used to display special
information, which can be selected and
looked at at any time and which overwrites
information already on the screen ◇ *Several remote stations are connected to the network and each has its own window onto
the hard disk.* **2.** a part of a document currently displayed on a screen ◇ *The operating system will allow other programs to be
displayed on-screen at the same time in
different windows.* **3.** an area of memory or
access to a storage device ■ *verb* to set up
a section of screen by defining the coordinates of its corners, allowing information
to be temporarily displayed and overwriting previous information without altering
information in the workspace

'…when an output window overlaps another, the interpreter does not save the contents of the obscured window' [*Personal Computer World*]

window, icon, mouse, pointer /ˌwɪndəʊ ˌaɪkɒn ˌmaʊs ˈpɔɪntə/ *noun* full form of **WIMP**

windowing /ˈwɪndəʊɪŋ/ *noun* **1.** the action of setting up a window to show information on the screen ○ *The network system uses the latest windowing techniques.* **2.** the process of displaying or accessing information via a window

'…windowing facilities make use of virtual screens as well as physical screens' [*Byte*]

'…the network system uses the latest windowing techniques' [*Desktop Publishing*]

'…the functions are integrated via a windowing system with pull-down menus used to select different operations' [*Byte*]

Windows /ˈwɪndəʊz/ a trade name for a family of operating systems developed by Microsoft that interacts with users through a Graphical User Interface. Windows is the operating system used by most of the world's PCs. Also called **Microsoft Windows, MS-Windows**

Windows 3.1 /ˌwɪndəʊz θriː ˌpɔɪnt ˈwʌn/ a trade name for the first of the new generation of Windows which provided features including OLE and drag and drop

Windows 3.1x /ˌwɪndəʊz θriː ˌpɔɪnt wʌn ˈeks/ a trade name for any version of Windows after version 3, including 3.1 and 3.11

Windows 3.11 /ˌwɪndəʊz θriː ˌpɔɪnt wʌn ˈwʌn/ same as **Windows for Workgroups**

Windows 95 /ˌwɪndəʊz ˌnaɪnti ˈfaɪv/ a trade name for a version of Windows that provides support for long filenames, an interface that is easier to use and better support for networks and the Internet

Windows 98 /ˌwɪndəʊz ˌnaɪnti ˈeɪt/ a trade name for an enhanced version of Windows 95 that provides more communications and Internet features and is easier to use and configure

Windows 2000 /ˌwɪndəʊz tuː ˈθaʊzənd/ a trade name for a version of the Windows operating system that improves on the speed and features of Windows 98, providing closer integration with the Internet, information sources and networks and better support for plug-and-play and error-detection and prevention

Windows API /ˌwɪndəʊz ˌeɪ piː ˈaɪ/ a trade name for a set of standard functions and commands, defined by Microsoft, that allow a programmer to control the Win-

dows operating system from a programming language

Windows CE /ˌwɪndəʊz siː ˈiː/ a trade name for a software operating system developed by Microsoft and designed to run on small PDA or palmtop computers that use either a pen input or a keyboard instead of a mouse

Windows Explorer /ˌwɪndəʊz ɪk ˈsplɔːrə/ a trade name for a software utility included with Windows that lets a user view the folders and files on the hard disk, floppy disk, CD-ROM and any shared network drives

Windows for Workgroups /ˌwɪndəʊz fə ˈwɜːkgruːps/ a trade name for a version of Windows that includes basic peer-to-peer file-sharing functions and email, fax and scheduler utilities. Also called **Windows 3.11**

Windows GDI /ˌwɪndəʊz dʒiː diː ˈaɪ/ a trade name for a set of standard functions, defined by Microsoft, that allow a programmer to draw images in windows within the Windows operating system

Windows Internet Naming Service /ˌwɪndəʊz ˌɪntənet ˈneɪmɪŋ ˌsɜːvɪs/ full form of **WINS**

Windows ME /ˌwɪndəʊz em ˈiː/ a trade name for a version of the Windows operating system designed for home users

Windows NT /ˌwɪndəʊz en ˈtiː/ a trade name for a high-performance GUI derived from Windows that does not use DOS as an operating system and features 32-bit code

Windows NT file system /ˌwɪndəʊz en tiː ˈfaɪl ˌsɪstəm/ full form of **NTFS**

Windows SDK /ˌwɪndəʊz es diː ˈkeɪ/ a trade name for a set of software tools, including definitions of the Windows API, that make it easier for a programmer to write applications that will work under the Windows operating system

Windows XP /ˌwɪndəʊz eks ˈpiː/ a trade name for a version of the Windows operating system designed for home and business users that provides a 32-bit multitasking operating system with the standard Windows graphical user interface together with improved network and Internet connectivity

WINS /wɪns/ *noun* a system that works with a network of computers running Windows and provides a database of the IP addresses of each computer on the network.

Full form Windows Internet Naming Service

COMMENT: This is more difficult than it sounds, since a computer is usually given a different IP address every time it is switched on. The WINS service provides 'name resolution' for Windows networks, DNS provides a similar service for networks with fixed IP addresses, including the public Internet.

Winsock /'wɪnsɒk/ *noun* a utility software that is required to control the modem when connecting to the Internet and allows the computer to communicate using the TCP/IP protocol. Also called **socket driver**

wipe /waɪp/ *verb* to clean data from a disk ○ *By reformatting you will wipe the disk clean.* (NOTE: **wipes – wiping – wiped**)

wire /'waɪə/ *noun* a thin metal conductor ■ *verb* to install wiring in something (NOTE: **wires – wiring – wired**)

wire frame model /ˌwaɪə freɪm 'mɒd(ə)l/ *noun* (*in graphics and CAD*) a method of displaying objects using lines and arcs rather than filled areas. Also called **wire mesh model, stick model**

wireless access point /ˌwaɪələs 'ækses ˌpɔɪnt/ *noun* full form of **WAP 2**

Wireless Application Protocol /ˌwaɪələs ˌæplɪ'keɪʃ(ə)n ˌprəʊtəʊkɒl/ *noun* full form of **WAP 1**

wireless markup language /ˌwaɪələs 'mɑːkʌp ˌlæŋgwɪdʒ/ *noun* a standardised system, based on XML, that is used for tagging text files and that specifies the interfaces of narrowband wireless devices

wireless modem /ˌwaɪələs 'məʊdem/ *noun* a modem that can be used with a wireless mobile telephone system (NOTE: A wireless modem normally includes the telephone hardware and an aerial, so does not need to be plugged into a separate mobile telephone.)

wireless network /ˌwaɪələs 'netwɜːk/, **wireless LAN** /læn/ *noun* a network that does not use cable to transmit data between computers, but instead uses radio signals to transmit signals, normally using the 802.11b or 802.11a transmission protocol. Also called **wireless LAN**

wire mesh model /ˌwaɪə meʃ 'mɒd(ə)l/ *noun* same as **wire frame model**

wire printer /'waɪə ˌprɪntə/ *noun* same as **dot-matrix printer**

wire wrap /'waɪə ræp/ *noun* a simple method of electrically connecting component terminals together using thin insulated wire wrapped around each terminal, which is then soldered into place, usually used for prototype systems

wiring /'waɪərɪŋ/ *noun* a series of wires ○ *The wiring in the system had to be replaced.*

wiring closet /'waɪərɪŋ ˌklɒzɪt/ *noun* a box in which the cabling for a network or part of network is terminated and interconnected

wiring frame /'waɪərɪŋ freɪm/ *noun* a metal structure used to support incoming cables and provide connectors to allow cables to be interconnected

WISC /wɪsk/ *noun* a CPU design that allows a programmer to add extra machine code instructions using microcode, to customise the instruction set. Full form **writable instruction set computer**

wizard /'wɪzəd/ *noun* a software utility that helps you create something

WML /ˌdʌb(ə)l juː em 'el/ *noun* a webpage formatting language that is similar to a very simple version of the standard HTML webpage coding system, but does not include many of the extra features that cannot be displayed on the small screen of a WAP handheld device or navigated with two or three buttons. Full form **WAP markup language**

WMLScript /ˌdʌb(ə)l juː em 'el ˌskrɪpt/ *noun* a scripting language similar to a very simple version of JavaScript that allows WML webpages to include scripting functions. Full form **WAP markup language script**

word /wɜːd/ *noun* **1.** a separate item of language, which is used with others to form speech or writing which can be understood **2.** a separate item of data on a computer, formed of a group of bits, stored in a single location in a memory

word break /'wɜːd breɪk/ *noun* the division of a word at the end of a line, where part of the word is left on one line with a hyphen and the rest of the word is taken over to begin the next line

word count /'wɜːd kaʊnt/ *noun* the number of words in a file or text

word length /'wɜːd leŋθ/ *noun* the length of a computer word, counted as the number of bits

word mark /'wɜːd mɑːk/ *noun* a symbol indicating the start of a word in a variable word length machine

word marker /'wɜːd ˌmɑːkə/ *noun* a symbol indicating the start of a word in a variable word length machine

WordPad /'wɜːdpæd/ a software utility included with versions of Microsoft Windows later than Windows 95 that provides the basic functions of Microsoft Word 6

WordPerfect /ˌwɜːd'pɜːfekt/ a trade name for a popular word-processing application developed by WordPerfect Corp. to run on a wide range of hardware platforms and operating systems.

word-process /wɜːd 'prəʊses/ *verb* to edit, store and manipulate text using a computer ○ *It is quite easy to read word-processed files.*

word-processing /ˌwɜːd 'prəʊsesɪŋ/ *noun* the process of using a computer to keyboard, edit and output text, in forms such as letters, labels and address lists ○ *Load the word-processing program before you start keyboarding.* Abbr **WP**

word-processing bureau /ˌwɜːd 'prəʊsesɪŋ ˌbjʊərəʊ/ *noun* an office which specialises in word-processing for other companies

word-processor /wɜːd 'prəʊˌsesə/ *noun* **1.** a small computer used for word-processing text and documents **2.** a word-processing package or program for a computer which allows the editing and manipulation and output of text, in forms such as letters, labels and address lists

word serial /wɜːd 'sɪəriəl/ *noun* a set of data words transmitted one after the other, along a parallel bus

words per minute /ˌwɜːdz pɜː 'mɪnɪt/ *noun* full form of **WPM**

WordStar /'wɜːdstɑː/ a trade name for an outdated word-processing application developed by MicroPro International for CP/M and IBM PC computers

word time /'wɜːd taɪm/ *noun* the time taken to transfer a word from one memory area or device to another

word wrap /'wɜːd ræp/ *noun* a system in word-processing in which the operator does not have to indicate the line endings, but can keyboard continuously, leaving the program to insert word breaks and to continue the text on the next line. Also called **wraparound**

work area /'wɜːk ˌeəriə/ *noun* the memory space which is being used by an operator

workaround /'wɜːkəˌraʊnd/ *noun* a technique that enables a user to continue using a computer program or system that has a fault or defect in it without actually putting the fault or defect right

'This is a known bug… the workaround is to get Outlook Express to prompt you to select an identity when you run it.' [*The Guardian*]

work disk /wɜːk dɪsk/ *noun* a disk on which current work is stored

work file /wɜːk faɪl/ *noun* a temporary work area which is being used for current work. Also called **scratch file**

workflow /'wɜːkfləʊ/ *noun* software designed to improve the flow of electronic documents around an office network, from user to user

workgroup /'wɜːkgruːp/ *noun* a small group of users who are working on a project or connected with a local area network

workgroup enabled /ˌwɜːkgruːp ɪn 'eɪb(ə)ld/ *adjective* referring to a feature added to standard software package to give it more appeal to a group of networked users ○ *This word-processor is workgroup enabled which adds an email gateway from the standard menus.*

workgroup software /'wɜːkgruːp ˌsɒftweə/ *noun* an application designed to be used by many users in a group to improve productivity, e.g. a diary or scheduler

working /'wɜːkɪŋ/ *adjective* operating correctly

working in tandem /ˌwɜːkɪŋ ɪn 'tændəm/ *noun* a situation in which two devices are working together

working store /'wɜːkɪŋ stɔː/ *noun* an area of high-speed memory used for temporary storage of data in current use

workload /'wɜːkˌləʊd/ *noun* the amount of work which a person or computer has to do

worksheet /'wɜːkˌʃiːt/ *noun* (*in a spreadsheet program*) a two-dimensional matrix of rows and columns that contains cells which can, themselves, contain equations

workspace /'wɜːkspeɪs/ *noun* a space on memory which is available for use or is being used currently by an operator

workstation /'wɜːkˌsteɪʃ(ə)n/ *noun* a place where a computer user works, with equipment such as a terminal, VDU, printer and modem ○ *The system includes five workstations linked together in a ring network.*

'...an image processing workstation must provide three basic facilities: the means to digitize, display and manipulate the image data' [*Byte*]

world /wɜːld/ *noun* a three-dimensional scene that is displayed on a website and allows a user to move around the scene exploring the objects visible

World Wide Web /ˌwɜːld ˌwaɪd 'web/ *noun* a collection of the millions of websites and webpages that together form the part of the Internet that is most often seen by users. Abbr **www, W3**. Also called **web**

COMMENT: Each website is a collection of webpages containing text, graphics and links to other websites. Each page is created using the HTML language and is viewed by a user with a web browser. Navigating between webpages and websites is called surfing; this requires a computer with a link to the Internet (usually using a modem) and a web browser to view the webpages stored on the remote web servers. The Internet itself includes email, Usenet and newsgroups as well as websites and webpages.

World Wide Web Consortium /ˌwɜːld waɪd 'web kənˌsɔːtiəm/ *noun* full form of **W3C**

WORM /wɜːm/ *noun* an optical disk storage system that allows the user to write data to the disk once, but the user can then read the data from the disk many times. Full form **write once read many times memory**

WP *abbr* word-processing

WPM, wpm *noun* a method of measuring the speed of a printer, the number of words printed in a minute. Full form **words per minute**

wraparound /'ræpəˌraʊnd/ *noun* same as **word wrap**

wrapper /'ræpə/ *noun* special software that is used to provide a single, convenient file that can be distributed over the Internet

COMMENT: Wrapper software often includes security features, to prevent unauthorised copying, and compression to reduce the size of the files. A user double-clicks the file and it automatically installs the software enclosed in the wrapper on the computer.

writable instruction set computer /ˌraɪtəb(ə)l ɪnˌstrʌkʃən set kəʊˈpjuːtə/ *noun* full form of **WISC**

write /raɪt/ *verb* to put text or data onto a disk ○ *Access time is the time taken to read from or write to a location in memory.*

(NOTE: **writes** – **writing** – **wrote** – **written**. You write data **to** a file.)

write-back cache /'raɪt bæk ˌkæʃ/, **write-behind cache** /ˌraɪt bɪˈhaɪnd ˌkæʃ/ *noun* same as **write cache**

write black printer /ˌraɪt 'blæk ˌprɪntə/ *noun* a printer in which toner sticks to the points hit by the laser beam when the image drum is scanned. Compare **white writer**

COMMENT: A write black printer produces sharp edges and graphics, but large areas of black are muddy.

write cache /'raɪt kæʃ/ *noun* temporary storage used to hold data intended for a storage device until the device is ready. Also called **write-back cache**

write error /raɪt 'erə/ *noun* an error reported when a user is trying to save data onto a magnetic storage medium

write head /raɪt hed/ *noun* same as **record head**

write once, read many times memory /ˌraɪt ˌwʌns riːd 'meni ˌtaɪmz ˌmem(ə)ri/ *noun* full form of **WORM**

write-permit ring /ˌraɪt pəˈmɪt rɪŋ/ *noun* a ring on a reel of magnetic tape which allows the tape to be overwritten or erased

write protect /raɪt prəˈtekt/ *verb* to make it impossible to write to a floppy disk or tape by moving a special write-protect tab

write-protect tab /ˌraɪt prəˈtekt tæb/ *noun* a tab on a floppy disk which if moved prevents any writing to or erasing from the disk

writer /'raɪtə/ *noun* ♦ **black writer, white writer**

write time /raɪt taɪm/ *noun* the time between requesting data transfer to a storage location and it being written

writing pad /'raɪtɪŋ pæd/ *noun* a special device which allows a computer to read in handwritten characters which have been written onto a special pad

www *abbr* World Wide Web

WYSIAYG /'wɪziːeɪg/ *noun* a program in which the output on screen cannot be printed out in any other form, as it contains no hidden print or formatting commands. Full form **What-You-See-Is-All-You-Get**

WYSIWYG /'wɪziːwɪg/ *noun* a program in which the output on the screen is exactly the same as the output on printout, including graphics and special fonts. Full form **What-You-See-Is-What-You-Get**

XYZ

X¹ /eks/ *noun* same as **X-Window System**

'X is the underlying technology which allows Unix applications to run under a multi-user, multitasking GUI. It has been adopted as the standard for the Common Open Software Environment, proposed recently by top Unix vendors including Digital, IBM and Sun.' [*Computing*]

X² /eks/ *abbr* extension

X2 *noun* a communications standard developed by US Robotics for its range of high-speed modems that can transfer data at 56,000 bits per second. ◊ **V series**

X.25 *noun* a CCITT standard that defines the connection between a terminal and a packet-switching network

X.400 *noun* a CCITT standard that defines an email transfer method

X.500 *noun* a CCITT standard that defines a method of global naming that allows every user to have a unique identity and allows any user to address an email message to any other user. ◊ **directory services**

XA ♦ **CD-ROM Extended Architecture** (*see*)

x-axis /ˌeks ˌaʊt 'æksɪs/ *noun* the horizontal axis of a graph

x-coordinate /eks kəʊ'ɔːdɪnət/ *noun* a horizontal axis position coordinate

x direction /ˌeks ˌaʊt dɪ'rekʃ(ə)n/ *noun* a movement horizontally

x distance /ˌeks ˌaʊt 'dɪstəns/ *noun* the distance along an x-axis from an origin

xerographic printer /ˌzɪərəgræfɪk 'prɪntə/ *noun* a printer such as a photocopier in which charged ink is attracted to areas of a charged picture

Xerox Network System /ˌzɪərɒks 'netwɜːk ˌsɪstəm/ a network protocol developed by Xerox that has provided the basis for the Novell IPX network protocols. Abbr **XNS**

Xerox PARC a Xerox development centre that has developed a wide range of important products including the mouse and GUI

XGA /ˌeks dʒiː 'eɪ/ *noun* a standard for colour video graphics adapter for PCs, developed by IBM, which has a resolution of 1,024 x 768 pixels with 256 colours on an interlaced display. Full form **extended graphics array**

XHTML /ˌeks eɪtʃ tiː em 'el/ *noun* a combination of the HTML and XML webpage markup languages. Full form **extensible hypertext markup language**

COMMENT: XHTML is actually written using the XML language and provides a simpler way of creating webpages that will be displayed in the same way over a wide range of web browser platforms.

XML /ˌeks em 'el/ *noun* a webpage markup language that is a simplified version of the SGML system and allows a designer to create his or her own customised markup tags to improve flexibility. Full form **extensible markup language**

XMODEM /'eks ˌməʊdem/ *noun* a standard file transfer and error-detecting protocol used in asynchronous, modem data transmissions

XMODEM 1K *noun* a version of XMODEM that transfers 1024-byte blocks of data

XMODEM CRC *noun* an enhanced version of XMODEM that includes error checking

XMS /ˌeks em 'es/ *noun* a set of rules that define how an MS-DOS program should access extended memory fitted in a PC. Full form **extended memory specification**

XNS *abbr* Xerox Network System

XON/XOFF /eks ˌɒn eks 'ɒf/ *noun* an asynchronous transmission protocol in which each end can regulate the data flow by transmitting special codes

X/OPEN /eks'əʊpən/ *noun* a group of vendors that are responsible for promoting open systems

XP *abbr* Windows XP

x punch /'eks pʌntʃ/ *noun* a card punch for column 11, often used to represent a negative number

X-series /ˌeks ˌaʊt 'sɪəriːz/ *noun* a set of recommendations for data communications over public data networks

XT /ˌeks 'tiː/ *noun* a trade name for a version of the original IBM PC, developed by IBM, that used an 8088 processor and included a hard disk

XT keyboard /ˌeks tiː 'kiːbɔːd/ *noun* a keyboard used with the IBM PC which had ten function keys running in two columns along the left-hand side of the keyboard

X-Window System, X-Windows a graphical interface, usually used on Unix workstation computers, made up of a set of API commands and display handling routines that provide a hardware-independent programming interface for applications

'X is the underlying technology which allows Unix applications to run under a multi-user, multitasking GUI. It has been adopted as the standard for the Common Open Software Environment, proposed recently by top Unix vendors including Digital, IBM and Sun.' [*Computing*]

COMMENT. Originally developed for UNIX workstations, it can also run on a PC or mini-computer terminals. The Open Software Foundation has a version of X-Windows called Motif; Sun and Hewlett Packard have a version called OpenLook.

x-y /ˌeks 'aʊt waɪ/ *noun* the set of coordinates for drawing a graph, where x is the horizontal and y the vertical value

x-y plotter /ˌeks waɪ 'plɒtə/ *noun* a plotter which plots to coordinates supplied, by moving the pen in two planes while the paper remains stationary

y-axis /waɪ 'æksɪs/ *noun* the vertical axis of a graph

Y/C /ˌwaɪ 'siː/ *noun* two parts of a video signal representing the luminance (Y) and the chrominance (C) parts of the image

Y/C delay /ˌwaɪ 'siː dɪˌleɪ/ *noun* an error caused by wrong synchronisation between the luma and chroma signals in a video transmission, seen as a colour halo around objects on the screen

y-coordinate /waɪ kəʊ'ɔːdɪnət/ *noun* the vertical axis position coordinate

Y/C video /ˌwaɪ siː 'vɪdiəʊ/ *noun* same as **S-Video**

y-direction /waɪ daɪ'rekʃən/ *noun* a vertical movement

y-distance /waɪ 'dɪstəns/ *noun* the distance along a y-axis from an origin

Yellow Book /'jeləʊ bʊk/ *noun* a formal specification for CD-ROM published by Philips, which includes data storage formats and has an extension to cover the CD-ROM XA standard

YMCK /ˌwaɪ em siː 'keɪ/ *noun* colour definition based on the four colours used in DTP software when creating separate colour film to use for printing. Full form **yellow, magenta, cyan, black**

YMODEM /'waɪ ˌməʊdem/ *noun* a variation of the XMODEM file transfer protocol that uses 1024-byte blocks and can send multiple files

y punch /'waɪ pʌntʃ/ *noun* a card punch for column 12, often used to indicate a positive number

YUV encoding /ˌwaɪ juː viː ɪn 'kaəʊdɪŋ/ *noun* a video encoding system in which the video luminance (Y) signal is recorded at full bandwidth but the chrominance signals (U&V) are recorded at half their bandwidth

Z *symbol* impedance

Z80 /ˌzed 'eɪti/ *noun* an 8-bit processor developed by Zilog, used in many early popular computers

zap /zæp/ *verb* to wipe off all data currently in the workspace ○ *He pressed CONTROL Z and zapped all the text.* (NOTE: zapping – zapped)

z-axis /zed 'æksɪs/ *noun* an axis for depth in a three-dimensional graph or plot

z buffer /zed 'bʌfə/ *noun* an area of memory used to store the z-axis information for a graphics object displayed on screen

zero /'zɪərəʊ/ *noun* **1.** the digit 0 ○ *The code for international calls is zero one zero (010).* **2.** the equivalent of logical off or false state (NOTE: The plural is **zeros** or **zeroes.**) ■ *verb* to erase or clear a file or the contents of a programmable device

zero compression /ˌzɪərəʊ kəm 'preʃ(ə)n/ *noun* the shortening of a file by the removal of unnecessary zeros. Also called **zero suppression**

zerofill /'zɪərəʊfɪl/ *verb* to fill empty storage space on a computer with zeros

zero flag /'zɪərəʊ flæg/ *noun* an indicator that the contents of a register or result is zero

zero insertion force socket /ˌzɪərəʊ ɪnˌsɜːʃ(ə)n fɔːs 'sɒkɪt/ *noun* a chip socket that has movable connection terminals, allowing the chip to be inserted without using any force, then a small lever is turned to grip the legs of the chip. Also called **ZIF socket**

zero-level address /ˌzɪərəʊ ˌlev(ə)l ə'dres/ *noun* an instruction in which the address is the operand

zero slot LAN /ˌzɪərəʊ slɒt 'læn/ *noun* a local area network that does not use internal expansion adapters, but instead the serial port or, sometimes, an external pocket network adapters connected to the printer port

zero suppression /ˌzɪərəʊ sə'preʃ(ə)n/ *noun* same as **zero compression**

zero wait state /ˌzɪərəʊ 'weɪt ˌsteɪt/ *noun* the state of a device (normally processor or memory chips) that is fast enough to run at the same speed as the other components in a computer, so does not have to be artificially slowed down by inserting wait states

zettabyte /'zetəbaɪt/ *noun* a unit of computer memory or disk storage space equal to one sextillion bytes or 1,024 exabytes

ZIF socket /'zɪf ˌsɒkɪt/ *noun* same as **zero insertion force socket**

zine /ziːn/ *noun* a paper, Internet magazine or other periodical published by its author, issued at irregular intervals and usually aimed at specialist readers

ZIP /zɪp/ *noun* a filename extension given to files that contain compressed data, usually generated by the PKZIP shareware utility program

Zip disk /'zɪp dɪsk/ *noun* a proprietary type of removable storage device, similar to a removable hard disk drive, manufactured by Iomega Corp. to provide a convenient backup and storage medium with 100 Mb or 1Gb disk capacity.

zip file /'zɪp faɪl/ *noun* a computer file with the extension .zip containing data that has been compressed for storage or transmission.

ZMODEM /'zed ˌməʊdem/ *noun* an enhanced version of the XMODEM file transfer protocol that includes error detection and the ability to restart a transfer where it left off if the connection is cut

zone /zəʊn/ *noun* a region or part of a screen defined for specialised printing

zoom /zuːm/ *verb* to enlarge an area of text or graphics to make it easier to work on

'…any window can be zoomed to full-screen size by pressing the F-5 function key' [*Byte*]

zooming /'zuːmɪŋ/ *noun* the process of enlarging an area of text or graphics ○ *Variable zooming from 25% to 400% of actual size.*

ZV Port /ˌzed 'viː ˌpɔːt/ *noun* an interface port that allows data to be transferred from a PC Card directly to the computer's video controller without passing through the computer's central processor. Full form **zoomed video port** (NOTE: It is used to allow a laptop computer to display live images from a video camera plugged into the computer's PC Card socket.)

SUPPLEMENT

HTML codes

The following is a list of the basic HTML codes (or tags) used to format webpages.

<a> ... </a>
creates a hyperlink target or source. For example,
```
<a href="www.bloomsbury.com">link to Bloomsbury</a>
```
will create a hyperlink to the Bloomsbury Publishing Plc webpage.

<address> ... </address>
enclosed text is formatted in smaller typeface as an address

<applet> ... </applet>
defines an applet within the document

<area>
defines the area of a graphic image that will respond to a mouse click using a client-side imagemap

<b> ... </b>
formats enclosed text in a bold typeface

<base>
defines the URL that is added in front of all relative URLs used within the document

<basefont>
defines the point size of the font used to format for the following text

<bgsound>
defines the audio file that is played as a background sound to the document (used in MS-IE)

<big> ... </big>
formats enclosed text in a bigger typeface

<blockquote> ... </blockquote>
formats the enclosed text as a quotation

<body> ... </body>
defines the start and finish of this document's body text; also used to define a graphic image used as a background, and to set the default colour of the text, hyperlinks and margins for the document

**
**
inserts a line break in the text; the <p> code also inserts a carriage return

<caption> ... </caption>
defines the caption for a table

<center> ... </center>
formats enclosed text to be centered across the line

<cite> ... </cite>
formats enclosed text as a citation

<code> ... </code>
formats enclosed text as program code, normally using the Courier typeface

<col>

defines the properties for a column that has been defined using <colgroup>

<colgroup>
defines a column

<comment> ... </comment>
defines the enclosed text to be a comment; only works in MS IE, with any other browser you should use the <!> comment <> tag format

<dd> ... </dd>
defines one element of a definition list

<dfn> ... </dfn>
formats enclosed text as a definition

<dir> ... </dir>
creates a directory list using the <li> to create entries

<div> ... </div>
divides the text within a document and formats each division

<dl> ... </dl>
creates a definition list using the <dd> and <dt> tags to create entries

<dt> ... </dt>
defines the definition part of an entry within a definition list

<em> ... </em>
formats enclosed text with emphasis (similar to bold typeface)

<embed> ... </embed>
points to an object to embed in a document

<font> ... </font>
defines the size, colour and typeface of the font to use for the enclosed text

<form> ... </form>
defines the following tags to be treated as one form; also defines how to process the form and where to send the encoded information

<frame> ... </frame>
defines a frame, including its border, colour, name and text

<frameset> ... </frameset>
defines a collection of frames

<h> ... </h>
defines a pre-set font size, such as <h1> for a large headings, <h4> for small headings

<hr>
breaks the current line of text and inserts a horizontal rule across the page

<html> ... </html>
defines the start and end of the entire html document

<i>... </i>
formats enclosed text using an italic typeface

<iframe> ... </iframe>
defines a floating frame

<img>

includes an image within a document, also defines a border for the image, size, alternative caption text and whether the image is a video clip

\<input type=checkbox\>
defines a checkbox button within a form

\<input type=file\>
defines a file-selection list within a form

\<input type=image\>
defines an image input element within a form

\<input type=password\>
defines a text input that displays an asterisk when text is entered

\<input type=radio\>
defines a radio button within a form

\<input type=reset\>
defines a button to reset the form's contents

\<input type=submit\>
defines a button to submit the form's contents to the named process

\<input type=text\>
defines a text input element to allow users to enter a line of text

\<isindex\>
defines the html document to be searchable by a defined search engine

\<kbd\> ... \</kbd\>
formats enclosed text as a keyboard input

\<li\> ... \</li\>
defines an item in a list; the list can be ordered using \<ol\> or unordered using \<ul\>

\<link\>
defines a link within a document header

\<listing\> ... \</listing\>
an old tag that is the same as the \<pre\> tag

\<map\> ... \</map\>
defines an image map that contains hotspots

\<marquee\> ... \</marquee\>
creates an animated scrolling text line, used in MS-IE

\<menu\> ... \</menu\>
defines a menu that has items created using the \<li\> tag

\<meta\>
allows the programmer to include extra information about the document

\<multicol\> ... \</multicol\>
defines multiple columns within the document; only used in Netscape Navigator

\<nextid\>
used by automated html document generators as a reference point within a file

<nobr> ... </nobr>
prevents the browser adding breaks within the enclosed text

<noframes> ... </noframes>
defines content that should be displayed if the browser does not support frames

<noscript> ... </noscript>
defines content that should be used if the browser does not support Java; only used in Netscape Navigator

<object> ... </object>
defines an object, applet or OLE object to be inserted into the document

<ol> ... </ol>
defines the start and end of a numbered list; items are inserted using the <li> tag

<option> ... </option>
defines one option within a <select> tag

<p> ... </p>
defines the start and end of a paragraph

<param> ... </param>
defines the parameters to be passed to an applet or object

<plaintext>
formats the rest of the document as plain text with spaces and breaks

<pre> ... </pre>
formats the enclosed text as plaintext with spaces and breaks

<s> ... </s>
formats enclosed text with a strikethrough (horizontal line)

<samp> ... </samp>
defines enclosed text as an example (sample)

<script> ... </script>
defines the start and end of a script written in a language such as JavaScript or VBScript

<select> ... </select>
defines a list of options within a form, each created using the <option> tag

<small> ... </small>
formats enclosed text in a small type size

<spacer>
inserts a character space within a line of text; only used in Netscape Navigator

<span> ... </span>
define a style sheet that formats text over several tags

<strike> ... </strike>
formats enclosed text with a strikethrough (horizontal line)

<strong> ... </strong>
formats enclosed text with emphasis, similar to bold typeface

<style> ... </style>
defines a collection of text formatting commands that can be referred to with this style command

<sub> ... </sub>
formats enclosed text as subscript

<sup> ... </sup>
formats enclosed text as superscript

<table> ... </table>
defines a table including border, colour, size and width; columns are added with <td> and rows with <tr>

<tbody>
a group of rows within a table

<td> ... </td>
defines a cell within a table, effectively adds a column to the table

<textarea> ... </textarea>
defines a multiple line text input element for a form

<tfoot>
defines rows within a table that are formatted as a footer to the table

<th> ... </th>
defines the header to each column in a table

<thead>
defines rows within a table that are formatted as a header to the table

<title> ... </title>
defines the title of an html document

<tr> ... </tr>
defines a row of cells within a table

<tt> ... </tt>
formats enclosed text in a monospaced typewriter-style font

<ul> ... </ul>
defines the start and end of a bulleted list of elements; each element is added using <li>

<var> ... </var>
enclosed text is the name of a variable

<wbr>
defines a possible point for a word break within a <nobr> line

<xmp> ... </xmp>
an old tag that formats enclosed text, similar to <pre>

Prefixes

T	tera-	10^{12}
G	giga-	10^{9}
M	mega-	10^{6}
k	kilo-	10^{3}
d	deci-	10^{-1}
c	centi-	10^{-2}
m	milli-	10^{-3}
μ	micro-	10^{-6}
n	nano-	10^{-9}
p	pico-	10^{-12}
f	femto-	10^{-15}
a	atto-	10^{-18}

Symbols

%	per cent
=	equals
≈	is approximately equal to
≠	is not equal to
<	is less than
>	is more than
+	plus
-	minus
÷	divided by
x	multiplied by
∴	therefore
&	and

Decimal Conversion Table

base	Decimal 10	BCD 2	Binary 2	Octal 8	Hexadecimal 16
	00	0000 0000	0000	00	0
	01	0000 0001	0001	01	1
	02	0000 0010	0010	02	2
	03	0000 0011	0011	03	3
	04	0000 0100	0100	04	4
	05	0000 0101	0101	05	5
	06	0000 0110	0110	06	6
	07	0000 0111	0111	07	7
	08	0000 1000	1000	10	8
	09	0000 1001	1001	11	9
	10	0001 0000	1010	12	A
	11	0001 0001	1011	13	B
	12	0001 0010	1100	14	C
	13	0001 0011	1101	15	D
	14	0001 0100	1110	16	E
	15	0001 0101	1111	17	F

Unicode Characters 0 - 255 in Decimal and Hexadecimal

dec	hex	char	dec	hex	char	dec	hex	char	dec	hex	char
0	0	NUL	52	34	4	104	68	h	156	9C	ST
1	1	SOH	53	35	5	105	69	i	157	9D	OSC
2	2	STX	54	36	6	106	6A	j	158	9E	PM
3	3	ETX	55	37	7	107	6B	k	159	9F	APC
4	4	EOT	56	38	8	108	6C	l	160	A0	NBSP
5	5	ENQ	57	39	9	109	6D	m	161	A1	¡
6	6	ACK	58	3A	:	110	6E	n	162	A2	¢
7	7	BEL	59	3B	;	111	6F	o	163	A3	£
8	8	BS	60	3C	<	112	70	p	164	A4	¤
9	9	HT	61	3D	=	113	71	q	165	A5	¥
10	0A	LF	62	3E	>	114	72	r	166	A6	¦
11	0B	VT	63	3F	?	115	73	s	167	A7	§
12	0C	FF	64	40	@	116	74	t	168	A8	¨
13	0D	CR	65	41	A	117	75	u	169	A9	©
14	0E	SO	66	42	B	118	76	v	170	AA	ª
15	0F	SI	67	43	C	119	77	w	171	AB	«
16	10	DLE	68	44	D	120	78	x	172	AC	¬
17	11	DC1	69	45	E	121	79	y	173	AD	SHY
18	12	DC2	70	46	F	122	7A	z	174	AE	®
19	13	DC3	71	47	G	123	7B	{	175	AF	¯
20	14	DC4	72	48	H	124	7C	|	176	B0	°
21	15	NAK	73	49	I	125	7D	}	177	B1	±
22	16	SYN	74	4A	J	126	7E	~	178	B2	²
23	17	ETB	75	4B	K	127	7F	DEL	179	B3	³
24	18	CAN	76	4C	L	128	80	xxx	180	B4	´
25	19	EM	77	4D	M	129	81	xxx	181	B5	µ
26	1A	SUB	78	4E	N	130	82	BPH	182	B6	¶
27	1B	ESC	79	4F	O	131	83	NBH	183	B7	·
28	1C	FS	80	50	P	132	84	IND	184	B8	¸
29	1D	GS	81	51	Q	133	85	NEL	185	B9	¹
30	1E	RS	82	52	R	134	86	SSA	186	BA	º
31	1F	US	83	53	S	135	87	ESA	187	BB	»
32	20	SP	84	54	T	136	88	HTS	188	BC	¼
33	21	!	85	55	U	137	89	HTJ	189	BD	½
34	22	"	86	56	V	138	8A	VTS	190	BE	¾
35	23	#	87	57	W	139	8B	PLD	191	BF	¿
36	24	$	88	58	X	140	8C	PLU	192	C0	À
37	25	%	89	59	Y	141	8D	RI	193	C1	Á
38	26	&	90	5A	Z	142	8E	SS2	194	C2	Â
39	27	'	91	5B	[	143	8F	SS3	195	C3	Ã
40	28	(	92	5C	\	144	90	DCS	196	C4	Ä
41	29	)	93	5D	]	145	91	PU1	197	C5	Å
42	2A	*	94	5E	^	146	92	PU2	198	C6	Æ
43	2B	+	95	5F	_	147	93	STS	199	C7	Ç
44	2C	,	96	60	`	148	94	CCH	200	C8	È
45	2D	-	97	61	a	149	95	MW	201	C9	É
46	2E	.	98	62	b	150	96	SPA	202	CA	Ê
47	2F	/	99	63	c	151	97	EPA	203	CB	Ë
48	30	0	100	64	d	152	98	SOS	204	CC	Ì
49	31	1	101	65	e	153	99	xxx	205	CD	Í
50	32	2	102	66	f	154	9A	SCI	206	CE	Î
51	33	3	103	67	g	155	9B	CSI	207	CF	Ï

dec	hex	char	dec	hex	char	dec	hex	char	dec	hex	char
208	D0	Ð	220	DC	Ü	232	E8	è	244	F4	ô
209	D1	Ñ	221	DD	Ý	233	E9	é	245	F5	õ
210	D2	Ò	222	DE	Þ	234	EA	ê	246	F6	ö
211	D3	Ó	223	DF	ß	235	EB	ë	247	F7	÷
212	D4	Ô	224	E0	à	236	EC	ì	248	F8	ø
213	D5	Õ	225	E1	á	237	ED	í	249	F9	ù
214	D6	Ö	226	E2	â	238	EE	î	250	FA	ú
215	D7	×	227	E3	ã	239	EF	ï	251	FB	û
216	D8	Ø	228	E4	ä	240	F0	ð	252	FC	ü
217	D9	Ù	229	E5	å	241	F1	ñ	253	FD	ý
218	DA	Ú	230	E6	æ	242	F2	ò	254	FE	þ
219	DB	Û	231	E7	ç	243	F3	ó	255	FF	ÿ

Notes:
1. Characters 0 - 127 form the ASCII character set.
2. Characters 32 - 127 and 160 - 255 are the same in the ANSI character set.

Unicode C0 and C1 controls

NUL null
SOH start of heading
SOT start of text
ETX end of text
EOT end of transmission
ENQ enquiry
ACK acknowledge
BEL bell
BS backspace
HT horizontal tab
LF line feed
VT vertical tab
FF form feed
CR carriage return
SO shift out
SI shift in
DLE data link escape
DC device control
NAK negative ack.
SYN synchronous idle
ETB end of transmission block
CAN cancel

EM end of medium
SUB substitute
ESC esape
FS file separator
GS group separator
RS record separator
US unit separator
SP space
DEL delete
BPH break permitted here
NBH no break here
IND indent
NEL next line
SSA start of selected area
OSC operating system command
ESA end of selected area
HTS character tabulation set
HTJ character tabulation with justification
VTS line tabulation set
PLD partial line forward
PLU partial line backward

RI reverse line feed
SS2 single shift two
SS3 single shift three
DCS device control string
PU1 private use one
PU2 private use two
STS set tranmit state
CCH cancel character
MW message waiting
SPA start of guarded area
EPA end of guarded area
SOS start of string
SCI single character introducer
CSI control sequence introducer
ST string terminator
PM privacy message
APC application program command
NBSP no-break space
SHY soft hyphen

Logic Function Tables

Written as	Drawn as	logic table		

A	A
0	0
1	1

A ──────

A	B	A·B
0	0	0
0	1	0
1	0	0
1	1	1

A AND B

A	B	A+B
0	0	0
0	1	1
1	0	1
1	1	1

A OR B

A	B	A exor B
0	0	0
0	1	1
1	0	1
1	1	0

A EXOR B

A	$\overline{A}$
0	1
1	0

NOT A ──────o

A	B	$\overline{A \cdot B}$
0	0	1
0	1	1
1	0	1
1	1	0

A NAND B

A	B	$\overline{A+B}$
0	0	1
0	1	0
1	0	0
1	1	0

A NOR B

A	B	A exnor B
0	0	1
0	1	0
1	0	0
1	1	1

A EXNOR B

Programming Languages

The following samples demonstrate the differences in programming languages for a similar function: an input, n, is requested from the user (defining the number of entries in a list); the program loop repeats itself n times, asking for an entry and comparing it with the current biggest number entered. The biggest entry entered is then displayed on screen.

BASIC

```
5       BIG=0
10      INPUT "How many numbers ";N
20      FOR I=1 TO N
30      INPUT X
40      IF X>BIG THEN BIG=X
50      NEXT I
60      PRINT BIG
70      END
```

FORTRAN

```
        INTEGER BIG
        BIG=0
        READ, N
        DO 2 I=1, N
        READ, C
2       IF (X.GT.BIG)BIG=X
        PRINT, BIG
        STOP
        END
```

C

```
#include <stdio.h>
main()
{
  int n, i, x, big;
  big=0;
  scanf("%d", &n);
  for (i=0; i<n; i++)
  {
     scanf("%d", &x);
     if (x>big)
        big=x;
  }
  printf("%d", big);
}
```

C++

```
#include <iostream>
using namespace std;
main()
{
    int n, x;
    int big = 0;
    cin >> n;
    for (int i = 0; i < n; i++)
    {
        cin >> x;
        if (x > big)
            big = x;
    }
    cout << big;
}
```